HORÆ BEATÆ MARIÆ VIRGINIS

OR

PRIMERS

HORÆ
BEATÆ MARIÆ VIRGINIS

OR

SARUM AND YORK PRIMERS

WITH

KINDRED BOOKS

AND

PRIMERS OF THE REFORMED ROMAN USE

TOGETHER WITH

AN INTRODUCTION

BY

EDGAR HOSKINS, M.A.

RECTOR OF ST. MARTIN AT LUDGATE IN THE CITY OF LONDON

LONGMANS, GREEN, AND CO.
39 PATERNOSTER ROW, LONDON
NEW YORK AND BOMBAY
1901

Andover-Harvard
Theological Library
Cambridge, Mass.

H 48,822

TABLE OF CONTENTS.

	PAGE
Introduction	vii
A Supplement to a Hand-List of Horæ or Primers	xxiii
A List of Printers and Booksellers with a List of places	571
A Concise List of Horæ or Primers	xli
A Concise List of Horæ or Primers according to the Roman Use	xlix
A Concise List of Horæ or Primers according to the Use of York	l
Variations in Horæ (Post Purificationem usque ad Adventum) according to the Uses of Sarum and York	li
Horæ or Primers in Regnal Periods	lii
Additions and Corrections in the Hand-List of Horæ or Primers and in the Summary of the Contents	liii
Additions and Corrections in the Indexes	lv
I. A Hand-List of Horæ or Primers	1
II. A Summary of the Contents of	
(a) The Hours or Primers according to Sarum and York uses in which the Hours are in Latin. A.D. 1478-A.D. 1558	107
(b) The Hours or Primers according to Sarum and York uses in which the Hours are in English and Latin or in English. A.D. 1536-A.D. 1558	159
III. A Summary of the Contents of	
(a) Primers and Goodly Primers printed chiefly for William Marshall. c. A.D. 1534-c. A.D. 1539	195
(b) Primers partly Sarum, partly those printed for William Marshall. A.D. 1536-A.D. 1540	213
(c) Manual of Prayers or Primer, Primer or Book of Prayers set forth by Bishop Hilsey. A.D. 1539-A.D. 1540	225
IV. A Summary of the Contents of	
The Primer set forth by the King's majesty and his Clergy, and of kindred Primers. A.D. 1545-A.D. 1671	237
V. A Summary of the Contents of	
A Primer or Book of private prayer authorized and set forth by the King's majesty, agreeable to the Book of Common prayer. A.D. 1553-A.D. 1825	290

TABLE OF CONTENTS.

	PAGE
VI. A Summary of the Contents of	
(*a*) John Austin's Devotions in the ancient way of Offices. A.D. 1668-A.D. 1789	311
(*b*) Theophilus Dorrington's reformed Devotions. A.D. 1686-A.D. 1727	317
(*c*) George Wheler's Protestant Monastery. A.D. 1698	322
(*d*) Devotions in the ancient way of Offices published by George Hickes. A.D. 1700-A.D. 1765	325
(*e*) A collection of Meditations and Devotions published by N. Spinckes. A.D. 1717	335
(*f*) Thomas Deacon's primitive method of daily private prayer. A.D. 1734-A.D. 1747	340
VII. A Summary of the Contents of	
The Primer or Office of the B. Virgin Mary according to the reformed Latin of the Roman use. A.D. 1571-A.D. 1867	349
VIII. Indexes	
(i.) Liturgical forms	383
(ii.) Hymns and Rhythms	445
(iii.) Names and Places	453
(iv.) General Index	498

INTRODUCTION.

THE book called the Primer which contains "Horæ beatæ Virginis Mariæ," whether of Salisbury,[1] York,[2] or a monastic use, and is known in its printed form by the title "Hore beate Marie Virginis" as well as, in the case of Salisbury use, by that of "The Primer,"[3] was formed in manuscript Psalters; it is found in Psalters up to the age of printing in the fifteenth century, although as early as the thirteenth century it was written as a separate book. For the purpose of tracing the formation of the Primer it will be found convenient to adopt the following classification of the Psalters:

I. Psalters which were written before the monastic revival in the tenth century.

II. Psalters which were written during the period of the monastic revival in the tenth, and the beginning of the eleventh century.

III. Psalters of the Norman period up to the commencement of the thirteenth century.

I. The additions which were made to the Psalter proper before the monastic revival afford sufficient evidence to show, that the book which comprised the one hundred and fifty psalms of David was the germ of the Divine service or Canonical Hours, commonly called the Breviary, and also the nucleus of the Primer; for some of the additions found in such manuscripts are common both to the Breviary and to the Primer, while some belong more especially to the

---

[1] Brit. Mus. C. 35. e. 6. See also page 5 Nº 10 of this book.
[2] York Minster xi. o. 28. See also page 19 Nº 51 of this book.
[3] Bodleian. Douce BB. 75. See also page 31 Nº 81 of this book.

INTRODUCTION.

Breviary and some more especially to the Primer. Among those which are common, at least in their general features, both to the Breviary and the Primer, the following may be quoted, "Kalendarium";[1] "Litania Sanctorum";[2] "Orationes Matutinales, Ad Primam, Terciam, Sextam, Nonam, Vesperam, Completorium";[3] "Orationes ad Angelos, Patriarchas, Prophetas, Apostolos, Martyres, Confessores, S. Mariam, et omnes Sanctos".[4] Among those which belong especially to the Breviary are the following Cantica; "Hymnus in die Dominica ad Matutinas";[5] "Hymnus ad Matutinas, Hymnus ad Vespertinam";[6] "Responsoria in Divino officio";[7] while such didactic matter as "Initium evangelii et Sequentie,"[8] and such devotional, as "Symbolum Apostolorum,"[9] "Oratio dominica,"[10] and "Gloria in excelsis,"[11] were probably inserted that they might be used privately by the laity, and also by members of monastic bodies, and thus can be claimed for the Primer.

When we turn from Psalters to other documents bearing on the point it is evident that such devotions as those in the Psalter which were subsequently part of the Primer were already being taught to the laity. The Venerable Bede writing in 734 to Egbert Bishop of York says; "Hoc præ ceteris omni instantia procurandum arbitror, ut fidem catholicam quæ Apostolorum symbolo continetur, et Dominicam orationem quam sancti Evangelii nos Scriptura edocet, omnium qui ad tuum regimen pertinent memoriæ radicitus

---

[1] Brit. Mus. Galba A. 18. fol. 3. Bodleian Junius 27. fol. 2.
[2] Brit. Mus. Galba A. 18. fol. 200. Bodl. Laud Lat. 81. fol. 144b.
[3] Brit. Mus. Galba A. 18. fol. 28b. C.C.C. Camb. 272.
[4] C.C.C. Camb. 411.
[5] Brit. Mus. Galba A. 18. fol. 172. Bodl. Douce 59. fol. 158.
[6] Brit. Mus. Vespasian A. 1. fol. 152 and 152b.
[7] C.C.C. Camb. 272.
[8] C.C.C. Camb. 411. See also page 118. No 10 of this book.
[9] Utrecht psalter in facsimile. fol. 178. Lambeth Palace 427. 198b.
[10] Utrecht psalter in facsimile. fol. 178. Lambeth Palace 427. 198b.
[11] Bodl. Douce 59. fol. 161. Utrecht Psalter in facsimile fol. 177.

INTRODUCTION.

infigere curis".[1] And a canon of the Council of Cloveshoo held in 747 under the presidency of Archbishop Cuthbert decrees: "Ut presbyteri Symbolum fidei ac Dominicam orationem, sed et sacrosancta quoque verba quæ in missæ celebratione et officio baptismi solemniter dicuntur, interpretari atque exponere posse propria lingua, qui nesciant discant".[2]

II. During the period of the monastic revival the Apostles creed, Lord's prayer and Gloria in excelsis continued to occupy a place in the Psalter,[3] the Creed and Lord's prayer being still ordered to be taught to the laity.[4] At this time too rules of devotion existed for the guidance of the laity and members of monastic bodies, which state that the Apostles creed and Lord's prayer were thus used; one rule of the year 994 " De mane et vespere orando" is as follows: " Christianis laicis etiam dicendum est, ut quisque bis saltem oret die, nisi sæpius queat, hoc est, mane et vesperi, nisi quis Pater noster et Credo possit, cantet et dicat," "Tu Domine qui me formavisti et creavisti miserere mei, Deus miserere mei peccatoris" . . . "invocet Dei sanctos et oret ut pro eo apud Deum intercedant, primo sanctam Mariam et omnes Dei sanctos."[5] Another of Hyde abbey or Newminster, a Benedictine house at Winchester, has these words; "Every Sunday take care that thou call upon the name of the Trinity, that is, Father and Son and the Holy Ghost, and sing 'Benedicite' and 'Gloria in excelsis Deo' and 'Credo in Deum,' and 'Pater noster' for Christ's sake, when all weeks shall turn out the better for thee".[6] But over and above these elementary private devotions, before the monastic period not only did many books exist which

---

[1] A. W. Haddan and W. Stubbs, Councils, Vol. 3. p. 316. sec. 3.
[2] Wilkins Conc. ed. 1747. Vol. 1. p. 96. sec. x.
[3] Brit. Mus. Vitellius E. 18. fol. 138b. Harl. 2904. fol. 205.
Arundel 60. fol. 128. Arundel 155. fol. 192b. Bodl. Douce 296. fol. 114b.
Camb. Univ. Ff. 1. 23. page 528.
[4] Wilkins Conc. ed. 1747. Vol. 1. page 272. sec. xxii. and page 304. sec. xxiii.
[5] Wilkins Conc. ed. 1747. Vol. 1. page 272. sec. xxiii.
[6] Brit. Mus. Titus D. xxvi. fol. 2. See also Royal Soc. of literature. Transac. Second Series, Vol. xi. p. 467.

INTRODUCTION.

though they did not formally contain the Hours of the Virgin supplied materials to form that section and other sections of the Primer;[1] while during that period the actual norm of the Hours of the Virgin and of other Hours occurs in some books which belonged to Benedictine houses; one book contains "Votiva laus in veneratione Sancte Marie Virginis," and "Hore de omnibus Sanctis ad Vesperam".[2] Another book which belonged to Hyde abbey has a form probably of Vespers (a) "In honore Sancte Marie," (b) "In honore sancte Crucis," and (c) "De Trinitate".[3] Psalters of this period also contained the Hours of the Virgin but without a title,[4] and the Hours of the Trinity with the title "Cursus de Sancta Trinitate,"[5] they also annexed devotions contained in the Breviary and Primer such as "Officium mortuorum"[6] "Litania de S. Maria"[7] "Orationes ad Patrem, Filium, ad Sanctum Spiritum"[8] and "Orationes ad Angelos et Sanctos".[9]

III. During the Norman period French as well as Latin was used in the Psalters,[10] and the Hours of the Virgin begin to appear in three portions; to be said at the different periods of the year (a) During Advent (b) From Christmas to the Purification (c) From the Purification to Advent. Other forms of Hours "In Sabbato ad Vesperas" and "In Laudibus" also occur.[11] A Psalter of the twelfth century

---

[1] Brit. Mus. Harl. 2965. Harl. 7653. Royal 2A.20. Stowe 944. Antiphonary of Bangor. Bradshaw Soc.
[2] Brit. Mus. Tiberius A. 3. fol. 107b. and fol. 57. See also Facsimiles of early Horæ de b. Maria V. Bradshaw Soc.
[3] Brit. Mus. Titus D. xxvii. fol. 76.
[4] Brit. Mus. Royal 2 B.V. fol. 1b.
[5] Bodl. Douce 296. fol. 127b.
[6] Brit. Mus. Vitellius E. 18. fol. 144.
[7] Brit. Mus. Vitellius E. 18. fol. 17b.
[8] Brit. Mus. Arundel 60. fol. 143. Arundel 155. fol. 171.
Bodl. Douce 296. fol. 124b. Camb. Univ. Ff. 1. 23. page 542.
[9] Bodl. Douce 296. fol. 125. Camb. Univ. Ff. 1. 23. page 546.
[10] Brit. Mus. Nero C. iv. Arundel 230. Add. 35283. Lansdowne 383. C.C.C. Coll. Camb. 53. Clare Coll. Camb. Kk. iii. 6.
[11] Brit. Mus. Harl. 863. fol. 117.

has "Commendatio anime".[1] Antiphons were appended to the Psalms.[2]

The thirteenth century witnessed a new departure in the history of the Primer; hitherto it had taken shape within the Psalter, but now the Psalter threw it off and it became available as a separate book, however still some Psalters continued to contain the Hours of the Virgin and to annex the devotions peculiar to the Primer; so that from the thirteenth century to the age of printing the Primer is found both in the Psalter, and as a separate book.

Six Primers of the thirteenth century which are known to exist[3] show that taking one book with another the Primer uniformly contained (a) A Kalendar, (b) The Hours of the Virgin from Purification to Advent, (c) The seven penitential psalms, (d) The Litany of the Saints, (e) The Office for the dead, (f) The Psalms of commendation, (g) The fifteen or gradual Psalms, and (h) The prayers of St. Bridget commonly called the Fifteen Oes; while either one Primer or another has, "Hore de S. Trinitate,"[4] " Hore de passione," or, "Heures del Nun Jesu,"[5] " Hore de S. Johanne Baptista,"[6] " Hore de S. Katherina,"[7] "Hore de S. Spiritu,"[8] Rubrics in French, and pictures with prayers on the sacred mysteries.[9]

Psalters of the thirteenth century with the Hours of the Virgin have in some cases the three variant forms for the three sections of the year,[10] in others only that which in the triple arrangement was assigned to the period from Purification

---

[1] Bodl. Rawl. G. 22. fol. 152b.
[2] Brit. Mus. Harl. 863.
[3] Brit. Mus. Harl. 928. Egerton 1151. Add. 35385. Bodl. Douce 231. Fitzwilliam Mus. 47 and 242. fol. 1. See also H. Bradshaw Hibernensis. page 55.
[4] Brit. Mus. Add. 33385. fol. 27. Fitzwilliam Mus. 242.
[5] Brit. Mus. Add. 33385. fol. 27. Brit. Mus. Egerton 1151. fol. 95.
[6] Brit. Mus. Add. 33385. fol. 107.
[7] Brit. Mus. Add. 33385. fol. 125.
[8] Brit. Mus. Add. 33385. fol. 42. Egerton 1151. fol. 184.
Fitzwilliam Mus. 242. fol. 43.
[9] Brit. Mus. Harl. 928. fol. 3-9.
[10] Brit. Mus. Arundel 305. fol. 271.

xii INTRODUCTION.

to Advent;[1] they are richer in private devotions than the Primers.

In the fourteenth century some Psalters with the Hours of the Virgin,[2] have the three variants above described and the public service of the commemoration of the Virgin as well, with the title "Plenum et non plenum Servitium de S. Maria": the portion from Purification to Advent also occurs in a Psalter, intermingled with "Hore de cruce" the Hours being "Secundum usum Sarum"; this book also has "Psalterium de passione Domini".[3] Fresh private devotions and some Hymns were added at this time to the Primer,[4] as well as "Psalterium B. Hieronymi,"[5] and "Psalmi S. Hilarii".[6]

Towards the end of the fourteenth, and at the beginning of the fifteenth century Psalters and Primers appeared in English; they contained important additions to the subjects in which the laity were instructed, and met the requirements of documents of the thirteenth century by supplying treatises on these additional subjects. Walter de Kirkham Bishop of Durham writing in 1255 says "Cum igitur in decalogi observatione salus animarum consistat, monemus ut unusquisque pastor animarum, ac quilibet sacerdos parochialis sciat decalogum hoc est decem mandata legis Mosaicæ quæ populo sibi credito frequenter ac diligenter exponat. Insuper sciat, quæ sunt septem criminalia ... sciat quoque saltem similiter septem ecclesiastica sacramenta. Habeat quoque unusquisque eorum simplicem intellectum fidei, sicut in Symbolo, tam majori quam minori, quod est in psalmo 'Quicunque vult' et etiam 'Credo in Deum' expressius continentur; necnon in Oratione dominica, quæ dicitur 'Pater noster,' ac 'Salutatione beatæ Mariæ,' et qualiter se debeant crucis charactere insignire."[7]

[1] Brit. Mus. Arundel 157. fol. 159b. St. John's Coll. Camb. D. 6. Duke of Rutland.
[2] Bodl. Laud. 85. fol. 7.
[3] St. John's Coll. Oxford 82.
[4] Brit. Mus. Harleian 1260. fol. 195b.
[5] Brit. Mus. Harleian 1260. fol. 197.
[6] Brit. Mus. Harleian 1260. fol. 103.
[7] Wilkins Conc. ed. 1747. Vol. 1. pages 704, 732.

Other documents of the thirteenth century already before this time had specified the times at which instruction should be given, in 1257; "Statuta Synodalia Walteri et Symonis Norwicensium episcoporum," thus decree "Statuimus præcipientes ut quilibet sacerdos parochialis singulis diebus ad Primam et ad Completorium Orationem dominicam et Symbolum dicat coram suis parochianis in audientia, distincte et aperte ad intelligendum,"[1] and Archbishop Peckham's constitutions in 1281 : "De informatione simplicium ". " Quilibet sacerdos plebi præsidens quater in anno, hoc est, semel in qualibet quarta anni die uno solenni vel pluribus vel per se vel per alium exponat populo vulgariter quatuor decem fidei articulos, decem mandata decalogi, duo præcepta evangelia, scilicet geminæ charitatis, septem opera misericordiæ, septem peccata capitalia cum sua progenie, septem virtutes principales, ac septem gratiæ sacramenta."[2]

The contents of the Psalters in English which contained additional subjects in which the laity were to be instructed may be thus summarised. One Psalter has an "A.B.C." technically so called, together with the Ten commandments, Seven works of bodily mercy, Five bodily wittes, Seven deadly sins and the contrary virtues, Seven gifts of the Holy Ghost, Four cardinal virtues, Four ghostly virtues, A short declaration of the Pater noster, The twelve articles of the Creed, together with Graces before and after meat, and before and after supper.[3] Another has the Parables of Solomon, the book of Ecclesiastes, the book of Sapience, and the book of Ecclesiasticus.[4] Another with the Hours of the Virgin from Purification to Advent has a Kalendar.[5] Another has The seven sacraments, The ten commandments, The seven deadly sins, The joys of the Virgin in English verse.[6]

[1] Wilkins Conc. ed. 1747. Vol. 1. page 732.
[2] Wilkins Conc. ed. 1747. Vol. 2. pages 54, 168, 297.
[3] Trin. Coll. Dublin. A. 4. 22.
[4] Brit. Mus. Add. 31044. fol. 109.
[5] Mr. H. Yates Thompson.
[6] Brit. Mus. Add. 17376. fol. 150.

xiv INTRODUCTION.

The contents of thirteen Primers in English of the end of the fourteenth and the beginning of the fifteenth centuries which are known to exist[1] are the Hours of the Virgin from Purification to Advent with the Hours of the Cross, a Kalendar, the Seven penitential psalms, the Fifteen or Gradual psalms, the Litany, the Office of the dead, the Psalms of commendation, devotions to the Virgin, the psalm De profundis, Psalms of the passion, A Christian man's confession, Misereatur, Pater noster, Ave Maria, Credo, Ten commandments, Six manners of conscience, Seven deadly sins, Five witts outward and inward, Seven works of mercy bodily and ghostly, Seven gifts of the Holy Ghost, Seven words, Sixteen properties of charity; together with instructions on many of the above subjects, and the words of Paul. One Primer contains an "A.B.C." technically so called.[2] Another Primer comprising a Latin portion of the fourteenth century and an English portion of the fifteenth should specially be mentioned; the Latin part has "Matutine de Virgine Maria per totum annum" with "Hore de cruce" and "Hore de compassione"; "Modus confitendi secundum dominum Robertum episcopum Lincolniensem," and a treatise "De fundatore sive auctore ordinis Carmelitani".[3] The English part consists of treatises on the Seven deadly sins, and the Ten commandments; it also has "Visitatio infirmorum" in English, and "Days of pardon for those who visit the Chapel of our Lady in Ely Cathedral":[4] the different dates of the Latin and English portions suggest that a Latin primer has been bound with an English treatise similar to Archbishop Thursby's manual of 1373,[5] for the repetition of the substance of Archbishop Peckham's constitutions of 1281[6] in a York provincial Council of 1466 points to the

[1] H. Littlehales, The Primer. Part ii. pages 1-10.
[2] Hunterian Mus. Glasgow. v. 6. 22. See also H. Bradshaw, Collected papers. page 333.
[3] Brit. Mus. Harl. 211. fol. 1. 102. 192.
[4] Brit. Mus. Harl. 211. fol. 35. 65. 101b.
[5] R. Thoresby Vicaria Leodiensis. page 196.
[6] Wilkins Conc. ed. 1727. Vol. 2. page 54.

INTRODUCTION.

existence of other treatises of a like character to this manual in the fifteenth century.[1]

By the time that printing was invented manuscript Psalters with the Hours of the Virgin and manuscript Primers had become rich storehouses out of which devotions both in Latin and in English could be taken; the earliest complete edition of a printed Primer which is known to exist drew largely upon these books, and bears striking evidence to the fact that the Primer was a Layman's book of devotions for private use either at home or in church: to prove this it is enough to quote some rubrics to the Latin prayers, such for instance as, "Ere ye depart out of your chamber at your uprising," "When thou enterest into the church," "When thou shalt receive the Sacrament".[2] No direction is given in this Primer for the use of the Hours of the Virgin, which in this book are the form for use from Purification to Advent, and are called "Matyns of our lady with pryme and the hours, with the Hours of the passion of our Lord, and the compassion of our Lady"; but a rule of devotion of about the same date as the Primer shows that the Hours formed a part of the private devotions which it was the custom of a layman to use at home; the rule is as follows;

> Afore all thing and principally
> In the morning when ye up rise
> To worship God have in memory;
> With Christ's cross, look ye, bless you thrice,
> Your Pater noster say in devout wise
> Ave Maria with the holy Creed,
> Then all the day the better shall ye speed.
>
> And while that ye be about honestly
> To dress yourself and do on your array,
> With your fellow well and tretably
> Our Lady matyns look that ye say;
> And this observance use ye every day
> With pryme and hours.[3]

---
[1] Wilkins Conc. ed. 1727. Vol. 3. page 599.
[2] See page 107. N⁰ 7. Lambeth Palace 25. 1. 23.
[3] Caxton's Book of curtesy, Early English Text. Soc. N⁰ 3. extra series. page 5.

INTRODUCTION.

That the Hours of the Virgin besides being used at home were used privately by lay people in church is also evident, for an Italian who was travelling in England in the fifteenth century says "That although Englishmen all attend mass every day, and say many Pater nosters in public, the women carrying long rosaries in their hands, and any who can read taking the Office of our Lady with them, and with some companion reciting it in the church verse by verse in a low voice after the manner of religious; they always hear mass on Sundays in their parish church".[1]

We know then that it was the custom of the laity to say the Hours from the Primer at home and also privately in church; but the further question arises, did they join in the church service when the Hours of the Virgin were said publicly by the clergy? We read of a distinguished lady who was in the habit in the early part of the fourteenth century of going to her accustomed place in church, "In vigilia assumptionis beatissime Virginis matris Dei ad audiendas vesperas:"[2] these Vespers were part of the Breviary. Again, the author of "The Myrrour of the church," writing in 1527, in a treatise on the ten commandments, of the way in which the Sabbaths and Holy days should be kept bids his reader, "rising in the morning go to the church and with devotion say his Matins without jangling, also sweetly hear Mass, and all the Hours of the day;"[3] although he advises attendance at the Hours of the Divine service, it is not clear what service is meant when he bids his reader "Say his Matins without jangling"; indeed no more would seem to be meant than the custom of the laity of reciting the Office of our Lady in church, verse by verse, in a low voice with some companion.

---

[1] Camden Soc. No 37 True account of the island of England. page 23.
[2] Early English Text Soc. No 20 Treatises of Richard Rolle. page xviii.
[3] Myrrour of the church. ed. 1527. Brit. Mus. C. 25. k. 19. Sign. B. 4b.

INTRODUCTION. xvii

We find, however, that bequests were made to the laity in the fourteenth and fifteenth centuries of Psalters, Primers[1] and Portuases or portable Breviaries[2] and it is plain from their contents that the owners of these books had it in their power to follow either the Hours of the Divine service, or the Hours of the Virgin when they were said publicly by the clergy in church; the fact too that the accustomed place in church which a layman occupied was now described as a pew, and that it was duly prepared for use points to regular attendance on the part of the laity at church services; the directions given to a servant for the preparation of a pew are very minute.

> Prince or prelate if it be, or any other potestate
> Or he enter into the church, be it early or late,
> Perceive all things for his pew that it be made preparate,
> Book, cushion, carpet, and curtain, bedes and book forget not that.[3]

The custom of the laity in using the Primer at home and in church may be further traced. George Cavendish the biographer of Wolsey relates that on Hallowen day in the year 1529 he came into the great chamber at Esher to give his attendance, and found Mr Cromwell leaning in the great window with a Primer in his hand saying our Lady Matyns.[4] But the Primer itself tells us what the custom of the laity was; a book published in 1530 has a rule of devotion called "The manner to live well and devoutly" it says, "When you have arrayed you say in your chamber or lodging Matyns, Prime, and Hours if ye may, then go to the church, or ye do any worldly business; if ye have no needful business, and abide in the church the space of a low mass, while there ye shall think and thank God of his benefits . . . and, when ye may, say Dirige and Commendations for all Christian souls, at the least

---

[1] R. R. Sharpe Kalendar of Wills. Part 1. page 669.
[2] Early English Text Soc. No 78. page 59.
[3] Early English Text Soc. No 32 Babees book, Book of nurture. page 178.
[4] J. Holmes, Cavendish Life of Wolsey. page 169.

way, on the holy days, and if ye have leisure say them on the holy days at least with three lessons".[1] One last piece of evidence which is forthcoming with regard to the use of the Primer is of the year 1570; at that time Arthur Chapman of Wolsingham a blacksmith was brought before a court at Durham for reading an English book or Primer in the church of Wolsingham at the time of the morning prayer while the Priest was saying his service not minding what the Priest read, but tending his own book and prayer, the Priest after the first lesson willed him to read more softly; he said that he would make amends for his fault.[2]

The Hours of the Virgin in the printed Primers are most commonly the form for use from Purification to Advent,[3] but all the three forms occur.[4] Although the Hours were not translated into English until about 1535 devotions in English are found in the earliest editions; from 1535 and up to the end of Queen Mary's reign they are found in English and Latin as well as in Latin. When the Hours were published in English and Latin, Latin prayers translated into English also appeared, except during the period between 1545 and 1551.

Three classes of Primers were published between 1534 and 1540, differing in some respects from those which preceded them.

I. Primers in which the Hours are either in English or in English and Latin printed for William Marshall, cum gratia et privilegio regali, with these titles "A Primer in English," "A goodly Primer in English," "The Primer with the pystles and gospels in English"; in this Primer the Hours are in English and Latin. This class of Primer is found between 1534 and 1539.[5]

---

[1] See page 147. No 92.
[2] Depositions in Court of Durham, page 231. Surtees Soc. No 21.
[3] See page 107-9. No 7.
[4] See page 125-8. No 39.
[5] See page 193.

INTRODUCTION. xix

II. Primers in which the Hours are in English and Latin partly of Sarum use and partly the Hours printed for William Marshall, cum gratia et privilegio regali. The edition of 1536 has the title "This Primer of Salisbury use," that of 1540 "The Primer". This class of Primer is found between 1536 and 1540.[1]

III. Primers in which the Hours are in English, or in English and Latin, set forth by John Hilsey, Bishop of Rochester, at the commandment of Lord Thomas Crumwell, Vice-gerent to the King's highness, cum privilegio ad imprimendum solum, with the titles "The Manual of prayers or the Primer" and "The Primer or Book of prayers". This class of Primer is found in 1539 and in 1540.[2]

The Primer which bears the title of "The Primer set forth by the King's majesty and his Clergy to be taught, learned and read, and none other to be used throughout all his dominions," the first edition of which was published on May 29, 1545, occupies a prominent position in the history of the Primers in the sixteenth century: it was published as the King's injunction for authorising the book states for the following reasons; "That much tendering the youth of our realms . . . and specially for that the youth by divers persons are taught the Pater noster, the Ave Maria, Creed, and Ten Commandments, all in Latin, and not in English, by means whereof the same are not brought up in the knowledge of their faith, duty and obedience . . . and for that our people and subjects which have no understanding in the Latin tongue, and yet have the knowledge of reading may pray in their vulgar tongue, which is to them best known . . . and for avoiding the diversity of primer books that are now abroad . . . and to have one uniform order of all such books throughout all our dominions . . . and that every schoolmaster and bringer up of young beginners in learning, next after

[1] See page 213.
[2] See page 225.

their A.B.C.[1] now by us also set forth do teach this Primer . . . in English, and that the youth use the same until they be of competent understanding and knowledge to perceive it in Latin. At what time they may . . . either use this Primer in English, or that which is by our authority likewise made in the Latin tongue, in all points correspondent unto this in English."[2]

Primers and Books of a kindred character and of the same class as the Primer of May 29 1545 which is known as the King's Primer appeared up to the reign of Charles the second: they were published with the following titles "The Primer," "Orarium seu libellus precationum per regiam majestatem latine æditus" 1560; "Preces privatæ in studiosorum gratiam collectæ et regia authoritate approbatæ . . . cum privilegio reginæ." 1564. "A collection of private devotions in the practice of the ancient church called the Hours of prayer. As they were much after this manner published by authority of Q. Elizabeth 1560." 1627; and "The King's Psalter." 1671, which was intended to succeed the King's Primer.[3]

The Books of the Common Prayer as they were published from 1549 and onwards are in touch with the contents of the class of books which originated with the King's Primer: but another class of Primers, the first of which was published in 1553 and was called "A Primmer or book of private prayer . . . authorised, and set forth by the King's majesty," actually claims in the King's privilege to the printer to be agreeable to the Book of Common prayers.[4] It was followed by other editions of this class of Primers; that of 1670 having as its title, "The Primer or Catechism set forth agreeable to the Book of Common Prayer authorised by the King's majesty to be used throughout his realms and dominions".[5]

---

[1] See page 153. No 161.
[2] See page 63. No 179. also page 65. No 186.
[3] See page 235.
[4] See page 289. No 200.
[5] See page 303. No 257.

INTRODUCTION. xxi

It has been already stated that Primers of Sarum and York uses were published with the Hours in Latin, and in Latin and English up to the end of Queen Mary's reign in 1558, with the exception of a break between 1545 and 1551. In the year 1571 the first edition of "Officium b. Mariæ Virginis nuper reformatum et Pii v. Pont. Max. jussu editum" was published in Latin, and in 1599 in Latin and English.[1]

Books of a kindred character to the Primers continued to be published in the seventeenth and eighteenth centuries.

They are [2]

 (a) John Austin's devotions in the ancient way of offices. Five editions from 1668 to 1789.

 (b) Theophilus Dorrington's reformed devotions. Nine editions. 1686-1727.[3]

 (c) George Wheler's Protestant Monastery. One edition. 1698.[4]

 (d) George Hickes: devotions in the ancient way of offices. Eight editions. 1700-1765.[5]

 (e) N. Spinckes: collection of meditations and devotions. One edition. 1717.[6]

 (f) Thomas Deacon's primitive method of daily private prayer. Two editions. 1734-1747.[7]

[1] See page 347.
[2] See page 309.
[3] See page 317.
[4] See page 322.
[5] See page 325.
[6] See page 335.
[7] See page 340.

INTRODUCTION.

The Editor desires to acknowledge the assistance which he has received from Mr. Falconer Madan's Summary Catalogue of manuscripts in the Bodleian Library, and from Dr. Montague R. James' descriptive catalogues of manuscripts. To the possessors of the valuable manuscripts and printed books which he has been allowed to consult he tenders his best thanks; and to Mr. Francis H. Jenkinson, the Rev. W. Howard Frere and Mr. E. Gordon Duff for the help which they have given him in the production of this book.

EDGAR HOSKINS.

20th May, 1901.

A SUPPLEMENT
TO A
HAND-LIST
OF
HORÆ OR PRIMERS.

₊ The contents of this Supplement are not included either in the concise List or in the Indexes or in the List of printers and booksellers, with a list of places.

9*. (c. 1494, *J. Herzog, Venice*) 16°.

Title not known. Sixteen lines to a full page with a border round the pages, except those which contain cuts. Printed in black and red. Two sizes of type are used. Without initials, signatures, catchwords or numbering.

Eleven fragments of this book are known, namely: Mr. F. H. Jenkinson; two leaves: three leaves. British Museum; a quire consisting of eight leaves: one leaf which is a duplicate of a leaf belonging to Mr. F. H. Jenkinson: five of one leaf each, all of which are duplicates of leaves at Eton College. Eton College Library; two copies of a fragment, containing two quires, each quire consisting of eight leaves.

Mr. F. H. Jenkinson. Three leaves; 2, 7, 8 of a quire containing the last part of Commendationes animarum, a cut of the cross, and a portion of the first of the Psalms of the Passion (Deus, Deus meus). Three leaves 5, 6, 8 of a quire containing portions of the following Psalms of the passion (Judica me Domine, Dominus illuminatio, Ad te Domine clamabo).

xxiv   SUPPLEMENT TO

Brit. Mus. A quire of eight leaves containing the four last Psalms of the passion (a portion of Ad te Domine clamabo, and of Afferte Domino, Exaltabo te Domine, In te Domine speravi) "Respice quesumus Domine . . ." "Sancte et individue Trinitati. . . ." Two little prayers which King Harry the sixth made (Domine Jesu Christe qui me creasti, Domine Jesu Christe qui solus). The preface to St. Jerome's psalter (Beatus Hieronymus ex omni psalterio). A cut of S. Jerome. A portion of St. Jeromes psalter. One leaf containing the last portion of "Admonitiones et orationes ad Jesum Christum," a cut of the Virgin and child on the reverse. One leaf containing a portion of the prayer (O intemerata et in eternum benedicta). One leaf containing the end of the prayer (Domine Jesu Christe qui hanc sacratissimam carnem), a cut of a Pieta on the reverse. One leaf containing Oratio Rome in ecclesia sancti Joannis laterani in quodam lapide (Domine Jesu Christe pater dilectissime rogo te), and a portion of Oratio ad Angelum custodem (Sancte angele Dei minister celestis imperii). One leaf containing the end of Oratio ad Angelum custodem and a portion of Suffragia De S. Christofero (An. Martyr Christophore).

Eton Coll. Two quires sixteen leaves containing a portion of the last of the Fifteen Oes (O Jesu vitis vera). Collecta (Deus qui per unigenitum filium). Admonitiones et orationes ad Dominum Jesum Christum (sima morte tua . . . per infinita secula seculorum Amen). Cut of the Virgin and Child. Oratio devota de Maria Virgine et Sancto Johanne euangelista (O intemerata et in eternum benedicta). Canticum Sanctorum Ambrosii et Augustini, transmutatum in laudem gloriose Virginis Marie (Te matrem Dei laudamus). Second quire. Oratio coram imaginem Marie Virginis (Ave sanctissima Maria mater Dei). Oratio devotissima de corpore (Ave verum). Ave Jesu fili Patris. Domine Jesu Christe qui hanc sacratissimam carnem. Cut of a Pieta. Oratio Rome in ecclesia sancti Joannis laterani in quodam lapide (Domine Jesu Christe pater dilectissime rogo te). Oratio ad Angelum custodem (Sancte Angele Dei minister celestis imperii). Suffragia. De S. Christophero (An. Martyr Christophore). De S. Sebastiano (An. O quam gloriosa refulsit gratia). De S. Georgio (An. Georgi martyr inclite). De S. Anthonio (An. O Anthoni pastor inclite). Colophon. Impressum venetiis per Iohannē hertzog. Impĕsis fam[os]orū vivoɹ Gerardi bar[revelt et Frederici Egmendt?]. On the reverse Device of J. Hamman in red as in the octavo Sarum missal of 1494.

Brit. Mus. I. A. 23043. Eton Coll. Fragm.
Mr. F. H. Jenkinson.
95 × 68. Latin.
*** See Robert Proctor, Indexes No. 5205.

11*. (*c.* 1495, *Jean Philippe, Paris, or Philippe Pigouchet, Paris*) 8°.
The title-page is wanting; the book begins on
A2. KL Februarius habet dies. xxviii. Luna vero. xxix.

Ends on 14[b]. vit et regnat deus. Per omnia secula seculorum. Amen. + Finis + (in prayer O intemerata et in eternum benedicta)

Mr. A. W. Pollard.
130 × 82. Latin.

12. (*c.* 1495, *Richard Pynson, London*) 8°.
Seventeen lines to a full page. Without signatures, catchwords or numbering. Printed entirely in black. Space left for 2-line initials

Two fragments of this book are known, namely: Mr. E. Gordon Duff; six leaves. Gonville and Caius Coll. Camb.; four leaves.

Mr. E. Gordon Duff. Six leaves; 1. 2. 3. 6. 7. 8 of a quire.

Begins. diat ītroitum tuū & exi tū tuū
All wanting after 8[b]. ex hoc

A⁴

Contents. A portion of Terce with Hours of the cross and of compassion. A portion of Sext, Nones, and Vespers with Hours of the cross and of compassion. A portion of Compline.

Gonville and Caius Coll. Camb. Four leaves 1. 4. 5. 8. of a quire. See No. 29. page 11.

Mr. E. Gordon Duff. Gonville and Caius Coll. Camb.

95 × 70. Latin.

⁎ Nos. 12 and 29 page 11 are parts of the same edition.

20*. 1499, *Paris*, 64°.

Horæ ad usum Sarum. Forma minima, very imperfect, but has end with imprint.

Sotheby's sale catalogue, 1867. No. 2733, George Offor's books.

⁎ A fire broke out while the sale was proceeding, and this book with others was destroyed.

72*. 1526, August 1, *Paris, for Jacques Cousin, Rouen,* 4°.

The title-page is wanting; the book begins on

A1. Poto KL Januarius habet dies xxxi. Luna xxx.

Colophon. Hore beate virginis marie secundum usum Sarų totaliter ad longum : cū multis pulcherrimis orationibus ᛐ indulgentiis iam ultimo adiectis . scđm exēplar : Parisius īpresse in edib⁹ Jacobi Cousin prope cordiferos ciuitatis Rothothomagi moram habētis. Anno dñi millesimo quingentesimo vigesimo sexto . die vero prima mensis Augusti.

Theological Coll., Edinburgh.

155 × 10. Latin.

74. 1526, *Wynkyn de Worde, London,* 4°.

Colophon. Expliciunt hore beatissime Marie virginis secūdum usum Sarų cū multis orationibus nuper circa finem adiectis. Impresse ac recognite ī ciuitate Londoñ. ꝑ me winādū de worde ī vico dicto ỹ fletestret ad signū solis ꝑmorātē. Anno dñi. M.d.xxvi . quarto nonas mēsis Aug.

Rev. L. E. Owen.

159 × 102. Latin.

A HAND-LIST. xxvii

170*. *c.* 1543, *Richard Kele, London*, 16°.

This is the Prymer in Englysh set out alonge with dyuers additions. (Cut of the Annunciation.)

Colophon. Imprynted at London by Rychard Kele, dwellynge at the longe shop in the Poultre under s. Mildredes churche.

Camb. Univ. Syn. 8. 54. 167.

84 × 53. English.

⁎⁎ "The Gospelles and Pystles of all ye Sõdayes and sayntes dayes that are rede in the churche," are bound with this book.

199*. 1552, *Richard Grafton, London*, 8°.

The title-page is wanting ; the book begins on

C 3. [Morning praier] of the father

Colophon. Imprinted at London by Rychard Grafton, Printer to the Kinges Maiestie. 1552. Cum privilegio ad Imprimendum solum.

Bishop of Cairo (Illinois).

113 × 60. English.

211*. 1555, *John Wayland, London*, 8°.

Hore beate Marie virginis secundum usum insignis ecclesie Sarisburieñ. Imprinted at Londõ by John Waylande at the signe of the sunne in Fletestrete ouer agaynste the greate conduit. Anno domini. M.D.L.V. Cum priuilegio per septennium.

Ends on K3ᵇ. vere tecuʒ flere crucifixo cõdolere.

Lincoln's Inn Library. 179. a.

127 × 76. Latin.

219*. (*c.* 1555, *Rouen, for Robert Valentin, Rouen*) 16°.

Twenty-six lines of a larger, and thirty lines of a smaller type to a full page. Known only from a fragment consisting of three leaves.

Begins. name, euer worlde with-nomen tuum ||

Ends. date eum oñes prayse ye hym, and ȳ wa ||

Contents. The last verses of the Te Deum at Matins. Cut of the meeting of the Virgin Mary and St. Elisabeth : on the two sides of the cut " Here begynneth the Laudes ", Psalms,

Dominus regnavit. Jubilate Deo. The latter part of the Benedicite, and a portion of the Psalm, Laudate Dominum de celis.

Brit. Mus. Harleian MS. 5936. Nos. 82. 83.
80 × 54. Latin and English.

222*. 1556, *London*, 16°.

The prymer in Englyshe for children, after the use of Salisburye.

Colophon. Imprynted at London M.D.L.VI.
Mr. Henry N. Stevens.
128 × 75. English.

⁎ This book, as well as No. 131, page 49 has on sign. B 1 "God savethe church, our King, and realm."

239*. *c.* 1559, *William Seres, London*, 4°.

The title-page is wanting; the book begins on

A1. [Graces.] Our father whiche art in heauen ha ||

Colophon. The ende of this Primer. ¶ Imprinted at London by Wyllyam Seres, dwellyng at the West ende of Poules, at the sygne of the Hedgehog.

Brit. Mus. 3406. c. 45. and C. 35. c. 19.
158 × 87. English.
⁎ See page 253.

260*. 1698, 8°.

The Protestant Monastery: or, Christian Œconomicks. Containing directions for the religious conduct of a family. Printed in the year 1698. (Sig. A 2.) Epistle to the readers (Signed) Geo. Wheler. (Sig. N 2, page 179.) Forms of prayer for the use of private families, for all the Hours of prayer both night and day. Taken out of the Common Prayer, with other inlargements. Which may be abbreviated, or inlarged, as more or less time and leisure will permit. (Sig. X 1.) Hymns suited to the several Hours of prayer, and other occasions, for the use of a private family. (Page 335.) Short Tunes to chant several of the Hymns.

Ends with "So longs my soul after the Lord."

Brit. Mus. 852. e. 20.
145 × 75. English.

263*. 1734, *London*, 8°.

A compleat Collection of Devotions,[1] both publick and private, taken from the Apostolical Constitutions, the Ancient Liturgies, and the Common Prayer Book of the Church of England. In two parts. Part I. Comprehending the publick Offices of the Church, humbly offered to the consideration of the present churches of Christendom, Greek, Roman, English, and all others. Part II. Being a primitive method of daily Private Prayer, containing devotions for the morning and evening, and for the Ancient Hours of prayer, Nine, Twelve, and Three, together with Hymns and Thanksgivings for the Lord's Day and Sabbath, and Prayers for Fasting days, as also, Devotions for the Altar, and Graces before and after meat. All taken from the Apostolical Constitutions and the Ancient Liturgies, with some additions; and recommended to the practice of all private Christians of every Communion. To which is added, an Appendix in justification of this undertaking, consisting of extracts and observations, taken from the writings of very eminent and learned Divines of different Communions. And to all is subjoind, in a Supplement, an Essay to procure Catholick Communion upon Catholick Principles. London, printed for the author; and sold by the booksellers of London and Westminster. M.DCC.XXXIV.

The Contents. Errata.
Brit. Mus. C. 52. f. 8.   Bodl. 8° Rawl. 1091.
175 × 95. English.

263**. 1747, *London*, 8°.

Devotions to be used by primitive Catholicks,[2] at church and at home. In two parts. Liverpool. Printed by J. Sadler in Harrington St. MDCCXLVII. Devotions to be

---

[1] See The Royalist. Vol. ix. No. 1. page 7. See also page 340 of this book.
[2] See The Royalist. Vol. ix. No. 1. page 13. See also page 346.

used by primitive Catholicks at church. Part I. Printed in the year . M.DCC.XLVII.

Bodl. 1399. e. 4. Mr. Henry Jenner.

149 × 90. English.

₊ This seems to be all that was ever published of a new edition of Thomas Deacon's " Compleat collection of devotions both publick and private, in two parts." No. 263* A.D. 1734.

264***. 1761, 8°.

The Divine Office,[1] Containing, Devotions for the Canonical Hours of Prayer, at Lauds, Tierce, Sext, None and Compline; to be used by all religious Societies where there is a Priest, and in the Houses of all the Clergy. Part I. Printed in the year 1761.

The book ends with "P. Depart in peace," then a cross.

Contents. Lauds, or Office for three in the morning. Tierce, or Office for the third Hour. Sext, or Office for the Sixth Hour. None, or Office for the Ninth Hour. The hymn, with the Proper Prefaces. Compline for Sunday, Compline for all Wednesdays that are Fast-days. Compline for Monday, Tuesday, Thursday, Friday, and Saturday.

Brit. Mus. C. 52. f. 7.

152 × 88. English.

₊ The verso of the title has. "N.B. Mattins and Vespers being publick Offices, at which all the faithful who have leisure ought to attend, are contained in the publick Offices of the Church.[2] If through any necessary avocation, the Priest is prevented from saying in community any of the Offices, at or near the hour appointed, that Office shall then be entirely omitted; and every one of the Society, or House, shall retire to their private devotion, according to the form prescribed in the second part of the collection of devotions."[3]

---

[1] See The Royalist. Vol. ix. No. 1. page 13.
[2] See A compleat collection of devotions both Publick and Private. page 340. (Brit. Mus. 3265. b. 27.)
[3] See page 346. (Bodleian.)

A HAND-LIST. xxxi

266*. 1573, *Plantin Press, Antwerp*, 8°.
Officium B. Mariæ Virginis, nuper reformatum, et Pii V. Pont. Max. jussu editum. Antwerpiæ, ex officina Christophori Plantini. M.D.LXXIII. Cum Priuilegio, & Indulgentiis.
Finis. Index eorum quæ in hoc volumine continentur.
✱ This book is bound with "Hymni per totum annum". "Orationes Dominicales & Feriales, cum suis Antiphonis & Versiculis per annum." "Orationes Propriæ de Sanctis, cum suis Antiphonis, & Versic." "Orationes Communes de Sanctis."
Colophon. Finis. Antwerpiæ excudebat Christopherus Plantinus, Architypographus regius, anno M.D.LXXIII. Idib. April.
Brit. Mus. 3365. bb. 21.
175 × 100. Latin.

266**. 1597, *Societas Typographica, Paris*, 8°.
Officium Beatæ Mariæ Virginis Nuper reformatum Et Pii V. Pont. Max. jussu editum. Cui accessit Kalendarium Gregorianum perpetuum, Parisiis, Apud Societatem Typographicam Librorum Officii Ecclesiastici, ex Decreto Concilii Tridentini via Jacobœa. Cum Privilegiis Pont. Max. & Franc. & Nauarræ Regis Christianiss. M.D.XC.VII. Finis. Index.
Rev. E. S. Dewick.
157 × 89. Latin.

267*. 1603, *Plantin Press, Antwerp, for John Moret (Antwerp)* 8°.
Officium Beatæ Mariæ Virginis, Pii V. Pont. Max. jussu editum. Cum Calendario Gregoriano, à Sixto P.P.V. & S.D.N. Clemente VIII. Pont. Max. aliquot Sanctorum festis aucto. Antverpiæ, Ex Officina Plantiniana, Apud Joannem Moretum. M.D.CIII. Cum gratia & priuilegio.
Colophon. Antwerpiæ, Ex Officina Plantiniana, Apud Joannem Moretum. M.D.CIII.
St. Gregory's Monastery, Downside.
125 × 65. Latin.

269*. 1614.

Office of the Blessed Virgin Marie with the Rubriques in English for the commoditie of those that doe not understand the Latin tongue. 1614. 644 pp. Not quite perfect.

Mr. C. Dolman's catalogue. June, 1853.

₊ The title of this book is almost similar to that of No. 277, 1633.

272*. c. 1619, (*John Heigham, St. Omers*) 12°.

The title-page is wanting; the book begins on

A 2. [Januarie] hath xxxi . dayes.

Ends on Ii 12ᵇ. Summa Privilegii. Albertus & Isabella, Clara Eugenia Archiduces Austriæ, Duces Burgundiæ, Brabantiæ, &c. . . . in literis datis Bruxellæ, I. Junii 1619. Signat. I. de Buschere.

Mr. Orby Shipley.

123 × 60. Latin and English.

₊ This book is the same as No. 271. A.D. 1616, except that "Litaniæ de D. Virgine in Æde Laurentana" is added; and on Gg11ᵇ. is omitted "An advertisement to the Reader, concerning this present edition, of the Office of our blessed Ladie in Latin, and Englishe. In the Calendar, of this edition, which ought to be thy truest tutor, when, and how, to serve the Saintes of the whole yeare, these severally are contained (following herein the laste Edition of the Roman Breviarie) which in all other English Primers, not set forth by me are wholie omitted. Their severall names doe here ensue. S. Romualdus Abbot, the 7 of Februarie . . . S. Eusebius Vercell. B. & mart. 15 of Deceb." The names of these Saints occur in the Calendar.

273*. 1627, *Paris, apud Gabrielem Clopejav*, 12°.

Officium B. Mariæ Virginis nuper reformatum, et Pii V. Pont. Max. jussu editum, ubi omnia suis locis sunt extensa. Cum indulgentiis et orationibus a Clemente VIII. ordinatis. Cum Kalendario Gregoriano. Parisius apud Gabrielem Clopejav via Jacobœa, sub signo Annuntiationis. M.DC.XXVII.

St. John's Coll. Oxford. Bc. 7. 5.

88 × 40. Latin.

A HAND-LIST. xxxiii

273**. 1630, *Jean le Boullenger, Rouen*, 12°.
The Primer, or Office of the Blessed Virgin Marie, in English. According to the last Edition of the Romane Breviarie. Printed at Rouen, by Jean le Boullenger. M.DC.XXX. Cum Gratia & privilegie.
Finis.
St. Gregory's Monastery, Downside.
122 × 63. English.

274*. 1631, *John Heigham, St. Omers*, 12°.
The Primer or Office of the Blessed Virgin Marie, in English. According to the last Edition of the Romaine Breviarie. Printed at S. Omers by John Heigham. Anno M.DC.XXXI. Cum Gratia & Priuilegio.
Finis.
Camb. Univ. Syn. 8. 63. 15.
95 × 53. English.

⁎ Some sheets of this edition are identical, as to letterpress, with No. 274. A.D. 1631; but without the copper cuts being printed in. Some are different and have woodcuts.

281*. *c.* 1665, 12°.
The title-page is wanting; the book begins on
A2. [January hath xxxi. dayes.] A1. Circumcision of our Lord (in red)
All wanting after Sign 7ᵇ. page 662.
Mr. Joseph Gillow.
114 × 59.

288*. 1700, *Nicolas Le Turner, Rouen*, 12°.
The Primer More Ample And In A New Order Containing The Three Offices of The B. Virgin Mary In Latin and English And all Offices and Devotions which were in former primers; last edition reviewed and corrected by P. R. with six Offices newly added. Rouen N. Le Turner 1700.
Mr. C. Dolman's catalogue June. 1853. Messrs. Bull and Auvache, catalogue c. 1890.
Latin and English.

⁎ The address to the reader is signed Thomas Fitzsimon. Priest. The title-page is engraved.

A⁵

288**. 1701, *Nicolas Le Turner, Rouen*, 12°.

The Primer More Ample, And in A New Order, Containing The Three Offices Of The B. Virgin Mary, In Latin and English. And all Offices and Devotions, which were in former primers, In this last Edition reviewed and corrected, by P. R. the Hymns are in a better verse and six Offices newly added. I. Of the holy Trinity : II. Of the B. Sacrament : III. Of the holy name of Jesus, with the Litany : IV. Of the Immaculate Conception of our B. Lady, with a Litany : V. Of the Angel-Guardian : VI. Of S. Joseph. And Sundry sweet Devotions, and Instructions taken out of the holy Scripture for to live a devout Christian life. A large and short examen of conscience. To the Calender are annexed many English and Irish Saints. Printed in Rouen, By Nicolas Le Turner, at the sign of the Turner in iron Cross street. With Permission. M.D.CCI.

Finis. It may please . . . he may happen to find. Then. A Table of the contents of this book.

St. Scholastica's Abbey, Teignmouth.

130 × 63. Latin and English.

291*. 1720, *London, for Thomas Meighan, London*, 12°.

The Office of the B. V. Mary in English. To which is added the Vespers, or Evensong, in Latin and English, As it is Sung in the Catholick Church. Upon all Sundays and principal Holydays throughout the whole Year. With the Compline, Rosary, Hymns and Prayers that are sung at the Benediction of the B. Sacrament. The Ordinary of the Holy Mass ; the Sequence, Dies iræ, dies illa, that is sung at solemn Mass for the Dead, and the Libera that is sung after Mass for the Dead : all in Latin and English. Together with several other Devout Prayers in English. London : Printed for Tho. Meighan, Bookseller in Drury-Lane. 1720.

Finis.

Mr. Joseph Gillow.

103 × 57. English.

A HAND-LIST.

294*. 1736, *London, for Thomas Meighan, London*, 12°.

The Office of the B. V. Mary in English. To which is added, The Ordinary of the Holy Mass in Latin and English ; the Sequence, Dies Iræ, and the Libera that is sung at Mass for the Dead. With the Vespers, or Even-Song, in Latin and English ; As it is Sung in the Catholick Church, Upon all Sundays and principal Holy-Days throughout the whole Year. The Compline, Rosary, Hymns and Prayers that are sung at the Benediction of the Blessed Sacrament. Together with several other Devout Prayers in English. London : Printed for Tho. Meighan, in Dury Lane. 1736.

Finis.

Rev^d. Reginald Tuke. St. Augustine's Priory, Newton Abbot. Mr. Cornish's Catalogue, Manchester, 1889.

102 × 54. English.

294**. 1737 (*London, for Thomas Meighan, London*), 12°.

The Second Part : containing The Holy Mass in Latin and English ; as also the Mass for the Dead, in English. The Vespers, or Evening-Song ; with the Antiphons, Psalms and Hymns, for all Sundays and Festivals of Obligation : The Method of saying the Rosary, in Latin and English. Printed in the Year MDCCXXXVII.

Finis.

Rev^d. Reginald Tuke.

102 × 54. Latin and English.

₊ This is the second part of No. 294*, A.D. 1736. It has a fresh pagination, and begins on sign. A 1. Another edition of this book was printed in 1750.

294***. 1750 (*London, for Thomas Meighan, London*), 12°.

The Second Part : containing The Holy Mass, in Latin and English ; as also the Mass for the Dead, in English. The Vespers, or Evening-Song ; with the Antiphons, Psalms, and Hymns, for all Sundays and Festivals of Obligation : The Method of saying the Rosary in Latin and English. Printed in the Year M.DCCL.

Finis.
St. Augustine's Priory, Newton Abbot.
105 × 32. Latin and English.
₊ This edition has a different English version of the offices and hymns from that in the edition of 1737. No. 294**.

296*. 1789, *James Haly, Cork*, 12°.
The Primer ; or, Office of the Blessed Virgin Mary. Cork : Printed by James Haly, at the King's Arms, North Main-street. M.DCC.LXXXIX.
Finis.
Camb. Univ. Syn. 8. 78. 41.
138 × 70. English.

296**. *c.* 1803, *published by R. Cross, Dublin*, 12°.
The Primer or, Office of the B. Virgin Mary, To which are added a New & Improved Version of the Church-Hymns, And the Remaining Hymns of the Roman Breviary ; With many useful Additions and Amendments. Dublin. Published by R. Cross, 28 Bridge Street.
Finis.
St. Mary's Convent, York.
146 × 76. English.

296***. 1804, *Ormskirk, for J. Fowler (Dublin)*, 12°.
The Lady's Primer ; or Office of the Blessed Virgin Mary, With a New and approved Version Of The Church Hymns. To which are added the remaining Hymns Of The Roman Breviary. Ormskirk : Printed for J. Fowler. 1804.
Finis.
Bodl. 138. i. 455. St. Mary's Abbey, Stanbrook.[1]
Mr. Joseph Gillow.
155 × 76. English.

296****. 1814, *Pickering and Co., Dublin*, 12°.
The Primer ; or Office of the Blessed Virgin Mary. Dublin : Printed by Wm. Pickering and Co. 8, Great Strand-Street. 1818.

---

[1] The Stanbrook copy has the date 1804 and measures 145 × 75.

A HAND-LIST. xxxvii

Finis.
Stonyhurst Coll.
120 × 70. English.

296*****. *c.* 1815, *Pickering and Son, Dublin*, 16°.

The Primer or Office of the B. Virgin Mary, To which are added a New and Improved Version Of The Church Hymns And the Remaining Hymns of the Roman Breviary. With many useful Additions & Amendments. Dublin, published by W. Pickering & Son, 8 Great Strand Street.

Finis.
St. Mary's Abbey, Stanbrook.
105 × 67. English.

297*. 1818, *Pickering and Co., Dublin*, 16°.

The Primer; or Office of the Blessed Virgin Mary. Dublin: Printed by Wm. Pickering and Co. 8, Great Strand-Street. 1818.

Finis.
St. Mary's Abbey, Stanbrook.
118 × 66. English.

297**. 1832, *Richard Grace and Son, Dublin*, 12°.

Officium parvum Beatæ Virginis Mariæ. With the english translation. Superiorum permissu, ac privilegio. Anno Domini 1832. Dublinii: Typis Ricardi Grace et Filii, 45, Capel-Street.

Ends on page 175. The Supper Grace is said at Dinner on Fast Days, on which the Vespers are said before Dinner.

Rev^d. Edgar Hoskins.
115 × 68. Latin and English.

297***. 1844, *P. J. Hanicq, Mechlin*, 8°.

The Office of the Blessed Virgin Mary, for the three times of the year, according to the Roman Breviary. Mechlin. P. J. Hanicq, Printer to the holy see, to the sacred congregation of the propaganda, and to the Archbishopric of Mechlin. Permissu Superiorum. 1844.

xxxviii SUPPLEMENT.

Colophon. Approbatio. Imprimatur. Mechliniæ 24 Septembris 1844. J. B. Pauwels. Vic. Gen.
Rev. Edgar Hoskins.
130 × 70. Latin.

297****. 1867, *John F. Fowler, Dublin,* 8°.
The Office of the Blessed Virgin Mary, and the Office for the Dead. Same as in the Evening Office Book of the St. John's Society, as established in Dublin. Dublin: John F. Fowler, 3 Crow Street, Dame Street. 1867.
The End.
Brit. Mus. 3433. bbbb. 42.
163 × 80. Latin and English.

A CONCISE LIST

OF

HORÆ OR PRIMERS.

EXPLANATIONS.

The measurement of the length and width of a page includes the head-line, the border, and the signature if they are there. The measurement is given in millimetres.

The form of the page, namely, folio, quarto, octavo, duodecimo, &c., is determined by the way in which the sheet of paper is folded; it is recognised by the direction of the wire marks, which are white lines occurring, as a rule, about an inch apart and running at right angles to the fine lines, and also by the position of the paper maker's device or water-mark. The wire-lines are perpendicular in a folio, octavo, 32mo, and horizontal in a quarto, 16mo. In a 12mo, as the name implies, the sheet is folded in twelve; and in the earlier part, at least, of the sixteenth century this was done in such a way that the wire-lines are perpendicular: the height of the sheet forming two pages, as is the case in an octavo, while the width is divided into six, instead of four as in an octavo. The later habit has been to fold the sheet differently, the height of the sheet forming the width of four pages, and the width of the sheet the height of three pages; consequently the wire-lines are horizontal.

Round brackets are used to distinguish suggestions as to the year in which the book was printed, the name of the printer, and the place at which the book was printed.

Square brackets are used to enclose head-lines and catch-words, as well as words or letters which are not clearly legible.

The letter "c" before a date stands for "circa".

The word "Language" in the concise list refers to "The Hours" but does not apply to all the contents of the book.

Three copies of each edition of a book have been given where it was possible to do so; when more than three copies are known to exist, preference has been given to a London, Oxford, and Cambridge Library.

The words "Apud," "Pro," "Impensis," and "Impensis et sumptibus" are rendered by the word "For"; the name that follows is that of the Bookseller.

A CONCISE LIST

OF

HORÆ OR PRIMERS.

Date	Printer	Place	Bookseller	Size of Page	Form	Language
c. 1478	(W. Caxton)	(Westminster)		80 × 57	8o	Lat.
c. 1480	(W. Caxton)	(Westminster)		130 × 85	4o	Lat.
c. 1485	(W. de Machlinia)	(London)		81 × 60	Vellum	Lat.
c. 1490	(W. Caxton)	(Westminster)		95 × 60	8o	Lat.
c. 1490	(W. Caxton)	(Westminster)		95 × 60	8o	Lat.
1491-2	(G. Leeu)	(Antwerp)			16o	Lat.
c. 1494	(W. de Worde)	(Westminster)		160 × 105	Vellum	Lat.
c. 1494	(W. de Worde)	(Westminster)		160 × 108	4o	Lat.
c. 1494	(W. de Worde)	(Westminster)		104 × 65	8o	Lat.
1495	(P. Pigouchet)	(Paris)		161 × 110	4o	Lat.
c. 1495	(J. Philippe)	(Paris)		124 × 79	Vellum	Lat.
c. 1495	(R. Pynson)	(London)		95 × 70	8o	Lat.
c. 1495	(P. Pigouchet)	(Paris)		133 × 84	8o	Lat.
1497	J. Barbier & J. H.	London	W. de Worde	120 × 80	8o	Lat.
1497	T. Kerver	(Paris)	J. Richard	140 × 90	8o	Lat.
c. 1497	R. Pynson	(London)		162 × 107	Vellum	Lat.
1498	P. Pigouchet	Paris	S. Vostre	143 × 91	Vellum	Lat.
1498	J. Jehannot	Paris	N. Lecomte	145 × 87	8o	Lat.
c. 1498		Paris	S. Vostre	143 × 93	Vellum	Lat.
c. 1498			J. Poitevin	145 × 90	8o	Lat.
1500	J. Notary	Westminster		85 × 27	32o	Lat.
c. 1500	(R. Pynson)	(London)		95 × 65	8o	Lat.
1501	P. Pigouchet	Paris	S. Vostre	172 × 110	Vellum	Lat.
1502	P. Pigouchet	Paris	S. Vostre	143 × 94	Vellum	Lat.
1502	W. de Worde	London		150 × 95	Vellum	Lat.
1503	W. de Worde	London		160 × 99	Vellum	Lat.
c. 1503	(W. de Worde)	(London)		154 × 92	Vellum	Lat.
c. 1503	J. Notary	London		162 × 102	Vellum	Lat.
c. 1503	(R. Pynson)	(London)		95 × 70	8o	Lat.
c. 1503		(Paris)	A. Verard	206 × 129	4o	Lat.

A CONCISE LIST OF

Date	Printer	Place	Bookseller	Size of Page	Form	Language
1506	W. Hopyl	Paris	W. Bretton	185 × 82	Vellum	Lat.
1506		Paris	A. Verard	159 × 88	Vellum	Lat.
c. 1507		Paris	S. Vostre	150 × 93	Vellum	Lat.
c. 1507		(Paris)	(S. Vostre)	152 × 92	8°	Lat.
c. 1507	(R. Pynson)	(London)		68 × 46	16°	Lat.
c. 1508	(W. de Worde)	(London)		108 × 70	8°	Lat.
1510	T. Kerver	Paris	W. Bretton	154 × 92	8°	Lat
c. 1510	(R. Pynson)	(London)		45 × 30	32°	Lat.
1511		Paris	F. Byrckman	160 × 97	4°	Lat.
c. 1512		(Paris)	S. Vostre	150 × 95	8°	Lat.
1513	W. de Worde	London		162 × 98	4°	Lat.
c. 1513	(R. Pynson)	(London)		161 × 96	4°	Lat.
1514		Paris	F. Byrckman	108 × 72	8°	Lat.
1514	R. Pynson	London		114 × 43	12°	Lat.
1514		Paris	F. Byrckman	158 × 96	4°	Lat.
1514	W. de Worde	London		114 × 42	12°	Lat.
c. 1514	(R. Pynson)	(London)		114 × 43	12°	Lat.
1515	(W. Hopyl)	Paris	F. Byrckman	158 × 95	4°	Lat.
c. 1515			P. Guerin	106 × 40	Vellum	Lat.
1516		Paris	F. Byrckman	160 × 101	4°	Lat.
c. 1516			(G. Bernard & J. Cousin)	185 × 121	4°	Lat.
1517			G. Bernard & J. Cousin	160 × 100	4°	Lat.
1519		Paris	F. Byrckman	160 × 100	4°	Lat.
1519	N. Higman	Paris	F. Regnault & F. Byrckman	215 × 130	4°	Lat.
1520		Paris	F. Byrckman	160 × 100	4°	Lat.
c. 1520	N. Higman	Paris	S. Vostre	199 × 114	4°	Lat.
c. 1520	N. Higman	Paris	S. Vostre	195 × 114	4°	Lat.
1521		Paris	F. Byrckman	165 × 102	4°	Lat.
1521		Paris	F. Byrckman	177 × 107	4°	Lat.
c. 1521	J. Bignon	Paris	R. Fakes	113 × 45	12°	Lat.
1522	R. Pynson	London		160 × 87	8°	Lat.
1523	W. de Worde	London		162 × 102	4°	Lat.
c. 1523	P. Kaetz	(London)		165 × 105	4°	Lat.
c. 1523	W. de Worde	London		120 × 45	12°	Lat.
1524		(Antwerp)		165 × 108	4°	Lat.
1524	C. Endoviensis	Antwerp	P. Kaetz	Width 45	16°	Lat.
1525	C. Endoviensis	Antwerp	F. Byrckman	164 × 102	4°	Lat.
1525		Rouen	J. Cousin	117 × 40	12°	Lat.

HORÆ OR PRIMERS.

Date	Printer	Place	Bookseller	Size of Page	Form	Language
c. 1525				118 × 45	12º	Lat.
1526	F. Regnault	Paris		145 × 58	12º	Lat.
1526	F. Regnault	Paris		215 × 130	4º	Lat.
1526	F. Regnault	Paris		161 × 99	Vellum	Lat.
c. 1526	(W. de Worde)	(London)		168 × 100	4º	Lat.
c. 1526	W. de Worde	London		159 × 102	4º	Lat.
c. 1526	(F. Regnault)	(Paris)		161 × 99	4º	Lat.
1527	F. Regnault	Paris		160 × 100	4º	Lat.
1527	F. Regnault	Paris		197 × 120	4º	Lat.
1527	F. Regnault	Paris		200 × 120	4º	Lat.
1527	N. Prevost	Paris	F. Byrckman	215 × 130	4º	Lat.
1527	F. Regnault	Paris		215 × 133	4º	Lat.
1527	F. Regnault	Paris		142 × 54	12º	Lat.
1527	Widow of T. Kerver	Paris	F. Byrckman	86 × 52	32º	Lat.
1528	Widow of T. Kerver	Paris	A. Plomier	87 × 47	Vellum	Lat.
c. 1528		Rouen	J. Cousin	118 × 45	12º	Lat.
c. 1528	G. Hardouyn	Paris		137 × 60	Vellum	Lat.
c. 1528				85 × 47	16º	Lat.
c. 1528				119 × 45	12º	Lat.
1530	C. Endoviensis	Antwerp		168 × 102	4º	Lat.
1530	F. Regnault	Paris		162 × 100	4º	Lat.
1530	F. Regnault	Paris		102 × 57	16º	Lat.
1530	G. Hardouyn	Paris		137 × 78	8º	Lat.
1530	C. Endoviensis	Antwerp		167 × 100	4º	Lat.
1530	F. Regnault	Paris		220 × 140	4º	Lat.
c. 1530	C. Endoviensis	Antwerp		205 × 140	4º	Lat.
1531	C. Ruremundensis	(Antwerp)		167 × 102	4º	Lat.
1531	F. Regnault	Paris		101 × 62	16º	Lat.
1531	F. Regnault	Paris		158 × 90	8º	Lat.
1531	F. Regnault	Paris		137 × 74	8º	Lat.
c. 1531	F. Regnault	Paris		137 × 74	8º	Lat.
c. 1531	(F. Regnault)	(Paris)		140 × 75	8º	Lat.
1532	W. Rastell	London		115 × 58	8º	Lat.
1532	F. Regnault	Paris		101 × 61	16º	Lat.
1532	Y. Bonhomme	Paris	J. Growte	103 × 55	16º	Lat.
1532	Y. Bonhomme	Paris	J. Growte	104 × 56	16º	Lat.
1532	F. Regnault	Paris		152 × 90	8º	Lat.
c. 1532				100 × 62	16º	Lat.
c. 1532				100 × 60	16º	Lat.

A CONCISE LIST OF

Date	Printer	Place	Bookseller	Size of Page	Form	Language
c. 1532				79 × 50	16º	Lat.
1533	F. Regnault	Paris		100 × 61	16º	Lat.
c. 1533	G. Hardouyn	Paris		120 × 78	8º	Lat.
c. 1533	R. Wyer	(London)		115 × 63	8º	Lat.
c. 1533				136 × 82	8º	Lat.
1534	F. Regnault	Paris		222 × 138	4º	Lat.
1534	Y. Bonhomme	Paris	J. Growte	102 × 55	16º	Lat.
c. 1534	J. Byddell	London	W. Marshall	110 × 63	8º	Eng.
1535	F. Regnault	Paris		198 × 125	4º	Lat.
1535	J. Byddell	London	W. Marshall	160 × 97	4º	Eng.
c. 1535	(N. Le Roux)	(Rouen)	(F. Regnault)	140 × 77	8º	Eng. Lat.
c. 1535	T. Godfray	London		117 × 64	8º	Eng.
c. 1535				79 × 48	16º	Eng.
c. 1535	(J. Byddell)	(London)		163 × 110	4º	Eng.
c. 1535	J. Byddell	London		123 × 80	8º	Eng. Lat.
1536	J. Byddell	London		87 × 50	16º	Lat.
1536	J. Gowghe	London		117 × 77	8º	Eng. Lat.
1536	N. Le Roux	Rouen	J. Groyat & J. Marchant	95 × 52	16º	Lat.
1536		Rouen		147 × 98	8º	Eng. Lat.
1537	N. Le Roux	Rouen	J. Cousin	140 × 78	Vellum	Lat.
1537		Rouen	F. Regnault	102 × 57	16º	Lat.
1537				117 × 47	12º	Lat.
c. 1537	(R. Redman)	(London)		164 × 115	4º	Eng. Lat.
c. 1537	(J. Byddell)	(London)		166 × 95	4º	Eng.
c. 1537	J. Byddell	London		124 × 78	8º	Eng. Lat.
c. 1537				127 × 75	8º	Eng.
1538	N. Le Roux	Rouen	F. Regnault	140 × 75	8º	Lat.
1538	F. Regnault	Paris		133 × 80	8º	Eng. Lat.
1538		Rouen	F. Regnault	136 × 74	8º	Lat.
1538	N. Le Roux	Rouen	F. Regnault	118 × 70	8º	Eng.
1538		Paris		147 × 92	8º	Eng. Lat.
1538		Rouen		152 × 90	8º	Lat.
1538	(N. Le Roux)	Rouen		141 × 80	8º	Eng. Lat.
1538	(N. Le Roux)	(Rouen)		140 × 87	8º	Eng. Lat.
1538	(R. Redman)	(London)		165 × 113	4º	Eng. Lat.
c. 1538	F. Regnault	Paris		136 × 70	8º	Lat.
1539	J. Wayland	London		158 × 109		Eng. Lat.
1539	J. Mayler	London	J. Wayland	156 × 98	8º	Eng.
c. 1539	J. Mayler	London	J. Wayland	128 × 79	8º	Eng.
c. 1539			H. Marshall	119 × 75	8º	Lat.

HORÆ OR PRIMERS.

Date	Printer	Place	Bookseller	Size of Page	Form	Language
c. 1539				102 × 73	8o	Eng.
c. 1539				128 × 80	8o	Lat.
c. 1539				75 × 60	8o	Eng.
c. 1539				147 × 82	8o	Eng. Lat.
c. 1539				84 × 55	16o	Eng.
1540	R. Grafton & E. Whitchurche	London		124 × 75	8o	Eng. Lat.
1540	N. Bourman	London		125 × 45	12o	Eng.
c. 1540				123 × 76	8o	Eng. Lat.
c. 1540				80 × 53	16o	Eng.
c. 1540				139 × 84	8o	Eng.
c. 1540				135 × 85	8o	Eng. Lat.
c. 1540				120 × 77	8o	Eng. Lat.
c. 1540	J. Mayler	London		150 × 92	8o	Eng. Lat.
1541	T. Petyt	London		60 × 36	32o	Lat.
1541	T. Petyt	London		141 × 90	8o	Eng. Lat.
c. 1541	J. Mayler	London		90 × 63	16o	Lat.
c. 1541	R. Toy	London		137 × 82	8o	Eng. Lat.
1542		(Antwerp)		149 × 80	8o	Lat.
1542		Rouen		113 × 65	8o	Lat.
1542	W. Bonham	London		162 × 113	4o	Eng. Lat.
1542	W. Bonham	London		162 × 112	4o	Eng. Lat.
1542	T. Petyt	London		130 × 82	8o	Eng. Lat.
1542	R. Toy	London		163 × 113	4o	Eng. Lat.
1543	T. Petyt	London		183 × 133	4o	Eng. Lat.
c. 1543	R. Grafton	London		58 × 35	32o	Eng.
1544	T. Petyt	London		83 × 53	16o	Lat.
1544	T. Petyt	London		129 × 84	8o	Eng. Lat.
1545	R. Grafton	London		114 × 57	8o	Eng.
1545	R. Grafton	London		157 × 90	4o	Eng.
1545	R. Grafton	London		110 × 57	8o	Eng.
1545	E. Whitchurche	London		155 × 87	4o	Eng.
1545	E. Whitchurche	London		110 × 58	8o	Eng.
1545	E. Whitchurche	London		115 × 61	8o	Eng.
1545	R. Grafton	London		152 × 100	4o	Eng. Lat.
1545	T. Petyt	London		83 × 53	16o	Lat.
1546	E. Whitchurche	London		125 × 80	8o	Eng. Lat.
1546	R. Grafton	London		66 × 34	16o	Eng.
1546	E. Whitchurche	London		75 × 48	16o	Eng.
1546	R. Grafton	London		160 × 88	4o	Eng.
1546	E. Whitchurche	London		112 × 60	8o	Eng.

Date	Printer	Place	Bookseller	Size of Page	Form	Language
1546	R. Grafton	(London)		115 × 56	8o	Lat.
1547	R. Grafton	London		158 × 86	4o	Eng.
1547	R. Grafton	London		160 × 88	4o	Eng.
1548	E. Whitchurche	London		120 × 68	8o	Eng. Lat.
c. 1548				82 × 47	16o	Eng.
c. 1548	R. Grafton	(London)		114 × 57	8o	Eng.
c. 1548				120 × 60	8o	Eng.
1549	R. Grafton	London		115 × 57	8o	Eng.
c. 1550	T. Gaultier	London	R. Toy	55 × 34	32o	Eng.
1551	R. Grafton	London		159 × 86	4o	Eng.
1551	R. Grafton	London		115 × 58	8o	Eng.
1551	N. Le Roux	Rouen	R. Valentin	143 × 76	8o	Lat.
1551			R. Valentin	96 × 55	16o	Lat.
1552	R. Grafton	London		113 × 59	8o	Eng.
1553	W. Seres	London		115 × 58	8o	Eng.
c. 1553	W. Seres	London		78 × 50	16o	Eng.
c. 1553				115 × 62	8o	Eng.
1554	J. Le Prest	Rouen	R. Valentin	142 × 77	8o	Lat.
1554	T. Petyt	London		126 × 80	8o	Lat.
1554		London		127 × 78	8o	Lat.
c. 1554				125 × 78	8o	Lat.
1555	J. Wayland	London		175 × 107	4o	Eng. Lat.
1555	R. Toy	London		125 × 78	8o	Lat.
1555	R. Caly	London		119 × 75	8o	Eng. Lat.
1555	R. Toy	London		126 × 76	8o	Lat.
1555	J. Wayland	London		120 × 71	8o	Eng.
1555	J. Wayland	London		167 × 107	4o	Eng. Lat
1555	J. Wayland	London		167 × 107	4o	Eng. Lat.
1555	J. Kyng	London	J. Waley	125 × 80	8o	Lat.
1555	J. Le Prest	Rouen	R. Valentin	140 × 77	8o	Lat.
1555			R. Valentin	97 × 54	16o	Lat.
1555		Rouen	R. Valentin	94 × 56	16o	Eng. Lat.
1555		Rouen	R. Valentin	112 × 66	8o	Lat.
1555		Rouen	R. Valentin	185 × 82	8o	Eng. Lat.
1556	R. Caly	London		118 × 76	8o	Eng. Lat.
1556	J. Kyngston & H. Sutton	London	J. Wight	127 × 77	8o	Lat.
1556	J. Kyng	London		118 × 65	8o	Eng.
1556		Rouen	R. Valentin	139 × 76	8o	Lat.
1556		Rouen	R. Valentin	138 × 84	8o	Eng. Lat.
1556		(Rouen)	F. Valentin	98 × 59	16o	Eng. Lat.

HORÆ OR PRIMERS.

Date	Printer	Place	Bookseller	Size of Page	Form	Language
c. 1556		London	J. Wight	126 × 80	8º	Lat.
c. 1556				118 × 75	8º	Eng. Lat.
c. 1556				125 × 75	8º	Lat.
c. 1556				115 × 68	8º	Lat.
c. 1556				125 × 78	8º	Lat.
1557	Assignes of J. Wayland	London		122 × 66	8º	Lat.
1557	Assignes of J. Wayland	London		124 × 75	8º	Eng. Lat.
1557	J. Kyngston & H. Sutton	London		167 × 113	4º	Eng. Lat.
1558	Assignes of J. Wayland	London		95 × 60	16º	Eng. Lat.
1558	Assignes of J. Wayland	London		93 × 59	16º	Eng. Lat.
1558	Assignes of J. Wayland	London		80 × 53	16º	Lat.
1558	Assignes of J. Wayland	London		125 × 74	8º	Eng. Lat.
1558	Assignes of J. Wayland	London		118 × 66	8º	Eng.
1559	Assignes of J. Wayland & W. Seres	London		158 × 87	4º	Eng.
c. 1559				114 × 57	8º	Eng.
c. 1559				110 × 65	8º	Eng.
1560	W. Seres	London		115 × 60	8º	Eng.
1560	W. Seres	London		120 × 58	8º	Lat.
c. 1560				114 × 59	8º	Eng.
c. 1560	(W. Seres)	(London)		115 × 60	8º	Eng.
1564	W. Seres	London		87 × 51	16º	Lat.
c. 1564				85 × 52	16º	Eng.
c. 1566	W. Seres	London		78 × 50	16º	Eng.
c. 1566				75 × 50	16º	Eng.
1568	W. Seres	London		110 × 58	8º	Eng.
1575	W. Seres	London		120 × 59	8º	Eng.
c. 1580	T. Purfoote	London		80 × 55	16º	(Eng.)
c. 1580				85 × 52	16º	Eng.
1627	R. Young	London		102 × 48	12º	Eng.
1668		Paris		130 × 73	8º	Eng.
c. 1670		London	Co. Stationers	80 × 55	16º	Eng.
1671		London	S. S.	135 × 74	8º	Eng.

xlviii A CONCISE LIST OF HORÆ OR PRIMERS.

Date	Printer	Place	Bookseller	Size of Page	Form	Language
c. 1685				88 × 58	16º	Eng.
1686		(London)	J. Watts	128 × 67	12º	Eng.
1700		London	W. Keble-white	144 × 68	12º	Eng.
c. 1710	R. Grafton	London		160 × 90	8º	Eng.
1717		(London)	D. Midwinter	165 × 84	8º	Eng.
1758		London	Co. Stationers	80 × 55	16º	Eng.
1825		London	C. & J. Rivington	135 × 72	12º	Eng.

A CONCISE LIST

OF

HORÆ OR PRIMERS ACCORDING TO THE ROMAN USE.

Date	Printer	Place	Bookseller	Size of Page	Form	Language
1571		Rome		123 × 60	12º	Lat.
1599	A. Conings	Antwerp		128 × 63	12º	Lat. Eng.
1604	A. Conings	Antwerp		129 × 63	12º	Lat. Eng.
1607	Plantinian Press	Antwerp	John Moret	125 × 65	8º	Lat.
1615	Henrie Jaey	Mackline		96 × 55	16º	Eng.
1616	John Heigham	St. Omers		119 × 64	12º	Lat. Eng.
1617	-			113 × 60	12º	Eng.
1621	John Heigham	St. Omers		127 × 63	12º	Lat. Eng.
1631	John Heigham	St. Omers		95 × 53	12º	Eng.
1632				124 × 64	12º	Eng.
1632				102 × 54	12º	Eng.
1633	J. Le Cousturier	(Rouen)		98 × 42	16º	Lat.
1633	J. Le Cousturier	(Rouen)		130 × 65	12º	Lat. Eng.
1644		Venice	ápud Cieras	254 × 172	4º	Lat.
1650	Widow of J. Cnobbaert	Antwerp	J. Thompson	113 × 60	12º	Lat. Eng.
1658	B. Moret	Antwerp		123 × 60	12º	Eng.
1669	D. Maurry	Rouen		129 × 62	12º	Lat. Eng.
1673		St. Omers		113 × 55	12º	Eng.
1684	N. Le Tourneur	Rouen		130 × 63	12º	Lat. Eng.
1685		Antwerp	T. D.	136 × 68	12º	Eng.
1687	H. Hills	London		105 × 53	8º	Eng.
c. 1687	H. Hills	London		94 × 48	16º	Lat.
1699				123 × 63	12º	Eng.
1706				142 × 70	12º	Eng.
1717		(London)	(T. Meighan)	140 × 70	12º	Eng.
1720	Widow of N. Le Turner	Rouen		128 × 62	12º	Lat. Eng.
1730	N. Le Turner	Rouen		130 × 64	12º	Lat. Eng.
1732		(London)	(T. Meighan)	144 × 72	12º	Eng.
1736					12º	Eng.
1770				133 × 70	12º	Eng.
1780	J. P. Coghlan	London		145 × 72	12º	Eng.
1817		Dublin	Coyne	115 × 65	12º	Eng.

A⁷

A CONCISE LIST

OF

HORÆ OR PRIMERS

ACCORDING TO

THE USE OF YORK.

Date	Printer	Place	Bookseller	Size of Page	Form	Language
c. 1510	(R. Pynson)	(London)		45 × 30	32º	Lat.
c. 1516			G. Bernard & J. Cousin	185 × 121	4º	Lat.
1517			G. Bernard & J. Cousin	160 × 100	4º	Lat.
1536	N. Le Roux	Rouen	J. Groyat & J. Marchant	95 × 52	16º	Lat.
1555	R. Toy	London		126 × 76	8º	Lat.
1556	J. Kyngston & H. Sutton	London	J. Wight	127 × 77	8º	Lat.
c. 1556		London	J. Wight	126 × 80	8º	Lat.
c. 1556				125 × 78	8º	Lat.

VARIATIONS IN
HORÆ BEATÆ MARIÆ VIRGINIS
Post Purificationem usque ad Adventum
ACCORDING TO
THE USES OF SARUM AND YORK.

SARUM USE.	YORK USE.
Ad Matutinas.	**Ad Matutinas.**
Resp. I. Sancta et immaculata virginitas ... Quia quem cæli ... *Versus.* Benedicta tu ... Quia quem cæli ...	*Resp. I.* Beata es virgo Maria quæ Dominum portasti ... Genuisti qui te ... *Versus.* Ave Maria ... Genuisti qui te ...
Resp. II. Beata es Maria quæ Dominum portasti ... Genuisti qui te ... *Versus.* Ave Maria ... Genuisti qui te ...	*Resp. II.* Sancta et immaculata virginitas ... Quia quem cæli ... *Versus.* Benedicta tu ... Quia quem cæli ...
Ad Laudes.	**Ad Laudes.**
Cap. Maria virgo semper lætare ... *Antiphona.* O gloriosa Dei genitrix ... *Canticum Zachariæ.* ℣. Ostende nobis Domine ... ℞. Et salutare tuum da nobis.	*Cap.* In omnibus requiem ... *Antiphona.* O gloriosa Dei genitrix ... *Canticum Zachariæ.* ℣. Domine exaudi ... ℞. Et clamor meus ...
Ad Primam.	**Ad Primam.**
Antiphona. O admirabile commercium ... *Psalmi.* Deus in nomine. Laudate Dominum. Confitemini Domino.	*Antiphona.* Quando natus es ... *Psalmi.* Beatus vir. Quare fremuerunt. Verba mea. Laudate Dominum.
Ad Tertiam.	**Ad Tertiam.**
Antiphona. Quando natus es ... *Psalmi.*	*Antiphona.* Rubum quem ... *Psalmi.*
Ad Sextam.	**Ad Sextam.**
Antiphona. Rubum quem ... *Psalmi.*	*Antiphona.* Germinavit radix ... *Psalmi.*
Ad Nonam.	**Ad Nonam.**
Antiphona. Germinavit radix ... *Psalmi.* *Cap.* Et radicavi ... ℣. Dignare me laudare ... ℞. Da mihi virtutem ...	*Antiphona.* Ecce Maria genuit ... *Psalmi.* *Cap.* Et radicavi ... ℣. Elegit eam Deus ... ℞. Et habitare facit ...
Ad Vesperas.	**Ad Vesperas.**
℣. Diffusa est gratia ... ℞. Propterea benedixit ... *An.* Sancta Maria ... *Canticum beatæ Mariæ.*	℣. Sancta Dei genitrix ... ℞. Intercede ... *An.* Sancta Maria ... *Canticum beatæ Mariæ.*
Ad Completorium.	**Ad Completorium.**
℣. Elegit eam Deus ... ℞. Et habitare facit ... *An.* Glorificamus te ... *Canticum Symeonis.*	℣. Ecce ancilla domini ... ℞. Fiat mihi ... *An.* Ecce completa sunt ... *Canticum Symeonis.*

HORÆ OR PRIMERS

IN

REGNAL PERIODS.

Edward IV.   Sarum Use.   A.D. 1478-1480, No. 1-2.

Henry VII.   Sarum Use.   A.D. 1485-1508, No. 3-36.

Henry VIII.   Sarum Use.   A.D. 1510, No. 37.
Sarum and York Uses.   A.D. 1510-1534, No. 38-114.
Sarum and York Uses and Reformed.   A.D. 1534-1544, No. 115-172.
Reformed.   A.D. 1545-1546, No. 173-186.

Edward VI.   Reformed.   A.D. 1547-1553, No. 187-202.
Sarum Use.   A.D. 1551, No. 197-198.

Queen Mary.   Reformed.   A.D. 1553, No. 201.
Sarum and York Uses.   A.D. 1554-1558, No. 203-238.

Queen Elizabeth.   Reformed.   A.D. 1559-1580, No. 239-254.
Roman Use.   A.D. 1571-1599, No. 266-267.

James I.   Roman Use.   A.D. 1604-1621, No. 268-273.

Charles I.   Reformed.   A.D. 1627, No. 255.
Roman Use.   A.D. 1631-1644, No. 274-279.

Commonwealth.   Roman Use.   A.D. 1650-1658, No. 280-281.

Charles II.   Reformed.   A.D. 1668-1671, No. 256-258.
Roman Use.   A.D. 1669-1684, No. 282-284.

James II.   Reformed.   A.D. 1685-1686, No. 259-260.
Roman Use.   A.D. 1685-1687, No. 285-287.

William and Mary.   Reformed.   A.D. 1700, No. 261.
Roman Use.   A.D. 1699, No. 288.

Queen Anne.   Reformed.   A.D. 1710, No. 262.
Roman Use.   A.D. 1706, No. 289.

George I.   Reformed.   A.D. 1717, No. 263.
Roman Use.   A.D. 1717-1720, No. 290-291.

George II.   Reformed.   A.D. 1758, No. 264.
Roman Use.   A.D. 1730-1736, No. 292-294.

George III.   Roman Use.   A.D. 1770-1817, No. 295-297.

George IV.   Reformed.   A.D. 1825, No. 265.

ADDITIONS AND CORRECTIONS IN THE HAND-LIST OF HORÆ OR PRIMERS, AND IN THE SUMMARY OF THE CONTENTS.

Page 7. No. 15. Rev. E. S. Dewick has a copy of this edition without the device of J. Philippe.

Page 8. No. 21. This fragment was sold at Sotheby's 1896. Feb. 14 No. 120 in an extra volume of Herbert's Ames Typographical Antiquities which contains specimen leaves of early English typography.

Page 11. No. 28. For "Impresse London . . . Saynt Clement parryshe . . . at the sygne of the thre kynges." Read "Impresse London . . . Saynt. Clements | paryshe."

Page 16. No. 43. 1514. Jan. 1. For "Francis Bryckman" read "Francis Byrckman."

Page 24. No. 62. For "Brit. Mus. C. 51. e. 2" Read "Brit. Mus. C. 52. e. 2."

Page 24. No. 63. For "Hore beate Marie virginis" read "Hore beate marie virginis."

Page 43. No. 115. For "The roya arms" read "The royal arms."

Page 48. No. 130. Last line. For "English" read "English and Latin."

Page 49. No. 131. This book as well as No. 222* 1556 has on Signature B.1. "God save the church our King and realm."

Page 50. No. 137. The title page of this book is a facsimile of the title page of No. 132, which is not the same edition as No. 137.

Page 51. No. 142. line 10. For "& the Kynges calling" read "at the Kynges calling."

Page 52. No. 144. line 6. For "Set forth by Tho. laet byshop of Rochester" read "Set forth by Jho. laet byshop of Rochester."

Page 56. No. 155. This book is the same as No. 162.

Page 58. No. 162. For "Colophon. Imprinted in Paules churcheyarde by Robert Toye." read "Colophon. Prynted in Pauls churcheyarde by Roberte Toye." This book is the same as No. 155.

liv ADDITIONS AND CORRECTIONS.

Page 67. No. 192 read

¶1. An iniūccyon ‖ gyuen by the kyng our souerei— ‖ gne lordes moste excellente ma ‖ iestie, for the autorysyng ⁊ ‖ establishyng the vse of ‖ this Prymer.

Page 68. No. 197. For "And be newly emprynted at Rouen" read "And be newly enprynted at Rouen."

Page 74. No. 216. For "Brit. Mus. C. 51. a. 6." read "Brit. Mus. C. 52. a, 6."

Page 75. No. 219. For "bibliopopolarū particulo" read "bibliopolarū porticulo."

Page 81. No. 239. Dele. "Brit. Mus. 3406. c. 45."

Page 86. No. 225. 9th Ed. 1693. After "Luke Meredith" add "at the Star in St. Paul's Church-yard."

Page 91. No. 261. 6th Ed 1730. Add "Bodl. Mason. AA. 327."

Page 92. No. 263. Dele. "6th ed. 1730." Bodl. Mason. AA. 327. (10).

Page 92. No. 264. line 6. For "1766" read "1758." line 8. After "Mr. Samuel Sandars" add "Bequest to Camb. Univ." also "Ed. 1766. Brit. Mus. 3408. aa. 44." All the other editions are in Camb. Univ. Library.

Page 95. No. 271. lines 1 and 6. For "John Heighan" read "John Heigham."

Page 102. No. 292. line 21. For "Rev: W. Holmes" read "Rev: T. S. Holmes."

Page 121. line 18. For "though" read "thorough."

Page 137. line 24. For "Nam et si" read "Nā & si."

Page 253. After "c. A.D. 1559. 4o English." add No. 239.*

Page 304. line 29. After "The sentences of holy Scripture" read "When the wicked man."

Page 309. line 19. For "A.D. 1700—A.D. 1758" read "A.D. 1700—A.D. 1765."

Page 316. last line. For "page 311" read "page 313."

Page 325. line 7. For "A.D. 1700—A.D. 1758" read "A.D. 1700—1765."

Page 347. line 9. For "A.D. 1571—A.D. 1844" read "A.D. 1571—A.D. 1867."

Page 365. last line. For "Tabula temporalia" read "Tabula temporalis."

ADDITIONS AND CORRECTIONS IN THE INDEXES.

Page
383. "A rod shall come" (*Lesson*) 253.   "Ad cœnam" 378.
389. "Ave salus" 78.   "Ave Sanguis" 78.
390. "Bless we the Lord" 164.
391. "Christus passus est pro nobis" 259.   "Christus resurgens a mortuis" 259.
392. "Commendo tibi Domine animam famuli tui" 146.
393. "Deliver us, save us, and justify us" 198.
394. "Deus servet ecclesiam regem vel reginam custodiat" 267.
394. "Deus in te speravi" 15.
397. "Domine ne in furore tuo" 260.   "Domine sic vel sic contra tuam voluntatem peccavi" 136.
399. "Domine Jesu Christe qui me creasti" 2. 111.
400. "Domine qui fons es sapientiæ omnis" add (*Psalmus*).
400. "Ecce mensurabiles posuisti dies meos" add (*Psalmus*).
401. "Et famulos tuos summum pontificem" 374.
401. "Ever glorious and blessed Mary" 380.   For "Exaudi quæsumus Dne. supplicum preces" 252, read "Exaudi . . . preces" 352.
404. "Grant we beseech thee Almighty God that we which believe." 178.
405. "Gratias tibi ago Dne. s. Pater omn. æterne Deus qui me indignum famulum tuum" 135.
407. "Holy Virgin Mary mother of God" 240.
407. "How hast thou O Lord humbled" add (*Psalm*).
407. "How hast thou O Lord humbled" add (*Psalm*).
409. "In the name of the Father" 344
411. "Laud be to the Lord King of eternal glory." 183.
412. "Legem pone" 280.
412. "Lord hear thou my words" add (*Psalm*).
414. "Magnus Dominus (*Psalm*)" 379.
415. "Most blessed redeemer I do most truly believe" 321
418. "O Domine Jesu qui es sola salus" 185.
423. "O Lord give us increase of faith" 247.
428. "O salutaris hostia" 78.   "O sanguis" 78.
428. "O sweet Jesu my only heart's desire" 223.

ADDITIONS AND CORRECTIONS.

Page
431. "Omnis anima potestatibus" add (*Lesson*).
432. "Our most gracious sovereign lord King Charles." 304.
434. "Qui pro alio orat pro seipso laborat" 130.
435. "Remember that thou keep holy." 304.
437. "Suscipe clementissime Deus." 354.
530. To "Office for the dead 379" add "313. 315."

A HAND-LIST
OF
HORÆ OR PRIMERS.

1. (*c.* 1478, *William Caxton, Westminster*) 8°.
Twelve lines to a full page. Without initials, signatures, catchwords or numbering. Printed entirely in black. Space left for 2-line initials. Known only from a fragment consisting of four leaves; 1, 2, 7, 8 of a quire.
  Begins. sue salutarem consequātur.
  Ends. Benedicam[9] dño Deo g̃s.
  Contents. A portion of the Suffragia at Lauds (St. Thomas of Canterbury, St. Nicholas, St. Mary Magdalen, St. Katharine, St. Margaret . . .) the Three Kings, St. Barbara.
  Bodl. Douce Fragm. 9.
  80 × 57. Latin.

2. (*c.* 1480, *William Caxton, Westminster*) 4°.
Twenty lines to a full page. Without initials, signatures, catchwords or numbering. Printed entirely in black. Space left for 2-line initials. Known only from two fragments consisting of two leaves and two pages, not consecutive, printed side by side on one side of a piece of paper, of which the other side is left blank; evidently a proof sheet.
  Contents. First leaf. The Antiphon to the Seven Psalms (Ne reminiscaris) and the Psalms (Domine ne in furore, Beati quorum). Second leaf. Suffragia (De tribus regibus). First page. Orationes S. Brigide. Second page. The Preces at the end of the Litany (Deus qui caritatis dona, Deus a quo sancta desideria). This description follows the order in which the fragments are at present bound.
  Brit. Mus. C. 40. l. 1. (4).
  130 × 85. Latin.

3. (c. 1485, *William de Machlinia, London*) on vellum. Seventeen lines to a full page. Two sizes of type are used. Without initials, signatures, catchwords or numbering. A border round the pages which contain the commencement of the Seven Psalms and the Psalms of the Passion.

Ten fragments of this book are known, namely: British Museum; three of two leaves each: one of one leaf. Lincoln Cathedral; two of two leaves each. Cambridge University; two of one leaf each, which are duplicates of two leaves at Lincoln. Corpus Christi College, Oxford; two of four leaves each.

Brit. Mus. Two leaves; 3, 6 of a quire. One leaf containing a portion of the Suffragia at Lauds (St. John Apostle, St. Lawrence, St. Stephen, St. Thomas of Canterbury). One leaf containing the concluding portion of Lauds (Collect for peace, Matins of the Cross).

Lincoln Cath. Four leaves; 2, 3, 6, 7 of a quire. Two leaves containing a portion of the Suffragia (Salve Regina, Gaude Virgo, Gaude flore). Two leaves containing the Antiphon to the Seven Psalms (Ne reminiscaris) and the three first of the Seven Psalms (Domine ne in furore, Beati quorum, Domine ne in furore).

Brit. Mus. Two leaves; 1, 8 of a quire. One leaf containing a portion of one of the Seven Psalms (Domine ne in furore). One leaf containing portions of two of the Fifteen Psalms (Memento Domine, Ecce quam bonum).

Brit. Mus. Three leaves. One leaf containing a portion of the first of the Psalms of the Passion (Deus, Deus meus). Two leaves, 2, 3, or 6, 7 of a quire, containing portions of the two last Psalms (Exaltabo te Domine, In te Domine speravi), the Prayer "Respice quæsumus," two little prayers which King Harry the Sixth made (Domine Jesu Christe qui me creasti, Domine Jesu Christe qui solus).

Corpus Christi Coll., Oxford. Four leaves; 2, 3, 6, 7 of a quire. Two leaves containing portions of the Psalms of the Dirige (Ad te Domine levavi, Dominus illuminatio mea). Two leaves containing portions of the Psalms of the Dirige (Quis mihi tribuat, Expectans expectavi).

Corpus Christi Coll., Oxford. Four leaves; 2, 3, 6, 7 of a quire. Two leaves containing portions of the Psalms of the Commendations (Iniquos odio, Feci judicium, Mirabilia testimonia, Justus es Domine, Clamavi in toto). Two leaves containing the concluding portion of the last Psalm of the Commendations (Domine probasti) and the Prayer (Tibi Domine commendamus).

Brit. Mus. Bagford Fragm. 463. h. 8. fo. 12.
Corpus Christi Coll. Oxford. Camb. Univ. Lincoln Cath.
81 × 60. Latin.

4. (*c.* 1490, *William Caxton, Westminster*) 8°.
Sixteen lines to a full page. Without catchwords or numbering. Printed entirely in black. Printed 2-line initials and cuts. Lombardic capitals in black. Known only from a fragment consisting of eight leaves; 1-8 of signature M.

Contents. A portion of Orationes S. Brigide. Oratio S. Gregorii. A devout prayer to our Lord (O pie crucifixe).

Brit. Mus. C. 35. a. 7. (2).
95 × 60. Latin.

5. (*c.* 1490, *William Caxton, Westminster*) 8°.
Sixteen lines to a full page. Without catchwords or numbering. Printed in black and red. Printed 2-line initials. Lombardic capitals in red. Known only from a fragment consisting of four leaves; 1, 2, 3, 4 of signature D.

Contents. The concluding portion of Lauds.

Brit. Mus. C. 35. a. 7. (1).
95 × 60. Latin.

6. (1491-92, *Gerard Leeu, Antwerp*) 16°.
This fragment cannot at present be found. Mr. Henry Bradshaw has left the following MS. note upon it:

"Horæ B.V.M. ad usum ecclesiæ Sarisburiensis Anglicanæ (Antwerp, Gerard Leeu, 1491-92) 16°. Eight leaves only remaining, being signature K; type, Holtrop 'Monumens typographiques des Pays Bas,' plate 102 (57) d; long lines.

"The first remaining leaf begins (in the suffrage de S. Georgio martyre): xp̄i miles ut hostes visibiles & in ‖.

"I found this, 10th January, 1883, while looking through the library of Brasenose College, Oxford, with Mr. Madan. The half-sheet forming sign. K in 16° was used for lining the end board of a 'Scriptores rei rusticæ' printed at Reggio, in the duchy of Modena, in 1496, and bound, while still new, in England. It was probably bound by the London stationer who imported the Horæ from Antwerp, as the sheet had never been folded, and the book consequently had never been sold and used."

7. (c. 1494, *Wynkyn de Worde, Westminster*) on vellum.
The book has no title-page; it begins at once on
    A1. KL Mensis Januarii habet dies xxxi
   Colophon. Thyse forsayd prayers as the . xv . oes in englysshe ⁊ yᵉ other folowyng ben enprynted by yᵉ cōmaūdemētys of yᵉ moost hye ⁊ vertuous pryncesse our lyege lady Elyzabeth by the grace of god quene of englond ⁊ of fraūce / ⁊ also of the ryght hye ⁊ moost noble pryncesse Margarete moḋ to our souerayn lord yᵉ kyng ⁊c.

    Lambeth Archiep. 25. 1. 23.   Bodl. Arch. Bodl. D. subt. 59.
    Camb. Univ. G. 4. 4. and G. 3. 61.
    160 × 105. Latin.

⁂ The Lambeth copy reads "prout tibi placet" instead of "prout tibi placeret" on sign F 8ᵇ, and the inner side of that sheet (pages F1ᵇ, F2ᵃ, F7ᵇ, F8ᵃ) has been set up afresh in order to "perfect" the corrected copies. See H. Bradshaw's "Collected Papers," Cambridge, 1889, page 345.

8. (c. 1494, *Wynkyn de Worde, Westminster*) 4°.
The book has no title-page: it begins, wanting A1, on
    A2. KL Mensis Marcii habet dies xxxi
   All wanting after p7ᵇ. q̄ sustinui te [L]ibera deus israel ex om. (in the Psalms of the Passion).

    Brit. Mus. C. 35. e. 5.
    160 × 108. Latin.

⁂ This is the only copy of this edition which is known; it agrees page for page with the preceding one, but is not identical.

9. (*c.* 1494, *Wynkyn de Worde, Westminster*) 8°.
Seventeen lines to a full page. Printed in black and red. Lombardic capitals in red. Known only from a fragment consisting of six leaves ; 1, 2, 3, 4, 6, 7 of signature Y.

Begins on y1. christū in colūbe specie : et supra.

All wanting after y7ᵇ (in the contents). The verses of saynt bernard ‖ with foure deuoute prayers fo ‖ wynge.

Contents. A portion of Oratio ad spiritum sanctum. A prayer late showed to a monk of Bynham (Deus propitius esto) with a collect to St. Michael (Deus qui miro ordine). A prayer to St. Erasmus (Sancte herasme martyr christi). A prayer to St. Rock (Confessor dei). Two leaves of contents.

Corpus Christi Coll. Oxford. fragments.

104 × 65. Latin.

*** The contents of this book are not one half of those of the quarto edition of the same date.

10. 1495 (*Philippe Pigouchet, Paris*) 4°.

Hore intemerate beatissime virginis Marie scđm usum Sarum. nouiter īpresse cum multis orationibus et suffragiis nouiter additis. A1.

Colophon. Expliciūt hore btē marie virginis secundū usū sarū nouiter impsse cū mītis orōib⁹ ꝛ suffragiis nouiter additis. Anno dñi. M.CCCC.xcv.

Brit. Mus. C. 35. e. 6. Bodl. Douce 24.

161 × 110. Latin.

11. (*c.* 1495, *Jean Philippe, Paris*) on vellum.

The book has no title-page ; it begins at once on

A1. KL Januarius habet dies . xxxi. Lu ‖ na vero . xxx. a.

B7ᵇ. Hore intemerate beate marie vir ‖ ginis secundum usum sarum.

Ends on m8ᵇ. us per omnia secula seculorum. Amen (in prayer O intemerata ꝛ in eternum benedicta).

Brit. Mus. C. 35. b. 1.

124 × 79. Latin.

12. (*c.* 1495, *Richard Pynson, London*) 8°.
Seventeen lines to a full page. Without initials, signatures, catchwords or numbering. Printed entirely in black. Lombardic capitals. Space left for 2-line initials. Known only from a fragment consisting of two leaves ; 4, 5 of a quire.

Begins. [D]ominus regit me ꞇ nihil mi.
Ends. ceciderunt. Si cōsistāt aduersū me.
Contents. Three Psalms of the Dirige (Dominus regit me, Ad te dñe leuaui, Dominus illuminatio).
Bodl. 8° Rawl. 586.
95 × 70. Latin.

13. (*c.* 1495, *Philippe Pigouchet, Paris*) 8°.
Twenty-seven lines to a full page. Printed in black and red. Known only from a fragment consisting of four leaves ; 1, 4, 5, 8 of signature G.

Begins. domine animas eorum. Pater Noster. Et.
Ends. manu inimicorū nostrorum liberati seruia.
Contents. A portion of Vigiliæ Mortuorum.
Bodl. Printed Fragment from Dr. Bliss's Papers.
133 × 84. Latin.

14. 1497, April 3, *Jean Barbier and J. H., London, for Wynkyn de Worde, Westminster*, 8°.
Twenty-one lines to a full page. Without catchwords or numbering. Printed in black and red. Lombardic capitals in red. Borders. Known only from a fragment consisting of four leaves ; 1, 4, 5, 8 of signature r.

Begins. esto dñe : ne tardauer?. In te dñe.
Colophon. Hore beate marie scdm usuȝ Saꝝ diligēter emēdate ac nouiꞇ impresse Londoñ. apud sanctū Thomam apostolū pro winando de worde expliciūt feliciter. Anno dñi mille° cccc° nonage° vii° tercia die mensis aprilis. (Mark of Jean Barbier and J. H.)
Contents. A portion of St. Jerome's Psalter, and the Rosary of our Lady.
Bodl. Douce Addˢ. f. 7.
120 × 80. Latin.

15. 1497, *Thielman Kerver (Paris), for Jean Richard, Rouen*, 8°.

Hore beate Marie ẙgīs secundū usum Sarum a (Mark of Thielman Kerver).

Colophon. Hoc presens officium beate marie cū multis deuotis suffragiis ad usum saruӡ finita sunt. Anno domini millesimo quadringentesimo nonagesimo septimo Pro iohanne ricardo mercatore librario rothomagi commoranti iuxta magnaӡ ecclesiam beate marie (Device of J. Philippe).

ꝛ1. Auxiliatrix sis michi trinitas sctā

Ends on ꝛ8ᵇ. Per omnia secula ‖ seculorum. Amen (in prayer Deus qui nos conceptionis).

Brit. Mus. C. 41. a. 17 (on vellum). Bodl. Douce 25.
Camb. Univ. AB. 5. 41.
140 × 90. Latin.

16. (*c.* 1497) *Richard Pynson (London)* on vellum.

Hore intemerate beatissime virginis Marie secundum usum Sarū nouiter impresse cū multis orationibus et suffragiis nouiter additis . feliciter incipiunt. A.

Colophon. Expliciunt hore beate marie virginis scdm usū Saru nouiter impresse cū multis orationibus ꝛ suffragiis nouiter additis. Per Ricardum Pynson.

Bodl. Douce BB. 128.
162 × 107. Latin.

17. 1498, May 16, *Philippe Pigouchet, Paris, for Simon Vostre, Paris*, on vellum.

Hore presentes ad usum Sarum impresse fuerūt Parisius per Philippū pigouchet Anno salutis . M.CCCC.xcviii . die vero . xvi . Maii . pro Symone vostre : librario cōmorante ibidē : in vico nuncupato nouo beate Marie . in intersignio sancti Iohannis euangeliste. S a. i.

Ends on q8ᵇ. The rosare (in the contents).

Brit. Mus. C. 41. a. 18. Bodl. Douce 23.
Camb. Univ. AB. 5. 33*b*.
143 × 91. Latin.

18. 1498, *Jean Jehannot, Paris, for Nicolas Lecomte, London*, 8°.

Hore beate marie virginis secundum usum Sarum J. Jehannot. A.

Colophon. Hoc presens officiũ beate marie virginis de nouo reuisũ ꝶ correctũ cum multis suffragiis ad usum insignis ecclesie sarisburiceñ ĩ p̄iclara uniũsitat͡ʠ parisieñ. Pro nicolao coïtis eiusdem uniuersitatis supposito pro nunc in anglia librorum mercatore. Anno dominice incarnationis nonagesimo octauo Per iohannem Iehannot.

ꝶ1. These prayers folowyng ought to be sayd or thou departe out of thy chambre at thyn uprisinge.

Ends on ꝶ8ᵇ. regnas deus. Per omnia secula seculoruȝ. Amen (in prayer Deus qui nos conceptionis).

Trin. Coll. Camb. VI*. 4. 3. (2). Rev. W. J. Blew.

145 × 87. Latin.

19. (*c.* 1498) *Paris, for Simon Vostre, Paris*, on vellum.

Incipiunt hore beate marie virginis secũdum usum sarum nouiter impresse parisii pro symone le vostre cõmorante in vico nouo beate marie virginis in intersignio sancti iohannis euangeliste.

Colophon. Expliciunt hore beate marie virginis secundũ usum sarum nouiter impresse parisii pro symone le vostre cõmorantem in vico nouo marie in intersignio sancti iohãnis euangeliste.

Earl Spencer No. 49.

143 × 93. Latin.

20. (*c.* 1498) *for Jean Poitevin, Paris*, 8°.

Hore ad usũ Sarrum impresse pro Iohãne Poitevin cõmorãte parisius in vico nouo beate Marie. a

Ends on q8ᵇ. The rosare (in the contents).

Trin. Coll. Dublin. Press B. 2. 13.

145 × 90. Latin.

21. 1500, April 2, *Julian Notary, Westminster*, 32°.

Printed in black and red. Known only from a fragment formerly in the possession of John Fenn, Esq., described in

Herbert's Ames (Typographical Antiquities, page 303). It consisted of a half-sheet, containing the two signatures i and k, sixteen leaves.

"¶ The contents conteyned in thys boke. Fyrst a Kalander. A prayer to say at your vprysynge, &c."

Colophon. Thys Emprynteth at Westmynster by me Julyan Notary. Dwellynge in kyng strete. Anno domini M.vC. ii. die mencis Aprilis.

1½ inches × 1 inch. Latin.

₊ Of a fragment of five lines in the Cambridge University Library Mr. H. Bradshaw has written the following note: "This is possibly a portion of that edition mentioned by Herbert". It contains a portion of De S. Sebastiano in Suffragia Sanctorum after Lauds.

22. (*c.* 1500, *Richard Pynson, London*) 8°.
Twenty lines to a full page. Without initials, signatures, catchwords or numbering. Printed entirely in black. Space left for 2-line initials. Known only from a fragment consisting of two leaves, 4, 5 of a quire.

Begins. tis pturbat me. Quia in

Ends. depcamur / ut aīas famuloɟ famula (in prayer Inclina dñe aurem).

Contents. Concluding portion of the Dirige.

Corpus Christi Coll. Camb. End paper to No. 82 of Archbishop Parker's books.

95 × 65. Latin.

23. 1501, October 20, *Philippe Pigouchet, Paris, for Simon Vostre, Paris*, on vellum.

Hore p̄sentes ad ūsū Sarū impresse fuerūt Parisius p Philippū pigouchet Anno dñi . M.V.C. prīo . die vero . xx . Octobris . pro Symone vostre: librario cōmorante ibidē: in vico nuncupato nouo btē marie. in ītersignio sctī Johīs euāgeliste. S a. i.

p6. The contentis of thys booke.

p7. line 26. Oratio dicenda die sabbati ad honorem in ‖ temerate dei genitricis virginis marie. ‖ Missus est gabriel.

Ends on p10ᵇ. Per omnia secula secu ǁ lorum. Amen (in prayer Interveniat pro nobis).

Brit. Mus. C. 29. h. 12.   Bodl. Arch. Bodl. D. subt. 70.
Mr. J. F. F. Horner.
172 × 110. Latin.

24. 1502, March 8, *Philippe Pigouchet, Paris, for Simon Vostre, Paris,* on vellum.

Hore presentes ad usum Sarum impresse fuerūt Parisius per Philippū pigouchet Anno dñi . M.CCCCC.ii die vero . viii . Marci . pro Symone vostre : librario cōmorante ibidē : in vico nuncupato nouo beate Marie . in intersignio sancti Johannis euangeliste. Sa. i.

Ends on q8ᵇ. The rosare (in the contents).

Bodl. Gough Missals 87.   Mr. A. H. Huth.
143 × 94. Latin.

25. 1502, *Wynkyn de Worde, London,* on vellum.

The book has no title-page ; it begins at once on
A1. KL Januarius habet dies . xxxi.

Colophon. Hore beate marie virginis ad usum insignis ecclesie Sarū finiunt feliciter / una cū multis sanctorᴀ ꝫ sanctaᴀ suffragiis / et multis aliis diuersis orationibus nouiter supadditis. Impresse Londonii per me wïnandum de worde commorantem in vico nūcupato de Fletestrete ad signum solis. Anno M.ccccii.

Bodl. Gough Missals 173.
150 × 95. Latin.

26. 1503, July 31, *Wynkyn de Worde, London,* on vellum.

Hore beate Marie virginis secundum usum Insignis ecclesie Sarum / totaliter ad longum ꝫ sine require.

Colophon. Hore beate marie virginis ad usum insignis ecclesie Sarū finiunt feliciter / una cū multis sanctoᴀ ꝫ sanctarū suffragiis / ꝫ multis aliis diuersis oratiōibus nouiter superadditꝫ : cū quattuor euangeliis ꝫ passione dñi / ꝫ cū horis dulcissimi nomīs Jesu. Impresse Londonii ꝑ me winandum de worde / commorantē in vico appellato the

Fletestrete ad signũ solis.   Anno . M.ccccc.iii ultima die mensis Julii.

aa. Incipiunt hore dulcissimi nominis Jesu.

Ends on aa6. dicat ꝛ custodiat corda ꝛ corpora nostra. Amen (in Horæ dulcissimi nominis Jesu).

Brit. Mus. C. 41. e. 8.
160 × 99. Latin.

27. (*c.* 1503, *Wynkyn de Worde, London*) on vellum.
The title-page is wanting; the book begins on
Aa2 ... sol in ariete. Eq̃noctiũ.
Aa3. xi A   Sancte marie egyptiace (in the Kalendar).
All wanting after A prayer of the fyue woundes of oure lorde (in the contents).

Lincoln Cath. RR. 5. 32.
154 × 92. Latin.

28. (*c.* 1503) *Julyan Notary, London*, on vellum.
Hore beate Marie virginis secundum usum Insignis ecclesie Sarum / totaliter ad longum ꝛ sine require.

Colophon. Hore beate marie virginis ad usum insignis ecclesie Sarũ finiunt feliciter / una cũ multis sanctoꝝ et sanctaꝝ suffragiis / et multis aliis diuersis oratiõibus nouiter superaddit̃ cũ quattuor euangeliis et passione dñi / et cũ horis dulcissimi nomĩs Jesu.   Impresse London without Tempell barre in. Saynt Clement / parryshe be me. Julyan / Notary dwellynge at the sygne of the thre kynges.

Duke of Devonshire.
162 × 102. Latin.

29. (*c.* 1503, *Richard Pynson, London*) 8°.
Seventeen lines to a full page. Without signatures, catchwords or numbering. Printed entirely in black. Space left for 2-line initials. Known only from a fragment consisting of four leaves; 1, 4, 5, 8 of a quire.

Begins. Amen.   Pater noster.   Aue maria ‖.   A deuoute prayer to the pyte of ‖ oure lorde iesu christe.

All wanting after 8ᵇ. sis testibus accusari colaphis cedi et
Contents. Portions of Oratio S. Gregorii, Orationes S. Brigide, Oratio S. Bernardini, A deuoute prayer to oure lorde crucifyed (O pie crucifixe).

Gonville and Caius Coll. Camb. fragments.
95 × 70. Latin.

30. (*c.* 1503) (*Paris*) *for Antoine Verard* (*Paris*) 4°.
Hore beate virginis Marie ad usum Sarum.
x8 Pro anthonio verard (after the contents).
Colophon. Hore intmerate diue virginis marie secundum usum. Sarum

Brit. Mus. C. 35 e. 4. Mr. James Toovey, 1885.
Mr. Samuel Sandars.
206 × 129. Latin.

31. 1506, Kal. ix Aprilis, *Wolfgang Hopyl, Paris, for William Bretton, London,* on vellum.
Hore beatissime ẙginis marie ad cõsuetudinẽ insignis ecclesie Sarũ nup emaculatissime ĩpresse : multis orationibᵠ pulcherrimis annexis. Impẽsis atq̃ sũptibus honesti mercatoris wilhelmi brettõ ciuis Lõd.
Colophon. Hore diue marie virginis ad usũ p̃clare eccl̃ie Sarũ : cum multis sanctorũ sctãrũq̃ suffragiis denuo superadditis. In alma Parrhisiorũ academia per wolffgangum hopylium impresse. Expensis et sumptibus honesti mercatoris Londoñ. wilhelmi Brettòn. Anno domini Mil. ccccvi. kal. ix. mẽsis Aprilis. Venales habent̃ Londoñ. apud bibliopolas In cimiterio scti Pauli sub intersignio sanctissime Trinitatis ⁊ sancte Anne.

Bodl. Arch Bodl. D. subt. 55.
135 × 82. Latin.

32. 1506, April 24, *Paris, for Antoine Verard* (*Paris*) on vellum.
Hore Diue Virginis Marie Secundum Usum. Insignis Ecclesie Saɤ.

Colophon. Expliciūt hore beate Marie virginis secundum usum insignis ecclesie Sarum impresse Parisius p Anthonio verard Anno dñi millesimo quingentesimo sexto. xxiiii. Aprilis.

Brit. Mus. C. 41. a. 19.
159 × 88. Latin.

33. (*c.* 1507) *Paris, for Simon Vostre, Paris*, on vellum.
Hore presentes ad usum Sarum impresse fuerūt Parisius pro Symone vostre : librario commorante ibidem : in vico nuncupato nouo beate Marie . in intersignio sancti Iohannis euangeliste. a.
Ends on q8^b. The rosare (in the contents).

Brit. Mus. C. 41. a. 20. Wadham Coll. Oxford.
150 × 93. Latin.

34. (*c.* 1507, *Paris, for Simon Vostre, Paris*) 8°.
The title-page is wanting ; the book begins
Cut of the anatomical man.
All wanting after q7^b. Prayers to ‖ the sacrament atte leuacion. Aue verum (in the contents).

Stonyhurst Coll. T. 5. 38.
152 × 92. Latin.

35. (*c.* 1507, *Richard Pynson, London*) 16°.
Twenty-one lines to a full page. Without initials, catchwords, or numbering. Printed entirely in black, with cuts. Space left for 4-line initials. Known only from a fragment consisting of four leaves, signature bb.
Begins on bb1. xii b sancti Bricii episcopi.
All wanting after bb4. Incipiunt hore beate marie. secundum usum Sarum. bb4^b. (A cut of the Annunciation.)
Contents. Portions of the Kalendar for November and December. "Auxiliatrix," "Piissime deus," Whan thou goste first oute (Crux triumphalis, Deus qui tres magos, Angele qui me) Whan thou entryst the churche (Dñe in

multitudine) Takyng holy vvater (Aqua bñdicta) Begynne thus to pray (Discedite a me).
Mr. F. J. H. Jenkinson.
68 × 46. Latin.

36. (*c.* 1508, *Wynkyn de Worde, London*) 8°.
Nineteen lines to a full page. Without catchwords or numbering. Printed in black and red, with cuts. 2-line initials in red. Known only from a fragment consisting of four leaves ; 1, 4, 5, 8 of a quire.
Begins. x e euurcii episcopi ꝛ ꝑfessoris
Ends on 8ᵇ. line 14. tus que tua sola bonitate michi
Contents. Portions of the Kalendar for September, October, December. Portions of " Initium " and " Sequentia sancti euangelii ". Portion of " Auxiliatrix ".
Mr. F. J. H. Jenkinson.
108 × 70. Latin.

37. 1510, September 5, *Thielman Kerver, Paris, for William Bretton, London*, 8°.
Hore beatissime ỹginis Marie ad usum Sarisburiēsis ecclesie accuratissime ĩpresse / cũ multis orationib⁹ pulcherrimis et indulgentiis iam ultimo recenter insertis.
Colophon. Finit officiũ beate virginis marie scđm usum Sarisburiensis ecclesie / Impressum parisius per Thielmannum Keruer impressorem ac librarium iuratum alme uniuersitatis parisiensis. Impensis ꝛ sumptibus prestantissimi wilhelmi bretton ciuis ꝛ mercatoris londoniēsis ꝛ stapul. ville calisie. Anno dñi millesimo quingentesimo decimo : die vero quinta mensis Septembris.
St. Paul's Cath. 38. D. 15. Bodl. 8°. H. 6. Th. BS.
Emman. Coll. Camb. MSS. 4. 3. 33.
154 × 92. Latin.

38. (*c.* 1510, *Richard Pynson, London*) 32°.
Fourteen lines to a full page. Printed in black and red. Lombardic capitals in red. Known only from a fragment

consisting of six leaves; 1, 2, 3, 4, 5, 8 of signature P. of a York Horæ, forming part of a sheet which has never been folded; it collates in eights, quarter sheets.

Begins on P1.   Omnes sancti innocen

All wanting after P8ᵇ. auxiliu . . . ut in ex (in collect Deus in te speravi).

Contents. A portion of the Litany.

Brit. Mus. Bagford fragments 463. h. 8. Fo. 22.

45 × 30. Latin.

39. 1511, Sept. 12, *Paris, for Francis Byrckman (London)* 4°.

Hore beatissime virginis Marie ad legitimũ Sarisburiensis ecclesie ritũ diligentissime accuratissimeq, impresse / cum multis orationibus pulcherrimis et indulgentiis iam ultimo de nouo adiectis Vendũtur Londoñ. apud bibliopolas in cimiterio sancti Pauli

Colophon. Hore beatissime virginis marie secundũ usum Sarum / totaliter ad lõgum: cu multis pulcherrimis orationibus et indulgentiis iam ultimo adiectis: ac in alma Parhisiorum Academia / impensis et sumptibus prestantissimi mercatoris Francisci byrckman ciuis Colonieñ impresse.   Anno domini Millesīo. cccccxi.   Die vero. xii. Septēbris

Mr. Samuel Sandars.

160 × 97. Latin.

40. (*c.* 1512, *Paris*) *for Simon Vostre, Paris,* 8°.

Officium beate Marie ỹginis ad usum Sarũ: cu plurib⁹ deuotis orationibus ꞇ cõtēplatiõibus impssũ caracteribus / figuris / ac mortis accidētia nouiter additis.   Expensis honesti viri Symonis vostre cõmorantis Parisius in vico nouo e regione diue virginis Marie: in intersignio sancti Johannis euangeliste.

Ends on q8ᵇ.   The rosare (in the contents).

Bodl. 8°. c. 143. Linc. (1).   Mr. Quaritch, 1888.

150 × 95. Latin.

41. 1513, *Wynkyn de Worde, London,* 4°.

The title-page is wanting; the book begins on

A1. Iesu lord for thyn holy [circumcisyon] (in the kalendar).

Colophon. Thus endeth the matyns of our lady with many a prayer and deuoute lessone with pryme ᵹ houres / vii. psalme Enlonged without inquysyon Newly corrected in the cyte of London Enprynted by me wynkyn de worde In the fletestrete at the sygne of the sonne The. M.CCCC. and. xiii yere of our lorde.

Brit. Mus. C. 35. e. 7.
162 × 98. Latin.

42. (*c.* 1513, *Richard Pynson, London*) 4º.

The title-page is wanting; the book begins on
aa2. The canon of ‖ Ebbes ᵹ Flodes.

B8ᵇ. Sequuntur hore beate marie virginis secū ‖ dum usum Sarum. Ad matutinas.

All wanting after A7ᵇ. This Epystell of our sauyoure . . . And he shall not perysshe with sodeyne deth / by the grace of god and our blessyd lady.

York Minster XI. N. 22.
161 × 96. Latin.

43. 1514, Jan. 1, *Paris, for Francis Bryckman (London)* 8º.

Hore btē marie viginis ad usū Sarū pro pueris / totaliter ad logū et sine require ī alma Parisiorū academia impensis Francisci byrckmā impresse. Anno millesimo. ccccxiiii. i. Ianuarii a. i.

Colophon. Hore beatissime marie viginis ad usum Sarum in alma Parisiorū academia / impensis Francisci byrckmam impresse. Anno millesimo quingentesimo. xiiii.

St. John's Coll. Camb. T. 10. 27.
108 × 72. Latin.

44. 1514, May 12, *Richard Pynson, London*, long 12º.

Hore beate marie virginis ad usum insignis ac preclare ecclesie Sarum. ai.

i5ᵇ. The contentes of this boke.

i7. Incipit rosariū bte marie ỹgīs.

i10. Vespere per aduentū de sancta maria usq̄ ad vigiliā natalis. dñi.

Colophon. Hore beate marie virginis secūdum usum Saꝝ finiunt feliciter cum orationibus ante et post sanctam cōmunionē dicendis in fine superadditis.   Impresse in ciuitate Londoñ per (Richardū Pynson) Regium Impressorem / in vico dicto the fletestrere / ad signum georgii commorantem.   Anno domini. M.CCCCC.xiiii. duo decima die mensis Mayus.

Clare Coll. Camb. KK. 8. 3 (2).
114 × 43. Latin.

45. 1514, July 12, *Paris, for Francis Byrckman (London)* 4°.
The title-page is wanting ; the book begins on

A2. KL Januari⁹ habet dies. xxxi. Luna vero. xxx.

Colophon. Hore beatissime virginis marie secūdum usum. Sarum / totaliter ad longum : cū multis pulcherrimis orationibus et indulgentiis iam ultimo adiectis : ac in alma Parhisiorum Academia / impensis et sumptibus prestantissimi mercatoris Francisci byrckman ciuis Colonicñ impresse Anno domini Millesimo. ccccxiiii. Die vero. xii. Iulii.

Gonville and Caius Coll. Camb. A. 3. 23.
158 × 96. Latin.

46. 1514, July 24, *Wynkyn de Worde, London,* long 12°.
Hore beate marie virginis ad usum insignis ac p̄clare ecclesie Sarū.

Colophon. Hore beate marie virginis secundū usum Saꝝ finiūt feliciter cū orationibus ante et post sanctā cōmunionē dicēdis in fine supadditis.   Impresse ĩ ciuitate London. per winandum de worde in vico dicto (the Fletestrete) ad signu solis commorantem. Anno dñi. M.ccccc.xiiii. die vero. xxiiii. Iulii.

Camb. Univ. AB. 5. 62.
114 × 42. Latin.

47. (*c.* 1514, *Richard Pynson, London*) long 12°.
The title-page is wanting ; the book begins on

D

A3. KL Martius habet dies ‖ xxxi. Luna vero xxx. ‖ Nox habet horas. xiiii. dies. x.

All wanting after I10ᵇ. Vespere per aduentū de sancta ‖ maria usq̨ ad vigiliam nati dñi.

Brit. Mus. C. 35. a. 2.
114 × 43. Latin.

48. 1515, October 12 (*Wolfgang Hopyl*) *Paris, for Francis Byrckman* (*London*) 4°.

Hore beatissime virginis Marie ad legitimum Sarisburiensis ecclesie ritum : diligētissime accuratissimeq̨ impresse / cum multis orationibus pulcherrimis et indulgentiis iam ultimo ac de nouo adiectis. Venduntur Londoñ. apud bibliopolas in cimiterio sancti Pauli. 1515. A. i.

Colophon. Hore beatissime virginis Marie secūdum usum Sarum / totaliter ad longum : cū multis pulcherrimis orationibus et indulgentiis iam ultimo adiectis : ac in alma Parhisiorum Academia / impensis et sumptibus prestantissimi mercatoris Francisci byrckman ciuis Colonieñ impresse Anno domini Millesimo. cccccxiiii. Die vero. xii. Octobris.

Bodl. Gough Missals 144.
158 × 95. Latin.

49. (*c.* 1515) *for Pierre Guerin* (*Rouen*) on vellum.

P G Hore beate marie virginis ad usum insignis ac preclare ecclesie Saɤ. Pour Pierres guerī demourāt en la paroisse saīt laurēs en la rue de leseureul. A1 Saɤ.

I12. The conteīg conteyned in ‖ thys boke.

K1ᵇ. Vespe p aduētū de sctā maria usq̨ ad vigiliā nati. dñi.

All wanting after K8ᵇ. sti. R. Post partū. ℣. Specio (in Matutine de sancta Maria a nativitate Domini usque ad purificationem).

Brit. Mus. C. 41. a. 21.
106 × 40. Latin.

50. 1516, Nov. 19, *Paris, for Francis Byrckman, London,* 4°.

Hore beatissime virginis Marie ad legitimū Sarisburiensis ecclesie ritū cū quindecī oronibus beate Brigitte in latino : ac multis aliis oronibus pulcherrimis et indulgētiis cū tabula aptissima iā ultimo adiectis.   Venduntur Londoñ. a Francisco byrckman ciuis Coloniēsis in cimiterio sctī pauli   A. i.

Colophon. Hore beatissime virginis Marie secundū usum Sarum / totaliter ad longū: cum orationibus beate brigitte : ac multis aliis orationibus ꝶ indulgentiis cum tabula aptissima iam ultimo adiectis : ac in alma Parhisiorum Academia / impensis et sumptibus prestantissimi mercatoris Francisci byrckmā ciuis Coloniēñ impresse.   Anno domini M.CCCC.xvi. Die vero xix. Nouembris.

r8ᵇ. Contenta in his horariis . . . Finis presentis tabule.

Bodl. 4°. H. 18. Th. Seld.   Bodl. Gough Missals 112.

160 × 101. Latin.

51. (*c.* 1516, *for Guillaume Bernard aud Jacques Cousin, Rouen*) 4°.

The title-page is wanting ; the book begins on

ci. [Euangeliū scđm matheū.] Fo. iii.

d8ᵇ. Sequuntur hore beate marie virginis secundū usū. Eboraceñ. Ad matutinas.

All wanting after C2ᵇ. sancti feliciter percipere : ꝶ libera me ī hora (in A devout prayer to our Saviour Domine Jesu Christe).

York Minster XI. O. 28.

185 × 121. Latin.

52. 1517, January 26, *for Guillaume Bernard and Jacques Cousin, Rouen,* 4°.

Hore beatissime virginis Marie ad legitimū Eboracensis ecclesie ritum diligētissime accuratissimeq̨, impresse cū multis orationibꝰ pulcherrimis et īdulgentiis iā ultimo de nouo adiectis. In conspectu altissimi immaculata permansi.   Venūdātur Rothomagi in officina Jacobi cousin in parrochia sancti nicolai ante atriū bibliopolarum moram habentis.   A. i.

Colophon. Hore beatissime virginis marie scđm morem āglicanū totaliter ad longū cum multis pulcherrimis orōníb⁹ et indulgētiis iā ultimo adiectis īpensis ⁊ sumptibus Guillermi bernard et Jacobi cousin ciuiū Rothomageñ. Parrochie sācti nicolai āte atriū et in atrio librarioʁ maioris ecclesie degētiū. Anno dñi. M.ccccc.xvii. die vero. xxvi. mensis Januarii. Laus deo.

St. John's Coll. Camb. T. 9. 26. St. Cuthbert's Coll. Ushaw. Earl of Carysfort.
160 × 100. Latin.

53. 1519, April 14, *Paris, for Francis Byrckman, London*, 4°.

Hore beatissime virginis Marie ad legitimū Sarisburiēsis ecclesie ritū cū quindecim orationibus beate Brigitte : ac multis aliis oratiōibus pulcherrimis et indulgētiis cum tabula aptissima iam ultimo adiectis. Venūdant Londoñ. a Frācisco byrckmā ciuis Coloniēsis / in cimiterio sancti Pauli. Saʁ. A i.

Colophon. Hore beatissime ỹginis Marie scđm usum Sarum / totaliter ad longum : cum orationibus beate brigitte : ac multis aliis orationibus et indulgentiis cū tabula aptissima iam ultimo adiectis : ac in alma Parrhisioʁ Academia / impensis et sumptibus prestātissimi mercatoris Francisci byrckman ciuis Colonisiensis īpresse. Anno domini. M.ccccc.xix. Die vero. xiiii. mensis Aprilis.

r8ᵇ. Contenta in his horariis . . . Finis presentis tabule.

Bodl. Douce BB. 141. (1). Bodl. c. 4. 10. Linc. (1).
160 × 100. Latin.

54. 1519, October 24, *Nicolas Higman, Paris, for François Regnault (Paris) and Francis Byrckman (London)* 4°.

Hore btīssime virginis Marie ad legitimū Sarisburēsis ecclesie ritum : cum quindecim orationibus beate Brigitte : ac multis aliis orationibus pulcherrimis ⁊ indulgētiis / cū tabula aptissima iā ultimo adiectis.

Colophon. Hore beatissime ỹginis Marie scđm usū Sarum totaliter ad longum : cum orationibus beate brigitte ac multis

aliis orationibus et indulgētiis cū tabula aptissima iam ultimo adiectis ac ī alma Parrhisiou̧ academia / impensis et sumptibus honesti viri Francisci regnault ciuis Parisiensis impresse : in vico sancti Iacobi in intersignio sancti Claudii cōmorantis. Anno domini M.ccccc.xix. Die ỹo. xxiiii. mēsis Octobris
ā1. Contenta in his horariis. . . . Finis presentis Tabule.

Colophon. Hore beatissime virginis Marie scd̃m usum Sau̧: totaliter ad longum / cum multis pulcherrimis orationibus et indulgentiis iam ultimo adiectis. Impresse Parisius per Nicolaum hicḡmā allemanū / Impensis et sumptib⁹ honesti viri Francisci Birckmā ciuis Coloniensis. Anno dñi Millesimo quingētesimo decimo nono. Die vero. xxiiii. Octobris.

Bodl. Douce BB. 194. Emman. Coll. Camb. MSS. 4. 2. 3.
Archbishop Marsh's Libr. Dublin. E. 3. 36.
215 × 130. Latin.

55. 1520, June 14, *Paris, for Francis Byrckman (London)* 4°.
Hore beatissime virginis Marie ad legitimum Sarisburiensis ecclesie ritum : diligētissime accuratissimeq̧, impresse cum multis orationibus pulcherrimis et indulgentiis iam ultimo ac de nouo adiectis. Venales habētur Londoñ. apud bibliopolas in cimiterio sctĩ Paulĩ. M.ccccc.l̃.xx. A i.

Colophon. Hore beatissime v̈ginis Marie scd̃ȝ usum Sarum / totaliter ad longum : cum orationibus beate brigitte : ac multis aliis orationibus et indulgentiis cū tabula aptissima iam ultimo adiectis : ac in alma Parrhisiorū Academia / irr̃pensis et sumptibus prestātissimi mercatoris Francisci byrckman ciuis Coloniensis impresse. Anno domini M.ccccc.xx. Die vero. xiiii. mensis Iunii.

r8ᵇ. Contenta in his horariis . . . Finis presentis tabule.
Bodl. Gough Missals 145.
160 × 100. Latin.

56. (*c.* 1520) *Nicolas Higman, Paris, for Simon Vostre, Paris,* 4°.
Hore beate virginis Marie : secundū usum Sarum : cū illius miraculis : unacū figuris apocalipsis : Thobie ꝛ Iudith. ac etiam

mortis accidentia / nouiter addita impresse fuerũt Parisiis opa ac arte Nicolai Hygmã. Impensis honesti viri Symonis vostre: cōmorantis ibidẽ in vico nouo. In intersignio sancti Iohannis euangeliste. S a

p4. The contentis of thys booke.

p5ᵇ. Oratio perpulchra . . . dicenda die sabbati ad honorem . . . virginis marie.

Ends on p8ᵇ. Per omnia secula seculorum. Amẽ (in prayer Interveniat pro nobis).

Brit. Mus. C. 41. e. 9. (on vellum). Bodl. Gough Missals 162. Stonyhurst Coll. T. 3. 48.

199 × 114. Latin.

57. (*c*. 1520) *Nicolas Higman, Paris, for Simon Vostre, Paris*, 4°.

Hore Marie virginis scdm usum Sarũ : cũ illius miraculis unacũ figuris apocalipsis post biblie hystorias insertis : ac etiã mortis accidẽtia nouiter addita impsse fuerũt Parisiis opa ac arte Nicolai higmã. Impesis honesti viri Symonis Vostre: cōmorãtis ibidẽ in vico nouo. In intersignio sancti Iohannis euangeliste.

p4. The contentis of thys booke.

p5ᵇ. Oratio perpulchra . . . dicenda die sabbati ad honorem . . . virginis marie.

Ends on p8ᵇ. Per omnia secula seculorum. Amen (in prayer Interveniat pro nobis).

Fitzwilliam Mus. Camb. 7. H. 1. (on vellum).
Stonyhurst Coll. T. 8. 1.
195 × 114. Latin.

58. 1521, January, *Paris, for Francis Byrckman, London*, 4°.

Hore beate Marie ad ritũ ecclesie Sarisburiensis. Venũdanĩ Londoñ. a Frãcisco byrckmã in cimiterio sctĩ pauli.

Colophon. Hore beatissime ỹginis marie scđm usum Sarum / totaliter ad longum : cum orationibus beate brigitte : ac multis aliis orationibus ⁊ indulgentiis cũ tabula aptissima iam ultimo adiectis : ac in alma Parrhisioᶉ Academia / impensis et sumptibus prestātissimi mercatoris Francisci byrckman ciuis Coloniensis impresse. Anno domini. M.ccccc.xxi. Mensis Januarii.

r8[b]. Contenta in his horariis . . . Finis presentis tabule.

Bodl. Tanner 867.
165 × 102. Latin.

59. 1521, April 9, *Paris, for Francis Byrckman, London*, 4°.

Hore beate Marie. ad ritum ecclesie Sarisburiēsis Venūdanī Londoñ. a Frācisco byrckmā in cimiterio sctī Pauli

Colophon. Hore / beatissime virginis marie : secundum usum Sarum / totaliter ad longum : cum orationibus beate Brigitte : ac multis aliis orationib^9 et indulgentiis. In alma Parrhisiorum Academia / impensis ꝉ sumptib^9 prestātissimi mercatoris Francisci byrckman ciuis Coloniēsis impresse. Anno domini. M.ccccc.xxi. ix. Mensis. Aprilis.

Bodl. Douce BB. 135. Queen's Coll. Oxford 79. cc.
Marquess of Bath.
177 × 107. Latin.

60. (*c.* 1521) *Jean Bignon, Paris, for Richard Fakes, London*, long 12°.

Hore beate marie virginis ad usum insignis ac preclare ecclesie Sarū cū figuris passionis mysteriū representātibus cecenter additis.

Colophon. Hore btē marie virginis secūdū usū īsignis eccłie Saꝝ puigili cura correcte hic felicit̄ termināt̄ / cū multis orōib^9 deuotissimis et p̄cipue aliqb^9 ī fine additis / ante et post eucharistie receptionē dicēdis. Impresse Parisius p̄ Iohānē bignon pro honesto viro Richard fakes Lōdoii librario / ꝉ ibidē cōmorāte in cymiterio sctī Pauli sub signo A B C

All wanting after L12[b]. under heuē ī erthis noo thyng stable (in The dance of death).

Bodl. Douce BB. 53 (1).
113 × 45. Latin.

※ The last four leaves of the book, L8-12, contain a portion of the Dance of death.

61. 1522, January 18, *Richard Pynson, London*, 8º.

Hore beatissime virginis Marie ad legitimum Sarisburiensis eccłie ritum : cū quindecim orationibus beate Brigitte : ac multis aliis orationibus pulcherrimis / cū tabula aptissima iam ultimo adiectis.

Colophon. Hore beatissime virginis Marie scđȝ usum Saƶ : totaliter ad longum / cū multis pulcherrimis orationibus et indulgētiis / cū tabula aptissīa iam ultimo adiectis. Impresse Londoñ : per Richardū Pynson regis impressor. Anno dñi. M.CCCCC.xxii. die vero. xviii. mēsis Ianuarii.

Bodl. Gough Missals 141.
160 × 87. Latin.

62. 1523, November 20, *Wynkyn de Worde, London*, 4º.

Hore beatissime virginis Marie ad cōsuetudinem insignis ecclesie Saƶ. Nuper emaculatissimi multis orationibus pulcherrimis annexis. Impresse Londoniis per wynādum de worde [in the Fletestrete] ad signum solis cōmorantem.

Colophon. Expliciunt hore beatissime Marie virginis secūdum usum Saƶ totaliter ad logū cū multis oratiōibus iam ultimo in fine adiectis impresse ī ciuitate Londoñ. p me winandū de worde in vico dicto yᵉ fletestrete ad signū solis cōmorātē. Anno dñi. M.ccccc.xxiii. die Ɏo. xx. mesis Nouēbris Laus deo detur.

Brit. Mus. C. 51. e. 2.   Salisbury Cath. L. 5. 12.
162 × 102. Latin.

63. (*c.* 1523) *Pieter Kaets (London)* 4º.

Hore beate Marie virginis secundum usum Sarum : cum variis orationibus / cuilibet deuoto ꝉ modis. (Device of Petrus Kaetz.)

All wanting after AA8ᵇ. sapientia patris. Amen (in Horæ dulcissimi nominis Jesu).

Stonyhurst Coll. T. 3. 22.
165 × 105. Latin.

64. (*c.* 1523) *Wynkyn de Worde, London*, long 12°.

Hore btē Marie virgīs ad usū īsignis ac p̄clare eccłie Saȝ totaliter ad lōgū.

Colophon. Expliciūt hore beatissime ma[rie] virginis scđm usum Saȝ [tota]liter: ad longum cum [ora]cionibus btē brigitte [ac m]ultis aliis orationibus iā ultimo in fine adiectis. Impresse in ciuitat[e Lon]doñ p me win[ando d]e worde in vico . . .

Emmanuel Coll. Camb. MSS. 4. 4. 3.
120 × 45. Latin.

65. 1524, August 19 (*Antwerp*) 4°.

The title-page is wanting; the book begins

K L. Januariᵒ habet dies. xxxi. Luna vero xx

Colophon. Expliciunt Hore diue virginis Marie / secundum ritum insignis ecclesie Sarū. Anno. M.ccccc.xxiiii. die vero. xix. Augusti.

St. Paul's Cath. 38. D. 12.   Earl of Ashburnham.
165 × 108. Latin.

66. 1524, November 22, *Christopher Endoviensis, Antwerp, for Pieter Kaetz* (*London*) 16°.

This edition is only known from a portion of the last page, which contains a portion of the contents and the Colophon.

Colophon. Expliciūt hore intemerate virginis secūdum usum Sarū: cū septem psalmis: letaniis: mortuoȝ vigiliis ꝛ recōmendationibᵒ ac multis aliis oratiūculis ꝛ utilitatibᵒ huic ultime editiōi insertis ꝛ in calce libelli annexis. Antuerpie quidē operi Christophori endouiensis impensis Petri kaetz mercatoris impressis. Anno. M.ccccc.xxiiii. die vero. xxii. Nouembris.

Brit. Mus. Bibl. Harl. 5918. No. 21. Latin.
Width of page 45.

67. 1525, May, *Christopher Endoviensis, Antwerp, for Francis Byrckman* (*London*) 4°.

Hore btē marie virginis ad usum Sarū: cū variis orōnibᵒ multū deuotis. Venūdantur per Franciscū byrckmā.

Colophon. Hore beatissime virginis marie secundum usum Sarum / totaliter ad longum : cum orationibus beate brigitte : ac multis aliis orationibus et indulgentiis cum tabula aptissima iam ultimo adiectis : Antwerpie per Christophorũ Endouieñ. / impensis et sumptibus prestantissimi mercatoris Francisci byrckman ciuis Coloniensis impresse. Anno domini. M.ccccc.xxv Mensis Maii.

FF8. Contenta in his horariis. . . . Finis presentis tabule.

Camb. Univ. A*. 10. 4.
164 × 102. Latin.

68. 1525, July 28, *Rouen, for Jacques Cousin, Rouen,* long 12°.

Hore btẽ Marie virginis secundum usum insignis ac preclare ecclesie Saɟ. totaliter ad longũ ℞ in tali volumine sicuti perãtea in ciuitate London impresse fuere atq̨ ordinate nuperrime. Impresse Rothomagi Impensis honesti viri Iacobi cousin bibliopole eadem in urbe ante edem fratrũ minorũ moram habentis. A. i. saɟ.

Colophon. Expliciũt hore beatissime Marie virginis scđm usũ Saɟ. totaliter ad longũ cum orationib⁹ btẽ brigitte ac multis aliis orationibus iã ultimo in fine adiectis Impresse Rothomagi p Iacobo cousin eadẽ ĩ urbe prope fratrũ minorũ conventum morã trahẽte. Anno salutis nostre. M.CCCCC.xxv. Die vero. xxviii. mẽsis Iulii. Laus Deo detur.

Camb. Univ. A•. 8. 16.
117 × 40. Latin.

69. (*c.* 1525) long 12°.

The title-page is wanting; the book begins on

D1 saɟ. [Ad ỹginẽ mariã.] fo xxxvii. feroɟ / quia pater seculoɟ / dabit te

All wanting after fo. cxx^b. hũc tam fortẽ / et per nati tui mor (in A prayer of the seven sorrows of our Lady).

Mr. F. J. H. Jenkinson.
118 × 45. Latin.

70. 1526, January 11, *François Regnault, Paris*, long 12°.
The title-page is wanting; the book begins on
A2. An almanacke for. xxii. yeres. f. ii.

Colophon. Expliciunt hore beatissime virginis Marie : scdm usum Sarum : totaliter ad longū : cum orationibus beate Brigitte : ac multis aliis orationibus. Parisius impresse : in edibus Francisci regnault : vici diui Jacobi. Ad signum Elephantis commorantis juxtà templum Mathurinorum. Anno salutifere dñi. M.ccccc.xxvi. Die vero. xi. Mensis Januarii.

Stonyhurst Coll. T. 7. 42.
145 × 53. Latin.

71. 1526, March 1, *François Regnault, Paris*, 4°.
Hore Beatissime virginis Marie ad legitimū Sarisburiensis Ecclesie ritum / cum quindecim orationibus beate Brigitte / ac multis aliis orationibus pulcherrimis / et indulgentiis / cum tabula aptissima iam ultimo adiectis. Venūdať Parisius a Frācisco Regnault In vico scti̇ Jacobi / sub signo Elephantis.

Colophon. Hore beatissime virginis Marie / secūdū usum Saɤ / totaliter ad longum / cum multis pulcherrimis orationibus ꝛ indulgētiis iam ultimo adiectis. Impresse Parisius per Frāciscū Regnault : Impe̊sis ꝛ sumptibus eiusdē almē uniuersitatis Parisieñ. librarii iurati. Anno dñi millesimo q̄ngentesimo vigesimo sexto. Die vero. i. Martii.

Brit. Mus. C. 35. h. 7. Bodl. Douce BB. 185.
Jesus Coll. Camb. B. 4. 6.
215 × 130. Latin.

72. 1526, March 17, *François Regnault, Paris*, on vellum.
Hore beatissime virginis Marie ad legitimum Sarisburiësis Ecclesie ritū / cū quindecim orationibus beate Brigitte / ac multis aliis orationibus pulcherrimis / et indulgētiis / cum tabula aptissima iam ultimo adiectis. Venundatur Parisius a Francisco regnault / in vico sancti Jacobi / sub signo Elephantis. M.D.xxvi.

Colophon. Hore beatissime virginis Marie / secūdum usum

Sa♃ / totaliter ad longum / cū multis pulcherrimis orationibus ⁊ indulgētiis iam ultimo adiectis. Impresse Parrhisiis in edibus Francisci Regnault. Alme uniuersitatis Parrhisiēsis librarii iurati. Anno domini millesimo quingētesimo vigesimo sexto. die vero. xvii. Martii.

Brit. Mus. C. 46. d. 9.
161 × 99. Latin.

73. (*c.* 1526, *Wynkyn de Worde, London*) 4°.
The title-page is wanting ; the book begins on
B2. Quoniam autem nonnulli queritant tempora incisio (in Aspectus duodecim signorum).
c8ᵇ. Sequuntur hore beate marie virginis secūdum usum Sa♃. Ad matutinas.
All wanting after ⁊2ᵇ. redemisti mūdum. Adiuua nos deus salutaris (in A devout prayer to our Saviour).

Mr. Samuel Sandars.
168 × 100. Latin.

74. (*c.* 1526) *Wynkyn de Worde, London*, 4°.
Hore beatissime virginis Marie ad consuetudinē insignis ecctie Sa♃. nuper emaculatissimi multis oratioibᵞ pulcherrimis annexis. Impresse Lōdoniis per me winādum de worde (in the fletestrete) ad signū solis ꝑmorantē. A. i.
All wanting after ⁊8ᵇ. heuynes of hert ⁊ delyted me ī ydle thoughtes (in The form of confession).

Lambeth Archiep. 39. 5. 35.
159 × 102. Latin.

75. (*c.* 1526, *François Regnault, Paris*) 4°.
The title-page is wanting ; the book begins on
B2. [Poto.] K L Ianuarius h₃ dies. xxxi. Luna xxx.
All wanting after AA6ᵇ. but with thy wyfe in wedloke onely (in The form of confession).

Queen's Coll. Oxford. 79. CC.
161 × 99. Latin.

76. 1527, March 17, *François Regnault, Paris*, 4º.
The title-page is wanting; the book begins on
Sa♃ B3. Initium sancti euangelii / secundum ‖ Iohannem. Gloria tibi domine.

Colophon. Hore beatissime virginis Marie / secũdum usum Sa♃ / totaliter ad longum / cũ multis pulcherrimis orationibus ⁊ indulgētiis iam ultimo adiectis. Impresse Parrhisiis in edibus Francisci Regnault Alme uniuersitatis Parrhisiēsis librarii iurati. Anno dñi millesimo quingentesimo vigesimo septimo. die vero. xvii. Martii.

Brit. Mus. C. 35. d. 9.
160 × 100. Latin.

77. 1527, June 27, *François Regnault, Paris*, 4º.
Hore Beatissime virginis Marie ad legitimũ Sarisburiēsis Ecclesie ritum / cum quindecim orationib⁹ beate Brigitte / ac multis aliis orationib⁹ pulcherrimis / et indulgentiis / cum tabula aptissima iam ultimo adiectis. 1527. Venũdāt Parisiis a Frãcisco Regnault In vico / sãcti Jacobi. sub signo Elephãtis.

Colophon. Hore beatissime virginis Marie / secundum usum Sa♃ / totaliter ad longum / cum multis pulcherrimis orationibus ⁊ indulgētiis iam ultimo adiectis. Impresse Parisius per Franciscum Regnault : Impensis ⁊ sumptibus eiusdem alme uniuersitatis Parisieñ. librarii iurati. Anno domini millesimo quingentesimo vigesimo septimo. Die vero. xxvii. Junii.

Brit. Mus. C. 42. e. 7. on vellum. Brit. Mus. C. 35. h. 9.
Brit. Mus. C. 23. b. 24. (2).
197 × 120. Latin.

78. 1527, June 27, *François Regnault, Paris*, 4º.
Hore beatissime virginis Marie ad legitimum Sarisburiēsis Ecclesie ritum / cum quindecim orationibus beate Brigitte / ac multis aliis orationib⁹ pulcherrimis / et indulgentiis / cum tabula aptissima iam ultimo adiectis. 1527. Venũdant Parisius a Frãcisco Regnault In vico sctĩ Jacobi / sub signo Elephantis.

30   A HAND-LIST OF   [1527-

Colophon. Hore beatissime virginis Marie / secundum usum Saꝝ / totaliter ad longum cum multis pulcherrimis orationibus ꝉ indulgentiis iam ultimo adiectis.   Impresse Parisius per Franciscum Regnault :   Impensis et sumptibus eiusdem alme universitatis Parisieñ. librarii iurati.   Anno domini millesimo quingentesimo vigesimo septimo. Die vero xxvii. Junii.

Brit. Mus. C. 25. i. 4.   Lambeth Archiep. 25*. 1. 23.
Earl Beauchamp.
200 × 120. Latin.

*** The Lambeth copy reads in the Colophon "ꝉ indulgētiis" for "ꝉ indulgentiis," and "Impensis ꝉ sumptibus" for "Impensis et sumptibus".

79. 1527, July 18, *Nicolas Prevost, Paris, for Francis Byrckman, London,* 4°.

Hore beatissime ỹginis Marie ad verū Sarisburiēsis ecclesie ritū : cū q̄ndecī orōnibus btē Brigitte et plerisq̧ aliis. sicuti index in calce earundem annexus edocet.

Colophon. Hore btissime ỹginis marie ad verū usum Sarū : ꝗ plurimis biblie historiis decorate : ac multis orationibus et iis quidē deuotissimis adaucte.   Impresse quidē Parisiis in officina industrii calcographi Nicolai Preuost.   Impēsis vero fidelissimi mercatoris Francisci Byrkman ciuis Coloniensis. Et apud eundē venundātur Londonii apud cimiteriū sancti Pauli.   Anno dñi. M.D.xxvii. die. xviii. Julii.

Brit. Mus. C. 35. h. 1.   Bodl. Gough Missals 176.
King's Coll. Camb. M. 33. 49.
215 × 130. Latin.

80. 1527, October 10, *François Regnault, Paris,* 4°.

Hore Beatissime virginis Marie ad legitimū Sarisburiēsis Ecclesie ritum / cum quindecim orationib⁹ beate Brigitte / ac multis aliis orationib⁹ pulcherrimis / et indulgentiis / cum tabula aptissima iam ultimo adiectis. 1527.   Venūdāt Parisiis a Frācisco Regnault In vico / sācti Iacobi. sub signo Elephātis.

Colophon. Hore beatissime virginis Marie / secūdum usum

Sa҉ / totaliter ad longum / cum multis pulcherrimis orationib̕
⁊ indulgentiis iam ultimo adiectis. Impresse Parisii p Franciscū Regnault alme uniuersitatis parisicñ. librariū iuratum. Impensis et sumptibus eiusdem. Anno domini Millesimo quingc̄tesimo vigesimo septimo. Die. vero. x. Octobris.

    Exeter Coll. Oxford. 171. G. 6. York Minster. XI. G. 21.
    Chetham. Libr. Manchester 21068.
    215 × 133. Latin.

    81. 1527, December 13, *François Regnault, Paris*, long 12°.
    This prymer of Salysbury use is set out a lōg wout ony serchyng / with many prayers / and goodly pyctures in the kalēder / in the matyns of our lady / in the houres of the crosse / in the. vii. psalmes / and in the dyryge. And be newly enprynted at Paris. 1527. Sa҉ A

    Colophon. Expliciunt hore beatissime virginis Marie scd̄m usum Sa҉ : totaliter ad longum : cum orationibus beate Brigitte : ac multis aliis orationibus. Parisiis impresse : in edibus Francisci regnault : vici diui Iacobi Ad signum Elephantis commorantis iuxta templū Maturinorum. Anno salutifere incarnationis domini. M.ccccc.xxvii. Die vero. xiii. mensis. Decembris.

    Bodl. Douce BB. 75.
    142 × 54. Latin.

    82. 1527, *Widow of Thielman Kerver, Paris, for Francis Byrckman London*, 32°.
The title-page is wanting; the book begins on
    A2. KL Ianuari̕ habet dies xxxi
    208. Parisiis in officina libraria viduc spectabil viri / Thielmāni Keruer Impensis quidem Francisci Byrckmā ciuis Coloniensis. Anno. 1527.

    Colophon. 1527 He hore venūdātur Londonii a Francisco byrckmā : apud cimiterium diui Pauli.

    Stonyhurst Coll. T. 10. 3. (1).
    86 × 52. Latin.

83. 1528, September 2, *Widow of Thielman Kerver, Paris, for Alard Plomier (Paris)* on vellum.

Enchiridion / p̄clare ecclesie Sarum : deuotissimis precationibus / ac venustissimis imaginib⁹ et iis quidem non paucis refertum. Parisiis Ex officina libraria vidue spectabilis viri Thielmanni Keruer. 1528

Colophon. Impressum est hoc orarium Parisiis in edibus vidue / spectabilis viri Thielmanni keruer in vico diui iacobi ad signū unicornis / Expensis quidem probi viri Alardi plomier mercatoris fidelissimi. Anno salutis nostre / millesimo quingentesimo vigesimo octauo. die. ii. septembris.

Brit. Mus. C. 17. a. 4. 5.   Bodl. Douce E. 2.
Emman. Coll. Camb. MSS. 4. 4. 13.
87 × 47. Latin.

84. (*c.* 1528) *Rouen, for Jacques Cousin, Rouen*, long 12°.

Hore beate marie virginis ad usum Saꝶ recc̄tissime impresse necnō emendate secundū exemplar Parrisius Impensis Iacobi cousin bibliopole benemeriti Rothomagi cōmorātis. A saꝶ.

Colophon. Expliciūt hore beatissime Marie virginis secundū usū Saꝶ totaliter ad lōgū cum orationibus btē brigide / ac multis aliis orationibus iā ultimo in fine adiectis. Imp̄sse Rothomagi impensis Iacobi cousin ī eadem ciuitate in parrochia diui Vincentii e regione fratrū minorum moram tenētis.

Bodl. Gough Missals 42.
118 × 45. Latin.

85. (*c.* 1528) *Germain Hardouyn, Paris*, on vellum.

Hore beate Marie virginis ad usum insignis ac preclare ecclesie Sarum / totaliter ad Longum sine require. Cum pluribus suffragiis ꝛ orationibus / Nouiter impressis parisius per Germanum Hardouyn / cōmorantem inter duas portas Palatii Rigis / ad inter signium diue Margarete.

Colophon. Expliciunt Hore beatissime virginis Marie secundum usum. Sarum totaliter ad longum. Cum pluribus suffragiis ꝛ Orationibus de nouo additis Nouiter impressis Parisius. per Germanum hardouyn / Cōmorantem inter duas portas Palatii Regis / ad intersigniuȝ Sancte Margarete.

Brit. Mus. C. 41. a. 22.   Bodl. Gough Missals 83.
Trin. Coll. Camb. VI^d. 6. 9.
137 × 60. Latin.

86. (*c.* 1528) 16°.

Hortulus anime recēter diuersis / ac odoriferis flosculis decoratus : cum additionibus variis pluriū deuotioni oportunis ꝛ necessariis nusꝙ sic impressis adiectis sc̄dm usum Saꝝ. horis beate Marie virginis / septē psalmis atꝗ vigiliis. In quo quidē hortulo : fidelis aīa christi amore lāguida : saluberrima sibi comperiet predicamenta.   Hortu. Saꝝ. a i

All wanting after P5^b. ꝑfer opē ꝛ depone : vite sortes ꝛ corone (in Suffragia de Wilhelmo).

Lambeth Archiep. 89. L. 16.
85 × 47. Latin.

87. (*c.* 1528) long 12°.

The title-page is wanting; the book begins

KL Martius habet dies. xxxi || Luna vero. xxx. || Nox habet horas. xii. Dies: xii.

All wanting after N4^b. regū. Deus q̄ tres magos. fol. xlvi. (in the contents).

Brit. Mus. C. 35. a. 3.
119 × 45. Latin.

88. 1530, January, *Christopher Endoviensis, Antwerp*, 4°.

The title-page is wanting; the book begins on

A1. Initium sancti euangelii secun || dum iohānem.

Colophon. Hore beatissime virginis marie / secundum usum insignis ecclesie Sarū / totaliter ad longum : cum orationibus beate brigitte / ac multis aliis orationibus et indulgentiis : cū tabula aptissima iam ultimo adiecta.   Antwerpie / per Christophorum Endouiensem impresse.   Anno a natiuitate domini / Millesimo / quingentesimo / tricesimo.   Mense Ianua.

DDi.   Contēta in his horariis.   Fo. cxciii.

All wanting after DD3ᵛ. Ad patriarchas et prophetas
... eodem (in the contents).

Jesus Coll. Cambridge. B. 4. 38.
168 × 102. Latin.

89. 1530, April 30, *François Regnault, Paris*, 4ᵒ.

Hore beate Marie ad usum ecclesie Sarisburiensis. Anno. M.ccccc.xxx. Venundatur Parisiis apud Franciscū Regnault / in vico sancti Iacobi / ad signū Elephantis.

Colophon. Expliciūt hore beate Marie secundū usum Sa℞ / totaliter ad longum cū multis pulcherrimis orationibus et indulgētiis iam ultimo adiectis. Impresse Parisiis in edibus Francisci Regnault Alme uniuersitatis parisiensis librarii iurati. Anno domini millesimo quingentesimo trigesimo Die ultima Aprilis.

Bodl. Gough Missals 117.
Sold at Sotheby's, 28th July, 1886. No. 485.
162 × 100. Latin.

90. 1530, April 30, *François Regnault, Paris*, 16ᵒ.

The title-page is wanting; the book begins on
Sar E1. [Secundum marcum.] Fo. xxxiii.

Colophon. Expliciunt hore beatissime virginis Marie secūdum usum Sa℞ totaliter ad longum : cum orationibus beate Brigitte ac multis aliis orationibus. Impresse Parisiis per Franciscum Regnault cōmorantē in vico Sancti Iacobi / iuxta templum maturinorum Ad signū Elephantis Anno dñi. M.ccccc.xxx. Die ultima Aprilis.

Stonyhurst Coll. T. 10. 12.
102 × 57. Latin.

91. 1530, May 6, *Germain Hardouyn, Paris*, 8ᵒ.

Enchiridion preclare ecclesie Sarum : deuotissimis precatiōibus : ac venustissimis imaginibus : ℞ iis quidem non paucis refertum.

Colophon. Impressum est hoc orarium Parisiis in edibus spectabilis viri Germani Harduoyn librarii iurati uniuersitatis

Parisieñ. apud palatiū cōmorantis ad signum diue Margarete. Anno salutis nostre millesimo quingentesimo trigesimo. Die vero. vi. Maii.

    Brit. Mus. C. 35. f. 11.   Bodl. Gough Missals 98.
    Camb. Univ. G. 3. 60.
    137 × 78. Latin.

92. 1530, Oct.,-1531, *Christopher Endoviensis, Antwerp, for sale in London*, 4°.

Hore btē marie virginis ad usū ecclesie Saɤ : cū multis ac variis orationibus multū deuotis. 1531   Venundantur: in cimiterio sancti pauli sub intersignio sancti Augustini.

Colophon. Hore beatissime virginis marie / secundum usum insignis ecclesie Sarū / totaliter ad longum : cum orationibus beate brigitte / ac multis aliis orationibus et indulgentiis iam ultimo adiectis. Antwerpie / per Christophorum Endouiensem impresse. Anno a natiuitate domini / Millesimo / quingentesimo / tricesimo. Mense Octobris.

    Brit. Mus. C. 35. d. 12.   Bodl. Douce BB. 127.
    167 × 100. Latin.

93. 1530, *François Regnault, Paris*, 4°.

Hore Beatissime virginis marie ad legitimum Sarisburiensis Ecclesie ritum / cum quindecim orationibus beate Brigitte / ac multis aliis orationibus pulcherrimis / et indulgentiis / cum tabula aptissima iam ultimo adiectis. 1530   Venundantur Parisiis a' Francisco Regnault In vico sancti Iacobi / sub signo Elephantis.

Colophon. Hore beatissime virginis Marie / secundū usum Sarisbu. totaliter ad lōgum / cum multis pulcherrimis orationibus et indulgētiis iam ultimo adiectis. Impresse Parisii per Franciscum Regnault alme uniuersitatis parisiensis librarium iuratum. Impensis et sumptibus eiusdem.

    Brit. Mus. C. 35. h. 11.   Bodl. Gough Missals 206. (1).
    Magdalen Coll. Camb. 1848.
    220 × 140. Latin.

94. (c. 1530, *Christopher Endoviensis, Antwerp*) 4°.
Twenty-six lines to a full page. Known only from a fragment, consisting of fourteen leaves : 2, 3, 7 of signature A ; 1, 2, 4, 5, 7 of signature B ; 3, 4, 8 of signature C ; 2, 7, 8 of signature D.

Begins on A2. Gloria p̄ri ꝉ filio ꝉ spiritui sctō : sicut erat
Ends on D8ᵇ. [Ad completorium.]

Contents. A2, 3, 7. ; B1. Portions of Matins and Lauds, B1ᵇ. 2, 4, 5, 7. Suffragia de S. Spiritu, S. Trinitate, S. Cruce, S. Michaele, S. Iohane B, SS. Petro et Paulo, S. Stephano, S. Thoma archiepō Cantuariensi ; then, A prayer to sante thomas and to all the holy sayntes howes relyques reste in the holy place of chrychurche wythī cātorbery. Then, añ. cū collecta sctorū patrū ī monasterio scī augustini angloꝝ apꝉī quiescētiū. Then, De sctō augustino angloꝝ apꝉ'o. orō. Then, Ad S. blasium, De S. Maria Magdalena, De S. Wilgefortis, A prayer to St. Katheryne C3, 4, 8 and D2, 7, 8. Portions of Prime, Terce, Sext and Vespers.

Brit. Mus. C. 35. g. 11.
205 × 140. Latin.

95. 1531, May 14, *Christopher Ruremundensis (Antwerp) for sale in London*, 4°.

Hore btē marie virginis ad usū ecclesie Saꝝ : cū multis ac variis orationibus multū deuotis. 1531 Venundantur in cimiterio sancti pauli sub intersignio sancti Augustini.

Colophon. Hore beatissime virginis marie / secundū usum insignis ecclesie Sarū / totaliter ad lōgum : cum multis ad diuersos sanctos ꝉ sanctas suffragiis / plurimū iis quos eorū oblectat deuotio cōmodis. Insuper ꝉ orationes beate brigitte multis indulgentiarū cētenis decorate / necnō gregoriane p̄catiūcule infarcite / que ꝉ eodē ferme quo et brigitte / indulgentiarū gaudēt priuilegio. Ex officina Christophori Ruremundeñ. Anno M.ccccc.xxxi. Die vero. xiiii. Maii.

Brit. Mus. C. 35. d. 13. Bodl. Gough Missals 118.
Mr. J. D. Chambers.
167 × 102. Latin.

96. 1531, June 10, *François Regnault, Paris*, 16°.

This prymer of Salysbury use is set out a long with out ony serchyng / with many prayers / ⁊ goodly pyctures in the kalender / in the matyns of our lady / in the houres of the crosse / in the vii. psalmes / and in the dyryge. And be newly enprynted at Parys. M.ccccc.xxxi. Saɹ. A

Colophon. Expliciunt hore beatissime virginis Marie secundum usum Saɹ totaliter ad longum : cum orationibus beate Brigitte ac multis aliis orōnibus. Impresse Parisiis per Franciscum Regnault commorantem in vico sancti Iacobi / iuxta tēplum maturinorum Ad signum Elephantis. Anno dñi. M.ccccc.xxxi. Die decima Iunii.

Bodl. 8°. B. 135. Linc. Bodl. Gough Missals 49.
Stonyhurst Coll. T. 10. 28.
101 × 62. Latin.

97. 1531, June 30, *François Regnault, Paris*, 8°.

This prymer of salysbury use is set out a lōg wout ony serchyng with many prayers / and goodly pyctures in the kalēder in the matyns of our lady / in the houres of the crosse / in the vii psalmes / ād ī the dyryge. And be newly enprynted at Parys. Venūdātur Parisiis apud Frāciscū Regnault / in vico sctī Iacobi / ad signū Elephātis.

Colophon. Explicịut Hore beate Marie / secundum usum Sar : totaliter ad longum cum multis pulcherrimis orationibus ⁊ indulgentiis iam ultimo adiectis. Impresse Parisiis in edibus Francisci regnault. Alme uniuersitatis parisiensis librarii iurati Anno domini millesimo quingētesimo trigesimo primo. Die ultima Iunii.

Sold at Sotheby's, 9th July, 1886. No. 1283.
153 × 90. Latin.

98. 1531, *François Regnault, Paris*, 8°.

This prymer of Salysbury use is set out a long wout ony serchyng / with many prayers / and goodly pyctures in the kalēder / in the matyns of our lady / in the houres of the crosse / in the. vii. psalmes / and in the dyryge. And be newly enprynted at Parys. M.ccccc.xxxi. Sa♃ Ai.

Colophon. Parisiis per Franciscum Regnault In vico sancti iacobi / E regione maturinorum. Ad signum Elephantis.

Brit. Mus. C. 12. e. 15 (on vellum).   Bodl. Arch. Bodl. D. subt. 57 (on vellum).   Camb. Univ. G. 5. 62.

137 × 74. Latin.

99. (*c.* 1531) *François Regnault, Paris*, 8°.

This prayer of Salisbury use is set out a long wout ony serchyng / with many prayers / and goodly pyctures in the kalender / in the matyns of our lady / in the houres of the crosse / in the. vii. psalmes / and in the dyryge. And be newly enprynted at Parys. Sa♃. A

Colophon. Parisiis per Franciscum Regnault In vico sancti iacobi / E regione maturinorum. Ad signum Elephantis.

Brit. Mus. G. 12.136 (on vellum).   Bodl. Douce BB. 89.

137 × 74. Latin.

100. (*c.* 1531, *François Regnault, Paris*) 8°.

The title-page is wanting; the book begins on

Sa♃ c1. [Thre verytees.] at that houre. Seke a good ꝯ faythfull frende of

All wanting after x8ᵇ. trinitas offerim⁹ tibi p oib⁹ gtificatis gīarū actio (in Oratio deuota ad sanctam trinitatem).

Bodl. 8°. C. 716. Linc. (2).

140 × 75. Latin.

101. 1532, April 30, *William Rastell, London*, 8°.

The title-page is wanting; the book begins

[Matyns. xiii.] humani animatum.

Colophon. Thus endyth thys prymer Newly impryntyd at London by. w. Rastell the. xxx. day of Apryll in yᵉ xxiiii. yere of the reyn of kyng Henry the. viii. and in yᵉ yere of our lorde. M.CCCCC.xxxii. Cum Priuilegio.

Camb. Univ. H. Bradshaw's collection.

115 × 58. Latin.

102. 1532, August 7, *François Regnault, Paris*, 16°.

This prymer of Salisbury use is set out a long without ony serchyng / with many prayers / ꝛ goodly pyctures in the kalender / in the matyns of our lady / in the houres of the crosse / in the vii. psalmes / and in the dyryge. And be newly enprynted at Parys. M.D.xxxii.

Colophon. Expliciunt hore beatissime Virginis Marie secundum usum Sau̴ totaliter ad longum : cum orationibus beate Brigitte ac multis aliis orationibus. Impresse Parisius per Franciscū Regnault commorantem in vico sancti Iacobi / iuxta templum maturinorum Ad signum Elephantie. Anno dñi M.ccccxxxii. Die septima Augusti.

Marquess of Bute.
101 × 61. Latin.

103. 1532, August, *Yoland Bonhomme, widow of Thielman Kerver, Paris, for John Growte (London)* 16°.

This prymer of Salysbury use is set out a long wout ony serchyng / with many prayers / and goodly pyctures in the kalender / in the matyns of our lady / in the houres of the crosse / in the. vii. psalmes / ꝛ in the dyryge. And be newly enprynted at Parys. M.D.xxxii.

Colophon. Expliciunt hore beatissime virginis Marie secūdum usum Sarum / totaliter ad longum / cum orationibus beate Brigitte / ac multis aliis / impresse Parisiis / impensis quidem honesti viri Ioannis Growte / librarii / opera autem cōspicue matrone yolande Bonhomme vidue defuncti Thielmanni Keruer / sub unicorni commorātis / in vico diui Iacobi. Anno dñi. M.D.xxxii. mense Augusto.

Brit. Mus. C. 35. a. 14 (1).   Bodl. Gough Missals 48. (1).
103 × 55. Latin.   Magd. Coll. Camb. 23. (1).

104. 1532-33, August, *Yoland Bonhomme, widow of Thielman Kerver, Paris, for John Growte, London*, 16°.

Thys prymer off salysburye use. is sett owght along. wythowght ony serchyng / wyth many prayers / and goodly pyctures yn the kalender / yn the matyns of owr lady / yn the houres off the crosse yn the vii. psalmes : ꝛ yn the dyryge / wyth the. xv. oos yn ynghlysh ꝛ the ꝑfessionall ꝛ Iesus psalter. newly enpryntyd yn Paris / wythyn the howse off Thylmā keruer att the expenses off Iohan growte bokeseller yn london dwellyng wythyn the blak freers next the churche doore. M.D.xxxiii.

Colophon. Expliciunt hore beatissime virginis Marie secūdum usum Sarum / totaliter ad longum / cum orationibus beate Brigitte / ac multis aliis / impresse Parisiis / impensis quidem honesti viri Ioannis Growte / librarii / opera autem cöspicue matrone yolande Bonhomme vidue defuncti Thielmanni Keruer / sub unicorni commorātis / in vico diui Iacobi Anno dñi. M.D.xxxii. mense Augusto.

Brit. Mus. C. 35. a. 13 (1).   Brit. Mus. C. 35. a. 12.
Lincoln Cath. Rr. 4. 21.
104 × 56. Latin.

105. 1532, October 31, *François Regnault, Paris*, 8°.

This prymer of salysbury use is set out a lōg wout ony serchyng with many prayers / and goodly pyctures in the kalēder in the matyns of our lady / in the houres of the crosse / in the. vii. psalmes / ād ī the dyryge. And be newly enprynted at Parys Venūdātur Parisiis apud Frāciscū Regnault / in vico sctī Iacobi / ad signū Elephātis.

Colophon. Expliciunt Hore beate Marie secūdum usum Saꝝ. totaliter ad longum cum multis pulcherrimis orationibus et indulgentiis iam ultimo adiectis. Impresse Parisiis in edibus Frācisci regnault. Alme uniuersitatis Parisiensis librarii iurati. Anno domini millesimo quingentesimo trigesimo secundo. Die ultima Octobris.

Bodl. Douce BB. 228.   Bodl. Gough Missals 78.
152 × 90. Latin.

106. (*c*. 1532) 16°.
The title-page is wanting; the book begins
[Octobre.] Fo. xvi.

All wanting after GG7ᵇ. A prayer of the god names Omnipo (in the contents).

Stonyhurst Coll. T. 10. 30.
100 × 62. Latin.

107. (*c.* 1532 F. Regnault) 16°.
The title-page is wanting; the book begins on
A2. [Almanacke] Fo. ii
All wanting after GG7ᵇ. terra gloria tua: osanna in excelsis. Amen (in Oratio ad sanctam trinitatem).

Mr. F. J. H. Jenkinson.
100 × 60. Latin.

108. (*c.* 1532) 16°.
The title-page is wanting; the book begins on
A2. KL Ianuarius habet dies xxxi
D1ᵇ. Sequuntur Horæ beate Marie virginis secundum usuȝ Ebor.
Finis.

York Minster. XV. R. 44.
79 × 50. Latin.

109. 1533, November 4, *François Regnault, Paris*, 16°.
This prymer of Salysbury use is set out a long without ony serchyng / with many prayers / & goodly pyctures in the kalender / in the matyns of our lady / in the houres of the crosse / in the vii. psalmes / and in the dyryge. And be newly enpryted at Parys. M.D.xxxiii.

Colophon. Expliciunt hore beatissime virginis Marie secūdū usum Sar. totaliter ad longū: cū orationibᵍ beate Brigitte ac multis aliis orationibᵍ. Impresse Parisus p Frāciscū Regnault cōmorantē in vico sancti Iacob / iuxta templum Maturinorum. Ad signum Elephantis. + Anno dni. M.D.xxxiii Die quarta Nouembris.

Lambeth Archiep. 89. L. 12.   Camb. Univ. G. 16. 48.
St. Gregory's Monastery, Downside.
100 × 61. Latin.

G

110. (*c.* 1533) *Germain Hardouyn, Paris*, 8º.

Enchiridiö preclare ecctie Sarisburicͤsis deuotissimis precationibus ac venustissimis imaginibus : ꝗ iis quidē non paucis refertū.

Colophon. Impressum est hoc orariū Parisiis in edibus spectabilis viri Germani Hardouyn librarii iurati uniuersitatis Parisieñ. apud palatiū cōmorantis ad signū diue Margarete.

Brit. Mus. C. 35. b. 11.   Bodl. Douce E. 42.
Camb. Fitzwilliam Mus. 7. H. 11. (on vellum).
120 × 78. Latin.

111. (*c.* 1533) *Robert Wyer (London)* 8º.

The title-page is wanting; the book begins on

a2. [Anno dñi M.D.xxxiii.] Daye. houre. mynute. sygne. degre.

c8ᵇ. Hore beate virginis Marie (ad usum sacrosancte ecclesie Sarum) iam sequuntur.

Colophon. Robertus Wyer me excudebat, in parochio diui Martini, moram trahenti sub intersigno sancti Joannis.

St. Paul's Cath. 38. D. 18.
115 × 63. Latin.

112. (*c.* 1533) 8º.

The title-page is wanting; the book begins on

KL. Februarius habet dies xxviii.

S7ᵇ. The Contentis of thys booke . . .

Ends on S8ᵇ. The rosare (in the contents)

St. Oswald's Church Library, Durham.
136 × 82. Latin.

113. 1534, *François Regnault, Paris*, 4º.

Hore Beatissime virginis marie ad legitimum Sarisburiensis Ecclesie ritum cum quindecim orationibus beate Brigitte / ac multis aliis orationibus pulcherrimis / et indulgentiis / cum tabula aptissima iam ultimo adiectis. M.D.xxxiiii. Venundantur Parisiis a Francisco Regnault In vico sancti Jacobi / sub signo Elephantis.

Colophon. Hore beatissime virginis Marie / secundū usum Sarisbu. totaliter ad logum / cum multis pulcherrimis orationibus et indulgētiis iam ultimo adiectis. Impresse Parisii per Frāciscum Regnault alme universitatis parisiensis librarium iuratum. Opera et impensis eiusdem.

Brit. Mus. C. 35. e. 11.   Bodl. Gough Missals 204.
Camb. Univ. C*. 3. 13.
222 × 138. Latin.

114. 1534, *Yoland Bonhomme, widow of Thielman Kerver, Paris, for John Growte, London,* 16°.

Thys prymer of salysbury use is set out a long without ony serchyng wyth many prayers and goodly pyctures in the kalēder in the matyns off our lady in the houres of the crosse in the vii / psalmes ꝯ in the dyryge wyth the . xv. oos ꝯ the confessionall. newly enpryntyd in Paris wythin the howse of Thylman karuer at the expenses off Johā growte bokeseller in London dwellyng wythyn the blak freers next the chyrche doore.   And be new corrected.   M.D.xxxiiii.

Colophon. Expliciunt hore beatissime virginis Marie secundum usum Saꝝ totalīt ad longum : cū orōnibus btē Brigitte / ac mīt? aliis orōnib⁹. Impresse Parisiis p honestā matronā yolandā bōhōme / viduā defuncti spectabilis viri Thielmāni keruer / sub signo unicornis in vico sctī Iacobi. Impensis q̄dē honesti viri ioānis growte librarii Lōdoñ. ꝑmorantis. in domo predicatorum.   Anno dñi. M.D.xxxiiii.

Brit. Mus. C. 35. a. 4. (1).   Bodl. Douce BB. 28. (1).
102 × 55. Latin.

115. (*c.* 1534) *John Byddell, London, for William Marshall* (*London*), 8°.

A Prymer in Englyshe, with certeyn prayers ꝯ godly meditations, very necessary for all people that understonde not the Latyne tongue. Cum priuilegio Regali. (The roya arms.)

Colophon. Thus endeth the prymer in Englysshe with many goodly and godly praiers. Imprented at London in Fletstrete by Johan Byddell. Dwellyng next to Flete Brydge at the signe of our Lady of pytye. for wyllyam Marshall. Cum gr̃a ⁊ priuilegio regali.

Bodl. Douce BB. 67 (1).
110 × 63. English.

116. 1535-36, May 25, *François Regnault, Paris*, 4°.

Hore beatissime virginis Marie ad legitimū Sarisburiensis Ecclesie ritum / cum quindecim·orationibus beate Brigitte / ac multis aliis orationibus pulcherrimis / ⁊ indulgētiis cum tabula aptissima iam ultimo adiectis. 1535. Venūdant Parisius a Frãcisco Regnault In vico Iacobi / sub signo Elephantis.

Colophon. Hore beatissime virginis Marie / secundum usum Saŋ / totaliter ad longum / cum multis pulcherrimis orationibus ⁊ indulgentiis iā ultimo adiectis. Impresse Parrhisiis per Frãciscum Regnault : impensis ⁊ sumptibus eiusdē : alme uniuersitatis Parrhisieñ. librarii iurati. Anno domini millesimo quingentesimo tricesimo sexto. Die vero. xxv. Maii.

Brit. Mus. C. 35. h. 15. Lambeth Archiep. 78. 1. 9.
Bodl. Gough Missals 200.
198 × 125. Latin.

117. 1535, June 16, *John Byddell, London, for William Marshall (London)*, 4°.

A goodly prymer in englyshe, newly corrected and printed, with certeyne godly meditations and prayers added to the same, very necessarie ⁊ profitable for all them that ryghte assuredly understande not yᵉ latine ⁊ greke tongues. (Arms of Henry the eighth and Anne Boleyn.) With the kyng⁊ most gracious priuilege for. vi. yeres.

Colophon. Imprynted at London in Fletestrete by Iohñ Byddell / dwellynge at the signe of the Sonne / nexte to the cundite / for wylliam Marshall / the yere of our lorde god M.D.xxxv. the xvi. day of Iune.

Bodl. Clar. Press E. 29ᵇ. Emman. Coll. Camb. MSS. 4. 2. 16. on vellum. Earl Spencer. No. 9840. on vellum.
160 × 97. English.

117*. (*c.* 1535) Rev. E. S. Dewick. 140 × 77. Eng. and Lat. see p. 93.

118. (c. 1535) *Thomas Godfray, London*, 8°.

A primer in Englysshe / with dyuers prayers ꝛ godly meditations.

Colophon. Printed at London by Thomas Godfray. Cum priuilegio Rygali.

Camb. Univ. G. 16. 3.
117 × 64. English.

118*. (c. 1535) 16°. Camb. Univ. 79 × 48. English. see. p. 82.

119. (c. 1535, *John Byddell, London*) 4°.

A goodly prymer in englyshe, newly corrected and printed, with certeyne godly meditations and prayers added to the same, very necessarie ꝛ profitable for all them that ryghte assuredly understande not yᵉ latine ꝛ greke tongues. (Arms of Henry the eighth and Anne Boleyn.) With the Kyngʒ most gracious priuilege for. vi. yeres.

All wanting after T3ᵇ. for the lorde cōmaunded || the fysshe, ꝛ anone he cast || out Ionas upon the || drye lande. (in The prayer of the prophet Jonas).

Balliol Coll. Oxford. Arch. c. 12. 4. (1).
163 × 110. English.

120. (c. 1535) *John Byddell, London*, 8°.

The title-page is wanting; the book begins on

A. [Matyns.] O Lorde open thou. Domine

Colophon. Imprynted at London in Flete strete, at the sygne of the Sonne, by me Johan Byddell.

Emman. Coll. Camb. MS. 4. 3. 15 (2).
123 × 80. English and Latin.

121. 1536, *John Byddell, London*, 16°.

The title-page is wanting; the book begins on

b1. [Octobris. fo. ix.] xv d nichasii cp̄i et marty. xi

Colophon. Imprinted at Londö in Fletestrete at the sygne of the Sonne / ouer agaynst the Condyth / by me Johñ Byddell. 1536

St. Paul's Cath. 38. D. 19.
87 × 50. Latin.

122. 1536, *John Gowghe, London*, 8°.

This prymer of Salysbery use / bothe in Englyshe and in Laten is set out a longe without any serchyng. And dyuerse expedient holsome exortatyons of crysten lyuynge The matyns. Pryme and houres the. vii salmes the lateny the salmys of the passion with the salme Beati immaculati ' and saynt Ieroms sauter \ And a confession general Also here unto Annexed a fruyt ful werck called (the paradyse of the soull) with dyuerce deuote meditations and prayers therin \ whiche hath not ben. usual sayd nor redde afore ꝫ al in englyshe. Also with Jhesus matyns with pryme and houres and euynsonge. ꝫ cetera. Cum gratia et priuelegio Regali. God saue our most noble kynge the. viii. Henry with his gratious quene Anne and all theyr progeny. Iohn Gowghe the prynter.

Colophon. Here endeth this prymer with The paradyse of the soule. Imprynted by Iohan Gowhe dwellynge in London in chepsyd next Paulys gate. 1536

Bodl. Douce B. 238 (1). Bodl. Gough Missals 65.

117 × 77. English and Latin.

123. 1536, *Nicolas Le Roux, Rouen, for Jean Groyat and Jean Marchant, Rouen*, 16°.

Hore bte Marie Virginis sedm usum Ebor totaliter ad longum sine require impresse pro Iohanne Marchant ante ecclesiā diui Macuti Rothomagen̄. sub intersignio duoꝝ unicorniū manente.

Colophon. Expliciut hore beatissime Marie virginis sedm usum Eboracen̄ cum multis aliis orationib⁹ iam ultimo in fine adiectis. Impresse Rothomagi / per Nicolaū le roux pro Iohāne groyat / et Iohane marchant in parochia sancti Macuti ad signum duarum unicornium manente. 1536.

Lincoln Cath. RR. 1. 20.

95 × 52. Latin.

124. 1536, *Rouen*, 8°.

Thys prymer in Englyshe and in Laten is newly trāslatyd after the Laten texte.

Colophon. Imprynted in Rowen the yere of our Lorde 1536

Bodl. Douce BB. 231 (1).
147 × 93. English and Latin.

125. 1537, *Nicolas Le Roux, Rouen, for Jacques Cousin, Rouen,* on vellum.

Thys Prymer of Salisbury use set out a long without ony serchyng / with many prayers / and goodly pyctures in the kalender in the matyns of our lady / in the houres of the crosse / ĩ the. vii. psal. and in the dyryge. And be newly emprynted at Rowen. M.D.xxxvii.

Colophon. Rothomagi Excussũ per me Nicolaũ le roux impensis honestissimi viri Iacobi cousin in parochia sancti vincentii huiusce verbis cõmoratis.

Bodl. Gough Missals 13. Rev. J. F. F. Bullock.
140 × 73. Latin.

126. 1537, *Rouen, for François Regnault (Paris)* 16°.

This prymer of Salysbury use is set out a long wout ony serchyng / with many prayers. And be newly emprynted at Rouen. 1537 Sa♃. A

Colophon. Expliciunt hore beatissime virginis Marie scdm usum Sa♃ totaliter ad longum : cum orationib^9 beate Brigitte ac multis aliis orationibus. Impresse pro Francisco Regnault cõmorante in vico diui Iacobi / iuxta templum Maturinorum / ad signũ Elephantis. 1537

Bodl. Gough Missals 46. Bodl. Douce BB. 16.
St. Mary's Coll. Blairs, Aberdeen.
102 × 57. Latin.

127. 1537, long 12°.

Hore beate Marie virginis / ad usum insignis ecclesie Sa♃ totaliter ad longum. Sa♃. A

Colophon. Expliciunt hore beatissime virginis Marie / secundum usum insignis ac preclare Ecclesie Sa♃ / totaliter ad longum / cũ orationibus beate Brigide / necnon multis aliis suffragiis et orationibus iam ultimo in fine adiectis Nouissime Impresse. .:. M.D.xxxvii.

Bodl. Douce BB. 46.
117 × 47. Latin.

128. (*c.* 1537, *Robert Redman, London*) 4".
This prymer in Englyshe and in Laten is newly translated after the Laten texte
Finis.

Lambeth Archiep. 39. 2. 6. (1). Balliol Coll. Oxford. Arch. c. 12. 5. (1). St. John's Coll. Camb. T. 9. 27 (1).
164 × 115. English and Latin.

129. (*c.* 1537, *John Byddell, London*) 4°.
A goodly prymer in Englysshe, newely corrected and prynted, with certeyne godly meditations ⁊ prayers added to the same, very necessarye and profytable for all them that ryghte assuredlye understande not the latine ⁊ greke tongues. Cum priuilegio regali.

Ends on Σ2. An ende of the exposicion of Hierome of Ferrarie ‖ . . . whiche, preuented by deathe, he ‖ coulde not fynysshe. (Verso) The arms of William Marshall.

Brit. Mus. C. 35. c. 12. Bodl. Linc. c. 2. 7.
Camb. Univ. G. 3. 39.
166 × 95. English.

130. (*c.* 1537) *John Byddell, London*, 8°.
The prymer with the pystles and gospels in Englysshe of euery sonday ⁊ holyday in the yere, reuised ⁊ diligētly corrected / and y⁰ forme of the new bedis / with diuers other thynges very necessary for yonge curates, and for all other men women and chyldren. Johñ Byddell.

Colophon. Imprynted at London in Fletestrete, at the sygne of the Sonne, by me Johan Byddell.

Balliol Coll. Oxford. Arch. c. 12. 13.
124 × 78. English.

131. (*c.* 1537) 8°.

The primer in English for children, after the use of Saɤ.

Ends on K8. them that bene bounden || with the chayne of || synnes, by Christe || oure Lorde. || Amen (in The litany).

Bodl. Douce B. 230 (1).

127 × 75. English.

132. 1538, *Nicolas Le Roux, Rouen, for François Regnault, Paris*, 8°.

This prymer of Salysbury use is set out a long wout ony serchyng / with many prayers / and goodly pyctures in te kalĕder / in the matyns of our lady / in the houres of the Crosse / in the. vii. psalmes / and in the dyryge. And be newly enprynted at Rowen. M.CCCCC.XXXVIII. Saɤ. Ai

Colophon. Rothomagi per Nicolaum le Roux impēsis honesti viri Frăcisci Regnault Parisiis In vico sancti Iacobi. E regione Maturinorŭ. Ad signŭ Elephātis degētis.

Brit. Mus. C. 35. c. 14.

140 × 75. Latin.

133. 1538, *François Regnault, Paris*, 8°.

Here after foloweth the Prymer in Engysshe and in latin sette out alonge : after the use of Sarum. M.D.XXXVIII.

Colophon. Imprynted in Paris be me Fransses regnault of our Lorde. Mil. d. xxxviii.

St. Paul's Cath. 38. D. 25. Aberdeen Univ.

133 × 80. English and Latin.

134. 1538, *Rouen, for François Regnault, Paris*, 8°.

This prymer of Salysbury use is set out a long wout ony serchyng / with many prayers / and goodly pyctures in te kalĕder / in the matyns of our lady / in the houres of the Crosse / in the. vii. psalmes / and in the dyryge. And be newly enprynted at Rowen. M.CCCCC.XXXVIII. Saɤ. Ai

Colophon. Parisiis per Franciscum Regnault In vico sancti iacobi / E regione maturinorum. Ad signum Elephantis.

Brit. Mus. C. 12. e. 14.

136 × 74. Latin.

135. 1538, *Nicolas Le Roux, Rouen, for François Regnault* (*Paris*) 8°.

Hereafter foloweth the Prymer in Englysshe sette out alonge / after the use of Sarum. 1538.

Colophon. Thus endeth the Prymer in Englysshe after the use of Salysbury / dilygētly correcte ꝉ newly imprynted at Rowen by Nycholas le Roux for Franchoys Regnault. M.D.xxxviii.

Brit. Mus. C. 35. b. 12.   Camb. Univ. H. Bradshaw's bequest.
Mr. H. H. Gibbs.
118 × 70. English.

136. 1538, *Paris*, 8°.

Thys prymer in Englyshe and in Laten is newly trāslatyd after the Laten texte.   Ai

Colophon. Imprynted in Parys the yere of our Lorde 1538
Brit. Mus. C. 35. c. 13. (1).   Bodl. Douce BB. 227 (1).
Camb. Univ. G. 4. 19. (1).
147 × 92. English and Latin.

137. 1538, *Rouen*, 8°.

This prymer of Salysbury use is set out a long wout ony serchyng / with many prayers / and goodly pyctures in te kalēder / in the matyns of our lady / in the houres of the Crosse / in the. vii. psaumes / and in the dyryge. And be newly enprynted at Rowen.   M.CCCC.XXXVIII.

All wanting after bb3ᵇ. Oratio Iesu filii Sirak   fo. cxvii. (in the contents).

Dr. C. Inglis.
152 × 90. Latin.

138. 1538 (*Nicolas Le Roux*) *Rouen*, 8°.

Thys Prymer in Englyshe and in Laten is newly translatyd after the Laten texte.

Colophon. Imprynted in Rowen the yere of our Lorde. M.CCCCC.XXX.viii.

Bodl. Gough Missals 15 (1).
Sold at Sotheby's June 26, 1885, No. 913.
141 × 80. English and Latin.

139. 1538 (*Nicolas Le Roux, Rouen*) 8°.

Thys prymer in Englyshe / and in Laten is newly translated after the Laten texte. M.D.xxxviii.+

Finis.

Lambeth Archiep. 24. 9. 1 (1).   Bodl. Gough Missals 89 (1).
Rev. W. J. Blew.
140 × 87. English and Latin.

140. 1538 (*Robert Redman, London*) 4°.

This prymer in Englyshe and in Latyn is newly correctyd thys presente yere of our Lorde M.CCCCC.XXXVIII.

Finis.

Bodl. Tanner 278 (1).   Lincoln Cath. RR. 4.
Mr. Samuel Sandars.
165 × 113. English and Latin.

141. (*c.* 1538) *François Regnault, Paris*, 8°.

The title-page is wanting; the book begins on

A3. [Ianuary.] Ianuary hath xxxi dayes. The mone hath

Colophon. Parisiis per Franciscum Regnault. In vico sancti iacobi / e regione maturinorum. Ad signum Elephantis.

Stonyhurst Coll. T. 7. 26.
136 × 70. Latin.

142. 1539, July 15, *John Wayland, London*, 4°.

The Manual of prayers / or the prymer in Englysh ⁊ Laten set out at length, whose contentes the reader by yͤ prologe next after the Kalēder, shal sone perceaue, and there in shall se brefly the order of the whole boke. To the Philippians. iiii. Be not carefull, but in all thynges shewe youre peticion unto God, in prayer, and supplication, and geuynge of thankes. James the fyrst. The prayer of a ryghteous man auayleth much, yf it be feruente. Set forth by Ihon by Goddes grace, ⁊ the Kynges callyng, Bysshoppe of Rochester at the cōmaundemente of the ryghte honorable lorde Thomas Crumwell, lorde Priuie seale, Vicegerent to the Kynges hygnes.

Colophon. Imprinted at Lōdō in fletestrete by me Iohñ

Wayland in saynt Dūstones parysh at the signe of the blewe Garland next to the Temple bare. In the yere of our Lorde. God a M.D.xxxix. the xv. daye of July. Cum priuilegio ad Imprimendum solum.

>Bodl. Mason H. 169.   Magdalen Coll. Camb. 1403.
>Mr. A. H. Huth.
>158 × 109. English and Latin.

143. 1539, *John Mayler, London, for John Wayland, London, sold by Andrew Hester, London, and Mychel Lobley, London,* 8°.

The Manuall of prayers, or the prymer in Englyshe, set out at lengthe, whose contentes the reader by the prologe next after the Kalender shal sone perceaue and there in shall se brefly the order of the whole boke. Set forth by Jhon late bysshoppe of Rochester at the cōmaundement of the ryght honorable Lorde Thomas Crūwel, Lord Priuie seale Vicegerent to the Kynges hygnes. The prayer of a ryghteous man. &c. Jacob i. Cum priuilegio ad imprimendum solum.

Colophon. Imprynted in botoll lane, at the sygne of the whyt beare by me Jhon Mayler for Jhon Waylande, and be to sell in powles churchyarde, by Andrewe Hester at the whyt horse, and also by Mychel Lobley, at the sygne of saynt Mychell. Cum priuilegio ad imprimendum solum. 1539.

>Brit. Mus. C. 12. e. 13 (1).   Bodl. Gough Missals 90.
>Archbishop Marsh's Libr. Dublin. E. 2. 7. 8.
>156 × 93. English.

144. (*c.* 1539) *John Mayler, London, for John Wayland, London, sold by Andrew Hester, London, and Mychel Lobley, London,* 8°.

The Primer in English moste necessary for the educacyon of chyldren extracted oute of the Manuall of prayers or Primer in Englishe and latē, set forth by Tho. laet byshop of Rochester, at the cōmaundement of the ryght honorable, Lord Thomas Crūwell, lord priuie seale, Vicegerent to the Kynges hygnes. Imprynted in fletestrete by Ihon waylande, at the signe of the blew garlande, ⁊ be to sell in Powles churcheyarde, by Andrew Hester at the whyt horse, and also by Mychell Lobley, at the sygne of saynte Mychell. Cum Priuilegio ad imprimendum solum.

Colophon. Imprynted by Ihon Maylart / for Ihon Waylande.

Brit. Mus. C. 35. b. 13.
128 × 79. English.

145. (*c.* 1539) *for Henry Marshall, Rouen,* 8°.
The title-page is wanting; the book begins on
A. + A. a. b. c. d. e. f. g. h. i. k. l. m. n. o. p. q.

Colophon. Expliciunt hore beate Marie virginis secundum usum Ecclesie Sarum. Venundātur Rothomagi apud Henricum Marescalum bibliopolam / commorantem in via magna horologii.

York Minster. X. Q. 6.
119 × 75. Latin.

146. (*c.* 1539) 8°.
Twenty-six lines to a full page. Known only from a fragment consisting of twelve leaves; L1-8, and 2, 3, 6, 7 of signature M.

Begins on L1. [The. vii. psalmes.] arte my refuge from tribulation that hath en

Ends on M7^b. alw-aye desyred. By Christ oure Lorde. So be it (in the Collect for the souls departed).

Contents. L1-4. A portion of the seven Penitential Psalms. L5-8 and M2. A portion of the Fifteen Psalms. M3, 6, 7. The beginning and end of the Litany.

Stonyhurst Coll. T. 10. 27.
102 × 73. English.

147. (*c.* 1539) 8°.
The title-page is wanting; the book begins on
Sarum. C Bestie ⁊ uniuersa pecora serpentes (in Lauds).

Colophon. Expliciunt hore beate Marie virginis scām usum ecclesie Sarum.

Brit. Mus. C. 35. b. 15. (1).
128 × 80. Latin.

148. (*c.* 1539) 8°.
The Primer in Englishe wyth ‖ the. A. B. C. for Chil ‖ dren after the use ‖ of Salisbu ‖ rye. ‖ Newlye Imprinted.

Brit. Mus. C. 35. b. 15 (2).
75 × 60. English.

⁎⁎* This is either a title-page or a colophon.

149. (*c.* 1539) 8°.
The title-page is wanting; the book begins on
A [Iohan.] Fo. ix. The begynnynge of the holy Inicium sancti
All wanting after S8ᵇ. putaui ocs pctō earth for offenders, therefore I haue [louyd.] (in The commendations).

Bodl. Auct. T. Infra. III. 20.
147 × 82. English and Latin.

150. (*c.* 1539) 16°.
The title-page is wanting; the book begins
To serue our lorde, with good (in Week Days moralysed).
All wanting after X6ᵇ. haue some good thoughtes there of (in Thoughts to have in the church).

St. Paul's Cath. 38. D. 20.
84 × 55. English.

151. 1540, *Richard Grafton and Edward Whitchurche, London*, 8°.
The prymer both in Englyshe and Latin Anno. M.D.XL. Prynted in the house late the graye freers by Rychard grafton and Edward whytchurche. Marke. xi. Whatsoeuer ye desyre in your prayer beleue ye shall receyue it and ye shall haue it. Cum priuilegio ad imprimendum solum.

Colophon. Imprynted in London in the house late the graye fryers by Rychard Grafton and Edward Whytchurche / and be to sell in Paules churche yearde at the sygne of the Byble. Cum priuilegio ad imprimendum solum. 1540.

Brit. Mus. C. 35. b. 14 (1).
124 × 75. English and Latin.

152. 1540, *Nicholas Bourman, London,* long 12°.

A Primer or boke of Prayers / set forth at longe, wherein are conteined the houres of our Lady, of the Passion, ꝛ of the holy gho[st] the. vii. Psalmes, the. [xv] Psalmes, the Diri[ge] with many other p[rayers] ꝛ ghostly medit[ations] Here unton is [added] Pistles ꝛ Gosp[els dayly] red in [the church. Anno 1540.]

Colophon. Imprynted at London in Aldersgate strete, by Nycholas Bourman.

Lambeth Archiep. 24. 9. 5.   Sir R. H. Paget, Bart.
Mr. H. H. Gibbs.

⁎⁎⁎ The title-page has been completed from Herbert's Ames, page 594.

125 × 45. English.

153. (*c.* 1540) 8°.

The title-page is wanting; the book begins

[A prologe.] My Lord fauour hath cōstrayned ꝛ bound

Ends on Y8ᵇ. whych lyuest and || reygneste God || worlde || wythout ende. || So be it. (in The dirige).

Dr. Edwin Freshfield.
123 × 76. English and Latin.

154. (*c.* 1540) 16°.

Seventeen lines to a full page. Known only from a fragment consisting of thirty-two leaves; signatures A, B.

Begins. The Manuall of prayers or Primer in englysh Set forth by Jhon by goddes gra[ce] late bysshop of Rochester at the cōmaūdement of the ryghte honorable Lorde Thomas

Crumwell, Lorde Priuie seale Vicegerent to the Kynges hygnes, for an uniuersall usage to his graces louyng subiectes.

Ends on 32^b. Thou shalt beare no false wit ‖ nesse agaynst thy neyghbour (in The ten commandments of almighty God).

Contents. Title-page. Almanack. Kalendar. Forme of byddynge of the bedes. Abrogacyon of the holy dayes. Pater Noster. Aue Maria. Crede. Ten Commandments.

Brit. Mus. C. 18. e. 1 (54).
80 × 53. English.

155. (*c.* 1540) 8°.
The title-page is wanting; the book begins on
T1. [called collettes] Fol. cxlvii.

All wanting after x.8^b. was sore aferde, and sodenly (in A meditation upon the 30th psalm).

Trin. Coll. Camb. VI*. 4. 3 (4).
139 × 84. English.

156. (*c.* 1540) 8°.
The title-page is wanting; the book begins
[Maye] KL The nyght is. viii. ‖ houres, the day. xvi

All wanting after U8^b. and to knowe thy iustyce ꝫ ‖ vertue, is the rote of ‖ immortalyte. Amen. (in A prayer. Sapien. xv.).

Camb. Univ. G. 6. 14.
135 × 85. English and Latin.

157. (*c.* 1540) 8°.
The title-page is wanting; the book begins on
B. [The Matyns] Domine la   O Lorde open thou my
The ende of the prymer.

St. Cuthbert's Coll. Ushaw.
120 × 77. English and Latin.

158. (*c.* 1540) *John Mayler, London,* 8°.
The Primer in Englisshe and Laten set oute at length with the exposicion of Miserere and In te domine speraui

and with the Epistles and Gospels thorowe out all the whole yere. Imprinted in London, by Ihon mayler at the signe of the whyte Beare in Botulph Lane.

Colophon. Imprynted in Botulph lane, at the sygne of the whyt beare, by me Jhon Mayler.

Bodl. Douce BB. 102. Bodl. 8°. c. 70. Th. Seld.
150 × 92. English and Latin.

159. 1541, *Thomas Petyt, London*, 32°.

Hore btē marie virginis secundum usū insignis ecclesie Sarisburiensis de nouo impresse, per Thomam Petit. Anno. M.DLXI.

Colophon. Expliciūt hore beatissime virginis marie secundum usum Sarum. Excusum Lòdini : in Cemiterio diui Pauli per Thomam Petit. Anno. M.D.XLI.

St. Marie's Seminary, Oscott. Case G. 8.
60 × 36. Latin.

160. 1541, *Thomas Petyt, London*, 8°.

The prymer in Englysshe and Laten. after the use of Sarum, set out at length with many goodly prayers, ꝛ with the exposicion of Miserere, ꝛ In te domine speraui with the Epystles and Gospels throughout the hoole yeare. M.D.XLI. Cum priuilegio ad imprimendum solum.

Colophon. Prynted at London in Paules church yerde / at the sygne of the Mayden's heade by Thomas Petyt. M.D.XLI.

Bodl. Gough Missals 94 (1). Stonyhurst Coll. Case 5.
141 × 90. English and Latin.

161. (*c.* 1541) *John Mayler, London*, 16°.

Hore beate marie virginis secundum usū insignis ecclesie Sariburisburium de nouo īpresse :

Colophon. Expliciunt hore beate Ma[rie] [virgini]s secundum u[sum S]arum . . . Johñ May[ler] . . . the whyte . . . [Boto]lph lane . . . ad im[primendum so]lū.

Brit. Mus. C. 35. a. 11.
90 × 63. Latin.

I

162. (c. 1541) *Robert Toy, London*, 8°.

A Prymar of Sālisbery use / set out a longe in Englyshe and Latyn and a prayer for euery sondaye and holy day in the yere / besydes these folowynge.

Colophon. Imprinted in Paules churcheyarde by Robert Toye.

Mr. J. F. F. Horner.
137 × 82. English and Latin.

163. 1542 (*Antwerp*) 8°.

Hore beate Marie virginis secundũ verum usum insignis ecclesie Sarisburiensis / cũ multis orationibus ad longum. Anno 1542

Finis (The royal arms).

Brit. Mus. C. 35. d. 16.
149 × 80. Latin.

164. 1542, *Rouen*, 8°.
The title-page is wanting; the book begins
[Ianuarius] KL January hath. xxxi. dayes.

Colophon. Expliciũt hore beatissime virginis Marie secundum usum / Sarum : totaliter ad longum cum orationibus beate Brigitte / ac multis aliis deuotis orationibus. Impresse / Rothomagi. Anno domini millesimo quingētesimo quadragesimo secundo.

Brit. Mus. C. 35. a. 1.
113 × 65. Latin.

165. 1542, *William Bonham, London*, 4°.

The Prymer in Englyshe, and Latyn wyth the Epystles and Gospelles: of euerye Sonday, ⁊ holye daye in the yere, and also the exposycion upon Miserere mei deus. wyth many other prayers + Prynted in London by Wyllyam Bonham Cum priuilegio Ad imprimendum solum. 1542.

Finis.

Earl Spencer. No. 19638. (1).
162 × 113. English and Latin.

166. 1542, *William Bonham, London*, 4°.

The Prymer in Englyshe, and Latyn wyth the Epystles and Gospelles : of euerye Sonday, ℞ holye daye in the yere, and also the exposycion upon Miserere mei deus. wyth many other prayers + Prynted in London by Wyllyam Bonham Cum priuilegio Ad imprimendum solum. 1542.

Ends on F4. kyngdome, whyche lyuest ‖ and raygnest for euer ‖ and euer. So be it. (in A fruitful prayer necessary for all men, called Deus propitius).

St. Paul's Cath. 38. D. 7. Camb. Univ. G. 3. 50.
St. John's Coll. Camb. T. 9. 19.
162 × 112. English and Latin.

167. 1542, *Thomas Petyt, London*, 8°.

The Prymer in Englysshe and Laten, after the use of Sarū set out at length with many goodly prayers With the Epystles and Gospels throughout the hoole yere. M.D.XLii. Cum priuilegio ad imprimendum solum.

Colophon. Prynted at london in paules churchyarde at the sygne of the maydens heed by Thomas Petyt. M.D.xlii.

Bodl. Gough Missals 67[A]. Mr. Christie Miller.
130 × 82. English and Latin.

168. 1542, *Robert Toy, London*, 4°.

The Prymer in Englyshe, and Latyn wyth the Epystles and Gospelles : of euerye Sonday, ℞ holye daye in the yere, and also the exposycion upon Miserere mei deus. with many other prayers + Prynted in London by Roberte Toye. Cum priuilegio Ad imprimendum solum. 1542.

Ends on F 4. a kyngdome, whyche lyuest ‖ and raygnest for euer ‖ and euer. So be it. (in A fruitful prayer necessary for all men, called Deus propitius).

Camb. Univ. B* 5. 55.
Sold at Sotheby's, 9th July, 1886. No. 1284.
163 × 113. English and Latin.

169. 1543, *Thomas Petyt, London*, 4º.

The prymer in Englysh and latyn, after the use of Sarum, set out at length with manye goodly prayers, with the exposicyon upon the Psalme called Miserere mei deus, and in te domine speraui, with the Epystels and Gospels on euery Sonday, and holye daye in the yeare. Cum priuilegio ad imprimendum solum.

Colophon after the prymer. Prynted at London in Paules churche yearde, at the sygne of the maydens heade, by Thomas Petyt. M.D.XLiii.

Colophon after the exposicyon. Prynted at London in Paules churche yearde, at the sygne of the Maydens heed, by Thomas petyt.

Colophon after the Epystels and Gospels. Imprinted at London in Paules church yarde at the sygne of the maydens heed, by Thomas Petyt.

Brit. Mus. C. 10. a. 14.   Bodl. 4º. P. 13. Th. Seld.
Camb. Univ. B* 5. 31.
183 × 133. English and Latin.

170. (*c.* 1543) *Richard Grafton, London*, 32º.
Seventeen lines to a full page. Known only from three fragments consisting of five leaves; 1, 2, 3, 6, 7, of signature T, and also signature U.

Begins on T 1. [The Dirige.] holde upon me, that I am.

Colophon. Imprynted in London by Rycharde Grafton dwellynge within the circuite of the late Gray fryers, prynter to the Prynces grace. Cum priuilegio ad imprimendū solum.

Contents. Portions of the Dirige.

Brit. Mus. C. 18. a. 23.   Camb. Univ. fragments.
58 × 35. English.

171. 1544, September 12, *Thomas Petyt, London*, 16º.

This prymer of Salysbury use is set out a longe without anye searchynge with many prayers. Imprynted at London the xii. day of Septembre M.D.XLiiii.

Colophon. Expliciunt hore beatissime virginis marie secundum usum sarum Excusū Londini in cemiterio diui Pauli per Thomam Petit. Año M.D.XLiiii.

Brit. Mus. C. 12. a. 8.
83 × 53. Latin.

172. 1544, *Thomas Petyt, London*, 8°.
The title-page is wanting ; the book begins on
   B. Thou shalt have none other god
Colophon. Printed at london in paules church yearde at the sygne of the maydens heed by Thomas petyt. M.D.xliiii

Brit. Mus. C. 35. b. 16 (2) Queen's Coll. Oxford. 283. A. 24 (2)
129 × 84. English and Latin.

173. 1545, May 29, *Richard Grafton, London*, 8°.
The title-page is wanting ; the book begins on
   A3. Kalender (mutilated)
   A4. KL Maye hath. xxxi. || daies.
Colophon. Imprinted at London within the precinct of the late dissolued house of the graye Friers, by Richard Grafton Printer to the Princes grace, the. xxix day of May, the yere of our Lorde. MDxlv. Cum priuilegio ad imprimendū solum.

Emman. Coll. Camb. MSS. 4. 3. 21 (1).
114 × 57. English.

174. 1545, May 29, *Richard Grafton, London*, 4°.

The Primer, Set Foorth by the Kynges maiestie and his Clergie, to be taught lerned, ⁊ read : and none other to be used throughout all his dominions. M.D.XLV.

Colophon. Imprinted at London within the precinct of the late dissolued house of the gray Friers, by Richard Grafton Printer to the Princes grace, the xxix. daye of May, the yere of our Lord, M.D.XLV. Cum priuilegio ad imprimendum solum.

Brit. Mus. C. 35. c. 15. Bodl. Douce BB. 123.
Keble Coll. Oxford.
157 × 90. English.

62   A HAND-LIST OF   [1545-

175. 1545, May 29, *Richard Grafton, London*, 8°.
The title-page is wanting; the book begins on
   A2. KL Ianuary hath. xxxi. || dayes.
   Colophon. Imprinted at London within the precinct of the late dissolued house of the gray Friers, by Richard Grafton Printer to the Princes grace, the. xxix. daye of May, the yere of our Lord, M.D.XLV. Cum priuilegio ad imprimendum solum.
   Bodl. Gough Missals 39 (1).
   110 × 57. English.

176. 1545, June 19, *Edward Whitchurche, London*, 4°.
   The Primer, Set Foorth by the Kynges maiestie and his Clergie, to be taüght lerned, ꝫ read: and none other to be used throughout all his dominions.   M.D.XLV.
   Colophon. Imprinted At London, in Fletestrete at the signe of the Sunne, ouer agaynst the conduyte, by Edward Whitchurche, the xix. day of June. M.D.XLV. Cum priuilegio ad imprimendum solum.
   Brit. Mus. C. 35. c. 16.   Bodl. 4°. P. 14 (1). Th. Seld.
   Trin. Coll. Camb. VI^d. 2. 4 (1).
   155 × 87. English.

177. 1545, June 20, *Edward Whitchurche, London*, 8°.
   The Primer set forth by ye kinges maieste and his Cleargy, and none other to be used through out his dominions. M.D.XLV.
   Colophon. Imprinted at London, in Fletestrete at the signe of the Sunne, ouer against the conduyte, by Edward Whitchurche the xx. day of Iune. M.D.XLV. Cum priuilegio ad imprimendum solum.
   Brit. Mus. C. 35. b. 17.
   110 × 58. English.

178. 1545, June 20, *Edward Whitchurche, London*, 8°.
The title-page is wanting; the book begins on
   A2 KL. Ianuary hath. xxxi dayes
   Colophon. Imprinted At London, in Fletestrete at the signe

of the Sunne, ouer against the conduyte, by Edward Whitchurche the xx. day of Iune. M.D.XLV. Cum priuilegio ad imprimendum solum.

Lincoln Cath. RR. 4. 24.
115 × 61. English.

179. 1545, September 6, *Richard Grafton, London,* 4°.

The Primer, In Englishe and Latyn, set foorth by the Kynges maiestie and his Clergie to be taught learned, and read : and none other to be used throughout all his dominions. Imprinted At London within the precinct of the late dissolued house of the Gray friers by Richard Grafton Printer to the Princes grace, the. vi. daye of Septembre, the yeare of our lorde. M.D.XLV. Cum priuilegio ad imprimendum solum.

Colophon. Imprinted At London within the precincte of the late dissolued house of the grey Friers by Richard Grafton Printer to the Princes grace, the. vi. daie of Septēber, the yere of our Lorde. M.D.XLV. Cum priuilegio ad imprimendum solum.

Brit. Mus. C. 25. h. 10 (1).   Queen's Coll. Oxford. 79. C (1).
Camb. Univ. 8. 3. 27. (1).
152 × 100. English and Latin.

180. 1545, November 25, *Thomas Petyt, London,* 16°.

This prymer of Sāylbury use is set out a longe without anye searchynge with many prayers. Imprynted at London the xxv. day of Nouēbre. M.D.XLV.

Colophon. Expliciunt hore beatissime virginis marie secūdum usum sarum. Excusū Londini in cemiterio diui Pauli per Thomam Petyt. Año M.D.XLV.

Dr. Edwin Freshfield.
83 × 53. Latin.

181. 1546, January 6, *Edward Whitchurche, London,* 8°.

The Primer, In Englishe ⁊ Latin, set forth by the kynges maieste ⁊ his Clergie to be taught learned, and read : and none other to be used thoughout all his dominions. 1546.

Colophon. Imprinted at London in Fletestrete at the sunne ouer against the conduyte by Edward Whitchurche the ix day of Januari MDXLVI. Cum priuilegio ad imprimendum solum.

 Brit. Mus. C. 25. c. 22. and C. 35. c. 17.
 125 × 80. English and Latin.
 ⁎ The Colophon is supplied from Herbert's Ames, page 542.

 182. 1546, March 16, *Richard Grafton, London*, 16°.
The title-page is wanting; the book begins on
 + i. [The Kalendar.]
Colophon. Imprinted at London within the precint of the late dissolued house of the Gray Friers by Richarde Graftō Printer to the Princes grace, the. xvi. day of March, the yere of our lord a thousande, D.xlvi. Cum priuilegio ad imprimendum solum.

 Mr. Samuel Sandars.
 66 × 34. English.

 183. 1546, April 1, *Edward Whitchurche, London*, 16°.
The title-page is wanting; the book begins on
 * 2. [The kalender.]
Colophon. Imprinted at Londō in Fletstrete at the signe of yᵉ Sunne ouer against the conduyte, by Edward Whitchurche, the first day of April. M.D.XLVI. Cum priuilegio, ad imprimendum solum.

 Dr. Edwin Freshfield.
 75 × 43. English.

 184. 1546, August 17, *Richard Grafton, London*, 4°.
 The Primer, Set Furth by the Kinges maiestie ⁊ his Clergie, to be taught lerned, and red : ⁊ none other to be used thorowout all his dominions. Imprinted At London within the precinct of the late dissolued house of the grayc Friers by Richard Grafton Printer to the Princes grace, the xvii. day of August, the yeare of our lorde M.D.XLVI. Cum priuilegio ad imprimendum solum.

The ende of the Primer. (verso) The copy of the Kynges highnes bil assigned. . . . God saue the Kyng.

Brit. Mus. C. 35. c. 18.   Bodl. 4°. P. 16. Th. Seld.
160 × 88. English.

185. 1546, August 20, *Edward Whitchurche, London*, 8°.

The Primer in Englysshe, set furth by the kynges maiestie and his Clergie, to be taught learned and red, thoroughout his dominions, all other set apart. M.D.XLVI.

Colophon. Imprinted at London in Flete strete at the signe of the Sunne ouer agaynst the conduyte By Edwarde Whit churche. The. xx. day of Auguste, the yere of our lorde : M.D.XLVI. Cum priuilegio ad imprimendum solum.

Brit. Mus. C. 35. a. 18.
112 × 60. English.

186. 1546, September 6, *Richard Grafton* (*London*) 8°.

Orarium seu libellus precationum per Regiam maiestatem & clerū latinè œditus. 1546. Cum priuilegio ad imprimendum solum.

Colophon. Ex officina Richardi Graftoni Clarissimo Principi Edouardo typographi. vi. die mensis Sep. Anno. M.D.XLV. Cum priuilegio ad imprimendum solum.

Brit. Mus. C. 35. b. 18.   Bodl. Douce BB. 38.
Camb. Univ. A* 8. 8.
115 × 56. Latin.

187. 1547, November 30, *Richard Grafton, London*, 4°.

The Primer set furth by the Kinges maiestie ⁊ his Clergie, to be taught lerned, and red : and none other to be used thorowout all his dominions. Imprinted at London, the laste daye of Nouember, in the fyrste yere of the reigne of our souereigne lorde kyng Edward the VI. By Richard Graftō printer to his moste royall Maiestie. Cum Priuilegio ad imprimendum solum.

Colophon. Imprinted at London, the laste daie of Nouëber, in the firste yere of the reigne of our souereigne lorde kyng

Edward the. vi: By Rychard Grafton printer to his moste royall Maiestie. In the yere of our Lorde. M.D.XLVII. Cum priuilegio ad imprimendum solum.

Brit. Mus. C. 25. h. 6 (1). Lincoln Cath. RR. 4. 29.
158 × 86. English.

188. 1547, November 30, *Richard Grafton, London*, 4°.

The Primer set furth by the Kinges maiestie ⁊ his Clergie, to be taught, lerned, and red: and none other to be used thorowout his highnes dominions. Cum priuilegio ad imprimendum solum.

Colophon. Imprinted at London, the last daie of Nouember, in the fyrste yere of the reigne of our souereigne lord kyng Edward the. VI. By Rychard Grafton. printer to his moste royall Maiestie. In the yere of our Lord. M.D.XLVII. Cum priuilegio ad imprimendum solum.

Bodl. Douce BB. 122.
160 × 88. English.

189. 1548, January 9, *Edward Whitchurche, London*, 8°.

The Primer in Englishe ⁊ Latin: set forth by the kynges maiestie ⁊ his Clergie to be taught learned, ⁊ read: ⁊ none other to be used thoughout all his dominiõs.

Colophon. Imprinted At London, in the Flete strete at the signe of the Sunne, ouer against the conduite, by Edward Whitchurche the ix. day of ianuarii, Anno m,d,x,l,uiii, Cum priuilegio ad imprimendum solum.

Brit. Mus. C. 35. b. 19.
120 × 68. English and Latin.

190. (*c.* 1548) 16°.

Fifteen lines to a full page. Known only from a fragment, of which there are two copies. Each copy consists of four leaves: 2, 3, 6, 7 of signature N.

Begins on N2. [The letany] That it maye please the to
Ends on N7[b]. The end of this Primer.

Camb. Univ. fragments.
82 × 47. English.

191. (*c.* 1548) *Richard Grafton, London*, 8º.

The title-page is wanting; the book begins on
A2. [Kalender.]

Colophon. Imprinted by Rychard Grafton Prynter to the Kynges Maiestie. Cum priuilegio ad imprimendum solum.

Marquess of Bath.
114 × 57. English.

192. (*c.* 1548) 8 .

The title-page is wanting; the book begins on

¶1. An iniūcyon ‖ gyuen by the kyng our souerei ‖ gne lordes moste excellente ma ‖ iestie, for the autorysyng ⁊ establishyng the use of this Prymer.

All wanting after R7ᵇ. The ende of the Primer.

Camb. Univ. G. 6. 55.
120 × 60. English.

193. 1549, *Richard Grafton, London*, 8º.

The Prymer set furth by the Kinges highnes and his Cleargye to be taught unto chyldren throughoute his dominions, all other set apart.

Colophon. Imprynted at London wythin the precincte of the late dissolued house of yᵉ grey Friers by Richard Grafton Printer to the Kynges grace. M.D.XLIX. Cum priuilegio ad imprimendum solum.

Bodl. Gough Missals 44. Emman. Coll. Camb. MSS. 4. 3. 16 (1).
115 × 57. English.

194. (*c.* 1550) *Thomas Gaultier, London, for Robert Toy, London*, 32º.

The title-page is wanting; the book begins on
C2. [A prayer.] fol. iiii. dementes, and so glorifie.

Colophon. Imprinted at London by Thomas Gaultier, at the costes and charges of Robert Toye, dwelling in Paules Churcheyarde, at the sygne of the Bell.

Mr. F. J. H. Jenkinson.
55 × 34. English.

195. 1551, *Richard Grafton, London*, 4°.

The Primer set furth by the Kynges hyghnes and hys Clergie, to be taught, learned and read, of all his louyng subiectes, all other set aparte, corrected accordynge to the Statute made in the third and. iiii. yere : of our souereigne Lorde the Kynges Maiesties reigne. Cum priuilegio ad imprimendum solum.

Colophon. Excusum Londini, in ædibus Richardi Graftoni Regii Impressoris. Anno. 1551.

Brit. Mus. C. 25. h. 9 (1). Exeter Coll. Oxford. 171. D. 10.
Routh Libr. Durham xvii. E 28.
159 × 86. English.

196. 1551, *Richard Grafton, London*, 8°.

The Primer, and Cathechisme, set furthe by the Kynges highnes and his Clergie, to bee taught, learned and read, of all his louyng subiectes, all other set apart, corrected accordyng to the Statute, mad in the third and iiii. yere, of our souereigne Lorde the Kynges Maiesties reigne. Anno domini. 1551.

Colophon. Imprinted at London, by Richard Grafton, Printer to the kynges Maiestie. 1551. Cum priuilegio ad imprimendum solum.

Brit. Mus. C. 35. b. 20 (1). Bodl. 8° c. 648. Linc.
Magd. Coll. Camb. A. 9. 29 (1).
115 × 58. English.

197. 1551, *Nicholas Le Roux, Rouen, for Robert Valentin, Rouen*, 8°.

This prymer of Salisbury use is se tout along with houtonyser chyng / with many prayers / ⁊ goodly pyctures in the Kalender, in the matins of our lady, in the houres of the crosse, in the. vii. psalmes, and in the dyryge. And be newly emprynted at Rouen. M.D.li. Sa⁊ A

Colophon. Expliciunt hore beatissime virginis Marie secundum usum Sa⁊ totaliter ad longum : cū orationibus beate Brigitte cum multis aliis orationib^9 Impresse per Nicolaum le

Roux pro Robertum Valentinum commorantem Bibliopola in porticu ecclesie beate Marie. M.D.li.

> Bodl. Gough Missals 91.   Bodl. 8°. Th. Seld. G. 16.
> 143 × 76. Latin.

198. 1551, *for Robert Valentin, Rouen*, 16°.
Hore beate Marie virginis secūdū usū Saɤ. Rothomagi apđ Robertū Valētinū, M.D.li.
All wanting after U7ᵇ. riculis / tentationib⁹ / ꞇ angustiis corpo (in Suffragia De nominibus dei).

> Bodl. Gough Missals 50.
> 96 × 55. Latin.

199. 1552, *Richard Grafton, London*, 8°.
The Primer, and Cathechisme, sette furthe by the Kynges highnes and his Clergie, to be taught, learned, and redde, of all his louing subiectes al other set apart corrected accordyng to the Statute, made in the thirde and iiii. yere, of our souereigne Lordes the Kynges Maiesties reigne. Cum Priuilegio ad Imprimendum solum. An. M.D.L.II.
Colophon. Imprinted at London by Rychard Grafton, Printer to the Kynges Maiestie. 1552. Cum Priuilegio ad Imprimendum solum.

> Canterbury Cath. H and Hᴬ Library.   Mr. H. H. Gibbs.
> Archbishop Marsh's Libr. Dublin F 2. 6. 10.
> 113 × 59. English.

200. 1553, *William Seres, London*, 8°.
A Prymmer or boke of priuate prayer nedeful to be used of al faythfull Christianes. Whiche boke is auctorysed and set fourth by the Kinges maiestie, to be taughte, learned, redde and used of al hys louynge subiectes. Continue in prayer. Rom. 12. Londini ex officina Wilhelmi Seres typographi. Cum priuilegio ad imprimendum solum. 1553.

Colophon. These bookes are to be solde, at the weste ende of Paules towarde Ludgate, at the sygne of the Hedgehogge.

Bodl. Douce BB. 41.
115 × 58. English.

201. (*c.* 1553) *William Seres, London*, 16°.

A Primmer or boke of private prayer nedefull to bee used of all faythfull Christians. Whiche boke is auctorised and set forth by the kynges Maiestye, to be taught, learned, read, and used be hys louynge Subiectes. Contynue in prayer. Ro. xii. Londini ex officina Wilhelmi Seres Tipographi. Cum priuilegio ad imprimendum solum.

Colophon. These bokes are to be solde, at the Weste ende of Paules towarde Ludgate at the signe of the Hedgehogge.

Brit. Mus. C. 35. a. 9.
78 × 50. English.

202. (*c.* 1553) 8°.

The title-page is wanting; the book begins on

☞ 2. [January] Hath. xxxi. days, the moone. xxxi

All wanting after N 6ᵇ. necessaries plentifully for me ℞ my [house] (in Sundry godly prayers for divers purposes).

Bodl. i. g. 59 (2).
115 × 62. English.

203. 1554, *Jean Le Prest, Rouen, for Robert Valentin, Rouen*, 8°.

This prymer of Salisbury use is se tout a long without ony serchyng / with many prayers / ℞ goodly pyctures in the Kalender / in the matins of our lady in the houres of the crosse / in the / vii. psalmes. and in the dyryge. And benewly enprynted at Rouen. M.D.Liiii. Saʀ. A

Colophon. Expliciunt hore beatissime virginis Marie secundum usum Saʀ / totaliter ad longum : cū orationibᵍ beate Brigitte cum multis aliis orationibᵍ Impresse per Iohannem le prest pro Robertūm Valentinum / commorantem Bibliopola in porticu ecclesie beate Marie. M.D.Liiii.

Brit. Mus. C. 35. c. 20. Bodl. Gough Missals 14.
Canterbury Cath. H and H^A Libr.
142 × 77. Latin.

204. 1554, *Thomas Petyt, London*, 8°.
Hore beate Marie, virginis secundum usum isignis ecclesie Sarisburiensis, de nouo Impresse. Anno Domini. M.D.L.iiii. Imprinted at London.

Colophon. Imprinted at Londö, by Thomas Petit, dwellynge in Paules Churchyarde. M.D.L.iiii.

Bodl. Gough Missals 62.
126 × 80. Latin.

205. 1554, *London*, 8°.
Hore beate Marie virginis secundum usum insignis ecclesie Sarisburiensis. Londini Anno, MD.Liiii.

Finis.

Rev. J. F. W. Bullock.
127 × 78. Latin.

206. (*c.* 1554) 8°.
The title-page is wanting; the book begins
[January] The nyght is. xvi houres
Finis.

Rev. J. F. W. Bullock.
125 × 78. Latin.

207. 1555, June 4, *John Wayland, London*, 4°.
An uniforme and Catholyke Prymer in Latin and Englishe, with many godly and deuout prayers, newly set forth by certayne of the cleargye with the assente of the moste reuerende father in god the Lorde Cardinall Pole hys grace: to be only used (al other sette a parte) of al the kyng and Quenes maiesties louinge subiectes throughe oute all their realmes and dominions, according to the Quenes hygnes letters patentes

in that behalf geuen. Imprinted at London, by Iohn Waylande the. iiii. daye of Iune. Anno domini. M.D.L.V. Cum priuilegio per septennium.

Colophon. Imprynted at London in Fletestrete at the sygne of the Sunne ouer against the Conduite by Iohn Wayland. Cum priuilegio per septennium.

Lambeth Archiep. 6. 1. 29.   Trin. Coll. Camb. vi^d. 2. 3.
Jesus Coll. Camb. B. 5. 14 (2).
175 × 107. English and Latin.

208. 1555, August 10, *Robert Toy, London*, 8°.

Hore beate Marie virginis secundum usum in signis ecclesie Sarum. nouo impres. Anno domini M.D.L.V. the x. of August. Londini in edibus Roberti Toy.

Finis.

Professor Middleton.

125 × 78. Latin.

209. 1555, October 1, *Robert Caly, London*, 8°.

The Primer in English and Latin, after Salisburie use : set out at length with manie Praiers and goodly pictures : Newly imprinted this present yeare. 1555. Excusum Londini in edibus Roberti Caly, Typographi, Primo Octobris Cum priuilegio.

Finis.

Earl of Ashburnham.

119 × 75. English and Latin.

210. 1555, *Robert Toy, London*, 8°.

Hore beate Marie virginis secundum usum insignis ecclesie Eboracensis.   M.D.LV.   Londini in edibus Roberti Toy.

Finis.

York Minster. X. P. 8.

126 × 76. Latin.

211. 1555, *John Wayland, London*, 8°.

The primer in Englishe (after the use of Sarum) with many godly and deuoute prayers, as in the contentes doth appeare. Wherunto is added a plaine and godly treatise concerning the Masse, and the blessed Sacrament of the aulter, for the instruccyon of the unlearned and symple people. Imprinted at Londō, by Iohn Wailande at the signe of the Sunne in Fletestrete ouer agaynst the great conduit. Anno domini. M.D.L.V. Cum priuilegio per septennium.

Finis. Cum Priuilegio per septennium.

Camb. Univ. A*. 8. 6. Emman. Coll. Camb. MSS. 4. 4. 5.
Peterborough Cath. S. 59.
120 × 71. English.

212. 1555, *John Wayland, London*, 4°.

This Primer in Latin and Englishe (after the use of Sarum) with many godlye and deuoute prayers, as in the contentes doth appere. Whereunto is added a playne and godly treatise concerning the Masse, and the blessed Sacramente of the Aulter, for the instruccion of the unlearned and simple people. Imprinted at London, by Iohn Waylande at the signe of the Sunne in Fletestrete ouer agaynste the great Conduit. Anno Domini. M.D.L.V. Cum priuilegio per septennium.

After the Primer. Finis.

Colophon (after "Godly Prayers"). Imprynted at London in Fletestrete at the sygne of the Sunne ouer against the Conduite by Iohn Wayland. Cum priuilegio per septennium.

Brit. Mus. C. 10. a. 12 (1). Routh Libr. Durham XVII. E. 29.
167 × 107. English and Latin.

213. 1555, *John Wayland, London*, 4°.

The Primer in Latin and Englishe (after the use of Sarum) with many godlye and deuoute prayers, as in the contentes doth appere. Whereunto is added a playne and godly treatise concerning the Masse, and the blessed Sacramente of the Aulter, for the instruccion of the unlearned and simple people. Imprinted at London, by Iohn Waylande at the signe of the Sunne in Fletestrete ouer agaynste the great Conduit. Anno domini. M D.L.V. Cum priuilegio per septennium.

After the Primer. Finis.

Colophon (after " Godly Prayers "). Imprynted at London in Fletestrete at the sygne of the Sunne ouer against the Conduite by John Wayland. Cum priuilegio per septennium.

After "A plaine and godly treatise". Finis.
Brit. Mus. C. 35. c. 22.   Bodl. Douce BB. 131.
Camb. Univ. B. 5. 54.
167 × 107. English and Latin.

214. 1555, *John Kyng, London, for John Waley* (*London*) 8°.
Hore beate Marie virginis secundum usum insignis ecclesie Sasburiensis de nouo Impresse.   Anno Domini. M.D.LV.   Imprinted at Londō by John Kyng, for Jhon Waley.
Finis.
Incorporated Law Society.
125 × 80. Latin.

215. 1555, *Jean Le Prest, Rouen, for Robert Valentin, Rouen*, 8°.
This prymer of Salisbury use is se tout a long with houtonyser chyng / with many prayers / ꝫ goodly pyctures in the Kalender / in the matins of our lady in the houres of the crosse / in thes / vii. psalmes and in the dyryge. And benewly enprynted at Rouen. M.D.L.V.   Saꝫ. A
Colophon. Expliciunt hore beatissime virginis Marie / secundū usū Sarum / totaliter ad longum : cū orationibus beate Brigide / cū multis aliis orationib^9 / Impresse per Iohannē le prest / impensis honestissimi viri Roberti valentini / suâ officinâ tenētis ī porticū bibliopolarū iuxta edē btē Marie. M.D.LV.
Brit. Mus. C. 35. c. 23.   Bodl. Gough Missals 7.
Camb. Univ. G. 5. 16.
140 × 77. Latin.

216. 1555, *for Robert Valentin, Rouen*, 16°.
Hore beate marie virginis / secūdum usum insignis ecclesie Sarum.   Venales habentur Rothomagi in porticu bibliopolarum / per Robertum Valentinum. M.D.L.V.
Finis.
Brit. Mus. C. 51. a. 6.
97 × 54. Latin.

217. 1555, *Rouen, for Robert Valentin, Rouen*, 16°.

Hereafter Foloweth the Prymer in Englysshe and in latin sette out alonge: after the use of Sarū. In edibus Roberti Valentini. M.D.lv.

Colophon. Rothomagi. Apud Robertum Valentinum.

Brit. Mus. C. 35. a. 10. Bodl. Gough Missals 51.
Earl Spencer No. 15469.
94 × 56. English and Latin.

218. 1555, *Rouen, for Robert Valentin, Rouen*, 8°.

This prymer of Sarysbury use is set out a long without ony serchyng / with many prayers / ꝛ goodly pyctures in the matyns of our lady. And benewly emprynted at Rouen. Venundantur Rothomagi apud Robertū Valentinū in porticu bibliopolarum / prope edem beate Marie. M.D.L.V.

Colophon. Expliciūt hore beatissime virginis Marie secundum usum Sacrum totaliter ad longum cum orationibus beate Brigitte / ac multis aliis deuotis orationibus. Impresse / Rothomagi. Anno domini millesimo quingētesimo quinguagesimo quinto. Sarum.

Lambeth. Archiep. 24. 9. 3 (1). Rev. W. J. Blew.
Earl Spencer No. 16578.
112 × 66. Latin.

219. 1555, *Rouen, for Robert Valentin, Rouen*, 8°.

Here after Foloweth the Prymer in Englysshe and in latin sette out alonge: after the use of Sarum. M.D.lv.

Colophon. Impressum rothomagi impensis honesti viri Roberti valentini bibliopolarū particulo morā teneñ. M.D.lv.

Bodl. Tanner 802. Bodl. Gough Missals 11.
Mr. A. Mackay.
135 × 82. English and Latin.

220. 1556, October 1, *Robert Caly, London*, 8°.

The Primer in English and Latin, after Salisburie use: set out at length with manie Praiers and goodly pictures: Newly

imprinted this present yeare. 1556. Excusum Londini in œdibus Roberti Caly, Typographi, Primo Octobris.
Finis.

Brit. Mus. C. 35. b. 21 (1). Bishop Cosin's Libr. Durham (with MSS.) Dv. 39.
118 × 76. English and Latin.

221. 1556, *John Kyngston and Henry Sutton, London, for John Wight* (*London*) 8°.

Hore beate Marie, virginis secundum usum insignis Ecclesie Eboracensis de Nouo Impress. Anno domini. 1556. Printed at London by Ihon Kingstone, and Henry Sutton.

Colophon. Imprinted at London by Iohn Kyngston and Henry Sutton for Iohn wyght.

Emman. Coll. Camb. MSS. 4. 3. 25.
127 × 77. Latin.

222. 1556, *John Kyng, London*, 8°.

The Primer in English after Salysburye use: sette out at lengthe with manye Godlye prayers: Newlye Imprinted thys presente yere. Anno domini. M.D.L.VI.

Colophon. Imprynted at London by John Kynge.

Camb. Univ. G. 6. 49.
118 × 65. English.

223. 1556, *Rouen, for Robert Valentin* (*Rouen*) 8°.

This prymer of Salisbury use is se tout along with houtonyser chyng / with many prayers / ꝫ goodly pyctures in the Kalender in the matins of our lady in the houres of the crosse. in the. vii. psalmes and in the dyryge. And benewly enprynted. at Rouen M.D.lvi. Sar₄. A

Colophon. Expliciunt hore beatissime virginis Marie / secundũ usũ Sarum / totaliter ad longum : cũ orationibus beate Brigide / ac multis aliis orationibus / Rothomagi / impresse impensis honestissimi viri Roberti valentini / suã officinã

tenentis ĩ porticu bibliopolarũ iuxta edẽ btẽ Marie.
M.D.L.vi.

    Lambeth Archiep. 24. 9. 2. Bodl. Auct. T. infra. iii. 13.
    Stonyhurst Coll. T. 7. 41.
    139 × 76. Latin.

    224. 1556, *Rouen, for Robert Valentin* (*Rouen*) 8°.

Here after Foloweth the prymer in Englysshe and in latin sette out alonge : after the use of Sarum. Robert Valentin. M.D.lvi.

Colophon. Impressum Rothomagi / impensis honesti viri Roberti valentini bibliopolarum porticulo moram teneñ.
M.D.lvi.

    Eton Coll. D. f. 4. 2. Stonyhurst Coll. V. 9. 42.
    138 × 84. English and Latin.

    225. 1556 (*Rouen*) *for Florence Valentin, Rouen*, 16°.

Hereafter Foloweth the Prymer in Englysshe, and in Latin sette out alonge : after the use of Sarum. In edibus Florenti Valentini. 1556. Sarum. A

Colophon. Rothomagi Apud Florentiũ Valentinũ.

    Bodl. Douce BB. 15.
    98 × 59. English and Latin.

    226. (*c.* 1556) *London, for John Wight* (*London*) 8°.

Hore beate Marie virginis, secundum usum insignis ecclesie. Eboriensis. de nouo Impres. Imprinted at London, for Jhon Wight.

    Finis.

    Magd. Coll. Camb. 136. L. York Minster. Fragments.
    126 × 80. Latin.

    227. (*c.* 1556) 8°.

The title-page is wanting ; the book begins on

    B1. [Iohn.] The beginning of the holy gos   Initium sa
    Finis.

    Lincoln Cath. RR. 4. 22 (1).
    118 × 75. English and Latin.

228. (*c.* 1556) 8°.
The title-page is wanting; the book begins
    KL. [Iulius] ‖ [ha]bet dies. [xxxi.] ‖ Luna ve[ro. xxx.]
All wanting after [Ne sim]ul tradas me cu pctorib̕ (in Psalms of the passion).

Camb. Univ. H. Bradshaw's collection.
125 × 75. Latin.

229. (*c.* 1556) 8°.
Twenty lines to a full page. Known only from two fragments consisting of two leaves each; 2, 7 of a quire and 4, 5 of a quire.
Begins on A2. Qui pceptus est de spũ san
Ends. am iustitiam faciĕdam no
Contents. Fragment 1. Leaf 1. Portion of the Apostles Creed. Grace (Benedicite) Leaf 2. Grace (Agimus tibi gratias). Precepta decalogi. Articuli fidei. Fragment 2. Leaves 1. 2. (O salutaris hostia) In elevatione sanguis. (Aue sanguis) (O sanguis) In ostensione eucharistie (Aue salus) Orationes dicende mane (In nomine patris) (Gratias ago tibi domine) (Omnipotens sempiterne deus).

Brasenose Coll. Oxford.
115 × 68. Latin.

230. (*c.* 1556) 8°.
Twenty-one lines to a full page. Known only from a fragment consisting of signature C. Eboɉ. is printed at the foot of C1.
Begins on C1. suũ sup nos ꝛ misereaꞇ nostri. Ut
Ends on C8ᵇ. sedes in iudicio sedes sup domũ da
Contents. Portions of Lauds, Prime and Terce.

York Minster, fragments.
125 × 78. Latin.

231. 1557, *Assignes of John Wayland, London,* 8°.
The Prymer in Latine, set forth after the use of Salis-

burye: enlarged wyth manye Prayers, and goodlye Pictures. Newelye Imprynted thys present yeare. 1557. At London by thassignes of Ihon Wayland, forbidding all other to Print this or any other Prymer. Eyther Latine or English.

Colophon. Imprinted at London by the assignes of Ihon Wayland, forbiddinge al other to Print this or any other Primer. Either in English or Latine. Cum priuilegio ad imprimendum solum.

Brit. Mus. C. 35. b. 23.   Bodl. Gough Missals 37.
Earl Spencer No. 19998.
122 × 66. Latin.

232. 1557, *Assignes of John Wayland, London,* 8°.

The Prymer in Englishe and Latine, after Salisbury use: set out at length wyth many Prayers and goodlye Pyctures. Newelye Imprynted thys present yeare. 1557. Imprinted at London by the assygnes of Jhon Wayland, forbyddynge all other to Prynt thys or any other Prymer.

Colophon. Imprynted at London by the assignes of Jhon Wayland, forbidding al other Persons to Print or cause to be Printed thys Prymer or any other in English or in Latyne.

Brit. Mus. C. 35. b. 22.   St. Cuthbert's Coll. Ushaw.
Mr. H. H. Gibbs.
124 × 75. English and Latin.

233. 1557, *John Kyngston and Henry Sutton, London,* 4°.

The Primer in Englishe and Latine, set out along, after the use of Saμ: with many godlie and deuoute praiers: as it appeareth in the table. Imprinted at London, by Jhon Kyngston, and Henry Sutton. 1557. Cum priuilegio ad imprimendum solum.

Finis.

Brit. Mus. C. 35. c. 24.
Bodl. Gough Missals 105 (1).   Charterhouse, London. B. h. 35.
167 × 113. English and Latin.

234. 1558, Aug. 22, *Assignes of John Wayland, London*, 16°.
The Primer in English and Latin after Salisburye use : set out at length with manye Godly prayers. Newly imprinted by the assignes of Iohn Wayland this presente yeare. An. 1558. Cum priuilegio ad Imprimendum solum.

Colophon. Imprinted at London by the assines of Iohn Wailand, forbiddyng all other to print or cause to be printed this primer, or anye other. An. 1558 The. xxii of August.

Mr. Samuel Sandars.
95 × 60. English and Latin.

235. 1558, Aug. 22, *Assignes of John Wayland, London*, 16°.
The prymer in English and Latin after Salisburye use : set out at length with manye Godly prayers. Newly imprinted by the assignes of Iohn Wayland this presente yeare. An. 1558. Cum priuilegio ad Imprimendum solum.

Colophon. Imprinted at London by the assines of Iohn Wailand, forbiddyng all other to print or cause to be printed this primer, or anye other. An. 1558 The. xxii of August.

Brit. Mus. C. 35. a. 17.   Christ Church, Oxford. NF. 10. 5.
Lincoln Cath. Rr. 4. 19.
93 × 59. English and Latin.

236. 1558, *Assignes of John Wayland, London*, 16°.
Hore Beate Marie virginis secundum usum insignis ecclesie Sarum. Imprinted At London by the assygnes of John Wayland, forbyddyng al other to Prynt, thys or any other Prymer. M.DLVIII.
Finis.

Bodl. Gough Missals 55.   Peterborough Cath. S. 58.
80 × 53. Latin.

237. 1558, *Assignes of John Wayland, London*, 8°.
The Prymer in English and Latine, after Salisbury use, set out at length wyth many prayers and goodly Pictures. Newelye Imprynted thys present yere. 1558. Imprinted at

London by the assygnes of Ihon Wayland, forbidding all other to Printe this or any other Primer.

Colophon. Imprynted at London by the assignes of Ihon Wayland, forbidding all other Persones to Prynt or cause to be prynted this Prymer or any other in Englyshe or in Latyne.

Brit. Mus. C. 35. b. 24. Bodl. Douce BB. 31.
York Minster. X. P. 26.
125 × 74. English and Latin.

238. 1558, *Assignes of John Wayland, London*, 8°.

The Primer in Englysh after Salysburie use : sette out at lengthe with manye Godlie prayers: Newlye Imprinted this presente yeare. Anno domini. M.D.L.VIII. Cum priuilegio ad imprimendum solum.

Colophon. Imprynted at London by the assygnes of Iohn Wayland, forbyddyng all other persons to prynt or cause to be prynted, thys prymer or any other in englyshe or Latin.

Bodl. CP. 1558. f. 1.
118 × 66. English.

239. 1559, *Assignes of John Wayland, London, and William Seres, London*, 4°.

The Primer set furth at large, with many godly and deuoute Prayers. Anno. 1559. Imprinted at London by the assignes of Iohn Wayland, forbyddyng all other to prynt this or any other Prymer. Cum priuilegio ad imprimendum solum.

Colophon. Imprinted at London, by Wyllyam Seres, dwellyng at the West ende of Poules, at the sygne of the Hedgehog.

Brit. Mus. 3406. c. 45. Christ Church, Oxford. WM. 6. 5 (1).
Jesus Coll. Camb. B. 6. 7 (1).
158 × 87. English.

240. (*c.* 1559) 8°.

The title-page is wanting ; the book begins on

A1. [A Cathechis ‖ me] that is to say, an instructiō, to Finis.

Mr. H. H. Gibbs.
114 × 57. English.

241. (*c.* 1559) 8°.
Twenty lines to a full page. Known only from a fragment consisting of eight leaves. Printers' waste. Four leaves unsigned. Four leaves of signature D.
Begins. [The Cathechisme.] mother.
D1. [The Laudes.] spire the hartes of them that be
Contents. Portions of the Catechism, Lauds, Prime and Third Hour.

Gonville and Caius Coll. Camb. fragments.
110 × 65. English.

242. (*c.* 1535) see No. 118*. page 45. 16°.
Sixteen lines to a full page. Known only from a fragment consisting of four leaves; 2, 3, 6, 7 of Signature B.
Begins on B2. art mi suster. And I called
All wanting after B 7ᵇ. That we beinge delyue[ryd]
Contents. Portions of Matins and Lauds.

Camb. Univ. H. Bradshaw's collection.
79 × 48. English.

243. 1560, *William Seres, London*, 8°.
A Primer or Boke of priuate praier nedeful to be used of all faythfull Christians. Whyche booke is to be used of all our louyng subiectes. Roma. xii. Continue in prayer. Londini ex officina Wilhelmi Seres typographi. Cum priuilegio ad imprimendum solum. 1560.
Finis.

Brit. Mus. G. 12, 139.
115 × 60. English.

244. 1560, *William Seres, London*, 8°.
Orarium Seu Libellus Precationum per Regiam maiestatem, Latinè æditus. 1560. Cum Priuilegio ad imprimendum solum.

Colophon. Londini ex officina Wilhelmi Seres typographi. Cum Priuilegio ad imprimendum solum. 1560.

Brit. Mus. C. 36. a. 5.   York Minster. X. P. 16.
St. Paul's Cath. 38. D. 16.
120 × 58. Latin.

245. (*c.* 1560) 8°.
The Primer and Cathechisme set forth at large, with many Godly Prayers, necessary for al faythful Christians to reade.
Finis.

Mr. H. H. Gibbs.
114 × 59. English.

246. (*c.* 1560, *William Seres, London*) 8°.
The title-page is wanting; the book begins on
B1. [Morning prayer for sondaye] Oure father
Finis.

Dr. Edwin Freshfield.
115 × 60. English.

247. 1564, *William Seres, London*, 16°.
Preces Privatæ, In Studiosorum Gratiam collecte, & Regiâ authoritate approbatæ.   Matth. 26. Vigilate & orate, ne intretis in tentationem.   Londini, Excudebat Guilelmus Seres: Anno Domini. 1564.   Cum priuilegio Reginæ.

Colophon. Londini Per Gulielmum Seres, sub signo Erinacei in cæmiterio Paulino.   Anno domini. 1564. & Reg. Reginæ nostræ Elizabethæ feliciss. memoriæ. 7. Cum Priuilegio ad imprimendum solum.

Brit. Mus. 3455. a. 27.   Bodl. Tanner 382.   Eton Coll. F. i. 9. 2.
87 × 51. Latin.

Ed. 1568, *William Seres, London*, 16°.

St. Paul's Cath. 38. D. 22.   Trin. Coll. Camb. VI°. 1. 8.
77 × 46. Latin.

Ed. 1573, *William Seres, London,* 16°.

Brit. Mus. 3455. a. 28.   Bodl. Wood 762.
Camb. Univ. G. 16. 63.
87 × 53. Latin.

248. (*c.* 1564) 16°.
The title-page is wanting; the book begins
[The Kalendar] xix A Focas.
All wanting after L 7ᵇ. of thine handes are the hea[uens] (in the Seven psalmes).

Brit. Mus. 3408. aa. 43.
85 × 52. English.

249. (*c.* 1566) *William Seres, London,* 16°.
A booke of Priuate Prayer, necessarye to be used of all Christians with manye Godlye Prayers. Imprinted at London by Wylliam Seres. Cum Priuilegio ad imprimendum solum.
Colophon. Imprinted at London by William Seres, dwelling at the Weast ende of Paules, at the signe of the Hedgehogge. Cum Priuilegio ad imprimendum solum.

Earl Spencer No. 4757.
78 × 50. English.

250. (*c.* 1566) 16°.
Nineteen lines to a full page. Known only from a fragment consisting of eight leaves of Signature A.
Begins on A1. [The catechisme] dead. I beleue in the holy ghost.
Ends on A8ᵇ. [Graces] nefites geuen vnto you.
Contents. Portions of the Catechism and of the Graces.

Mr. F. J. H. Jenkinson.
75 × 50. English.

251. 1568, *William Seres, London,* 8°.
A Primer, or booke of priuate prayer, needefull to be used of all faythfull Christians, which Booke is to be used of al our

louing subiects. Rom. xii. Continue in prayer. Londini, ex officina Gulielmi Seresii Typographi. Cum priuilegio. An. 1568.
Finis.

Camb. Univ. A*. 10. 46.
110 × 58. English.

252. 1575, *William Seres, London*, 8°.

The Primer, and Cathechisme, set forth at large, wyth many godly praiers necessarie for all faithfull Christians to reade. Imprinted at London, by Willyam Seres. Anno. 1566.

Colophon. Imprinted at London, by William Seres, dwelling at the West ende of Paules Church, at the signe of the Hedgehogge. Cum priuilegio ad imprimendum solum. Anno. 1575.

Bodl. Tanner 63.   Bodl. 8°. C. 85. Linc.
Balliol Coll. Arch. C. 12. 14.
120 × 59. English.

253. (*c.* 1580) *Thomas Purfoote, London, assigned by William Seres, London*, 16°.

A primer and a Cathechisme, and also the notable fayres in the Kalender set forth by the Quenes maiesty to be taught unto children. Imprinted at London by Thomas Purfoote. assigned by William Seres. Cum priuilegio ad imprimendum solum. (verso) [The Kalender.] K.L. January hath. xxx.

Brit. Mus. Bibl. Harl. 5937. No. 117.
80 × 55. inclusive of a border which surrounds the letterpress.

⁎⁎* This edition is only known by the title-page.

254. (*c.* 1580) 16°.
The title-page is wanting; the book begins
[June] 13 d xiiii chester, at Reading, at
All wanting after thou not despise. [O] (in the Seven psalms).

Mr. F. J. H. Jenkinson.
85 × 52. English.

255. 1627, *R. Young, London*, 12°.

A Collection of Private Deuotions: in the Practice of the Ancient Church, Called The Houres of Prayer. As they were much after this maner published by Authoritie of Q. Eliz. 1560. Taken out of the Holy Scriptures, the Ancient Fathers, and the diuine Service of our owne Church. London, Printed by R. Young. 1627.

Finis.

Brit. Mus. C. 46. c. 34.   Rev. W. J. Blew.
Univ. Libr. Durham. H. vi. 72.
102 × 48. English.

Ed. 1627, *R. Young, London*, 12°.

Brit. Mus. 3405. aa. 20.   Univ. Libr. Durham. H. vi. 72ª.
102 × 47. English.

5th Ed. 1638, *R. Young, London*, 12°.

Brit. Mus. 1220. a. 7.   Christ Church, Oxford. M. 2. 8. 25.
95 × 42. English.

Ed. 1655, *London, for Richard Royston (London)* 12°.

Brit. Mus. 843. g. 11.   Sion College.
Mr. E. Gordon Duff.
135 × 70. English.

5th Ed. 1664, *J. F., London, for R. Royston (London)* 12°.

Brit. Mus. 3455. a. 55.   Rev. Dr. E. C. Lowe.   Mr. E. Gordon Duff.
120 × 60. English.

Ed. 1672, *London, for R. Royston, and sold by Will. Cademan, London*, 12°.

Rev. W. J. Blew.
120 × 50. English.

7th Ed. 1676, *J. Grover, London, for R. Royston, London*, 12°.
Christ Church, Oxford. N. 2. 8. 3.
132 × 68. English.

8th Ed. 1681, *London, by R. N., for Rich. Royston*, 12°.
Camb. Univ. G. 6. 41.
132 × 70. English.

9th Ed. 1693, *W. H., for Luke Meredith, London*, 12°.
Camb. Univ. G. 5. 66 (now missing).   Mr. W. R. Richardson.
134 × 68. English.

10th Ed. 1719, *London, for T. Horne, J. Knapton, R. Knaplock, J. Wyat, D. Midwinter, R. Robinson, W. Taylor, J. Bowyer, H. Clements, W. Meers, R. Gostling, W. Innys, W. Churchil, and B. Cowse*, 12°.
King's Coll. Camb. c. 75. 34.
130 × 70. English.

256. 1668, *Paris*, 8°.
Devotions in the Ancient Way of Offices : With Psalms Hymns, and Prayers ; for every day in the Week, and every Holiday in the Year. Tho. a Kempis. Mind not who speaks, but what is said. Paris, MDCLXVIII.
Finis.
Brit. Mus. 3395. aa. 4.   Camb. Univ. G. 6. 10.
130 × 73. English.

2nd Ed. 1672, *Rouen*, 12°.
Brit. Mus. 3456. c. 14.   Bodl. 138. g. 232.
Camb. Univ. G. 6. 11.
130 × 67. English.

3rd Ed. 1684, *Rouen*, 12°.
Bodl. 8°. y. 25. B S.   Camb. Univ. G. 6. 12.
Rev. W. Cooke.
141 × 77. English.

4th Ed. 1685, *Rouen*, 12°.
Camb. Univ. G. 16. 13.   Peterborough Cath. C. 5. 24.
Rev. W. J. Blew.
135 × 75. English.

Ed. 1789, *Mundell and Son, Edinburgh, for J. P. Coghlan, London, and D. Downie, Edinburgh*, 8°.
Brit. Mus. 3455. d. 38.   St. Paul's Cath. 45. H. 10.
Rev. W. J. Blew.
173 × 90. English.

257. *c.* 1670, *London, for Company of Stationers, London,* 16°.

The Primer, Or, Catechism set forth agreeable to the Book of Common Prayer, Authorized by the Kings Majesty to be used throughout His Realms & Dominions wherein is contained godlie prayers, and graces : very mete and necessary for the instruction of youth. Cum priuilegio.

Colophon. London : Printed for the Company of Stationers. Finis.

Brit. Mus. C. 36. a. 37.
80 × 55. English.

258. 1671, *London, for S.S. sold by Thomas Hartley, London,* 8°.

The Kings Psalter Containing Psalms and Hymns, With Easie and Delightful Directions to all Learners, whether Children, Youths, or others, for their better reading of the English Tongue. Also Prayers for every Day of the Week, beginning with the Letters of the Name of our Soveraign Lord King Charles ; and Other observable Varieties, fit either for the School, or for the Closet ; all which are profitable, plain, and pleasant. London, Printed for S.S. and sold by Tho. Hartley at the Black-Boy behinde St. Albans Church in Wood street, 1671.

Finis.

Bodl. Bliss 1534. Mr. Samuel Sandars.
130 × 74. English.

259. (*c.* 1685) 16°.

The Primer, Or Catechism, Set forth agreeable to the Book of Common Prayer, Authorized by the Kings Majesty to be used throughout His Realms and Dominions. Wherein is contained Godly Prayers and Graces, very meet and necessary for the instruction of Youth. Cum Priuilegio.

Finis.

Mr. H. H. Gibbs.
83 × 53. English.

260. 1686 (*London*) *for Joseph Watts, London,* 12°.

Reform'd Devotions, in Meditations, Hymns and Petitions, For Every Day in the Week, and Every Holiday in the Year. Divided into Two Parts. The Second Edition. Ex ædibus Lambeth. May 7. 1686. Imprimatur, Jo. Battely. London, Printed for Joseph Watts at the Half-Moon in St. Paul's Church-Yard, 1686.

Finis.

128 × 67. English.
Magd. Coll. Oxford. n. 1. 18.

2nd Ed. 1687, *J. A.* (*London*) *for Joseph Watts, London,* 12°.

Bodl. 8°. B. 102. Th.
128 × 67. English.

3rd Ed. 1693, *H. Clark, London, for Richard Cumberland, London,* 12°.

Christ Church. Oxford. K. 2. 8. 18.
135 × 70. English.

4th Ed. 1696, *H. Clark* (*London*) *for Richard Cumberland, London,* 12°.

Brit. Mus. 4404. cc.
138 × 68. English.

5th Ed. 1700, *London, for A. Roper, London, and for R. Basset, London,* 12°.

Brit. Mus. 3456. e. 11.
135 × 67. English.

6th Ed. 1704 (*London*) *for A. Roper, London, and for R. Basset, London,* 8°.

Brit. Mus. 3455. e. 36. St. Paul's Cath. 39. H. 30.
164 × 85. English.

8th Ed. 1724, *London, for Joseph Hazard, London, and John Brotherton, London,* 12°.

Rev. W. Cooke.
135 × 70. English.

9th Ed. 1727, *London, for Joseph Hazard, London, and for J. Brotherton, London,* 12°.

Brit. Mus. 3456. bb. 37. Rev. W. J. Blew.
145 × 73. English.

⁂ All editions after the fourth edition contain: "An Holy Office, Before, At, and After Receiving the Holy Sacrament. By Dr. Edward Lake."

261. 1700, *London, for W. Keblewhite, London, and J. Jones, London,* 12°.

Devotions in the ancient Way of Offices. With Psalms, Hymns, and Prayers For Every Day of the Week, And Every Holiday in the Year. Reformed by a Person of Quality, and Published by George Hickes, D.D. London, Printed for W. Keblewhite at the Swan, and J. Jones at the Bell, in St. Paul's Church-Yard, 1700.

Finis.

Lambeth Archiep. 65*. A. 21.   Bodl. 138. i. 513.
Camb. Univ. G. 5. 36.
144 × 68. English.

2nd Ed. 1701, *T. Mead, London, for John Nicholson, London, and John Sprint, London,* 12°.

Brit. Mus. 3456. d. 38.   Bodl. 8°. N. 59. Linc.
Magd. Coll. Oxford. T^A. 1. 14.
145 × 70. English.

3rd Ed. 1706, *E. Mead, London, for John Nicholson, London, and John Sprint, London,* 8°.

Brit. Mus. 3456. g. 34.
Bodl. Mason. AA. 369.   New Coll. Oxford. B. 9. 39.
145 × 70. English.

4th Ed. 1712, *M. Jenour, London, for John Nicholson, London, and J. and B. Sprint, London,* 12°.

Rev. W. Cooke. Rev. W. J. Blew.
150 × 75. English.

5th Ed. 1717, *London, for J. and B. Sprint, London, and Executors of J. Nicholson, London,* 8°.

Brit. Mus. 3456. d. 56. St. Paul's Cath. 39. H. 27.
Bodl. 138. i. 113.
150 × 77. English.

6th Ed. 1730, *London, for D. Midwinter, London; B. Sprint, London; W. Innys, London; and J. Osborn and T. Longman, London.* 12°.

Brit. Mus. 3456. d. 57.
155 × 77. English.

Ed. 1765, *Edinburgh, for T. Longman, London, and Drummond, Edinburgh,* 12°.

Brit. Mus. 3456. e. 44. Rev. W. J. Blew.
153 × 80. English.

Ed. 1758, *Wal. Ruddiman & Co., Edinburgh; sold by the Booksellers in Town,* 12°.

Rev. W. J. Blew.
135 × 68. English.

262. *c.* 1710, August 17, *R. Grafton, London,* 8°.

The Primer Set Furth By the kinges maicstie ⁊ his Clergie, to be taught lerned, and red : ⁊ none other to be used thorowout all his Dominions. Imprinted at London within the precinct of the late dissolued house of the graye Friers by Richard Grafton Printer to the Princes grace, the xvii. day of August, the yeare of our lorde M,D.XLVI. Cum priuilegio ad imprimendum solum. Reprinted without any Alteration.

The ende of the Primer.

U 4. The copy of the Kynges highnes bil assigned.

U 4ᵇ. The Contents of this Primer . . . Certain godly Praiers for sundry purposes.

Brit. Mus. 1219. e. 6.   Lambeth Archiep. 46. f. 27.
Bodl. Gough Missals 5.
160 × 90. English.

⁎ This book is a reprint.

263. 1717 (*London*) *for D. Midwinter, London*, 8°.
A Collection of Meditations and Devotions, In Three Parts. I. Meditations on the Creation. II. Meditations and Devotions on the Life of Christ. III. Daily Devotions and Thanksgivings, &c. By the First Reformer of the Devotions In the Ancient Way of Offices; Afterwards reviewed and set forth By the late Learned Dr. Hickes. Published by N. Spinckes, M.A. London : Printed for D. Midwinter, at the Three Crowns in St. Paul's Church-Yard. 1717.
Finis.

Brit. Mus. 3455. d. 29.   Bodl. 8°. S. 240. Th.
Camb. Univ. 1. 49. 56.
165 × 84. English.

6th Ed. 1730.

Bodl. Mason. AA 327 (10).

264. 1758, *London, for Company of Stationers, London*, 16°.
The Primer, Or, Catechism, Set forth agreeable to the Book of Common-Prayer, Authorized by the King, to be used throughout his Dominions. Containing godly Prayers and Graces. London : Printed for the Company of Stationers. 1766.
Finis.

Mr. Samuel Sandars.
80 × 55. English.

⁎ The other editions which are known are those of 1764, 1766, 1769, 1772, 1775, 1777, 1783.

265. 1825, *London, for C. and J. Rivington, London, Deighton and Sons (Cambridge) and J. Nicholson, Cambridge*, 12 .

The Primer: A Book of Private Prayer, Needful To Be Used of All Christians. Which Book Was Authorized And Set Forth By Order Of King Edward VI. To Be Taught, Learned, Read And Used, Of All His Subjects. Edited By The Rev. Henry Walter, B.D. F.R.S. Late Fellow Of St. John's College, Cambridge. London: Printed For C. And J. Rivington, St. Paul's Church-Yard, And Waterloo-Place, Pall-Mall : Deighton And Sons; And J. Nicholson, Cambridge. 1825.

The end.

Brit. Mus. 1018 e. 27.   Bodl. Douce E. 114.
135 × 72. English.

117*. (*c.* 1535, *Nicolas Le Roux, Rouen, for François Regnault, Paris*) 8°.

The title-page is wanting; the book begins on

E 2. [An exhortacyon. Fo. xx.] maner of loue and pacyence we ought to use to

All wanting after D6^b. in his owne strengthe and puissance: and yet he was [nat] (in A meditacion upon the. xxx. Psalme).

Rev. E. S. Dewick.

140 × 77. English and Latin.

HAND-LIST OF PRIMERS

OR

OFFICES OF THE BLESSED VIRGIN MARY

ACCORDING TO

THE REFORMED LATIN OF THE ROMAN USE.

266. 1571, *Rome*, 12°.
Officium B. Mariæ Virginis, nuper reformatum, & Pii V. Pont. Max. iussu editum. Cum Priuilegio & Indulgentiis. Romæ, In Ædibus Populi Romani. M.D.LXXI.
Ends. Series Chartarum. A B C D E F G H I K L M N O P Q R S. Omnia sunt integra folia.

Brit. Mus. C. 27. d.
123 × 60. Latin.

267. 1599, *Arnold Conings, Antwerp*, 12°.
The Primer, or Office of The Blessed Virgin Marie, in Latin and English : According to the reformed Latin : and with lyke graces Priuileged. Printed, At Antwerp by Arnold Conings. Anno M.D.XCIX.
Finis. It may please . . . he may happen to fynde.

Lambeth Archiep. A. 4. 36.   Brasenose Coll. Oxford.
Duke of Norfolk. G. 9. 1.
128 × 63. Latin and English.

268. 1604, *Arnold Conings, Antwerp*, 12°.
The Primer, or Office of The Blessed Virgin Marie, in Latin and English : According to the reformed Latin : and

with lyke graces Priuileged. Printed At Antwerp by Arnold Conings, Anno M.DC.IIII.

Finis. It may please . . . he may happen to fynde.

Brit. Mus. 1219. a. 3.   Bodl. Douce BB. 48.
Camb. Univ. G. 6. 39.
129 × 63. Latin and English.

269. 1607, *Plantinian Press, Antwerp, for John Moret,* (*Antwerp*) 8°.

Officium Beatæ Mariæ Virginis. Pii V. Pont. Max. iussu editum. Cum Calendario Gregoriano, à Sixto PP.V. & S.D.N. Clemente VIII. Pont. Max. aliquot Sanctorum festis aucto. Antwerpiæ, Ex Officina Plantiniana, Apud Ioannem Moretum. M.DC.VII. Cum gratia & priuilegio.

Colophon. Antwerpiæ, Ex Officina Plantiniana, Apud Ioannem Moretum. M.DC.VII.

Lambeth Archiep. 96. A. 7.   Stonyhurst Coll. cc. 8. 50.
125 × 65. Latin.

270. 1615, *Henrie Iaey, Mackline*, 16°.

The Primer, or Office of the Blessed Virgin Marie, in English. According to the last Edition of the Romane Breuiarie. Printed at Mackline by Henrie Iaey, Anno M.DC.XV. Cum Gratia & Priuilegio.

Finis.

Brit. Mus. 3356. b. 6.
96 × 55. English.

271. 1616, *John Heighan, St. Omers*, 12°.

The Primer or Office of the Blessed Virgin Marie, in Latin and English : According to the reformed Latin : Set foorth by the commaundement of Pope Pius the fifth. With the calendar of Pope Gregorie. And with lyke graces Priuileged. Printed. At S Omers by Iohn Heighan. Anno 1616.

All wanting after Gg.11ᵇ. S. Eusebius Vercell. B. & mart. 15. of Decēb [In] (in An advertisement to the Reader).

Incorporated Law Society.
119 × 64. Latin and English.

272. 1617, 12°.
The Primer According to the last Edition of the Roman Breuiarie. Printed with Licence. 1617. Newly reviewed and corrected.
Finis.

Camb. Univ. G. 6. 122. Incorporated Law Society.
113 × 60. English.

273. 1621, *John Heighan, St. Omers*, 12°.
The Primer, or Office of the Blessed Virgin Marie, in Latin and English : According to the reformed Latin. and with like graces Priuileged. At S. Omers, By Iohn Heighan Anno 1621.
Finis.

Pembroke Coll. Camb.
127 × 63. Latin and English.

274. 1631, *John Heighan, St. Omers*, 12°.
The Primer or Office of the Blessed Virgin Marie, in English. According to the last Edition of the Romaine Breviarie. Printed. At S. Omers by Iohn Heighan Anno M.DC.XXXI. Cum Gratia & Priuilegio.
Finis.

Camb. Univ. G. 16. 93.
95 × 53. English.

275. 1632, 12°.
The Primer, or Office of the Blessed Virgin Marie, in English. According to the last Editiō of the Romaine Breviarie. Permissu Superiorum. M.DC.XXXII.
Finis.

Brit. Mus. 3366. a. 35.
124 × 64. English.

276. 1632, *Rouen*, 12°.

The Primer, or Office of the Blessed Virgin Marie, in English. According to the Roman use. At Roan, M.DC.XXXII. Finis.

Corpus Christi Coll. Oxford. W. I. 3. 15.
102 × 54. English.

277. 1633, *John Le Cousturier (Rouen)* 16°.

The Office of the Blessed Virgin Marie in Latin. with the Rubrikes in English, for the cōmoditie of those that doe not understand the Latin tongue. By John Le Cousturier. Permissu Superiorum. M.DC.XXXIII.
Finis.

D. dd². 699. Litaniæ de D. Virgine in æde Lauretana.
D. dd 4. Index eorum quæ hoc volumine continentur.
All wanting after D dd 4ᵇ. 704. Litania B. Mariæ. 681.

York Minster. X. Q. 25. Rev. Christopher Wordsworth.
98 × 42. Latin.

278. 1633, *John le Cousturier (Rouen)* 12°.

The Primer or Office of the Blessed Virgin Marie in Latin and English : According to the reformed Latin : and with like graces Priuiledged. By John le Cousturier. Permissu Superiorum. M.DC.XXXIII.
Finis.

St. John's Coll. Oxford. Bc. 6. 6.
130 × 65. Latin and English.

279. 1644, *Venice, apud Cieras*, 4°.

Officium B. Mariæ Virginis nuper reformatum, & Pii Quinti Pont. Max. Iussu Editum. Ad instar Breuiarii Romani sub Urbano VIII. recogniti. Cum Indulgentiis. Venetiis apud Cieras. M.DCXXXXIIII

Colophon. Venetiis, M.DC.XLIIII. Apud Cieras. Sub Signo Europæ.

Brit. Mus. C. 47. i. 3.
254 × 172. Latin.

280. 1650, *Widow of John Cnobbaert, Antwerp, for James Thompson (London)* 12°.

The Primer, Or Office Of The blessed Virgin Marie, in Latin and English. According to the reformed Latin : And With lyke graces Priuileged. At Antwerp, By the Widow of John Cnobbaert, for James Thompson, 1650

Ends on Pp 5ᵇ. It may please . . . he may happen to ‖ fynde.

Stonyhurst Coll. cc. 8. 25a.   Mr. Orby Shipley.
113 × 60. Latin and English.

281. 1658, *Balthasar Moret, Antwerp*, 12°.

The Primer, or Office of the Blessed Virgin Mary. According to the Reformed Latin ; And With like graces Priviledged. At Antwerpe, Printed by Balthasar Moret.   1658.

Finis.

Lambeth Archiep. 50. L. 10.   Camb. Univ. G.
123 × 60. English.

282. 1669, *David Maurry, Rouen*, 12°.

The Primer more ample, and in a new Order, containing the three offices of the B. Virgin Mary, in Latin and English. And al Offices and Devotions, which were in former primers. In this last Edition the Hymns are in a better verse, and six Offices newly added.   I. Of the Holy Trinity.   II. Of the B. Sacrament.   III. Of the holy name of Iesus, with a Letany. IV. Of the Immaculate Conception of our B. Lady, with a Letany.   V. Of the Angel-Guardian.   VI. Of S. Joseph. And Sundry sweet Devotions, and Instructions taken out of the holy Scripture for to liue a deuout Christian life.   A large and short examen of conscience.   To the Calender are annexed many English and Irish Saints.   Printed at Rouen, By David Maurry.   1669.   With permission.

Finis.

Incorporated Law Society.   Mr. E. Gordon Duff.
129 × 62. Latin and English.

283. 1673, *St. Omers*, 12°.

The Primer or, Office of the Blessed Virgin Mary in English : Exactly revised, and the new Hymnes and Prayers added, according to the Reformation of Pope Urban 8. Printed at S. Omers 1673.

Finis.

Bodl. 8°. R. 138. Th.

113 × 55. English.

284. 1684, *Nicolas Le Tourneur, Rouen*, 12°.

The Primer more ample, and in a new Order, containing the Three Offices of the B. Virgin Mary, in Latin and English, and al Offices and Devotions, which were in former primers. In this last Edition the Hymns are in a better verse, and six Offices newly added. I. Of the holy Trinity. II. Of the B. Sacrament. III. Of the holy name of Iesus, with a Letany. IV. Of the Immaculate Conception of our B. Lady, with a Letany. V. Of the Angel-Guardian. VI. Of S. Joseph. And Sundry sweet Devotions, and Instructions taken out of the holy Scripture for to live a devout Christian life. A large and short examen of conscience. To the Calender are annexed many English and Irish Saints. Printed at Rouen, By Nicolas Le Tourneur, rue S. Lo, vis à vis la porte du Palais, au Tourneur. With Permission. 1684.

Finis. It may please . . . he may happen to fynde.

Brit. Mus. 844. C. 9. 1.   Exeter Coll. Oxford. 16. c. 10.

Bodl. Arch. Bodl. B. I. 112.

130 × 63. Latin and English.

285. 1685, *Antwerp, for T. D. (Antwerp)* 12°.

The Primer or, Office of the Blessed Virgin Mary in English : exactly Revised, and the new Hymns and Prayers added, according to the Reformation of Pope Urbans. Printed at Antwerp for T. D. 1685.

Finis.

Brit. Mus. 3355. aa. 31.   Stonyhurst Coll. cc. 8. 33.

Rev. W. Cooke.

136 × 68. English

286. 1687, *Henry Hills, London*, 8°.

The Office of the B. V. Mary in English. To which is added the Vespers, or Even-Song, in Latin and English, As it is Sung in the Catholic Church Upon all Sundays and principal Holy days throughout the whole Year. With the Compline, Rosary, Hymn and Prayers that are sung at the Benediction of the B. Sacrament. The Prayers for the King, Queen, &c. The Ordinary of the Holy Mass; the Sequence, Dies iræ, dies illa, that is sung at solemn Mass for the Dead, and the Libera that is sung after Mass for the Dead: all in Latin and English. Together with several other Devout Prayers in English. London: Printed by Henry Hills, Printer to the King's Most Excellent Majesty for his Houshold and Chappel; And are to be sold at his Printing-house on the Ditch side in Black Fryars. 1687.

Finis.

Brit. Mus. 3355. a. 27. Magd. Coll. Oxford. d. 2. 9.
Incorporated Law Society.
105 × 53. English.

287. (*c.* 1687) *Henry Hills, London*, 16°.

Officium B. Mariæ Virg Nuper reformatum et Pii V. Pont Max. Iussu Editum. Ad instar Breviarii Romani sub Urbano VIII recogniti Cum Indulgentiis, Orationibus, Hymnis et hujusmodi aliis quæ in Indice notantur. Londini. Typis Henrici Hills S. Regiæ Majestati pro Familia et Sacello Typographi.

Finis.

Brit. Mus. 1220. a. 1. Earl Beauchamp.
Mr. Joseph Gillow.
94 × 48. Latin.

288. 1699, 12°.

The Primer, or, Office of the Blessed Virgin Mary. Printed in the Year 1699.

Finis.

Rev. W. J. Blew.
123 × 63. English.

289. 1706, 12°.

The Primer, or, Office of the B. Virgin Mary, revis'd : with a new and approv'd Version of the Church-Hymns throughout the Year : to which are added the remaining Hymns of the Roman Breviary. Printed in the Year 1706.

Finis.

Brit. Mus. 3395. a. 25.   Mr. Joseph Gillow.
142 × 70. English.

290. 1717 (*London, for Thomas Meighan, London*), 12°.

The Primer, or Office Of The B. Virgin Mary, Revis'd : With a New and Approv'd Version Of The Church-Hymns. Throughout the Year : To which Are Added the Remaining Hymns of the Roman Breviary. Faithfully Corrected. Printed in the Year, 1717.

Finis.

Mr. Orby Shipley.
140 × 70. English.

291. 1720, *Widow of Nicolas Le Turner, Rouen*, 12°.

The Primer More Ample, And In A New Order, Containing The Three Offices Of The B. Virgin Mary, In Latin and English, And all Offices and Devotions, which were in former primers. In this last Edition reviewed and corrected, by P. R. the Hymns are in a better verse and six Offices newly added. I. Of the holy Trinity : II. Of the B. Sacrament : III. Of the holy name of Jesus with the Litany : IV. Of the Immaculate Conception of our B. Lady, with a Litany : V. Of the Angel Guardian. VI. Of S. Joseph. And Sundry sweet Devotions, and Instructions taken out of the holy Scripture for to live a devout Christian life. A large and short examen of conscience. To the Calender are annexed many English and Irish Saints. Printed in Rouen, by the Widdois Nicolas Le Turner, at the Sign of the Turner in iron Cross street. With Permission. M.DCC.XX.

Ends on Y 12^b. [Permission du Roy.] Louis par la Grace

de Dieu Roi de France et de Navarre . . . Registré sur le Registre IV. de la Commun. des Libraires & Imprimeurs de Paris . . . a Paris le 30. Octobre 1719. Delaulne, Syndic. Registré sur le Registre de la Commun. des Libraires & Imprimeurs de Rouen . . . le 28. de Fevrier 1720. N. Le Boucher.

Rev. W. J. Blew.
128 × 62. Latin and English.

292. 1730, *Nicolas Le Turner, Rouen*, 12°.

The Primer More Ample, And In A New Order, Containing The Three Offices of the B. Virgin Mary, In Latin and English, And all Offices and Devotions, Which were in former primers. In this last Edition reviewed & corrected, by P. R. the Hymns are in a better verse and six Offices newly added. I. Of the holy Trinity : II. Of the B. Sacrament III. Of the holy name of Jesus, with the Litany. IV. Of the Immaculate Conception of our B. Lady, with a Litany : V. Of the Angel-Guardian. VI. Of S. Joseph. And Sundry sweet Devotions and Instructions taken out of the holy Scripture for to live a devout Christian life. A large and short examen of conscience. To the Calender are annexed many English and Irish Saints. Printed in Rouen, By Nicolas Le Turner, at the Sing of the Turner in iron Cross street. With Permission. M.D.CC.XXX.

Ends on Y 12[b]. [Permission du Roy.] Louis par la Grace de Dieu Roy de France et de Navarre . . . Registré sur le Registre IV de la Commun des Libraires & Imprimeurs de Paris . . . le 28 de Fevrier 1720. N. Le Boucher.

Rev. W. Holmes.
130 × 64. Latin and English.

293. 1732 (*London, for Thomas Meighan, London*) 12°.

The Primer ; or, Office of the B. Virgin Mary, With a New and Approv'd Version of the Church Hymns. To which are added the Remaining Hymns of the Roman Breviary. Printed for T. Meighan in the Year M.DCC.XXXII.

Ends on Bb 12⁰. A Table of the Contents . . . Christian every Day.

Lambeth Archiep. 103. I. 24. Rev. W. Cooke.
Mr. Joseph Gillow.
144 × 72. English.

294. 1736, 12°.
The Office of the B. V. Mary in English. With the Ordinary of the H. Mass in Latin and English, the Sequence, Dies Iræ, and the Libera. With the Vespers in Latin and English. The Compline, Rosary, Hymns and Prayers. 1736.

Mr. Cornish's Catalogue, Manchester. 1889.
English.

295. 1770, 12°.
The Office of the B. V. Mary. To which is added the Method of saying the Rosary of our Blessed Lady, and the Manner how to serve at Mass. Printed in the Year MDCCLXX.
Finis.

Brit. Mus. 3366. a. 31. Mr. Joseph Gillow.
Sold at Puttick and Simpson, 25th June, 1890.
133 × 70. English.

296. 1780, *J. P. Coghlan, London*, 12°.
The Primer; or Office of the Blessed Virgin Mary, With a New and Approved Version of the Church-Hymns. Translated from the Roman Breviary. To which is added A Table, according to the New Regulations, of the Festivals of Obligation, Days of Devotion, Fasting, and Abstinence, as observed by the Catholics in England. A New Impression. London. Printed by J. P Coghlan, Duke-Street Grosvenor Square, M,DCC,LXXX.
Finis.

Bodl. Mason. A A. 410. Rev. W. J. Blew.
145 × 72. English.

104   A HAND-LIST OF HORÆ OR PRIMERS.   [1817.

297. 1817, *Dublin, published by Coyne, Dublin*, 12°.
The Primer or Office of the B. Virgin Mary. To which are added a New & Improved Version Of The Church Hymns and the Remaining Hymns of the Roman Breviary: With many useful Additions & Amendments Dublin Published by Coyne Parliament Street 1817.
Finis.

Incorporated Law Society.
115 × 65. English.

A SUMMARY OF THE CONTENTS

OF THE

HORÆ OR PRIMERS,

IN WHICH THE HOURS ARE IN LATIN,

ACCORDING TO

THE USES OF SARUM AND YORK,

A.D. 1478—A.D. 1558.

EXPLANATIONS.

1. A summary of all the contents of No. 7, c., A.D. 1494 is given as a standard of comparison for those Horæ of Sarum and York uses, in which the Hours are in Latin. This book is the first complete printed edition of a Sarum Horæ which is known to exist.

2. The contents of the fragments Nos. 2-6 are not given because they are all to be found in No. 7. The suffrage "De S. Barbara" in fragment No. 1 is given, as it is not to be found in No. 7.

3. The Hours of the blessed Virgin Mary occur in three different forms, which are analogous to though not identical with the three forms of "Non plenum Servitium de sancta Maria" in the Sarum Breviary; they are (a) "Post Purificationem usque ad Adventum Domini." (b) "Per Adventum usque ad vigiliam Natalis Domini." (c) "A Nativitate Domini usque ad Purificationem." The first form "Post Purificationem usque ad Adventum Domini," which is the usual one, occurs in the first complete printed edition of the Horæ which is known to exist and is the only one which was translated into english, No. 124, A.D. 1536. The other two forms "Per Adventum usque ad vigiliam Natalis Domini," and "A nativitate Domini usque ad Purificationem," occur for the first time, so far as is known, in No. 39, A.D. 1511, and are not known to have been translated. Other forms of Horæ occur, they are "Horæ de cruce," and "Horæ de compassione," No. 7, c., A.D. 1494. "Officium de Sancto Spiritu," No. 17, A.D. 1498. "Horæ dulcissimi nominis Jesu." No. 26, A.D. 1503. "Horæ conceptionis beatæ Mariæ," No. 63, c., A.D. 1523. "Horæ de passione Christi." "Officium sanctissimæ Trinitatis." "Horæ pro defunctis." "Officium de omnibus Sanctis." "Horæ de sacramento." "Horæ die Sabbati de beata virgine Maria," No. 83, A.D. 1528.

4. A list of Horæ or Primers, according to the Use of York is given at the beginning of the book before the Hand-List.

5. All fresh words in the titles and all fresh devotions after No. 7, are given as they occur, as well as any variation in the component parts of a devotion. So far as the text of the actual Horæ goes, there is nothing new to index except "Suffragia Sanctorum ad Laudes," which is the only variable part of the Sarum Hours in Latin only.

6. An index is given of the prayers, psalms and benedictions. Groups of psalms such as the seven penitential psalms, or those in the Hours are not indexed separately. Another index gives all the hymns and rhythms. A general index refers to other matters of liturgical, devotional and general interest.

A SUMMARY OF THE CONTENTS

OF THE

HORÆ OR PRIMERS,

IN WHICH THE HOURS ARE IN LATIN,

ACCORDING TO

THE USES OF SARUM AND YORK,

A.D. 1478—A.D. 1558.

c. A.D. 1478. (William Caxton, Westminster.) 8o. No. 1.
Ad Laudes. Suffragia Sanctorum. De S. Barbara. Añ. O pulchra præcipuum rosa . . . ℣. Ora pro nobis . . . ℟. Ut digni . . . Oremus. Intercessio, quæsumus, beatæ Barbaræ . . . Amen. ℣. Benedicamus Domino. ℟. Deo gratias.

₊ *All the other contents of this fragment and the fragments, Nos. 1-6, except this devotion are found in*

c. A.D. 1494. (Wynkyn de Worde, Westminster), on vellum. No. 7.
₊ *The colophon has "These foresaid prayers as the XV. oes in english and the other following ben enprynted . . ."* [1]

₊ *The titles of the devotions in this book are taken from the contents at the end of the book, as well as from the words at the head of the devotion in the body of the book. Some titles are supplied from later editions.*

The book has no title-page, it begins with the Kalender, then:

These prayers following ought for to be said or ye depart out of your chamber at your uprising. A prayer to the Trinity, Auxiliatrix, another Piissime Deus. Auxiliatrix sis mihi Trinitas . . . Crux triumphalis passionis . . . Jesus Nazarenus rex Judæorum fili Dei . . . In nomine. Per signum sanctæ crucis . . . Piissime Deus et clementissime pater . . . Amen.

When thou goest first out of thy house bless thee, saying thus: Crux triumphalis with the collect of the three kings. Crux triumphalis Domini . . . In nomine. Deus qui tres magos . . . Amen. Angele qui meus es custos . . .

Ad crucem. To the cross. Crucem tuam adoramus . . . Amen.

When the priest turneth after the lavatory. To answer the priest at mass, when he saith: Orate pro me fratres. Spiritus sancti gratia illustret . . .

At the levation of our Lord. Anima Christi sanctifica me . . . Amen.

---

[1] See Fuller: Church Hist., ed. 1845. Vol. 4, page 21; also C. H. Cooper: Memoir of Margaret, Countess of Richmond and Derby.

When thou enterest into the church, say thus: Domine in multitudine misericordiæ tuæ . . .
When thou takest holy water, say thus: Aqua benedicta sit mihi salus . . . Amen.
When thou beginnest to pray, thus begin kneeling: Discedite a me maligni . . . O bone Jesu tu novisti . . . Amen. Ascendat ad te Domine Deus oratio mea . . . Amen. Jesus, Jesus, Jesus, esto mihi Jesus. Amen.
Pro carnali dilectione. A prayer for carnal delectation. Domine libera animam meam . . . Amen.
Pro temptatione carnis. A prayer for temptation of the flesh. Domine Jesu Christe rex virginum . . . Amen.
Pro vera pænitentia. A prayer for very penance. Omnipotens sempiterne Deus precor te . . . Amen.
A prayer for diverse hours of the day. Hora prima. Domine Deus qui nos ad principium hujus diei . . . Amen. Domine Deus omnipotens qui me in hanc horam secundam . . . Amen. Hora tertia. Domine Jesu Christe qui hora tertia diei . . . Amen. Hora sexta. Domine Jesu Christe qui dum hora sexta . . . Amen. Hora nona. Domine Jesu Christe qui hora nona . . . Amen. Hora vespertina. Gratias tibi ago domine Deus omnipotens . . . Amen. Domine Deus dominator omnium . . . Amen.
Oratio S. Augustini in nocte. A prayer of Saint Austyn in the night. Deus pater noster qui ut oremus hortaris . . .
Oratio S. Ancelmi. A prayer of Saint Ancelme. Domine Deus meus si feci . . . Amen.
Pater noster. Ave Maria and Credo.[1] In nomine. Pater noster . . . libera nos a malo. Amen. Ave Maria . . . benedictus fructus ventris tui Jesus. Amen. Credo in Deum . . . et vitam æternam. Amen.
A confession general. Confiteor tibi Domine Jesu Christe omnia peccata mea . . .
Suscipere digneris. Suscipere dignare Domine Deus omnipotens has orationes . . . Amen.
When thou receivest the pax say. Da pacem Domine in diebus nostris . . .
When thou shalt receive the sacrament. Domine non sum dignus ut intres . . . Amen.
When thou hast received. Vera perceptio corporis et sanguinis . . . Amen.
To get grace for sins. Exaudi quæsumus Domine supplicium preces . . . Amen.
Against evil thoughts. Omnipotens mitissime Deus respice propitius ad preces nostras . . . Amen.
For the king. Deus regnorum et Christiane maxime protector . . . Amen.
For thy friend living. Deus qui justificas impium . . . Amen.
For wayfaring men. Adesto Domine supplicationibus nostris . . . Amen.
For friends in sickness or in necessity. Omnipotens sempiterne Deus salus æterna credentium . . . Amen.

[1] See Wilkins Conc., ed. 1787. Vol. 3, page 59.

For thy father and mother dead. Deus qui nos patrem et matrem honorare præcepisti . . . Amen.

For thy friend that is dead. Suscipe piissime Deus in sinu patriarchæ tui Abrahæ . . . Amen.

For the living and dead. Omnipotens sempiterne Deus qui vivorum dominaris . . . Amen.

₊ *The title " Orationes quotidianæ " is given in No. 31, A.D. 1506, to all the preceding devotions in the book.*

Hic incipiunt horæ Beatæ Mariæ secundum usum Sarum. Matyns of our lady with pryme and the hours, with the hours of the passion of our Lord and of the compassion of our lady.

₊ *As the following Suffragia are not the same in every edition, any fresh one is given as it occurs.*

Ad Laudes. Suffragia Sanctorum. De S. Spiritu. Añ. Veni Sancte Spiritus . . . ℣. Emitte Spiritum tuum . . . ℟. Et renovabis . . . Oremus. Deus qui corda fidelium . . . Amen.

De S. Trinitate. Añ. Libera nos, salva nos . . . ℣. Sit nomen Domini benedictum. ℟. Ex hoc nunc . . . Oremus. Omnipotens sempiterne Deus qui dedisti famulis tuis . . . Amen.

De S. Cruce. Añ. Nos autem gloriari oportet . . . ℣. Omnis terra adoret . . . ℟. Psalmum dicat . . . Oremus. Deus qui sanctam crucem tuam ascendisti . . . Amen.

De S. Michaele archangelo. Añ. Michael archangele veni . . . ℣. In conspectu angelorum . . . ℟. Adorabo ad templum . . . Oremus. Deus qui miro ordine angelorum ministeria . . . Amen.

De S. Johanne baptista. Añ. Inter natos mulierum . . . ℣. Fuit homo missus . . . ℟. Cui nomen . . . Oremus. Perpetuis nos Domine Sancti Joannis Baptistæ tuere . . . Amen.

De SS. Petro et Paulo. Añ. Petrus apostolus et Paulus doctor gentium . . . ℣. In omnem terram . . . ℟. Et in fines orbis terræ . . . Oremus. Deus cujus dextera beatum Petrum apostolum ambulantem . . . Amen.

De S. Andrea. Añ. Andreas Christi famulus . . . ℣. Dilexit Andream Dominus. ℟. In odorem suavitatis. Oremus. Majestatem tuam Domine suppliciter exoramus . . . Amen.

De S. Johanne evangelista. Añ. Iste est Johannes qui supra pectus Domini . . . ℣. Valde honorandus est . . . ℟. Qui supra pectus Domini . . . Oremus. Ecclesiam tuam quæsumus Domine benignus illustra . . . Amen.

De S. Laurentio. Añ. Laurentius bonum opus operatus est . . . ℣. Dispersit, dedit . . . ℟. Justitia ejus manet . . . Oremus. Da nobis quæsumus omnipotens Deus vitiorum nostrorum flammas extinguere . . . Amen.

De S. Stephano. Añ. Stephanus vidit cælos apertos . . . ℣. Gloria et honore . . . ℟. Et constituisti . . . Oremus. Da nobis quæsumus Domine imitari quod colimus . . . Amen.

De S. Thoma Archiepiscopo Cantuariensi. Añ. Tu per Thomæ sanguinem
... ℣. Gloria et honore ... ℟. Et constituisti ... Oremus. Deus
pro cujus ecclesia ... Amen.
De S. Nicolao. Añ. Beatus Nicolaus adhuc puerulus ... ℣. Ora pro nobis
... ℟. Ut digni ... Oremus. Deus qui beatum Nicolaum pium
pontificem tuum ... Amen.
De S. Maria Magdalena. Añ. Maria ergo ... ℣. Dimissa sunt ... ℟.
Quoniam dilexit ... Oratio. Largire nobis clementissime pater ...
Amen.
De S. Katherina. Añ. Virgo sancta Katherina ... ℣. Ora pro nobis ...
℟. Ut digni ... Oremus. Omnipotens sempiterne Deus qui gloriosæ
virginis et martyris tuæ Katherinæ ... Amen.
De S. Margareta. Añ. Erat autem Margareta ... ℣. Specie tua ... ℟.
Intende prospere ... Oremus. Deus qui beatam virginem Margaretam
... Amen.
De omnibus sanctis. Añ. Omnes sancti et electi Dei ... ℣. Lætamini in
Domino ... ℟. Et gloriamini ... Oremus. Omnium sanctorum
tuorum, quæsumus Domine, intercessione placatus ... Amen.
Pro pace. Añ. Da pacem Domine in diebus nostris ... ℣. Domine fiat pax
... ℟. Et abundantia ... Oremus. Deus a quo sancta desideria ...
Amen. Benedicamus Domino. Deo gratias.

₊ *The several " Hours of the passion of our Lord, and of the compassion of
our Lady" occur, in this book, after each of the corresponding " Hours of our
Lady," from Lauds to Compline.*

₊ *The title " Orationes de beata Maria," is given as a Head line in No. 81,
A.D. 1506, to the following devotions down to " A prayer to our blessed Lady
against the pestilence. Stella cæli."*

Salve regina with the verses. Añ. Salve Regina misericordiæ ... ℣. Ave
Maria ... ℟. Benedicta tu ... Oremus. Omnipotens sempiterne
Deus qui gloriosæ virginis et matris Mariæ ... Amen.
The five corporal joys of our Lady. Añ. Gaude virgo mater Christi ... ℣.
Benedicta es ... ℟. Quia per te fructum ... Oremus. Deus qui
beatissimam virginem Mariam ... Amen.
The seven spiritual joys of our Lady. Añ. Gaude flore virginali ... Añ. O
sponsa sancta et humilis virgo ... Amen. ℣. Exaltata es ... ℟.
Super choros angelorum ... Oremus. Dulcissime Domine Jesu Christe
fili Dei vivi qui beatissimam ... Amen.
De profundis for all christian souls. Psalmus. De profundis. Kyrie eleyson.
Pater noster. ℣. Requiem æternam ... ℟. Et lux perpetua ... ℣.
A porta inferi. ℟. Erue Domine ... ℣. Credo videre ... ℟. In
terra viventium. ℣. Domine exaudi ... ℟. Et clamor meus ...
Oremus. Absolve quæsumus Domine animas famulorum ... Amen.
Et animæ omnium fidelium defunctorum ... Amen. God have mercy
on all christian souls. Amen. God save the King and bring us to the
bliss that never shall have ending.

A prayer to our Lady and St. John the evangelist. O intemerata et in æternum benedicta ... Amen.
Another to our Lady and St. John the evangelist. Sancta Maria Dei genitrix semperque virgo benedicta ... Amen.
Before our Lady of pity. Obsecro te Domina sancta Maria mater Dei ... Amen.
De beata virgine Maria pro vitæ incolumitate. Sancta Maria regina cæli et terræ, mater Domini nostri Jesu Christi ... Amen.
To our blessed Lady against the pestilence. Añ. Stella cæli extirpavit, quæ lactavit Dominum ... ℣. Ora pro nobis ... ℟. Ut digni ... Oremus. Deus misericordiæ, Deus pietatis ... Amen.

₊ *The particular titles of the several devotions, as well as the general one of "Oratio" occur as head lines, in No. 31, A.D. 1506, to the following devotions, down to "Oratio ad S. Iheronimum".*

Ad elevationem corporis Christi. Prayers to the sacrament at levation. Ave verum corpus natum de Maria virgine ... Ave Jesu Christe verbum Patris ... Amen. In præsentia sacrosancti corporis et sanguinis tui Domine Jesu Christe ... Amen. Oremus. Domine Jesu Christe qui hanc sacratissimam carnem tuam ... Amen.
A prayer to the Trinity. Sancta Trinitas unus Deus: miserere nobis. O beata et gloriosa ... Amen.
Deus qui superbis. Deus qui superbis resistis et humilibus das gratiam ... Pater noster. Ave.
Deus qui liberasti. Deus qui liberasti Susannam de falso crimine ... Amen.
Two little prayers which King Harry the sixth made. Domine Jesu Christe qui me creasti ... Domine Jesu Christe qui solus es sapientia ... Amen. Pater noster. Ave.
Two prayers with two collects to the three Kings of Cologne. Rex Jaspar, rex Melchior, rex Balthasar ... Amen. ℣. Reges Tharsis et insulæ munera offerent. ℟. Reges Arabum et Saba dona adducent. Oremus. Deus illuminator omnium gentium ... Amen. Trium regum trinum munus ... ℣. Vidimus stellam ... ℟. Et venimus ... Oremus. Deus qui tres Magos ... Amen.
The xv hours of the passion of our Lord. O Domine Jesu Christe æterna dulcedo ... Amen. Pater noster. Ave. O Jesu vera libertas angelorum ... Amen. Pater noster. Ave. O Jesu mundi fabricator ... Amen. Pater noster. Ave. O Jesu cælestis medice ... Amen. Pater noster. Ave. O Jesu speculum claritatis divinæ ... Amen. Pater noster. Ave. O Jesu rex amabilis ... Amen. Pater noster. Ave. O Jesu fons inexhaustæ pietatis ... Amen. Pater noster. Ave. O Jesu dulcedo cordium ... Amen. Pater noster. Ave. O Jesu regalis virtus ... Amen. Pater noster. Ave. O Jesu Alpha et Omega ... Amen. Pater noster. Ave. O Jesu abyssus profundissime ... Amen. Pater noster. Ave. O Jesu veritatis speculum ... Amen. Pater noster.

112   SUMMARY OF CONTENTS.   [1494-

Ave. O Jesu leo fortissime . . . Amen. Pater noster. Ave. O Jesu unigenite . . . Amen. Pater noster. Ave. O Jesu vitis vera . . . Amen. Pater noster. Ave. Credo.

To them that before this image of pity[1] devoutly say: v. Pater noster. v. Aves, and a Credo; piteously beholding these arms of Christ's passion are granted xxxii. M. VII hundred and lv years of pardon. Prayers to the pity of our Lord with indulgences. Adoro te Domine Jesu Christe in cruce pendentem . . . Amen. Pater noster. Adoro te Domine Jesu Christe in cruce vulneratum . . . Amen. Pater noster. Adoro te Domine Jesu Christe in sepulchro positum . . . Amen. Pater noster. Adoro te Domine Jesu Christe descendentem ad inferos . . . Amen. Pater noster. Adoro te Domine Jesu Christe resurgentem a mortuis . . . Amen. Pater noster. O Domine Jesu Christe pastor bone . . . Amen. Pater noster. O Domine Jesu Christe rogo te propter illam maximam amaritudinem . . . Amen. Pater noster. Ave. Credo. ℣. Adoramus te Christe . . . ℟. Quia per sanctam crucem . . . Oremus. Benignissime Domine Jesu Christe respice super me miserum peccatorem . . . Amen. Dominus papa sixtus quartus composuit quartam et quintam prædictorum suffragiorum oratiunculas. Et cum hoc omnes indulgentias hæc legentibus per ante concessas duplicavit.

A devout prayer to our Lord crucified, and to His five wounds. O pie crucifixe redemptor omnium populorum . . . Amen. Pater noster. Ave. Domine Jesu Christe qui gloriosum caput tuum . . . Amen. Pater noster. Ave. Domine Jesu Christe qui gloriosas manus tuas . . . Amen. Pater noster. Ave. Domine Jesu Christe qui pretiosum latus tuum . . . Amen. Pater noster. Ave. Domine Jesu Christe qui pretiosos pedes tuos . . . Amen. Pater noster. Ave. Domine Jesu Christe qui totum corpus tuum . . . Amen. Pater noster. Ave. Credo. ℣. Adoramus te Christe . . . ℟. Quia per sanctam crucem . . . ℣. Domine exaudi . . . ℟. Et clamor meus . . . Oremus. Deus qui voluisti pro perditione mundi . . . Amen.

Oratio S. Bernardini confessoris ordinis minorum. The prayer of St. Bernardyn, O bone Jesu with anthem and collect. O rex gloriose. O bone Jesu, O dulcis Jesu . . . Amen. Añ. O rex gloriose inter sanctos tuos . . . ℣. Sit nomen . . . ℟. Ex hoc nunc . . . Oremus. Deus qui gloriosissimum nomen Jesu Christi . . . Amen.

To the Cross. Sanctifica me Domine Jesu Christe signaculo tuæ sanctæ crucis . . . Amen.

To the proper angel. Añ. Angele qui meus es custos . . . ℣. O beate angele . . . ℟ Actus meos regula . . . Oremus. Deus qui sanctorum angelorum tuorum . . . Amen. Oratio. O sancte angele Dei, minister cælestis imperii . . . Amen.

Oratio ad S. Jacobum apostolum fratrem S. Johannis evangelistæ. Diverse commemorations to these Saints following. To St. James the more.

---

[1] See Henry Bradshaw's Collected papers, page 84.

Añ. O lux et decus Hispaniæ . . . ℣. Ora pro nobis . . . ℟. Ut digni . . . Oremus. Protector in te sperantium Deus . . . Amen. Alia antiphona. Gaude felix tota Hispania . . . ℣. Ora pro nobis . . . ℟. Ut digni . . . Oremus. Deus cujus dispositione mirabili . . . Amen.

De S. Jacobo minori Alphæi. To St. James the less. Añ. O candor perpetue puræ castitatis . . . ℣. Ora pro nobis . . . ℟. Ut digni . . . Oremus. Deus qui justum apostolum tuum Jacobum . . . Amen.

De S. Sebastiano. To St. Sebastian. Añ. O quam gloriosa refulget gratia . . . ℣. Ora pro nobis . . . ℟. Ut digni mereamur pestem . . . Oremus. Deus qui beatum Sebastianum gloriosum martyrem tuum . . . Amen.

De S. Christofero. To St. Christopher. Añ. Martyr Christofore pro salvatoris honore . . . Amen. ℣. Ora pro nobis . . . ℟. Ut digni . . . Oremus. Concede quæsumus omnipotens et misericors Deus ut qui beati Christofori . . . Amen.

De S. Georgio. To St. George. Añ. Georgi martyr inclite te decet laus et gloria . . . ℣. Ora pro nobis . . . ℟. Ut hostes visibiles . . . Oremus. Omnipotens sempiterne Deus qui deprecantium voces . . . Amen.

De S. Martino. To St. Martin. Añ. O Martine, O pie, quam pium est gaudere de te . . . ℣. Ora pro nobis . . . ℟. Ut digni . . . Oremus. Deus qui conspicis quia ex nulla nostra virtute . . . Amen.

De S. Anthonio. To St. Anthony. Añ. O Anthoni pastor inclite qui cruciatos reficis . . . ℣. Ora pro nobis . . . ℟. Ut digni . . . Oremus. Deus qui concedis obtentu beati Anthonii confessoris tui . . . Amen.

De S. Francisco. To St. Franciscus. Añ. Franciscus vir catholicus et totus apostolicus . . . ℣. Ora pro nobis . . . ℟. Ut digni . . Oremus. Deus qui ecclesiam tuam beati Francisci meritis . . . Amen.

De S. Anna. To St. Anne. Añ. Cæleste beneficium introivit in Annam . . . ℣. Ora pro nobis . . . ℟. Ut digni . . . Oremus. Deus qui beatæ Annæ tantam gratiam donare dignatus es . . . Amen.

De S. Barbara. To St. Barbara. Añ. Gaude Barbara beata, summe pollens . . . ℣. Ora pro nobis . . . ℟. Ut digni . . . Oremus. Intercessio, quæsumus Domine, beatæ Barbaræ virginis . . . Amen.

De undecim millia virginum. To the xi thousand virgins. Añ. O vos undena millia, puellæ gloriosæ . . . ℣. Orate pro nobis sponsæ . . . ℟. Ut ad vestrum consortium . . . Oremus. O dulcissime Domine Jesu Christe qui es sponsus virginum . . . Amen.

De S. Apollonia. To St. Appollyn. Añ. Virgo Christi egregia, pro nobis Apollonia . . . ℣. Specie tua . . . ℟. Intende prospere . . . Oremus. Omnipotens sempiterne Deus spes et corona . . . Amen.

Ad omnes Sanctos. To all Saints. Oratio. O vos omnes sancti et electi Dei quibus Deus . . . Amen.

Two devout prayers in English to Jesu. O glorious Jesu, O meekest Jesu, . . . Amen. The holy body of Christ Jesu . . . Amen. The glorious blood of Christ Jesu . . . Amen. I cry God mercy . . . O the most sweetest spouse of my soul Christ Jesu . . . Amen.

Istæ orationes debent dici in agonia mortis per sacerdotem pro infirmo in mutando verba. Et quilibet potest dicere pro semetipso, sicut hic stat. Devout prayers to be said in the agony of death and also daily. Dic primo. Kyrieleyson. Domine miserere nostri. Pater noster. Ave. Salvator mundi, salva nos . . . Auxiliare nos deprecamur Deus noster. Oremus. Domine Jesu Christe per agoniam . . . Amen. Secundo dic. Kyrieleyson. Pater noster. Ave. Domine miserere nobis. Sanctifica nos Domine signaculo sanctæ crucis . . . Oremus. Domine Jesu Christe qui pro nobis mori dignatus es in cruce . . . Amen. Tertio dic. Kyrieleyson. Domine miserere nobis. Pater noster. Ave. Protege et salva, benedic, sanctifica Domine . . . Amen. Oremus. Domine Jesu Christe qui per os prophetæ tui dixisti . . . Amen. Oremus. Domine Jesu Christe qui redemisti nos pretioso sanguine tuo . . . Amen.

Oratio ad Patrem. Pater de cælis Deus, miserere nobis. Domine sancte Pater omnipotens æterne Deus qui coæqualem . . . Amen.

Oratio ad Filium. Fili redemptor mundi Deus, miserere nobis. Domine Jesu Christe fili Dei vivi qui es verus et omnipotens Deus . . . Amen.

Oratio ad Spiritum Sanctum. Domine Spiritus sancte Deus qui coæqualis . . . Amen.

Oratio bona quotidie dicentibus revelatione divina transmissa uni monacho de Bynham, circa annum Domini Millesimo ccclxxxv, quinque Pater noster, v. Ave Maria et Credo in Deum. A special prayer late shewed to a monk of Bynham. Deus propitius esto with a collect to Saint Mychell. Deus propitius esto mihi peccatori et esto custos mei . . . Amen. ℣. Ora pro nobis . . . ℞. Ut digni . . . Oremus. Deus qui miro ordine angelorum ministeria . . . Amen.

Oratio ad S. Gabrielem. An anthem with a collect to St. Gabriel. Precor te et princeps egregie Gabriel . . . Amen.

Oratio ad S. Raphaelem. Auxiliare mihi et tu princeps obsecro eximie Raphael . . . Amen.

A devout blessing. Benedicat me imperialis majestas . . . Amen.

Two devout prayers in english. O blessed Trinity, Father, Son and Holy Ghost, three Persons and one God . . . Amen. O Lord God almighty, all seeing all things . . . Amen. Credo in Deum.

Hic incipiunt septem Psalmi pænitentiales. Añ. Ne reminiscaris. Psalmi. Domine, ne in furore. Beati, quorum. Domine, ne in furore. Miserere mei, Deus. Domine, exaudi. De profundis. Domine, exaudi.

Quindecim psalmi. Ad Dominum. Levavi oculos. Lætatus sum. Ad te levavi oculos meos. Nisi quia Dominus. Qui confidunt. In convertendo. Nisi Dominus. Beati omnes. Sæpe expugnaverunt. De profundis. Domine, non est. Memento, Domine. Ecce, quam bonum. Ecce nunc.

The Litany and suffrages.

Versus S. Bernardi. The viii verses of St. Bernard. Illumina oculos meos ne unquam obdormiam in morte.

The short prayers taught by our Lady to St. Brygytte. Jesu fili Dei omnium conditor adjuva me . . . Pater noster. Ave. Jesu fili Dei qui coram judice tacuisti . . . Pater noster. Ave. Jesu fili Dei qui ligatus fuisti . . . Pater noster. Ave.

A prayer against thunder and tempest shewed by an angel to St. Edward. Titulus triumphalis, Jesus Nazarenus rex Judæorum crucifixus, Ecce vivificæ crucis dominicum signum . . . Alleluya. Kyrieleyson. Pater noster. Ave. Credo. ℣. Esto nobis Domine . . . ℟. A facie inimici. ℣. Domine exaudi . . . ℟. Et clamor meus . . . Oremus. Omnipotens sempiterne Deus parce metuentibus . . . Amen. Peto Domine Jesu Christe largire mihi . . . Amen. Domine Jesu Christe ego cognosco me graviter peccasse . . . Amen. Pater noster. Ave. Credo.

Hic incipiunt Vigiliæ mortuorum.

Hic incipiunt Commendationes animarum.

Oratio ad S. Crucem. A devout prayer to the cross. Salve, salve Rex sanctorum . . . Amen.

Psalmi de passione Christi. Psalms of the passion. Psalmi. Deus deus meus. Dominus regit me. Domini est terra. Ad te Domine levavi. Judica me Domine. Dominus illuminatio mea. Ad te Domine clamabo Afferte Domino filii Dei. Exaltabo te Domine. In te Domine speravi. Añ. Christus factus est . . . ℣. Ora pro nobis . . . ℟. Ut digni . . . ℣. Valde honorandus est beatus Johannes. ℟. Qui supra pectus . . . Oratio. Respice quæsumus Domine super hanc familiam tuam . . . Amen. Interveniat pro nobis Domine Jesu Christe apud tuam clementiam . . . Amen. Beati Johannis apostoli tui . . . Amen. Gloriosa passio . . . Amen. Benedictum sit dulce nomen Domini nostri . . . Amen. Sanctæ et individuæ Trinitati . . . Amen. Ave benigne Jesu gratia plenus . . . Amen.

Beatus Iheronomus in hoc modo disposuit hoc psalterium ubi angelus Domini docuit eum per Spiritum Sanctum porro propter hoc abbreviatum est, quod hi qui solicitudinem habent, vel qui in infirmitate jacent, aut qui in operibus occupantur, vel iter agunt, vel longinquam viam seu per mare navigatum, aut qui bellum contra hostes committunt, seu contra invidiam diabolorum qui militant contra animas Christianorum assidue, aut qui verum votum voverunt Deo quotidie psallere psalterium integrum et minime possunt hoc facere, vel qui jejunant fortiter et debilitatem habent, et pro piis qui festas solemnes custodiunt eo quod minime possunt psalterium canere illud unumquemque ergo ex his quos superius diximus si volunt animam suam salvam facere, et vitam æternam habere, assidue oportet canere hoc psalterium et possidebunt regnum Dei. Psalterium Iheronimi . . . Oratio. Dona mihi quæso omnipotens Deus ut per hanc sacrosanctam psalterii cælestis melodiam . . . Amen.

Oratio ad S. Iheronimum. An anthem with a collect of St. Iherom. Añ. Ave amator quam famose Iheronime gloriose . . . ℣. Ora pro nobis . . . ℟. Ut Deum diligamus . . . Oremus. Deus qui gloriosum confessorem tuum Iheronimum . . . Amen.

116 SUMMARY OF CONTENTS. [1494-

Oratio S. Gregorii. A devout prayer to the Trinity made by St. Gregory. Dominator domine Deus omnipotens qui es trinitas . . . Amen.

₊ *The rest of the devotions in this book had been previously printed separately, see Brit. Mus. C. 25. c., the book has a colophon similar to the one in this book, but no title-page, and is commonly called " The fifteen Oes and other prayers," it was printed at Westminster by W. Caxton c. 1490-91 (see Henry Bradshaw's Collected papers, page 333).*

The xv Ooes in english. O Jesu, endless sweetness of loving souls . . . Amen. Pater noster. Ave. O blessed Jesu, maker of all the world . . . Amen. Pater noster. Ave. O Jesu, heavenly leach . . . Amen. Pater noster. Ave. O Jesu, very freedom of angels . . . Amen. Pater noster. Ave. O Jesu, blessed mirror of endless clearness . . . Amen. Pater noster. Ave. O blessed Jesu, loveable King . . . Amen. Pater noster. Ave. O Blessed Jesu, well of endless pity . . . Amen. Pater noster. Ave. O blessed Jesu, sweetness of hearts . . . Amen. Pater noster. Ave. O blessed Jesu, royal strength . . . Amen. Pater noster. Ave. O blessed Jesu, beginning and ending . . . Amen. Pater noster. Ave. O blessed Jesu, deepness of endless mercy . . . Amen. Pater noster. Ave. O blessed mirror of truth . . . Amen. Pater noster. Ave. O blessed Jesu, most meekest lion . . . Amen. Pater noster. Ave. O blessed Jesu, the only begotten Son . . . Amen. Pater noster. Ave. O blessed Jesu, very and true plenteous vine . . . Amen. Pater noster. Ave. Credo.

Three devout prayers in english to our Saviour Jesu with devout orisons in Latin. O my sovereign Lord Jesu, the very son of almighty God . . . Deus propitius esto mihi peccatori vel peccatrici. I thank Thee also with all my heart . . . Non nobis Domine non nobis, sed nomini tuo da gloriam. Adonai domine Deus magne rex admirabilis . . . Amen. Psalmus. Domine Dominus noster. ℣. Ab inimicis nostris . . . ℟. Afflictionem nostram . . . ℣. Dolorem cordis nostri . . . ℟. Peccata populi tui . . . ℣. Orationes nostras . . . ℟. Fili Dei vivi . . . Hic et in perpetuum nos custodire digneris Christe. Exaudi nos, exaudi, exaudi nos Christe. Oratio. Infirmitatem nostram quæsumus Domine propitius respice . . . Amen. Jesu for thy holy Name and for thy bitter passion . . . Amen. O most dear Lord and Saviour sweet Jesu . . . Amen.

A prayer to our Lady in english. O blessed Lady, mother of Jesu and Virgin immaculate . . . Amen.

A prayer in english to the proper angel with certain orisons and verses. O glorious angel to whom our blessed Lord . . . Amen. Resp. Spem in alium nunquam habui . . . Qui irasceris et propitius eris . . . In tribulatione . . . ℣. Domine Deus cæli et terræ . . . ℟. Qui irasceris . . . ℣. Gloria Patri. ℟. In tribulatione. ℣. Sit nomen Domini. ℟. Ex hoc nunc . . . Oremus. Protector in te sperantium Deus . . . Amen.

Ad S. Trinitatem. To the holy Trinity a prayer in Latin with certain Psalms. Domine Deus omnipotens, Pater et Filius et Spiritus Sanctus . . . Amen.

In nomine. Pater noster. Ave. Psalmi. Deus in nomine. Deus misereatur. De profundis. Voce mea ad Dominum. Ad te levavi oculos meos. Levavi oculos. Beati omnes. Jesus autem transiens per medium illorum ibat.

Oratio ad patrem. Domine sancte Pater omnipotens æterne Deus in illa sancta custodia . . . Amen.

Orationes ad Dominum. Two devout prayers to our Saviour and to the holy company of heaven. Deus propitius esto mihi peccatori N. vel peccatrici N. istam orationem ferenti . . . Amen. Domine Jesu Christe fili Dei vivi Deus omnipotens, rex gloriæ . . . Amen. Pater noster. Ave.

Oratio S. Crucis. A blessing by the virtue of the holy cross with the psalm, Inclina Domine aurem tuam, and an orison. Signum sanctæ crucis defendat me . . . Amen. Psalmus. Inclina Domine aurem tuum. Kyrie eleyson. Pater noster. Ave. ℣. Adoremus crucis signaculum. ℟. Per quod salutis sumpsimus sacramentum. Oremus. Sanctifica quæsumus Domine famulum tuum . . . Amen.

Oratio ad Dominum. A prayer to our Saviour and the archangels. Domine Jesu Christe apud me sis ut me defendas . . . Amen. Sancte Michael esto mihi lorica . . . Amen. Dulcissime Jesu inspira cordi meo . . . Amen.

Ad crucem. A prayer to the holy cross. Añ. Quicquid inimicus meus alligaverit in me . . . ℣. Omnis terra adoret . . . ℟. Psalmum dicat . . . Oremus. Deus qui per crucem passionis tuæ . . . Amen.

Oratio ad Dominum. A prayer to our Saviour. Vita viventium Christe ab iniqua et subitanea morte libera me . . . Amen. Kyrieleyson. Pater noster. Ave. Oremus. Omnipotens sempiterne Deus non me permittas perire . . . Amen.

Oratio contra temptationes. A prayer against temptations. Deus qui contritorum non despicis gemitum . . . Amen.

Contra mortalitatem hominum. A prayer against the pestilence. Añ. Per signum tau a peste epidimiæ libera nos Jesu . . . ℣. Miserere nostri . . . ℟. Ut a peste epidimiæ . . . Oremus. Visita nos quæsumus Domine et habitationem istam . . . Amen.

Oratio de beato rege Henrico. A prayer to holy King Henry. Añ. Rex Henricus sis amicus nobis in angustia . . . ℣. Ora pro nobis . . . ℟. Ut per te cuncti . . . Oremus. Præsta quæsumus omnipotens et misericors Deus ut qui devotissimi regis . . . Amen.

Ad S. Rochum. A prayer to St. Rocke Añ. O quam magnificum est nomen tuum beate Roche . . . ℣. Ora pro nobis . . . ℟. Ut digni . . . Oremus. Omnipotens sempiterne Deus qui meritis et precibus beatissimi Rochi . . . Amen.

To every christian creature able to receive pardon saying this anthem and collect following within the church or churchyard is granted for every christian creature there buried xl days of pardon and xiii lents. A prayer for all christian souls. Avete fideles omnes animæ in sancta Dei pace . . . Amen. Oremus. Miserere Domine per tuam gloriosam resurrectionem . . . Amen. Requiescant in pace. Amen.

Colophon " *These foresaid prayers as the XV. oes in english and the other following ben enprynted* . . ."

c. A.D. 1494. (Wynkyn de Worde, Westminster). No. 9.

A prayer to Saint Erasmus. Sancte Herasme martyr Christi preciose . . . Amen. Whoso saith this prayer following in the worship of God and Saint Rock, shall not die of the pestilence by the grace of God. Raphael archangelus ad beatum Rochum. Añ. Confessor Dei venerande . . . ℣. Ora pro nobis . . . ℞. Ut digni . . . Oratio. Omnipotens sempiterne Deus qui meritis et precibus beatissimi Rochi . . . Amen.

A.D. 1495 (Philippe Pigouchet, Paris). 4º. No. 10.

⁂ This book has a title-page, which has " *Horæ . . . cum multis orationibus et suffragiis noviter additis* . . ."

A stanza of four lines in Latin occurs at the end of each month of the Kalender.

⁂ The words " *Cum quatuor evangeliis et passione Domini* " *in the title of No. 26, A.D. 1503 describe the following.*

Initium sancti evangelii, secundum Johannem. Gloria tibi Domine. In principio erat verbum . . . Añ. Te invocamus, te adoramus . . . ℣. Sit nomen . . . ℞. Ex hoc nunc . . . Oratio. Protector in te sperantium Deus sine quo nihil est validum . . . Amen.

Sequentia S. Evangelii, secundum Lucam. Gloria tibi Domine. In illo tempore. Missus est Gabriel . . . Deo gratias.

Sequentia S. Evangelii, secundum Matthæum. Gloria tibi Domine. In il o tempore. Cum natus esset Jesus . . . Deo gratias.

Sequentia S. Evangelii secundum Marcum. Gloria tibi Domine. In illo tempore. Recumbentibus undecim discipulis . . . Deo gratias.

Passio domini nostri Jesu Christi secundum Johannem. Egressus est dominus Jesus . . . Deo gratias.

Ad laudes. Suffragia sanctorum. De S. Apostolis. Añ. Dum steteritis ante reges . . . ℣. In omnem terram . . . ℞. Et in fines . . . Oremus. Concede quæsumus omnipotens Deus ut sicut apostolorum tuorum . . . Amen.

A prayer against thunder and tempest. Titulus triumphalis . . . (as on page 115) with this addition. Deus qui culpa offenderis pænitentia placaris . . . Amen. Pater noster. Ave. Credo.

The rosare. Ave Maria . . . benedictus fructus ventris tui Jesus Christus Amen. Jesus. Quem de Spiritu sancto, angelo nunciante concepisti. Ave.

c. A.D. 1495. (Jean Philippe, Paris), on vellum. No. 11.

Oratio ante imaginem corporis Christi. Conditor cæli et terræ rex regum . . . Amen.

A.D. 1497, April 3, Jean Barbier and J. H., London, for Wynkyn de Worde, Westminster, 8º. No. 14.

⁎ *The colophon has "Horæ . . . diligenter emendatæ . . ."*

A.D. 1497. Thielman Kerver for Jean Richard, Rouen, 8º. No. 15.

⁎ *The colophon has "Officium beatæ Mariæ . . ."*

Almanach pro xxvii. Annis. Cut of anatomical man.
Passio domini nostri Jesu Christi secundum Johannem. Egressus est (as on page 118) with this addition. Oremus. Deus qui manus tuas et pedes tuos . . . Amen.
Oratio de beata virgine Maria. Añ. Ave cujus conceptio . . . ℣. Ora pro nobis . . . ℟. Ut digni . . . Oratio. Deus qui nos conceptionis . . . Amen.

⁎ *A copy of this book, without the device of J. Philippe beneath the colophon, is in the possession of the Rev. E. S. Dewick.*

A.D. 1498, May 16. Philippe Pigouchet, Paris, for Simon Vostre, Paris, on vellum. No. 17.

Officium de Sancto Spiritu.

A.D. 1498, Jean Jehannot, Paris, for Nicolas Lecomte, London, 8º. No. 18.

⁎ *The title has "Hoc præsens officium . . . de novo revisum et correctum cum multis suffragiis . . ."*

A.D. 1501, October 20. Philippe Pigouchet, Paris, for Simon Vostre, Paris, on vellum. No. 23.

A stanza of four lines in french occurs at the end of each month of the Kalender.
Oratio dicenda die sabbati ad honorem intemeratæ Dei genitricis virginis Mariæ. Missus est Gabriel angelus ad Mariam virginem . . . Oremus. Te deprecor ergo mitissimam . . . Amen. Pater noster. Ave.
Devota contemplatio beatæ Mariæ virginis juxta crucem filii sui lachrymantis: et ad compassionem Salvatoris singulos invitantis. Stabat mater dolorosa . . . Amen. ℣. Tuam ipsius animam . . . ℟. Ut revelentur . . . Oremus. Interveniat pro nobis quæsumus Domine Jesu Christe nunc et in hora mortis . . . Amen.

A.D. 1502. Wynkyn de Worde, London, on vellum. No. 25.

⁎ *This book has no title-page, the Colophon has "Horæ . . . una cum multis sanctorum et sanctarum suffragiis, et multis aliis diversis orationibus noviter suppcradditis . . ."*

Psalmi de passione Christi, (as on page 115) with this addition. Nos cum prole pia benedicat virgo Maria. Amen.
Quædam orationes speciales, primo.

Oratio ad Patrem. Kyrieleyson. Pater de cælis Deus: miserere nobis. Qui mundum mirabiliter de nihilo creasti: miserere nobis . . .
Oratio ad Filium. Kyrieleyson. Fili redemptor mundi Deus: miserere nobis. Qui de virgine Maria incarnari voluisti: miserere nobis . . .
Oratio ad Spiritum sanctum. Kyrieleyson. Spiritus sancte Deus: miserere nobis. Qui in columbæ specie super Christum descendisti: miserere nobis . . .
Oratio ad beatam Trinitatem Sancta Trinitas unus Deus: miserere nobis. O beata et benedicta et gloriosa Trinitas: miserere nobis . . . Memento mei Deus meus in bonum . . . Amen.
Oratio ad sanctam Mariam. Sancta Maria mater Dei: ora pro nobis. Sancta Maria regina cæli: ora pro nobis . . . Amen.
Oratio ad sanctos Angelos. Omnes sancti beatorum ordines: orate pro nobis . . . Amen.
Oratio ad sanctos Patriarchas et Prophetas. Omnes sancti Patriarchæ et Prophetæ: orate pro nobis . . . Amen.
Oratio ad sanctos Innocentes. Omnes sancti Innocentes: orate pro nobis . . . Amen.
Oratio ad sanctos Apostolos et Discipulos Domini. Omnes sancti Apostoli et electi discipuli Domini: orate pro nobis . . . Amen.
Oratio de Martyribus. Omnes sancti Martyres: orate pro nobis . . . Amen.
Oratio de Confessoribus. Omnes sancti Confessores: orate pro nobis . . . Amen.
Oratio de sanctis Virginibus. Omnes sanctæ Virgines et Matronæ: orate pro nobis . . . Amen.
Oratio de omnibus Sanctis. Omnes sancti: orate pro nobis . . . Amen.
For women in travailing of child. Psalmus. Beatus vir qui non abiit. Maria peperit Christum. Anna Mariam . . . Amen.
De S. Maria. Oratio. Añ. Sub tuam protectionem confugimus . . . ℣. Sancta Dei genitrix . . . ℟. Intercede pro nobis . . . Oremus. Gratiam tuam quæsumus Domine mentibus nostris infunde . . . Amen.
De corpore Christi. Oratio. Añ. O sacrum convivium in quo Christus . . . ℣. Panem de cælo . . . ℟. Omne delectamentum . . . Oremus. Deus qui nobis sub sacramento mirabili passionis tuæ . . . Amen.
Ad invocandam gratiam Spiritus sancti. Oratio, primo dicitur. Hymnus. Veni creator Spiritus . . . ℣. Emitte spiritum tuum . . . ℟. Et renovabis . . . Oremus. Deus cui omne cor patet . . . Amen.
De nominibus Dei. Oratio. Omnipotens Dominus ✠ Christus. Messias ✠ Sother . . . Amen. O Domine Jesu Christe in tuam protectionem . . . Amen.
Oratio de sancta Maria. O gloriosissima, O optima, O sacratissima virgo Maria . . . Amen.
Si quis istam orationem sequentem devote frequentando dixerit: quicquid debite et juste petierit obtinebit. Añ. Sancti per fidem vicerunt regna . . . ℣. Exultent justi . . . ℟. Et delectentur . . . Oremus. Omnipotens et misericors Deus qui sanctorum tuorum Dyonisii . . . Amen.

The prayer of Loth, Jacob, and Moses, and it is for them that have taken any new great thing upon them, that they would have brought to good end. Oratio prima legislatoris. Exodi. xxxiiii. Dominator domine Deus misericors et clemens . . . Amen.

This prayer following is to thank God of His gracious gifts sent to us, and to ask mercy and grace to keep them continually. Oratio Moysi et populi. Exodi. xv. Fortitudo mea et laus mea Dominus . . . Eleazar. Genesis xxiiii. Benedictus Dominus Deus qui non abstulisti misericordiam . . . Numeri vi. Benedictio. Benedic igitur et nunc mihi et custodi me . . .

This prayer following is for them that have labour in temptation, or have any other disease with governance of the people. Josue lxxiii. Oratio Josue ducis populi. Numeri. xvi. Fortissime Deus spirituum universæ carnis . . . Amen.

This prayer following is to thank God of His gifts, asking them to be continued in us, and in all His people. Oratio David ii Regum vii. Quis ergo Domine Deus et quæ domus mea . . . Amen.

This prayer following is for a soul falling into sin, as well of great estate as of low, where, though he or the people be punished, to purchase grace thereof. Oratio David et Ezechie et aliorum. Regum xix. Domine Deus rex Israel qui sedes super cherubin . . . Amen.

This prayer following is the prayer of the sinful King Manasses, that shed the blood of Innocents and of Prophets, and did many other sins, as Scripture witnesseth, more than any other that was afore him or after following, reigning. And yet after all this, he besought God of mercy entirely, and did penance, and had mercy ii Paralipomenon ultimo. Oratio devota Manasses regis filii regis Ezechie. Domine Deus omnipotens patrum nostrorum Abraham, Isaac et Jacob . . . Amen.

This prayer following is for any that falleth in dysclaunder, reproof, or any manner of tribulation, as the blessed elder Thobye, and Sara Raguellis daughter were, and delivered graciously through God and this prayer. Oratio Thobie senioris et Sare filiæ Raguelis. Thobie iii. Justus es Domine et omnia judicia tua justa sunt . . . Amen.

This prayer following is to thank God of deliverance out of tribulation, or dysclaunder, reproof or other disease, and that also he is brought by God's help to much comfort, grace, and peace as the elder Thobye was. Thobie xiii. Oratio Thobie senioris Deo regratiatoria. Magnus es Domine in æternum et in omnia sæcula regnum tuum . . . Amen.

This prayer following is for them that intend to be married, or be new married, to pray God that they may love together singularly, and finally to bring forth fruit betwixt them two, as the younger Thobie did and Sara his wife. Thobie viii. iiii. ix. Oratio Thobie junioris et Sara uxoris ejus. Domine Deus patrum nostrorum benedicant te cæli et terra . . . Amen.

This prayer following is to thank God of victory of enemies. Oratio Judith xiii. ii. xvi. capitulis. Laudate dominum Deum nostrum quem non deseruit . . . Amen.

122   SUMMARY OF CONTENTS.   [1503-

This prayer following is for them that have sickness or adversity, to thank God and to pray all the days of their life to make satisfaction for their sins. Oratio sancti Job in tempore suæ probationis. Parce mihi Domine, nihil enim sunt dies mei ... Amen.

This prayer following is for them that will praise God, both of his goodness and also of his right wiseness, and for to ask time of repentance. Oratio regis Salomonis capitulo xii. O quam bonus et suavis est Domine spiritus tuus in nobis ... Amen.

This prayer following is for them that be laboured with sundry vices, and namely with the sin of lechery and desire grace to withstand them. Prima oratio Jesus filii Sirak. Ecclesiastici xxiii. Domine pater et dominator vitæ meæ ne derelinquas me ... Amen.

This prayer accordeth for them that be maliciously accused, and in great danger and disease, yet let them ever hope and trust in God to be delivered, as Susan the true wife was by this prayer. Oratio Susanne. xiii. Deus æterne qui absconditorum cognitor es ... Amen.

This prayer following is according to them that stand in disease and distress unlikely to be delivered, and yet let them trust to be delivered and to come out of their peril and jeopardy, as Jonas that was cast into the deepness of the sea trusted yet in the great goodness of God to be saved, and to praise him therefore in his temple, and so it was. Jone primo. Oratio Jone prophetæ in ventre ceti et in profundo maris. Clamavi de tribulatione mea ad dominum et exaudivit me ... Amen.

This prayer following is for them that be in disease, or have their friends diseased, or imprisoned, or fall in some great sin, to pray God to deliver them well out, as the good duke Neemye he prayed for them that were in the captivity of Babylon, the which were delivered. Oratio Neemiæ ducis. Neemie primo. Quæso domine Deus cæli, fortis, magne, atque terribilis ... Amen.

Innocentius papa secundus concessit cuilibet hanc orationem sequentem devote dicenti, quattuor millia dierum indulgentiæ. Ave vulnus lateris nostri salvatoris ... Pater noster. Ave. Credo.

Rosarium beatæ Mariæ virginis. Suscipe rosarium virgo deauratum ... Ave Maria. Quem virgo carens vitio de flamine concepisti ... Ave. ℣. In omni tribulatione ... ℟. Succurrat nobis ... Oremus. Interveniat pro nobis quæsumus Domine Jesu Christe apud tuam clementiam ... Amen. Oratio. O domine Jesu Christe pater dulcissime rogo te amore illius gaudii ... Amen. Pater noster. Ave.

Quinque devotissimæ orationes ad quinque plagas Domini nostri Jesu Christi, dicendæ ante crucifixum genibus flexis. Laus honor et gloria et gratiarum actio sit tibi pro sacratissimo vulnere ... Amen.

A.D. 1503, July 31. Wynkyn de Worde, London, on vellum. No. 26.

Oratio bona, unicuique dicenti perutilis, et pro suis benefactoribus. Hanc quidem orationem composuit S. Augustinus. Añ. Deprecamur te domine Jesu ... ℣. Adoramus te Christe ... ℟. Quia per sanctam crucem

... Clementer qui passus es pro nobis. Oremus. Domine Jesu Christe
fili Dei vivi pone passionem . . . Amen. Gloriosa passio . . . Amen.
Johannes papa. xii. concessit omnibus dicentibus orationem sequentem, transeundo per cymiterium, tot annos indulgentiarum quot fuerunt ibi corpora
inhumata a constitutione ipsius cymiterii. Añ. Avete omnes animæ
fideles quarum corpora . . . ℣. Non intres in judicium . . . ℟. Quoniam
non justificabitur . . . Oremus. Domine Jesu Christe salus et liberatio
fidelium . . . Amen.
Oratio devota de plagis Christi. Ave caput Christi gratum, duris spinis coro-
natum . . . Amen.
Quicunque hanc orationem sequentem devote quotidie dixerit, genibus flexis,
non morietur sine confessione: nullus hostis visibilis neque invisibilis
ei nocere potest illa die: et gloriossimam virginem Mariam videbit ante
diem exitus sui in adjutorium sibi. Domine Jesu Christe qui septem
verba . . . Amen.
Horæ dulcissimi nominis Jesu.

c. A.D. 1503 Julyan Notary, London, on vellum. No. 28.

This prayer following ought for to be said at mass, when the priest hath said the
gospel. Per hæc sancta evangelica dicta, deleantur universa nostra
delicta.

A.D. 1506, Kal. IX. Aprilis. Wolfgang Hopyl, Paris, for William Bretton, London, on vellum. No. 31.

⁎ *Head lines to the pages occur in this edition.*

Oratio coram imagine crucifixi dicenda quam qui devote dixerit, tot dies indulgentiarum meretur, quot erant vulnera in corpore Jesu tempore
passionis ejus, quas indulgentias contulit Gregorius papa tertius ad
petitionem reginæ Angliæ. Precor te amantissime domine Jesu Christe
. . . Amen. ℣. Proprio filio . . . ℟. Sed pro nobis . . . Oremus.
Omnipotens sempiterne Deus qui ex nimia charitate . . . Amen.
Subscriptam orationem edidit Sixtus papa quartus, et concessit eam devote
dicentibus coram imagine beatæ Mariæ Virginis in sole, undecim milia
annorum indulgentiarum. Oratio. Ave sanctissima Maria, mater Dei
. . . Amen.

A.D. 1506, April 24, Paris for Antoine Verard (Paris) on vellum. No. 32.

Oratio. Añ. Ave regina cælorum, ave domina angelorum . . . ℣. Post partum
virgo . . . ℟. Dei genitrix intercede . . . Oratio. Famulorum tuorum
quæsumus Domine delictis ignosce . . . Amen.

A.D. 1510, September 5. Thielman Kerver, Paris, for William Bretton, London, 8°. No. 37.

*The title has "Horæ . . . cum multis orationibus pulcherrimis et indulgen-
tiis jam ultimo recenter insertis".*

Tabula ad inveniendum perpetue omnia festa mobilia. The Canon of ebbs and floods. The Canon for letting of blood. Tabula præsens indicat locum lunæ . . . et in qua parte humani corporis ipsa luna dominatur in signis correspondentibus illis membris corporis. Aspectus signorum with a cut of the anatomical man. Distinctiones quatuor complexionum hominum.

Ad beatam Mariam post communionem. Oratio. O serenissima et inclita mater domini nostri Jesu Christi . . . Amen.

Ad Laudes. Suffragia Sanctorum. De S. Erkenwaldo episcopo. Añ. O decus insigne nostrum, pastorque benigne . . . ℣. Ora pro nobis .·. . ℞. Ut digni . . . Oremus. Omnipotens sempiterne Deus apud quem est continua . . . Amen.

This prayer showed our Lady to a devout parson, saying that this golden prayer is the most sweetest and acceptablest to me, and in her appearing she had this salutation and prayer written with letters of gold in her breast. Ave rosa sine spinis, tu quam pater in divinis . . . Amen.

Our holy father Bonifacius pope of Rome hath granted unto all them that say devoutly this prayer L days of pardon. Oratio. Ave Maria alta stirps, lilii castitatis . . . Amen.

This prayer was showed to Saint Bernard by the messenger of God, saying that as gold is most precious of all other metal so exceedeth this prayer all other prayers, and who that devoutly saith it shall have a singular reward of our blessed Lady and her sweet son Jesus. Ave Maria ancilla, Trinitatis humilissima . . . Amen.

This epistle of our Saviour sendeth our holy father pope Leo unto the emperor Carolo magno, of the which we find written who that beareth this blessing upon him and says it once a day shall obtain xl years of pardon and lxxx. lettys (lents). And he shall not perish with sudden death. Crux ✠ Christi sit mecum, Crux Christi ✠ est quam semper adoro . . . Amen.

This prayer was showed unto Saint Augustine by revelation of the Holy Ghost, and who that devoutly say this prayer, or hear her read, or heareth about them shall not perish in fire or water, neither in battle or judgment. And he shall die no sudden death, and no venom shall poison him that day. And what he asketh of God he shall obtain if it be to the salvation of his soul, and when thy soul shall depart from thy body it shall not enter to hell. Oratio. Deus propitius esto mihi peccatori et custos meus sis . . . Amen.

These v petitions and prayers made Saint Gregory, and hath granted unto all them that devoutly say these v prayers with v Pater noster, v Ave Maria and a Credo, v hundred years of pardon. Oratio. Ave manus dextera Christi perforata plaga tristi . . . Pater noster. Ave. Credo. ℣. Vulneratus est . . . ℞. Attritus est . . . Oremus. Concede quæsumus omnipotens Deus ut sanctissima vulnera . . . Amen.

This prayer shall ye say in the worship of all the blessed members of Christ devoutly, and ye shall have ccc days of pardon for every salve. Oratio. Salve tremendum cunctis potestatibus caput salvatoris . . . Amen.

This prayer is made by our holy father the pope John the xxii, and he hath granted unto all them that devoutly say this prayer beholding the glorious visage or vernacle of our Lord v thousand days of pardon. And he that cannot say this prayer, let them say v Pater noster. v Aves. and a Credo. Añ. Salve sancta facies nostri redemptoris . . . Amen.

This prayer made the holy doctor Saint Ambrose of all the articles of Christus passion. And our holy father Anastasius the pope hath granted to all them that devoutly say it hundred days of pardon. Oratio. Domine Jesu Christe fili Dei vivi creator et resuscitator . . . Amen.

Ad omnes choros angelorum. Oratio. O inflammati seraphin ardentes dilectione . . . ℣. Benedicite Domino . . . ℟. Potentes virtute . . . Oremus. Deus qui novem spirituum ordines . . . Amen.

De S. Wilhelmo episcopo et confessore. Añ. O Wilhelme pastor bone . . . ℣. Ora pro nobis . . . ℟. Ut digni . . . Oremus. Deus qui nos beati Wilhelmi confessoris tui . . . Amen.

De S. Edwardo rege et martyre. Añ. Ave sancte rex Edwarde, inter cæli lilia . . . ℣. Ora pro nobis . . . ℟. Ut digni . . . Oremus. Omnipotens sempiterne Deus qui donasti beatissimo regi Edwardo . . . Amen.

Alexander the vi pope of Rome hath granted to all them that say this prayer devoutly, in the worship of Saint Anna and our Lady and her son Jesus, v thousand years of pardon for deadly sins, and xx years for venial sins, totiens quotiens. Oratio. Ave Maria gratia plena . . . et benedicta sit sancta Anna mater tua ex qua sine macula et peccato processisti virgo Maria . . . Amen.

Another devout prayer to be said before the image of Saint Anna, Maria, and Jesus, of the which Raymund the cardinal and legate hath granted a hundred days of pardon, totiens quotiens. Oratio. Quotquot maris sunt guttæ, et arenæ terræ granæ . . . Amen.

De S. Dorothea. Añ. Salve virgo Dorothea, audi quæso vota mea . . . ℣. Diffusa est . . . ℟. Propterea benedixit . . . Oremus. Omnipotens sempiterne Deus in cujus nomine gloriosa virgo . . . Amen.

Pius the ii pope of Rome hath granted to all them that say this prayer following for the salvation of all Christian souls, totiens quotiens, a hundred days of pardon. And also Johannes the iiii. pope hath granted as many days of pardon as there be bodies of christian people buried. Pater noster. Ave. Oratio. Miserere mi Domine animabus quæ singulares . . . Amen. Pater noster.

When ye enter into the churchyard say this prayer. Salvete vos omnes fideles animæ quarum corpora . . . Amen.

A.D. 1511, Sept. 12. Paris, for Francis Byrckman (London). 4º. No. 39.

Ad Laudes Suffragia Sanctorum. De S. Wilgefortis virginis et martyris. Añ. Ave sancta famula Wilgefortis . . . ℣. Diffusa est . . . ℟. Propterea benedixit . . . Oremus. Famulam tuam quæsumus Domine beate Wilgefortis . . . Amen. Pater noster. Ave.

De S. Sitha virgine. Añ. Ave sancta famula Sitha . . . ℣. Ora pro nobis . . .

126   SUMMARY OF CONTENTS.   [1511-

℞. Ut mundemur . . . Oremus. Deus qui beatam Sitham virginem . . . Amen. Pater noster. Ave.

A devout prayer to our blessed Lady. O domina gloriæ, O regina lætitiæ . . . Amen. Pater noster.

A devout prayer of the vii sorrows of our blessed Lady. Ave dulcis mater Christi, quæ dolebas cordi tristi . . . Pater noster. Ave.

A devout prayer of the great sorrow that our Lady had when our Lord Jesu Christ was dead on the cross. Memento obsecro dulcissima mater . . . Pater noster. Ave.

Celestinus the pope hath granted to all them that devoutly say this prayer in the honour and worship of our blessed Lady iii hundred days of pardon. Pater noster. Ave. Oratio. Ave mundi spes Maria, Ave mitis, Ave pia . . . Amen. Pater noster. Ave.

Our holy father [pope] Sixtus hath granted at the instance of the high most and excellent princess Elisabeth, late Queen of England and wife to our sovereign liege lord King Harry the seventh, God have mercy on her sweet soul and all christian souls, that every day in the morning after iii tollings of the Ave bell, say iii times the whole salutation of our Lady, Ave Maria; that is to say at vi the klock in the morning iii Ave Maria, at xii the clock, at none iii Ave Maria. And at vi the klock at even, for every time so doing is granted of the spiritual treasure of holy church iii hundred days of pardon totiens quotiens. And also our holy fathers the Archbishop of Canterbury and York with other ix Bishops of this realm have granted iii times in the day xl days of pardon to all them that be in the state of grace able to receive pardon the which begun the xxvi day of March anno. m.cccc.xcii. anno. Henrici septimi vii. and the sum of the indulgence and pardon for every Ave Maria viii hundred days and lx, totiens quotiens. This prayer shall be said at the tolling of the Ave bell. Suscipe verbum virgo Maria . . . Ave. Say this iii times. And afterward say thy collect following. ℣. Dilexisti justitiam . . . ℞. Propterea unxit . . . Oratio. Deus qui de beatæ Mariæ virginis utero . . . Amen. Pater noster. Ave.

Say this prayer devoutly at the tolling of the Ave bell at none, for a memory and remembrance of the passion and death of Christ. Resp. Tenebræ factæ sunt dum crucifixissent Jesum Judæi . . . Et inclinato capite . . . Tunc unus ex militibus . . . ℣. Et velum templi scissum est. ℞. Et inclinato capite . . . ℣. Proprio filio suo non pepercit . . . ℞. Sed pro nobis . . . Oratio. Domine Jesu Christe fili Dei vivi qui pro salute mundi . . . Amen. Pater noster. Ave.

A general and devout prayer for the good state of our mother the holy church militant here in earth. Omnipotens et misericors Deus rex cæli et terræ . . . Amen. Pater noster. Ave.

Our holy father pope John the xxii hath granted a hundred days of pardon to all them that say this prayer at the elevation of our Lord Jesu Christ. Oratio. Ave caro Christi cara, immolata crucis ara . . . Pater noster. Ave.

Our holy father Innocent the II, pope of Rome, hath granted VII years of pardon to all them that say this prayer devoutly at the elevation of our Lord in the mass. Oratio. Salve lux mundi: verbum Patris . . . Amen. Alia oratio. Sanguis tuus Domine Jesu Christe pro nobis effusus . . . Amen. Pater noster. Ave.

Another devout prayer to say at the sacring of the mass. Ave in ævum sanctissima et preciosissima caro . . . Amen. Pater noster. Ave.

Post communionem et potest esse secretum missæ. Auxilientur nobis pie domine Jesu Christe omnes passiones tuæ . . . Amen.

These iii prayers be written in the chapel of the holy cross in Rome, otherwise called sacellum sanctæ crucis septem romanorum; who that devoutly saith them shall obtain xc.m. years of pardon for deadly sins granted of our holy father. Jhoñ. xxii pope of rome. Pater noster. Ave. Oratio. Domine Jesu Christe: ego miser peccator rogo . . . Pater noster. Ave. Domine Jesu Christe salvator et redemptor . . . Pater noster. Ave. Domine Jesu Christe rogo et ammoneo te . . . Amen. Pater noster. Ave.

A devout orison to the blessed vernacle of our Lord; who that saith it devoutly shall have iii years of pardon granted by our holy father the pope Innocentius. Ave facies præclara, quæ pro nobis in crucis ara . . . Amen. Fac mecum signum in bonum ut videant . . . ℣. Domine exaudi . . . ℟. Et clamor . . . Oremus. Deus qui nobis signatis lumine vultus . . . Amen.

Who that devoutly beholdeth these arms of our Lord Jesu Christ shall obtain VI thousand years of pardon of our holy father Saint Peter the first pope of Rome and of xxx other popes of the church of Rome successors after him, and our holy father pope John the XXII hath granted unto all them, very contrite and truly confessed, that say these devout prayers following in the commemoration of the bitter passion of our Lord Jesus Christ iii thousand years of pardon for deadly sins, and other iii thousand for venial sins, and say first a Pater noster. Ave Maria. Oratio. Dirupisti domine vincula mea . . . Amen. Pater noster. Ave. Auxilientur mihi Domine Jesu Christe omnes passiones tuæ . . . Amen. Pater noster. Ave. O bone Jesu duo in me cognosco . . . Amen. Pater noster. Ave. Domine Jesu Christe fili Dei vivi te deprecor . . . Amen. Pater noster. Ave. Domine Jesu Christe fili Dei vivi salvator mundi . . . Amen. Pater noster. Ave.

Psalmus lxxxv. in quo monet ad orationem. Inclina Domine aurem tuam. Kyrieleyson. Pater noster. Ave. ℣. Adoramus crucis signaculum. ℟. Per quod salutis . . . Oremus. Sanctifica quæsumus Domine famulum tuum . . . Amen.

Ante sumptionem corporis Christi. Salve salutaris hostia . . . Amen.

Post sumptionem corporis. Gratias ago tibi omnipotens et misericors Deus meus . . . Amen.

When ye go out of the churchyard say this prayer. Valete vos omnes fideles

animæ quæ jacetis . . . Amen. Oremus. Respice quæsumus omnipotens
Deus super animas famulorum . . . Amen. Pater noster. Ave. Credo.
Vesperæ per adventum de Sancta Maria usque ad vigiliam natalis Domini.
Matutinæ de Sancta Maria, a nativitate Domini usque ad purificationem.

c. A.D. 1512 (Paris) for Simon Vostre, Paris. 8º. No. 40.

*** *The title has "Officium . . . cum pluribus devotis orationibus et contemplationibus impressum caracteribus, figuris, ac mortis accidentia noviter additis . . ."*

A.D. 1513. Wynkyn de Worde, London. 4º. No. 41.

*** *The title-page is wanting, the colophon has "Thus endeth the matyns of our Lady, with many a prayer and devout lesson, with pryme and hours, vii psalms. Enlonged without inquysyon newly corrected . . ."*

The Kalender has prayers to the Saints in rhyme.
A glorious orison to the holy cross and to all the saints of heaven. O glorious
   cross that with holy blood . . .
The x commandments of the law. Thou shalt worship one God only . . .

c. A.D. 1513. (Richard Pynson, London.) 4º. No. 42.

A devout prayer to our blessed Lady. O illustrissima excellentissima et
   gloriosissima mater . . . Amen.
Salutatio ad Virginem Mariam. A prayer to our Lady. Ave fuit prima salus
   . . . ℣. Ora pro nobis . . . ℟. Ut digni . . . Oremus. Famulorum
   tuorum quæsumus Domine delictis agnosce . . . Amen.
Septem salutationes ad beatam Mariam virginem nostram mediatricem efficacissimam. Ave Dei patris filia nobilissima . . . Amen.

A.D. 1514, Jan. 1, Paris, for Francis Byrckman (London). 8º. No. 43.

*** *The title has " Horæ . . . pro pueris totaliter ad longum et sine require . . ."*

Hanc orationem compilavit papa Johannes xii, concedens cuilibet transeunti
   cimīterium sive ecclesiam, et orationem eandem devote legenti, tot dierum
   indulgentias, quot Christi fidelium corpora ibi sunt sepulta. Oratio
   Avete omnes Christi fideles animæ, det vobis requiem ille . . . Amen.
Invocatio S. Trinitatis cum aliquid vis incipere. Domine Dei patris et filii et
   Spiritus sancti . . . Amen.
Pro peste evitanda. Añ. Regina cæli lætare. Alleluia. ℣. Ego sum resurrectio . . . Alleluia. ℟. Qui credit in me . . . Alleluia. Oratio. O
   clementissime Deus, qui vitæ et mortis . . . Amen.
✠ A. a. b. c. d. e. f. g. h. i. k. l. m. n. o. p. q. r. s. t. v. u. x. y. z.[1]
Pater noster. Ave Maria. Credo in Deum. Confiteor. Suscipere dignare.
Salutatio vulnerum Christi. O salutifera vulnera dulcissimi amatoris mei
   Jesu Christi . . . Amen.
Orationes dicendæ in infirmitate. O summa deitas . . . Domine Jesu Christe

---
[1] See Henry Bradshaw's Collected papers, page 333.

paradisum tuum postulo . . . ℣. Dirupisti Domine . . . ℟. Tibi
sacrificabo . . . Oratio. Domine Jesu Christe propter illam amaritudinem . . . Oratio. Pax domini nostri Jesu Christi . . . Amen.
Largire clarum vespere . . . ℣. In manus tuas . . . ℟. Redemisti
me Domine . . .

Oratio ad beatam Virginem. O regina cælorum, mater misericordiæ . . . Amen.

Oratio ad omnes angelos et præsertim ad proprium. O spiritus cælorum
angeli beatissimi assistite mihi . . . Amen.

Inquiratur ab infirmo, cui sanctorum vel sanctarum magis devotus exstiterit, ut
illi precationem offerat dicendo. O gloriosissime Sancte vel Sancta N.
singularem in te . . . Amen.

Orationes circa infirmos dicendæ. Deus sub cujus nutibus vitæ nostræ momenta
. . . Amen. Oratio. Omnipotens sempiterne Deus qui subvenis . . .
Amen. Respice domine famulum tuum in infirmitate . . . Amen.
Benedictio. Benedicat te Deus pater qui in principio . . . Amen. Oratio.
Dominus noster Jesus Christus apud te sit . . . Amen.

Orationes circa agonizantes. ℣. Esto ei Domine turris . . . ℟. A facie inimici.
Oratio. Omnipotens sempiterne Deus conservator animarum . . . Amen.
Oratio. Absolve domine animam famuli tui . . . Amen. Omnipotens
sempiterne Deus qui subvenis in periculis . . . Amen.

A.D. 1514, May 12. Richard Pynson, London. Long 12º. No. 44.

The title-page has on it. God be in my head, and in mine understanding . . .

₊ *The colophon has "Horæ . . . cum orationibus ante et post sanctam
communionem dicendis in fine superadditis . . ."*

Oratio devotissima dicenda die sabbati ad honorem intemeratæ Dei genitricis
Virginis Mariæ. Missus est Gabriel angelus ad Mariam Virginem (as on
page 119) with this addition. Et benedicta sit sancta Anna mater tua . . .
Credo in Deum. O Domine Jesu Christe pater dulcissime . . . Amen.

Passio domini nostri Jesu Christi secundum Johannem. In illo tempore.
Apprehendit Pylatus Jesum et flagellavit eum . . . et scimus quia verum
est testimonium ejus. Oratio. Deus qui manus tuas et pedes tuos . . .
Amen.

Quinque devotissimæ orationes ad quinque plagas domini nostri Jesu Christi
dicendæ ante crucifixum genibus flexis Laus honor (as on page 122) with
this addition. Saucia domine Jesu Christe cor meum vulneribus tuis
sanctis . . . Amen.

A.D. 1514, July 12, Paris, for Francis Byrckman (London). 4º. No. 45.

Ad Laudes. Suffragia Sanctorum. De S. Panthaleone Martyre. Añ. Sancte
Panthaleon martyr Christi . . . ℣. O sancte Panthaleon . . . ℟. Ut
ab omnibus liberemur febribus. Oratio. Deus qui humilium vota
respicis . . . Amen.

De S. Armigillo Confessore. Añ. Sancte Dei preciose advocate . . . ℣. Ora pro nobis . . . ℟. Ut per te liberemur . . . Oremus. Deus qui beatum Armigillum confessorem . . . Amen.

This prayer made Saint Augustine affirming who that says it daily kneeling shall not die in sin and after this life everlasting joy and bliss. Respice ad me infelicem pietas immensa . . . Amen.

A.D. 1514, July 24. Wynkyn de Worde, London. Long 12º. No. 46.

Qui pro alio orat pro seipso laborat. Oratio pro defunctis non habentibus orantem pro ipsis. Miserere piissime Jesu per gloriosam resurrectionem tuam . . . Amen.

Oratio ad idem. Reminiscere clementissime Deus miserationum tuarum . . . Respice quæsumus domine Jesu Christe animas omnium fidelium christianorum . . . Deus in cujus miseratione animæ omnium fidelium defunctorum requiescunt . . . Amen. Requiescant in pace. Amen.

Oratio S. Thomæ de Aquino. Concede mihi misericors Deus quæ tibi placita sunt ardenter recupiscere . . . Amen. Domine Jesu Christe fac quod amem te ardenter et perseveranter . . . Amen. O bone Jesu sint coram te præterita valde mala . . . Amen.

Quicunque orationem sequentem devote dixerit promeretur xi. M. annorum indulgentiarum. Et per tot dies videbit beatam Virginem ante diem exitus sui per quot annos continuaverit. Ave domina sancta Maria mater Dei, regina cæli, porta Paradisi, domina mundi . . . Amen.

Oratio multum devota ante sacram communionem. O fons totius misericordiæ, qui nunquam manare cessas . . . Amen.

Quicunque, devote dixerit istam orationem, habebit tria millia dierum indulgentiarum criminalium peccatorum, et viginti millia dierum venialium a domino Johanne papa XXII ut in antidotario animæ [1] habetur. Oratio post communionem. Hæc sunt convivia quæ tibi placent, qui nobis orphanis . . . Amen.

c. A.D. 1514 (Richard Pynson, London). Long 12º. No. 47.

A good blessing. Benedicat me Deus pater, qui cuncta creavit ex nihilo . . . Amen. Domine Jesu Christe exaudi orationem meam . . . Amen. Ave.

c. A.D. 1515 for Pierre Guerin (Rouen), on vellum. No. 49.

A devout prayer in english. Lord God in good mind in which I hold me now with Thy grace . . . Amen.

c. A.D. 1516, (for Guillaume Bernard and Jacques Cousin, Rouen.) 4º. No. 51.

Prætereundo imaginem crucifixi dic. Añ. Salva nos Christe salvator . . . ℣. Omnis terra . . . ℟. Psalmum dicat . . . Oratio. Deus qui sanctam crucem ascendisti . . . Amen.

Horæ beatæ Mariæ virginis secundum usum Eboracensem.

---

[1] See Nicolaus de Saliceto. Antidotarius animæ, 1494, Brit. Mus. C. 30. c. 9. (2).

Oratio de beata virgine Maria. Ave Maria ancilla sanctæ Trinitatis . . . Amen. Pater noster. Ave.

A.D. 1517, January 26, for Guillaume Bernard and Jacques Cousin, Rouen. 4º. No. 52.

₊ *The title has "Horæ . . . ad legitinum Eboracensis ecclesiæ ritum . . ."
The colophon has "Horæ secundum morem anglicanum totaliter ad longum cum
multis pulcherrimis orationibus et indulgentiis jam ultimo adjectis . . ."*

A prayer which may be said before the epistle. Domine Jesu Christe fili Dei vivi qui pro redemptione nostra . . . Amen.

A.D. 1519, Oct. 24, Nicolas Higman, Paris, for François Regnault (Paris) and Francis Byrckman (London). 4º. No. 54.

Oratio devota ante divinum officium dicenda. O pater misericordiarum scio et vere cognosco . . . Amen.

Sixtus papa quartus, omnibus vere contritis sequentem orationem sive laudationem post officium divinum dicentibus, remittit omnes defectus et negligentias in divino officio commissas. Sanctissimæ ac individuæ Trinitati, Jesu Christi domini nostri sacratissimæ humanitati . . . Amen.

c. A.D. 1520, Nicolas Higman, Paris, for Simon Vostre, Paris. 4º. No. 57.

₊ *The title has "Horæ . . . cum illius miraculis, unacum figuris apocalipsis, post bibliæ historias insertis, ac etiam mortis accidentia noviter addita . . ."*

A.D. 1521, April 9, Paris, for Francis Byrckman, London. 4º. No. 59.

Two stanzas in Latin, one of four lines, the other of three, are found at the end of each month of the Kalender; between the stanzas there is a weather prognostication, according to the signs of the Zodiac.

A.D. 1523, November 20, Wynkyn de Worde, London. 4º. No. 62.

The Kalender has prayers to the Saints in rhyme, and is the same as that in No. 41, A.D. 1518.

Here beginneth the Pater noster in english.[1] Our Father that art in heaven . . . deliver us from evil. Amen.

The declaration of the Ave Maria. Hail Mary full of grace . . . Holy Mary mother of God pray for us sinners. Amen.

Here followeth the Credo as it ought to be said. I believe in God father almighty . . . so be it.

Ad Laudes. Suffragia Sanctorum. De S. Paulo. An. O gloriosum lumen omnium ecclesiarum . . . ℣. In omnem terram . . . ℟. Et in fines . . . Oratio. Deus qui universum mundum beati Pauli apostoli prædicatione . . . Amen.

Prayer to S. Herasme. An. Sancte Herasme martyr Christi preciose . . . Amen. ℣. Ora pro nobis . . . ℟. Ut tecum regnum . . . Oremus. Præsta quæsumus omnipotens Deus ut qui beati Herasmi . . . Amen.

[1] See Burnet. Hist. of Reformation, ed. 1865. Vol. 1. page 68.

Oratio devotissima ad Jesum Christum. O domine Jesu Christe rogo te amore illius gaudii . . . Amen.
Oratio devota, mandatum domini Wilhelmi Cantuariensis Archiepiscopi. Misericors et miserator Deus, qui et barbaros salvari vis . . . Amen.
Invocatio S. Trinitatis cum aliquid vis incipere. Nomen Dei patris et filii et Spiritus Sancti sit benedictum . . . Amen.
Super quolibet bono opere finito. Benedictum sit dulce nomen Domini nostri Jesu Christi . . . Amen. Divinum auxilium maneat semper nobiscum. Amen.
Pro peccatis. Añ. Media vita in morte sumus . . . ℣. Peccavimus cum patribus nostris . . . ℟. Injuste egimus . . . Oremus. Deus qui sperantibus in te misereri potius eligis . . . Amen.
Alia oratio pro peccatis. Resp. Peccavi super numerum arenæ maris . . . Et malum coram te feci. ℣. Quam iniquitatem meam cognosco . . . ℟. Et malum . . . ℣. Erravi sicut ovis . . . ℟. Require servum tuum . . . Oratio. Omnipotens sempiterne Deus misericordiam tuam concede . . . Amen. Alia oratio. Omnipotens mitissime Deus qui sitienti populo . . . Amen.
Pro pace dic trina vice. Añ. Da pacem Domine in diebus nostris . . . ℣. Fiat pax . . . ℟. Et abundantia . . . Oratio. Deus auctor pacis et amator . . . Amen. Alia oratio. Deus a quo sancta desideria . . . Amen. Alia oratio. Protector in te sperantium Deus sine quo nihil est validum . . . Amen.
Pro cogitatione mundi. Resp. Domine pater et Deus vitæ meæ . . . Domine aufer a me concupiscentiam ℣. Fiat cor meum immaculatum . . . ℟. Domine aufer a me concupiscentiam . . . ℣. Domine exaudi . . . ℟. Et clamor meus . . . Oratio. Omnipotens mitissime Deus respice propitius preces nostras . . . Amen. Oratio. Deus a quo bona cuncta procedunt . . . Amen.
Pro locutione accepta. Resp. Verbum iniquum et dolosum . . . Sed tantum victui meo . . . ℣. Ne forte satiatus . . . ℟. Sed tantum . . . ℣. Dixi custodiam . . . ℟. Ut non delinquas . . . Oratio. Linguam fidelium tuorum et vota . . . Amen.
Pro operatione justa. Resp. Ne derelinquas me Domine pater . . . Ne gaudeat de me inimicus meus. ℣. Apprehende arma et scutum et exsurge . . . ℟. Ne gaudeat . . . ℣. Laudans invocabo Dominum . . . ℟. Et ab inimicis meis salvus ero . . . Oratio. Actiones nostras quæsumus Domine . . . Amen.
Pro charitate dic. Añ. Ubi charitas et dilectio, ibi sanctorum est congregatio. ℣. Mandatum novum . . . ℟. Ut diligatis . . . Oratio. Deus pacis charitatisque amator . . . Amen.
Pro humilitate. Oratio. Deus qui superbis resistis et gratiam paras humilibus . . . Amen.
Pro castitate. Oratio. Ure igne sancti Spiritus renes nostros . . . Amen.
Contra tempestates et tonitrua. Oratio. A domo tuo quæsumus Dominę nequitiæ repellantur . . . Amen,

Ad beatam Mariam. Saluto te sancta virgo Maria, domina cælorum . . . Amen.
Has videas laudes, qui sacra virgine gaudens. Et venerando piam studeas laudare Mariam . . . Añ. Salve virgo virginum stella matutina . . . ℣. Ora pro nobis . . . ℟. Ut digni . . . Oratio. Deus qui de beatæ Mariæ virginis utero . . . Amen.
A prayer and desire alway to live and to do the pleasure of God. O Thou most benign Jesu, grant me I beseech Thee of Thy grace . . . Amen.
A prayer against evil thoughts. Lord God, I beseech Thee, not to be long absent from me . . .
A devout prayer for the illumination of man's mind. O Thou good Jesu clarify me with the clerete of everlasting light . . .
The form of confession. First, I knowledge myself guilty unto almighty God . . . I have offended my Lord grievously and specially in the vii deadly sins . . . The x commandments . . . The v wyttes . . . The vii works of mercy bodily . . . The vii works of mercy ghostly . . . The vii gifts of the Holy Ghost . . . The vii sacraments . . . The viii beatitudes.[1]

c. A.D. 1523 Pieter Kaetz (London). 4°. No. 63.

⁎ *The title has "Horæ . . . cum variis orationibus cuilibet devoto et modis . . ."*

The x commandments. One God only Thou shalt love, and worship perfectly . . .

Horæ conceptionis beatæ Mariæ.

A.D. 1524, August 19 (Antwerp). 4°. No. 65.

De laudando Deo, præsertim ab his qui ecclesiastico sunt ministerio addicti, et imminente nocturno tempore. Ps. cxxxiii. Ecce nunc benedicite Dominum.
Oratio Christi in cruce pendentis, et descriptio passionis ejus, ut ex assidua illius meditatione patientiam comparemus. Psalmus xxi. Deus deus meus. Dulcissime Domine da mihi cor mundum . . . Pater noster. Ave.

A.D. 1525, July 28, Rouen, for Jacques Cousin, Rouen. Long 12°. No. 68.

Certain questions what sin is with the form of confession. First what is penitence. Penitence is the emendation . . . And then begin your confession after this manner. The form of confession (see page 133).

A.D. 1526, March 1, François Regnault, Paris. 4°. No. 71.[2]

Pro fidelibus defunctis. Oratio. Deus qui hominem de limo terræ . . . Amen. Fidelium animæ per misericordiam Dei . . . Amen. Animæ eorum in bonis demorentur . . .

c. A.D. 1526 Wynkyn de Worde, London. 4°. No. 74.

In festo nativitatis beatæ Mariæ virginis. Añ. Nativitas tua Dei genitrix . . .

---

[1] See Articles of our Faith, Ten Commandments, &c. R. Pynson. Brit. Mus. G. 11, 907.
[2] See Burnet. Hist. of Reformation, ed. 1865. Vol. 2. page 135. Vol. 5. pages 218, 228.

℣. Dilexisti justitiam . . . ℟. Propterea benedixit . . . Oratio. Famulis tuis quæsumus Domine cælestis gratiæ munus . . . Amen.

A.D. 1527, June 27, François Regnault, Paris. 4⁰. No. 78.

A stanza in english of four lines at the end of each month of the Kalender.

Pro cunctis fidelibus defunctis. Collecta. Animabus quæsumus Domine omnium famulorum . . . Fidelium Deus omnium conditor . . . Amen. Requiescant in pace. Amen. Pater noster. Ave.

A.D. 1527, July 18, Nicolas Prevost, Paris, for Francis Byrckman, London. 4⁰. No. 79.

⁎ *The colophon has, "Horæ . . . quamplurimis bibliæ historiis decoratæ, ac multis orationibus et iis quidem devotissimis adauctæ . . ."*

Precatio ad sanctam Trinitatem. Benedicta sit summa et incomprehensibilis Trinitas . . . Amen.
Precatio ad sanctam Trinitatem. Adoramus te sancta Trinitas pater et fili et Spiritus sancte . . . Amen.
Precatio ad Jesum dicenda, vel cum levatur Eucharistia vel ante crucifixum. Jesu qui post innumeros corporis tui cruciatus . . . miserere nostri.
Precatio ad Jesum. Respice clementissime domine Jesu Christe nos miseros peccatores . . . Amen.
Precatio ad Jesum. Domine Jesu Christe qui Deus immortalis . . . Amen.
Precatio ad divam virginem Mariam. Salve intemerata virgo Maria filii Dei genitrix . . . Amen.
Confessio peccatorum generalis. O creator et gubernator cæli et terræ . . . Amen.

A.D. 1527, December 13, François Regnault, Paris. Long 12⁰. No. 81.

⁎ *The title has, "This prymer of Salisbury use is set out a long without any searching with many prayers and goodly pictures in the Kalender, in the matyns of our lady, in the hours of the cross, in the vii psalms and in the dirige . . ." The colophon has, "Horæ . . . totaliter ad longum, cum orationibus beatæ Brigittæ ac multis aliis orationibus . . ." The book has stanzas of four lines in english before the Hours of the cross and of compassion, each one of the seven psalms and in the dirige.*

A.D. 1528, September 2, widow of Thielman Kerver, Paris, for Alard Plomier, (Paris), on vellum. No. 83.

⁎ *The title has "Enchiridion . . . devotissimis precationibus ac venustissimis imaginibus et iis quidem non paucis refertum . . ." The colophon has "Orarium . . ."*

Psalmus contra omnia adversa. Qui habitat in adjutorio.
Horæ de passione Christi. Officium sanctissimæ Trinitatis. Horæ pro defunctis. Officium de omnibus sanctis. Horæ de sacramento. Horæ die Sabbati de beata virgine Maria.

Oratio de singulis articulis passionis Jesu Christi multum devota. Ave Jesu splendor paternæ gloriæ, flosculus virginitatis . . .
Cum vadis dormitum sequentem præmitte confessionem, ac orationes subsequentes. Confiteor tibi domine Deus omnipotens creator . . . Amen. Oratio dormituro. O Jesu, dulcissime Jesu . . . Amen. Alia oratio dormi turo. Omnipotens sempiterne Deus tibi gratias ago quia me ex tua gratia . . . Amen. Alia oratio dormituro. Gratias tibi ago Domine sancte pater omnipotens æterne Deus qui me . . . Amen. Hymnus. Christus qui lux es et dies. ℣. Custodi nos domine . . . ℟. Sub umbra . . . Oratio. Illumina quæsumus Domine tenebras nostras . . . Amen. Alia oratio non minus devota. Deus qui illuminas noctem et lucem post tenebras facis . . .
Quicunque subscriptam orationem tribus diebus devote dixerit in honore sacratissimæ passionis Domini nostri Jesu Christi ; et in honore beatissimæ virginis Mariæ matris ejus, quæcunque licita petierit misericorditer obtinebit, sicut a pluribus devotis est sæpissime expertum. Sancta Maria, perpetua Virgo virginum, mater misericordiæ . . . Amen.
Oratio ante sacram communionem. Ad mensam dulcissimi convivii tui pie Domine . . . Amen.
Oratio post sacram communionem. Gratias tibi ago Domine sancte Pater omnipotens æterne Deus qui me . . . Amen.
De facie nostri redemptoris. Añ. Salve sancta facies nostri redemptoris . . . ℣. Adoramus te Christe . . . ℟. Quia per sanctam crucem . . . Oratio. Deus qui nobis famulis tuis lumine vultus . . . Amen.
Quicunque verba subscripta quotidie dixerit : subitanea morte non peribit ut scribitur in miraculis Cæsarii, de sancto Edmundo archiepiscopo Cantuariensi. Jesus Nazarenus rex Judæorum. Titulus triumphalis defendat nos ab omnibus malis . . . Sancte Deus, sancte fortis, sancte et immortalis, miserere nobis.
Gratiarum actiones pro variis donis et beneficiis a Deo perceptis : ac a multis periculis animæ et corporis liberatis. Gratias tibi ago et laudes tibi refero, Domine Deus meus . . . Amen.
Ad lectorem. Habes candide lector hoc præsens orarium nonnullis imaginum figuris nuper adornatum . . . Pictura est laicorum scriptura . . .

c. A.D. 1528. 16º. No. 86.

*** *The title has,* "*Hortulus animæ recenter diversis ac odoriferis flosculis decoratus, cum additionibus variis . . . adjectis secundum usum Sarum horis beatæ Mariæ virginis, septem psalmis, atque vigiliis . . .*" *The book is similar to the* "*Hortulus animæ*" *printed abroad in the fifteenth and sixteenth centuries. A full summary of the contents of orationes* "*De Apostolis,*" "*De Martyribus*" "*De Confessoribus*" "*De Virginibus et Viduis,*" *and* "*De Festis*" *is given.*

Tabula ad cognoscendum in quo signo sit luna omni die. Rota literæ dominicalis. Rota numeri aurei. Tabula signorum et festorum mobilium. Declaratio tabulæ præcedentis. Aliqua notabilia et primo de quatuor partibus anni. Distinctiones quatuor complexionum. De minutione notabili.

De qualitate signorum. De quatuor ventis. De luna quæ est temporum mutationis significativa. De comestione notabili.

Missa de nomine Jesu. Officium . . . Per totas octavas dicitur missa prædicta quando de octava fit servitium, sed fine (sine) Credo. Sequentia per octavas. Jesus pulcher in decore.

Cursus S. Bonaventuræ de passione Christi : ante horas de passione Christi. Adoramus te domine Jesu Christe et benedicimus tibi . . . Gratias ago tibi domine, Jesu Christe cujus gratia sum id quod sum . . . Dignare me laudare te benignissime Jesu Christe . . .

Orationes dicendæ ante imaginem pietatis.[1] Innocentius VIII addidit orationes sequentes, secundam, octavam et nonam, et duplicavit indulgentias antedictas. O amantissime Domine sancte pater, ego offero tibi innocentem mortem . . . Amen. Pater noster. Ave. O Domine Jesu Christe fili Dei vivi qui mysterium . . . Amen. Pater noster. Ave.

Leo papa decimus modernus apprehendit prædictas orationes et adjunxit orationem sequentem. O domine Jesu Christe, adoro te ad judicium progredientem . . . Amen. Pater noster. Ave. Credo. Et ad devotionem.

Papa Clemens concessit remissionem defectuum cum trecentis diebus indulgentiarum dicentibus orationem sequentem. Obsecro te domine Jesu Christe ut passio tua sit virtus mea . . . Amen.

Oratio ante imaginem pietatis dicenda: de qua, ut fertur, concessit beatus Gregorius omnium peccatorum remissionem. In mei sint memoria, Jesu pie signacula . . . Amen. ℣. Adoramus te Christe . . . ℟. Quia per crucem . . .

Oratio de armis passionis Christi devotissima, multis indulgentiis a summis pontificibus dotata. Culter qui circumcidisti : sacrosanctam carnem Christi : refera nocentia . . .

Oratio. Passio domini nostri Jesu Christi (as on page 118) with this addition. Rogo te dilectissime Deus ut mors tua amarissima . . . Amen.

Oratio dormituro. Veritas tua quæsumus Domine semper maneat . . . Amen.

Oratio dormituro. Visita quæsumus Domine habitationem istam . . . Amen. Benedictio. Benedicat et custodiat nos omnipotens et misericors Dominus . . . Amen.

Versiculus sequens est profecto tantæ virtutis. Ego autem constitutus sum rex ab eo super Syon montem ejus, prædicans præceptum ejus.

Tres veritates Gersonis nocte et mane ab omnibus dicendæ, quibus quilibet homo potest certo scire, se esse in statu gratiæ, si pure et fidis actione dixerit.[2] Prima veritas est. Domine sic vel sic contra tuam voluntatem peccavi . . .

Orationes cum mane surgis. In nomine Domini nostri Jesu Christi crucifixi surgo . . . Amen. Gratias tibi ago Domine sancte Pater omnipotens æterne Deus qui me dignatus es . . . Amen. O dulcissime Domine Jesu Christe omnipotens Deus aperi cor meum . . . Amen.

[1] See Henry Bradshaw's Collected papers, page 888.
[2] See A very behoveful teaching, page 149.

Gratiarum actio pro acceptis a Deo beneficiis. Laudo et glorifico te domine Deus meus qui ab æterno . . . Amen.

Gratiarum actio sanctæ et individuæ Trinitatis. Tibi ago laudes et gratias, O summa sanctissima et individua Trinitas . . . Amen.

Benedictio et recommendatio ad Deum. Benedictio Dei patris et filii et Spiritus Sancti . . . Amen.

Recommendatio ad Deum. In manus ineffabilis misericordiæ tuæ commendo animam meam . . . Amen.

Recommendatio sub protectione et custodia beatissimæ virginis Mariæ. O domina mea sancta Maria, me in tuam benedictam fidem . . . Amen.

Alia commendatio ad beatam Mariam virginem. Spes animæ meæ post Deum, virgo Maria . . . Amen.

Alia commendatio devotissima. In sanctas ac venerabiles manus tuas Domine Jesu Christe . . . Amen.

Oratio ad Deum, quam si quis dicat ut scribitur, non morietur absque vera confessione, et ante horam mortis absque digna sacramentorum perceptione. Jesus Nazarenus, rex Judæorum, rex omnium populorum semperque amabilis . . . Amen.

Oratio ad Deum pro bono fine. O domine Jesu Christe, fili Dei vivi crucifixe . . . Amen.

Oratio ad beatam Virginem pro bono fine impetrando. O domina dulcissima visceribus misericordiæ plena . . . Amen.

Exeundo domum dic. Vias tuas Domine demonstra mihi . . .

Versus dicendi pro tribulatione evitanda. Nam et si ambulavero in medio umbræ mortis . . .

Post ingressum ecclesiæ, dic. Salve sancta civitas, benedicat te tota Trinitas . . . Alia. Ave rex noster, Ave fili David . . . Avete omnes sancti et electi Dei quorum reliquiæ . . . ℣. Sancti Dei omnes. ℟. Intercedite pro nostra omniumque salute. Collecta. Omnipotens sempiterne Deus per istorum et omnium Sanctorum merita . . . Amen.

Oratio ad totam Trinitatem. Sancta Trinitas unus Deus. Miserere nobis. Te Deum patrem unigenitum . . . Amen. ℣. Benedicamus Patrem . . . ℟. Laudemus et superexaltemus . . . Collecta. Omnipotens sempiterne Deus qui dedisti famulis tuis . . . Amen.

Oratio de æterna sapientia. Añ. Ego diligentes me diligo . . . ℣. Initium sapientiæ, timor Domini. ℟. Intellectus bonus omnibus facientibus eum. Collecta. Fragilitatem nostram quæsumus Domine propitius respice . . . Amen.

Oratio ad beatam virginem Mariam excellentissima. O excellentissima, gloriosissima, atque sanctissima semper virgo Maria . . . Amen.

De S. Michaele archangelo. Añ. Sancte Michael archangele Domini nostri Jesu Christi . . . ℣. Ascendit fumus aromatum. ℟. In conspectu Domini . . . Oratio. Deus cujus claritatis fulgore beatus Michael . . . Amen.

Ad proprium angelum oratio brevis in carmine. Añ. Obsecro te angelice spiritus . . . ℣. Gloriosus apparuisti . . . ℟. Propterea decorem induit te.

Oratio. Omnipotens et misericors Deus qui hominem ad imaginem tuam
. . . Amen.
De S. Johanne Baptista. Añ. Sancte Johannes Baptista electe Dei . . . Amen.
℣. Fuit homo . . . ℟. Cui nomen . . . Collecta. Omnipotens sempiterne Deus da cordibus nostris . . . Amen.
Ad omnes Patriarchas et Prophetas. Sancti patriarchæ, sancti prophetæ quibus ab initio mundi . . . Amen.
De sancto patriarcha Joachim, avo Domini nostri Jesu Christi secundum temporalem propagationem. Añ. Ave flos patriarcharum Joachim . . . ℣. Amavit eum Dominus . . . ℟. Stola gloriæ induit eum. Oratio. Clementissime Deus qui per beati patriarchæ Joachim gloriosissimum progeniem tuam . . . Amen.
De S. Joseph orationuncula. Salve Joseph, nutricie Christi pater . . . Amen. Jesus. Maria.
De S. Disma bono latrone. Salve Disma, fur optime, defendens benignissime a consortis injuria . . . Amen.
De conversione S. Pauli. Sancte Paule apostole, prædicator veritatis . . . Amen. Alia oratio ad S. Paulum. Celebremus conversionem sancti Pauli apostoli . . . ℣. Ora pro nobis . . . ℟. Ut digni . . .
Orationes de omnibus Apostolis, secundum ordinem Kalendarii. Et primo de S. Matthia, qui fuit electus ad locum Judæ traditoris Domini. Añ. Sancte Matthia qui Domino disponente . . . ℣. In omnem terram . . . ℟. Et in fines . . . Oratio. Deus qui beatum Matthiam . . . Amen.
De S. Philipo apostolo. Añ. Domine ostende nobis patrem . . . ℣. Dedisti hæreditatem. ℟. Timentibus nomen tuum Domine. Oratio. S. Philippe apostole Domine . . . Amen.
De S. Jacobo minore. Añ. S. Jacobe Alphæi per gratiam quam frater Domini . . . ℣. In omnem terram . . . ℟. Et in fines . . . Oratio. Deus qui nos annua apostolorum tuorum . . . Amen.
De S. Petro apostolo. Añ. O beate Petre claviger æthereæ . . . ℣. Solve jubente Deo . . . ℟. Qui facis ut pateant . . . Oratio. Deus qui beato Petro apostolo tuo collatis clavibus regni . . . Amen.
De S. Paulo (as on page 131).
De S. Jacobo majore. Añ. O lux et decus Hispaniæ . . . ℣. Ora pro nobis . . . ℟. Ut digni . . . Oratio. Deus qui beatum Jacobum apostolum tuum . . . Amen.
De S. Bartholomæo. Añ. Sancte Bartholomee per gratiam quam meruisti . . . ℣. Annunciaverunt opera Dei. ℟. Et facta ejus intellexerunt. Oratio. Præsta quæsumus omnipotens Deus ut beatus Bartholomæus . . . Amen.
De S. Matheo apostolo et evangelista. Añ. Sancte Mathee apostole per illam omnipotentis Dei gratiam . . . ℣. In omnem terram . . . ℟. Et in fines . . . Oratio. Beati Mathæi apostoli tui et evangelistæ . . . Amen.
De S. Symone caturiens (chananeo)[1] apostolo. Añ. Ecce ego mitto vos . . . ℣. Dedisti hæreditatem. ℟. Timentibus nomen tuum Domine. Collecta. Sancte Symon per gratiam illius qui te elegit . . . Amen.

[1] See Hortulus animæ. Nuremberg. 1518. Brit. Mus. 1219. b. 4.

De S. Juda apostolo. Añ. Sancte Juda apostole per illum qui te sibi in amicum ascivit . . . ℣. Constitues eos principes . . . ℟. Memores erunt nominis tui . . . Oremus. Deus qui nos per beatos apostolos tuos Symonem et Judam . . . Amen.

De S. Andrea apostolo. Añ. Sancte Andrea apostole Dei qui dimissa navi . . . ℣. O sacer Andrea . . . ℟. Salve clavigeri frater amande Petri . . . Oratio. Majestatem tuam Domine suppliciter exoramus . . . Amen.

De S. Thoma apostolo. Añ. O gloriose tactor vulnerum Domini Jesu . . . ℣. Quia vidisti me Thoma . . . ℟. Beati qui non viderunt . . . Oratio. Sancte Thoma qui propriis manibus latus redemptoris . . . Amen.

De S. Johanne apostolo et evangelista qui fuit frater sancti Jacobi majoris et filius Zebedæi et Mariæ Salome. Añ. Valde honorandus est beatus Johannes . . . ℣. Cibavit eum Dominus . . . ℟. Et aqua sapientiæ . . . Oratio. Sit Domine quæsumus beatus Johannes apostolus et evangelista . . . Amen.

De S. Marco evangelista. Añ. Beati martyris Marci evangelistæ . . . ℣. In omnem terram . . . ℟. Et in fines . . . Collecta. Deus qui beatum Marcum evangelistam tuum . . . Amen.

De S. Luca evangelista. Añ. In medio ecclesiæ aperuit os ejus . . . ℣. Implevit eum Dominus . . . ℟. Et aqua sapientiæ salvatoris . . . Oratio. Deus qui per os beati Lucæ evangelistæ . . . Amen.

De omnibus apostolis et evangelistis aliisque, &c., pulcherrima. O Petre beatissime apostolorum maxime . . . Amen. Spes nostra. Jesus. Maria.

Orationes de Martyribus et primo de S. Sebastiano. ℣. Exora summum martyr . . . ℟. Liberet ut famulos peste . . . Añ. O magne fidei sanctissime Sebastiane . . . ℣. Ora pro nobis . . . ℟. Ut mereamur pestem . . . Oratio. Omnipotens sempiterne Deus qui meritis et precibus Sancti Sebastiani . . . Amen.

De S. Vincentio. Añ. Jam tibi charissime divini ubi curam commiseram . . . ℣. Corona aurea . . . ℟. Expressa signo sanctitatis. Oratio. Adesto Domine supplicationibus nostris . . . Amen.

De S. Blasio episcopo et martyre. Añ. Ave præsul honestatis martyr magnæ sanctitatis . . . ℣. Ora pro nobis . . . ℟. Ut digni . . . Oratio. Deus qui per orationem beati Blasii . . . Amen.

De S. Valentino presbytero et martyre. Añ. O beate Valentine magna est fides tua . . . ℣. Ora pro nobis . . . ℟. Ut digni . . . Oratio. Deus cujus charitatis ardore beatus Valentinus . . . Amen.

De S. Georgio milite et martyre. Añ. O Georgi miles Christi Palestinum devixisti . . . ℣. Ora pro nobis . . . ℟. Ut hostes visibiles . . . Oratio. Deus pro cujus legis defensione beatus Georgius miles strenuus . . . Amen.

De S. Erasmo episcopo et martyre. Añ. Gaude Erasme martyr Christi dilectissime . . . ℣. Ora pro nobis . . . ℟. Ut digni . . . Oratio. Deus cujus gratia beatus Erasmus martyr et pontifex . . . Amen.

Ad decem millia martyrum. Añ. O bone Jesu Christe per merita decem millia martyrum tuorum . . . ℣. Justi autem . . . ℟. Et apud Dominum . . . Oratio. Deus qui ad imitandum passionis tuæ exemplum . . . Amen.

Ad decem millia Martyrum. Añ. Gaudent in cælis animæ martyrum . . . ℣. Orate pro nobis . . . ℟. Ut digni . . . Oratio. Omnipotens et misericors sanctorum exercituum Deus . . . Amen.

Ad eosdem sanctos Martyres quorum festivitas celebratur xxii. die Junii cum jejunio magnæ efficaciæ. Et etiam ad sanctam legionem Thebæorum. Añ. O decem mille martyres cum legione Thebæorum . . . ℣. Lætamini in Domino . . . ℟. Et gloriamini . . . Oratio. Omnipotens sempiterne Deus qui per gloriosi bella certaminis . . . Amen.

De S. Christofero. Añ. Sancte Christofore martyr Dei preciose . . . ℣. Gloria et honore . . . ℟. Et constituisti. Oratio. Præsta quæsumus omnipotens Deus ut qui beati Christofori . . . Amen.

De S. Laurentio. Añ. Beatus Laurentius dum in craticula suprapositus . . . ℣. Dispersit dedit . . . ℟. Justitia ejus manet . . . Oratio. Da quæsumus omnipotens Deus vitiorum nostrorum flammas extinguere . . . Amen.

Ad S. Mauricium et socios ejus. Añ. O fidelis miles Christi sanctissime Maurici . . . Amen. ℣. Justi autem . . . ℟. Et apud Dominum . . . Oratio. Præsta quæsumus omnipotens Deus ut sicut beatus Mauricius . . . Amen.

De S. Dionysio. Añ. Sancte Dionysii Galliæ doctor et inclite martyr . . . ℣. Ora pro nobis . . . ℟. Ut digni . . . Oratio. Deus qui beatum Dionysium martyrem tuum . . . Amen.

De S. Stephano protomartyre. Añ. O Stephane martyr invictissime Christi . . . ℣. Ecce video cælos . . . ℟. Et Jesum stantem . . . Oratio. Omnipotens sempiterne Deus qui primitias martyrum , . . Amen.

Ad quatuordecim auxiliatores. Añ. Gaudent in cælis animæ sanctorum . . . ℣. Gloriosus Deus in sanctis suis . . . ℟. Mirabilis in majestate sua. Oratio. Omnipotens et mitissime Deus qui electos sanctos tuos . . . Amen.

De Confessoribus, et primo De S. Erhardo. Añ. O pastor bone, O pater egregie Erharde . . . ℣. Amavit eum Deus . . . ℟. Et ornavit eum. Oratio. Deus qui per electos famulos tuos . . . Amen.

De S. Anthonio. Añ. O Anthoni heremita, infirmorum spes et vita . . . ℣. Ora pro nobis . . . ℟. Ut digni . . . Oratio. Deus qui concedis obtentu beati Anthonii confessoris tui . . . Amen.

De S. Gregorio. Añ. O Gregorii dulcissimum sancti Spiritus organum . . . ℣. Justus ut palma . . . ℟. Sicut cedrus Libani . . . Oratio. Deus qui nos beati Gregorii confessoris tui atque pontificis . . . Amen.

De S. Benedicto. Añ. O sanctissime confessor Domini monachorum pater . . . ℣. Ora pro nobis . . . ℟. Ut digni . . . Oratio. Omnipotens sempiterne Deus qui hodierna die . . . Amen.

De S. Ambrosio episcopo et doctore. Añ. O præsul beatissime Ambrosi doctor maxime . . . ℣. Ecce sacerdos magnus . . . ℟. Et inventus est justus.

Oratio. Deus qui populo tuo æternæ salutis beatum Ambrosium . . . Amen.

De S. Alexio. Añ. Viam qui liquisti pro Christo dulcis Alexi . . . ℣. Ora pro nobis . . . ℞. Ut digni . . . Oratio. Omnipotens et misericors Deus qui manus ineffabiles . . . Amen.

De S. Dominico. Añ. O sancte Dominice amator pacis . . . ℣. Justus ut palma . . . ℞. Sicut cedrus Libani . . . Oratio. Deus qui ecclesiam tuam beati Dominici . . . Amen.

De S. Bernardo abbate. Añ. Charitate vulneratus castitate dealbatus . . . ℣. Ora pro nobis . . . ℞. Ut digni . . . Oratio. Intercessio, nos quæsumus Domine, beati Bernardi abbatis commendet . . . Amen.

De S. Augustino. Añ. O gloriosum lumen ecclesiæ sole splendidius . . . ℣. Justum deduxit Dominus . . . ℞. Et ostendit illi regnum Dei. Oratio. Deus qui beatum Augustinum pontificem tuum . . . Amen.

De S. Hieronymo. Añ. Ave gemma clericorum . . . ℣. Ora pro nobis . . . ℞. Ut digni . . . Oratio. Deus qui beatum Hieronymum hæreticorum malleum . . . Amen.

De S. Francisco. Añ. Cælorum candor splenduit, novum sidus emicuit . . . ℣. Signasti Domine servum tuum . . . ℞. Signis redemptionis nostræ. Oratio. Deus qui mira crucis mysteria . . . Amen.

De S. Gallo. Añ. Venerabilis Gallus diaconus . . . ℣. Ora pro nobis . . . ℞. Ut digni . . . Oratio. Deus qui nos annua beati Galli confessoris solemnitate . . . Amen.

De S. Wolfgango. Añ. Gaudet tota mater ecclesiæ egregii præsulis Wolfgangi meritis . . . ℣. Ora pro nobis . . . ℞. Ut digni . . . Collecta. Deus qui nobis eternæ salutis beatum Wolfgangum pontificem . . . Amen.

De S. Leonardo. Añ. O Leonarde pater venerande nos tibi devotos . . . ℣. Justum deduxit Dominus. ℞. Per vias rectas. Oratio. Omnipotens sempiterne Deus immensam clementiam tuam humiliter imploramus . . . Amen.

De S. Martino episcopo. Añ. Domine Deus noster cujus gratia beatus Martinus . . . ℣. Ecce sacerdos . . . ℞. Et inventus est . . . Oratio. Deus qui conspicis, quia ex nulla nostra virtute . . . Amen.

De S. Nicolao. Añ. O pastor æterne, O clemens et bone custos . . . ℣. Ora pro nobis . . . ℞. Ut digni . . . Oremus. Deus qui beatum Nicolaum pontificem tuum . . . Amen.

Orationes de Virginibus et Viduis et primo de S. Agnete virgine. Añ. Beata Agnes in medio flammarum, expansis manibus, orabat . . . ℣. Agno nos Christo junges. ℞. Pia quæsumus Agnes. Oratio. Omnipotens sempiterne Deus qui infirma mundi eligis . . . Amen.

De S. Brigitta. Añ. O beata Brigitta late collaudata . . . ℣. Multæ filiæ regum . . . ℞. Tu supergressa es . . . Oratio. Domine Jesu Christe qui beatam Brigittam . . . Amen.

De S. Agatha. Añ. Salve sancta Agatha virgo et martyr Dei inclyta . . . ℣. Diffusa est . . . ℞. Propterea . . . Oratio. Intercessionibus beatæ

Agathæ . . Amen. Ista sunt verba quæ super candelas festo Purificationis Mariæ benedictas, scribi solent in die S. Agathæ. Mentem sanctam spontaneam honorem Deo et patriæ liberationem.

De S. Dorothæa (as on page 125).

De S. Apollonia. Añ. Virgo Christi egregia pro nobis Apollonia . . . ℣. Specie tua . . . ℞. Intende . . . Oratio. Deus pro cujus sanctissimi nominis honore . . . Amen.

De S. Gertrude. Añ. Ave Gertrudis virgo grata, ex regali stirpe nata . . . ℣. Ora pro nobis . . . ℞. Ut ad hospitium æternum . . . Oratio. Deus qui beatam Gertrudam piam virginem . . . Amen.

De S. Sophia et ejus filiabus. Añ. Pulchra es et decora, filia Hierusalem Sophia. ℣. Adducentur regi virgines . . . ℞. Proxime ejus afferentur tibi. Oratio. Deus qui recta petentibus jugiter effectum impedis . . . Amen.

De S. Margareta. Añ. Ave stella radiosa, solis luce clarior . . . ℣. Diffusa est . . . ℞. Propterea benedixit . . . Oratio. Omnipotens et mitissime Deus te humiliter imploro ut me miserum . . . Amen.

De S. Maria Magdalena. Añ. Gaude pia Magdalena, spes salutis vitæ vena . . . ℣. Dimissa sunt . . . ℞. Quoniam dilexit . . . Oratio. Deus qui beatæ Mariæ Magdalenæ pænitentiam . . . Amen.

De S. Martha. Añ. Exultet urbs Bethania, quæ contulit immania . . . ℣. Ora pro nobis . . . ℞. Ut digni . . . Oratio. Omnipotens sempiterne Deus cujus filius sumpta carne . . . Amen.

Ad undecim mille Virgines. Añ. O præclaræ vos puellæ, nunc implere meum velle . . . ℣. Pia martyr Ursula . . . ℞. Cum tuis sodalibus . . . Oratio. Deus qui affluentissimæ bonitatis tuæ prudentiam . . . Amen.

De S. Elizabeth. Añ. Ave gemma speciosa, mulierum sidus, rosa . . . ℣. Ora pro nobis . . . ℞. Ut digni . . . Oratio. Tuorum corda fidelium Deus miserator illustra . . . Amen.

De S. Katherina. Añ. Gaude virgo Katherina, quam refecit lux divina . . . Amen. ℣. Ora pro nobis . . . ℞. Ut digni . . . Oratio. Deus qui dedisti legem Moysi . . . Amen.

De S. Barbara. Añ. Ave martyr gloriosa, Barbara quam generosa . . . ℣. Specie tua . . . ℞. Intende . . . Oratio. Intercessio nos quæsumus Domine beatæ Barbaræ . . . Amen.

De S. Odilia. Añ. O præclara Christi sponsa, insignis Odilia . . . ℣. Diffusa est . . . ℞. Propterea . . . Collecta. Deus qui Spiritus Sancti gratia almam virginem Odiliam . . . Amen.

Ad unum sanctum specialem Patronum cujuscunque fuerit status. Oratio. Sancte (N) martyr vel confessor Dei preces meas . . . ℣. Ora pro nobis . . . ℞. Ut digni . . . Collecta. Deus tuorum gloria sanctorum præsta . . . Amen.

Ad plures sanctos cujuscunque status seu gradus existant. Añ. O vos omnes preciosi viri sancti . . . ℣. Exultent justi . . . ℞. Et delectentur . . . Collecta. Tua me Domine quæso gratia semper et præveniat . . . Amen.

Orationes de principalioribus festis secundum ordinem Kalendarii. Et primo in die circumcisionis Domini. Añ. O Jesu clementissime qui de Virgine natus . . . ℣. Tecum principium in die virtutis tuæ . . . ℟. In splendoribus Sanctorum . . . Oratio. Deus qui nobis nati Salvatoris die concedis celebrare octavam . . . Amen.

In die Epiphaniæ Domini. Añ. Tribus miraculis ornatum diem sanctum colimus . . . ℣. Vidimus stellam . . . ℟. Et cum muneribus venimus . . . Collecta. Deus qui hodierna die unigenitum tuum . . . Amen. Eodem die. De tribus regibus Rex Jaspar, rex Melchior, rex Balthasar (as on page 111).

In festo Purificationis beatæ Mariæ. Añ. Hodie beata virgo Maria puerum Jesum præsentavit . . . ℣. Responsum accepit Symeon . . . ℟. Non visurum se mortem . . . Oratio. Omnipotens sempiterne Deus majestatem tuam supplices exoramus . . . Amen.

De Festo Annunciationis beatæ Mariæ. Añ. Hæc dies quam fecit Dominus . . . ℣. Ave Maria . . . ℟. Benedicta tu . . . Oratio. Deus qui de beatæ Mariæ virginis utero . . . Amen.

In festo sancto Paschæ de resurrectione Domini. Añ. Salve dies sanctitatis lætitiæ . . . ℣. Surrexit Dominus . . . ℟. Qui pro nobis pependit . . . Oratio. Deus qui hodierna die per unigenitum tuum . . . Amen.

De sancta Cruce. Añ. O crux splendidior cunctis astris . . . ℣. Hoc signum crucis erit in cælo. ℟. Cum Dominus adjuvandum . . . Oratio. Deus qui in vexillo sanctæ crucis . . . Amen.

In diebus rogationibus. Añ. Petite et dabitur vobis . . . ℣. Surrexit Christus . . . ℟. Quem redemit . . . Collecta. Deus a quo cuncta bona procedunt . . . Amen.

Ad beatam virginem Mariam in carmine. Da mihi dona tria, sanctissima virgo Maria . . . Amen.

In die Ascensionis Domini. Añ. O rex gloriæ, Domine virtutum . . . ℣. Ascendens Christus in altum. ℟. Captivam duxit . . . Collecta. Concede quæsumus omnipotens Deus ut qui hodierna die unigenitum tuum . . . Amen.

In die sancto Penthecostes (De S. Spiritu as on page 109). Alia añ. Veni sancte Spiritus reple tuorum corda fidelium . . . ℣. Emitte spiritum tuum . . . ℟. Et renovabis . . . Oratio. Omnipotens sempiterne Deus da nobis illam sancti Spiritus gratiam . . . Amen.

In die corporis Christi. Añ. O sacrum convivium in quo Christus sumitur . . . ℣. Cibavit eos . . . ℟. Et de petra melle. Oratio. Deus qui nobis sub sacramento mirabili passionis tuæ . . . Amen.

In festo Visitationis beatæ Mariæ. Añ. Jesu redemptor optime, ad Mariam nos imprime . . . ℣. Dilexisti justitiam . . . ℟. Propterea unxit . . . Collecta. Omnipotens sempiterne Deus qui ex abundantia charitatis. . . Amen.

In divisione Apostolorum. Añ. Euntes in mundum universum prædicate . . . ℣. In omnem terram . . . ℟. Et in fines . . . Oratio. Deus qui in tuorum divisione Apostolorum . . . Amen.

In festo Assumptionis beatæ Mariæ. Añ. Virgo prudentissima quo progrederis . . . ℣. Elegit eam . . . ℟. Et habitare . . . Oratio. Veneranda nobis, quæsumus Domine, hujus diei festivitas . . . Amen.
In festo Nativitatis beatæ Mariæ (as on page 133).
 Ad virginem Mariam. Añ. Dulcis amica Dei, rosa vernans, stella decora . . . Amen. Spes nostra. Jesus. Maria.
In festo omnium Sanctorum. Añ. Omnes supernæ virtutes atque angelicæ potestates . . . ℣. Beati qui habitant . . . ℟. Quem in sæcula sæculorum laudabunt te. Collecta. Domine Jesu Christe qui omne genus humanum . . . Amen.
In festo Præsentationis beatæ Mariæ. Añ. Novæ laudis adest festivitas . . . ℣. Diffusa est . . . ℟. Propterea benedixit . . . Oratio. Omnipotens sempiterne Deus qui sanctam filii tui genitricem . . . Amen.
In adventu Domini. Añ. Ecce Dominus veniet . . . ℣. Ecce apparebit Dominus . . . ℟. Et cum eo Sanctorum millia. Collecta. Conscientias nostras, quæsumus Domine, visitando purifica . . . Amen.
In festo Conceptionis beatæ Mariæ virginis. Añ. Maria plena gratia, stirpe concepta regia . . . ℣. Audi filia . . . ℟. Et inclina aurem tuam. Collecta. Supplicationem servorum tuorum Deus miserator . . . Amen.
In festo Nativitatis Domini. Añ. Hodie Christus natus est . . . ℣. Verbum caro factum est. ℟. Et habitavit . . . Collecta. Concede quæsumus omnipotens Deus ut nos unigeniti tui nova . . . Amen.
In festo Sanctorum Innocentium. Añ. Ambulabunt mecum in albis . . . ℣. Lætamini in Domino . . . ℟. Et gloriamini . . . Collecta. Deus cujus præconium innocentes Martyres . . . Amen.
In dedicatione ecclesiæ pro indulgentiis consequendis. Añ. Præsta Domine ut si quis in hoc templum . . . ℣. Hæc est domus Domini . . . ℟. Quæ fundata est . . . Oratio. Domine Deus pater omnipotens immensæ pietatis . . . Amen. Oratio. Deus qui de vivis et electis lapidibus . . . Amen.
In dedicatione altaris. Oratio. Omnipotens sempiterne Deus altare hoc nomini tuo dedicatum . . . Amen.
Confessio generalis vel meditatio de peccatis commissis et bonis omissis. O Creator et Domine cæli et terræ, maris et omnis creaturæ . . . Amen.
Qualis debeat esse confessio . . . Cum tua peccata dicis, confessio quæ sit . . .
Oratio ante confessionem dicenda. Per sanctorum omnium angelorum . . . Amen.
Modus et forma confitendi. Primo confitens accedens ad confessorem sancto signo sanctæ crucis . . . De peccato cordis, hoc est de cogitatione. De peccato oris, id est de locutione. De operum peccatis, scilicet septem peccatis mortalibus. Virtutes et remedia contra vitia septem capitalia. De decem præceptis. Decem prosagiæ (plagæ)[1] Egyptiacæ. De omnibus membris et sensibus. De peccatis omissionis . . .
De septem operibus misericordiæ corporalibus. De septem operibus misericordiæ spiritualibus.

---

[1] See Hortulus animæ. Nuremberg. 1518. Brit. Mus. 1219. b. 4.

De xii articulis fidei. Divisio Symboli per xii articulos. Petrus. Credo in
    Deum . . . Matthias. Et vitam æternam. Amen.
De septem Sacramentis ecclesiæ. De septem Virtutibus theologicalibus et
    cardinalibus. De septem donis Spiritus Sancti. Duodecim sunt fructus
    Spiritus Sancti. Octo Beatitudines. De octo Beatitudinibus.
De ix Peccatis alienis. Peccata in Spiritum Sanctum. De Peccatis crimina-
    libus[1] (clamantibus) in cælum. De peccatis mutis vel sodomiticis.
Forma absolutionis Gersonis. Dominus noster Jesus Christus per suam
    misericordiam . . . Amen.
Oratio post confessionem dicenda. Omnipotens sempiterne Deus miseri-
    cordissime qui venisti . . . Amen.
Casus papales. Casus episcopales.
Orationes ante communionem. Omnipotens et misericors Deus ecce accedo ad
    sacramentum . . . Amen. Alia oratio. O dulcissime atque amantissime
    Domine Jesu Christe . . . Amen.
Orationes post sacram communionem, et primo. Ave sanctissima caro, summa
    vitæ dulcedo . . . Amen. Alia oratio. Ineffabilem misericordiam tuam
    Domine Jesu Christe humiliter exoro . . . Amen. Alia oratio. O
    benignissime Domine Jesu Christe respice super me indignum . . . Amen.
Oratio S. Thomæ de Aquino in elevatione corporis Christi dicenda. Adoro te
    devote latens Deitas, quæ sub his figuris vere latitas . . . Amen.
De missa, et primo unde exordium sumpserit, et quis eam auxerit. Missam
    imprimis Dominus noster Jesus Christus sacerdos secundum ordinem
    Melchisedech instituit . . .
Jubilus S. Bernardi abbatis de glorioso nomine Jesu. Jesu dulcis memoria, dans
    cordi vera gaudia . . . Amen.
Pro iter agentibus. Deduc me Domine in vita tua . . . Psalmus. Benedictus
    Dominus Deus. Añ. In via pacis . . . Kyrie. Pater noster. Preces.
    Benedictus Dominus die quotidie. Prosperum iter faciat nobis . . . Deus
    noster deus . . . Et Domini exitus mortis. Nihil perficiat inimicus in
    nobis. Et filius iniquitatis non apponat . . . Esto nobis Domine . . .
    A facie inimici . . . Domine exaudi . . . Et clamor . . . Oratio. Deus
    qui es Sanctorum tuorum ductor . . . Amen.
Pro amico tribulato. Præsta quæsumus Domine famulo tuo N consolationis
    auxilium . . . Amen.
Oratio ante phlebotomiam sive minutionem dicenda. Mediator Dei et hominum,
    bone Jesu Christe . . . Amen.
Pro peste. Añ. Regina cæli lætare. Alleluia. Quia quem meruisti portare.
    Alleluia . . . Oratio. O clementissime Deus qui te vitæ et mortis ordi-
    nariam habes potestatem . . . Amen. Tetrastichon. Per tua Christe
    Jesu merita et crucis ampla trophæa. Respice custodi protege plasma
    tuum . . . Amen.
Oratio. O Domine Jesu Christe fili Dei vivi, suscipe hanc orationem in amore
    . . . Amen.

[1] See Hortulus animæ. Nuremberg. 1518. Brit. Mus. 1219. b. 4.

Quatuor exhortationes Gersonis apud morientes faciendæ. Prima. Amice dilecte aut dilecta considera nos omnes subjectos esse potenti manui Dei . . . Secunda. Recognosce diligenter cum gratiarum actione . . . Tertia. Sollicite cogita te in vita tua plurima delicta perpetrasse . . . Quarta. Super omnia in hac extrema hora constitutus . . .

Interrogationes apud morientes faciendæ. Dilecte vel dilecta. Credis tu omnes principales articulos fidei Christianæ . . . Ultimo dicat. In manus tuas commendo spiritum meum.

Cautela servanda circa morituros. Plurimum dicatur infirmo de morte . . . Sex observanda per moriturum. Solutio debiti ab obligationibus . . .

Si infirmus anxiatur et obitus ejus prolongatur, dicantur Psalmi. Confitemini. (Qui legitur dominica die ad laudes.) Beati immaculati. Ad Dominum cum tribularer et Psalmi penitentiales vel passionis. Oratio. Commendo tibi Domine animam famuli tui te devotissime deprecando . . . Amen.

Postquam infirmus contulit (conclusit)[1]: dicatur cum devotione. Kyrie. Pater noster. Requiem æternam . . . Et lux . . . ℣. A porta inferi. ℟. Erue Domine animas eorum. Oratio. Deus cui omnia vivunt et cui non pereunt . . . Amen. Oratio. Suscipe Domine animam servi tui . . . Amen.

De extremo judicio. Añ. Dies Domini sicut fur in nocte ita veniet . . . ℣. Timebunt gentes . . . ℟. Et omnes reges terræ . . . Oratio. Præsta quæsumus omnipotens Deus ut qui pro peccatis nostris . . . Amen.

Ad S. Raphaelem. Añ. Auxiliare mihi, O tu princeps obsecro eximie Raphael . . . ℣. Ora pro nobis . . . ℟. Ut digni . . . Oremus. Deus qui miro ordine angelorum ministeria . . . Amen. Pater noster. Ave.

De S. Lamberto episcopo. Añ. Magna vox laude sonora . . . ℣. Justus ut palma . . . ℟. Et sicut cedrus . . . Oratio. Deus qui beatum Lambertum . . . Amen.

De S. Adriano. Añ. Ave martyr Adriane . . . ℣. O beate Christi martyr . . . ℟. Libera nos ab omni peste . . . Oratio. Omnipotens sempiterne Deus qui nos beati Adriani martyris . . . Amen.

De S. Theobaldo. Añ. Operibus Dei vir Dei insistens . . . ℣. Ora pro nobis . . . ℟. Ut digni . . . Collecta. Deus qui nos beati egregii confessoris tui Theobaldi . . . Amen.

De S. Servatio. Añ. Servatius servavit fidem . . . ℣. Ora pro nobis . . . ℟. Ut digni . . . Oratio. Deus qui nobis dedisti beatum Servatium prædicatorem . . . Amen.

De S. Huberto. Añ. Sacerdos et pontifex et virtutum opifex . . . ℣. Amavit eum Dominus . . . ℟. Stola gloriæ induit eum. Oremus. Da quæsumus omnipotens Deus ut qui beati Huberti confessoris . . . Amen.

De S. Machabæis martyribus, cum indulgentiis centum dierum. Añ. O inexpugnabiles Machabæi portum salutis . . . ℣. Mirabilis Deus . . . ℟. Et gloriosus . . . Oratio. Fraterna nos Domine sanctorum Martyrum tuorum . . . Amen.

---

[1] See Hortulus animæ. Nuremberg. 1518. Brit. Mus. 1219. b. 4.

De beato rege Henrico (as on page 117). De S. Rocho (as on page 117). De S.
    Edwardo (as on page 125).
De S. Joseph. Omnipotens sempiterne Deus intercessione beatissimi Joseph
    nutricii tui . . . Amen.
De S. Quirino. Añ. Filiæ Hierusalem venite et videte . . . ℣. Ora pro nobis
    . . . ℟. Ut digni . . . Oratio. Quæsumus omnipotens sempiterne
    Deus sicut precibus . . . Amen.
De S. Severino. Añ. Gaude sacer Severine pie præsul Agripine . . . ℣. Amavit
    eum . . . ℟. Stola gratiæ . . . Oratio. Deus qui nobis sanctam hujus
    diei solemnitatem . . . Amen.
De S. Materno episcopo. Añ. Iste homo ab adolescentia sua . . . ℣. Amavit
    eum . . . ℟. Stola gratiæ. Collecta. Deus qui universarum nationum
    populos . . . Amen.
De S. Cornelio et Cypriano. Añ. Insigniorum virorum miracula . . . ℣. Sancti
    et justi . . . ℟. Nos elegit Deus . . . Oratio. Infirmitatem nostram
    quæsumus Domine propitius respice . . . Amen.
De S. Wilhelmo episcopo et confessore. Añ. O Wilhelme pastor bone, cleri
    pater et patrone, Munda nobis in agone, confer opem et depone, Vitæ
    sortes et coronæ (all the rest of the book is wanting).

c. A.D. 1528. Long 12º. No. 87.

A Stanza of four lines in english occurs at the end of each month of the Kalender.
Ad Laudes. Suffragia Sanctorum. De Sanctis quorum reliquiæ continentur
    in universali ecclesia. Añ. Corpora Sanctorum in pace sepulta sunt . . .
    ℣. Beati qui habitant . . . ℟. In sæcula sæculorum laudabunt te . . .
    Oratio. Præsta quæsumus omnipotens Deus ut sanctæ Dei genitricis
    . . . Amen.

A.D. 1530, Oct., 1531, Christopher Endoviensis, Antwerp, for sale in London. 4º. No. 92.

The days of the week moralysed. Sunday. I am Sunday honourable. The
    head of all the week days . . .
The manner to live well devoutly and salutarily every day for all persons of
    mean estate. Compiled by Master John Quentin Doctor in divinity at
    Parys. Translated out of french into english by Robert Copland printer
    at London.[1] For to begin the manner of salutary or healthful living.
    And to come to perfection . . . keep these small doctrines here following
    to your powers. First. Rise up at VI of the clock in the morning in all
    seasons, and in your uprising do as followeth. Thank our Lord of the
    rest that he gave you that night. Commend you to God, to our B.
    Lady St. Mary, and to that Saint which is feasted that day, and to all
    the Saints of heaven. Secondly. Beseech God that he preserve thee
    that day from deadly sin and at all other times. And pray him, that
    all the works that other doth for you may be accept to the laud of
    his name, of his glorious mother, and of all the company of heaven.
    Thirdly. When you have arrayed you, say in your chamber or lodging,

[1] See J. C. Brunet. Manuel du libraire. ed. 1863, sub Quentin.

Matyns, Prime and Hours if ye may. Then go to the church or ye do any worldly works; if ye have no needful business, and abide in the church the space of a low mass, while there ye shall think and thank God of his benefits. Think a while on the goodness of God, on his divine might and virtue . . . Think also what grace he hath done to you in the sacrament of baptism, cleansing your soul from sin. Think how many times you have offended him since you were christened . . . Think how ill you have bestowed the time that he hath given you to do penance. Think how many times he hath forgiven you in shrift, and how many times ye have fallen to sin again . . . Think then, what shall become of the worldly goods that ye have gathered and spared with great labour, and how lothe ye shall be to leave them and all your friends and kinsfolk . . . And these be the thoughts that I will that ye have in the church.

And if by any other reasonable business ye may not be so long in the church as it is said here afore, yield thanks to God of his goodness, and think on the residue in your houses in the day or in the night if ye may. When ye are come from the church, take heed to your household or occupation till dinner time[1] . . . Then take your refection or meal reasonably, without excess or overmuch forbearing of your meat . . . if ye fast once in a week it is enough, beside Vigils et ymbre days out of lenten. And if ye think the fasting be not good nor profitable do by councell. Rest you after dinner an hour or half an hour as ye think best . . . The residue of the day bestow in your business to the pleasure of God.

As touching your service, say unto tiers afore dinner, and make an end of all before supper. And when ye may, say Dirige and Commendations for all christian souls, at the least way on the holy days, and if ye have leafer say them on other days at the least with three lessons. Shrive you every week to your curate, except ye have great let. And beware ye pass not a fortnight, except very great let. If ye be of power, refuse not your alms to the first poor body that axeth it of you that day if ye think it needful. Take pain to hear and keep the Word of God. Confess you every day to God without fail of such sins as ye know that ye have done that day. Consider often either by day or night, when ye do awake, what our Lord did . . . Seek a good and faithful friend of good conversation to whom ye may discover your mind secrets . . . Say little and follow virtuous company . . . After all work praise and thank God, love him above all things, and serve him and his glorious mother diligently. Do to none other but that ye would were done to you, love the wealth of another as your own. And in going to your bed, have some good thoughts either of the passion of our Lord or of your sin . . . and then, I hope, your living shall be acceptable and pleasing to God.

See Collection of ordinances for Royal households. A.D. 1526. p. 151. Soc. Antiquaries, also Holinshed Chronicle, ed. 1807. Vol. 1. p. 388.

c. A.D. 1530, (Christopher Endoviensis, Antwerp). 4°. No. 94.

Ad Laudes. Suffragia Sanctorum. A prayer to St. Thomas and to all the holy Saints, whose relyques rest in the holy place of Chrychurche within Cantorbery, is granted a c and xl days of pardon. Añ. Sol Anglorum splendens Thoma . . . ℣. Gloriosi martyres . . . ℟. Ut digni . . . Oratio. Omnipotens sempiterne Deus cujus ineffabili providentia gloriosi martyres, Thomas, Alphegus . . . Amen. Pater noster. Ave.

Añ. cum collecta Sanctorum Patrum in monasterio Sancti Augustini Anglorum apostoli quiescentium. Alme pater Augustine cum tuo collegio . . . ℣. Sancte Augustine cum sociis tuis . . . ℟. Ut digni . . . Oratio. Sanctorum confessorum tuorum Augustini Anglorum apostoli . . . Amen.

De S. Augustino Anglorum apostolo. Oratio. Summe præsul Augustine, prothodoctor Angliæ . . . ℣. Sacerdos Dei Augustine. ℟. Pastor egregie . . . Oratio. Deus qui per prothodoctorem nostrum Augustinum . . . Amen.

Ad S. Blasium martyrem atque pontificem. Añ. Hic est vere martyr qui pro Christi nomine . . . ℣. Gloria et honore . . . ℟. Et constituisti . . . Oratio. Omnipotens sempiterne Deus qui beatum Blasium . . . Alia Añ. Ave cohæres cælorum, ave lux an (mutilated).

A.D. 1531, May 14, Christopher Ruremundensis (Antwerp), for sale in London. 4°. No. 95.

₊ *The colophon has, "Horæ . . . totaliter ad longum cum multis ad diversos Sanctos et Sanctas suffragiis plurimum iis quos eorum oblectat devotio commodis . . . In super et orationes beatæ Brigittæ multis indulgentiarum centenis decoratæ necnon Gregorianæ præcatiunculæ infarcitæ quæ et eodem ferme quo et Brigittæ indulgentiarum gaudent privilegio."*

A.D. 1531, François Regnault, Paris. 8°. No. 98.

A very behoveful teaching and remedy for every man and woman daily to come out of sin, and to come soon into the state of health, after the doctrine of Master John Gerson, Chanceler of Paris, and Doctor in divinity. God our sovereign Lord knowledging the great fragility . . . The first verity. My God I knowledge and confess . . .[1]

When thou enterest into the church. Introibo in domum tuam Domine . . . Aufer a nobis Domine cunctas iniquitates . . . ℣. Lætamini in Domino . . . ℟. Et gloriamini . . . Oremus. Deus qui per unigeniti tui passionem . . . Amen. Alia oratio. Sancti Dei quorum corpora et reliquiæ . . . Amen.

A prayer at the elevation. Ave Domine Jesu Christe verbum Patris . . . Amen.

At the elevation of the chalice. Ave vere sanguis Domini nostri Jesu Christi . . . Amen.

A devout prayer to our Lord. O dulcissime Domine Jesu Christe, qui pro me indignissimo peccatore . . . Amen.

---
[1] See Tres veritates Gersonis. page 136.

Devout prayer and contemplation of the names of Jesus. O Jesu salus mea ...
℣. Jesu rex clementissime ... ℟. Ut tibi laudes debitas ... Oratio.
Sancti nominis tui Domine timorem ... Omnipotens sempiterne Deus
dirige actus nostros ... Amen. O Jesu, Intra pectus meum ... Amen.

A.D. 1532, April 30, William Rastell, London. 8º. No. 101.

*** *"Horæ de Cruce" and "Horæ compassionis, beatæ Mariæ" are in this book in English as well as Latin.*

Certain devout prayers made by the right reverend Father in God Lord Cuthbert Bishop of Durham.

A prayer to Jesus to be said either at the levation time, or before the crucifix.
O Jesu qui post innumeros corporis tui cruciatus pendens in cruce ... Amen.

Prayers to the Holy Trinity. Sancta Trinitas, unus Deus: miserere nostri.
Domine Deus omnipotens qui ad imaginem ... Domine Deus omnipotens, a quo omnis est ... Amen.

A prayer to our Lord God. Dominator domine Deus omnipotens qui es personarum trinitas ... Amen.

A.D. 1532, August, Yoland Bonhomme, widow of Thielman Kerver, Paris, for John Growte (London). 16º. No. 103.

The changes of the moon, eclipses, dates of moveable feasts, as well as the golden number and dominical letter for the years A.D. 1533-A.D. 1588 are given in a table for each year.

After Agnus Dei, say. Deus pius et propitius, agnus immolatus ... Amen.

Oratio dicenda post quatuor evangelia. Dulcissime salvator ac redemptor noster Jesu Christe ... Amen. Oremus. Deus qui beatos evangelistas tuos ... Amen.

In elevatione corporis Christi. Domine Jesu Christe qui cum discipulis tuis cænans ... Amen.

Quando tu es in cæmiterio, dic. Da requiem cunctis Deus ... Amen.
Animæ omnium fidelium defunctorum per misericordiam Dei ... Amen.
Sit laus Deo, pax vivis, et requies defunctis. Amen. Pater noster. Ave.

A prayer to God for them that be departed, having none to pray for them. Miserere quæsumus domine Deus per preciosam mortem ... Amen.

The seven petitions of the Pater noster by John Colet dean of Poules. The first petition. O Father in heaven halowed be thy name among men in earth ... The VII petition. But O Father deliver us from all evils. Amen.[1]

A.D. 1532-33, August, Yoland Bonhomme, widow of Thielman Kerver, Paris, for John Growte, London. 16º. No. 104.

*** *The title has "This Primer ... is set out a long without any serching, with many prayers and goodly pictures ... with the xv oos in english and the confessional and Jesus psalter ..."*[2]

---

[1] See Tyndale's answer to More. Parker Soc. page 168; also Grafton's Chronicle, ed. 1569. page 954; also J. H. Lupton life of Colet, ed. 1887, page 203.
[2] See Psalter of Jesus, 1885. London: Pickering and Co.

A.D. 1533, November 4, François Regnault, Paris. 16º. No. 109.

First ye shall say, in the morning when ye do arise from your bed, this prayer following. In matutinis Domine meditabor in te ... Oremus. Gratias ago tibi domine omnipotens æterne Deus qui me in hac nocte ... Amen.

To the relykes in the church. Añ. Corpora sanctorum in pace sepulta sunt ... ℣. Lætamini in domino ... ℟. Et gloriamini ... Oratio. Propitiare nobis Domine famulis tuis ... Amen. Oratio. Sanctæ Dei genitricis Mariæ semper virginis gloriosæ ... Amen.

Oratio devotissima ad sanctam Trinitatem. Adoro te sancta et individua Trinitas, Deus ineffabilis ... Amen.

c. A.D. 1533, Robert Wyer, (London). 8º. No. 111.

A lesson for children. When the child is come to discretion, first, he ought to know what God is. God is might ... Secondarily, he ought to know himself, that is to say, what man is. Man is create ... And then when the time cometh that he shall give him to any manner estate, he shall say. Lord grant us to know the way and estate in the which we ought to walk.

A.D. 1536, John Byddell, London. 16o. No. 121.

Prayer to the sacrament. Salve sancta caro Dei, per quam salvi fiunt rei ... Amen.

A.D. 1536, Nicolas Le Roux, Rouen, for Jean Groyat and Jean Marchant, Rouen. 16º. No. 123.

Oratio ad beatam virginem Mariam. Regina cæli lætare. Alleluia. Quia quem meruisti portare. Alleluia. Ora pro nobis ... Alleluia.

Oratio ad levationem. Salve sanguis preciosi domini nostri Jesu Christi ... Amen. Te igitur Deus rogo te, ut sicut hic te video præsentem ... Amen.

De S. Erasmo. Añ. Sancte Erasme martyr Jesu qui die dominico ... Amen. ℣. Ora pro nobis ... ℟. Ut digni ... Oremus. Deus qui beatum Erasmum martyrem ... Amen. Domine Deus gloriosæ ecclesiæ salus et veritas ... Amen.

Commemoratio de S. Sebastiano. Añ. Sancte Sebastiane semper vespere et mane ... ℣. Ora pro nobis ... ℟. Ut mereamur pestem epidimiæ ... Omnipotens sempiterne Deus qui meritis beati Sebastiani ... Amen.

Commemoratio de S. Rocho. Añ. O beate Confessor Roche quam magna apud Deum sunt merita tua ... ℣. Ora pro nobis ... ℟. Ut digni ... Oremus. Sacro munere sacrati supplices ... Amen.

Commemoratio de S. Christoforo. Añ. Sancte Christofore martyr Jesu Christi qui pro ejus nomine ... ℣. Gloria et honore ... ℟. Et constituisti ... Oremus. Concede quæsumus omnipotens et misericors Deus ut qui beati Christofori ... Amen.

Commemoratio de S. Henrico. Añ. Rex Henricus pauperum et ecclesiæ defensor ... ℣. Ora pro nobis ... ℟. Ut digni ... Oratio. Deus sub cujus ineffabili providentia universi reges ... Amen.

A.D. 1537, Nicolas Le Roux, Rouen, for Jacques Cousin, Rouen, on vellum. No. 125.

Pope Benedict the XII. made this prayer and gave to all them that devoutly sayeth it as many days of pardon as our Lord had wounds, that is, VI. M. VI. C. LXVI. Oratio. Gratias ago tibi domine Jesu Christe qui voluisti pro redemptione mundi ... Amen.

A.D. 1537, Rouen, for François Regnault (Paris). 16º. No. 126.[1]

Angelica salutatio. Ave Maria ... Sancta Maria, mater Dei, ora pro nobis peccatoribus. Amen.
De S. Laurentio martyre. Añ. Levita Laurentius bonum opus operatus est ... ℣. Dispersit dedit ... ℟. Justitia ejus ... Oratio. Da nobis, quæsumus, omnipotens Deus vitiorum nostrorum ... Amen.

A.D. 1538, Rouen. 8º. No. 137.

The Kalender has St. Thomas of Canterbury on January 5, July 7, December 29 and also in the Litany.
Oratio tertia post communionem in missa. Domine Deus de Deo, lumen de lumine qui humanum genus ... Amen.
Oratio ad S. Gabrielem. Protector et princeps egregie Gabriel fortissime agonista ... Pater noster. Ave ... Amen.
Versus S. Bernardi. O bone Jesu. Illumina oculos meos ne unquam obdormiam ... Kyrie. Pater noster. ℣. Confiteantur ... ℟. Et sancti ... ℣. Domine exaudi ... ℟. Et clamor ... Oratio. Omnipotens sempiterne Deus qui Ezekiæ regi Judæ cum lacrimis ... Pater noster. Ave.

c. A.D. 1539, for Henry Marshall, Rouen. 8º. No. 145.

*** St. Thomas of Canterbury does not occur either in the Kalender or in the Litany.[2]

✠ A. a. b. c. Oratio dominica. La salutation angelique. Credo. In manus tuas. Per crucem hoc fugiat procul ... In nomine. Confitemini domino. Quoniam in sæculum. Confiteor Deo cæli ... Adjutorium nostrum. Qui fecit. Sit nomen. Ex hoc. Kyrie. Sequentia S. Evangelii secundum Johannem. Gloria tibi domine. Benedictiones mensæ.
Hoc modo incipiuntur præfationes ad missam per totum annum tam in feriis quam in festis. ℣. Per omnia sæcula sæculorum ... Amen. Dominus vobiscum ... Et cum spiritu tuo. ℣. Sursum corda. ℟. Habemus ad Dominum. ℣. Gratias agamus domino Deo nostro. ℟. Dignum et justum est. Præfatio quotidiana. Vere dignum et justum est ...

---

[1] See State Papers. Domestic. Vol. xi. No. 1488, and Vol. xiii. Pt. 2 No. 836.
[2] See Wilkins Conc. ed. 1737. Vol. 3. pages 835, 847.

Sanctus. Sanctus. Sanctus . . . Benedictus qui venit . . . Osanna in excelsis. Agnus Dei, qui tollis peccata mundi.
In fine missæ dicitur. Ite missa est.

A.D. 1541, Thomas Petyt, London, 32o. No. 159.[1]

In the name. The seven petitions of the Pater noster. The first petition. Our Father which art in heaven, hallowed be thy name. The Ave Maria. Hail Mary full of grace . . . fruit of thy womb. So be it. The Creed or the xii articles of the christian faith. The first article. I believe in God the Father almighty, maker of heaven and earth. The x commandments. The first commandment. Thou shalt have none other Gods but me.

c. A.D. 1541, John Mayler, London. 16o. No. 161.[2]

The King's highness greatly tendering the wealth of his realm hath suffered heretofore the Pater noster, Ave, Creed, and Ten commandments of God to be had in the english tongue, but his grace perceiving now the great diversity of the translations hath willed them all to be taken up, and instead of them hath caused an uniform translation of the said Pater noster, Ave, Creed, and the Ten Commandments to be set forth as hereafter followeth; willing all his loving subjects to learn and use the same; and straightly commandeth every Parson, Vicar and Curate to read and teach the same to their parishioners, and that no man imprint or set forth any other translation upon pain of his high displeasure. God save the king.

In the name. The seven petitions of the Pater noster. The first petition. Our Father which art in heaven hallowed be thy name.

The salutation of the angel called the Ave Maria. Hail Mary full of grace . . . fruit of thy womb. Amen.

The Creed or xii Articles of the christian faith. The first article. I believe in God the Father almighty, maker of heaven and earth.

The x Commandments of Almighty God. The first commandment. Thou shalt have none other Gods but me . . .

The symbol or creed of Athanasius dayly read in the church. Whosoever will be saved . . .

A prayer. O God which hast instructed the hearts of the faithful . . . So be it.

✠ A. a. b. c. In nomine. Pater noster. Ave Maria. Credo. In manus tuas commendo . . . Amen. Per crucis hoc signum fugiat procul . . . In nomine. Confitemini Domino . . . Quoniam in sæculum . . . Confiteor Deo, beatæ Mariæ, omnibus Sanctis et vobis quia peccavi . . . Misereatur vestri omnipotens Deus et dimittat vobis . . . Amen. Adjutorium nostrum . . . Qui fecit cœlum . . . Sit nomen . . . Ex hoc nunc . . . Kyrie eleyson . . .

---

[1] See Wilkins Conc. ed. 1737. Vol. 3. pages 813-816; also The Institution of a christian man, 1537; also A necessary doctrine and erudition for any christian man, 1543.

[2] See Wilkins Conc. ed. 1737. Vol. 3. page 861; also, Collier. Eccles. Hist. ed. 1840. Vol. 5. page 96.

*** *The words in italics, as well as the letters ℣ and ℟, are supplied from* "*Benedictiones Mensæ*," *in the Sarum Manual.*

Benedictiones mensæ. Ante prandium. Benedicite. ℟. *Dominus. Psalmus.* Oculi omnium . . . Et tu das escam . . . Aperis tu manum . . . Et imples . . . Gloria Patri . . . Sicut erat . . . Kyrie eleyson. Pater noster. *Sacerdos.* Oremus. Benedic Domine nos et dona tua . . . ℟. Amen. *Lector.* Jube Domine . . . *Sacerdos. Benedictio.* Mensæ cælestis participes . . . ℟. Amen. *Lector.* Deus charitas est . . . ℟. Amen.

Post prandium. *Sacerdos.* Deus pacis et dilectionis . . . Amen. ℣. Tu autem Domine . . . ℟. Deo gratias. *Psalmus.* Confiteantur tibi . . . Et sancti tui . . . Gloria Patri . . . Sicut erat . . . *Sacerdos. Capitulum.* Agimus tibi gratias omnipotens Deus pro universis beneficiis . . . Amen. *Psalmus.* Laudate Dominum omnes gentes . . . Quoniam confirmata est . . . Gloria Patri. Sicut erat. Kyrie eleyson. Pater noster. ℣. Dispersit . . . ℟. Justitia ejus . . . ℣. Benedicam Dominum . . . ℟. Semper laus . . . ℣. In Domino lætabitur . . . ℟. Audiant mansueti . . . ℣. Magnificate Dominum . . . ℟. Et exaltemus nomen ejus . . . ℣. Sit nomen . . . ℟. Ex hoc nunc . . . *Sacerdos.* Oremus. Retribuere dignare Domine . . . Amen. ℣. Benedicamus Domino. ℟. Deo gratias. Mater ora filium . . . Ave. Meritis et precibus suæ piæ matris . . . Amen. Animæ omnium fidelium . . . Amen.

Ante prandium. Benedicite. ℟. *Dominus. Psalmus.* Edent pauperes . . . ℣. Gloria Patri . . . ℟. Sicut erat . . . Kyrie eleyson. Pater noster. Jube Domine . . . *Sacerdos. Benedictio.* Cibo spiritualis . . . Amen. *Lectio.* Gratia domini nostri . . . Amen. *Lectio.* Frange esurienti panem tuum . . .

Post prandium. *Sacerdos.* Deus pacis et dilectionis . . . *Psalmus.* Memoriam fecit mirabilium . . . ℣. Gloria Patri . . . ℟. Sicut erat . . . *Capitulum.* Agimus tibi.

Ante prandium. Benedicite. ℟. *Dominus. Sacerdos. Benedictio.* Apposita et apponenda benedicat Dei dextera. In nomine.

Post prandium. Pro tali convivio benedicamus domino. Deo gratias. Mater ora filium ut post hoc exilium . . . Amen.

Ante cænam. Benedicite. ℟. *Dominus. Sacerdos.* Cænam sanctificet qui nobis omnia præbet In nomine.

Post cænam. *Psalmus.* Benedictus Deus in donis tuis . . . ℟. Et sanctus in omnibus operibus suis. ℣. Adjutorium . . . ℣. Sit nomen. Oremus. Retribuere. Benedicite. ℟. *Dominus. Sacerdos. Benedictio.* Votum servorum benedicat rex angelorum. In nomine.

In vigilia Paschæ. Benedicite. ℟. *Dominus. Psalmus.* Edent . . . Gloria patri. Sicut erat . . . Kyrie eleyson. Pater noster. Oremus. Benedic. Jube domine benedicere. *Sacerdos. Benedictio.* Cibo spiritualis. *Lectio.* Si consurrexistis cum Christo . . .

Post prandium. *Sacerdos.* Deus pacis. *Psalmus.* Memoriam. Gloria patri. Sicut erat. *Capitulum.* Agimus tibi. *Psalmus.* Laudate dominum . . .

Quoniam confirmata . . . Gloria patri . . . Sicut erat . . . ℣. Dominus
vobiscum. ℟. Et cum spiritu tuo. Oremus. Spiritum in nobis domine
tuæ charitatis infunde . . . Amen.
In die Pascæ. Benedicite. ℟. *Dominus.* ℣. Hæc est dies . . . ℟. Exul-
temus et lætemur in ea. Gloria patri. Sicut erat . . . Kyrie eleyson.
Pater noster. Oremus. Benedic domine. Jube Domine. *Benedictio.*
Mensæ celestis. *Lectio.* Expurgate vetus fermentum . . .
Post prandium. *Sacerdos.* ℣. Qui dat escam omni carni. ℣. Tu autem.
℟. Deo gratias. *Psalmus.* Laudate dominum. Quoniam confirmata.
Gloria patri. Sicut erat . . . ℣. In resurrectione tua Christe. ℟.
Cælum et terra lætentur. Alleluya. Oremus. Spiritum in nobis . . .
Amen. ℣. Dominus vobiscum. ℟. Et cum spiritu tuo. ℣. Benedi-
camus Domino. ℟. Deo gratias. Eodem modo dicitur per totam
ebdomadam. Retribuere. Post cænam. Hæc dies. ℣. In resurrectione.
℟. Cæli et terra.
Psalmus. De profundis. Kyrie eleyson. Pater noster. ℣. Requiem æternam.
℟. Et lux . . . ℣. A porta . . . ℟. Erue . . . ℣. Credo videre . . .
℟. In terra . . . ℣. Domine exandi . . . ℟. Et clamor . . . Oremus.
Inclina Domine aurem . . . Amen. Animæ omnium fidelium defunctorum . . . Amen.
O Lord which hast displayed thine hands and feet, and all Thy body on the
cross . . . So be it.
An order and form of bidding the beads by the King's commandment. Ye
shall pray for the whole congregation of Christ's church and specially for
this church of England wherein first, I commend to your devout prayers
the King's most excellent majesty, supreme head immediately under God
of the spirituality and temporality of the same church. And for the
prosperity of the noble Prince Edward his son. Secondly ye shall pray
for the clergy the Lords temporal and commons of this realm beseeching
almighty God to give everyone of them in his degree grace to use themselves in such wise as may be to his contentation, the king's honour and
the weal of this realm. Thirdly. Ye shall pray for the souls that be
departed abiding the mercy of God almighty that it may please him
rather at the contemplation of our prayers to grant them the fruition of
his presence.[1]
A prayer unto Christ. O maker of heaven and earth King of kings and Lord
of lords . . . So be it.
The office of all estates. Rulers. Sapi. i. Ye that are rulers . . .

⁎ *The index has " The whole A B C for to learn children all in Latin ".*

A.D. 1542 (Antwerp). 8o. No. 163.[2]

✠ A. a. b. c. Oratio dominica. Pater noster. Salutatio angelica. Ave Maria.
Duodecim articuli fidei. Credo in Deum. Confiteor tibi domine Jesu

---
[1] See Wilkins Conc. ed. 1737. Vol. 3. pages 783. 807 ; also C. H. O. Forms of Bidding Prayer
[2] See Wilkins Conc. ed. 1737. Vol. 3. pages 863. 864.

Christe omnia peccata mea . . . Amen.   Suscipere dignare domine
Deus omnipotens has orationes . . . Amen.

A.D. 1544, September 12, Thomas Petyt, London.   16º.   No. 171.

An order and form of bidding of the beads by the King's commandment. Ye shall pray for the whole congregation of Christ's church and specially for this church of England wherein first I commend unto your devout prayers the King's most excellent majesty, supreme head immediately under God of the spirituality and temporality of the same church. Also ye shall pray for Queen Katherine that now is, and for our most noble Prince Edward. Secondly ye shall pray for the clergy, the Lords temporal and the commons of this realm . . . Thirdly. Ye shall pray for the souls that be departed abiding the mercy of God . . .[1]

A.D. 1555, John Kyng, London, for John Waley (London).   8º.   No. 214.

✠ A. a. b. c. Pater noster. Ave Maria. Credo.[2]

. . . Requiescant in pace. Amen. Benedictiones mensæ. (as on page 153, but "Ave regina cælorum" for "Mater ora filium".)

A.D. 1557, Assignees of John Wayland, London.   8º.   Latin.   No. 231.

Precatio in aurora.   Domine Deus omnipotens cui omnia exposita . . . Amen.
Precatio cum surgis.   Domine Jesu Christe qui es clarus mundi sol . . . Amen.
Precatio antequam petas lectum.   Domine qui es unus Deus verus benignus . . . Amen.
Precatio pro fiducia in Deum.   Initium ruinæ hominis, sibi fidere . . .
Precatio regis Asa in tempore belli.   Domine non est apud te ulla distantia . . .
Precatio pro concordia ecclesiæ Christi.   Surge Domine ut dissipentur inimici . . . Amen.
Precatio pro obtinenda sapientia.   Sapientia ix.   Deus patrum meorum, et Domine misericordiæ . . . Amen.
Precatio pro bona fama conservanda.   Sapiens ille, qui tibi a secretis fuit, pater cælestis . . . Amen.
Precatio contra curam mundanam.   Benignissime et indulgentissime pater defensor noster . . . Amen.
Precatio contra superbiam et libidinem.   Domine pater et Deus vitæ meæ ne derelinquas . . .
Fructuosa precatio quovis tempore dicenda.   Misericors Deus, concede, ut quæ tibi placita sunt . . . Amen.
Precatio contra diabolum.   Domine Jesu Christe qui per os Sancti Petri . . .
Pro alterius vitæ cupiditate.   Animæ obscurus, teterque carcer hoc corpus est . . . Amen.

---

[1] See Wilkins Conc. ed. 1787. Vol. 3. pages 783. 807; also C. H. O. Forms of Bidding Prayer.

[2] See Wilkins Conc. ed. 1787. Vol. 4. pages 145. 169; also Collier Eccles. Hist. ed. 1841. Vol. 9. page 316.

A SUMMARY OF THE CONTENTS

OF THE

HORÆ OR PRIMERS,

IN WHICH THE HOURS ARE IN ENGLISH AND LATIN, OR IN ENGLISH,

ACCORDING TO

THE USES OF SARUM AND YORK,

A.D. 1536.—A.D. 1558.

EXPLANATIONS.

1. A summary of all the contents of No. 124 A.D. 1536 is given as a standard of comparison for those Horæ of Sarum use in which the Hours, as well as other devotions in latin, are translated into english. This is the first edition which is known in which the translation of the Hours into english occurs.

2. The Hours of the blessed Virgin Mary which are translated into english, all belong to that form of the Hours which is commonest in the latin Horæ, (see Explanations, page 106, No. 8), and which is analogous to though not identical with the corresponding form given in the Sarum Breviary as, "Non-plenum Servitium de sancta Maria," "Post Purificationem usque ad Adventum Domini". The other two forms of the Horæ "Per Adventum usque ad vigiliam Natalis Domini," and "A nativitate Domini usque ad Purificationem," are not known to have been translated.

3. No translation of the Hours of the blessed Virgin Mary into english, according to the Use of York, is known to exist.

4. The latin title of a devotion, when one occurs, as well as the english translation of it is given, and also the latin and english of the first words of the collect, but only the english of each of the component parts of the devotion.

5. The various known editions of the Epistles and Gospels in english are given as they occur, they were first printed A.D. 1538. They are found either as separate books or forming a part of the Primer.

6. All fresh words in the titles and all fresh devotions after No. 124 are given as they occur, as well as any variation in the component parts of a devotion. So far as the text of the actual Hours goes there is nothing new to index except "The collects at Lauds," for these are the only variable portion of the Hours in english and latin or in english apart from the substitution at the beginning of all the Hours between Septuagesima and Easter of "Laud be to the Lord, King of eternal glory" for "Praise ye the Lord" and also at Matins of the "Fifty-first psalm" for the "Te Deum".

7. An index is given of the prayers, psalms and benedictions. Groups of psalms such as the seven penitential psalms, or those in the Hours are not indexed separately. Another index gives all the hymns and rhythms. A general index refers to other matters of liturgical, devotional and general interest.

A SUMMARY OF THE CONTENTS

OF THE

HORÆ OR PRIMERS,

IN WHICH THE HOURS ARE IN ENGLISH AND LATIN, OR IN ENGLISH,

ACCORDING TO

THE USES OF SARUM AND YORK,

A.D. 1536—A.D. 1558.

A.D. 1536, Rouen, 8º. English and Latin, No. 124.

*** *The title is " This Prymer in english and in latin is newly translated after the Latin text". St. Thomas of Canterbury occurs in the Kalender on January 5, July 7 and December 29 and also in the Litany.*

Title-page containing the contents of the book. Then an Almanack. Then the Kalender, each page having two months.

A preface advertising the reader of certain things contained in this book following. Our master Christ in his holy gospel teacheth a certain form of praying, which in itself, I dare well say, containeth all petitions necessary for man's salvation, and that is the Pater noster. Howbeit we have many devout prayers of holy fathers, both in the old and the new testament[1] by the which, because christian people may be moved unto virtue and devotion, they are not to be rejected, but to be had in great price and estimation. After whose ensample many good men and doctors of holy church have since that time devised forms of good prayers and suffrages to the honour of God and memory of his blessed Saints for to move and stir the hearts of people to virtue and contemplation, which in mine opinion are well to be allowed and suffered, so long as they give us none occasion to withdraw from God his due honour and reverence. The due honour to God, as me seemeth, is; that we should neither worship fear nor serve nothing but him only, which opinion I would not that men should interpret so straitly as though mine intent were to withdraw from saints and temporal rulers their due worship and obedience.

[1] See Prayers of the Bible. Lambeth. Archiep. 24. 9. 11. (1). c. A.D. 1534.

For my mind is that if we worship fear or serve either Saint Angel Prince, father or mother we should do it for the respect of God only which neither would his Saints to be dishonoured, nor princes to be disobeyed neither our parents to be despised. Yet am I not ignorant that some people have been greatly deluded of long time about the veneration of Saints and such like things, partly by ignorance and partly through impure persuasions of false preachers. For the reformation whereof almighty God of his eternal providence hath put in the minds of his elect princes, and true pastors of his flock to purge the filthiness of false doctrine out of the hearts of them that have been seduced by blind guides, so that no man shall have cause to err, but only those which are at a point to stop their ears at the truth. And for the more increase of virtue and advancement of true doctrine they have now permitted and admitted such prayers and suffrages as were wont to be said and pronounced only in Latin (which heretofore none did understand, but only those that had the knowledge of the same tongue) to be translated into english. And of their blessed zeal unto the increase of virtue and devotion among people, whereas heretofore none of the Prymers yet emprinted in English hath been according in all things unto the common usage (to the intent that no man should be ignorant what he hath said before time in Latin) have suffered the same to go abroad, not omitting any part of the ordinary service that hath been used to be said. In the setting forth whereof, albeit that neither the translatour neither the printour have done their part so well as might have been, if learned men had taken the matter in hand; yet they most entirely desire the readers to be contented with their good purpose and endeavour, which herein have regarded nothing so much as the honour and glory of God and edifying of the readers. First there is to be noted in the hours of the Matyns, in the four chapters, that is to wit, "In omnibus requiem." "Ab initio." "Et sic in Syon." "Et radicavi ". which as they stand there do seem to be spoken in praise of our Lady, where indeed they are meant and were made only to the laud and commendation of the wisdom of God as it shall appear by the reading of the Bible in the book of Ecclesiastic. ca. 24, which I think no man will deny except it be such as either be ignorant of the Scripture, or else wily wresters of Scripture. Moreover in Salve regina we call our Lady our life and hope ; that is not to be suffered, for these three theological virtues, Faith, Hope, and Charity are so merely appropried unto the Godhead, that it is damnable sin to ascribe any of them to any power either in heaven or earth, how high how holy or how much exalted so ever they be, yea though the same hath been persuaded by never so great doctors, by never so holy men and by never so long process of time. And yet the worship of our Lady and the holy Saints of heaven is no wit the more diminished thereby, but rather the better augmented and increased, for the most acceptable worship that can be done to them is to follow their virtuous life and good examples. And nothing is more displeasant unto them than when we be so curious in the worshipping of them, that God is defrauded thereby of his due honour. Wherefore it were very expedient to the christian congregation that the preachours of God's word and curates of mens souls should instruct unlearned people in the right form of worshipping God and his Saints according to the rule of scripture, which teacheth us to give all honour and glory unto God putting our whole faith, hope, and confidence in him only and to worship our Lady and his Saints as his elect and well-beloved servants and not as Gods nor as equal to God for that were cursed idolatry, but that we should pray to them as petitioners with us and for us, referring all things to the honour and glory of God, which heareth and accepteth our just prayers much more favourably and sooner than any Saint in heaven. Wherefore in my judgment the Litany deserveth singular commendation which expresseth unto us an evident diversity between the honoring of God and his Saints, for in all places where anything is referred to the person of God it saith on this wise, "Have mercy on us," and if it touch our Lady or any other Saint it is always "Pray for us," whereby we may learn that to have mercy on us or to save us, lieth only in the power of God, but to help us with prayer may lie in the power of our Lady and other blessed Saints whom God listeth to accept. And in such wise it is lawful for us to pray to any good man, whom we suppose to be in the favour of God. In consideration whereof most benign readers, I thought it right expedient to give you admonition and warning before all such things that might cause you to be offended in reading of this book, which how necessary it is to them that have mind to be occupied in godly meditation, I will not speak any further at this time, lest I should seem to be a boaster of mine own works. And if there be any like faults in this work escaped either by negligence or by ignorance, whereof I have given no warning, I humbly beseech you most benign readers charitably to reform them after the rule which I have shewed you before, whereby ye may merit highly in Christ who preserve you. So be it.

A very devout prayer of the seven words which our Lord spake hanging on the cross. Oratio devotissima de septem verbis quæ dominus Jesus in cruce pendens dixit. Omnipotent Lord Jesu Christ, that yet hanging on the Cross . . . So be it. Domine Jesu Christe qui septem verba . . . Amen.

The beginning of the holy gospel after S. Johan. i. Initium S. Evangelii secundum Johannem i. Glory be to the Lord. In the beginning was the word . . . In principio erat verbum . . . Deo gratias. Anty. We do call upon Thee . . . Versicle. Blessed be the Lord's name . . . Answer. From this time forth . . . O God the protector of all that trust in Thee . . . Amen. Protector in te sperantium Deus . . . Amen.

Luke i. The angel Gabriel was sent from God. In illo tempore. Missus est Gabriel . . . Deo gratias.

Matthew the second Chapter. When Jesus was born in Bethlehem . . . Cum natus esset Jesus in Bethlehem . . . Deo gratias.
Mark xvi. After that He appeared unto the eleven. . . . In illo tempore. Recumbentibus undecim discipulis apparuit illis Jesus . . . Deo gratias.
The passion written by Saint Johan Evangelist. Passio Domini nostri Jesu Christi secundum Johannem. When Jesus had spoken these words He went forth with His disciples . . . Egressus est dominus Jesus cum discipulis suis . . . Deo gratias. ℣. Thou that suffered'st for us . . . A. Lord have mercy on us. O Lord which hast displayed Thine hands and feet . . . So be it. Deus qui manus tuas et pedes tuos . . . Amen.
O Lord, for Thy great mercy and grace, Help thy people that so fain would have Thy holy gospel preached in every place . . . So be it. Populo tuo domine qui sacrosancti evangelii tui prædicationem ubique tam ardentibus votis affectant . . . Amen.
The Pater noster. Oratio dominica. The first petition. O Father in heaven.[1]
The salutation of the angel Gabriel. Salutatio angelica. Hail Mary . . . blessed be the fruit of thy womb Jesus Christ. So be it. Ave Maria gratia plena . . . Amen.
The XII. articles of the faith. Duodecim articuli fidei. The first article. I believe in God the Father almighty . . . Credo in Deum . . .
The x. commandments. Deutero v. chapter. Decem præcepta. Deuteron v. Thou shalt not have strange Gods in my sight . . . Non habebis Deos alienos . . .
The ten commandments in metre. Decem præcepta. One God only thou shalt love and worship perfectly . . . Unum crede Deum ne jures vana per ipsum . . .
A little metre containing the duty of a christian man. Iambicum carmen quid deceat Christianum perstringens . . . To believe that Christ hath for us merited . . . Credere meruisse Christum ut æterni patris . . .
An invocation unto the holy Trinity to be said in the morning when Thou shalt rise up. Invocatio S. Trinitatis mane, cum exsurrectus fueris, dicenda. Holy Trinity be helping unto me . . . So be it. Auxiliatrix sis mihi Trinitas . . . Amen.
The Matyns, Laudes. Matyns of the Cross and of the Compassion of our Lady. Matutinæ. Ad Laudes. Ad Matutinas de Cruce. De Compassione.
Laudes. The collects. Of the Holy Ghost. De S. Spiritu. Anty. Come Holy Spirit of God . . . ℣. Send forth thy Spirit . . . A. And the face of the earth . . . Let us pray. O God which hast instructed the hearts . . . So be it. Oremus. Deus qui corda fidelium . . . Amen.
Of the Holy Trinity. De S. Trinitate. Anty. Deliver us, save us . . . ℣. The Lord's name be blessed . . . A. From this time forth . . . Let us pray. Almighty and everlasting God which hast granted to thy

---

[1] See Burnet. Hist. Reform. ed. 1865. Vol. 6. pages 199, 206, 210.

servants . . . So be it. Oremus. Omnipotens sempiterne Deus qui dedisti . . . Amen.

Of the holy Cross. De S. Cruce. Anty. Verily we ought to rejoice . . . ℣. All the earth worshippeth . . . A. And praiseth . . . Let us pray. O God which hast ascended Thy most holy cross . . . So be it. Oremus. Deus qui sanctam crucem tuam ascendisti . . . Amen.

Of St Michael the archangel. De S. Michaele archangelo. Anthem. O archangel Michael come for to succour . . . ℣. In thy holy temple . . . A. And thy blessed name confess . . . Let us pray. O God which by a wonderful order dost appoint . . . So be it. Oremus. Deus qui miro ordine angelorum ministeria . . . Amen.

Of St John Baptist. De S. Johanne Baptista. Anthem. Among the sons of women . . . ℣. From God there was a man sent . . . A. Whose name was John . . . Let us pray. O Lord defend us alway through the continual succours of Saint John Baptist . . . So be it. Oremus. Perpetuis nos Domine S. Johannis Baptistæ tuere . . . Amen.

Of St Peter and Paul. De S. Petro et Paulo. Anty. Peter the apostle and Paul the doctor . . . ℣. In all the earth . . . A. And in the coasts of the world . . . Let us pray. O God whose right hand did lift up blessed Peter . . . So be it. Oremus. Deus cujus dextera beatum Petrum apostolum ambulantem . . . Amen.

Of St Andrew. De S. Andrea. Anthem. Andrew was the servant of Christ . . . ℣. The Lord loved Andrew . . . A. With a savour . . . Let us pray. Lord we humbly beseech Thy majesty . . . So be it. Oremus. Majestatem tuam Domine suppliciter exoramus . . . Amen.

Of St John Evangelist. De S. Johanne Evangelista. Anthem. This is the same John . . . ℣. Greatly to be praised . . . A. Which leaned on the breast . . . Let us pray. We beseech Thee Lord of Thy benignity . . . So be it. Oremus. Ecclesiam tuam quæsumus Domine benignus illustra . . . Amen.

Of St. Laurence. De S. Laurentio. Anty. Saint Laurence the deacon . . . ℣. He distributed . . . A. His righteousness . . . Let us pray. Lord we beseech Thee to give us grace for to quench . . . So be it. Oremus. Da nobis quæsumus omnipotens Deus vitiorum nostrorum flammas extinguere . . . Amen.

Of St Stevyn. De S. Stephano. Anty. Stevyn saw the heavens open . . . ℣. Thou hast him crowned . . . A. And hast him set . . . Let us pray. Grant good Lord that we may perfectly follow him . . . So be it. Oremus. Da nobis quæsumus Domine imitari quod colimus . . . Amen.

Of St. Nycolas. De S. Nicolao. Antyphona. Blessed Saint Nycolas being yet a child . . . ℣. Blessed Nycolas for us make petition . . . A. That we be enabled . . . Let us pray. O God which hast glorified . . . So be it. Oremus. Deus qui beatum Nicolaum pium pontificem tuum . . . Amen.

Of Mary Magdalene. De S. Maria Magdalena. Añ. Mary Magdalen did anoint . . . ℣. Many sins were forgiven her . . . A. Because her love was entire . . . Let us pray. Grant unto us most merciful Father . . . So be it. Oremus. Largire nobis clementissime pater . . . Amen.

Of St. Katheryne. De S. Katherina. Añ. The virgin Saint Katheryne . . . ℣. Holy Katheryne . . . A. That we be enabled . . . Let us pray. Almighty and eternal God, which hast commanded . . . So be it. Oremus. Omnipotens sempiterne Deus qui gloriosæ virginis . . . Amen.

Of St. Margarete. De S. Margareta. Añ. Saint Margarete was but xv years old . . . ℣. For thy beauty . . . A. Proceed prosperously . . . Let us pray. God that hast caused the blessed virgin Margarete . . . So be it. Oremus. Deus qui beatam virginem Margaretam . . . Amen.

Of the Saints whose relykes remain in the holy church. De Sanctis quorum reliquiæ continentur in universali ecclesia. Anthem. The bodies of holy Saints . . . ℣. Blessed be they that dwell . . . A. They praise Him . . . Let us pray. Almighty God we beseech Thee vouchsafe that the merits . . . So be it. Oremus. Præsta quæsumus omnipotens Deus ut sanctæ Dei genitricis . . . Amen.

Of all Saints. De omnibus Sanctis. Anthem. All ye blessed Saints . . . ℣. Rejoice in the Lord . . . A. And all you that in heart . . . Let us pray. We beseech Thee good Lord, that Thou being pleased . . . So be it. Oremus. Omnium sanctorum tuorum quæsumus Domine intercessione placatus . . . Amen.

For peace. Pro pace. Anthem. Lord send us peace . . . ℣. Lord send peace . . . A. And great abundance . . . Let us pray. O God from whom all holy desires . . . So be it. Oremus. Deus a quo sancta desideria . . . Amen. Bless we the Lord. Thank we God.

How the saying of Hours first began, and why they are so called. De origine celebrandi horas, et cur ita vocantur. At certain hours unto God for to pray, Was first begun by the prophet Daniel . . . Daniel vi. Statis horis Deum orare, a Daniele propheta primam traxit originem . . .

Prime and the Hours of our Lady, with the Hours of the Cross and of the Compassion of our Lady. Horæ deiparæ Virginis.

A prayer in the praise of our Lady. Oratio ad laudem deiparæ Virginis. Anthem. Hail Queen, mother of mercy . . . Salve regina, mater misericordiæ . . . ℣. Hail Mary . . . A. Blessed be thou . . . Prayer. Almighty eternal God, which by the operation of the holy Ghost . . . Amen. Oremus. Omnipotens sempiterne Deus qui gloriosæ virginis et matris Mariæ . . . Amen.

Of the five corporal joys of our Lady. De gaudiis beatæ Mariæ virginis corporalibus. Anthem. Rejoice, O virgin, Christ's mother dear . . . Gaude virgo, mater Christi . . . ℣. Thou art blessed of Thy son . . . A. For the fruit of life we received by thee . . . Prayer. O God which with double joy . . . So be it. Oremus. Deus qui beatissimam virginem Mariam . . . Amen.

Of the vii spiritual joys of our Lady. De septem gaudiis deiparæ Virginis spiritualibus. Anthem. Rejoice, O flower of virgins all . . . Gaude flore virginali . . . Anty. O most holy and humble spouse . . . ℣. O mother of God, thou art exalted . . . A. Above the orders of angels . . . Prayer. Most sweet Lord Jesu, Son of the living God . . . So be it. Oremus. Dulcissime Domine Jesu Christe fili Dei vivi qui beatissimam . . . Amen.

A prayer to our blessed Lady for the pestilence. Oratio ad beatam Virginem Mariam contra pestem. The star of the sea which the Lord fostered . . . Stella cæli extirpavit . . . ℣. Holy mother of God, pray to Thy Son . . . A. That we may deserve . . . Prayer. O God, merciful, pitiful and sufferable . . . So be it. Oremus. Deus misericordiæ, Deus pietatis . . . Amen.

A prayer for them that be dead. Oratio pro defunctis. Out of the bottomless pit of my heavy trouble . . . De profundis clamavi . . . Lord have mercy on us. Our Father. ℣. Lord give them eternal rest. ℟. And continual light . . . ℣. From the gates of hell. ℟. Lord deliver their souls. ℣. I trust to see . . . ℟. In the land . . . ℣. Lord God hear . . . ℟. And give hearing . . . Prayer. Lord incline Thine ear . . . So be it. Oremus. Inclina Domine aurem tuam . . . Amen. The souls of all true believers . . . So be it. Animæ omnium fidelium defunctorum . . . Amen.

A prayer to be said at the elevation of the sacrament. In elevatione corporis Christi. Hail very body incarnate of a Virgin . . . Ave verum corpus natum de Maria Virgine . . .

The fifteen Oos in english. Quindecim orationes S. Brigittæ. O Jesu endless sweetness . . . O Domine Jesu Christe, eterna dulcedo . . . (see pages 111-116).

The seven psalms penitential. Septem psalmi pænitentiales. Anthem. Remember not. Añ. Ne reminiscaris. Psalms. 6. Lord, rebuke me not in thy fury . . . 31. Blessed are they, whose iniquities be forgiven. 37. Lord reprove me not in Thy fury. 50. Have mercy upon me, oh God, according to Thy great mercy. 101. Lord hear my prayer, and let my clamour come unto thee. 129. Out of the bottomless pit of my heavy trouble. 142. Lord hear my prayer, with thine ears perceive my desire.

The xv psalms. Quindecim psalmi. Psalms. 119. I cried unto the Lord, when I was in trouble. 120. I lifted up mine eyes unto the hills. 121. I rejoiced in those things that were said unto me. 122. Unto Thee have I lift up mine eyes, O God. 123. Unless the Lord had been among us. 124. They that trust in the Lord as a mountain of Sion. 125. When the Lord turned the captivity of Sion. 126. Unless the Lord have builded the house. 127. Blessed be all that fear the Lord. 128. Eftsones have they assailed me, even from my youth. 129. Out of the bottomless pit of my heavy trouble I call unto Thee. 130. Lord my heart is not exalted. 131. Lord have mind of David. 132. Behold how good and

pleasant it is for two brethren to dwell together. 133. Lo now bless ye the Lord, all the servants of the Lord.
Lateny. Letania.
The verses of Saint Bernard. Versus Sancti Bernardi. Illuminate mine eyes to the end I never sleep in darkness . . . Glory be to the Father. Illumina oculos meos ne unquam obdormiam in morte . . . Gloria Patri.
Jesu Son of God, maker of all things help me . . . Our Father. Hail Mary. Jesu fili Dei omnium conditor, adjuva me . . . Pater noster. Ave. Jesu Son of God, which heldest thy peace before a Judge . . . Our Father. Hail Mary. Jesu fili Dei qui coram judice tacuisti . . . Pater noster. Ave. Jesu Son of God, which wast bounden rule mine hands . . . Our Father. Hail Mary. Jesu fili Dei, qui ligatus fuisti . . . Pater noster. Ave. ℣. Arise Lord and help us. A. And for Thy name's sake deliver us. Prayer. I beseech Thee Lord Jesu cause me to have . . . So be it. Oremus. Peto Domine Jesu largire mihi . . . Amen. Our Father. Hail Mary. I believe in God the Father.
The Dirige and first The Evensong.
The Commendations of the souls.
A prayer to God for them that be departed, having none to pray for them. Oratio pro his qui vitam migraverunt quibus desunt intercessores apud Deum. Have mercy we beseech Thee Lord God through the precious passion . . . So be it. Miserere quæsumus Domine Deus per preciosam mortem . . . Amen.
The psalms of Christ's passion. Psalmi de passione Christi. Anty. Christ was made obedient . . . Añ. Christus factus est. Psalms. 21. O God, my God, look toward me. 22. The Lord ruleth me. 23. The earth is the Lord's. 24. Unto Thee, Lord, have I lift up my soul. 25. Judge me good Lord, for I have entered in mine innocency. 26. The Lord is my light and my health. 27. O Lord, I shall cry to Thee, O God, my God. 28. Bring to the Lord, O ye sons of God. 29. I shall exalt Thee, O Lord, for Thou hast defended me. 30. In Thee, Lord, have I trusted, let me not be confounded for ever. Anty. Christ was made obedient. ℣. Holy mother of God . . . A. That we be enabled . . . ℣. Greatly to be praised is John . . . A. Which leaned . . . Regard we beseech Thee Lord this thy household . . . Respice quæsumus Domine super hanc familiam tuam . . . Lord Jesu Christ, we beseech Thee of Thy goodness . . . Interveniat pro nobis Domine Jesu Christe apud tuam clementiam . . . Lord God we pray Thee that the prayer of blessed St John . . . So be it. Beati Johannis apostoli tui et evangelistæ . . . Amen. The glorious passion . . . So be it. Gloriosa passio . . . Amen. The Virgin Mary with her holy Son . . . So be it. Nos cum prole pia . . . Amen. To the holy and indivisible Trinity . . . So be it. Sanctæ et individuæ Trinitati . . . Amen. All hail most benign Jesu, full of mercy and grace . . . So be it. Ave benigne Jesu gratia plenus . . . Amen.

The Psalter of Saint Hierome. Psalterium beati Hieronymi. O good Lord receive my words in Thine ears . . . Verba mea auribus . . . The prayer. Grant I beseech Thee, Lord God, that by the holy melody . . . So be it. Oremus. Dona mihi quæso omnipotens Deus ut per hanc sacrosanctam psalterii cælestis melodiam . . . Amen.

When thou shalt receive the sacrament. In sumptione corporis Christi. O merciful Lord, I am not worthy . . . So be it. Domine non sum dignus ut intres . . . Amen.

When thou hast received it. Post sumptionem corporis Christi. The very true receiving of Thy glorious body . . . So be it. Vera perceptio corporis et sanguinis . . . Amen.

A devout prayer of Saint Bernard. Oratio Sancti Bernardini. O bountiful Jesu, O sweet Jesu . . . Amen. O bone Jesu, O dulcis Jesu . . . Amen. O glorious King which amongst Thy saints . . . So be it. O rex gloriose inter sanctos tuos . . . Amen.

A prayer unto the image of the body of Christ. Oratio ad imaginem corporis Christi. O maker of heaven and earth, King of kings . . . So be it. Conditor cæli et terræ rex regum . . . Amen.

A prayer to obtain wisdom. Sapience the ix Chap. Oratio pro impetranda sapientia. Sapi. ix. O the God of our fathers, God of mercy . . . So be it. Deus patrum nostrorum et domine misericordiæ . . . Amen.[1]

The prayer of Salomon for wisdom to the intent to govern the people rightly to be daily pronounced of all princes which be set in authority iii Regum the iii chapter. Oratio pro sapientia ad populum recte gubernandum omnibus quotidie Principibus in potestate constitutis pronuncianda. 3 Regum. 3. Thou hast made Lord with thy servant David my father great mercy . . . Tu fecisti Domine, cum servo tuo David patre meo . . .[1]

For a competency of living, the prayer of Salomon. Proverbs the xxx. chapter. Pro vitæ competentia oratio Salomonis Proverbiorum. xxx. Two things, Lord, I demanded that thou wouldest not deny me . . . So be it. Duo rogavi te ne deneges mihi . . . Amen.[1]

Colophon. Imprynted in Rowen the yere of our Lorde 1536.

⁎ *Then follows in english and latin with a fresh pagination.*

An exposicyon after the manner of a contemplacyon upon the. li. Psalm, called Miserere mei Deus, which Hierom of Farrarye made at the latter end of his days. Expositio ac meditatio in psalmum Miserere mei, fratris Hieronymi de Ferraria, quam in ultimis vitæ suæ edidit.[2]

A meditacyon of the same Jerom upon the psalm of In te Domine speravi, which prevented by death he could not finish. Meditatio ejusdem Hieronymi in Psalmum In te Domine speravi, quam preventus morte implere non potuit.[2]

Colophon. Imprynted in Rowen the yere of our Lorde 1536.

[1] Præcationes Biblicæ. Brit. Mus. 843. c. 6. A.D, 1531; also Prayers of the Bible. Lambeth. Archiep. 24. 9. 11. (1). c. A.D. 1534.
[2] Lambeth. Archiep. 24. 9. 11. (3). c. A.D. 1534; also Fratris Hieronymi Ferrariensis expositiones in psalmos. A.D. 1505.

c. A.D. 1537, Robert Redman, London.   40.   No. 128.   English and Latin.

₊ *The title is, "This Prymer in english and in latin is newly translated after the Latin text". St. Thomas of Canterbury occurs in the Kalender, on January 5, July 7 and December 29 and also in the Litany.*

The days of the week moralysed (as on page 147).

The commandments of God given by Moses and expounded by Christ, in our mother tongue, very necessary and expedient for youth and all other to learn and know. The first table. I am the Lord thy God, which have brought thee out of the land of Egypt . . . Christ. Hear Israel our Lord God . . .

The Symbol or Creed of the great doctor Athanasius dayly read in the church. Symbolum Athanasii. Whosoever will be saved . . . Quicunque vult salvus esse . . .

The office of all estates. A bishop must be faultless . . . Rulers . . . The comens . . . Husbands . . . Wives . . . Fathers and mothers . . . Children . . . Masters . . . Servants . . . Widows . . . The sum of all . . . So be it.

A preface advertising the reader of certain things contained in this book following. "Our master Christ in his holy gospel teacheth" down to "nor princes to be disobeyed neither our parents to be despised" (as on page 159). Then. Howbeit in the judgment of these and such like indifferent things there be right many that by avoiding of one extremity fall into another. For even as it is a point of Christian prudence and circumspection not to receive anything for certain and undoubted, which is not expressed in manifest scripture, so contrary-wise is it a point of presumptuous perversity and arrogance proudly to reject that thing which the religious contemplation of good and godly men have either taught, to the solace and comfort of them that believe or left to the instruction of the unlearned multitude, of which sort all these prescript forms of prayers, worshippings of Saints and such like, which, as me seemeth, ought meekly to be received as mens tradition, so long as they vary not from that only and singular precedent, after which all things ought and must be fashioned, I mean the word of God. And since that, all wise and well learned men heretofore have been and yet are of the same opinion, is it not marvel that many be so set from all indifferency of judgment frowardly to refuse every thing that hath been commended to us by tradition of our elders, without any respect had of the use and commodity thereof which is a most evident proof and clear token of rashness and temerity. And this they do with an extreme zeal, but not according to knowledge, but rather because they have not that same pure and lightsome eye that is spoken of Mat. 6. the lack whereof causeth them to stand in their own light, darkeneth their understanding, and finally maketh their judgments sinister and corrupt. This do I here touch the more apertly by occasion of this english Prymar of Sarum use which when it was first imprinted, like as it lacked not the vituperation and dispraise of some, so had it again the favour and commendation of the more learned sort. Howbeit when it came so to pass that it was not utterly misliked of the better party, but that also it seemed to men of authority not inconvenient to pass among the common people, it hath animated the setters forth thereof not a little, to communicate the same eftsones again to the reading of other, being more diligently corrected, more purely imprinted, and meetly well purged of many things that seemed no small faults therein. In the setting forth whereof albeit that neither the Translatour nor the Printer have done their part so well, as might have been, if better learned had taken the matter in hand; yet they most entirely desire the readers to be contented with their good purpose and endeavour which herein have regarded nothing so much as the honour of God and edifying of the people. And if it so be that any manifest fault hath escaped them, let it be ascribed either to negligence, or ignorance and not unto any malice or seditious intent. For if men of excellent learning have not stand so much in their own conceit, as to think that no fault could escape them in their works, much less then ought I, being far from the knowledge requisite in a learned man, vindicate any such perfection of learning or clear judgment, but that I do and may lightly stand in mine own light and be deceived, except I would account myself wiser than S. Austine, which in one of his epistles rebuketh certain his friends because they defended diverse errors contained in his writings, whereas his adversaries had founden fault, as they might justly do, affirming these words. You that are my friends and ascribe so perfect knowledge to me, that I did never err in all my writings, have taken a wrong quarrel in hand, your opinion is false. And if I should so think myself, I might rather be reputed mad than wise. For never to err is to be equal with God, but man's judgment is both deceived and deceiveth, according to David that saith, "Omnis homo mendax, Every man is a liar." "Yet am I not ignorant" down to "not omitting any part of the ordinary service that hath been used to be said" (as on page 160). Then. In the which albeit that many things are contained that seem not to have their whole ground of the Scriptures, yet doth Christian charity require that every thing should be construed to the best. As for example, when many things are ascribed to the Virgin Mary beside the testimony of Scripture of which sort be these. First, in the Matyns in the third Lesson these words, "Per te redempti," i, redeemed by Thee make an evident error. For we are only redeemed by Christ's blood, and not by our Lady, either any Saint or angel in heaven. Item in the chapter before Benedictus these words, "Meruisti Christum portare i. thou hast deserved to bear Christ." "Threnosa compassio &c. i. the sorrowful compassion of the mother of God bring us unto heaven." The four chapters in the hours "i In omnibus requiem." "Ab initio" down to "By never so long process of time" (as on page 160). Then. Also in the anthem before "Nunc dimittis" that beginneth "Glorificamus" these words "Salva omnes qui te glorificant i. Save all them that glorify Thee" are prejudicial to Christ for there we make our Lady a saviour. Likewise in "Stella cæli extirpavit, quæ lactavit Dominum, mortis pestem quam plantavit primus parens hominum," i that our Lady hath extirped the mortal pestilence which our first father hath planted, with divers other things applied to the praise of Saints and their merits, which have proceeded of to immoderate affection of some men towards Saints, and therefore ought not to be admitted into any part of our belief, because they seem to derogate the due honour of God not a little and the faith that we should have in him. And though this opinion concerning veneration of Saints doth seem to abrogate and take away some part of the accustomed devotion, as some call it. "And yet the worship of our Lady and the holy saints of heaven" down to "putting our whole faith hope and confidence in Him only" (as on page 160). Then. And in the blood of His only begotten Son Christ which is our chief and special advocate and reconciliator unto God his Father. And as for Saints though we have no commandments of scripture to pray to them, yet since that we have example of scripture that angels may pray for us, I think it no impiety nor diffidence in God's promise either to pray to them or to worship them, so that it be done none otherwise but as to the elect and well beloved servants of God, and not as to gods nor as equal to God, for that were cursed idolatry, but that we should pray to them as petitioners with us and for us, referring all things to the honour and glory of God which heareth and accepteth our just prayers much more favourably, and sooner than any Saint in heaven. "Wherefore in my judgment the Litany" . . . down to "So be it" (as on page 161).

When thou entrest into the church. Oratio ad ingressum templi. Lord by the abundance of Thy mercy I will enter into Thy house . . . Domine in multitudine misericordiæ tuæ . . .

A declaration of the Matyns. For the more evident explanation and understanding of this Primar it is to be noted, that this word Matyns is as much to say as the morning hours, or morning service, and so is called, because the same is and hath been always accustomed to be said and songen in the morning. And forasmuch as the whole process thereof doth specially bring to our remembrance the Nativity and birth of Christ conceived and born of the most inviolate virgin Mary, it is called the Matyns of our Lady. In whose most worthy praise and commendation, many solemn hymns, divine collects, and pleasant anthems are herein written.

The Laudes. This word Laudes is as much to say as praises, and the service following is called so, because it containeth only the mere laudes and praises of Christ and the virgin His mother.

How the saying of Hours first began and why they are so called. The first that ever we find in scripture to have used the worshipping of God at certain set hours of the day was Daniel the prophet, as it appeareth in his vi chapter. And in the new testament in the Acts of the Apostles, the x chapter, we read that Saint Peter the apostle accustomed himself to certain hours of prayer. By which examples, as Saint Cipriane testifieth the catholick church of Christ did first receive and admit such manner of praying. Whereupon the same usual service that we call Pryme and hours was first instituted to be said and songen here in the churches of England according to the custom and use of the diocese, somewhere after the use of Sarum and somewhere after the use of Yorke. And therefore when we read Hora prima, tertia, sexta and nona, that is, the first, the third, the sixth and the ninth hour, even as they make mention of several hours, so were they and may be used at several times of the day, to be said in remembrance of Christ's passion and the compassion of the virgin His mother.

The Evynsonge of our Lady. What is meant by this word Evynsong. Like as the service that we be daily accustomed to say in the morning is called Matyns, even so is the service used to be said or songen toward evening called Evynsonge. And this is the true signification and meaning of the same word, which we call Evynsong of our Lady, because it is specially done in the laud and praising of her.

The Complyn. What is meant by this word Complyn. This word Complyn is no more to say but an accomplishment or fulfilling. And for so much, as of all the services that are daily done in the church, this is the last, therefore is it called Complyn, as who should say, that in the same, all the whole service of the day is fully complete and ended.

The xv prayers of Saint Brygyde. These xv prayers following, called commonly the. xv. oos are set forth in divers Latin prymers, with goodly painted prefaces, promising to the sayers thereof many things both foolish and false, as the deliverance of xv souls out of Purgatory, with other like vanities, yet are the prayers self right good and virtuous, if they be said without any such superstitious trust or blind confidence. And therefore are they called the prayers of S. Brygide, because that holy virgin used daily to say them, as many write, before the image of the Cross, in Saint Paul's church at Rome.

The seven penitential psalms. Why that these vii psalms following are called penitential, and be chiefly noted above other, the common opinion and mind of many writers is and hath been, that the king and prophet David compunct and stricken with hearty repentance . . .

The Letany. The signification of this word Letany. Mamercus bishop of Vienne, what time that a terrible earthquake fell in his province, Leo the first then being bishop of Rome, caused the people to assemble and to go together in a long array, praying and calling upon God, which thing we now call procession . . .

The beginning of the Dirige, and praying for the dead. The making of this service that we call Dirige, some do ascribe to Saint Isidore and some to Saint Gregorie, but whether of them it was forceth not much, for certain it is, that all that is contained therein, the collects except, may as well be applied for the living as for the dead . . . I think it very charitable and to proceed of a good and godly mind, in that we use any worldly obsequies about the dead or do pray for them . . .

The argument of the Commendations. This psalm following according to the number of the Hebrew letters is divided into xxii parts, which are called Octonaries, because every of them containeth eight verses. But why it is called the Commendation of souls I much marvel . . .

The prayer of the prophet Jonas delivered out of the whales belly. Oratio Jone prophetæ de ventre piscis erepti. In my affliction I cried unto the Lord . . . Clamavi de tribulatione mea ad dominum . . . Amen. [1]

The argument of the Psalms of the passion. Forasmuch as in these psalms following diverse prophecies concerning the passion, death and resurrection of our Saviour Christ are contained, therefore are they called Psalms of the passion . . .

The argument of the Saint Hierom's Psalter. Because it is unknown who first gathered all these verses together, that we call Saint Hierom's Psalter, therefore of the beginning and purpose of the service, I can declare nothing for certain . . .

A prayer to St. Hierome. Precatio ad divum Hieronymum. O God the lover of mankind, which by Thine elect servant . . . So be it. Amator humani generis Deus . . . Amen.[2]

A prayer of the church of the faithful for the word of God to be spoken with boldness of heart. Acts the xiiii. Chap. Oratio ecclesiæ fidelium ad verbum Dei cum fiducia loquendum. Actu. xiiii. Lord Thou hast made heaven and earth . . . Domine tu fecisti cœlum et terram . . . Amen.[1]

A prayer of Christ before His passion for His church in this world. Joh. xvii. Chap. Father the hour is come, glorify Thy Son . . . So be it. Pater venit hora, clarifica filium tuum . . .[1]

The prayer of the church for sins. Sapi. the xv. chapter. Oratio ecclesiæ pro peccatis. Sap. xv. Thou our God art gentle and true . . . Tu Deus noster suavis et verus es . . .[1]

The prayer and blessing of Job in his most tribulation and taking away of his goods. Job. ii. chap. Oratio et benedictio Job in maxima sua tribulatione, et bonorum ereptione. Job ii. Job, his head clipped, falling flat on the ground . . . So be it. Job tonso capite corruens in terram . . . Amen.[1]

When we be scourged of God either for our sins or that we may be proved by Him, the prayer of Tobie. the iii. Chap. Thou art just Lord, and all Thy judgments are true . . . Justus es Domine, et omnia judicia tua . . .[1]

Another prayer of Hieremie the prophet. Hie. xvii. Chap. Alia Hieremiæ oratio. Hiere. xvii. Heal me Lord, and I shall be healed . . . Sana me Domine et sanabor . . .[1][2]

---

[1] Præcationes biblicæ. Brit. Mus. 843. c. 6. A.D. 1531; also Prayers of the Bible. Lambeth Archiep. 24. 9. 11. (1). c. A.D. 1534.

[2] Præcationes Erasmi. Brit. Mus. 3224. a. 58. (3). A.D. 1535.

-1537]   HOURS IN ENGLISH AND LATIN.   173

₊ "*The Pystles and Gospels of every Sunday and holy day in the year. Imprinted at London by me Robert Redman dwelling at the sign of the George next to Saynt Dunston's churche,*" *are bound with this book, they are in english only and begin with the first Sunday in Advent. The Holy days are selected from the Sarum missal, and include St Thomas day of Canterbury, as well as his Translation also the Dedication day* [1] *and Saint George.*

c. A.D. 1537, 8°.   English.   No. 131.

₊ *The title is* "*The Primer in english for children after the use of Sarum*". *A summary of all the contents of this book is given. St. Thomas occurs in the Kalender on December 29. and also in the Litany.*

The A. B. C. + A. a. b. c. d. e. f. g. . . . In the name.[2]

The prayer of the Lord. Our Father which art in heaven . . .

The salutation of the angel to the blessed virgin Mary. Hail Mary full of grace . . . fruit of thy womb. So be it.

The Creed or xii articles of the christian faith. I believe in God the Father almighty . . . Amen.

The ten commandments of Almighty God. Thou shalt have none other gods but me . . . Lord into thy hands . . . Thou hast redeemed me . . .

Grace before dinner. The eyes of all things look up and trust in Thee, O Lord . . . Amen. The King of eternal glory . . . So be it. God is charity and he that dwelleth in charity . . . Amen.

Grace after dinner. The God of peace and love . . . So be it. Lord have mercy. Our Father. Lord hear my prayer. And let my cry . . . From the fiery darts of the devil . . . So be it.

Grace before supper. O Lord Jesu Christ without whom nothing is sweet . . . Amen.

Grace after supper. Blessed is God in all His gifts . . . Our help . . . Who hath made . . . Blessed be the name . . . From henceforth . . . Most mighty Lord and merciful Father . . . Amen. God save the church, our King and realm and God have mercy upon all christian souls. Amen.

De profundis clamavi. From the depth I called on Thee, O Lord . . . Lord have mercy. Our Father. Lord give Thy people eternal rest. And everlasting light shine upon them. From the gates of hell. Lord deliver their souls. I trust to see . . . In the land . . . Lord hear my prayer . . . And let my cry . . . Almighty God and most holy Father . . . Amen.

The works of mercy. Refresh the hungry and thirsty both . . .

₊ *Here ends the A. B. C. It is here given in full.*

The Matins. The Prime and hours of our Lady. The third hour. The sixth hour. The ninth hour. The evensong of our Lady. The complin. The

---

[1] See Act for abrogation of certain holidays. A.D. 1536. Wilkins Concilia, ed. 1737. Vol. 3. page 823; also Burnet. Hist. Reform. ed. 1865. Vol. 6. pages 199, 210.

[2] See Henry Bradshaw's Collected papers, page 333, also Burnet. Hist. Reform. ed. 1865 Vol. 6. pages 199, 206, 210. Wilkins Conc., ed. 1737. Vol. 3. page 843.

Hours of the cross and of the compassion of our Lady are attached to Matins and to each succeeding hour.

⁎ *The collects at Lauds are the same as those in No. 124. A.D., 1536, with the following addition.*

Collects at Lauds. Of S. Thomas Archbishop of Canterbury. Anthem. By the blood of Thomas which for Thee . . . ℣. Thou hast him crowned . . . A. And hast set him . . . Let us pray. O God to whose church thy glorious martyr . . . So be it.

After Complin. O blessed Christ these hours canonical . . .

Hail queen mother of mercy our life . . . ℣. Hail Mary full of grace . . . A. Blessed art thou . . . Let us pray. Almighty and eternal God which by the operation of the Holy Ghost . . . So be it.

Of the five corporal joys of our Lady. Rejoice O virgin Christ's mother dear . . . ℣. Thou art blessed . . . A. For the fruit of life . . . Let us pray. O God which with double joy . . . Amen.

Seven psalms penitential.

The Litany.

A.D. 1538, François Regnault, Paris, 8º. English and Latin. No. 133.

⁎ *The title is "Here after followeth the Prymer in english and in latin set out along after the use of Sarum". St. Thomas of Canterbury occurs in the Kalender on January 5, July 7 and December 29, and also in the Litany.*

The preface and the manner to live well (as on page 147).

A.D. 1538, Nicolas Le Roux, Rouen, for François Regnault (Paris), 8º. English. No. 135.

⁎ *The title of this book is "Hereafter followeth the Prymer in english set out along after the use of Sarum". The colophon has "The Primer in english after the use of Salisbury diligently correct . . .". St. Thomas of Canterbury occurs in the Kalender on January 5, July 7, and December 29 and also in the Litany. The prayers, for the most part the psalms, the Litany and other portions of the book are in english, a few prayers for use in church and at mass are in Latin only. Many of the prayers in english as well as the psalms which are in english have latin titles.*

On the reverse of the title-page. God be in my head, And in mine understanding.

A very behoveful teaching and remedy for every man and woman daily to come out of sin and to come soon into the state of health after the doctrine of Master Johan Gerson Chanceler of Parys, and doctor in divinity (as on page 149).

To the relykes in the church. Añ. Corpora sanctorum in pace sepulta sunt . . . ℣. Lætamini in domino . . . ℟. Et gloriamini . . . Oremus. Propitiare nobis Domine famulis tuis . . . Amen. Oratio. Sanctæ Dei genitricis Mariæ semper virginis . . . Amen.

At the elevation of the sacrament. Anima Christi sanctifica me . . . Amen.

Another prayer at the elevation. Ave domine Jesu Christe verbum Patris . . . Amen.

At the elevation of the chalice. Ave vere sanguis Domini nostri . . . Amen.

A prayer to our Lord.   Salve sancte caro Dei, per quam salvi fiunt rei . . .
    Amen.
When thou goest to receive the body of our Lord.   Domine non sum dignus ut
    intres . . . Amen.
When thou hast received.   Vera perceptio corporis et sanguinis . . . Amen.

A.D. 1538, Paris, 8º.   English and Latin.   No. 136.

₊ *The title is " This Primer in english and in latin is newly translated after the Latin text ". St. Thomas of Canterbury occurs in the Kalender on January 5, but neither on July 7 nor December 29. St. Thomas of Canterbury occurs in the Litany. The book has a cut of the anatomical man.*

A.D. 1538 (Nicolas Le Roux), Rouen, 8º.   English and Latin.   No. 138.

₊ *The title is " This Primer in English and in Latin is newly translated after the Latin text ". St. Thomas of Canterbury occurs in the Kalender on January 5, July 7 and December 29, and also in the Litany.*

An order and form of bidding of the beads by the king's commandment.   First.
    Ye shall pray for the whole congregation of Christ's church, and specially
    for this church of England wherein first, I commend to your devout
    prayers the king's most excellent majesty, supreme head immediately
    under God of the spirituality and temporality of the same church, and
    for the good estate of our noble Prince Edward.   Secondly, ye shall pray
    for the clergy, the Lord's temporal and commons of this realm . . .[1]
    Thirdly, ye shall pray for the souls that are departed abiding the mercy
    of almighty God, that it may please him the rather at the contemplation
    of our prayers to grant them the fruition of his presence.
The abrogation of the holy days.   First, that the feast of the dedication of the
    church shall in all places throughout this realm be celebrated and kept
    on the first Sunday of the month of October, for ever and upon none
    other day. . . .[2]
The rule of charity is this.   Do as thou wouldest be done to, for charity holdeth
    all alike . . .
A comparison between faith, hope and charity.   Faith cometh of the word of
    God, hope cometh of faith, and charity springeth of them both . . .

A.D. 1538 (Nicolas le Roux, Rouen), 8º.   English and Latin.   No. 139.

₊ *The title is " This Primer in english and in latin is newly translated after the Latin text ". St. Thomas of Canterbury occurs in the Kalender on January 5, July 7, and December 29 and also in the Litany. The book has a Stansa in english of four lines at the end of each month.*

₊ *" The Pystles and Gospels of every Sunday and holy day in the year. M.D. xxxviii." are bound with this book, they are in english only and are the same as those in No. 128. c. A.D. 1537.*

---

[1] See Wilkins Conc. ed. 1737.   Vol. 3. pages 783, 844.

[2] See Wilkins Conc. ed. 1737.   Vol. 3. page 823.

176   SUMMARY OF CONTENTS.   [1538-

A.D. 1538 (Robert Redman, London), 4º.   English and Latin.   No. 140.

⁎ *The title is "This Primer in english and in latin is newly corrected this present year of our Lord". St. Thomas of Canterbury does not occur either in the Kalender or in the Litany.*[1]

A prayer to Christ our Saviour. Oratio ad Christum salvatorem. Hail heavenly king, father of mercy, our life . . .[2] Salve cælorum, rex pater misericordiæ . . . Almighty eternal God, which by the operation of the Holy Ghost . . . So be it. Omnipotens sempiterne Deus qui gloriosæ virginis et matris Mariæ . . . Amen.

The Prayer of Anna. i. Regum, the second chapter. Oratio Anne. 1. Regum. Capitulo 2. My heart hath rejoiced in the Lord . . . Exultavit cor meum in Domino . . .[3]

⁎ *"The Pystles and Gospels of every Sunday and holy day in the year. Imprinted at London in Fleet Street by me Roberte Redman dwelling at the sign of the George next to Saint Dunston's church," are bound with this book, they are in english only. The Holy days do not include the days of Saint Thomas of Canterbury, they are otherwise the same as those in No. 128. c. A.D. 1537.*

c. A.D. 1539, 8º.   English.   No. 148.

⁎ *All that is known of this book is a single leaf which is either a title-page or a colophon, it has on one side of it "The Primer in english with the A.B.C. for children after the use of Salisbury. Newly imprinted." The other side of the leaf is blank.*[4]

c. A.D. 1540, 8º.   English and Latin.   No. 156.

⁎ *The title-page is wanting. St. Thomas of Canterbury does not occur either in the Kalender or the Litany.*

Certain godly prayers throughout the year commonly called collects.[5]

The first Sunday of Advent. Verse. Shew Thy ways Lord to us . . . And teach us Thy paths. Stir up we beseech Thee Lord Thy power . . . Amen.

The second Sunday. ℣. Out of Syon is the appearance of His beauty. Our God shall come openly. Stir up, O Lord, our hearts . . . Amen.

The third Sunday in Advent. ℣. Remember us Lord . . . And visit us with Thy health . . . Apply Thy ears to our prayers . . . Amen.

The fourth Sunday in Advent. ℣. Fear not, O ye weak hearted. Our God shall come . . . Raise up we beseech Thee Lord thy power . . . Amen.

In the day of the Nativity of Christ. ℣. A child is born to us. A son is given to us. O God which madest the most holy night to wax clear . . . Amen. Grant we beseech Thee almighty God that the new nativity . . . Amen.

---

[1] See Wilkins Conc. ed. 1737. Vol. 3. pages 815, 835, 847.
[2] See John Hollybush, "Exposition upon Salve regina". Bodl. Tanner. 23.
[3] Præcationes biblicæ. Brit. Mus. 843. c. 6. A.D. 1531; also Prayers of the Bible. Lambeth. Archiep. 24. 9. 11. (1). c. A.D. 1534.
[4] See Henry Bradshaw's Collected papers, page 333, also No. 161. c. A.D. 1541. page. 57.
[5] See "Psalter of David in english," Brit. Mus. c. 24. b. 4 (2). St. Paul's Cathedral, 38. D. 41.

The first Sunday after the Nativity of Christ. ℣. The Lord reigneth . . . The Lord hath put on strength . . . Almighty everlasting God guide our doings in Thy pleasure . . . Amen.

On the day of the Epiphany or appearing. ℣. They shall come to Thee . . . And shall worship . . . God the illuminator of all heathen . . . Amen.

The first Sunday after the Epiphany. ℣. The Lord hath shewed forth . . . In the sight of the heathen . . . O Lord favour with the heavenly mercy . . . Amen.

The second Sunday. ℣. All the earth mought worship . . . And sing psalms to Thy name . . . Almighty everlasting God which governest . . . Amen.

The third Sunday. ℣. The Lord reigneth . . . Many isles mought be glad. Almighty and eternal God look mercifully . . . Amen.

The fourth Sunday. ℣. Lord hear my prayer. And let my cry come unto Thee. O God which knowest that we being set . . . Amen.

The fifth Sunday. ℣. Lord hear my prayer. And let my cry come unto Thee. We beseech Thee, O Lord, keep thy family . . . Amen.

The sixth Sunday. ℣. Lord hear my prayer. And let my cry come unto Thee. Save thy people, O God . . . Amen.

The Sunday of Septuagesima. ℣. I will love Thee, O Lord, my strength. The Lord is my sure hold . . . We beseech Thee, O Lord, hear mercifully the prayers of thy people . . . Amen.

The Sunday of Sexagesima. ℣. Rise God, help us. And redeem us . . . O God which seest that we have confidence in no doing of ours . . . Amen.

The Sunday of Quinquagesima. ℣. In the Lord I trust . . . Deliver me in Thy justice. Hear our prayers we beseech Thee Lord favourably . . . Amen.

The second Sunday in Lent. ℣. To the Lord I have lift up my soul . . . My God I trust in Thee . . . O God which seest us to want all strength . . . Amen. O God which suffrest not them that sin to perish . . . Amen.

The third Sunday in Lent. ℣. To Thee I have lift up mine eyes. Which dwellest in the heavens. We beseech Thee almighty God behold the wishes of the humble . . . Amen.

The fourth Sunday in Lent. ℣. Cleanse me Lord . . . From presumptuous faults keep Thy servant. Grant we beseech Thee almighty God that we which be punished . . . Amen.

The fifth Sunday in Lent. ℣. The heavens shew forth . . . And the firmament declareth . . . O God which renewest the world with unspeakable sacraments . . . Amen.

The sixth Sunday. ℣. Lord hold not of Thine help from me. Have a regard to my defence. Almighty everlasting God, which wouldest that our Saviour . . . Amen.

Collects in the Passion week. The first. ℣. Revenge, O God, them that hurt me. Subdue them that oppress me. Grant, we beseech Thee, almighty God that we which fain . . . Amen. ii ℣. Deliver me Lord

... Lord I fly to Thee. Almighty eternal God grant that we may so use the mysteries of the Lord's passion ... Amen. iii ℣. Lord hear my prayer. And let my cry come unto Thee. O God which wouldest that Thy Son should hang on the cross ... Amen. iiii ℣. My flesh verily is meat. My blood verily is drink. God which hast left the remembrance of thy passion ... Amen. v ℣. God spared not his own Son. But for us all delivered Him. Lord Jesu Christ which nailed and hanged for the redemption of mankind ... Amen. vi ℣. The Lord destroying battle. The Lord is His name. O God which teachest us in the books of the testaments ... Amen.

On Easter day. ℣. In Thy resurrection, O Christ. Heaven and earth mought rejoice ... O God which through Thy only-begotten hast opened unto us the way ... Amen. God which brightenest this day with the glory of the Lord's resurrection ... Amen.

The first Sunday after Easter. ℣. Our Easter Christ is offered. Let us fast (feast)[1] in unleavened bread ... O God which always makest Thy church merry and glad with some new birth ... Amen.

The second Sunday after Easter. ℣. O give thanks to the Lord ... Because His mercy ... O God which in the humility of Thy Son diddest lift up the depressed world ... Amen.

The third Sunday after Easter. ℣. Make mirth to the Lord all the earth ... Sing psalms to His name ... O God which shewest the light of Thy truth ... Amen.

The fourth Sunday after Easter. ℣. Sing to the Lord a new song. Because He hath done ... O God which makest the souls of the faithful ... Amen.

The fifth Sunday after Easter. ℣. Declare the voice of mirth. For the Lord hath delivered ... O God from whom all good things proceed ... So be it.

On Ascension day. ℣. All people clap your hands. Make mirth to God ... Grant we beseech Thee almighty God, that we which believe ... O God whose Son ascended mightily into heaven ... Amen.

The Sunday after the Ascension. ℣. The Lord is my light ... Whom shall I fear. Almighty eternal God, grant that we may bear ever a devout mind ... Amen.

On Whytsonday. ℣. The Apostles spake with sundry tongues. The glorious things of God. Grant we beseech Thee almighty God that the brightness of Thy clearness ... Amen.

On Trinity Sunday. ℣. Let us bless the Father ... Let us praise Him and exalt Him for ever. Almighty eternal God which hast given to Thy servants ... So be it.

The Sunday after Trinity. ℣. Lord in Thy mercy have I trusted. And mine heart hath rejoyced ... O God the strength of hopers, come favourably to our callings ... Amen.

[1] Psalter of David. Brit. Mus. C. 25. b. 4. (2).

The second Sunday after Trinity. ℣. I will love Thee, O God, my strength. The Lord is my sure hold . . . O Lord let us have perpetual love and also fear of Thy holy name . . . Amen.

The third Sunday after Trinity. ℣. Look towards me and have mercy on me. Because I am alone and poor. O God the defender of them that trust in Thee . . . Amen.

The fourth Sunday after Trinity. ℣. Help us God, our saving health. And for the honour of Thy name . . . Grant we beseech Thee that both the course of this world . . . Amen.

The v Sunday after Trinity. ℣. O God our defender behold. And look upon Thy servants. O God which hast prepared invisible things to them that love Thee . . . Amen.

The vi Sunday after Trinity. ℣. The Lord is the strength of His people. And the defender of the health of His church. O God of powers, whose are all things that be good . . . Amen.

The vii Sunday after Trinity. ℣. O all ye heathen, clap your hands. Make mirth to the Lord . . . O God whose providence in disposition of things . . . Amen.

The viii Sunday after Trinity. ℣. O God we have received Thy mercy. In the midst of Thy temple. Give us alway, O Lord, for Thy mercy and spirit to think and to do . . . Amen.

The ix Sunday after Trinity. ℣. Behold, God helpeth me. And God is the receiver of my soul. O Lord let the ears of Thy mercy be open to Thine humble petitioners . . . Amen.

The x Sunday after Trinity. ℣. When I cried to the Lord. He heard my voice. O God which declarest Thy power chiefly in sparing and having mercy . . . Amen.

The xi Sunday after Trinity. ℣. O Lord, I have cried to Thee my God . . . Depart not from me. Almighty everlasting God, which in the abundance of Thy goodness . . . Amen.

The xii Sunday after Trinity. ℣. I will bless the Lord always. His praise shall be always . . . Almighty and merciful God of whose gift it becometh . . . Amen.

The xiii Sunday after Trinity. ℣. God, the God of my health . . . In the day have I cried . . . Almighty everlasting God, give to us increase of faith . . . Amen.

The xiiii Sunday after Trinity. ℣. Lord, Thou art my Saviour. From generation to generation. Lord, we beseech Thee, keep Thy church with perpetual mercy . . . Amen.

The xv Sunday after Trinity. ℣. It is a good thing to praise the Lord. And to sing to Thy name . . . O Lord, let Thy continual mercy cleanse and defend Thy church . . . Amen.

The xvi Sunday after Trinity. ℣. Lord look to my help. Let them be confounded that seek my soul. We beseech Thee Lord, let Thy grace prevent . . . Amen.

The xvii Sunday after Trinity Sunday. ℣. Thou art just, O Lord. And Thy judgment is right. Grant we beseech Thee, Lord, to Thy people . . . Amen.

The xviii Sunday after Trinity Sunday. ℣. Let my prayer be directed. As incense in Thy sight. Let the operation of Thy mercy, O Lord, guide our hearts . . . Amen.

The xix Sunday after Trinity. ℣. If I shall walk in the middle of the shadow of death. I will fear no evil. Almighty and merciful God having pity on us . . . Amen.

The xx Sunday after Trinity Sunday. ℣. The eyes of all look to the Lord. And Thou givest to them meat in their time. O Lord, we beseech Thee, being pacified, grant pardon and peace . . . Amen.

The xxi Sunday after Trinity Sunday. ℣. My soul in Thy saving health. And in Thy word hath greatly trusted. Keep Thy family with continual mercy . . . Amen.

The xxii Sunday after Trinity Sunday. ℣. Shew to us Lord Thy mercy. And give us Thy saving health. O God our succour and strength, be present at the godly prayers of Thy church . . . Amen.

The xxiii Sunday after Trinity Sunday. ℣. We will praise God all the day long. And we will worship His name . . . Raise up we beseech Thee, Lord, the wills of Thy faithful . . . Amen.

The xxiiii Sunday after Trinity. ℣. O Lord, if Thou wilt observe iniquities. Who shall be able to abide them. Assoyle, we beseech Thee, the faults of Thy people . . . Amen.

The xxv Sunday after Trinity. ℣. Lord, Thou hast blessed Thy land. Thou hast turned away the captivity of Jacob. Almighty everlasting God, which through Thy grace healest both bodies and souls . . . Amen.

On Midsummer Day. ℣. There was a man sent from God. Whose name was John. Grant, we beseech Thee almighty God, that the family may walk in the way of health . . . Amen.

Upon the day of Peter and Paul. ℣. Into all the earth went forth their sound. And their words into all the ends of the earth. O God which hast consecrated Thy church in the faith of Peter thine Apostle . . . Amen.

On Mary Magdalene's day. ℣. Many sins were forgiven her. For she loved much. Grant to us most merciful God that as Mary Magdalene . . . Amen.

On Saint Laurence day. ℣. Thou hast crowned Him with glory and honour. And hast set Him over thy works of Thy hands. Grant to us almighty God that we may quench the flames of our vices . . . Amen.

On the assumption of Mary. ℣. Hail Mary full of grace, the Lord &c. Blessed be thou amongst women &c. O Lord let the venerable feast of blessed Mary . . . Amen.

Of Saint Bartholomew. ℣. Thy friends are very honourable O God. The dominion of them is greatly strengthened. Almighty everlasting God which hast granted a generable (venerable)[1] and holy mirth . . . Amen.

[1] Psalter of David. Brit. Mus. C. 25. b. 4. (2

On the nativity of Mary. ℣ Hail Mary full of grace, the Lord &c. Blessed art thou among women. Grant Lord to Thy servants the gift of heavenly grace . . . Amen.
On Saint Michael's day. ℣. Bless the Lord all ye His angels. Mighty in strength which do His commandment. O God which with a marvellous order dispensest . . . So be it.
On Saint Luke's day. ℣. Into all the earth is their voice gone. And their words unto the ends of the earth. Grant we beseech Thee almighty God, that as thy people devoutly observeth . . . Amen.
On Simon and Jude's day. ℣. Thou shalt make them princes . . . They shall be mindful . . . O God which hast granted us to come to Thy knowledge . . . Amen.
On Alhalowen day. ℣. Let the just rejoice in the sight of God. And be delighted in mirth. Almighty everlasting God, which hast granted us godly to praise . . . Amen.
On all Souls day. ℣. The souls of the righteous be in the hand of God. And the torment of malice shall not touch them. O God which hast taught us by the mouth of holy Paul . . . Amen.
On Saint Stephen's day. ℣. They waited for the soul of the just. And condemned innocent blood. Grant we beseech Thee Lord, that we may follow that that we greatly esteem . . . Amen.
On Saint John the Evangelist day. ℣. God fed him with the bread of life . . . And gave him to drink the water of healthful wisdom. Varnish and brighten the church abundantly we beseech Thee . . . Amen.
On Childermas Day. ℣. The souls of the just be in the hands of God. And the punishment of evil shall not come nigh them. O God whose praise this day innocent martyrs not in speaking but in dying confessed . . . Amen.
On the Conversion of Paul. ℣. Into all the earth is their voice gone. And their words unto the ends of the earth. O God which hast taught the whole world by the preaching of blessed Paul . . . Amen.
On the day of the Purification. ℣. Great is the Lord and greatly to be praised. In the city of our God, in His holy hill. Almighty God we humbly beseech Thy majesty, that as Thy only begotten Son . . . Amen.
On the Annunciation. ℣. Hail Mary full of grace &c. O God which wouldest that Thy word should receive flesh . . . Amen.
On Saint Mark's day. ℣. Thou shalt make them princes. And they shall be mindful of Thy name, O Lord. O God which hast extolled Mark thine evangelist . . . Amen.
On Philippe and Jacobes day. ℣. Rejoice in the Lord O ye just. Praising becometh the right persons. O God which makest us merry with the yearly solemnity . . . Amen.
On the Apostles. ℣. The heavens shew forth the glory of God. And the firmament . . . Grant to us we beseech Thee eternal God to rejoice . . . Amen.

Of Martyrs. ℣. They seemed in the sight of the unwise to die. But they are in peace. Grant we beseech Thee almighty God, that we which have known . . . Amen.

Of Confessors. ℣. The Lord hath guided the just . . . And hath shewed to him . . . Hear, O Lord, our prayers which we bring to Thee . . . Amen.

Of Virgins. ℣. With Thy beauty . . . Go forth prosperously . . . Almighty God which choosest the weak things . . . Amen.

Prayers sundry things. For the forgiveness of sins. ℣. From the deep I have cried . . . Lord hear my prayers . . . Hear we beseech Thee, Lord, the prayers of the humble . . . Amen. Spare, O Lord, spare our sins . . . Amen.

For the health of our neighbour. ℣. Thou art just, O God . . . Do with Thy servant according to Thy mercy . . . Almighty God, have mercy on Thy servant . . . Amen.

For peace. ℣. Let peace be in Thy strength. And abundance in Thy towers. O God of whom holy desires . . . Amen.

For to acknowledge the truth. ℣. To Thee I have lift up mine eyes. Which dwellest in heaven. We beseech Thee Lord, pour into Thy servants the spirit of truth . . . Amen.

Against adversities. ℣. Redeem us, O God of Israel. From all our iniquities. O God which despisest not the groaning . . . Amen.

Against sudden death. ℣. Thou which rulest Israel . . . Which leddest Joseph . . . Almighty and merciful God behold mercifully Thy people . . . Amen.

For prisoners. ℣. Lord hear my prayer . . . And let my cry . . . O God which diddest loose from bonds . . . Amen.

For them which be a dying. ℣. According to the multitude . . . Do away our iniquities. Almighty God the Saviour of souls . . . Amen.

For our enemies. ℣. Lord hear my prayer. And let my cry . . . O God the lover and keeper of peace . . . Amen.

For charity. ℣. Let God arise . . . And they that hate Him . . . O God which makest all things to profit them . . . Amen.

For chastity. ℣. Make a clean heart in us . . . And renew a right spirit . . . Burn our reins and thoughts . . . Amen.

For humility. ℣. Lord hear my prayer. And let my cry . . . O God which resistest the proud . . . Amen.

Against the adversities of the church. God we beseech Thee being pacified . . . Amen. We beseech Thee Lord admit, being pacified, our prayers . . . Amen.

Divers godly and necessary prayers to be said most specially at the hour of death. O Lord Jesu, which art the only health of all men living . . . Amen.

A prayer and thanksgiving to the heavenly Father for all His benefits shewed to us. O most highest almighty and eternal God whose glory replenisheth heaven . . . Amen.

A prayer for meekness and chastity. Ecclesiastici. xxiii. O Lord thou father and God of my life . . . Amen.[1]

For a sweet and ill (still) heart. Psalmus xli. This favour, this grace, O Lord, shew me that all my life long . . . Amen.[2]

Another prayer. I confess and re-knowledge here before Thee, O heavenly Father . . . Amen.

c. A.D. 1540, John Mayler, London, 8°. English and Latin. No. 158.

₊ *The title has " The primer in english and latin set out at length with the exposition of Miserere and In te domine speravi and with the Epistles and Gospels throughout all the whole year . . .". St. Thomas of Canterbury does not occur either in the Kalender or the Litany. The Bidding of the beads has the words " Queen Anne". (Henry the eighth married Anne of Cleves January 6, 1540, and was divorced on July 7 in the same year.) The book corresponds in some particulars with Bishop Hilsey's Manual of prayers, No. 148, A.D. 1539.*

An order and form of bidding of the beads by the king's commandment. This is the same as that in No. 138. A.D. 1538, except that the words "and Queen Anne his wife and for the prosperity of the noble Prince Edward his son"[3] occur after the word "church".

The gospel of St. Matthew mentioning the incarnation of Jesus Christ.[4] The birth of Christ was on this wise . . . Matt. i. Christi autem generatio . . .

A lesson of the gospel of St. John declaring the passion of our Master, Christ. John xviii. Passio domini nostri Jesu Christi secundum Johannem. When Jesus had spoken these words [4] (as on page 162).

A lesson of the gospel of St. Luke mentioning the resurrection of Christ.[4] Luke xxiii. But upon one of the Sabbaths . . . Caput xxiii. Una autem sabbati . . .

A lesson of the gospel of St. Mark mentioning the ascension of Christ.[4] Mark xvi. At the last as the eleven . . . Secundum Marcum Caput xvi. Discipulis autem recumbentibus . . .

₊ *In the Hours: " Laud be to the Lord, King of eternal glory " is said between Septuagesima and Easter, for, " Praise ye the Lord," according to the use of Sarum, in those Hours which are in english and latin, or english; but Psalm li is not said at Matins instead of " Te Deum". At the end of Compline: " A memory of the compassion of our Lady," and, " A memory of our Lady," are the same as in Bishop Hilsey's Manual No. 148, A.D. 1539, except the rhythm " At complin time this mother of mercy," which is from Sarum use of " Compline of the compassion of our Lady " and occurs in this book in " A memory of the compassion of our Lady ".*

The third part of this primer treating of works.[4] Works are divers, some right good and necessary . . .

₊ *" The Pystles and Gospels of the Sundays and festival holy-days, newly corrected and amended " which are contained in this book are in english only, and begin with New Year's day. The Holy-days do not include the days of Saint Thomas of Canterbury, and are fewer than those in No. 140, A.D. 1538.[5]*

---

[1] Præcationes e sacris biblicis. Brit. Mus. 1410. a. 30. (1). A.D. 1528; also, Præcationes biblicæ. Brit. Mus. 843. c. 6. A.D. 1531; also, Prayers of the Bible. Lambeth. Archiep. 24. 11. (1). c. A.D. 1534.

[2] Præcationes Christianæ. Brit. Mus. 843. b. 6. A.D. 1536; also, Epitome of the Psalms, R Taverner. A.D. 1539. Brit. Mus. 1219. a. 34.

[3] See Wilkins Conc. ed. 1737. Vol. 3. page 783.

[4] See Bishop Hilsey's manual of prayers. A.D. 1539. Brit. Mus. c. 12. e. 13.

[5] See Domestic State Papers. Vol. xiii. Pt. 1. No. 1150.

184   SUMMARY OF CONTENTS.   [1541-

A.D. 1541, John Mayler, London, 8°. English and Latin. No. 160.

*** *The title has "The Primer in english and latin . . . set out at length with many goodly prayers and with the exposition of Miserere and In te domine speravi with the Epistles and Gospels throughout the whole year". St. Thomas of Canterbury does not occur either in the Kalender or in the Litany.*

The King's commandment. The King's highness greatly tendering the wealth of this realm hath suffered heretofore the Pater noster, Ave, Creed and the Ten Commandments of God to be had in the english tongue. But his grace perceiving now the great diversity of the translations hath willed them all to be taken up and instead of them hath caused an uniform translation of the said Pater Noster, Ave, Creed and x Commandments to be set forth, as hereafter followeth, willing all his loving subjects to learn and use the same, and straightly commandeth every Person, Vicar and Curate to read and teach the same to their parishioners. And that no man imprint, or set forth any other translation upon pain at his high displeasure.

A devout prayer for the grace and mercy of God. Almighty God, King and Lord of glory eternal, which art so full of goodness and mercy . . . So be it.

*** "*The Pystles and Gospels of the Sundays and festival holy-days, newly corrected and amended. Imprynted in Botulph Lane at the sygne of the whyt beare by me Jhon Mayler*" *which are contained in this book, are in english only and begin with New Years Day. The Holy-days do not include the days of St. Thomas of Canterbury, and are fewer than those in No.* 158. *c. A.D.* 1540.[1]

c. A.D. 1541, Robert Toy, London, 8°. English and Latin. No. 162.

*** *The title is "A Prymar of Salisbury use set out a long in english and latin and a prayer for every Sunday and Holy Day in the year . . .". St. Thomas of Canterbury does not occur either in the Kalender or the Litany.*

A prayer at thy uprising. In the morning at thy uprising. Into this day do I enter all things for to do . . . Pater noster. Credo.

A prayer when thou goest to bed. I lay me down to rest in the name . . . Pater noster. Credo. I thank Thee my heavenly Father by Thy dearly beloved Son . . .

A.D. 1542, William Bonham, London, 4°. English and Latin. No. 166.

*** *The title is, "The Prymer in english and latin with the Epistles and Gospels of every Sunday and Holy Day in the year, and also the exposition upon Miserere mei Deus with many other prayers".*

A prayer to Christ. Oratio ad Christum. Hail Jesu Christ, King of mercy our life[2] . . . Salve rex Jesu Christe, rex misericordiæ . . . ℣. In all our trouble . . . ℣. In omnibus tribulationibus . . . A. O Jesu our health . . . ℟. Jesu Christe succurre nobis. The prayer. O Jesu Christ, the Son of God, our redeemer which dejectedst . . . So be it. Oratio. Domine Jesu Christe, fili Dei ac redemptor noster, qui temetipsum . . . Amen.

---

[1] See Wilkins. Conc. ed. 1787. Vol. 3. page 859.
[2] See note. page 176 John Hollybush, Exposition upon Salve regina. Bodl. Tanner. 23.

Goodly and necessary prayers to be said most specially at the hour of death. Piæ ac necessariæ precationes dicendæ præcipue in hora mortis. O domine Jesu, qui es sola salus . . . O Lord Jesu which art the only health . . . In manus tuas . . . That is to say. O Lord into Thy hands . . . Domine Jesu accipe spiritum meum. Lord Jesu receive my soul unto thee. So be it.

A prayer for the reader, expressing after what sort scripture should be read. O most merciful and ever good, of whose incomparable goodness we receive all things necessary . . . Amen. Then. God save the king.

⁎ *The Epistles and Gospels which are contained in this book are in english only and are the same as those in No. 140, A.D. 1538 except that the Holy-days do not include, " The Visitation of our Lady ".*

A.D. 1542, Thomas Petyt, London, 8°. English and Latin. No. 167.

⁎ *The title has " The Prymer in english and latin, after the use of Sarum set out at length with many goodly prayers with the Epistles and Gospels throughout the whole year. Cum privilegio ad imprimendum solum." St. Thomas of Canterbury does not occur in the Kalender, but is found in the Litany.*

The ten commandments. Thou shalt have none other Gods but me . . .

A general confession for all times in the year. O my most merciful Father, the father of all mercies . . . Amen. Then say the li Psalm, called Miserere mei Deus.

⁎ *The Epistles and Gospels which are contained in this book are in english only and begin with the First Sunday in Advent. The Holy days do not include the days of Saint Thomas of Canterbury, and are fewer than those in No. 160, c. A.D. 1541.*

A.D. 1542, Robert Toy, London, 4°. English and Latin. No. 168.

⁎ *The title has " The Prymer in english and latin with the Epistles and Gospels of every Sunday and Holy Day in the year, and also the exposition upon Miserere mei Deus with many other prayers . . .".*

A prayer at the receiving of the sacrament. Oratio ad perceptionem sacramenti. What tongue or what mind may worthily . . . So be it. Quæ lingua aut qui mens . . . Amen.

A.D. 1543, Thomas Petyt, London, 4°. English and Latin. No. 169.

⁎ *The title has " The Prymer in English and Latin after the use of Sarum set out at length with many goodly prayers. With the exposition upon the Psalm called Miserere mei Deus, and in te Domine speravi, with the Epistles and Gospels on every Sunday and Holy day in the year . . ." St. Thomas of Canterbury does not occur in the Kalender, but is found in the Litany.*

⁎ *The Epistles and Gospels which are contained in this book are in english only and are the same as those in No. 166, A.D. 1542.*

186   SUMMARY OF CONTENTS.   [1544-

A.D. 1544, Thomas Petyt, London, 8º.   English and Latin.   No. 172.

₊ *The title page and Kalender are wanting. St. Thomas of Canterbury occurs in the Litany.*

₊ *The first edition of the Horæ which is known to have been printed in the reign of Queen Mary is in latin No. 208. A.D. 1554 and has this title, " This prymer of Salisbury use is set out along without any searching with many prayers and goodly pictures . . .". St. Thomas of Canterbury occurs in the Kalender on January 5, July 7, and December 29 and also in the Litany.*

A.D. 1555, June 4, John Wayland, London, 4º.   English and Latin.
No. 207.[1]

₊ *The title has "An uniform and Catholick Primer in latin and english with many godly and devout prayers newly set forth by certain of the clergy with the assent of the most reverend father in God the Lord Cardinal Pole his grace . . . ". St. Thomas of Canterbury occurs in this and in all the editions of the Horæ in Queen Mary's reign both in the Kalender on January 5, July 7, and December 29 as well as in the Litany.*

A right godly rule how all faithful christians ought to occupy and exercise themselves in their daily prayers. Luke xxii. Matthew vi.

Christ teacheth us in his gospel saying, pray that ye fall not into temptation. How a man shall behave himself in the morning, when he riseth. When thou risest in the morning . . . In manus tuas Domine commendo spiritum meum . . . In nomine. For Sunday in the morning. Holy Trinity be helping unto me . . . Amen. For Monday. A morning prayer. O most loving and gentle God . . . Amen. For Tuesday. A morning prayer. Seeing that Thou, O heavenly Father, art that one and alone almighty God . . . Amen. For Wednesday. A morning prayer. O Lord Jesus Christ which art the bright sun of the world . . . Amen.[2] For Thursday. A morning prayer. O Lord Jesus Christ, to whom and before whom all things . . . Amen. For Friday. A morning prayer. O merciful Lord God and heavenly Father, I render most high lauds . . . Amen. For Saturday. A morning prayer. O heavenly Father, which like a diligent watchman . . . Amen. A general morning prayer. O almighty God, our heavenly Father, I confess and knowledge that I am a miserable sinner . . . Our Father.

After that thou hast prayed on this manner, seeing that we be all sinners, it shall be expedient if thou hast convenient leisure thereunto, to confess thyself on this manner, remembering the publican.

A general confession of sins unto God daily to be said. O most merciful Lord God, and most tender and dear father . . . Amen.[3]

Prayers of the passion of our Saviour Christ. Blessed be the Father the Son . . . Let us praise Him . . . Almighty God our heavenly Father Thy mercy and goodness is infinite . . . Almighty God our heavenly Father we beseech Thy

---

[1] See Wilkins Conc. ed. 1737. Vol. 4. pages 105-115, and 145, 169.
[2] Præcationes Erasmi. Diluculo ad Christum. A.D. 1535. Brit. Mus. 3224. a. 58. (3).
[3] Epitome of the Psalms. R. Taverner. A.D. 1539. Brit. Mus. 1219. a. 34.

gracious goodness . . . Amen. Our Saviour and redeemer Jesu Christ which in Thy last supper with Thy apostles diddest consecrate . . . Amen. Almighty God our heavenly Father which suffered'st Peter Thy apostle . . . Amen. Our blessed Saviour Jesus Christ which in that great heaviness of Thy soul . . . Amen. Almighty God, eternal Father, we do remember that in the condemnation . . . Amen.

At Lauds. The collects. Of St. Thomas Archbishop of Canterbury. De S. Thoma archiepiscopo Cantuariensi. Añ. We pray Thee through St. Thomas blood . . . ℣. O Lord Thou crownedst him . . . ℟. And over Thy handy works hast made him governor. Let us pray. O God for whose church sake Thomas . . . Amen. Oremus. Deus pro cujus ecclesia . . . Amen.

₊ *The following prayers down to " A godly prayer to desire" . . . are in english only.*

Godly prayers. Prayer called Ave rex. Hail heavenly King, father of mercy . . . ℣. In all our troubles . . . ℟. O Jesu our health . . . Let us pray. O Jesu Christ the Son of God our redeemer which dejectedst . . . Amen.

Prayer against evil thoughts. O pitiful Lord God alway showing Thy mercy upon me . . . Amen.

Another prayer. Omnipotent and merciful God the Father eternal which dost not despise . . . Amen.

Devout prayers to our Saviour Jesus Christ. Jesu have mercy on me, and forgive me the great offences . . . Amen. The holy Trinity one very God have mercy on me. Amen.

For thoughts say this prayer. Jesu the Son of God, and maker of all things, help me now . . .

For speech say thus. Jesu the Son of God, which kept silence before the Judge hold my tongue . . .

For works say thus. Jesu the Son of God, which was bounden, govern my members . . .

For keeping of the sight say thus. O Lord Jesu Christ, I commend my sight both inward and outward . . .

For hearing say thus. O Lord Jesu Christ, I commend my hearing . . .

For the mouth and speech say thus. O good Lord Jesu Christ, I pray Thee to open my mouth . . .

For the hands say thus. O Lord Jesu Christ, I commend and betake my hands to Thy holiness . . .

For the heart say thus. O Lord Jesu Christ, I commend my heart to Thy love . . .

If you will salute Jesu Christ, our redeemer say thus. I salute Thee Saviour of the world, word and wisdom of the Father . . . Amen.

A devout prayer to our Lord Jesus Christ. O glorious Jesu, O meekest Jesu, O most sweet Jesu . . . Amen.

A devout prayer to our Lord Jesus Christ. O my sovereign Lord Jesu the very Son of almighty God . . .

188   SUMMARY OF CONTENTS.   [1555-

Another prayer. O Lord God almighty our heavenly Father, and most merciful Lord, Thou art my life . . . Amen.
A prayer for trust in God. The beginning of the fall of man was trust in himself . . . Amen.
The prayer of any captive according to the form of David, when he was hid in the cave. Psal. cxxxxii. With my voice I cry to Thee, afore Thee I open my lamentation . . . Amen.[1] [2]
A prayer for patience in trouble. Psal. lx. How hast Thou, O Lord, humbled and plucked me down . . . Amen.[1] [3]
The oration of Job, in his most grievous adversity and loss of goods. Job i. Naked I came out of my mother's womb, and naked shall I return again . . .[2]
In great trouble of conscience. Psalm cxxxxiii. Lord hear my prayer, receive my supplication . . .[1] [3]
A prayer in adversity. O Lord God, without whose will and pleasure a sparrow doth not fall to the ground . . . Amen.
A prayer in prosperity. I give thanks unto Thee, O God almighty, which not only hast endued me . . . Amen.
The prayer of Manasses king of Juda. ii. Paralipo. xxxvi. O Lord almighty, God of our fathers Abraham, Isaac and Jacob . . .[2]
A prayer of Jeremie. Jerem. xvii. Heal me, O Lord, and I shall be whole . . . Amen.[4]
A prayer of Jeremy. Jerem. 31. O Lord Thou hast chastened me, and Thy chastening have I received as an untamed calf . . .[1] [2]
The prayer of Jesus the son of Sirack in necessity, and for wisdom. Eccle. the last Chapter. I thank Thee, O Lord and King, and praise Thee . . . Amen.[2] [5]
The comfort of all troubles and diseases is to pray to our Lord Jesu Christ. Most merciful Lord Jesus Christ, which was sent from the most highest tower . . . Amen. O great and marvellous Lord, Adonai, which diddest give health . . . Amen. Laud be to God.
A fruitful meditation not to be said with the mouth lightly; but to be cried with heart and mind oft and mightily. O most excellent goodness, withdraw not Thy mercy, O most mighty Maker . . . Amen.
A goodly devout prayer. Grant me merciful Lord God, to desire fervently . . . Amen.
A godly prayer to desire the life to come. This my body is the very dark and filthy prison of my soul . . . Amen.
An intercession and prayer unto our Saviour Jesu Christ. O most merciful Jesu my sweet Saviour and most gracious Lord God . . . Amen. Pater

[1] Epitome of the Psalms, R. Taverner, Brit. Mus. 1219. a. 34. A.D. 1539.
[2] Præcationes biblicæ. Brit. Mus. 843. c. 6. A.D. 1531; also, Prayers of the Bible. Lambeth Archiep. 24. 9. 11. (1). c. A.D. 1534.
[3] Præcationes Christianæ. Brit. Mus. 843. b. 6. A.D. 1536.
[4] Præcationes Erasmi. Brit. Mus. 3224. a. 58. A.D. 1535.
  Præcationes e sacris biblicis. Brit. Mus. 1410. a. 30. A.D. 1528.

noster. Ave. Credo. Jesus Nazarenus rex Judæorum. Titulus triumphalis defendat nos . . . Amen. Sancte Deus, sancte fortis . . . We worship Thee Christ . . . For Thou redeemest . . . Lord Jesu Christ God's Son of heaven set Thy passion . . . Amen. The joyful passion of our Lord . . . Amen. Deus propitius esto mihi peccatori . . . Sancta Maria, mater Dei. Ora pro nobis . . . Amen.

Another prayer unto our Saviour Jesu Christ, called Conditor cœli. O maker of heaven and earth, King of kings . . . Amen.

Another prayer called. O bone Jesu. O bountiful Jesu, O sweet Jesu, O Jesu the Son of the pure virgin Mary . . . Amen.

Another prayer called, O rex gloriose. O glorious King which amongst thy saints . . . Amen.

And ye be sick or in tribulation, say thus. Lord God, which dost punish and scourge Thy people . . . Amen.

Five godly necessary prayers, to be said most specially at the hour of death. O Lord Jesu Christ which art the health of all men living . . . Amen.

The prayer of Solomon for to obtain wisdom. Thou hast made Lord with Thy servant David . . .[1][3]

A prayer for obtaining of wisdom. Sapi. ix. God of our fathers, and Lord of mercy . . . Amen.[1][4]

A prayer for a competent living. Two things Lord, I demand, that Thou wilt not deny me . . .[1]

A preparation to meditation and prayer. Good Lord God, and sweet Saviour Jesu Christ . . . Amen.

A devout prayer to our Lord God. O Lord which hast vouchsafed of Thy unspeakable goodness . . . Amen.

A prayer that we may have the fear of God before our eyes in all our doings. O almighty and everlasting God, thy holy word teacheth us . . . Amen.

A prayer against the enemies of Christ's truth. Psal. cxxxix. Deliver me, O Lord, from the ungodly and stiffnecked persons . . . Amen.[2]

A prayer to keep the tongue, and to eschew the infection of the world. Psal. cxl. To Thee, I cry, O Lord, hear me speedily . . . Amen.[1][2]

A prayer of the church against sins. Sapien. xv. Thou, O our God art sweet, long-suffering and true . . .[1]

In the wars, the prayer of king Asa. ii. Parali. viii. Lord it is all one with Thee, to help them that have need . . . Amen.[1]

A prayer for keeping of a good name. That wise man, which was privy of Thy secrets, O heavenly Father . . . Amen.[2]

A prayer against worldly carefulness. O most dear and tender Father, our defender and nourisher . . . Amen.

---

[1] Præcationes biblicæ. Brit. Mus. 848. c. 6. A.D. 1531; also, Prayers of the Bible. Lambeth Archiep. 24. 9. 11. (1). c. A.D. 1534.
[2] Epitome of the Psalms, R. Taverner. Brit. Mus. 1219. a. 34. A.D. 1539.
[3] Præcationes Erasmi. Brit. Mus. 3224. a. 58. A.D. 1535.
[4] Præcationes e sacris biblicis. Brit. Mus. 1410. a. 30. A.D. 1528.

A prayer against the devil. Jesu Christ, our Lord, which by the mouth of Thy holy Apostle Saint Peter diddest say . . . Amen.

A thanksgiving unto God for all his benefits. We most heartily thank Thee, O Lord God, our heavenly Father for thy manifold and inestimable benefits . . . Amen.

A devout prayer to be daily said. O almighty and eternal God which vouch safest that we as it were heavenly children . . . Amen.

Another prayer to our Lord God. O heavenly Father, God almighty, I pray and beseech Thy mercy . . . Amen.

A devout prayer. Lord, hearken to my words, consider the thought of my heart . . . Amen.

A prayer of Esay in the lxiii. and the lxiiii. chap. Lord look down from heaven, and behold from thy holy habitation . . . Amen.[1]

Before the receiving of the Sacrament say thus. Lord, although I be not worthy to receive Thee . . . Amen.

After the receiving of the Sacrament say thus. I thank Thee good Lord of Thine infinite goodness . . . Amen.

A devout prayer. O my Lord Jesu, with all my mind . . . Amen.

A prayer and thanksgiving to the heavenly father for all his benefits shewed unto us. O most highest almighty and eternal God whose glory replenisheth . . . Amen.

The form of confession. First I knowledge myself guilty unto almighty God (as on page 188).

The copy of the Queen's Majesty's letters patents.

Mary by the grace of God, Queen of England, France and Ireland, &c. To all printers of books, and to all other our officers, ministers and subjects, these our letters patents hearing or seeing, greeting. Know ye . . . that we . . . have given . . . full power license and authority and privilege unto our well-beloved subject John Wayland, Citizen and Scrivener of London. That he and his assignes only . . . shall from henceforth have authority and liberty to print all and every such usual Primers or Manual of prayers . . . which by us our heirs, successors or by our clergy by our assent shall be authorised set forth and devised for to be used of all our loving subjects . . . during the full time and term of vii years next ensuing the date of these letters patents . . . Witness our self at Westminster the xxiiii. day of October in the first year of our reign. God save the King and Queen.

„ "*The Pystels and Gospels of every Sonday and holy Daye in the yere. Venales habentur Rothomagi in officina Roberti Valentini bibliopole illius civitatis prope templum beate Marie virginis. M.D.L.V. Imprynted at Rouen by Jhon Prest for Roberte Valentin dwellynge be our Lady churche.*" *These Epistles and Gospels are bound with No. 207, they are in english only and are the same as No. 128. c. A.D. 1537 except that the* "*Translation of St. Thomas of Canterbury*" *is omitted.*

[1] Præcationes biblicæ. Brit. Mus. 843. c. 6. A.D. 1531; also, Præcationes e sacris biblicis. Brit. Mus. 1410. a. 30. A.D. 1528; also, Prayers of the Bible. Lambeth Archiep. 24. 9. 11. (1). c. A.D. 1534.

1555, October 1, Robert Caly, London, 8º. English and Latin. No. 209.

₊ *The title has "The Primer in english and latin, after Salisburie use, set out at length with many prayers and goodly pictures, newly imprinted this present year* 1555 . . .".

A.D. 1555, John Wayland, London, 4º. English. No. 211.

₊ *The title has, "The Primer in english after the use of Sarum, with many godly and devout prayers . . . Whereunto is added a plain and godly treatise concerning the Mass and the blessed Sacrament of the altar for the instruction of the unlearned and simple people . . ."*

A prayer to all Saints. O all ye blessed Saints of God and blessed Spirits angelical . . . Amen.

A plain and godly treatise concerning the Mass and the blessed Sacrament of the Altar, for the instruction of the simple and unlearned people.

A.D. 1555, John Wayland, London, 4º. English and Latin. No. 213.

A prayer to the holy and blessed Trinity. Oratio ad sanctam Trinitatem. To the holy and indivisible Trinity . . . Amen. Sanctæ et individuæ Trinitati . . . Amen. Blessed be the sweet name of our Lord Jesu Christ . . . Benedictum sit dulce nomen domini nostri Jesu Christi . . . Amen.

A prayer to our Lady and Saint John the Evangelist. Oratio ad virginem Mariam et ad sanctum Johannem evangelistam. O undefiled and blessed for ever . . . Amen. O intemerata et in æternum benedicta . . . Amen. Holy Mary, mother of God, blessed Virgin for ever . . . Amen. Sancta Maria, Dei genitrix, semperque Virgo benedicta . . . Amen.

Of the most holy Trinity. De sanctissima Trinitate. O holy Trinity, one God, have mercy upon us, O blessed and glorious Trinity . . . Sancta Trinitas unus Deus : miserere nobis. O beata et gloriosa Trinitas . . . O God which resistest the proud . . . Amen. Deus qui superbis resistis . . . Amen.

A prayer to the proper angel. Ad proprium angelum. Anthem. O angel which art my keeper . . . Angele qui meus es custos . . . ℣. O blessed angel . . . A. Direct or rule my doings . . . Let us pray. O God whose pleasure is to have certain of the holy angels . . . Amen. Oratio. Deus qui sanctorum angelorum tuorum . . . Amen. Let us pray. O holy angel of God, the minister of the heavenly empire . . . Amen. O sancte angele Dei minister cælestis . . . Amen.

Of St. George. De S. Georgio. Anthem. George the famous martyr . . . ℣. Pray for us . . . A. That both our visible and invisible enemies . . . Let us pray. O almighty and everlasting God which being benign . . . Amen. Oremus. Omnipotens sempiterne Deus qui deprecantium voces . . . Amen.

A prayer unto all Saints. Oratio ad omnes Sanctos. O all you Saints, the elect and chosen of God . . . Amen. O vos omnes sancti et electi Dei . . . Amen.

1555, Rouen for Robert Valentin, Rouen, 16º. English and Latin. No. 217.

₊ *The title has " The Prymer in english and in latin set out along after the use of Sarum . . .".*

A.D. 1556, John Kyng, London, 8º. English. No. 222.

₊ *The title has " The Primer in english after Salisbury use, set out at length with many godly prayers . . .".*

When thou hast received the sacrament. Suffer me not to receive Thy glorious body and blood my sovereign Lord . . . Amen.

A.D., 1557, John Kyngston and Henry Sutton, London, 4º. English and Latin. No. 233.[1]

₊ *The title has " The Primer in english and latin, set out along after the use of Sarum, with many godly and devout prayers . . .".*

₊ *The following prayers are in english only.*

Grace before dinner. The eyes of all things trust in Thee, O Lord . . . Amen. The King of eternal glory . . . Amen. God is charity, and he that dwelleth in charity . . . Amen.

Grace after dinner. The God of peace and love . . . Glory, honour and praise be to Thee, O God . . . Amen. Lord have mercy upon us. Our Father. ℣. Lord hear my prayer. A. And let my cry come to Thee. From the fiery darts of the devil both in weal and woe . . . Amen. God save the church, our King, Queen, and realm . . . Amen.

Grace before supper. O Lord, Jesu Christ, without whom nothing is sweet . . . Amen.

Grace after supper. Blessed is God in all His gifts. And holy in all His works. . . . Most mighty Lord and merciful Father . . . Amen. God save the church, our King, Queen, and realm, and God have mercy on all Christian souls. Amen.

Godly prayers. A preparation to meditation and prayer. Sweet Saviour and good Lord God Jesu Christ the Son of the living God . . . Amen.

A devout prayer to be daily said. Almighty and eternal God which vouchsafest that we as it were heavenly children . . . Amen.

A prayer of the seven words that our Lord spake hanging upon the Cross. Jesu Christ omnipotent Lord, that yet hanging on the cross spakest these words . . . Amen.

[1] See Wilkins. Conc. ed. 1787. Vol. 4. page 157.

A SUMMARY OF THE CONTENTS

OF THE

PRIMERS: AND GOODLY PRIMERS:

PRINTED CUM PRIVILEGIO REGALI,

CHIEFLY FOR WILLIAM MARSHALL.

C. A.D. 1534—C. A.D. 1539.

AND OF THE

PRIMERS

IN WHICH THE HOURS ARE PARTLY SARUM, AND PARTLY
THOSE PRINTED CHIEFLY FOR WILLIAM MARSHALL.

CUM PRIVILEGIO REGALI.

A.D. 1536—A.D. 1540.

ALSO OF THE

MANUAL OF PRAYERS OR PRIMER: PRIMER:
AND PRIMER OR BOOK OF PRAYERS:

SET FORTH BY BISHOP HILSEY.

CUM PRIVILEGIO AD IMPRIMENDUM SOLUM.

A.D. 1539—A.D. 1540.

THE HOURS IN THE BOOKS NAMED ABOVE ARE EITHER IN
ENGLISH, OR IN ENGLISH AND LATIN.

EXPLANATIONS.

1. This portion of the Summary of the contents is in three divisions and includes those books in which (a) The Hours are either in english, or in english and latin, printed cum privilegio regali, chiefly for William Marshall. (b) The Hours are printed cum privilegio regali ; and compounded partly of Sarum use, and partly of those hours printed chiefly for William Marshall. (c) The Hours are in english, or in english and latin, set forth by John Hilsey, bishop of Rochester, at the commandment of Lord Thomas Crumwell, Vicegerent to the King's highness. A summary of all the contents of one of the Primers in each of these three divisions is given as a standard of comparison for each of the other books in the same division.

2. The latin title of a devotion is given, when one occurs, as well as the english translation of it; and also both the latin and english of the first words of the collect, but only the english of each of the other component parts of the devotion.

3. The various known editions of the Epistles and Gospels in english are given as they occur; they were first printed A.D. 1538. They are found either as separate books or forming a part of the Primer.

4. All fresh matter, as it occurs in the various successive books, is given in each division after the summary of the contents of the book which serves as a standard of comparison.

5. An index is given of the prayers, psalms, and benedictions. Groups of psalms, such as the seven penitential psalms or those in the Hours, are not indexed separately. Another index gives all the hymns and rhythms. A general index refers to other matters of liturgical, devotional, and general interest.

6. There existed formerly one or more books, akin to the books in these divisions, which cannot now be found; they are described as follows: " Hortulus animæ in sermone anglicano " mentioned in 1529 in a list of books (Wilkins Conc. Vol. 3. p. 721). Erroneous opinions are quoted in 1530, " Out of the Prymar" (*Ibid.* Vol. 3. p. 733). In the same year " Hortulus animæ in english " occurs amongst prohibited books (*Ibid.* Vol. 3. p. 739). In 1531 " Ortulus animæ in english " and " The Primer in english " were proclaimed at Paul's cross (State papers domestic Vol. 5. p. 768). In the same year Richard Bayfield was charged with bringing " The Primer in english into England." (Fox ed. 1870 Vol. 4. p. 680). A Primer by George Joye is described in 1532 as having Thomas Hytton in the Kalender on the eve of St. Matthias by the name of St. Thomas the martyr (More's works ed. 1557. p. 343). George Joye writes in 1533, that he did not translate the prayer of Esaie alike, in the Hortulus and the prophet (State papers Vol. 6. p. 183). " The subversion of More's false doctrine " by George Joye, published in the same year, mentions the Hortulus. Tunstal, in 1537, writes about a book in english called " Ortulus animæ," and says that it contains a manifest declaration against the late Act of Succession, see Kalender, August, Decollation of St. John Baptist. (State Papers Vol. 8. p. 399). Bonners injunctions of 1542 mention " Ortulus animæ in english " in a list of prohibited books. (Burnet ed. 1865. Vol. 4. p. 517).

A SUMMARY OF THE CONTENTS

OF THE

PRIMERS: AND GOODLY PRIMERS:

IN WHICH THE HOURS ARE EITHER IN ENGLISH, OR IN ENGLISH AND LATIN,

PRINTED CUM PRIVILEGIO REGALI,

CHIEFLY FOR WILLIAM MARSHALL.[1]

C. A.D. 1534—C. A.D. 1539.

c. A.D. 1534. John Byddell for William Marshall, London. 8o. English.
No. 115.

*** *The title of the book is "A Primer in english with certain prayers and godly meditations, very necessary for all people that understand not the latin tongue. Cum privilegio regali".*[2] *Beneath the title the royal arms. The colophon has "The primer in english with many goodly and godly prayers. Imprinted by Johan Byddell . . . for William Marshall. Cum gratia et privilegio regali."*

Almanake for xv. years. It begins A.D. 1534. Easter Day. 5 April.

The Kalender has a few of the Saints days from the Sarum Kalender. It has "The translation of St. Thomas" on July 7. "Thomas the archbishop" on December 29, and frequent references and quotations from Holy Scripture.

A general confession for every sinner brought in to knowledge of his sins, to confess himself with penitent and sorrowful heart before God at all times. O my most merciful Father, the father of mercies . . . Amen. Then say the one and fifty psalm, called Miserere mei Deus, the fourth among the vii Psalms.

The preface unto the reader.[3] Among other innumerable pestilent infections of books and learnings, with the which christian people have been piteously seduced and deceived, brought up in divers kinds of diffidence and false hope, I may judge and that chiefly those to be pernicious on whom they be wont in every place to pray, and have also learned, by heart, both curiously and with great scrupulosity to make rehearsal of their sins.

---

[1] See State Papers. Foreign and Domestic. Henry 8. Vol. 7, Nos. 422, 423, and Vol. 9, Nos. 345, 357; also Tanner, Bibliotheca, ed. 1748, page 513, sub Marshal Gulielmus.

[2] See Wilkins Conc., ed. 1737. Vol. 3, pages 769, 770, 776, 804; and Joyce Sacred Synods, pages 379, 380.

[3] See John Gau. The right way to the kingdom of heaven. A.D. 1533. (Scottish Text Soc.) page 3; and Wilkins Conc., ed. 1737. Vol. 3, page 867; also Burnet, ed. 1865. Vol. 4, page 517.

These books though they abounded in every place with infinite errours and taught prayers, made with wicked foolishness both to God and also to his saints, yet by cause they were garnished with glorious titles and with red letters, promising much grace and pardon, though it were but vanity, have sore deceived the unlearned multitude. One is called the Garden of the soul,[1] another the Paradise of the soul, and by cause I will be short, look thou thyself what diverse and glorious names be given unto them. Wherefore here needeth sharp reformation, yea, and many of them be worthy to be utterly destroyed. The same judgment and reformation is also to be had of the books of passions and saints lives called Legends,[2] for in these are also many things added, whereof Satan is author. Howbeit since neither time sufficient is given to one man neither the burthen of this reformation of one may be sustained, I thought it enough in this place only to have monished you, trusting that God in time coming shall add to those things both time convenient and also light. Therefore here as entering my matter, first, I will declare after a simple and plain manner by the which even as by a glass thou shalt know what the knowledge of sin is, and how we ought truly to pray following the rehearsal of the commandments and of the Pater noster, and I doubt not but this one prayer is sufficient enough to them that pray how often soever it be, or whatsoever they require . . . Therefore I desire all persons that from henceforth they forget such prayers as be Saint Brigitte's and other like, which great promises and pardons have falsely advanced . . . Such virtue hath the Pater noster that the longer and the more thou use it, the sweeter and more acceptable it is, which I desire that the master of this prayer confirm, Jesus Christ, which is blessed eternally. So be it.

It was never ordained, without the singular providence of God, that the multitude of christian people should learn by heart the Ten commandments, the Creed, and the Pater noster. For truly he that understandeth these hath the pith of all those things which Holy Scripture doth contain, and whatsoever may be taught necessary unto the christian . . . Wherefore it is expedient to begin at the commandments, so that we may by them learn to knowledge our sin and malice as the spiritual infirmity which maketh us feeble and weak, so that we can neither do, neither leave that which we be bound to do or to leave.[3]

The ten commandments.[4] The first and most excellent table of Moses containeth three commandments . . . The second table. The second and last table of Moses containeth seven precepts . . . A short conclusion of the ten commandments . . . Of the transgression of the commandments . . . The fulfilling of the commandments . . .

[1] Ortulus animæ in duytsche. Antwerp. Hochstraten. (Bodl. i. c. 28). A.D. 1528.
[2] Legenda aurea, editions from 1483 to 1527.
[3] See Precationes biblicæ. (Brit. Mus. 843, c. 6.) A.D. 1531, page 186.
[4] Opera Lutheri, ed. 1558. Vol. 7, pages 119-122; and John Gau. The right way to the kingdom of heaven. A.D. 1533. (Scottish Text Soc.) page 8.

The Creed or Belief.[1] The effect of our faith standeth in three parts, as in it are rehearsed three persons of the godly Trinity . . . The first part of the Belief . . . The second part of the Belief . . . The third part of the Belief . . .

The prayer of the Lord, called the Pater noster. Our Father which art in heaven, hallowed be thy name . . . So be it.

A goodly interpretation or declaration of the Pater noster.[1] Our Father which art in heaven, look mercifully upon us thy wretched children here in earth . . . Amen.

The prayer of the Lord called the Pater noster, wherein are contained vii petitions.[2] The preface and introduction to ask these vii petitions is contained in these words. Our Father which art in heaven. The understanding of the words. Almighty God syth thou of thine infinite benevolence and mercy . . . The seventh petition. But deliver us from evil. This petition prayeth for all the evils of pains and punishments as doth the church in the Litany. O Father deliver us from thy everlasting wrath . . . Amen. Grant us good Lord that all these prayers may be obtained of us . . . Amen, that is to say, stable, constant, true, and sure be it.

The salutation of our most blessed Lady Saint Mary the Virgin.[2] Hail Mary full of grace. Here first of all take heed no man put his sure trust and hope in the Mother of God . . .

An oration or sermon how and in what manner we ought to pray to almighty God.[3] First of all, two things are necessarily required to thee that our prayer may be a very prayer . . .

The passion of our Saviour Christ.[4] Our Saviour Christ at his last supper . . . Adoramus te, etc. The verse. We worship thee, O Christ . . . The answer. For by thy holy cross . . . Oremus. Domine Jesu Christe, etc. O Lord Jesu Christ the Son of the living God put thy passion . . . Amen. Gloriosa passio, etc. The glorious passion . . . Amen. God setteth forth His incomparable love that he beareth unto us . . .

A devout fruitful and godly remembrance of the passion of our Saviour Jesu Christ.[5] There are certain which when they exercise themselves in the meditation or remembrance of the passion . . .

A fruitful and a very christian instruction for children.[6] In the morning at thy uprising thou shalt make the sign of the cross over thee saying thus. Into this day do I enter all things to do. In the name. Then kneel down upon thy knees, or else standing say this prayer following. With

---

[1] Precationes biblicæ. (Brit. Mus. 843, c. 6.) A.D. 1531, page 209; and John Gau. The right way to the kingdom of heaven. A.D. 1533. (Scottish Text Soc.) page 26; also, Institution of a christian man, ed. 1537. October (Emman. Coll. Camb. MSS. 4. 3. 29. (1)); and Opera Lutheri, ed. 1558. Vol. 7, page 122b.

[2] See Opera Lutheri, ed. 1558. Vol. 7, pages 129, 129b; and John Gau. The right way to the kingdom of heaven. A.D. 1533, (Scottish Text Soc.) page 102.

[3] Opera Lutheri, ed. 1582. Vol. 1, page 70b.

[4] Passio domini Jesu Christi ex quatuor evangelistis collecta. (Lambeth. Archiep. 14. 9. 13. (3).) no date.

[5] Certain prayers and godly meditations. (Brit. Mus. c. 17. a. 31.) A.D. 1538.

[6] Precationes biblicæ. (Brit. Mus. 843, c. 6.) A.D. 1531. page 275.

an humble and a contrite heart, with a sorrowful and a repenting spirit
... Amen. The Pater noster. The Ave Maria. The Creed.

The grace or blessing of the table to be said of children standing before it, their hands elevated and joined together, saying thus devoutly and sadly.[1] The eyes of all things look up and wait upon thee ... Thou openest thy hand and replenishest all things ... Our Father. O Lord God our heavenly Father, bless thou us and these thy gifts ... Amen.

After dinner. Let us give thanks unto the Lord for he is right good ... Amen. Our Father. We thank thee O Lord God our father by thy Son Jesus Christ our Lord for all thy benefits ... Amen. Our Father.

The grace to be said before supper. Christ which at his last supper gave himself unto us ... Amen. Our Father.

The grace to be said after supper. Honour and praise be unto God the King everlasting ... Amen. Our Father. God almighty father of all mercy and God of all consolation ... So be it.

Grace to be said before dinner or supper indifferently. He which of his inestimable goodness feedeth every creature ... Amen.

Grace to be said after dinner or supper indifferently. We thank thee, O heavenly Father, which of thine infinite power ... Amen.

Grace to be said before dinner or supper indifferently. Blessed be thou, O God, which feedest us from our youth ... Amen.

Grace to be said after dinner or supper indifferently. Glory be to thee, O Lord ... Amen. Praise ye the Lord all gentiles ... Glory be to the Father.

When thou shalt go to bed, say thus. I lay me down to rest. In the name. Then say these two prayers following. I thank thee my heavenly Father by thy most dear beloved Son Jesu Christ that this day of thy plenteous rich mercy ... Amen. O above all blessed and almighty Lord God my Father I thy sinful creatnre ... Amen. Then as thou diddest in the morning, say The Pater noster, The Ave Maria, and The Creed (see page 184).

The Matins. The Prime and Hours. The Third Hour. The Sixth Hour. The Ninth Hour. The Evensong in english. The Complene.

At Matins. Prayers. A prayer to the Holy Ghost. Come Holy Spirit, replenish the hearts ... Versicle. Send forth thy spirit ... Answer. For so renewest thou ... Prayer. O God which hast instructed the hearts of the faithful men ... Amen. A prayer to the Trinity. Deliver us, save us and justify us ... The name of God be blessed ... From age to age ... Prayer. O almighty everlasting God, which hast given us thy servants to knowledge ... Amen. (See page 162).

₊ *The Hours are those known as Marshall's; and are found in those Primers which were printed "cum privilegio regali" chiefly for William Marshall. The framework of the Hours as well as the commencement of each Hour is Sarum. The Psalms except those for Evensong are Sarum. The Canticles are Sarum. The Blessings at Matins and the Suffragia at Lauds are Sarum. The Ave Maria occurs at Matins but not as the Invitatory. The Hymns, Antiphons, Lessons, Responds, Chapters, and Collects are not Sarum. The chapters in the Hours from Prime to the Ninth Hour are omitted.*

[1] See Precationes biblicæ. (Brit. Mus. 843, c. 6.) A.D. 1531, page 277.

Salve rex.[1] Hail Jesu Christ, King of mercy, our life, our sweetness . . . In all our trouble . . . O Jesu our health and glory . . . Prayer. Jesu O Christ the Son of God, our Redeemer, which dejectedest and humblest thyself . . . Amen (see page 184).

The seven Psalms in english. Domine ne in furore. The first. Psalm sextus. Ah, Lord rebuke me not in thy wrath. Beati quorum. Psalm xxxii. Blessed is he whose ungodliness is forgiven. Domine ne. The second. Psalm xxxvii. Punish me not Lord, of indignation. Miserere mei Deus. Psalm li. Have mercy upon me, God, for thy favourable goodness. Domine exaudi. Psalm cii. Lord hear my prayer and suffer my deep desire. De profundis. Psalm cxxx. From my most deepest painful troubles. Domine exaudi. The ii. Psalm cxliii. O Lord, hear my prayer, listen unto my fervent beseeching.

The Commendations are Sarum omitting Psalm. Domine probasti. The argument before Psalm cxix is different. What follows after Psalm cxix is also different.

The Psalms of the passion of Christ. An argument is appended to each Psalm. Deus Deus meus respice. Psalm xxii. My God, my God, lo, wherefore forsakest thou me. Dominus regit me. Psalm xxiii. The Lord is my pastor and feeder. Domini est terra. Psalm xxiiii. The earth is the Lord's and all that is contained in it. Ad te Domine levavi. Psalm xxv. Unto thee, O Lord, I lift up my mind. Judica me, Domine. Psalm xxvi. Be judge for me, Lord, for I am purposed to live innocently. Dominus illuminatio mea. Psalm xxvii. The Lord is my light and my saving health. Ad te Domine clamabo. Psalm xxviii. Upon thee Lord do I call. Afferte Domino filii Dei. Psalm xxix. Give unto the Lord, ye that excel in mighty power. Exaltabo te Domine. Psalm xxx. I shall exalt thee, Lord, for thou hast exalted me. In te Domine speravi. Psalm xxxi. In thee, O Lord, have I trusted, let me never be shamed . . . Praise ye the Lord.

The prayer of the prophet Jonas delivered out of the whale's belly.[2] Jonas prayed unto the Lord his God in the whale's belly . . .

A dialogue wherein the child, asked certain questions, answereth to the same.[3] The question. Speak my dear child, what art thou? The answer. As concerning my first birth I am a creature of God endued with wit and reason, the son of Adam, and as touching my new and second birth, I knowledge myself to be a christian . . . (see page 151).

A prayer for the molifying and suppling of our hard hearts, the lightening of our blind hearts, and the true converting of our impenitent hearts. O most merciful Father which by the mouth of our sweet Saviour Jesu Christ . . . Amen.

[1] See John Hollybush, Exposition upon Salve regina. (Bodl. Tanner. 23; and Christ Church, Oxford) also State Papers, Foreign and Domestic, Henry 8 Vol. 8. page 121. No. 52.
[2] Precationes biblicæ. (Brit. Mus. 843. c. 6.) A.D. 1531 (page 46); and Prayers of the Bible. (Lambeth. Archiep. 24. 9. 11. (1).) c. A.D. 1534.
[3] See A lesson for Children, c. A.D. 1533. No. 111. page 151.

An effectuous prayer very needful in these last and perilous days to be said with tears and deep sighs from the bottom of our heart ; the prayer of the prophet Esaye in the lxiii and lxiiii chapters of his prophecies for the restoring of Christ's poor church scattered abroad with persecution forsaken and brente.[1] Lord look out from heaven and behold from thy holy habitation . . .

The song of Anna Helcanas wife i. Regum, ii. wherein she praiseth God, for that he gave her a son called Samuel, after that she had been long barren.[1] My heart is pleasantly set at rest in the Lord . . .

The prayer of the prophet Daniel for the restoring of Christ's church under the figure of Jerusalem, and the children of Israel being in captivity at the Babylonites. Daniel ix.[1] Haste thee, Lord God, which art great and reverently to be feared . . .

Prayer peaseth God's wrath[2] . . . Forasmuch as we have now grievously offended our Lord God . . . Amen.

Colophon. Thus endeth the prymer in english with many goodly and godly prayers . . . Cum gratia et privilegio regali.

An exposition after the manner of a contemplation upon the li. psalm called Miserere mei Deus[3] (see page 167).

To fill up the leaf we have touched certain places which we thought most necessary to edify the congregation of Christ. Of faith. First dear brethren we ought to give diligent heed . . . The power of faith is to justify us . . . The work of faith. Faith worketh by charity . . . Good works. Among good works the chief are to be obedient . . .[4]

Colophon. Here endeth the Exposition upon the li Psalm, called Miserere mei Deus. Imprinted at London in Fleetstreet by John Byddell, dwelling next to Flete Bridge at the sign of our Lady of pity, for William Marshall. Cum privilegio regali.

A.D. 1535, June 16. John Byddell, London. 4º. English. No. 117.

_{*} *The title of the book is "A goodly prymer in english newly corrected and printed, with certain godly meditations and prayers added to the same, very necessary and profitable for all them that right assuredly understand not the latin and greek tongues". Then the arms of Henry the eighth impaled with those of Anne Bullen, crowned, having H and A in the upper corners. A rose in one corner at the bottom, and a pomegranate in the other corner at the bottom. Underneath the arms the words " With the King's most gracious privilege for vi years". On the reverse of the title-page an emblematic cut, above the cut the word "Hipocrisy," on the proper right side " Time revealeth all things," on the proper left " Truth the daughter of time". Underneath the cut " Matth. x. Nothing is covered that shall not be discovered. And nothing is hid that shall not be revealed."*

[1] Precationes e sacris bibliis desumptæ. (Brit. Mus. 1410. a. 30. (1).) A.D. 1528.; Precationes biblicæ. (Brit. Mus. 843. c. 6.) A.D. 1681 (page 40); and Prayers of the Bible. (Lambeth. Archiep. 24. 9. 11. (1).) c. A.D. 1534.

[2] See Preface to Prayers of the Bible. (Lambeth. Archiep. 24. 9. 11. (1).) c. A.D. 1534.

[3] Fratris Hieronymi [G. Savonarola] Ferrariensis expositiones in psalmos. A.D. 1505. 8o. Venice.

[4] Precationes christianæ. (Brit. Mus. C. 53. a. 36 (1).) A.D. 1536; Certain prayers and godly meditations. (Brit. Mus. C. 17. a. 31.) A.D. 1538; and State Papers, Foreign and Domestic, Henry 8 Vol. 7. No. 423.

An admonition to the reader.[1] This with verbal differences is the same as "The preface unto the reader" (page 195) down to "Have sore deceived the unlearned multitude". Then. As for an example, what vanity is promised in the superscription or title before "Obsecro te, domina sancta Maria," where it is written, that whosoever saith that prayer daily before the image, called the image of our Lady of pity, shall see the visage of our most blessed Lady, and be warned both of the day, and also of the hour of his death, before he depart out of this world. I pray you what fondness or rather madness is this. Is not the prayer of the Lord, called the Pater noster, as good a prayer as that, of as great antiquity, of as great commodities, and made by as great an author as that . . . Such another foolish title, but not the same, is before "Ave rosa sine spinis" where they have brought in our Lady and made her to speak as they lust to imagine, and to say, that the golden prayer is most acceptable and sweetest to her of all other.[2] And then methink it should be sweeter unto her than the most sweetest, holy, and charitable prayer of her sweet Son Jesu Christ, made unto his blessed Father and ours, for the health, salvation, redemption, and conservation of all his elect and most entirely beloved children of eternal inheritance. And yet me thinketh, yea and I am sure that so it is, that whatsoever doth most please her heavenly Father and ours, and her Son and Saviour Jesu Christ, doth also please her most, and is to her most acceptable. But the most fondness or madness of all is, that they make our Lady to give and deliver the said prayer by revelation, and that at the time of the same revelation it was written with letters of gold in her breast. Oh almighty God, who did ever hear tell of such blindness, and yet is nothing said to it, nor yet hitherto any convocations have been holden to call in, or to forbid and inhibit such blasphemous slanders, both against God and also our blessed Lady. More such blasphemies and vain promises shalt thou find in the titles before the prayers, called "Ave Maria, ancilla Trinitatis"; there be two prayers that begin after that manner. Item before the xv Oos in latin, where it is granted that whosoever saith them an whole year shall deliver xv souls out of purgatory of his next kindred, and convert other xv sinners to good life, and preserve other xv of his kin in grace. Before "Crux Christi sit mecum," before "Respice ad me infelicem, pietas immensa," before "Deus propitius esto mihi peccatori," before "Domine Jesu Christe qui septem verba," before the verses, as they be called, of St. Barnard, which begin "Illumina oculos meos". And finally to speak of such false titles and untrue promises, I beseech you, what an abomination is it to think of the title and promise written before the mass of the five wounds in the mass-book. . . . Here I omit and let pass many abominable heresies against Christ and his most blessed blood, contained in some parts of some of the prayers above

---

[1] See John Gau. The right way to the kingdom of heaven. A.D. 1533. (Scottish Text Soc.) page 3.
[2] See No. 37. A.D. 1510. page 124; and Burnet. ed. 1865. Vol. 5. pages 213, 228.

alleged, for I do not condemn every word in every of them, which not only men unlearned and of small reputation and authority, but also bishops and doctors in divinity can wink at well enough. I omit also the shame, rebuke, and slander done unto the redemption which we have in Jesu Christ, commonly comprised in all collects of saints, and some of their anthems and versicles, as, "Tu per Thomæ sanguinem," "Salve regina, Mater misericordiæ," and "Deus qui beatum Nicolaum," with such other almost innumerable. . . . And because we will not be over tedious and long, I let pass many other books of superstitious prayers which I could recite, if I delighted in much rigorous rehearsals, as the "Garden of the soul,"[1] "The Paradise of the soul," with other of the same hue and colour. Wherefore here needeth sharp reformation, yea and many of them be worthy to be clean put out of memory. The same judgment and reformation that is meant of the books before named, is also to be had of the books of passions and saints lives, called "Legendaries,"[2] of "Festivals,"[3] of "Manipulus curatorum,"[4] of "Eccius,"[5] of "Cocleus,"[6] and of "Hocstratus" books,[7] with such like dregs and draff, wherein the Pope's false usurped power, and his most wicked laws be maintained and defended, to the great and dangerous infection of our most gracious sovereign Lord the King's liege people, and the unlawful withdrawing of their hearts from his Grace's majesty by such mischievous books. Besides that, that many things be mingled in the said book of John Eccius,[5] whereof I fear me sore that the devil is the very author. . . . It is not meet, comely, nor fitting, that in our prayers we should make a God and Saviour of any Saint in heaven, no not of our blessed Lady. Neither is it meet to make them check with our Saviour Christ, much less than to make them checkmate. I would they that be learned, should here call to mind the honour of Latria, wherewith they were wont to say and preach, and in disputations to declare and teach, that it was both sin and shame to honour any creature. Their distinction of Latria, Dulia, and Hyperdulia, in contentious disputation, swimmeth ever in their lips. But when they come to practise the matter in their petitions and prayers, then seemeth it as clean forgotten with them as they had never spoken it, read it, nor heard of it in their lives. Such is the blindness of nature without the Spirit of God. I pray God ones amend that is amiss. . . . Truly the high blasphemy of the most holy name of God, most good and almighty, the defiling and defacing of the precious blood

---

[1] See John Gau. The right way to the kingdom of heaven. A.D. 1533. (Scottish Text Soc.) pages 3. 4. and Introduction page 38; and Ortulus animæ in duytsche. Antwerp, Hochstraten. (Bodl. i. c. 28.). A.D. 1528.
[2] Aurea legenda, editions from 1483-1527.
[3] Liber festivalis. London. 1502.
[4] Guido di monte Rotherii. Manipulus curatorum. London. 1509.
[5] J. Eckius. Enchiridion. 1525. and Panzer. Annales typographici. Johannes Eckius. Vol. 10. page 302.
[6] See Panzer. Annales typographici. Johannes Cochlæus. Vol. 10. page 256.
[7] See Panzer. Annales typographici. Jacobus Hochstratus. Vol. 10. page 413.

of our Saviour Jesu Christ, the contemning of the most gracious inspiration of the Holy Ghost, and finally, so abominable idolatry as more can never be; from the which he defend us, that redeemed us with his most precious blood. So be it.

An Almanake for xx years. It begins A.D. 1535. Easter Day 28 March.

The Kalender is Sarum. It has "Oct. S. Thomas martyr" on January 5. "Translation of Thomas Cantor" on July 7. "S. Thomas martyr" on December 29. St. Thomas of Canterbury does not occur in the Litany.

Preface.[1] It was never ordained, O good reader . . . This preface occurs before with verbal differences in "The preface unto the reader" No. 115. c. A.D. 1534 (page 196).

An instruction how and in what manner we ought to pray to almighty God.[2] First of all, two things are necessarily required to thee, that our prayer may be a very prayer . . . The prayer of the Lord called the Pater noster. Our Father which art in heaven hallowed be thy name . . . A goodly brief interpretation or declaration of the prayer of the Lord. Our Father which art in heaven look mercifully upon us thy wretched children here in earth . . . A more large exposition of the prayer of the Lord wherein are contained seven petitions. The preface and introduction to ask the seven petitions is contained in these words. Our Father which art in heaven, etc. The understanding of the words. Almighty God since thou of thine infinite benevolence and mercy hast not only admitted us but also taught . . .

Conditor cæli et terræ. O maker of heaven and earth, King of kings and Lord of lords . . . So be it (as on pages 155, 167).

The office of all estates (as on pages 155. 168).

Good works. Among good works, the chief are to be obedient in all things unto kings, princes, judges and such other officers as far as they command civil things . . .

Persecution. After these and such other works let every man bolden and comfort his brethren to suffer the cross that God will lay on them . . .

₊ *The Hours are those commonly known as Marshall's; and are the same as those in No. 115. c. A.D. 1534.*

A preface to the Litany. Forasmuch good christian reader as I am certainly persuaded, that divers persons, of small judgment and knowledge in holy scripture, have been offended for that that in the english Primer[3] which I lately set forth, I did omit and leave out the Letany which, I take God to witness, I did not of any perverse mind or opinion, thinking that our blessed Lady and holy Saints might in nowise be prayed unto, but rather because I was not ignorant of the wicked opinion and vain superstitious manner, that divers and many persons have not only used in worshipping

---

[1] See John Gau Right way to the kingdom of heaven. A.D. 1533. (Scottish Text Soc.) page 7.
[2] Opera Lutheri. ed. 1582. Vol. 1. page 70b Vol. 7. pages 129. 125; Precationes biblicæ. (Brit. Mus. 843. c. 6.) A.D. 1531. page 222.
[3] No. 115. c. A.D. 1534. page 105.

of them, but also thinking that God by Christ would none otherwise gladly hear and accept their petitions and prayers, but by his blessed mother and saints . . . and although it be nothing like nor true, as concerning the necessity, that we by the commandment of holy Scripture must of necessity pray to our blessed Lady and Saints, or that otherwise we cannot be heard; yet is it true, as concerning that we must needs have a peace maker and mediator to our heavenly Father, which is his only Son, and our only sufficient and eternal mediator Jesu Christ. Wherefore for the contentation of such weak minds and somewhat to bear their infirmities, I have now, at this my second edition of the said Primer, caused the Litany to be printed and put into the same, trusting that they by their old untrue opinion before alledged, nor yet by any other like will abuse the same. Right doubtful it is, as I think, to pray unto all those that be mentioned, named, and called saints in the common primers in latin. For although many of them, by what authority I cannot tell, have been canonised and made saints, by such as have been bishops of Rome; yet whether they be saints or no I commit to the secret judgment of God.

The Litany has Invocations of Saints and Angels, arranged according to the classification in the Sarum use. It has "Our most gracious sovereign Lord and King Henry the eighth, his most gracious Queen Anne, all their posterity, aiders, helpers, and true subjects".

O bone Jesu. O bountiful Jesu, O sweet Jesu, O Jesu the Son of the pure virgin Mary . . . So be it. O glorious King which amongst Thy Saints art laudable . . . Amen (as on pages 167. 189).

An admonition or warning to the reader necessary to be had and read for the true understanding and meaning of the Dirige hereafter following.[1] Our Saviour Jesu Christ, good christian reader, in the gospel of John commandeth us whiles we have light to walk in light: for he that walketh in darkness, seeth not whither he goeth, nor where he walketh. Amongst all other works of darkness and deep ignorance, wherein we have blindly wandered, following a sort of blind guides, many days and years, I account not this one of the least, that we have rung and sung, mumbled, murmured, and piteously puled forth a certain sort of psalms hereafter ensuing with response, versicles, and lessons to the same, for the souls of our christian brethren and sistern that be departed out of this world: which psalms and lessons (I beseech God I die) and if they make any more for any such use and purpose, that is to say, that they ought or may be used any rather for them that be departed, than for them that be in life and in good bodily health than may "Te Deum" or "Gloria in excelsis" . . . And as for the ix lessons in the said Dirige, taken out of the prophet Job, I wonder sore of what intent they were ordained to be sung or said for the souls of the dead . . . So be it.

---

[1] See Preface to Dirige. No. 128. c. A.D. 1537. page 171.

The Dirige is Sarum except that "Lord give them eternal rest and let continual light shine unto them" is omitted at the end of each Psalm and elsewhere. The only collect at the end of the Evensong which is retained from Sarum use is "Deus cui proprium est". The psalm "Deus misereatur" and "The Song of Zachary" are omitted in the Mattins. All the collects at the end of the Dirige which are found in Sarum use are omitted, and "Deus cui proprium est" is substituted.

The Commendations are the same as in No. 115. c. A.D. 1534 down to the end of Psalm 119, but the rest is different.

Be it known to all men by these presents, that it is prohibited by our sovereign Lord the King by his letters patents, to all printers, booksellers, and merchants and all others, that (without license had of him, that at his costs and charges printed this book) they in no wise do print, or utter in sale or otherwise, at any place within our said sovereign Lord's dominions, this book, entitled and called the English Primer, at any time within six years next after the printing hereof, as they will answer at their perils, and avoid the penalties mentioned in the privilege hereunto granted.

Colophon. Imprinted at London, in Fleet Street, by John Byddell . . . for William Marshall, the year of our Lord God M.D. xxxv. the xvi. day of June.

c. A.D. 1535, Thomas Godfray, London, 8º. English. No. 118.

₀ *The title is "A Primer in english with divers prayers and godly meditations. Cum privilegio regali". The contents of the book are on the title-page. The Litany and Dirige do not occur in the book.*

An Almanake for xiiii years. It begins A.D. 1535. Easter day. 28 March.

The Kalender is Sarum, it has "Octava S. Thomæ mar." on January 5. "Translatio S. Tho. mart." on July 7. "Thomæ martyris." on December 29.

A christian man's learning divided in three parts. The prologue. Ye have desired me oft and many times dear brother and friend truly and faithfully to write unto you the sum and effect of a christian mans learning, that is to say the principal thing that a christian man is bound to know . . . The x commandments . . . The creed or belief . . . The Pater noster . . .

An exhortation for them that receiveth the blessed sacrament of the altar. Most dearly beloved in God ye shall understand how that the gospel of Christ putteth us alway in remembrance that of ourselves we are but ignorant poor and wretched sinners. . .

Grace for fish days. Benedicite. *Dominus.* That meat that goeth into the mouth, saith Christ, Matt. xv. defileth not a man . . . Praise ye the Lord. Our Father.

After dinner. These are the very words of the Holy Ghost in the first epistle to Timothy the fourth cap. In the latter days some shall depart from the faith . . . Amen.

*** *The Hours are those commonly known as Marshall's; and are the same as those in No.* 115. *c. A.D.* 1534. *The Passion of our Saviour Christ and the Resurrection of our Lord come after Lauds and before Prime and Hours.*

The passion of our Saviour Christ (as on page 197)

The resurrection of our Lord. Now for because the sum of our salvation and life perpetual consisteth in the faith in Christ's death, his resurrection, and ascension, I shall continue the story of this gospel . . .

The commendations are the same as in No. 115. c. A.D. 1534.

c. A.D. 1535 (John Byddell, London) 4°. English. No. 119.

*** *The title page as well as the reverse of it is the same as that in No.* 117. *A.D.* 1535. *June* 16.

An almanake for xx years. It begins A.D. 1535. Easter day. 28 March.

The Kalender is the same as that in No. 117. A.D. 1535. June 16. It has "Oct. S. Thomas martyr" on January 5. "Translation S. Thomas" on July 7. "S. Thomas martyr" on December 29. St. Thomas of Canterbury does not occur in the Litany.

*** *The Hours are those commonly known as Marshall's; and are the same as those in No.* 115, *c. A.D.* 1534.

The Litany is the same as that in No. 117. A.D. 1535. June 16. It has "Our most gracious Sovereign Lord and King, Henry the eighth, his most gracious Queen Anne, all their posterity, aiders, helpers, and true subjects".

The Dirige is the same as that in No. 117. A.D. 1535. June 16.

The Commendations are the same as in No. 117. A.D. 1535. June 16.

c. A.D. 1537 (John Byddell, London) 4°. English. No. 129.[1]

*** *The title is the same as that of No.* 117. *A.D.* 1535. *June* 16. *It has* "*Cum privilegio regali*". *The title-page has no coat of arms. The reverse of the title-page is the same as that of No.* 117.

The Kalender is the same as that in No. 117. A.D. 1535. June 16, except that on July 12, instead of "S. Nabor and Felix," it has "Erasmus of Rotterdam deceased 1536".

*** *The Hours are those commonly known as Marshall's; and are the same as those in No.* 115. *c. A.D.* 1534.

The Litany is the same as that in No. 117. A.D. 1535. June 16. It has "Our most gracious Sovereign Lord and King, Henry the eighth, his most gracious son Prince Edward, all their posterity, aiders, helpers, and true subjects".

The Dirige is the same as that in No. 117. A.D. 1535. June 16.

The Commendations are the same as in No. 117. A.D. 1535. June 16.

On the reverse of "The table of the book". The prophets as they were all taught, stirred up and thrusted forth of one spirit to preach . . .[2] Even

---

[1] See H. J. Todd, Life of Cranmer. Vol. 1. page 129. Crumwell was appointed Privy Seal, A.D. 1536. July 2. Rymer. Fœdera. ed. 1728. Vol. xiv. page 571.

[2] See Preface to Jeremy the prophet translated into english by George Joye. A.D. 1534.

by the same Spirit hath God, the Father of our Saviour Jesu Christ, raised up our most gracious Prince, Henry the viii, to set forth his most holy will . . . Amen.

A goodly exposition upon the xxx Psalm, In te Domine speravi.[1]

The arms of William Marshall are on the reverse of the last leaf of the book.

₊ *The book has no colophon.*

c. A.D. 1537, John Byddell, London, 8º. English and Latin. No. 130.

₊ *The title is "The prymer with the pystles and gospels in english of every Sunday and Holy-day in the year, revised and diligently corrected, and the form of the new bedes with divers other things very necessary for young curates, and for all other men women and children".*

The Prologe. Forasmuch as the laws and decrees of the very Antichrist and great enemy of God the Bishop of Rome, which named himself Pope, have been preached and taught many years unto the people by the Bishops and clergy of this realm of England; and the very scripture of the Gospel, which is God's word and the life of the soul, hath been hid and shut up, so that no man for fear of that Antichrist durst open or shew the very truth of it, until now of late days our sovereign Lord the King took upon him his old title and right to be supreme head in earth immediately under God of the Church of England,[2] which title of supreme head was given always of God to Emperors, Kings, Princes, and Rulers, as it appeareth in many and divers places of Scripture. To the which both the Bishops and Clergy of this realm have not only in convocation assembled, consented, recognised, and approved lawfully and justly to appertain to the Kings highness, but also by word, oath, confession, and writing under their signs and seals have confessed, ratified, corroborated, and confirmed the same.[5] And also all the nobles and commons both spiritual and temporal by the authority of parliament by one assent have granted, annexed, knit, and unied to the crown imperial of the same realm the title, dignity, and style of supreme head in earth immediately under God of the church of England.[5] Wherefore the King's grace calling to his remembrance the power, charge, and commission given to him of almighty God, and upon a vehement love and affection towards his loving and faithful subjects, and that they should not perish or faint for lack of spiritual food, hath straightly charged and commanded all his said Bishops, and other of his clergy to declare, teach, and preach unto the people every Sunday and other high feasts through the year, the true mete and sincere word of God without any manner colour or dissimulation,[3] and that the said title, style, and jurisdiction of supreme head appertaineth to the King's crown and dignity royal; and also to publish and declare the great and innumerable enormities and abuses, which the said Bishop of Rome as

[1] Fratris Hieronymi [G. Savonarola] Ferrariensis expositiones in psalmos. A.D. 1505. Venice.

[2] See Wilkins Conc. ed. 1737. Vol. 3. page 725, and Joyce England's sacred Synods. ed. 1855. page 335.

[3] See Wilkins Conc. ed. 1737. Vol. 3. pages 807. 810. 815. 825. 830.

well in the title, and style, as also in authority, and jurisdiction of long time, unlawfully and unjustly hath usurped upon the King's grace and his progenitors and all other christian Princes, which word of God is now of late well set forth and preached in divers places of this realm. And the very Christians of the same are greatly desirous to have the said word of God in their mother tongue; and specially the Pystles and Gospels[1] which are read every Sunday and other Holy Days in the church, that they may thereby the better understand the preacher in his sermon.

And because the word of God may the better go forward, and forasmuch as the price of the whole New Testament[2] is somewhat high, and specially for them that have little money; and also that children and other having little cunning or experience cannot briefly find the said Pystles and Gospels in the said New Testament, therefore I have set forth and compiled in this book all the Pystles and Gospels together that are read in the church every Sunday and other Holy-days in the year, beginning first with the Sunday at Advent Sunday and so forth, and afterwards with the Feast of St. Andrew's day, which every man woman or child that can read shall briefly find by the table in the end of this book, which table shall shew you in what leaf ye shall find every Pystle and Gospel in the year.

The form of the new beads.[3] Ye shall pray for the whole congregation of Christ's church and specially for this church of England; wherein first I commend to your devout prayers the King's most excellent majesty supreme head immediately under God of the spirituality and temporality of the same church; and for the declaration of the truth thereof ye shall understand, that the unlawful jurisdiction power and authority of long time usurped by the Bishop of Rome in this realm, who then was called Pope, is now by God's law justly, lawfully and upon good grounds, reasons and causes by authority of Parliament, and by and with the whole consent and agreement of all the Bishops, Prelates, and both the Universities of Oxford and Cambridge, and also the whole clergy of this realm extinct and ceased for ever, as of no strength value or effect in this realm of England, in which realm the said whole clergy, Bishops, prelates, and either of the Convocations of both Provinces,[4] with also the Universities of Oxford and Cambridge, have, according to God's laws and upon good and lawful reasons and grounds, knowledged the King's highness to be supreme Head in earth immediately under God of the church of England.

An almanack for xxi years. It begins A.D. 1537. Easter Day 1st April.

A general rule to know when Alleluia goeth out. A general rule for Easter day. A general rule to know Advent Sunday. A general rule to know

---

[1] See Wilkins Conc. ed. 1737. Vol. 3. page 844.
[2] See Wilkins Conc. ed. 1737. Vol. 3 page 811.
[3] See Wilkins Conc. ed. 1737. Vol. 3. page 783, and Cranmer's writings. Parker Soc. page 460.
[4] See Wilkins Conc. ed. 1737. Vol 3. page 725, and Joyce, England's sacred Synods, ed. 1855. page 335.

the Ymbre days. A general rule to know what time of the year it is lawful to marry, and what time it is not lawful.

The Kalender is Sarum. It has "Transla. Thomæ martyris" on July 7. "S. Thomæ martyris" on December 29. St. Thomas of Canterbury does not occur in the Litany. The Kalender has one stanza of four lines in english at the head of each month, also one in english, and one in latin at the end. In January the stanza at the head of the month begins "The first six years of man's birth and age": the stanzas at the end "Cir. cfi. stat. ly. iii. kings. came by night" and "In jano claris calidisque cibo potiaris".

‸ *The Hours are those commonly known as Marshall's; and are the same as those in No. 115. c. A.D. 1534. The portions common to the use of Sarum, as well as those taken from Holy Scripture are in latin as well as english. The other portions of the Hours are in english only. The Hours in No. 120 c. A.D. 1585 are treated in the same way.*

The Seven psalms are in latin as well as english; this is also the case in No. 120. c. A.D. 1535 (page 45).

The Litany is the same as that in No. 117. A.D. 1535. It is in latin and english down to "In the day of judgment," the rest is in english only. It has "Our most gracious Sovereign Lord and King, Henry the eight, and all his true subjects".

The Dirige is the same as that in No. 117. A.D. 1535; it is for the most part in latin as well as english; this is also the case in No. 120. c. A.D. 1535.

The Commendations are the same as those in No. 117. A.D. 1535; they are in latin as well as english; this is also the case in No. 120. c. A.D. 1535.

‸ *The Pystles and Gospels on the Sundays and on Saints days which are contained in this book are in english only; and are the same as those in No. 128. c. A.D. 1537. (see page 173.)* [1]

c. A.D. 1539, 16º., English. No. 150.

‸ *The title-page and colophon of this book are wanting.*

The days of the week moralysed (as on page 147).

A little metre containing the duty of a christian man. To believe that Christ hath for us merited . . . (as on page 162).

The x commandments of God, given by Moses and expounded by Christ. The first table. Exod. xx. Deuteronomi vi. I am thy Lord God which hath brought thee . . . Christ. Hear Israel, our Lord God is one Lord . . . (as on page 168).

The gospel of Saint John i. In the beginning was the word . . . Añ. We do call upon thee . . . ℣. Blessed be the Lord's name . . . ℟. From this time forth . . . Amen. Prayer. O God the protector of all that trust in thee . . . Amen (as on page 162).

The gospel of Saint Luke. i. The angel Gabriel was sent down from heaven . . . (as on page 161).

Matthew the. ii. Chapter. When Jesus was born in Bethlehem a town of Jurye . . . Thanks be to God (as on page 162).

[1] Wilkins Conc. ed. 1737. Vol. 3. page 844.

The passion of our Lord Jesu Christ, written by Saint John the Evangelist. When Jesus had spoken these words, he went forth . . . ℣. Thou that suffered for us. ℟. Lord have mercy on us (as on page 162).

Auxiliatrix. Holy Trinity be helping unto me. O God in thy name . . . So be it (as on page 162).

A prayer to say when thou enterest into the church. Lord by the abundance of thy mercy I will enter into thy house . . . Amen (as on page 170).

Matyns in english. The Laudes. Pryme and Hours. The iii Hour. The vi Hour. The ix Hour. The Evensong. The Complyn.

₊ *The Hours are those commonly known as Marshall's; and are the same as those in No. 115. c. A.D. 1534, except that at Prime the rendering of the hymn "Veni creator Spiritus" agrees with Sarum use, "Come Holy Ghost O creator eternal" except in the last verse.*

The Litany is very imperfect; it consists of the latter portion only, and has "That thou vouchsafe to give peace to our King (Henry) and among all Kings universal".

The prophet Esai the lix Chapter. Lo, the Lord is yet alive whose power is not so minished . . .

Psalms of the passion (as in No. 115. c. A.D. 1534) adding (as on page 166). Añ. Christ was made obedient for us unto death . . . ℣. Holy mother of God pray for us . . . ℟. That we may able to his promission. ℣. Greatly to be praised is John . . . ℟. Which leaneth on the breast . . . The prayer. Regard we beseech thee Lord this thy household . . . Lord Jesu Christ we beseech thee ot thy goodness . . . Lord God we pray thee that the prayer of blessed St. John . . . Amen. The glorious passion of our Lord Jesu Christ . . . The Virgin Mary with her holy Son give to us their benediction. To the holy and indivisible Trinity . . . Amen. All hail most benign Jesu full of mercy . . . Amen.

A ghostly Psalm of the Catholick Faith, made by Athanasius called Quicunque vult. Whosoever he be, that will be saved . . . (as on pages 158. 168).

A prayer of the seven words that our Lord spake hanging on the cross. Omnipotent Lord Jesu Christ, that yet hanging upon the cross . . . Amen (as on page 161).

A prayer against ill thoughts. O pitiful Lord God alway shewing thy mercy . . . Amen (as on page 187).

The rule of charity. Do as thou wouldest be done to for charity holdeth all alike . . . (as on page 175).

A comparison between faith, hope, and charity. Faith cometh of the word ot God, hope cometh of faith, and charity springeth of them both . . .

A prayer to S. Hierome. O God the lover of mankind, which by thy elect servant . . . So be it (as on page 172).

A prayer when thou shalt receive the Sacrament. Domine non sum dignus . . . O merciful Lord, I am not worthy . . . So be it (as on page 167).

When thou hast received it. Vera perceptio corporis. The very true receiving of thy glorious body of flesh and blood . . . (as on page 167).

A prayer for wisdom. Sapyence ix chapiter. Deus patrum nostrorum. O the God of our fathers, God of mercy which hast made all with thy word . . . (as on page 167).

The prayer of Salomon for wisdom. Thou hast done Lord with thy servant David my father great mercy . . . (as on page 167).

For a competent living the Prayer of Salomon Prouerbi xxx. Duo rogavi te ne deneges. Two things, Lord, have I required thee that thou wouldest not deny me . . . (as on page 167).

A prayer of the church of the faithful for the word of God to be spoken with boldness of heart. Acts xiiii. Domine tu fecisti cœlum. Lord thou hast made heaven and earth, sea and all that are in them . . . (as on page 172).

The prayer of Christ before His passion for his church in this world. John xiii. chap. Pater venit hora ; clarifica filium. Father the hour is come glorify thy son . . . Amen (as on page 172)

The prayer of the church for sinners. Sapience. xv. Tu Deus noster suavis. Thou our God art gentle and true, patient, and with mercy ordering . . . (as on page 172)

The prayer and blessing of Job in his most tribulation and taking away of his goods. Job ii. cha. In tonso capite corruens. Job, his head clipped, falling flat on the ground, worshipped God . . . So be it (as on page 172).

When we are scourged of God either for our sins, or that we may be proved by him. The prayer of Thobie the iiii. chapiter. Justus es Domine. Thou are just Lord, and all thy judgments are true . . . (as on page 172).

A prayer of Jeremy xviii. Chap. Sana me Domine et sanabor. Heal me good Lord, and I shall be healed . . . Finis (as on page 172).

He that loveth God, loveth his neighbour. John iii. If a man say, I love God and yet hateth his neighbour, he is a liar.

An order and form of bidding of the beads by the King's commandment[1] (as on page 175) but for " For the good estate of our noble Prince Edward" read "And for the most noble and royal estate of our prince Prince Edward."

The abrogation of the Holydays (as on page 175).

The xv. Oes in english (as on pages 116, 171).

A devout prayer. O my sovereign Lord Jesu, the very Son of almighty God . . . Deus propitius esto mihi peccatori vel peccatrici. I thank thee also with all my heart and most gracious Lord for the benefits and grace . . . So be it (as on pages 116, 187).

A devout prayer. Jesu for thy holy name and for thy bitter passion, save us from sin . . . So be it (as on page 116).

A devout prayer. Most dear Lord and Saviour sweet Jesu, I beseech thy most courteous goodness . . . So be it (as on page 116).

---

[1] See Wilkins Conc. ed. 1737. Vol. 3. page 783.

A devout prayer. O blessed lady, mother of Jesu and Virgin immaculate, that art well of comfort . . . (as on page 116).

A devout prayer. O glorious Angel unto whom our blessed Lord of his most merciful grace . . . So be it (as on page 116).

The manner to live well, devoutly, and salutarily every day, for all christian persons of mean estate for to read. Compiled by Master Johan Quentin, doctor in divinity at Paris, diligently translated into our english tongue (as on page 147) but omits from " Rest you after dinner " to " And beware ye pass not a fortnight except very great let ". Also for, " Rise up at vi of the clock in the morning in all seasons " read " When you rise up in the morning at all seasons ". And for " Think how many times he hath forgiven you in shrift " read " Think how many times he hath forgiven you in trust".

₄ *The book has neither Dirige nor Commendations.*

A SUMMARY OF THE CONTENTS

OF THE

PRIMERS IN ENGLISH AND LATIN:

IN WHICH THE HOURS ARE COMPOUNDED PARTLY OF SARUM USE;
AND PARTLY OF THOSE HOURS PRINTED CHIEFLY FOR
WILLIAM MARSHALL.

PRINTED CUM PRIVILEGIO REGALI.

A.D. 1536—A.D. 1540.

A.D. 1536, John Gowghe,[1] **London, 8º. English and Latin. No. 122.**

⁎ *The title of the book has " This prymer of Salisbury use both in english and in latin . . . Hereunto annexed a fruitful work called the Paradise of the soul . . . also Jesus matyns with prime and hours and evensong. Cum gratia et privilegio regali." The contents of this book are almost the same as those of No. 117* page* 93.

An Almanacke for xx years. It begins A.D. 1535. Easter. 28 March.

The Kalender is Sarum. It has on January 5. " Oct. S. Thomæ," on July 7. " Transl. S. Thomæ," on December 29. " S. Thomas."

✠ A. b. c. d. e. f. g. h. i. k. l. m. n. o. p. q. r. s. t. v. u. x. y. z.

In nomine . . . In the name. Oratio dominica. Pater noster.

Seven petitions of the Pater noster by John Colet, Dean of Poules. O Father in heaven hallowed be thy name among men in earth . . . Amen (as on page 150).

Salutatio angelica. Ave Maria . . . Jesus Christus. Amen. The salutation of the angel. Hail Mary . . . fruit of thy womb. Jesus. Amen.

Duodecim articuli fidei. Credo in Deum . . . Amen. The xii articles of the faith, the which every true christian man and woman be bound to believe. I believe in God the Father almighty creator of heaven and earth . . . Amen.

The x commandments. One God only thou shalt love and worship perfectly . . . (as on page 162).

A dialogue of christian living wherein the child asketh certain questions and answereth to the same. The question. Speak my dear child, what art thou. The answer. As concerning my first birth. I am a creature of God endued with wit and reason the son of Adam, and as touching my new and second birth, I knowledge myself to be a christian . . . Then

---

[1] See State papers. Foreign and Domestic. Henry 8. Vol. 5. No. 896, and Vol. 7. No. 805.

214   SUMMARY OF CONTENTS.   [1536-

> when the child is come to discretion, let him be induced to know what God is. God is might, wisdom, and infinite goodness, without beginning . . . It is also necessary to know what man is. Man is created after the likeness of the image of God . . . (see pages 151, 199).

Grace afore dinner. Blessed be the Lord omnipotent with all faithful eyes that trust in him . . . Amen.

Grace after dinner. Blessed be the Lord omnipotent that sendeth us plenty . . . Amen. The holy name of our Lord Jesu be ever blessed . . . The souls that be hence passed in Christ Jesu. Rest they in peace at his will and pleasure. Amen.

Grace afore dinner. Break thou the bread and food to the poor . . . Amen.

Grace after dinner.˙ Our bountiful Lord God hath made unto us all a remembrance . . . Amen. God save our noble worthy King Henry and his gracious Queen Anne with all their progeny. The faithful souls that are hence passed rest they in Christ Jesu. Amen.

Grace. Good Lord for thy grace meekly we call . . . In nomine.

After grace. Bless we our Lord which of his grace . . . All christian souls rest in peace. Amen.

The x commandments of the old and new law. These are the words of the Lord God omnipotent and saith, I am thy Lord God . . .

An introduction to all persons to fulfil the commandments to their power. My most dearly beloved christian people that are fixed in faith and in the love of Christ Jesu . . . Amen.

The comfortable words and sayings of Christ at the high day of judgment. The evangelist witnesseth that He saith to them that shall be saved . . .

The vii works of mercy ghostly . . . The v bodily wyttes . . . The v ghostly wyttes . . . (see page 133).

Our Father which art in heaven hallowed be thy name . . . Amen. Because ye may understand the Pater noster the better, ye shall mark . . .

Our Father which art in heaven, this is the meaning. Even as a child when he goeth to his father to have anything of him . . .

Hail Mary full of grace, the Lord is with thee, blessed art thou among women, and blessed is the fruit of thy womb, Jesus Christ. So be it. Here thou seest that in these words no petition but pure praises . . . (as on page 197).

O maker of heaven and earth, king of kings . . . So be it (as on page 203).

Office of all estates. Good works. Acts v. Persecution (as on page 203).

A general confession for every sinner brought in to knowledge of his sins to confess himself with penitent and sorrowful heart before God at all times. O my most merciful Father, the father of mercies and God of all consolation . . . So be it. Furthermore. I have not given meat to the hungry . . . So be it (as on page 195).

An exhortation for them that receiveth the blessed sacrament of the altar. Most dearly beloved in God ye shall understand how that the gospel of Christ . . . Amen (as on page 205).

-1536] HOURS, SARUM, AND MARSHALL. 215

If thou have grace of the Holy Ghost in thee thou shalt not need to dread any peril of these sins following, Pride, Envy, Wrath, Covetous, Sloth, and Gluttony, and Lechery. Pride cometh only of man's high arrogant will . . .

The four gospels in english. In the beginning was the word . . . Anty. We do call upon thee . . . ℣. Blessed be the name of the Lord . . . A. From henceforth and evermore . . . O God the protector of all that trust in thee . . . Amen (as on page 209).

Luke i. The angel Gabriel was sent from God unto a city of Galilee . . .

Matthew the second chapter. When Jesus was born in Bethlehem a town of Jury . . .

Mark xvi. After that He appeared unto the eleven as they sat at meat . . .[1]

A prayer concerning the vii petitions that the sinner prayeth to God for the vii times that Christ spake on the cross. Omnipotent Lord Jesu Christ that the hanging on the cross . . . Amen (as on page 210).

The passion written by Saint Johan Evangelist. When Jesus had spoken these words, He went forth . . . ℣. Thou that suffered'st for us. A. Lord have mercy on us. O Lord which hast displayed thine hands and feet . . . Amen (as on page 210).

Matyns of our Lady. Prime and Hours of our Lady. The third Hour of our Lady. The sixth Hour of our Lady. The ninth Hour of our Lady. Evensong of our Lady. Compline of our Lady.

₊ *The Hours are in english and latin. Matins and Lauds are the same as those printed chiefly for William Marshall; as in No. 115. c. A.D. 1534. The First, Third, Sixth, Ninth Hours, and Evensong are according to the use of Sarum, as in No. 124. A.D. 1536, but without any invocation of the Virgin Mary. Compline is Sarum except the Antiphon to the psalms, the Chapter, and the Hymn. The Hours of the cross are appended; they are Sarum and are in english and latin, as in No. 124. A.D. 1536, with the addition of a collect in english at the end of each Hour.*

At Lauds.[1] The collects. Of the Holy Ghost. De S. Spiritu. Añ. Come Holy Spirit of God . . . Versicle. Send forth thy Spirit . . . Answer. And the face of the earth . . . Let us pray. O God which hast instructed the hearts of the faithful . . . So be it. Oremus. Deus qui corda fidelium . . . Amen.

Of the Holy Trinity. De S. Trinitate. Anty. Deliver us, save us . . . ℣. The Lord's name be blessed . . . A. From this time forth . . . Let us pray. Almighty and everlasting God which hast granted . . . Amen. Oremus. Omnipotens sempiterne Deus qui dedisti . . . Amen.

Of the holy Cross. De S. Cruce. Añ. Truly we ought to rejoice . . . ℣. All the earth worshippeth . . . Respo. And praiseth his name . . . Let us pray. O God which hast ascended thy most holy cross . . . Oremus. Deus qui sanctam crucem ascendisti . . . Amen.

Of St John Baptist. De S. Johanne Baptista. Añ. Amongst the sons of women . . . ℣. From God there was a man sent . . . A. Whose name

[1] See Sarum Hours. English and Latin. A.D. 1536. No. 124. page 162

was John . . . Let us pray. O Lord defend us alway through the continual succour . . . So be it. Oremus. Perpetuis nos Domine sancti Johannis Baptistæ tuere . . . Amen.

Of St Peter and Paul. De Sanctis Petro et Paulo. Añ. Peter the apostle and Paul the doctor . . . ℣. In all the earth . . . A. And in the coasts of the world . . . Let us pray. O God whose right hand did lift up blessed Peter . . . So be it. Oremus. Deus cujus dextera beatum Petrum apostolum . . . Amen.

Of St Andrew. De S. Andrea. Anty. Andrew was the servant of Christ . . . ℣. The Lord loved Andrew . . . A. With a savour sweet . . . Let us pray. Lord we humbly beseech thy majesty . . . So be it. Oremus. Majestatem tuam Domine suppliciter exoramus . . . Amen.

Of St John evangelist. De S. Johanne evangelista. Añ. This is the same John . . . ℣. Greatly to be praised . . . A. For he leaned on the breast . . . Let us pray. We beseech thee Lord of thy benignity . . . So be it. Oremus. Ecclesiam tuam fidelem quæsumus Domine . . . Amen.

Of St Laurence. De S. Laurentio. Anty. Saint Laurence the deacon . . . ℣. He distributed . . . A. His righteousness remaineth . . . Let us pray. Lord we beseech thee to give us grace . . . So be it. Oremus. Da nobis quæsumus omnipotens Deus vitiorum nostrorum . . . Amen.

Of St. Steven. De S. Stephano. Anty. Stevyn saw the gates of heaven . . . ℣ Thou hast him crowned . . . A. And hast set him . . . Let us pray. Grant good Lord that we may perfectly follow him that we do worship . . . Amen. Oremus. Da nobis quæsumus Domine imitari . . . Amen.

Of Mary Magdalen. De S. Maria Magdalena. Añ. Mary Magdalen did anoint . . . ℣. Many sins were forgiven her. A. Because her love . . . Let us pray. Grant unto us most merciful Father that like as blessed Mary Magdalen . . . Amen. Oremus. Largire nobis clementissime pater . . . Amen.

Of St. Margarete. De S. Margareta. Añ. Saint Margarete was but xv years old . . . ℣. For thy beauty . . . A. Proceed prosperously . . . Let us pray. God that hast caused the blessed virgin Margarete . . . Amen. Oremus. Deus qui beatam virginem Margaretam . . . Amen.

Of the Saints whose relikes remain in the holy church. De sanctis quorum reliquiæ continentur in universali ecclesia. Anthem. All ye blessed Saints . . . ℣. Rejoice in the Lord . . . A. And all you that in heart . . . Let us pray. We beseech thee good Lord that thou being pleased . . . Amen. Oremus. Omnium sanctorum tuorum quæsumus Domine . . . Amen.

For peace. De pace. Anthem. Lord send us peace in our time . . . ℣. Lord send peace . . . A. And great abundance . . . Let us pray. O God from whom all holy desires . . . Amen. Deus a quo sancta desideria . . . Amen. Bless we the Lord. Thank we God.

Hail Jesu Christ, King of mercy, our life, our sweetness . . . ℣. In all our trouble . . . ℟. O Jesu our health and glory . . . The prayer. O Jesu Christ the Son of God our redeemer, which dejected'st and humblest thyself . . . Amen (as on page 199).

Of the v corporal joys of our Lady. De gaudiis beatæ Mariæ virginis corporalibus. Rejoice, O virgin . . . Gaude virgo . . . ℣. Thou art blessed . . . A. For the fruit of life . . . Let us pray. O God which with double joy . . . So be it. Oremus. Deus qui beatissimam Virginem Mariam . . . Amen (as on page 164).

Out of the bottomless pit of my heavy troubles. De profundis. Lord pray for us. Our Father. ℣. Lord give them eternal rest. A. And continual light. ℣. From the gates . . . A. Lord deliver . . . ℣. I trust to see . . . A. In the land . . . ℣. Lord God hear . . . A. And give hearing . . . Let us pray. Lord incline thine ear . . . So be it. Oremus. Inclina Domine aurem tuam . . . Amen. God have mercy of all christian souls. So be it. Animæ omnium fidelium defunctorum . . . Amen (as on page 165).

A prayer to be said at the levation of the sacrament. Hail very body incarnate of a virgin . . . Ave verum corpus . . . (as on page 165).

The seven psalms.

The Litany of Jesus Christ's acts and mercy for all sinners cordially of him axing.

₊ *The Litany has this invocation " All holy saints and the elect creatures of God. Pray ye for us". It has " That thou vouchsafe to give universal peace to Cæsar and among all kings universal". "That thou vouchsafe to preserve our King Henry and all his aiders and helpers." "That the ministers and governors may catholically rule thy people." The acts of Jesus Christ, showing his mercy, are in this Litany in the place of the invocations of saints in the Litany according to Sarum use.*

Whosoever willeth to be saved . . . Quicumque vult salvus esse . . . Deliver us, save us, justify us, O blessed Trinity. ℣. The Lord's name be blessed . . . A. From this time forth . . . Let us pray. Almighty and everlasting God, which hast granted to us thy servants through confession of the true faith . . . Amen. Oremus. Omnipotens sempiterne Deus qui dedisti nobis famulis tuis . . . Amen (see page 210).

₊ *The book has no Dirige.*

The Commendations are Sarum; as in No. 124. A.D. 1536, (page 166) but with the addition of the argument as in No. 174. A.D. 1545 (page 237).

The Psalms of Christ's passion.

The Psalter of St Hierom. Psalterium beati Hieronymi (as on page 167).

When thou shalt receive the sacrament. In sumptione corporis Christi. O merciful Lord I am not worthy . . . Amen. Domine non sum dignus . . . (as on page 167).

When thou hast received it. Post sumptionem corporis Christi. The very true receiving of thy glorious body . . . Vera perceptio corporis . . . Amen. (as on page 167).

A devout prayer of St. Bernard. Oratio sancti Bernardini confessoris ordinis minorum. O bountiful Jesu ... So be it. O bone Jesu ... Amen. O glorious King ... O rex gloriose ... (as on page 167).

For a competency of living the prayer of Solomon. Proverbs the xxx. chapter. Pro vitæ competentia. Oratio Salomonis. Prover. xxx. Two things Lord I demanded that thou wouldest not deny me ... So be it. Duo rogavi te ne deneges ... Amen (as on page 167).

The Matyns in the honor of the blessed name of Jesu. Lauds of Jesus. Pryme and Hours of Jesus. The first Hour. The third Hour. The vi. Hour. The ninth Hour. The Evensong of the name of Jesus. The Complene or burying time.

₊ *These Hours are, with some variations, a translation of " Horæ dulcissimi nominis Jesu " (see No. 26. A.D. 1508. page 10).*

Devout meditations and prayers with contemplations called the Paradise of the soul.

₊ *This devotion is printed in full on pages 220-224.*

Colophon. Here endeth this prymer with the Paradise of the soul. Imprinted by Johan Gowhe dwelling in London in Chepsyd next Paulys gate 1536.

₊ *The reverse of the leaf on which the colophon is printed has, A cut of the King's arms encompassed with the garter; the arms are crowned, and supported by a dragon and a greyhound: over the arms is a riband with the motto " Dieu et mon droit," on the right a rose, on the left a pomegranate: beneath the arms, on the right a fleur de lis, on the left a portcullis. The words " Johan Gowghe, the printer. Cum privilegio," are below the cut.*

An exposition after the manner of a contemplation upon the li psalme called Miserere mei Deus[1] (as on page 200).

A devout short prayer to Jesus. Jesu Lord that madest me, And with thy blessed blood hast me bought ... Amen.

The Pater noster spoken of the sinner, God answering Him at every petition. The sinner. Our Father which art in heaven, what a great space is between thee and us ... Amen.

A prayer for the King and the Queen. O Lord God, which art the very high imperial protector ... Amen.

A meditation of Jerom de Fararia upon the psalm of In te Domine speravi, which prevented by death he could not finish[2] (as on page 207).

Colophon. An end of the meditation of Hierom of Ferrarie upon the psalm In te domine speravi which prevented by death he could not finish.

A.D. 1540, Richard Grafton and Edward Whitchurche,[3] London. 8º. English and Latin No. 151.

₊ *The title of the book is " The Primer both in english and latin ... Cum privilegio ad imprimendum solum ".*

[1] Fratris Hieronymi [G. Savonarola] Ferrariensis expositiones in psalmos A.D. 1505.
[2] Fratris Hieronymi [G. Savonarola] Ferrariensis expositiones in psalmos A.D. 1505.
[3] See Rymers Fœdera, ed. 1728, Vol 14. page 766; and Acts of privy council Vol 1. new series, A.D. 1890, pages 107. 117. 121.

-1540] HOURS, SARUM, AND MARSHALL.   219

An Almanacke for. xvii. years. It begins 1539. Easter day, 6 April.

The Kalender is the same as that in Hilsey's Primer No. 143. A.D. 1539 except that St Katherine is commemorated on November 20.

A lesson of the gospel of S. John declaring the passion of our master Christ. John xviii. When Jesus had spoken these words . . . ℣. Thou that sufferedest for us. A. Lord have mercy on us. A prayer. O Lord which hast displayed thine hands and feet . . . O Lord for thy great mercy and grace. Help thy people that so fain would have . . . So be it (as on page 162).

A lesson of the gospel of St Luke mentioning the resurrection of Christ. Luke xxiiii. But upon one of the Sabbaths very early in the morning . . . Thanks be to God (as on page 183).

A lesson of the gospel of St. Mark mentioning the ascension of Christ. Marke xvi. At the last as the eleven sat at the table . . . (as on page 183).

An order and form of bidding of the beads by the King's commandments (as on page 175).

The Symbol or Creed of the great doctor Athanasius daily read in the church. Whosoever will be saved before all things . . . (as on page 210).

The abrogation of the holydays (as on page 211).

A preface to the Matyns and the other Hours declaring the first institution of them, and for what cause they be received and accustomed to be said in the church and among other christians. Of long time christian reader it hath been used in the church of God certain hours to be appointed to the service of God and to prayer . . . God save the King (see pages 170, 229).

Matyns of our Lady. Prime and Hours of our Lady. Third, Sixth, and Ninth Hours of our Lady. Evensong of our Lady. Complyn of our Lady. The Hours of the Cross are appended to each Hour except Compline.

⁎ *The Hours in the case of Matins and Lauds are the same as those printed chiefly for William Marshall as in No. 122. A.D. 1536, (page 213) and No. 115. c. A.D. 1534 (page 195). In the case of the First, Third, Sixth, and Ninth Hours they are according to the use of Sarum, as in No. 124. A.D. 1536 (page 159) and like No. 122. A.D. 1536. omitting the chapters with their responds, and any invocation of the Virgin Mary.*

The xv Psalms.

The signification of the word Letany. Mamercus bishop of Vienne what time that a terrible earthquake . . .

The Letany wants all but the last part; it begins ℣. Lord save the King and the realm.

The prologe to the Dirige. We read in sundry places of the Bible most dear reader, that the antique people the Hebrews had a certain manner of lamentation for the dead . . . (see page 231).

The Dirige, as well as the translation of it into english, is the same as that in Bishop Hilsey's Primer No. 143. A.D. 1539, (page 232).

⁎ *The book has not " The Commendations ".*

The third part of the Prymer treating of works. Works are diverse some right and necessary which must needed be observed . . . (see page 232).

Certain godly prayers to be used, and first in the morning when you arise. I thank thee my heavenly Father by thy dearly beloved Son Jesus Christ that this night . . . Amen (as on page 184).

The grace to be said afore dinner. The eyes of all things look up and wait upon thee . . . Our Father. O Lord God our heavenly Father bless thou us and these thy gifts . . . Amen (as on page 198).

Grace after dinner. We thank thee, O Lord our Father, by thy son Jesus Christ our Lord . . . Amen (as on page 198).

Grace before supper. Christ which at the last supper gave himself unto us . . . . Amen (as on page 198).

Grace after supper. Honour and praise be to God the King everlasting . . . Amen. God almighty Father of all mercy . . . Amen (as on page 198).

When thou shalt go to bed say thus. I lay me down to rest. In the name. I thank thee my heavenly Father by thy dear beloved Son Jesus Christ . . . Amen (as on page 198).

Prayer and thanksgiving to the heavenly Father for all his benefits shewed to us. O most highest almighty and eternal God whose glory replenisheth heaven . . . Amen (as on page 182).

Prayer for true faith. I will love thee O Lord my strength. The Lord is my stablishment and refuge. O Lord, make us to have a perpetual fear and love . . . O God defender of all that trust in thee . . . Amen (as on page 179).

⁎ "*The Pystels and Gospels of the Sundays and festival Holy-days newly corrected and amended. Printed in London in the house late the Grey Friars by Richard Grafton and Edward Whitchurche.* 1540. *Cum privilegio ad imprimendum solum*"[1] *are bound with this book; they are in english only and begin with New Year's day. The Holy days do not include the days of St. Thomas of Canterbury; and are fewer than those in No.* 140. *A.D.* 1538 (*page* 183).

The Paradise of the soul.

⁎ *This devotion occurs in No.* 122. *A.D.* 1536 (*page* 218).

Here followeth devout meditations and prayers with contemplations called the paradyse of the soul. When I conceived in my mind the great danger of hypocrisy and loss of prayer which Matthew reciteth in the vi. and xv and xxiii chapters . . . Amen.

Devota et brevis oratio penetrat cælos. First when thou intendest to prayer or devotion, which is stirred of the Holy Ghost, if thou mayest, get thee into a quiet place . . . Amen.

If thou wylt thou may'st use these prayers for every day in the week. A prayer for the Sunday. Sweet merciful and bountiful Lord Jesu this day I beseech thee . . . Pater noster. The Monday. Lord God I beseech thee that my heart may be inflamed with the love . . . Tuesday. Lord God eternal I humbly beseech thee that by thy great virtue of patience

---

[1] See Wilkins Conc. ed. 737. Vol. 3. page 776.

... Wednesday. Bountiful Lord God I pray thee that this day my heart may be illuminate . . . Pater noster. Thursday. Merciful Lord God omnipotent this day I recordially beseech thee that I may have fervent love . . . A Pater noster. Friday. This day good Lord, I beseech thee, by thy great virtue and grace . . . Saturday. This day pitiful Lord I beseech thee by the merits of thy painful passion . . .

A devout prayer to the Trinity. O mighty and dreadful and most merciful Lord, yea though I am a wretched and a miserable sinner that so uteren and grievously hath offended thy high majesty . . . Pater noster.

A special devout prayer. O my Lord and maker omnipotent through whose righteousness Lucifer fell from heaven . . . Amen. Pater noster.

When thou shalt receive the sacrament. O merciful Lord I am not worthy that thou shouldest enter in my sinful house . . . Amen (as on page 210).

When thou hast received. The very true receiving of thy glorious body of flesh and blood . . . (as on page 210).

To get grace for sin. O my Lord God I beseech Thee humbly of thy benign grace to hear me praying . . .

Against all evil thoughts. O pitiful Lord God, alway shewing thy mercy upon me . . . Amen. Pater noster (as on page 210).

For the King and the Queen. O Lord God which art the very high imperial protector of all christian realms I humbly beseech thee of thy pitiful mercy to enlumine our King N and his council with thy most holy Spirit of grace, sapience, and of understanding, and to preserve him therein and his Queen with their succession . . . Amen (see page 218).

For thy friend living. O Lord God that of thy mere mercy dost daily justify the wicked . . . Amen.

A devout contemplation. O Jesu the very son of almighty God and of the pure Virgin Mary . . . Non nobis Domine non nobis, sed nomini tuo da gloriam. O my sovereign Lord and Creator of all things on earth . . . O blessed Lord God look not at my defaults . . . Amen.

A lively contemplation to all them that have devotion in the saying of our Ladyes Sauter; at every Pater noster and x. Aves. The first Pater noster. O blessed Lord God omnipotent, by whose wisdom all things ben created . . . Say x. Aves. The 2 Pater noster. O most high and meek Lord, which by thy goodness only did'st vouchsafe to come . . . Say x Aves. The 8. Pater noster. Sweet and bountiful Lord God I meekly pray thee that like as thou chose Peter John and James . . . Say x Aves. The 4 Pater noster. Most meek Lord and Saviour which kneeled at the feet of thy disciples and washed them also . . . Say x Aves. The 5 Pater noster. O glorious Lord that straight after thy expiration on the cross . . . Amen. Say x Aves. The 6 Pater noster. Most mighty Lord, which after thine ascension did'st send down the Holy Ghost . . . The Credo.

A good exhortation. Above all things love God with all thy heart, desire his honor more than the health of thine own soul . . . Amen.

A devout contemplation. Thus most merciful Lord that doest all of thy exceeding charity and not of my merits . . .

A devout prayer how the soul desireth the favour and grace of God for his offences. My sovereign Lord Jesu Christ I humbly beseech thee not to be long absent from me . . . Amen.

A devout prayer. My high and most sovereign Lord Jesu Christ when I do remember the saying of the holy prophet Job . . . Amen.

A brief meditation of Christ's passion. O sovereign Lord God that wouldest vouchsafe for our sins and trespasses come to redeem the world . . . Amen.

A devout prayer for the grace and mercy of God. Almighty God King and Lord of glory eternal which art so full of goodness and mercy . . . Amen (as on page 184).

A devout prayer to Christ the second person in Trinity our only redeemer God and Man. O Lord Jesu thou art the very Lamb of God and very God and Man most meek and kind . . . Also, Lord Jesu Christ king of mercy and of pity I believe and knowledge that thou sufferedest in thy blessed feet to be nailed . . . Also, Lord Jesu King of glory I believe and I knowledge that when thou sawest the city of Jerusalem given to horrible sins . . . Also, Lord Jesu I believe and knowledge that when thou hung nailed on the cross thou heardest thy enemies report . . . Also, Lord Jesu King of glory I believe and knowledge that when thou were yet hanging on the cross thou Lord openest thy most holy mouth and prayed for thine enemies . . . Also, Lord Jesu King of glory, I believe and knowledge that thou thirsted full sore on the cross and said'st I thirst . . . Also, Lord Jesu King of glory and omnipotent, I believe and knowledge that thou Lord wast crowned with a sharp garland of thorns . . . Also, Lord Jesu King of mercy and pity I steadfastly believe and knowledge, that thou Lord sufferedst thy blessed body to be beaten rent and torn . . . Also, Sweet Jesu I do knowledge and believe that while thou were yet hanging on the cross thou sufferedest thy most blessed side to be pierced . . . Amen. Almighty Jesu and God in Trinity three persons and one God for thine endless mercy and pity give me grace Lord to keep clean my soul . . .

A devout short prayer to Jesu. Jesu Lord that madest me, And with thy blessed blood hast me bought . . (as on page 218).

A devout prayer for to avoid the dangers of this miserable life that daily fall to us. O my special and most gracious Lord Jesu my heart Lord is in manner confounded for sorrow . . .

A devout prayer against the vain glory of this world. O thou my most special Lord God and most principal precious jewel of my soul . . .

How the soul of man desireth of God our Father eternal his favour and grace against all tribulations. O Lord God I am sick and weak in my spirit and almost comfortless . . . Amen.

A consolation of comfort in faith for a man being in a great agony of a secret heart. O good Lord Jesu hearken to my words and mark well my prayer . . .

Another devout contemplation in a faithful soul. When I considered in my mind the penitential psalms of David . . . Amen.

A contemplation of a faithful man against malicious injuries or despites. O Lord God all my hope hath been even in thee save me therefore from all mine enemies . . .

A good devout prayer to withstand the unstability of man's mind against vain glory. Conform me my high sovereign Lord Jesu Christ by thy inestimable grace and goodness . . . Amen.

The xv oos or prayers of Saint Bryget as it is written in Rome of Saint Johans in a table.[1] O the most delectable and quietness of my soul sweet Jesu Christ that art Verus salus omnium in te sperantium . . . Pater noster. The second petition. O sweet Jesu the very solatious comfort of all creatures . . . Pater noster. The third petition. O the very former and creator of all this world Jesu Christ . . . Pater noster. The fourth petition. O the most delicious rose and sweetness to all mankind sweet Jesu . . . Pater noster. The fifth petition. O the most highest sapience divine that ever was . . . Pater noster. The sixth petition. O the very fountain and sweet spring of eternal life . . . Pater noster. The vii petition. O the very celestial joy and liberty of angels sweet Jesu Christ . . . Pater noster. The viii petition. O good Jesu the very solatious comfort of all them that are laden and oppressed with tribulations . . . Pater noster. The ix petition. O my sweet love and potential Lord Jesu Christ . . . Pater noster. The x petition. O the very plentiful of all goodness and grace my high sovereign Lord God . . . Pater noster. The xi petition. O Jesu the very victorious and triumphant crown of eternal glory . . . Pater noster. The xii petition. O the most high eternal consummation and finisher of God's works . . . Pater noster. The xiii petition. O the very hope and glory of all that believe and trust in thee . . . Pater noster. The xiiii petition. O Jesu the very repairer and edifier of all mankind . . . Pater noster. The xv petition. O sweet Jesu my only heart's desire and comfort . . . Amen. Pater noster. Ave. Credo. Finis. (see pages 116, 171, 211.)

The nosegay or posee of light to lead and comfort all sinners that walk in darkness, gathered out of the New Testament. Qui ambulat in tenebris . . . The law of God is a doctrine that biddeth good . . . He that loveth God and his neighbour keepeth all the commandments of God . . . He that loveth God loveth his neighbour . . . He that loveth God keepeth all the commandments . . . He that hath the christian faith loveth God . . . It is not in our power to keep any of the commandments of God without God's grace . . . The law was given to show us our sins . . . Of the gospel and what it signifieth . . . The nature of the law, and of the virtue of the gospel . . . A disputation

[1] See Edward VI. Homilies. Of works. A.D. 1547.

between the law and the gospel . . . Of faith . . . He that believeth his word . . . He that believeth not God's word believeth not God Himself . . . Faith is the gift of God . . . Faith is not in our power . . . Without faith it is impossible to please God . . . He that hath the faith wotteth well that he pleaseth God . . . Of faith . . . He that believeth in Christ shall be saved . . . He that believeth not the gospel believeth not God . . . He that believeth the gospel shall be safe . . . A comparison between faith, and unfaithfulness or incredulity . . . Of hope . . . We should put our hope and trust in God only and in no other thing nor creature . . . Of charity[1] . . . The rule of charity is this . . . A comparison between faith, hope, and charity . . . Of works . . . Every man's works are either good or evil . . .

[1] See pages 175, 210.

A SUMMARY OF THE CONTENTS
OF THE
BOOKS VARIOUSLY CALLED
MANUAL OF PRAYERS OR PRIMER:
PRIMER: PRIMER OR BOOK OF
PRAYERS:
IN WHICH THE HOURS ARE IN ENGLISH, OR IN ENGLISH AND
LATIN, SET FORTH BY JOHN HILSEY BISHOP OF ROCHESTER,
AT THE COMMANDMENT OF LORD THOMAS CRUMWELL, VICE-
GERENT TO THE KING'S HIGHNESS.
CUM PRIVILEGIO AD IMPRIMENDUM SOLUM.[1]
A.D. 1539—A.D. 1540.

A.D. 1539, John Mayler, London, for John Wayland, London, sold by Andrew Hester, London, and Mychel Lobley, London, 8o. English.

No. 143.[2]

₊ *The title of the book has "The Manual of prayers or the primer in english set out at length . . . Set forth by John late Bishop of Rochester at the commandment of the right honorable Lord Thomas Crumwell, Lord Privy seal, Vice-gerent to the King's highness . . . Cum privilegio ad imprimendum solum."*

John late Bishop of Rochester unto the Right Honorable Thomas Lord Crumwell Lord Privy seal, Vice-gerent to the King's highness, wisheth and desireth grace, peace, and health in God the Father by the Holy Ghost, through our Lord Jesus Christ. Although that the sundry and divers sorts of prymers (my special good Lord and singular friend) here before set forth, as well in many things superstitious as derogative unto the true honor of God, might have enforced (and did indeed) me to have desired a sincere correction herein; yet the fervent desire that I perceive in your Lordship to the true honor of God, the unity and weal of the christian commonalty hath much more (as the proverb saith) set the spur unto the hasty runner, and in manner compelled me to show some token of my due service toward God's honor, and toward your favourable goodness in setting forth this rude and simple work . . . committing it to the most wisest judgment of the King's most sapient council, whereof ye are, that if so be it should seem unto the same a thing worthy or meet to be had in common usage, then by the judgment of the same approved, it might the rather, and with the more avidity be received of the people . . .

[1] Wilkins Conc. ed. 1737. Vol. 3. page 776.

[2] See Primer. No. 158. c, A.D. 1540. page 183; and State papers, foreign and domestic, Henry 8. Vol. 14. Pt. 1. No. 1329.

The prologe to the Kalender. The strangeness of this Kalender, gentle reader, shall not move thee to marvel very much, the cause ones known; for the new fashion hereof hath a double commodity. The one is briefness, for where the other Kalender had a great number of Saints without profit to the unlearned, this hath but only such feasts which are kept holyday, and the Epistle and Gospel that are read in the church on such holy days, set forth in the Kalender. The second is, that where the number of Saints were set, there have we appointed weekly certain places of the Scripture, which the church doth use to read at Matins, that the Reader may know what Scripture the church doth use throughout the year, and to study and use the same.

An Almanacke for xvii years. It begins 1539. Easter Day. 6 April.

The Kalender. The contents are described above in the Prologe. The days of St. Thomas of Canterbury do not occur either in the Kalender or in the Litany. The Epistles and Gospels referred to are bound with the copy of this book in the British Museum C. 12. e. 13.

The prologue to the whole work. I have here set forth most dear reader a rude work whom it hath pleased me to call the Manual of prayers, because it is so commonly had in hand with the people, which before was called the Primer, because I suppose that it is the first book that the tender youth was instructed in. And in this Primer were contained a great number of unnecessary prayers and some very superstitious, but in especial therein was the chief suffrages, that is to say, the Matins with the Hours, Evensong with Complene, appointed to be of our Lady; for this cause so called, as some unlearned hath both feigned and taught, that she should use to say it, but how false and foolish this is, let the learned judge; but rather it was so called, because that all the Anthems, Hymns, Lessons, Responses, Chapters, and Collects were thought to be of our Lady; yet were there many Scriptures distorted unto our Lady, which in their own native sense are nothing meant of her, but of Christ, the Wisdom of the Father. As for an example at the first, how the chapter is " In omnibus requiem quæsivi " written Ecclesiastici. xxiv.[1] with the chapters of the Hours and of Complene. For this cause have I thought it my bounden duty towards God's true and sincere honour, to set forth such a manner of Primer; wherein might be no such distorted Scripture or false honour of that most immaculate Mother of God, lest the youth should learn to take such Scriptures to be of our Lady which are of God, and to give such praise to her as should only be given to God, but to know first the true honour of God, and to know the honour that belongeth to that blessed Virgin Mary, and to the Holy Saints. And forasmuch as the Primer is not had in hand of so many, but all they, yea every Christian is bound first to learn to lead a christian life, therefore have I here in the process of this Primer in manner pointed and set forth the true life of a Christian,

[1] See Preface to Primer c. A.D. 1537. No. 128. page 169.

that as oft as he shall handle his Primer, he may so often learn and remember the true life toward God, which life consisteth principally and wholly in faith, in prayer, and in good works; and these three are not only taught in the three lessons of Matins, but also in the three parts of this Primer so divided . . . But where there shall seem to the reader in the Psalms any difference between the Latin and English, let the same remember that the English is accordant to the Hebraical psalter translated by St Jerome, and the Latin is the usual psalter, which in some places are not correspondent in all things; and thus have I joined them, that such as delighteth in the English might have the plainer sentence, and that the other that readeth the Latin should not think that we should bring in any strange psalmody.

Moreover where as the psalms, and anthems, hymns, lessons, which were right good, are now changed; this did I, not that I should think them worthy of rejection, other that I would be noted to be of such rare and excellent judgment, that I would correct the use of the church so long continued; but rather thus have I enterprised, because that the said anthems, hymns, and lessons are such sentences, and in the said psalms is such obscurity and darkness, that the rude and the unlearned which hath most the use of such kind of books as this is, might not comprehend the mysteries of them, and hereby had the less devotion; having therefore now psalms, anthems, lessons, and hymns of more plain sentence, they may better understand the same, and in understanding shall have more contemplation and devotion. To avoid prolixity, which often time decayeth devotion, the great number of memories of the Saints used in the Matins, of the which some doth plainly derogate the honour of God, is omitted.

I omitted also the great number of Saints commonly set forth in other Primers in the Litany; not because that I would go about to teach herein the people that they should not pray to Saints, other that I do mistrust the holiness of the Saints that are here omitted, but that they, according to the King's grace's injunction,[1] should have the greater devotion in the suffrages that followeth in the litany than in numbering so many Saints.

In the Dirige set forth in other Primers, were made anthems, responses, and lessons applied for the dead, which seemed more to be lamentations of the misery of man's life than the prayers for the dead. I thought it convenient to change the same, and to declare by the three first lessons, and responses, the miserable state of man's life; by the second, the condition of the sepulture, and by the three last lessons, to declare the resurrection general, that the devout reader, encumbered with the misery of this present life, by faith and hope of the last resurrection, might with the more patience tolerate this journey, abiding Christ the Judge of quick and dead, which liveth and reigneth everlasting. So be it.

[1] See Wilkins Conc. ed. 1737. Vol. 3. pages 813-816.

The Symbol or Creed of the great Doctor Athanasius. Daily read in the Church. Whosoever will be saved, before all things it is necessary that he hold the catholic faith . . . (as on page 210).

The Creed, or the twelve articles of the Christian Faith. The first article. I believe in God the Father Almighty, maker of heaven and earth . . .

The gospel of St. Matthew mentioning the incarnation of Jesus Christ. The birth of Christ was on this wise . . . (see page 183).

A lesson of the gospel of St John declaring the passion of our Master Christ, John xviii. When Jesus had spoken these words . . . ℣. Thou that suffredest for us. A. Lord have mercy on us. A prayer. O Lord which hast displayed Thine hands and feet . . . Amen. O Lord, for Thy great mercy and grace, Help Thy people, that so fain would have Thy holy gospel preached in every place . . . So be it (as on page 188).

A lesson of the gospel of St Luke mentioning the resurrection of Christ. Luc. xxiiii. But upon one of the sabbaths very early in the morning . . . Thanks be to God (see page 188).

A lesson of the gospel of St Mark mentioning the ascension of Christ. Mar. xvi. At the last, as the eleven sat at the table, He shewed Himself unto them . . . (see page 188)

The second part of this Manual called Prayer.

An order and form of bidding of the beads by the King's commandment. Ye shall pray for the whole congregation of Christ's church, and specially for this church of England; wherein first I commend to your devout prayers the King's most excellent Majesty supreme Head immediately under God of the spirituality and temporality of the same church, and for the prosperity of the noble Prince Edward his son. Secondly. Ye shall pray for the clergy, the Lord's temporal and commons of this realm . . . Thirdly. Ye shall pray for the souls that be departed . . .[1] (see page 211).

The seven petitions of the Pater noster. The first petition. Our Father which art in heaven, hallowed be thy name . . .

The salutation of the Angel, called the Ave Maria. Hail Mary, full of grace; the Lord is with thee . . . And blessed is the fruit of thy womb. Amen.

A prayer to be said in the morning when you arise. I thank thee, my heavenly Father, by thy dearly beloved Son Jesus Christ, that this night thou hast given me sleep and rest . . . Amen (see page 198).

The grace to be said afore dinner. The eyes of all things look up and wait upon thee . . . Thou openest thy hand, and replenishest all things . . . Our Father. O Lord God our heavenly Father, bless thou us, and these Thy gifts . . . Amen (as on page 198).

Grace after dinner. We thank Thee, O Lord, our Father, by thy Son Jesus Christ our Lord for all thy benefits . . . Amen (as on page 198).

Grace before supper. Christ which at the last supper gave himself unto us . . . Amen (as on page 198).

---

[1] Wilkins. Conc. ed. 1737. Vol. 3. pages 783, 844.

-1539] HOURS SET FORTH BY BP. HILSEY. 229

Grace after supper. Honour and praise be to God the King everlasting . . . Amen. God almighty, Father of all mercy . . . Amen (as on page 198).

When thou shalt go to bed say this. I lay me down to rest. In the name. I thank thee, my heavenly Father, by thy dear beloved son Jesus Christ . . . Amen (as on page 198).

The abrogation of the Holydays.[1] First, that the feast of dedication of the church shall in all places throughout this realm be celebrated and kept on the first Sunday of the month of October for ever, and upon none other day. Item, that the feast of the patron of every church within this realm, called commonly the Church holyday, shall not from henceforth be kept or observed as a holyday as heretofore hath been used; but that it shall be lawful to all and singular persons, resident or dwelling within this realm, to go to their work, occupation, or mystery, and the same truly to exercise and occupy upon the said feast, as upon any other work day, except the said feast of Church holyday be such as must be else universally observed as a holyday by this ordinance following. Also, that all those feasts or holy days which shall happen to occur, either in the harvest time, which is to be counted from the first day of July unto the twenty ninth day of September, or else in the term time at Westminster, shall not be kept or observed from henceforth as holidays, but that it may be lawful for every man to go to his work or occupation upon the same, as upon any other work-day, except always the feasts of the Apostles, of our blessed Lady, and of St George, and the four Evangelists, and Mary Magdalene. And also, such feasts as wherein the Kings Judges at Westminster Hall do not use to sit in judgment, all which shall be kept holy and solemn of every man, as in time past hath been accustomed. Provided always, that it may be lawful unto all priests, and clerks, as well secular as regular, in the foresaid holydays now abrogate, to sing or say their accustomed service for those holydays in their churches, so that they do not the same solemnly, nor do ring to the same, after the manner used in high holydays, nor do command or indict the same to be kept or observed as holydays . . .

₊ *The abrogation of the Holydays is the same as that in No. 136. A.D. 1538 (page 175.) but adds the words " And the four Evangelists, and Mary Magdalene" after " Except always the feasts of the Apostles, of our blessed Lady, and of St. George ".*

A preface to the Matins and the other Hours, declaring the first institution of them, and for what cause they be received and accustomed to be said in the church, and among other christians. Of long time christian reader, it hath been used in the church of God certain hours to be appointed to the service of God and to prayer, in the which, among other business, man should of his Lord and God have a hearty and fervent meditation and contemplation, and a remembrance of the manifold benefits and bountiful goodness of God shewed to him . . . (see page 219).

[1] See Wilkins Conc. ed. 1737. Vol. 3. page 823.

Matyns, the Laudes, the Prime, the Third Hour, the Sixth hour, the Ninth hour, the Evensong, the Compline. "A memory of the passion of Christ" which is the "Hours of the cross" according to Sarum use, and "A memory of the compassion of our Lady" which is modelled on the "Hours of the compassion of our Lady" according to Sarum use, are appended to each one of the Hours from Lauds to Compline.

⁎ *The Hours are those known as Hilsey's, and are found in those Primers which were set forth by Bishop Hilsey at the commandment of Lord Thomas Crumwell. The framework of the Hours as well as the commencement of each Hour is Sarum. The Psalms at Lauds and Prime are Sarum, but not those in the other Hours. The Canticles are Sarum. The Blessings at Matins and the Suffragia at Lauds are Sarum. The Ave Maria does not occur at all at Matins. The Hymns from Prime to the ninth Hour are Sarum, but not those at Matins, Lauds, Evensong, and Compline. The Antiphons, Lessons, Responds, Chapters, and Collects are not Sarum. The Chapters in the Hours from Prime to the ninth Hour are omitted.*

The Laudes, This word Laudes is as much to say as praise. And the service following is called so, because it containeth only the mere lauds and praise of Christ and the Virgin his mother (as on page 170).

The Evensong. What is meant by this word Evensong. Like as the service that we be daily accustomed to say in the morning is called Lauds, even so is the service used to be said or sung toward evening called Evensong (as on page 171).

The Complene. What is meant by this word Complene, This word Complene is no more to say but an accomplishment or fulfilling. And for so much as of all the services that are daily done in the church this is the last, therefore it is called Complene; as who should say that in the same all the holy service of the day is full and complete (as on page 171).

At Lauds and Evensong. The memory of the Holy Ghost. Anthem. Come Holy Spirit of God, inspire Thou the hearts . . . ℣. Send forth Thy Spirit . . . A. For so renewest Thou . . . The prayer. O God which hast instructed the hearts . . . So be it (see pages 162, 198).

A memory of the most holy Trinity. Anthem. Deliver us, save us . . . ℣. Bless we the Father . . . A. Praise we Him . . . Prayer. Almighty and everlasting God which hast granted to Thy servants . . . So be it (see pages 162, 198).

A memory of our Lady. Anthem. O glorious mother of God . . . ℣. O holy mother of God . . . A. Pray for us . . . Prayer. Grant we beseech Thee O Lord God, that Thy servants may enjoy . . . So be it.

A memory of All Saints. Anthem. All ye blessed Saints and elect servants of God . . . ℣. Rejoice in the Lord . . . A. And be you all glad . . . Prayer. We beseech Thee good Lord that Thou being pleased with the prayer of all thine holy Saints . . . So be it (as on page 216).

A prayer of Christ our Saviour.[1] Hail heavenly King, father of mercy, our life . . . Prayer. Almighty eternal God, which by the operation of the Holy

[1] See John Hollybush. Exposition upon Salve regina. (Bodl. Tanner, 23. and Christ Church Oxford.)

-1539] HOURS SET FORTH BY BP. HILSEY. 231

Ghost . . . So be it. To the holy and indivisible Trinity . . . So be it. Blessed be the sweet name of our Lord Jesu Christ . . . And the souls of all true believers being departed . . . So be it. Praising be to God, peace unto the living . . . So be it (as on page 199).

A devout prayer unto Jesus our Saviour. O bountiful Jesu, O sweet Jesu, O Jesu the son of the pure Virgin Mary . . . So be it. The anthem. O glorious King, which amongst thy saints art laudable . . . (as on page 204).

A prayer unto Christ. O maker of heaven and earth, King of kings . . . So be it (as on page 208).

The fifteen prayers called the xv. Oes.[1] The xv. prayers following, called commonly the xv. Oes, are set forth in divers Latin primers with goodly painted prefaces, promising to the sayers thereof many things both foolish and false, as the deliverance of xv. souls out of purgatory, with other like vanities; yet are the prayers self right good and virtuous, if they be said without any such superstitious trust or blind confidence. And forasmuch as these prayers are a goodly and godly meditation of Christ's passion, we have not thought it neither to us grievous, neither to this primer superfluous, to set them in this place. The i. prayer. O Jesu, endless sweetness to all that love thee . . . So be it. Our Father. (see page 223).

The seven penitential psalms. Why that these vii psalms following are called penitential . . . (as on page 171).

The fifteen psalms (See Prologue to the whole work. page 227).

The signification of this word Litany. Mamercus, bishop of Vienne what time that a terrible earthquake (as on page 171).

The Litany has invocations of saints and angels classified, according to the order in Sarum use. It has " That thou give peace, concord, and victory to our King and princes " (see prologue to the whole work, page 227).

An instruction of the manner in hearing of the Mass, shewing how and to what intent it should be heard; the which instruction I have, by occasion, prevented with a declaration to the instablishment of the christian faith concerning the Sacrament of the altar which is consecrated in the Mass.

The order taken of me in this Primer, most dear reader, setteth here following certain meditations to be said at the sacring, as we call it, of the mass, and in the mass time : . . .

A prayer to be said before mass. O Lord Jesu Christ, which art our very bishop, and did'st offer thyself unto God the Father . . . So be it.

A prayer to be said at the elevation time. Hail, very body, incarnate of a virgin, Nailed on a cross, and offered for man's sins . . . (as on pages 165, 217).

A prayer to be said after the mass. O Lord God omnipotent, which not of our deserts . . . So be it.

Prologue to the Dirige. We read in sundry places of the Bible, most dear reader, that the antique people the Hebrews had a certain manner of

[1] See Edward VI. Homilies. Of works. A.D. 1547.

lamentation for the dead . . . of these old Jewish customs hath there crept into the church a custom to have a certain suffrages for the dead, called Dirige of Dirige the first anthem hereof; but by whom or when these suffrages were made we have no sure evidence of writing . . . And as for such suffrages as are set forth in the Dirige, the collects excepted, they are no more to be applied for the dead than for the quick. But whether these were ordained at the first to be said for the souls departed or no, I will make no doctrine of it ; but this I know well, that the reader of these may have a great learning and knowledge of the miseries and shortness of the life of man, and may learn hereby to die well, and to have a hope and trust of the last resurrection. . . .

The Dirige is Sarum, except that "Lord give them eternal rest, And let continual light shine unto them" is omitted at the end of each psalm and elsewhere, also the Ave Maria. The nine Lessons are different from those in Sarum use. (see prologue to the whole work page 227).

₊ *The book has not "The Commendations".*

The third part of the Primer treating of works.

Works are divers, some right good and necessary, which must needs be observed as the commandments of God . . . Some are works of mens tradition, yet agreeable and consonant to God's word, and these ought to be observed . . . Some works are traditions of men not agreeable to God's word, but repugnant . . . Of these briefly shall be somewhat said . . .

The commandments of God given by Moses, and expounded by Christ sententially taken . . .[1] The first table. I am the Lord thy God, which have brought thee out of the land of Egypt . . . Christ. Hear Israel our Lord God is one Lord . . . (as on page 209).

The ten commandments compendiously extracted and briefly set forth according to the form of the last setting furth.[1] I. Thou shalt have none other Gods but me. II. Thou shalt not take the name . . .[2]

The second state of works is of man's tradition, which be with God's words, or at the least not repugnant to God's word; they are to be received, as the prescription of certain days to be kept holy, or to be fasted . . .

The third sort of works are of the tradition of man, which are not in the scripture of God, nor yet consonant to the scripture of God, but plainly repugnant, as pardons, pilgrimages, kissing of images, offering of candles, kneeling and crouching to stocks and stones . . .

The office of all estates. Be wise now therefore, O ye kings . . . To the liege people of all estates unto their prince. Let every soul submit himself to the auctority of the higher powers . . . The Bishops. A bishop must be blameless . . . The Elders or Parsons . . . Rulers . . . Every Christian to his even Christian . . . Husbands . . . Wives . . . Fathers and Mothers . . . Children . . . Masters . . . Servants . . . Widows

[1] The Pater noster, Ave, Creed, and 10 Commandments. (Brit. Mus. c. 25. b. 24) A.D. 1539. Camb. Univ. and Emman: Coll. Camb. no date.

[2] The order of the commandments is Sarum, see No. 124. page 162.

-1539] HOURS SET FORTH BY BP. HILSEY. 233

... The sum of all ... The conclusion of St. Peter upon all states. In conclusion, be ye all of one mind ... (see page 214).

The bishop of Rome with his adherences, destroyers of all estates. There were false prophets also among the people, even as there shall be false teachers among you likewise ...

Colophon. Imprinted in botoll lane ... Cum privilegio ad imprimendum solum. 1539.

₀ " *The Pystels and Gospels of the Sundays and festival Holy Days newly corrected and amended* " *are bound with this book; they are in english only and begin with New Year's day; they are the same as those in No.* 140. *A.D.* 1538.

c. A.D. 1539, John Mayler, London, for John Wayland, London, sold by Andrew Hester, London, and Mychel Lobley, London. 8o. No. 144.

₀ *The title has* " *The Primer in english most necessary for the education of children extracted out of the Manual of prayers or Primer in english and latin, set forth by Jho. late Bishop of Rochester at the commandment of the right honorable Lord Thomas Crumwell, Lord privy seal, Vice-gerent to the king's highness ... Cum privilegio ad imprimendum solum.*"

₀ *The Manual of prayers from which this book is extracted is No.* 142, *A.D.* 1539. *July* 15 (*page* 51). *It is the same book as No.* 143. *A.D.* 1539, (*page* 225,) *but the Hours are in Latin as well as English; the other parts of the book are also for the most part in Latin and English.*

The Kalender is the same as that in No. 143. A.D. 1539 (page 225) except that St Katherine is commemorated on November 20.

✠ a. b. c ... Seven petitions of the Pater noster. Salutation of the angel called the Ave Maria. Crede or the xii articles of the christen faith. The x commandments of almighty God. The Symbole or Crede of Athanasius daily read in the church. Prayer to be said in the morning when you arise. I thank thee my heavenly father ... Amen. Grace afore dinner. The eyes of all things ... Our Father. O Lord God our heavenly father bless thou us ... Amen. Grace after dinner. We thank thee O Lord our father ... Amen. Grace before supper. Christ which at the last supper ... Amen. Grace after supper. Honour and praise be to God the king ... Amen. God almighty father of all mercy ... Amen. When thou shalt go to bed say this. I lay me down to rest ... Amen. I thank thee my heavenly father ... Amen. Devout prayer unto Jesus our Saviour. O bountiful Jesu, O sweet Jesu, O Jesu the Son of the pure Virgin Mary ... So be it. Anthem. O glorious king which amongst thy saints ... Prayer for peace. O God from whom all holy desires ... Amen.

₀ *Here ends the A. B. C. It is here given in full.*

₀ *The Hours are in english; they are the same as in No.* 143. *A.D.* 1539.

The Litany has invocations of Saints and Angels classified, according to the order in the Sarum use. It has " That thou give peace, concord and victory to our King and princes ".

₀ *The book has neither Dirige nor Commendations.*

EE

A.D. 1540, Nicholas Bourman, London, long 12º.   English and Latin.
No. 152.

⁂ *The title has "A Primer or boke of Prayers . . . Hereunton is added Pistles and Gospels daily read in the church".*

An Almanacke for xvi. years. It begins 1540. Easter day, 18 March.

The Kalender is Sarum.   St Thomas of Canterbury is not commemorated.

A Cathechismus, or childish instruction, which all parents are bound to see their children to know by rote, set forth question and answer wise. This Catechismus consisteth in the three chief points of the whole scripture, namely faith, works, and prayer; whereout all parents may teach their children, what they ought to believe, what they ought to do and leave undone, and how they ought to pray. Question. What art thou. Answer. As concerning my first birth I am a reasonable creature created of God, but as concerning my second birth I am a christian . . . (see pages 151, 213).

How men ought to bless themselves in the morning and at even, with the grace both before and after dinner or supper. In the morning when a man riseth, he ought to bless himself with the sign of the holy cross, and say. I thank thee my heavenly Father by thy dearly beloved Son Jesus Christ, that this night . . . Amen. At even going to bed, bless you as is above and say thus. I thank thee my heavenly Father, by thy dear beloved Son Jesus Christ that this day . . . Amen (as on page 198).

Grace after dinner or supper. O give thanks unto the Lord, for he is gracious . . . A prayer. We thank thee O Lord our Father by thy Son Jesus Christ our Lord . . . Amen (as on page 220).

An order and form of bidding of the bedes by the king's commandment [1] (as on page 219).

Matyns. The Laudes. The Prime. The third Hour. The sixth Hour. The ninth Hour. The Evensong. The Compline. A memory of the Passion of Christ, and a memory of the Compassion of our Lady are appended to each of the Hours from Lauds to Compline.

⁂ *The Hours are the same as those in No. 143. A.D. 1539, page 225.*

The Litany has invocations of Saints and Angels classified, according to the order in Sarum use. It has "That thou give peace, concord and victory to our King and princes".

The Dirige is the same as that in No. 143. A.D. 1539.

⁂ *This book has not "The Commendations".*

⁂ *"The Pistles and Gospels daily read in the church" which are contained in this book are in english only, and are the same as those in No. 158, c. A.D. 1540. page 188.*

[1] See Wilkins Conc. ed. 1737. Vol. 3. page 783.

A SUMMARY OF THE CONTENTS
OF
THE PRIMER, SET FORTH BY THE KING'S
MAJESTY AND HIS CLERGY:
IN THE REIGNS OF HENRY VIII. AND EDWARD VI.
AND OF KINDRED PRIMERS:
IN THE REIGNS OF ELIZABETH. CHARLES I. AND CHARLES II.
A.D. 1545—A.D. 1671.

EXPLANATIONS.

1. The various books in this class consist of five main types; the descriptions of them, which are printed below, are drawn up in view of this classification; but note that No. 194 c., A.D. 1550, is placed in chronological order, and not according to its logical position.

The first type is as follows:

(a) A summary is given of all the contents of No. 174. A.D. 1545. as a standard of comparison for "The Primer[s] set forth by the King's majesty and his clergy" during the reigns of Henry the eighth and Edward the sixth: and for a number of Primers which directly follow this model; it also serves as a standard of comparison for (1). "The Primer[s] set forth at large with many godly and devout prayers" during the reign of Elizabeth, see No. 239 A.D. 1559, and its kindred books. (2). Orarium seu libellus precationum per regiam majestatem latinè æditus. 1560. No. 244. A summary is given of all the contents of both of these books.

The four remaining types are these:

(b) A summary is given of all the contents of No. 194. c. A.D. 1550. as the framework and contents of the Hours materially differ from those of any other book: this book is imperfect, and stands alone.

(c) A summary is given of all the contents of No. 247. A.D. 1564 "Preces privatæ in studiosorum gratiam collectæ et regia authoritate approbatæ" with the variations which occur in the edition of 1573. as the Hours mark a fresh departure in connection with No. 244. A.D. 1560 "Orarium seu libellus precationum." and "Liber precum publicarum in ecclesia anglicana. 1560." the Prayer Book in Latin in the reign of Elizabeth. Three editions of this type are known.

(d) A summary is given of all the contents of No. 255. A.D. 1627 "A collection of private devotions in the practice of the ancient church, called the Hours of prayer." as the book was published after the manner of the "Orarium seu libellus precationum." No. 244. A.D. 1560. Ten editions of this type are known.

(e) A summary is given of all the contents of No. 258. A.D. 1671 "The King's Psalter" as it was; "composed on purpose to succeed the King's Primer". Only one edition of this book is known, and only two copies of the edition, which vary in some particulars.

2. The various known editions of the Epistles and Gospels in english are given as they occur; they were first printed A.D. 1538; they are found either as separate books, or as forming a part of the Primer.

3. All fresh matter is given as it occurs, and all variations from the book which is in any case the standard of comparison: in some cases however, the same matter is repeated on account of the summary of contents of the standard book as well as that of others in the group being printed in full: this is the case with No. 239. A.D. 1559. and No. 244. A.D. 1560.

4. An index is given of the prayers and psalms. Groups of psalms such as the seven penitential psalms or those in the Hours are not indexed separately. Another index gives all the hymns. A general index refers to other matters of liturgical, devotional and general interest.

A SUMMARY OF THE CONTENTS
OF
THE PRIMER, SET FORTH BY THE KING'S MAJESTY AND HIS CLERGY:

IN THE REIGNS OF HENRY VIII. AND EDWARD VI.:

AND OF KINDRED PRIMERS:

IN THE REIGNS OF ELIZABETH. CHARLES I. AND CHARLES II.

A.D. 1545—A.D. 1671.

A.D. 1545, May 29. Richard Grafton, London. 4º. English. No. 174.

*** The title is "*The Primer set forth by the King's majesty, and his clergy; to be taught, learned, and read, and none other to be used throughout all his dominions*". The colophon has "*Cum privilegio ad imprimendum solum*".

*** This book was also printed in english and latin, No. 179. A.D. 1545; and in latin, No. 186. A.D. 1546, September 6. "*Orarium seu libellus precationum per regiam majestatem et clerum latine æditus. Cum privilegio ad imprimendum solum.*"[1]

The contents of this book.

The Kalender has " S. George " on April 23. " Peter and Paul apostles." on June 29. " Mary Magdalen." on July 22. " Assumption of our Lady " on August 15. " Nativity of our Lady " on September 8. " Conception of our Lady " on December 8. The Saints days, some of which are printed in red and some in black, are all in the Kalender of Marshall's primer No. 117. A.D. 1535. June 16. with the exception of " S. Alphege " on April 19. " S. Marke and Marcelliane " on June 18. " Prothe and Hiacynthe " on September 11. and " S. Dionise and his fellows martyrs." on October 9.

An Almanacke for xxii. years. It begins A.D. 1545.

An Injunction given by the King our Sovereign Lord's most excellent majesty, for the authorising and establishing the use of this Primer.[2] Henry the viiith, by the grace of God King of England, France, and Ireland, Defender of the faith, and of the church of England and also of Ireland, in earth the supreme Head. To all and singular our subjects, as well Archbishops, Bishops, Deans, Archdeacons, Provosts, persons, vicars, curates, priests, and all other of the clergy; as also all estates

[1] See T. Tanner Bibliotheca ed. 1748. sub voce Cranmerus Thomas.

[2] See Wilkins Conc. ed. 1737. Vol. 3 page 875: and Preface to Primer. A.D. 1559. No. 239, page 250.

and degrees of the lay fee, and teachers of youth within any our realms, dominions, and countries, greeting. Among the manifold business, and most weighty affairs appertaining to our regal authority and office, we much tendering the youth of our realms, whose good education and virtuous bringing up redoundeth most highly to the honour and praise of almighty God, for divers good considerations and specially for that the youth by divers persons are taught the Pater noster, the Ave Maria, Creed, and Ten Commandments all in Latin and not in English, by means whereof the same are not brought up in the knowledge of their faith, duty, and obedience, wherein no christian person ought to be ignorant; and for that our people and subjects, which have no understanding in the Latin tongue, and yet have the knowledge of reading may pray in their vulgar tongue, which is to them best known, that by the mean thereof they should be the more provoked to true devotion, and the better set their hearts upon those things that they pray for; and finally, for the avoiding of the diversity of primer books that are now abroad, whereof are almost innumerable sorts, which minister occasion of contentions and vain disputations rather than to edify; and to have one uniform order of all such books throughout all our dominions, both to be taught unto children, and also to be used for ordinary prayers of all our people not learned in the latin tongue, have set forth this Primer or book of prayers in english, to be frequented and used in and throughout all places of our said realms and dominions, as well of the elder people, as also of the youth, for their common and ordinary prayers; willing, commanding, and straightly charging, that for the better bringing up of youth in the knowledge of their duty towards God, their prince, and all other in their degree, every schoolmaster and bringer up of young beginners in learning, next after their A, B, C,[1] now by us also set forth, do teach this Primer or book of ordinary prayers unto them in english; and that the youth customably and ordinarily use the same, until they be of competent understanding and knowledge to perceive it in latin; at what time they may at their liberty either use this Primer in english, or that which is by our authority likewise made in the latin tongue,[2] in all points correspondent unto this in english. And furthermore, we straightly charge and command as well all and singular our subjects, and sellers of books, as also all schoolmasters, and teachers of young children within this our realm, and other our dominions, as they intend to have our favour and avoid our displeasure by the contrary, that immediately after this our said Primer is published, and imprinted, that they, nor any of them, buy, sell, occupy, use nor teach privily or apertly any other Primer, either in english or latin, than this now by us published; which with no small study, travail, and labour, we have

[1] See Henry Bradshaw's Collected papers, page 333: and the A. B. C. c. A.D. 1537, No. 131, page 173.

[2] No. 186, A.D. 1546, page 65. See T. Tanner. Bibliotheca. ed. 1748. page 207. sub voce Cranmerus Thomas.

-1545] PRIMER OF THE KING AND CLERGY. 239

purposely made to the high honour and glory of almighty God, and to the commodity of our loving and obedient subjects, and edifying of the same in godly contemplation, and virtuous exercise of prayer. Given at our palace of Westminster, the vi day of May, in the xxxvii year of our reign.

The prayer of our Lord.[1] Our Father which art in heaven, hallowed be thy name . . . Amen.

The salutation of the angel to the blessed Virgin Mary.[1] Hail Mary full of grace . . . blessed is the fruit of thy womb. Amen.

The Creed or xii articles of the christian faith.[1] I believe in God, the Father almighty, maker of heaven and earth . . . Amen.

The x Commandments of Almighty God.[1] Thou shalt have none other Gods but me . . . Lord into thy hands . . . Thou hast redeemed me . . .

Grace before dinner.[1] The eyes of all things trust in thee, O Lord . . . Amen. The King of eternal glory make us partners of the heavenly table. Amen. God is charity, and he that dwelleth in charity dwelleth in God . . . Amen.

Grace after dinner.[1] The God of peace and love, vouchsafe alway to dwell with us. And thou Lord have mercy upon us. Glory, honour, and praise be to thee O God . . . Amen. Lord have mercy upon us. Our Father. Lord hear my prayer . . . And let my cry . . . From the fiery darts of the devil . . . Amen. God save the church, our King, and realm; and God have mercy upon all christian souls. Amen.

Grace before supper.[1] O Lord Jesu Christ, without whom nothing is sweet nor savoury . . . Amen.

Grace after supper.[1] Blessed is God in all his gifts. And holy in all his works. Our help . . . Who hath made . . . Blessed be the name . . . From henceforth . . . Most mighty Lord and merciful Father, we yield thee hearty thanks . . . Amen. God save the church, our King, and realm, and God have mercy upon all christian souls. Amen.

The Matyns. The Laudes. The Prime. The third Hour. The sixth Hour. The nynth Hour. The Evensong. The Compline.

₊ *The Hours are those found in the Primers set forth by the Kings' majesty and his clergy during the reign of Henry the eighth and the commencement of the reign of Edward the sixth. The framework as well as some of the component parts of each Hour are Sarum. The Ave Maria occurs at Matins as the invitatory, The hymns are from the Sarum Breviary with the exception of that at Compline.*

At Lauds. The Collects. Of the Holy Ghost. Come Holy Spirit of God, inspire the hearts . . . Let us pray. O God which by the information of the Holy Ghost . . . Amen. Of the Holy Trinity. Deliver us, save us . . . Let us pray. Almighty and everlasting God, which hast granted to us thy servants . . . Amen. Of the cross of Christ. We ought to glory in the cross . . . Let us pray. O God which hast ascended thy most holy cross . . . Amen. Of the holy Apostles. Ye be they that have

---

[1] See the A. B. C. c. A.D. 1537, No. 131, page 173.

left all things . . . Let us pray. Almighty God, regard our infirmity . . . Amen. Of the holy Martyrs. The souls of Saints rejoice in heaven . . . Let us pray. Grant to us, almighty God, that we which know that thy glorious martyrs . . . Amen. For peace. Lord, send us peace in our days . . . Let us pray. O God, from whom all holy desires . . . Amen. (See No. 124. A.D. 1536, page 162 and pages 198, 230.)

A prayer of the passion. Christ suffered for us . . . The versicle. We worship thee, Christ . . . The answer. For thou hast redeemed the world . . . Let us pray. Lord Jesu Christ, son of the living God set thy holy passion . . . Amen. The glorious passion of our Lord Jesu Christ . . . Amen. (See No. 26, A.D. 1503. page 122.)

The seven psalms. An argument is appended to each psalm. Psalms 6. Domine ne in furore. Lord, rebuke me not in thy rage. 31. Beati quorum. Blessed are they whose iniquities are forgiven. 37. Domine ne, &c. Lord, rebuke me not in thy rage. 50. Miserere mei deus. Have mercy upon me, O God, according to thy great mercy. 101. Domine exaudi orationem meam. Lord, hear my prayer, and let my cry come unto thee. 129. De profundis clamavi. From the depth I called on thee, O Lord. 141. Domine exaudi. Lord, hear my prayer, with thine ears perceive my desire. The anthem. Remember not, O Lord God, our old iniquities . . . Amen.

The Litany and suffrages.[1] As these holy prayers and suffrages following, are set forth of most godly zeal for edifying, and stirring of devotion of all true faithful christian hearts, so is it thought convenient in this common prayer of procession, to have it set forth, and used in the vulgar tongue for stirring the people to more devotion; and it shall be every christian man's part, reverently to use the same to the honour and glory of almighty God, and the profit of their own souls. And such among the people as have books and can read, may read them quietly and softly to themselfe; and such as cannot read, let them quietly and attentively give audience in time of the said prayers, having their minds erect to almighty God, and devoutly praying in their hearts the same petitions which do enter in at their ears; so that with one sound of the heart and one accord, God may be glorified in his church. And it is to be remembered, that that which is printed in black letters is to be said or sung of the priest with an audible voice, that is to say so loud and so plainly, that it may well be understand of the hearers. And that which is in the red is to be answered of the quier, soberly and devoutly.

The Litany has invocations of saints and angels as follows "Holy Virgin Mary, mother of God our Saviour, Jesu Christ. Pray for us. All holy angels, and archangels, and all holy orders of blessed spirits. Pray for us. All holy patriarchs, and prophets, apostles, and martyrs, confessors, and

---
[1] See "An exhortation unto prayer . . . also a Litany". Parker Soc. Q. Elizabeth. Private Prayers: and "Letter of Cranmer to Henry 8. Oct. 7, A.D. 1544," Parker Soc. Cranmers writings; also. "Enchiridion piarum precationum. D. Martini Lutheri. A.D. 1543.

-1545] PRIMER OF THE KING AND CLERGY. 241

virgins, and all the blessed company of heaven. Pray for us." It has " From the tyranny of the Bishop of Rome and all his detestable enormities". It has " Henry the eight, thy servant, and our king and governor . . . Our noble Queen Catherine . . . Our noble prince Edward, and all the King's majesty's children ". The collects at the end of the Litany are " We humbly beseech thee, O Father, mercifully to look upon our infirmities . . . Amen. O God whose nature and property is ever to have mercy . . . Amen. Almighty and everliving God, which only workest great marvels . . . Amen. We beseech thee, O Lord, to shew upon us thine exceeding great mercy . . . Amen. Grant we beseech thee, O almighty God, that we in our trouble . . . Amen. A prayer of Chrysostome. Almighty God which hast given us grace . . . Amen.

The Dirige is different in its construction from that of Sarum use; it has only three lessons with anthems, so called; the lessons are different from those of Sarum; there are fewer psalms, but these with the exception of "In te Domine speravi" are Sarum. The versicles and responses, as well as the collects at the end of the Dirige are Sarum. An argument is appended to each psalm.

The Commendations. This psalm is the A.B.C. of godly love, the paradise of learning, the shop of the Holy Ghost, the school of truth. In which appeareth, how the saints of God esteem his holy laws, how fervently they be given unto them, how it grieveth them that they should be despised, how fervently they desire to learn them, to walk in them, and to fulfil them; finally, how the transgressors and adversaries of them shall be punished and destroyed.

₀ *The Commendations are the same as those of Sarum use, except that Psalm 188, Domine probasti me, and the V. and R. and collect which follow are omitted.*

The psalms of the passion. An argument is appended to each psalm. Psalms. 21. Deus, deus meus. O God, my God, look toward me. 69. Salvum me fac Deus. Save me, O God, for the waters are entered unto my soul. 87. Deus, deus salutis. O Lord God of my health, I have cried day and night before thee. 2. Quare fremuerunt gentes. Why hath the heathen raged. 58. Eripe de inimicis. Deliver me from mine enemies, O my God.

The passion of our Saviour Jesu Christ, written by Sainct John. Jesus went forth with his disciples over the brook Cedron (see No. 124. A.D. 1536, page 162, and pages 210, 215, 228.)

Prayers of the passion of our Saviour Christ. Blessed be the Father, and the Son . . . Let us praise him, and exalt him . . . Almighty God, our heavenly father, thy mercy and goodness is infinite . . . Amen. Almighty God, our heavenly father, we beseech thy gracious goodness . . . Amen. Our Saviour and redeemer Jesu Christ, which in thy last supper with thine apostles diddest consecrate thy blessed body and blood under the form of bread and wine . . . Amen.[1] Almighty God, our

[1] See Strype Eccles. Mem. ed. 1822. Vol. 1. Pt. 2. page 444. Articulus 3. De eucharistia: and "Cranmers writings" Parker Soc. page 475.

heavenly father, which sufferedest Peter the apostle . . . Amen. Our blessed Saviour Jesu Christ, which in that great heaviness of thy soul . . . Amen. Almighty God, eternal father, we do remember that in the condemnation of thine own dearly beloved son . . . Amen. (as in No. 207. A.D. 1555, page 186).

A prayer in the morning. O Lord God almighty, to whom and before whom all things are manifest and plain . . . Amen (as in No. 231. A.D. 1557, page 156. and No. 207. A.D. 1555, page 187).

A prayer at your uprising. O Lord Jesu Christ, which art the very bright sun of the world . . . Amen[1] (as on pages 156. 186).

A prayer before ye go to bed. O Lord, which art only God, true, gracious, and merciful . . . Amen (as on page 156).

A prayer for trust in God. The beginning of the fall of man was trust in himself . . . Amen[2] (as on pages 156, 188).

A prayer for patience in trouble. Psalm lx. How hast thou, O Lord, humbled and plucked me down . . . Amen[3,4] (as on page 188).

A prayer for concord of Christ's church. Psal. lxviii. Arise, Lord, let thine enemies be scattered . . . Amen[3,4] (as on page 156).

A prayer against the enemies of Christ's truth. Psal. cxxxix. Deliver me, O Lord, from the ungodly and stiff-necked persons . . . Amen[3,4] (as on page 189).

A prayer to keep the tongue, and to eschew the infection of the world. Psal. cxl. To thee, I cry, O Lord, hear me speedily . . .[3,4] (as on page 189).

The prayer of any captive according to the form of David when he was hid in the cave. Psal. cxlii. With my voice I cry to thee, afore thee I open my lamentations . . .[3,4] (as on page 188).

In great trouble of conscience. Psal. cxxxiiii. Lord hear my prayer, receive my supplication . . .[3,4] (as on page 188).

A prayer of the church against sins. Sapien. xv. Thou, O our God, art sweet, long suffering and true . . .[6,7] (as on pages 172, 189).

In wars, the prayers of King Asa. ii Paralipo. xiiii. Lord it is all one with thee to help them that have need . . . Amen[6,7] (as on page 156, 189).

The prayer of Manasses, King of Juda ii Parali. xxxvi. O Lord almighty, God of our fathers, Abraham, Isahac, and Jacob . . . Amen.[5,6,7,8] (as on pages 121, 188).

The oration of Job in his most grievous adversity and loss of goods. Job. i. Naked came I out of my mother's womb . . . Amen.[4,6,7] (as on page 188).

---

[1] Precationes Erasmi. (Brit. Mus. 3224. a. 58. (3).) A.D. 1537. page 20.
[2] J. Ludovicus Vives, Preces. (Brit. Mus. 1019. a. 6.) A.D. 1539.
[3] Precationes christianæ. (Brit. Mus. 843. b. 6.) A.D. 1536.
[4] Epitome of the Psalms, R. Taverner. (Brit. Mus. 1219. a. 34.) A.D. 1539.
[5] Lutheri opera. ed. 1558. Vol. 7, page 155.
[6] Precationes biblicæ. (Brit. Mus. 843. c. 6.) A.D. 1531. (Sion Coll.) A.D. 1529.
[7] Prayers of the Bible. (Lambeth Archiep. 249. 11 (1).) c. A.D. 1534.
[8] S. Augustine, Meditationes. ed. 1510. Brit. Mus. 3670.

-1545] PRIMER OF THE KING AND CLERGY. 243

A prayer of Hieremy. Hieremy xvii. Heal me, O Lord, and I shall be whole . . . Amen.[1][3][4][5] (as on page 188).

A prayer of Hieremy. Hieremy xxxi. O Lord, thou hast chastened me, and thy chastening . . .[3][4][5] (as on page 188).

A prayer of Solomon for a competent living. Proverbes xxx. Two things I require of thee, that thou wilt not deny me . . .[3][4][5] (as on pages 167, 189).

A prayer for obtaining of wisdom. Sapience. ix. God of our fathers, and lord of mercy . . . Amen.[3][4][5] (as on pages 156, 167, 189).

The prayer of Jesus, the son of Syrach in necessity, and for wisdom. Ecclesi, the last chapter. I thank thee, O Lord and king, and praise thee, O God my Saviour . . .[3][4][5][6] (as on page 188).

A prayer to speak the word of God boldly. Act. iiii. Lord, thou art God which hast made heaven and earth . . .[3][4][5] (as in No. 128. c. A.D. 1537, page 172; and No. 150. c. A.D. 1539. page 211).

A prayer for the peace of the church. Lord Jesus Christ, which of thine almightiness madest all creatures . . . Amen.[1][3]

A prayer for the keeping of a good name. That wise man which was privy of thy secrets, O heavenly father . . . Amen[3] (as on pages 156. 189).

A prayer against worldly carefulness. O most dear and tender father, our defender . . . Amen[2] (as on pages 156. 189).

A prayer against pride and unchasteness. Eccle. xxiii. O thou Lord, father and God of my life . . . Amen[3][4][5] (as in No. 25. A.D. 1502, page 122 and page 156).

Another prayer against pride. O Lord Christ in most mighty power most meek . . . Amen.[2]

A prayer against envy. Lord, the inventor and maker of all things . . . Amen.[3]

A prayer against anger. Lord Jesu Christ, which saydest whosoever is angry with his brother . . . Amen.

A prayer in adversity. O Lord God, without whose will and pleasure a sparrow doth not fall . . . Amen (as on page 188).

A prayer in prosperity. I give thee thanks, O God almighty, which not alonely hast endued me . . . Amen (as on page 188).

A fruitful prayer to be said at all times. O merciful God, grant me to covet with a fervent mind . . . Amen (as on page 156).

A devout prayer unto Jesu Christ, called, O bone Jesu. O bountiful Jesu, O sweet Jesu, O Jesu the son of the pure Virgin Mary . . . Amen (as in No. 7 c. A.D. 1494, page 112, and pages 167, 189).

A prayer to be said at the hour of death. O Lord Jesu, which art the only health of all men living . . . Amen[1] (as on page 189).

---

[1] Precationes Erasmi. (Brit. Mus. 3224. a. 58. (3).) A.D. 1537. page 20.
[2] J. Ludovicus Vives, Preces. (Brit. Mus. 1019. a. 6.) A.D. 1539.
[3] Epitome of the Psalms, R. Taverner. (Brit. Mus. 1219. a. 34.) A.D. 1539.
[4] Precationes biblicæ. (Brit. Mus. 843. c. 6.) A.D. 1531. (Sion Coll.) A.D. 1529.
[5] Prayers of the Bible. (Lambeth Archiep. 249. 11. (1).) c. A.D. 1534.
[6] Precationes e sacris biblicis. (Brit. Mus. 1410. a. 30.) A.D. 1528.

A general confession of sins unto God. O most merciful Lord God and most tender and dear father . . . Amen [1] (as on page 186).

A prayer against the devil. Jesu Christ our Lord, which by the mouth of the holy apostle Seinte Peter . . . Amen [2] (as on pages 156, 190).

For the desire of the life to come. This my body is the very dark and filthy prison of the soul . . . Amen [2] (as on pages 156, 188).

The ende of the Primer.

The copy of the King's Highness bill assigned. Henry the viiith by the grace of God of England, France, and Ireland King, Defender of the faith, and of the churches of England and Ireland in earth the supreme head. To all printers and booksellers, and to all other our officers, ministers, and subjects. We do you to understand, that of our grace especial we have granted and given privilege and licence to our well-beloved subject, Richard Grafton, printer and servant to our most dearest son Prince Edward; and Edward Whitchurch, citizen of London, to print or cause to be printed our Primer, now by us and our clergy set forth, both in english and latin . . . and the assignes of any of them . . . Given at our Manor of Greenwich the xxviiith day of May, in the xxxviith year of our reign. God save the King.

Colophon. A cut of the Prince of Wales plume with the motto "Ich dien" in a flamed circle: the letters E and P being on either side of the plume; the whole set in a rectangle with E and P on either side. Underneath the cut the words: " Imprinted at London . . . by Richard Grafton printer to the Princes grace, the xxix day of May, the year of our Lord, MDXLV. Cum privilegio ad imprimendum solum.

A.D. 1545, May 29. Richard Grafton, London. 4°. English. No. 175.

₊ *The contents of this book are the same as those in No. 174, A.D. 1545, it is bound with "Here foloweth the Epystels and Gospels of the Sondayes and festyvall dayes, as they are red in the church through the whole yere:" the Epistles and Gospels are in English only, and are the same as those in No. 151, A.D. 1540, page 220.*

A.D. 1547, November 30. Richard Grafton, London. 4°. English. No. 187.

₊ *The title has "The Primers set forth by the King's majesty and his clergy to be taught, learned, and read, and none other to be used throughout all his dominions. Imprinted at London, the last day of November, in the first year of the reign of our sovereign lord King Edward the VI. . . . Cum privilegio ad imprimendum solum."*

An Almanacke for xv. years. It begins 1547. 10 April.

The Kalender has two months on each page: it has the same Saints days printed in red as in No. 174, A.D. 1545 (page 237). The other Saints days printed in black are not the same.

---

[1] Epitome of the Psalms, R. Taverner. (Brit. Mus. 1219. a. 34.) A.D. 1539.

[2] J. Ludovicus Vives, Preces. (Brit. Mus. 1019. a. 6.) A.D. 1539.

[3] See Edward VI. Injunctions. 1547. July 31st, and Visitation Articles: also Wilkins Conc. ed. 1737. Vol. 4. page 3.

The contents of the book are the same as those of No. 174, A.D. 1545.

The Litany is the same as that in No. 174, A.D. 1545: it has "Edward the sixte, thy servant, and our King and governor. Our noble Queen Katherine dowager. The Lady Marie's grace, the Lady Elizabeth's grace, and the Lord Protector's grace."

A.D. 1547, November 30. Richard Grafton, London. 4°. English. No. 188.

⁎ *The title of the book is the same as that of No. 187, A.D. 1547, except that it has "And none other to be used throughout his highness dominion" instead of "And none other to be used throughout all his dominions . . . Cum privilegio ad imprimendum solum."*

An Almanacke for xv. years. It begins A.D. 1547.

The Kalender wants all after August; it has the same Saints days printed in red, as in No. 174, A.D. 1545 (page 237), with the addition of "St. Barnabas" on June 11th; it omits "St. George" on April 23rd, "St. Mary Magdalen" on July 21st, and "Assumption of our Lady" on August 15th; it has no Saints days printed in black.

The contents of the book are the same as those of No. 174, A.D. 1545, with the exception of the Litany.

The Litany is the same as that in No. 174, A.D. 1545, except that it has no Invocations of saints: it has in the deprecations "From the tyranny of the Bishop of Rome and all his detestable enormities": it has "Edward the sixt thy servant our king and governor". The collects at the end of the Litany are "We humbly beseech thee, O Father, mercifully to look upon our infirmities . . . Amen," and "Almighty God, which hast given us grace . . . Amen".

A.D. 1549. Richard Grafton, London. 8°. English. No. 193.

⁎ *The title is "The Prymer set forth by the Kings highness and his clergy to be taught unto children throughout his dominions, all other set apart". The colophon has "Cum privilegio ad imprimendum solum".*

The Kalender is the same as that in No. 174, A.D. 1545 (page 237) except that St. George on April 23rd is printed in black.

An Almanacke for xx years. It begins A.D. 1549. Easter. 21 April.

The contents of the book are the same as in No. 174, A.D. 1545, with the exception of the Litany: it has "Edward the sixth thy servant, and our King and governor".

The Litany is the same as that in No. 188, A.D. 1547, except that the collects at the end are the same as those in No. 174, A.D. 1545.

c. A.D. 1550. Thomas Gaultier, London, for Robert Toy, London. 32°. English. No. 194.

⁎ *The title-page and Kalender are wanting. A summary is given of all the contents of this book.*

The book begins on c. 2. fo. iiii. [A prayer.] commandments, and so glorify and praise thee everlastingly . . . And from the very bottom of my heart I cry and say: O our Father which art in heaven, &c., this done, I add this prayer for the morning.[1] O merciful Lord God heavenly father, I render most high lauds, praise, and thanks unto thee, that thou hast preserved me both this night . . . Amen (as in No. 207, A. D. 1555, page 186 and No. 200. A.D. 1553. page 291).

Or thus more briefly. O merciful Lord God heavenly father, I laud and praise thee that thou hast preserved me this night from all peril, danger and evil . . . Amen.

Prayer to be said at night going to bed.[1] O merciful Lord God, our heavenly father, whether we sleep or wake, live or die, we are always thine . . . Amen.

Or thus more briefly. O merciful Lord God, our heavenly father, I laud and thank thee most heartily for that thou hast so graciously kept and preserved me this day . . . Amen.

Prayer for grace to observe the commandments of God. Most gracious, loving, and merciful father, which diddest write thy law in the heart of our first father Adam . . .

The x commandments of God, given by Moses and expounded by Christ. The first table. i. Thou shalt have none other gods but me. Exod. xx. and Deut. vi. I am the Lord thy God . . . Christ. Marke xii. Hear Israel our Lord God is one Lord . . . (as in No. 128. c. A.D. 1537. page 168. and No. 150. c. A.D. 1539. page 209).

A declaration upon the Creed. I believe in God the Father almighty, maker of heaven and earth . . . First, we believe in one God, Deut vi, and father of our Lord Jesus Christ . . .

The seven petitions of the Pater noster with a brief declaration of the same. Our Father which art in heaven. We have, saith Paul, one Lord, one faith, one baptism, one God, and father of all. Ephe iiii. . . .

The Ave Maria. Hail Mary full of grace, &c., Luc. i. The angel Gabriel was sent from God . . . Hail full of grace, the Lord is with thee . . . fruit of thy womb. Amen.

Conditor cœli et terræ. O maker of heaven and earth, King of kings . . . Amen (as in No. 161. c. A.D. 1541. page 155, and on pages 167, 189).

A general confession of sins unto God, daily to be said of the christian person. O most merciful Lord God, and most tender and dear father . . . Amen (as in No. 207. A.D. 1555. page 186. and No. 174 A.D. 1545. page 244).

Prayer upon the psalm of Miserere. Have mercy on me God, according of thy great tenderness to heart . . . Amen.

First hour of prayer. Third hour of prayer. Sixt hour of prayer. Ninth hour of prayer. Evening prayer. Complyn.

˙ *First hour to the Ninth hour and Evening prayer. Each of these Hours begins with a hymn: then paraphrases of the psalms, then a text of holy Scripture with a collect. Compline begins with a hymn, then paraphrases of psalms, then "Save us, O Lord, waking . . . Our Father. Hail Mary. I believe, &c.," to the end of Compline in the Sarum Breviary. The hymns are those in the "Hours printed chiefly for William Marshall". The collects are translations of collects in the Sarum Breviary for the first, fourth, and fifteenth Sundays after Trinity,*

[1] See Godly Prayers. Book of Common Prayer. A.D. 1552. E. Whitchurche. 4°.

for the Trinity Ember season; and of the collect "Visita nos quæsumus Domine" in No. 7. c. A.D. 1494. page 117.

A fruitful and most necessary prayer, to be said of all men and at all times. O merciful God, grant me to covet with an ardent mind those things which may please thee . . . Amen (as in No. 231. A.D. 1557. page 156. and No. 174. A.D. 1545. page 243).

Prayer and thanksgiving to the heavenly father, for all his benefits shewed to us. O most highest, almighty, and eternal God whose glory . . . Amen (as in No. 156. c. A.D. 1540. page 182 and on page 190).

For meekness and chastity. Ecclesiasti. xxiii. O Lord, thou father and God of my life, let me not have a proud look . . . Amen (as in No. 25. A.D. 1502. No. 231. A.D. 1557. page 156. No. 156. c. A.D. 1540. page 183, and No. 174. A.D. 1545. page 243).

For true faith. I will love thee, O Lord my strength . . . O Lord, make us to have the perpetual fear and love of thy holy name . . . Amen (as in No. 156. c. A.D. 1540. page 179). O Lord give us increase of faith . . . Amen.

For our enemies. Arise, O God, and let the enemies be scattered . . . O God, the lover and keeper of peace and love, give to all our enemies . . . Amen (as in No. 156. c. A.D. 1540. page 182).

For the forgiveness of sins. We have sinned with our fathers, we have dealt unrighteously . . . O God which suffered'st not sinners to perish . . . Amen (as in No. 156. c. A.D. 1540. page 177). Another prayer. Enter not into judgment with thy servant . . . O almighty God which knowest that we sit in so great jeopardies . . . (as in No. 156. c. A.D. 1540. page 177).

Against temptation. Lord Jesu Christ, the only guardian of our mortality, our only hope . . .

In trouble. O most merciful redemptor which art alway bowed to pity . . .

O bone Jesu. O bountiful Jesu, O sweet Jesu, O Jesu the son of the Virgin Mary . . . So be it (as in No. 7. c. A.D. 1494. page 112. No. 124. A.D. 1536. page 167 and on page 189).

Prayer. O rex gloriose. O glorious King, which amongst thy Saints art praised . . . (as in No. 7. c. A.D. 1494. page 112 and on pages 167. 189. 218. 231. 233).

For such as are in jeopardy of death. According to the multitude of thy mercies, O Lord, put away our iniquity . . . O almighty God, the keeper of souls which correctest such as thou lovest . . . Amen (as in No. 43. A.D. 1514. page 129).

A godly and necessary prayer to be said most specially at the hour of death. O Lord Jesu which art the only health of all men living . . . Amen (as in No. 156. c. A.D. 1540. page 182 and on pages 185. 189).

The first hour. Psalm 5. Lord, hear thou my words, mark my crying O my King and my God . . .

Prayer for the peace of the congregation. Give us peace, O Lord, in our days for there is none that fighteth for us . . . Prayer. O God, of whom are all desires, right counsells . . . Amen (as in No. 124. A.D. 1536. page 164 and on page 182).

Prayer. Lord hear my prayer. And let my cry come unto thee. Prayer. O God which would that thy Son should hang upon the cross for us . . . (as in No. 156. c. A.D. 1540. page 178). To the Lord have I lifted up my soul. My God I trust in thee . . . O God which seest us to want all strength . . . Amen (as in No. 156. c. A.D. 1540. page 177).

Prayer for the King and for peace. O most high and mighty Lord God, and King of peace, which when thou tookest thy most holy humanity upon thee . . . (Collect in Litany, No. 117. A.D. 1535. page 204).

The Litany is the same as that in No. 188, A.D. 1547: it has "Edwarde the syxte thy servaunte, our King, and governor".

Certain Graces to be said before and after meat.

₀ *The Graces are the same as in No. 174. A.D. 1545 (page 239), except that "God save our King, and the realm ; and send us peace in Christ. Amen." occurs instead of " God save the church, our King, and realm, and God have mercy upon all christian souls. Amen."*

The contents of this book . . . Finis tabulæ.

A.D. 1551. Richard Grafton, London. 8º. English. No. 195.

₀ *The title is " The Primer set forth by the King's highness, and his clergy ; to be taught, learned, and read of all his loving subjects, all other set apart ; corrected according to the statute, made in the third and iiii. year of our sovereign Lord the King's Majesty's reign.[1] Cum privilegio ad imprimendum solum."*

An Almanacke for xix years. It begins 1550. 6 April.

The Kalender has two months on each page : it has those Saints days printed in red, for which there is an Epistle and Gospel in the Book of the Common Prayer of 1549 ; "Peter and Paul, Apost." occurs on June 29 : it has no other Saints days.

The salutation of the angel to the blessed Virgin Mary is omitted at the beginning of the book after " The prayer of our Lord" and before "The Creed " (see No. 174. A.D. 1545, page 239).

The Graces before and after meat are the same (as in No. 174. A.D. 1545), except that " God save our King, and realm, and send us peace in Christ. Amen " occurs instead of " God save the church, our King, and realm, and God have mercy upon all christian souls. Amen."

The Hours are the same as those in No. 174, A.D. 1545 with these differences. Matins. The Ave Maria is omitted. the V and A. " The earth, O Lord, is full of thy riches. O teach me thy statutes." occurs instead of " Pray for us holy mother of God. That we may be made worthy to attain the promises of Christ." Lauds. The anthem to the Psalms "Behold the eyes of all wait upon thee . . ." instead of " O wonderful exchange . . ." Chapter. " Thus saith the Lord . . ." instead of " Virgin Mary rejoice alway . . ." Anthem to the Song of Zachary. " The kindness and love of God . . ." instead of " Blessed be they that hear the word of

[1] See Statutes at large. ed. 1763, Vol. 2. p. 434. cap. 10. sec. v. An act for the abolishing and putting away of divers books and images.

-1551] PRIMER OF THE KING AND CLERGY. 249

God . . ." V and A. "Confirm the same . . . And protect us . . ." instead of "O Lord shew thy mercy . . . And give to us thy salvation . . ." Prime. Third hour. Sixth hour. Ninth hour are the same as in No. 174. Evensong. Anthem to the psalms "Now therefore being justified . . ." instead of " Blessed be the name . . ." Chapter. " Be glad Jerusalem . . ." instead of " Blessed art thou, O Virgin . . ." V and A. " Make me a clean heart . . . And renew . . ." instead of " Blessed is Mary . . . And blessed is the fruit . . ." Anthem to the Song of Mary. " If God be on our side . . ." instead of " Lo all things be fulfilled . . ." Collect. " Lord of all power and might who art the author and giver of all good . . . Amen." instead of " Holy Lord, almighty Father, everlasting God, which did'st replenish the blessed Virgin Mary . . . Amen. Complin. V and A. He that dwelleth in the help . . . Shall abide in the protection . . . instead of " Behold the handmaid . . . Be it done to me . . ."

The Litany is the same as in No. 188. A.D. 1547. (page 245).

The Dirige is the same as in No. 174. A.D. 1545 with these differences. After Psalm 145. Lauda anima mea Dominum and the V and A; the collects; "O God whose nature and property . . . Amen, We beseech thee O Lord, to show upon us thine exceeding great mercy . . . Amen." occur instead of "God to whom it is appropried to be merciful and to spare, be merciful to the souls of thy servants . . . Amen. O God, the Lord of pardon grant unto the soul of N thy servant . . . Amen. O God, that art Creator and redeemer of all faithful people, grant unto the souls of all true believers, being dead, remission of all their sins . . . God have mercy on all christian souls. Amen." The following collect is omitted at the end of the Dirige. " We beseech thee, Lord, that the prayer of thy suppliants may avail to the souls of thy servants . . . Amen. God have mercy on all christian souls."

Prayers of the passion are the same as in No. 174. A. D. 1545 except that in the prayer, " Our Saviour and Redeemer Jesu Christ, which in thy last supper with thine apostles did'st consecrate thy blessed body and blood under the form of bread and wine . . ." the words " diddest deliver " occur instead of " diddest consecrate ".

The rest of the prayers in the book are the same as in No. 174. A.D. 1545. page 242.

A.D. 1551. Richard Grafton, London. 8º. English. No. 196.

*** *The title has "The Primer and Catechism, set forth by the King's highness, and his clergy ; to be taught, learned, and read of all his loving subjects, all other set apart ; corrected according to the statute, made on the third and iiii. year of our sovereign Lord the King's majesty's reign* . . .[1] *The colophon has, "Cum privilegio ad imprimendum solum".*

The Kalender has those Saints days printed in red, for which there is an Epistle and Gospel in the Book of Common prayer of 1552; it has not any other Saints days.

[1] See Statutes at large. ed. 1763. Vol. 2. p. 434. cap. 10. sec. v. An act for the abolishing and putting away of divers books and images.

250   SUMMARY OF CONTENTS.   [1559-

An Almanacke for xix years. It begins A.D. 1550. Easter day. 6. April.
A general rule to know when the Leap year shall be.
The Catechism for children.[1]

    ⁎ *This Catechism is the same as that in the Book of the Common prayer A.D. 1549.*

"The Graces before and after meat" are the same as in No. 195, A.D. 1551. (page 248).
The Hours are the same as in No. 195. A.D. 1551.
The Litany is the same as in No. 188 A.D. 1547. (page 245).
The Dirige is the same as in No. 195 A.D. 1551.
The prayers of the passion are the same as in No. 195 A.D. 1551.
The rest of the prayers in the book are the same as in No. 174. A.D. 1545.

    ⁎ *"The Epystles and Gospels of every Sundaye and holy daye thorow out the hole yeare, after the Churche of England. Cum privilegio ad imprimendum solum." are bound with this book: they are in english only, and are the same as those in "The Book of the Common Prayer" A.D. 1549. A separate copy of these Epistles and Gospels has "Imprinted at London in Paules Churchyarde, at the Sygne of the Starre, By Thomas Raynalde. M.D. and L. the xxviii daye of January. This book is in St. Paul's Cath. Library. 38. D. 84.*

A.D. 1559. Assignes of John Wayland, London, and William Seres, London. 4°. English. No. 239.

    ⁎ *The title has "The Primer set forth at large with many godly and devout prayers. Anno 1559 . . . Cum privilegio ad imprimendum solum." A summary is given of all the contents of this book.*

An Almanacke for xvi. years. It begins A.D. 1559. Easter day 26 March.
The Kalender has those Saints days printed in red, with the exception of S.
    Bartholomew, for which there is an Epistle and Gospel in the Book of
    the Common prayer of 1549: it has not any other Saints days. "Peter
    and Paule apost" occurs on June 29.
A preface made by the King's most excellent majesty unto this his Primer book[2]
    Henry the viiith, by the grace of God King of England, France, and
    Ireland, defender of the faith, and in earth supreme Head of the church
    of England and Ireland; to all and singular our subjects, as well of the
    clergy as also of the lay fee, within any our dominions whatsoever they
    be, greeting. It is the part of Kings, whom the Lord hath constituted
    and set for pastors of his people, not only to procure, that a quiet and
    peaceable life may be led of all his universal subjects, but also that the
    same life may be passed over godly, devoutly, and virtuously in the true
    worshipping and service of God, to the honour of him, and to the sancti-
    fying of his name, and to the everlasting salvation of their own selves . . .
    In consideration whereof, we have set out and given to our subjects a
    determinate form of praying in their own mother tongue; to the intent
    that such, as are ignorant of any strange or foreign speech, may have
    what to pray in their own acquainted, and familiar language with fruit

---

[1] See Bishop Ridley's Visitation articles. A.D. 1550. Wilkins Conc. ed. 1737. Vol. 4. page 60.
[2] Wilkins Conc. ed. 1787. Vol. 3. page 873.

and understanding; and to the end that they shall not offer unto God, being the searcher of the reins and hearts, neither things standing clean against true religion and godliness, nor yet words far out of their intelligence and understanding. Nevertheless, to the intent that such as have understanding of the Latin tongue, and think that they can with a more fervent spirit make their prayers in that tongue, may have wherein to do their devotion to God, being none acceptor neither of any person nor tongue, we have provided the selfsame form of praying to be set forth in Latin also [1] which we had afore published in english, to the intent that we should be all things to all persons, and that all parties may at large be satisfied, and as well the wills and desire of them that perceive both tongues, as also the necessity and lack of them that do not understand the Latin. And we have judged it to be of no small force, for the avoiding of strife and contention, to have one uniform manner or course of praying throughout all our dominions . . .

An injunction given by the King our sovereign Lord's most excellent majesty, for the authorising and establishing the use of this Primer (as in No. 174. A.D. 1545. page 237).

An order for Morning prayer daily through the year.[2]

At what time soever a sinner doth repent . . . Ezech. xviii . . . If we say that we have no sin . . . 1 John i. Dearly beloved brethren, the Scripture moveth us in sundry places . . .

A general confession to be said of the whole congregation after the minister, kneeling. Almighty and most merciful Father, we have erred and strayed from thy ways like lost sheep . . . Amen.

The absolution to be pronounced by the minister alone. Almighty God, the Father of our Lord Jesus Christ, which desireth not the death of a sinner . . . Amen.

The collects for the Queen. Almighty God, whose kingdom is everlasting and power infinite, have mercy upon the whole congregation and so rule the heart of thy chosen servant Elizabeth . . . Amen. Almighty and everlasting God, we be taught by thy holy word . . . Amen.

A general confession to be made before we receive the Holy Communion. Almighty God, Father of our Lord Jesus Christ, maker of all things . . . Amen.

Prayer to be said before the receiving of the Holy Communion. We do not presume to come to this thy table, O merciful Lord . . . Amen.

Thanksgiving unto God after receiving of the Holy Communion. Almighty and everlasting God, we most heartily thank thee, for that thou dost vouchsafe to feed us . . . Amen.

The blessing at the departure of the people. The peace of God, which passeth all understanding . . . Amen.

Our Father which art in heaven . . .[3] but deliver us from evil . . . Amen.

[1] Orarium. No. 186. A.D. 1546.
[2] See The Books of Common Prayer. of A.D. 1552 and A.D. 1559.
[3] See Visitation articles. A.D. 1559: Wilkins Conc. ed. 1737. Vol. 4. page 189.

The Creed or xii Articles of the christian faith. I believe in God the father almighty . . . Amen.

The x Commandments of almighty God. Thou shalt have none other Gods but me . . . Lord into thy hands I commit my spirit. Thou hast redeemed me Lord God of truth.

Grace before and after dinner, and before and after supper is the same as in No. 195, A.D. 1551 (page 248).

Matins. The Lauds. The Prime. The third Hour. The sixth Hour. The ninth Hour. The Evensong. The Complin.

₊ *The Hours are the same as those in No. 195 A.D. 1551.*

The Seven psalms are the same as in No. 174. A.D. 1545 (page 240).

The Litany is the same as in No. 188. A.D. 1547 (page 245) except that it omits in the deprecations " From the tyranny of the Bishop of Rome, and all his detestable enormities ". It has " Elizabeth thy servant, our Queen and governor ".

The Dirige is the same as that in No. 195. A.D. 1551.

The Commendations are the same as in No. 174. A.D. 1545.

The Psalms of the passion are the same as in No. 174. A.D. 1545.

The Passion of our Saviour Jesu Christ, written by St. John as in No. 174. A.D. 1545.

Prayers of the passion are the same as in No. 195, A.D. 1551.

The rest of the prayers in the book are the same as in No. 174. A.D. 1545, beginning with " A prayer in the morning. O Lord God almighty, to whom and before whom all things are manifest and plain . . . Amen."

c. A.D. 1559. 8º. English. No. 240.

₊ *The title-page is wanting, the book begins on A1.*

A Catechism, that is to say, an instruction to be learned of every child before he be brought to be confirmed of the Bishop.

₊ *This catechism is the same as that in the Book of the Common prayer A.D. 1549.*

The Graces before and after dinner, and before and after supper, are the same as in No. 195. A.D. 1551, except that " Lord save thy church, our Queen, and realm, and send us peace in Christ ". occurs instead of " God save our King, and realm, and send us peace in Christ. Amen." The following occur in addition.

Grace before meat. At the beginning of this refection let us reverently . . . Answer. Laud, praise, and glory be unto God . . . So be it (as in No. 200. A.D. 1553. page 290).

Thanks after meat. Forasmuch as you have well refreshed your bodies . . . Answer. Praise and thanks be to God . . . Amen (as in No. 200. A.D. 1553. page 290).

Grace after supper. Christ which at his last supper promised his body to be crucified . . . Amen (as in No. 200. A.D. 1553. page 290).

The Hours are the same as in No. 195. A.D. 1551. (page 248).

The Litany is the same as in No. 188. A.D. 1547 (page 245). It has "Thy servant Elizabeth, our most gracious Queen and governour".
The Dirige is the same as in No. 195. A.D. 1551. (page 248).
The Commendations are the same as in No. 174. A.D. 1545. (page 241).
Psalms of the passion are the same as in No. 174. A.D. 1545.
Prayers of the passion are the same as in No. 195. A.D. 1551.
The rest of the prayers in the book are the same as in No. 174. A.D. 1545.

c. A.D. 1559. 4°. English.

₊ *The title-page is wanting, the book begins on A*1.
The contents are the same as those of No. 195. A.D. 1551 (page 248). The Litany has "Elizabeth thy servant our Queen and governour". The known copies of the book are Brit. Mus. 3406. c. 45. and C. 35. c. 19.

A.D. 1560, William Seres, London, 8°. Latin. No. 244.

₊ *The title is "Orarium seu libellus precationum, per regiam majestatem latine æditus. 1560. Cum privilegio ad imprimendum solum". A summary is given of all the contents of this book.*

The Kalender has those Saints days printed in red for which there is an Epistle and Gospel in the Book of Common Prayer A.D. 1559: it also has other Saints days printed in black.

Cathechismus, hoc est, instructio a singulis infantibus perdiscenda priusquam per episcopum confirmentur.[1]

₊ *The catechism is a latin version of that in the Book of the Common Prayer A.D. 1549.*

Precatio matutina.[2] Deus mi, Pater mi et Servator, qui gratia erga me tua effecisti . . . Amen.
Sub noctem, quum itur dormitum. Domine Deus, qui noctem destinasti hominis quieti . . . Amen.
Benedictio mensæ. Omnia ad te respiciunt Domine, et tu das illis escam tempore . . . Amen.
Post pastum gratiarum actio.[2] Gratias agimus, Deus ac Pater, de tot beneficiis . . . Amen.
Generalis confessio ab universa congregatione dicenda, genibus flexis.[3] Omnipotens et clementissime Pater, tanquam oves perditæ . . . Amen.
Absolutio per Ministrum solum pronuncianda.[3] Omnipotens Deus, Pater domini nostri Jesu Christi, qui non vult mortem peccatoris . . . Amen.
Preces matutinæ. Prima hora. Tertia hora. Hora sexta. Hora nona. Preces vespertinæ. Completorium.

₊ *The Hours are the same as those in No. 195. A.D. 1551, but with these chief points of difference. The antiphons to the psalms from Preces matutinæ down to the Ninth hour comprise the eight beatitudes instead of from Prime to the Ninth hour. Preces matutinæ. First lesson. "Timor domini initium" instead of "A rod shall come". Third lesson. "Omnis anima potestatibus" instead of "Then said Mary". Lauds. No chapter. Collect.*

[1] See Wilkins Conc. ed. 1737. Vol. 4. page 186.
[2] See H. Bull Christian prayers. A.D. 1566. pages 47, 55. Parker Soc.
[3] Liber precum publicarum. A.D. 1560.

"*Omnipotens sempiterne Deus qui dedisti nobis filium tuum.*" *instead of* "*Grant we beseech thee Lord God that thy servants may enjoy*". *Prime. Collect.* "*Domine sancte pater omnipotens æterne Deus qui nos ad principium hujus diei.*" *instead of* "*Lord Jesus Christ most poor and mild of spirit*". *Preces vespertinæ. Antiphon to psalms.* "*Mandatum novum.*" *instead of* "*Now therefore being justified*". *Antiphon to Magnificat.* "*Qui dicit se nosse Deum.*" *instead of* "*If God be on our side*". *Collect.* "*Omnipotens domine Deus ex cujus ordine.*" *instead of* "*Lord of all power and might which art the author*".

Septem Psalmi.

*** *These psalms are the same as The seven psalms in No.* 174. *A.D.* 1545 (*page* 240). *and are found in No.* 186. *A.D.* 1546 (*page* 65). *The following Psalmi selecti are incorporated with them.* Psalmi. 36. Noli æmulari. 88. Dixi, custodium. 41. Quemadmodum. 52. Dixit insipiens.

Litania. Antiphona. Ne reminiscaris.

*** *The Litany is the same as that in No.* 188. *A.D.* 1547. (*page* 245). *with these exceptions: it omits* "*From the tyranny of the Bishop of Rome, and all his detestable enormities*": *it has* "*Reginam nostram et gubernatorem, Elizabetham*": *it adds the following collects.*

Pro docilitate.[1] Audi preces meas æterna Patris sapientia . . . Amen.
Pro regina.[2] Domine pater cælestis, rex regum et dominator dominantium . . . Amen.

Psalmi selecti de passione Christi.

*** *These psalms are the same as* "*The Psalms of the passion*" *in No.* 174. *A.D.* 1545 (*page* 241). *and are found in No.* 186. *A.D.* 1546 (*page* 65).

Passio servatoris nostri Jesu Christi secundum Johannem.

*** *This is the same as* "*The passion of our Saviour Jesu Christ, written by St. John*" *in No.* 174. *A.D.* 1545 (*page* 241). *and is found in No.* 186. *A.D.* 1546.

Precationes de passione servatoris nostri Christi.

*** *These prayers are the same as* "*Prayers of the passion of our Saviour Christ*" *in No.* 174. *A.D.* 1545 (*page* 241). *and are found in No.* 186. *A.D.* 1546 (*page* 65). *omitting the two following prayers.* "*Almighty God, our heavenly Father, we beseech thy gracious goodness . . . Amen. Our Saviour and redeemer, Jesus Christ, which in thy last supper . . . Amen.*"

*** *The following prayers are the same as No.* 174. *A.D.* 1545 (*page* 242). *and are found in No.* 186. *A.D.* 1546 (*page* 65).

Precatio in aurora petens protectionem Domini. Domine Deus omnipotens, cui omnia exposita . . . Amen. Precatio cum surgis. Domine Jesu Christe, qui es clarus mundi sol . . . Amen. Precatio antequam petas lectum. Domine, qui es unus Deus, verus . . . Amen. Precatio pro fiducia in Deum. Initium ruinæ hominis, sibi fidere . . . Precatio pro patientia. Ut tu Domine humiliasti et afflixisti me . . . Precatio pro concordia ecclesiæ Christi. Exsurge, Domine, ut dissipentur inimici . . . Amen. Precatio contra inimicos veritatis Christi. Eripe me, Domine, a viris iniquis . . .

[1] Precationes Erasmi (Brit. Mus. 3224. a. 58 (3).) A.D. 1535. and S. Knight. Life of Dean Colet. ed. 1823. page 129.
[2] Liber precum publicarum. Litania. A.D. 1560.

*** *The following prayers are not found in No.* 174. *A.D.* 1545.

Adversus consilia inimicorum Dei et divinæ illius veritatis. Ah Domine Deus fortis, qui consilia impiorum . . . Amen.[1]

Ad Spiritum sanctum. Veni sancte Spiritus, unicum solatium afflictorum, Spiritus sanctificator . . . Amen.[1]

Ad Spiritum sanctum. Veni sancte Spiritus, unicum solatium, verus doctor veritatis . . . Amen.[1]

Pro gratia et misericordia. Domine omnipotens Deus, miserere nostri . . . Amen.[1]

Pro augmento et constantia in vera fide. Omnipotens sempiterne Deus, benignissime domine, ac Pater domini nostri Jesu Christi . . . Amen.[1]

Ad Spiritum, ut corda nostra sibi in templum dedicatum inhabitet. Ad te sancte Spiritus, qui es Spiritus solatii . . . Amen.[1]

Pro fidelibus ministris, et fructu Evangelii. Misericordia, domine Jesu Christe, erga nos te commoveat . . . Amen.[1]

Pro concordia et consensu, tum judicii, tum voluntatum, in rebus divinis. Œterne ac misericors Deus, qui es Deus pacis . . . Amen.[1]

Pro vere Christiano amore. Domine omnipotens Deus, qui es charitas . . . Amen.[1]

In tristitia, morbis, et adversitatibus. Misericors Pater, gratiam tuam nobis impertire . . . Amen.[1]

In afflictione. Clementissime redemptor, qui semper es misericors . . . Amen.[2]

Apud ægrotum, dum invisitur. Omnipotens, sempiterne, et clementissime Deus, inter multiplices disciplinas . . . Amen.[1]

In gravi morbo. Domine Jesu, unica salus viventium . . . Amen.[2]

*** *The following prayers are the same as No.* 174. *A.D.* 1545 (*page* 242) *and are found in No.* 186. *A.D.* 1546 (*page* 65).

Precatio ecclesiæ contra peccata. Sapi. xv. 1-4. Tu Deus noster, sauvis es et patiens . . . Precatio regis Asa in tempore belli. ii. Para. xiiii. 11. Domine non est apud te ulla distantia . . . Amen. Precatio Manassæ regis Juda. ii. Para. xxxvi. Domine omnipotens Deus patrum nostrorum Abraam . . . Amen. Oratio Job graviter afflicti Job. i. 21. Nudus egressus sum de utero . . . Amen. Precatio Hieremiæ. Hiere. xvii. 14. 17. 18. Sana me, Domine, et sanabor . . . Amen. Altera precatio. Hie. xxxi. 18. 19. Castigasti me, Domine, et eruditus sum . . . Precatio Salomonis pro moderato victu. Prover. xxx. 7-10. Duo rogavi te, ne deneges mihi . . . Amen. Precatio pro obtinenda sapientia. Sapien. ix. 1-7. 10-12. Deus Patrum meorum, et Domine misericordiæ qui fecisti omnia . . . Amen. Precatio Jesu filii Sirach. Ecclesi. ultimo. Confitebor tibi, Domine rex, et collaudabo te . . . Precatio pro annunciando verbum Domini confidenter. Actu. iiii. 24-31. Domine, tu es Deus, qui fecisti cælum ac terram . . . Amen. Precatio pro bona fama conservanda. Sapiens ille, qui tibi a secretis fuit . . . Amen. Precatio contra curam

---

[1] Precationes christianæ (Brit. Mus. 843 b. 6) A.D. 1536.
[2] Precationes Erasmi. (Brit. Mus. 3224. a. 58 (3).) A.D. 1537.

mundanam. Benignissime et indulgentissime pater, defensor noster . . . Amen. Precatio contra superbiam et libidinem. Eccl. xxiii. 4-7. Domine pater, et Deus vitæ meæ ne derelinquas me . . . Alia precatio contra superbiam. Domine Jesu Christe, in summa potentia mitissime . . . Amen. Precatio contra invidiam. Domine inventor factorque omnium . . . Amen. Contra iram. Domine Jesu Christe, qui dixeras unumquemque irascentem fratri . . . Amen. In rebus adversis. Domine Deus, sine cujus voluntate ne passer . . . Amen. In rebus prosperis. Gratias ago tibi, Deus omnipotens qui non solum donis naturæ . . . Amen. Fructuosa precatio quovis tempore dicenda. Misericors Deus, concede, ut quæ tibi placita sunt . . . Amen. Devota oratio ad Jesum Christum. O bone Jesu, O dulcis Jesu, O Jesu, fili Mariæ virginis . . . Amen. Precatio dicenda in hora mortis. Domine Jesu, qui es unica salus viventium . . . Amen. Generalis confessio peccatorum. Domine Jesu Christe, qui solus es medicus ægrotarum animarum . . . Amen. Precatio contra diabolum. Domine Jesu Christe, qui per os sancti Petri apostoli . . . Amen. Pro alterius vitæ cupiditate. Animæ obscurus teterque carcer hoc corpus est . . . Amen.

₊ *The following prayers are not found in No. 174. A.D. 1545.*

Quum adeunda est schola. Ex psalmo cxix. 9, 10. In quo instituet adolescens viam suam . . . Domine qui fons es sapientiæ. omnis et doctrinæ · · · ¹
Communis gratiarum actio pro cognitione donorum Dei accepta. Nos miseri et egeni homines, domine Deus omnipotens . . . Amen.²

c. A.D. 1560, 8°. English. No. 245.

₊ *The title is.* "*The Primer and Catechism, set forth at large, with many godly prayers, necessary for all faithful christians to read*".

The Kalender has those Saints days printed in red, for which there is an Epistle and Gospel in the Book of Common prayer A.D. 1552 : it has not any other Saints days.

An Almanacke for xvi. years. It begins A.D. 1559. Easter day. 26 March.

A general rule to know when the Leap Year shall be as in No. 196. A.D. 1551. (page 250).

A Catechism, that is to say, an instruction to be learned of every child before he be brought to be confirmed of the Bishop.³

₊ *This catechism is the same as that in the Book of the Common prayer A.D. 1549.*

The Graces are the same as in No. 240. c. A.D. 1559 (page 252).

The Hours are the same as in No. 195. A.D. 1551 (page 248).

The Litany is the same as in No. 188. A.D. 1547 (page 245). it has " Elizabeth our most gracious Queen and Governour ".

The Dirige is the same as in No. 195. A.D. 1551, but omits at the end the collect " Almighty eternal God to whom there is never any prayer made

---
[1] See Short Catechism. A.D. 1553. Parker Soc. Liturgies of Edward VI. page 539.
[2] Precationes christianæ. (Brit. Mus. 843. b. 6). A.D. 1536.
[3] See Wilkins Concilia. ed. 1737. Vol. 4. page 186.

without hope of mercy, be merciful to the souls of thy servants . . . Amen.

The Prayers of the passion are the same as in No. 195. A.D. 1551 (page 249).

The rest of the prayers in the book are the same as in No. 174. A.D. 1545. (page 242).

A.D. 1564, William Seres, London, 16o. Latin. No. 247.

. *The title has* "*Preces privatæ, in studiosorum gratiam collectæ et regia authoritate approbatæ* . . . *Cum privilegio reginæ*". *The colophon has.* "*Cum privilegio ad imprimendum solum*". *A summary is given of all the contents of this book.*

Typographus lectori. Latinis his precibus edendis non id agimus, candide Lector, ut Romanæ linguæ rudes atque ignari eas non intellectas recitent, atque demurmurent. Id enim longissime abest a nostro instituto. Verum illas in studiosorum tantum, et Latinæ linguæ peritorum (si qui his uti velint) gratiam excudi curavimus. Alios vero istius idiomatis imperitos hortamur atque admonemus, ut sese precibus vernacula lingua conscriptis assuescant, iis instent, easque sibi familiares habeant: Ne dum ignota lingua (ut Paulus inquit) orare velle videantur, mens interim ipsorum omni fructu vacet. Quod ne fiat, etiam atque etiam caveto, amice Lector, teque de ea re paucis a me præmonitum ne ægre feras, quæso, Vale.

Index contentorum in hoc libello.

The Kalender assigns each day of the month to a particular saint, some of the days are printed in red, and some in black. Two stanzas, one of two lines, and another of four lines are appended to each month; they are taken from Precationes christianæ (Brit. Mus. 843. b. 6). A.D. 1536. the stanza of two lines is also found in Precationes biblicæ (Brit. Mus. 843. c. 6.) A.D. 1531. The stanza of two lines appended to January begins "Carnes torreo Janus en trementes": that of four lines. "Circumcisio. Magos mittit".

De anno et ejus partibus. De festis mobilibus. De festis immobilibus.[1]

Tabula æconomica, in qua quisque sui officii commonetur in quocunque tandem vitæ sit genere.[2] Magistratus officium. Subditorum officium. Episcoporum et Pastorum officium. Quid debeant auditores Episcopis suis. Conjugum officium. Parentum erga liberos officium. Liberorum erga parentes officium. Servorum, Ancillarum, Mercenariorum, et Operariorum officium erga dominos. Patrum et Matrum familias officium erga servos. Adolescentes. Viduæ. Tota congregatio. I. Cor. ii. 9. Oculus non vidit, nec auris audivit . . . (pages 155. 168. 203. 214. 232.)

Carmina. Ad Jesum Christum precatio. J. Park.[3] Dulcis Jesu, Cælica nutu. Regna gubernans . . . Ira Dei adversus pios brevis.[3] Numinis ira brevis, bonitas pia gaudia præbet . . . Ad Deum Opt. Max. precatio.[3] Dolos maligne qui struunt . . .

---

[1] Liber precum publicarum. A.D. 1560.
[2] See Precationes christianæ (Brit. Mus. 843. b. 6). A.D. 1536.
[3] J. Parkhursti ludicra. ed. 1573.

258   SUMMARY OF CONTENTS.   [1564-

*** *Ed. 1573 has here, Admonitio, ad lectorem (page 269).*

Cathechismus, hoc est, instructio a singulis infantibus perdiscenda, priusquam per Episcopum confirmentur.

*** *This Catechism is a Latin version of that in the Book of the Common prayer A.D. 1549. and the same as that in No. 244. A.D. 1560.*

Orationes mane in aurora dicendæ, cum e lecto te erigis. In nomine Patris et Filii et Spiritus sancti. Amen. Oratio. In nomine Domini nostri Jesu Christi surgo . . . Amen.[1] Alia. Gratias ago tibi, domine Jesu Christe, quod hanc noctem mihi volueris esse prosperam . . . Amen.[1,2] Alia. Deus mi, Pater mi et Servator, qui gratia erga me tua effecisti . . . Amen[3] (as in No. 244. A.D. 1560. page 253). Alia. Dignare me, domine, die isto sine peccatis custodire . . . Amen. Oratio inter vestiendum. Tua me, domine Deus, cælesti armatura hodie contra hostes meos indue . . . Amen. Inter lavandum manus. Ablue, domine Deus, aqua tuæ divinæ gratiæ animum meum . . . Amen.

Pia meditatio ante preces. Omnipotens, æterne, ac cælestis Pater, qui per filium tuum unigenitum . . . Amen.[4]

Preces matutinæ. Litania. Preces vespertinæ.

*** *Preces matutinæ is composed of Matins and Lauds. Preces vespertinæ of Vespers and Compline: they begin and end in the same way as Matutinæ preces and Vespertinæ preces in "Liber precum publicarum in ecclesia anglicana. 1560:" beginning with Sententiæ. Pia confessio. Omnipotens et clementissime Pater, tanquam oves perditæ . . . Amen. Oratio. Omnipotens Deus, Pater domini nostri, Jesu Christi, qui non vis mortem peccatoris . . . Amen. Oratio dominica. V and R. Domine, labia mea aperies. Et os meum . . . ending with Credo. Kyrie. Pater noster. Vs. and Rs. Ostende nobis, Domine, misericordiam tuam. R. Et salutare tuum da nobis, &c. and collects. In other respects they mainly follow the Hours in No. 244. A.D. 1560, (page 253) but with these chief points of difference. Matins. No benediction. Lauds. "Psalm 99. Jubilate Deo." instead of "Psalm 67. Deus misereatur". A lesson. "Sic Deus dilexit mundum." is introduced. Hymn. "Consors paterni luminis." instead of "Ales diei nuncius". No antiphon to the Benedictus. Suffragia. "Pro pace, Deus auctor pacis et concordiæ amator . . . Amen." instead of "Deus a quo sancta desideria . . . Amen." adding "Domine sancte Pater, omnipotens æterne Deus qui nos ad principium hujus diei . . . Amen". Vespers. Antiphon to psalms. "Qui dicit se Deum nosse." instead of "Mandatum novum". Psalms are Compline psalms as in No. 244. A.D. 1560, adding Psalm 14. "Domine quis habitabit". Hymn, Compline hymn as in No. 244. "Rerum creator omnium" instead of "Salvator mundi". A lesson "Tobias senior cum putaret" is introduced. No collect. Compline. Antiphon to psalms. "Mandatum novum" instead of "Salva nos". Psalms are the Vesper psalms as in No. 244. A lesson. "Dilectio sit inter vos." is introduced. Hymn. "Christe qui lux es." instead of "Rerum creator omnium". The Litany which comes after Preces matutinæ is the same as that in Liber precum publicarum. 1560.*

Preces dicendæ, cum itur cubitum. In nomine. Pater noster. Hymnus. Salvator mundi, Domine.[5] Oratio. Gratias ago tibi, Pater omnipotens æterne

---

[1] Hortulus animæ. Nuremberg (Brit. Mus. 1219. b. 4). ed. 1518.
[2] Precationes Erasmi. (Brit. Mus. 3224. a. 58. (3).) A.D. 1537.
[3] See H. Bull. Christian prayers. A.D. 1566. page 47. Parker Soc.
[4] Precationes christianæ. (Brit. Mus. 843. b. 6.) A.D. 1536.
[5] Sarum Brev. Ad completorium.

Deus, qui pro infinita bonitate tua . . . Amen.[1] Illumina quæsumus, domine Deus, tenebras nostras . . . Amen. Psal. 120. 4-7. Ecce non dormitabit, neque dormiet, qui custodit Israel . . .[2]

Noctu si forte expergisceris, ad hunc modum tecum meditare. In noctibus extollam manus tuas in sancta, et benedicam Domino . . . Paternoster Ex Psal. 50. Averte faciem tuam Domine . . . Oratio. Illumina oculos meos Domine, ne unquam obdormiam in morte . . . (pages 114, 166).

Cum ad somnum te rursus componis dic. Salva me, Domine, vigilantem, custodi me dormientem . . . Amen.[5] In manus tuas Domine, commendo spiritum meum . . .

Psalmi, Lectiones, et Preces selectæ, de Nativitate, Passione, Resurrectione, et Ascensione Christi; ac etiam de Missione Spiritus sancti, et sancta Trinitate; in festis Natalis Domini, Parasceves, Paschæ, Ascensionis, Pentecostes, et Trinitatis; necnon aliis, quibus visum fuerit, temporibus recitandæ. De Nativitate Domini nostri Jesu Christi.[3] Psalmi. 84. Benedixisti, Domine, terram tuam. 109. Dixit Dominus. 131. Memento Domine, David. Lectio. Luke i. 26-86. et. ii. 6-21. Missus est angelus Gabriel. John i. 14. Verbum caro factum est. Oremus. Omnipotens Deus, qui unigenitum Filium tuum nobis dedisti . . . Amen. De passione Domini.[3][4] Psalmi. 2. Quare fremuerunt gentes. 21. Deus, Deus meus. 87. Domine, Deus salutis meæ. Lectio quæ continet historiam passionis. John cap xviii. and xix. Egressus est Jesus cum discipulis suis. i. Petri. ii. 21, 22. Christus passus est pro nobis. Oremus. Omnipotens, sempiterne Deus, qui salvatorem nostrum tradi . . . Amen. Alia oratio. Omnipotens Deus et cælestis pater quem nulla nostra dignitas . . . Amen. De resurrectione Domini.[3] Psalmi. 29. Exaltabo te Domine. 56. Miserere mei, Deus. 97. Cantate Domino canticum novum. Lectio. Johan. cap. xx. quæ continet historiam resurrectionis Domini. Uno die sabbatorum Maria Magdalene venit mane. Rom. vi. 9. 11. Christus, resurgens a mortuis . . . Precatio. Deus, qui per unigeniti tui gloriosam resurrectionem . . . Amen. De ascensione Domini.[3] Psalmi. 46. Omnes gentes, plaudite manibus. 67. Exsurgat Deus. 96. Dominus regnavit. Lectio. Marc. cap. xvi. 14-20. Actus Apost. cap, 1. 10. 11. Apparuit Jesus undecim discipulis. Joha, xvi. 28. Exivi a Patre, et veni in mundum . . . Precatio. Deus rex gloriæ, qui unigenitum filium tuum redemptorem nostrum . . . Amen. De missione Spiritus sancti.[3] Psalmi. 47. Magnus Dominus. 103. Benedic anima mea. 144. Exaltabo te Deus. Lectio. Actus Apost. cap. ii. 1-22. Et cum complerentur dies Pentecostes. Johan. xvi. 7. 13. Expedit vobis ut ego vadam. Precatio. Deus, qui corda fidelium . . . Amen. Veni, sancte Spiritus, reple tuorum corda fidelium . . . Amen. De sancta Trinitate.[3] Psalmi. 66. Deus misereatur. 145. Lauda,

---

[1] Hortulus animæ (Brit. Mus. 1219. b. 4). ed. 1518.
[2] Enchiridion preclaræ ecclesiæ Sarum. A.D. 1528. No. 83. page 135.
[3] Liber precum publicarum. Psalmi proprii festorum A.D. 1560.
[4] See Orarium. A.D. 1560. Psalmi de passione. page 254.
[5] Sarum Brev. Ad completorium.

anima mea. Symbolum Athanasii. Lectio. 1 Johan cap. v. 1-15. Omnis, qui credit Jesum esse Christum. i John v. 7. Tres sunt, qui testimonium dant in cælo . . . Præcatio. Omnipotens sempiterne Deus qui dedisti nobis famulis tuis . . . Amen.

Septem psalmi, quos vulgo vocant pænitentiales, una cum succinctis orationibus, Psalmi uniuscujusque summam breviter complectentibus. Psalmus 6. Peccator morbum curari ac hostes prosterni exoptat. Domine ne in furore tuo. Oratio. Domine, qui in terribili et tremenda majestate tua . . . Amen. Psalmus 31. Quomodo lugenda peccata, orandus Deus, et in ipso exultandum. Beati quorum. Oratio. Quæsumus, Domine, intellectum sapientiæ tuæ divinæ . . . Amen. Psalmus 37. Peccator peccatorum pondere pressus implorat opem Dei, cujus misericordiæ sese committit. Domine, ne in furore tuo. Oratio, Domine, ne in furore tuo excandescenti arguas nos . . . Amen. Psalmus 50. Peccator agnoscit ac dolet sceleratam vitam, quærit purgari, implorat spiritum Dei, ut renovetur ac confirmetur. Miserere mei Deus. Oratio. Dele, quæso, iniquitates nostras Domine . . . Amen. Psalmus 101. Querela pii ad Deum ab impiis graviter vexati. Domine, exaudi orationem meam. Oratio. Benigne salvator, sinum tuæ pietatis nobis aperi . . . Amen. Psalmus 129. Peccator ob peccata mulctatus petit solvi a peccato et peccati pæna. De profundis. Oratio. De profundis cordis clamamus ad te Domine . . . Amen. Psalmus 142. Justus malis affectus orat, ut eripiatur a malis. Domine exaudi orationem meam. Oratio. Non avertas, Domine, tanquam offensus faciem . . . Amen. Conclusio Psalmi pænitentialis.[1] Ne reminiscaris Domine . . . Amen.

Psalmi aliquot selecti, qui quotidianæ orationi maxime idonei videntur. Psalmi 3. Pro ope divina in adversis. Domine quid multiplicati sunt. 24. Oratio in tribulatione. Ad te, Domine, levavi animam meam. 30. Oratio viri afflicti. In te Domine speravi. 33. Laus Dei et gratiarum actio. Benedicam Dominum. 111. Piorum commendatio et e contra. Beatus vir. 120. Petitio divini auxilii. Levavi oculos meos. 122. Implorat divinam misericordiam. Ad te levavi oculos meos. 124. De fiducia in Deum. Qui confidunt in Domino. 130. Contra superbiam. Domine non est exaltatum cor meum. 132. Movet ad unitatem fraternam. Ecce quam bonum. 133. Movet ad laudandum Deum. Ecce nunc benedicite Dominum.

Psalmi selecti et peculiares pro Rege vel Regina. Psalmi. 19. In quo mystice agitur de Christi regno. Exaudiat te Dominus in die tribulationis. 20. Mystice de Christo. Domine in virtute tua lætabitur Rex. 71. Mystice de Christi regno. Deus judicium tuum Regi da. Precatio ad exemplar orationis Salomonis pro Regina.[2] Domine Deus, qui serenissimam nostram Reginam regnare super nos fecisti . . . Amen. Salvam fac, Domine, Reginam . . . Amen.

---

[1] Ed. 1573. has "Conclusio psalmorum pænitentialium."
[2] Precationes biblicæ (Brit. Mus. 843. c. 6). A.D. 1531. (Sion Coll.) A.D. 1529

Flores psalmorum, quos Psalterium Hieronymi appellant, precandi studiosis valde jucundi et familiares.

⁎ *This is the same as in No. 7. c. A.D. 1494. page 115, but with some verses omitted and others added: the collect: " Dona mihi quæso omnipotens Deus " is omitted.*

⁎ *Ed. 1573 has the following fifteen Precationes from " Psalmi, seu Precationes D. Joan. Fisheri Episcopi Roffensis (Brit. Mus. G. 12, 149). n. d. An english translation of this book was published in 1544 ". Psalms or Prayers taken out of holy scripture. (Exeter Coll. Oxford. 171. c. 14).*

Psalmus primus, ad impetrandam remissionem peccatorum. O dominator Domine, deus omnipotens, magne et terribilis . . . Psalmus 2. Pro peccatorum remissione. Fortissime Deus spirituum, et universæ carnis . . . Psalmus 3. Pro peccatorum remissione. Deus æterne, juste et sancte qui custodis pactum . . . Psalmus 4. Quæritur, quod a peccatis premitur et superatur. Dominator Domine Deus, misericors et clemens . . . Psalmus 5. Pro impetranda sapientia divina. Domine Deus misericordiæ, qui omnia verbo tuo fecisti . . . Psalmus 6. Ut exaudiatur a Deo. Domine exaudi preces meas . . . Psalmus 7. Pro recte vivendi directione. Ad te domine Deus, animum meum levo . . . Psalmus 8. Ut protegatur ab inimicis. Deus omnipotens, serva me ab inimicis meis . . . Psalmus 9. Contra inimicos. Domine, ecce quam multi sunt . . . Psalmus 10. Quum usque adeo inimici sæviant, ut ferre non possit. Miserere mei, Deus, quoniam conculcat me inimicus . . . Psalmus 11. De fiducia in Deum. Domine, lux mea, et salus mea . . . Psalmus 12. Si Deus paulo diutius auxilium suum differat. Deus meus, Deus meus, ecquare me derelinquis . . . Psalmus 13. In quo gratias agit Deo, quod non prævaluerunt hostes. Laudibus te celebrabo, domine Deus . . . Psalmus 14. In quo divina laudatur bonitas. Domine, dominus noster, quam admiranda est majestas tua . . . Psalmus 15. De beneficiis Dei, cum gratiarum actione. Collaudat te anima mea, O Deus et omnia . . . Psalmus 22. Deus, Deus meus, cur deseruisti me . . . Psalmus 100. Jubilate Deo omnis terra. Gratiarum actio. Jubilate in honorem domini . . . Psalmus 12. Petitio adventus Christi accelerandi, propter superborum principum et hypocritarum in populo multitudinem invalescentem. Salvum me fac, Domine, quoniam deficit sanctus . . .

⁎ *Ed. 1573 has the following " Precationes ex novo testamento " from ed. 1572 of " Psalms or Prayers taken out of holy scripture ". (St. Paul's Cath. 38. E. 27.)*

Precationes ex novo testamento. Matth. vi. 9. 14. Precatio dominica. Pater noster. Matth. xi. 25. 26. Jesu. Ago tibi gratias, Pater, cæli terræque Domine . . . Matth. xxvi. 39. Jesu. Mi Pater, si fieri potest, evadam hoc poculum . . . Et paulo post. 42. Mi Pater, si hoc evadere poculum non possum. Lucæ i. 46-56. Agit Deo gratias Maria . . . Mariæ, Jesu matris, carmen. Magnificat animus meus Dominum . . . Luc. i. 68-80. Deo gratias agit, qui promissum miserit Servatorem . . . Zachariæ

Joannis carmen Baptistæ patris. Grates Domino Israelitarum Deo . . . Lucæ ii. 14. Laudant genii Deum, nato Christo. Deo gloria supremis in locis . . . Lucæ ii. 29-33. Agit Simeon Deo gratias ob missum Servatorem. Nunc dimittis . . . Lucæ xviii. 11. 12. Pharisæi precatio, sed superba et vitiosa. Deus, ago tibi gratias, quod non sum quales . . . Lucæ xviii. 18. Publicani precatio, modesta et bona. Deus, propitius esto mihi sonti. Lucæ xxiii. 42. Latronis cum Christo crucifixi. Memento mei, Domine, . . . Lucæ xxiii. 46. Jesu expirantis. Pater, tibi in manus . . . Joannis xi. 41. 42. Jesu Lazarum in vitam revocaturi. Pater ago tibi gratias, qui me audias . . . Actorum i. 24. 25. Apostolorum super subrogatione Josephi Barsabæ, aut Matthiæ, in Judæ locum. Tu, Domine, qui omnium mentes perspicis . . . Actorum iv. 24-31. Precantur Apostoli Deum, ut se contra adversarios confirmet ad docendum evangelium. Domine, tu Deus es, qui cælum . . . Actorum vii. 58. 59. Stephani morientis. Domine Jesu, accipe spiritum meum. Tum demissis genibus. Domine, noli in eos hoc vindicare peccatum. Ex Epistolis. Rom. i. 8. Ago Deo meo gratias per Jesum Christum . . . Rom. xvi. 25-27. Ei qui vos confirmare potest . . . 1 Corinth. i. 4. Ago Deo meo semper de vobis gratias . . . 1 Corinth. xvi. 23. 24. Gratia Domini Jesu Christi vobis adsit . . . 2 Corinth. i. 2. 3. Gratia vobis, et pax, a Deo patre nostro . . . 2 Corinth. xiii. 13. Gratia Domini Jesu Christi et Dei caritas . . . Galat. vi. 18. Gratia Domini nostri Jesu Christi adsit animo vestro . . . Ephes. vi. 24. Adsit omnibus gratia. 1 Tim. i. 2. Gratia, misericordia, pax . . . Tit. i. 4. Gratia, misericordia . . . 1 Pet. i. 2. 3. Gratia vobis et pax multa sit . . . Ex Apocalypsi. Apocal. v. 8 - 14. Cum cepisset Agnus librum . . . Apocal. vii. 9-13. Postea animadverti tantam turbam . . .

Piæ meditationes de vitæ hujus fragilitate, et spe resurrectionis vitæque eternæ.[1] De vitæ hujus fragilitate. Psalm xxxviii. 6. 7. Ecce mensurabiles posuisti dies meos . . . Lectio ex historia Job. Job vii. Militia est vita hominis super terram . . . Oratio. Media vita in morte sumus . . . Amen. De spe resurrectionis et vitæ æternæ.[1] Job. xix. 25-28. Scio quod redemptor meus vivit . . . Lectio i. Ep. Pauli ad Cor. cap. xv. 20-58. Christus resurrexit ex mortuis . . . Job. xi. 25. 26. Ego sum resurrectio et vita . . . Pater noster. Oratio. Omnipotens et misericors Deus, Pater domini nostri Jesu Christi, qui est resurrectio et vita . . . Amen. Apoca. xiv. 13. Audivi vocem de cælo . . . Item Psal. cxv. 15. Pretiosa in conspectu Domini mors sanctorum ejus.

Precationes aliquot biblicæ sanctorum patrum &c. utriusque testamenti.[2] Oratio Neemiæ pro peccatis populi. Neem. i. Domine Deus cæli, fortis, magne, et terribilis qui custodis pactum . . . Amen. Oratio Moseh. Num. xiv. pro peccato populi. Num. xiv. 18. 19. Patiens Dominus, et multæ misericordiæ auferens iniquitatem . . . Amen. Confessio peccatorum ex xv Sap. Tu, Deus noster, suavis, et verus es, patiens . . . Oratio

[1] See Liber precum publicarum. Sepultura. A.D. 1560.
[2] Precationes biblicæ. (Brit. Mus. 843. c. 6.) A.D. 1531. (Sion Coll.) A.D. 1529.

Danielis. cap. ix. pro peccatorum remissione. Obsecro, Domine Deus,
magne et terribilis, custodiens pactum . . . Amen. Precatio Manassis
pro peccatorum remissione. 2 Para. xxxvi.[1] [2] Domine omnipotens, Deus
patrum nostrorum, Abraham . . . Amen. Oratio populi ut liberetur ab
hoste. Judic. x. 10. 15. Peccavimus tibi, quia dereliquimus te . . .
Oratio regis Asa contra hostes veritatis, aut patriæ impugnatores. 2
Para. xiv. 11. O Domine, non est apud te ulla distantia . . . Oratio
Tobiæ in afflictione. Tobi. iii. 2-7. Justus es, Domine, et omnia judicia
tua vera sunt . . . Oratio et benedictio Job graviter afflicti. Job. i. 21.
Nudus egressus sum de utero matris meæ . . . Ut liberemur ab
adversariis. Isai. xxxvii. 16. 17. 20. Exercituum, Domine, Deus Israel,
tu es Deus solus . . . Amen. Pia Susannæ meditatio quum ab impudicis
senibus solicitaretur. Dan. xiii. 22. 23. Angustiæ mihi sunt undique, si
enim hoc egero . . . Eleazari pia deliberatio de vitanda simulatione. 2
Mach. vi. 24. Non est ætati nostræ dignum fingere . . . Formula
benedictionis filiorum Israel. Nume. vi. 23-27. Sic benedicetis filiis Israel
et dicetis, benedicat tibi Dominus . . . Oratio Salomonis pro necessariis
vitæ subsidiis. Prov. xxx. 7-10. Duo rogavi te, ne deneges mihi antequam
moriar . . . Contra superbiam et impudicitiam. Eccle. xxiii. 4. 7.
Domine pater, et Deus vitæ meæ, ne derelinquas me in cogitatu
malorum . . . Oratio domini nostri Jesu Christi quam docuit discipulos
suos. Matth. vi. 9-14. Pater noster qui es in cælis . . . Amen. Quia
tuum est regnum . . . Canticum Annæ, quo gratias agit Deo pro illius
in se beneficiis. i Reg. ii. 1-11. Exultavit cor meum in Domino . . .
Gratiarum actio Pauli pro conversione sua. 1 Tim 1. 17. Regi
sæculorum immortali, invisibili . . . Amen. Alia ex Apoc. Apoc. xi. 17.
Gratias agimus tibi, domine Deus omnipotens, qui es, et qui eras . . .
Alia ex Apoc. Apoc. xv. 3. 4. Magna et mirabilia sunt opera tua, domine
Deus omnipotens . . .

Aliæ Præces, vel potius Ejaculationes piæ, e sacris Scripturis excerptæ.[3]

Pro timore pio. Da domine, ut tuis præceptis eruditus tibi serviam . . .
Contra desperationem. Multi dicunt animæ meæ, non est salus ipsi in
Deo ejus . . . In mortis periculo. Servator benignissime, illumina
oculos meos ne unquam obdormiam . . . Alia de eodem. Circum
dederunt me dolores mortis et torrentes iniquitatis . . . Pro docilitate
pietatis. Servus tuus ego sum, da mihi intellectum domine . . . Alia
pro eadem. Vias tuas, Domine, demonstra mihi . . . Pro venia
delictorum. Erravi sicut ovis quæ periit, require servum tuum . . .
Pro munditia cordis. Cor mundum crea in me, Deus et spiritum rectum
innova . . . In afflictione. Domine, da nobis auxilium de tribulatione . . . Pro devicta tentatione. Transivimus per ignem et aquam, et

---

[1] Precationes biblicæ. (Brit. Mus. 843. c. 6.) A.D. 1531. (Sion Coll.) A.D. 1529.
[2] S. Augustini meditationes. ed. 1510: and No. 124. A.D. 1536. page 167: also c. A.D. 1534.
No. 115. page 199. and No. 244. A.D. 1560. page 253.
[3] Precationes Erasmi. (Brit. Mus. 3224. a. 58.) A.D. 1537.

eduxisti nos in refrigerium . . . Alia pro eadem. Tu factus es fortitudo pauperi, domine . . . Contra malorum insectationem. Esto mihi, Domine, in Deum protectorem . . . Pro divina misericordia. Sit, obsecro, misericordia tua ad consolandum me . . . In morbo. Sana me, Domine, et sanabor, salvum me fac . . . Revalescentis. Castigans castigavit me Dominus, et morti non tradidit me . . . Resipiscentis. Si iniquitates observaveris, Domine. Domine quis sustinebit . . . Alia pro eodem. Hierem. xxxi. 18, 19. Castigasti me, Domine, et eruditus sum . . . Amen. Pro statu ecclesiastico. Sacerdotes tui induant justitiam . . . Pro principe adolescente, ex oratione Solomonis. Domine Deus, tu regnare fecisti servum tuum . . . Quum recitatur locus Pauli. 1 Cor. v. 7. Expurgate vetus fermentum, ut sitis nova conspersio, sicut estis azymi sic tecum loquere apud Christum. Utinam vere sim azymus, purus ab omni fermento malitiæ . . . Amen. Quum legitur evangelium de seminante semen suum, sic tecum ora. Felix ille, qui meretur esse terra bona . . . Amen. Quum legitur evangelium de nuptiis in Cana Galileæ, sic ora. Jesu, fons bonorum omnium, qui aqua conversa in vinum . . . Benedictio, et claritas et sapientia . . . Amen.

Præcationes piæ variis usibus, temporibus et personis accomodatæ.

Diluculo ad Christum.[1] Domine Jesu Christe, qui verus es mundi sol, semper oriens . . . Amen.

Sub noctem.[1] Domine Jesu Christe, cujus inexhaustæ bonitatis debemus omnia . . . Amen.

Pro docilitate.[1][5] Audi preces meas, æterna Patris sapientia, Domine Jesu . . . Amen.

Succincta confessio peccatorum.[2] Omnipotens et clementissime Deus, qui es medicus unicus . . . Amen.

Pænitentis et divinam misericordiam implorantis, ex Augustino.[3] Ecce, plasmator mei, multa rogavi, qui nec pauca promerui . . . Amen.

Alia ex eodem Augustino.[4] En, ad ostium tuum, summe Paterfamilias, mendicus pulso . . . Amen.

Ad Deum patrem precatio.[2] Omnipotens Deus, cælestis Pater, creator cæli et terræ . . . Amen.

Ad Deum filium.[2] Jesu Christe, dux æternæ felicitatis, cui Pater omnem dedit potestatem . . . Amen.

Ad Deum spiritum sanctum.[2] Veni, sancte Spiritus, unicum solatium afflictorum . . . Amen.

Pro vera pietate.[1] Precor, Jesu Christe, ut quando ex nobis ipsi nihil possumus . . . Amen.

Pro consensu dogmatum et contra adversarios veræ fidei.[1] Amator humani generis, Deus, qui donum linguarum . . . Amen.

[1] Precationes Erasmi. (Brit. Mus. 3224. a. 58 (3). A.D. 1537.
[2] Precationes Christianæ. (Brit. Mus. 843. b. 6.) A.D. 1536.
[3] S. Augustini liber meditationum. (Brit. Mus. 3670. a.) ed. 1510.
[4] S. Augustini liber soliloquiorum. (Brit. Mus. 3670. a.) ed. 1510.
[5] See S. Knight life of Colet, page 129.

Pro gaudio spirituali.[1] Domine Jesu, redemptor et consolator humani generis . . . Amen.

Pro concordia et unitate ecclesiæ Christi.[2] Æterne ac misericors Deus, qui es Deus pacis . . . Amen.

Pro fiducia in Deum.[3] Initium ruinæ hominis sibi fidere . . . Amen.

Pro vera fide.[4] Sancte Pater omnipotens, æterne et clemens Deus, te oro . . . Amen.

Pro veræ fidei augmento.[2] Omnipotens sempiterne Deus et Pater benignissime, eramus nos equidem rebelles . . . Amen.

Pro vere christiano amore.[2] Domine Deus omnipotens, qui caritas es, in qua qui manet . . . Amen.

Pro fide, spe et caritate.[5] Domine Jesu Christe, clemens ac misericors Deus, te oro supplex . . . Amen.

Pro christiana perfectione.[5] Dulcissime Domine Jesu, qui splendor es Patris . . . Amen.

Pro tollenda morum pravitate, et vita melius instituenda ex Augustino.[5] Domine Deus meus, da cordi meo pænitentiam . . . Amen.

Brevis, sed efficax oratio.[6] O Domine Deus meus, meipsum mihi eripe . . . Amen.

Viri fidelis oratio de se humiliter sentientis, ex Augustino.[6] Scio, Domine, et fateor quod non sum dignus quem diligas . . . Amen.

Oratio afflicti in tribulatione ex Augustino.[6] Miserere, Domine, miserere pie et omnipotens Deus . . . Amen.

Oratio qua nos Deo commendamus et gratiam ab eo poscimus ex Augustino.[5] Ne memineris, dulcissime Jesu, tuæ justitiæ adversus peccatorem tuum . . . Amen.

Precatio adversus curam mundanam.[3] Benignissime et indulgentissime Pater, defensor noster . . . Amen.

Contra superbiam pro humilitate.[3] Domine Jesu Christe, in summa potentia mitissime . . . Amen.

Contra invidiam.[3] Domine Deus, creator omnium, bonorumque immensorum dispensator . . . Amen.

Contra iram.[3] Domine Jesu Christe, qui dixeras unumquemque fratri suo irascentem . . . Amen.

Ante sacram communionem.[1] Ago tibi gratias, Jesu Christe, pro ineffabili caritate tua . . . Amen.

Gratiarum actio post communionem.[1] Omnipotens ac benignissime Pater non possumus agere tibi . . . Amen.

Oratio ante concionem. Mitissime Domine Jesu Christe, qui ex mera atque singulari gratia tua . . . Amen.

---

[1] Precationes Erasmi. (Brit. Mus. 3224. a. 58 (3).) A.D. 1537.
[2] Precationes Christianæ. (Brit. Mus. 843. b. 6.) A.D. 1536.
[3] J. Ludovicus Vives, Preces. (Brit. Mus. 1019. a. 6). A.D. 1539.
[4] S. Verrepæus. Precationum piarum enchiridion. (Camb. Univ. A.* 7. 20). ed. 1571.
[5] J. Lanspergius. Pharetra divini amoris. A.D. 1533.
[6] S. Augustini liber meditationum. (Brit. Mus. 3670. a.) ed. 1510.

Post auditam concionem. Domine Jesu Christe, æterne salvator, gratias tibi ago quod cibo verbi tui me pavisti . . . Amen.

Oratio in angustiis et extremis periculis dicenda.[1] Deus qui Susannam matronam honestam calumniose circumventam . . . Amen.

Pro christianis Magistratibus. Misericors Deus ac cælestis Pater, in cujus manu . . . Amen.

Pro Ministris verbi et fructu evangelii.[2] Nos miseri peccatores, qui ope alia destituti . . . Amen.

In rebus adversis.[3] Domine Deus, sine cujus voluntate ne passer quidem in terram cadit . . . Amen.

In rebus prosperis.[3] Gratias ago tibi, Domine Deus omnipotens, qui non solum donis naturæ . . . Amen.

Oratio dicenda tempore veris.[4] Omnipotens rerum omnium innovator, Domine Jesu . . . Amen.

In Æstate.[4] Sapientissime gubernator ac moderator universi, Jesu Christe . . . Amen.

In Autumno.[4] Agimus tibi gratias, indulgentissime Pater, conditor cæli et terræ . . . Amen.

In hyeme.[4] Sapientissime mundi conditor et gubernator Deus . . . Amen.

Tempore pestilentiæ.[4] Non est mirum, O justissime Pater si variis modis . . .

Pro custodia pudicitiæ.[4] Divine Spiritus, qui abhorres ab omni spurcitia . . . Amen.

Pro felici conjugio.[4] Omnipotens Deus, unice prosperator actionum humanarum omnium . . . Amen.

Pro tuenda bona fama.[4] Docuit nos, O Pater cælestis, sapiens ille . . . Amen.

Pro parentibus nostris.[4] Domine Deus, qui nos secundum te plurimum honoris . . . Amen.

Templum ingrediens sic ora. Domine, in multitudine misericordiæ tuæ introibo in domum tuam . . .

Quoties horam sonare audis, dic. Concede mihi, Domine Deus, felicem ac salutarem . . .

Iter ingressurus sic ora. Tibi, Domine Jesu Christe, commendo egressum meum . . . Amen.

Dum es in via aut itinere, sic ora. Deduc me in via tua, ingrediar in veritate tua . . .

Reversus domum, aut ad itineris finem perductus, dic. Gratias tibi ago, benignissime Jesu Christe, quod me ex infinita bonitate tua . . . Amen.

In hostium periculo constitutus dic. Incute, Domine Jesu, terrorem hostibus meis . . . Amen.

De vitæ hujus miseriis querela, ex Augustino.[5] Tædet me, omnipotens ac misericors Deus, et valde tædet hujus vitæ . . . Amen.

[1] Enchiridion preclaræ ecclesiæ Sarum. A.D. 1528. No. 83. page 135.
[2] Precationes Christianæ. (Brit. Mus. 843. b. 6.) A.D. 1536.
[3] Primer. A.D. 1555. No 207. page 188: and A.D. 1545. No. 174. page 243: also A.D. 1560. No. 214. page 256.
[4] Precationes Erasmi. (Brit. Mus. 3224. a. 58. (3). A.D. 1537.
[5] S. Augustini liber meditationum, (Brit. Mus. 3670. a.) ed. 1510.

Præcatio efficacissima, quovis tempore et a quibusvis sæpe dicenda.[1]
Clementissime et misericors Deus, concede mihi quæso . . . Amen.
Præcatio contra diabolum.[2] Domine Jesu Christe, qui per os sancti Petri apostoli . . . Amen.
Adversus avaritiam. Inclina cor meum, Deus, in testimonia tua . . .
Pro alterius vitæ cupiditate.[2] Animæ obscurus teterque carcer hoc corpus est . . . Amen.
In gravi morbo vel in hora mortis.[3] Domine Jesu, qui es unica salus viventium . . . Amen.
Gratiarum actio pro divinis in nos donis et beneficiis.[4] Nos miseri et egeni homines, Domine Deus omnipotens . . . Amen.
Præcationes ante cibum, quas Consecrationes vel Benedictiones mensæ dicimus. Oculi omnium in te sperant Domine . . .[5] Amen. Pater noster. Alia. Creavit Deus cibos ad sumendum . . . Pater noster. Alia. Quicquid appositum est et quicquid apponetur . . . Amen.[3] Pater noster. Alia. Exhilirator omnium, Christe, sine quo nihil vere suave est . . . Amen.[3] Alia carmine reddita a Phil. Melancthone. His epulis donisque tuis benedicito, Christe . . . Alia. Quæ nunc sumemus membris alimenta caducis. Alia. O Deus, appositis apponendisque, precamur. Gratiarum actiones a cibo. Benedictus Deus in donis suis. Oremus. Benignissime Deus, qui nos pascis a juventute nostra . . . Amen.[3] Alia. Misericors Deus, qui alis nos indies ex largis donis tuis . . . Amen. Alia. Omnipotens, æterne Deus, qui escam das timentibus te . . . Amen. Alia ex Chrysostomo. Gloria tibi, Domine, gloria tibi Sancte, gloria tibi Rex . . . Amen.[3] Alia. Omnes gentes laudent Dominum . . . Oremus. Gratias agimus tibi, Pater cœlestis . . . Amen.[5] Alia car. reddita. Corpora qui solito satiasti nostra cibatu . . . Alia. Quod sumus utilibus dapibus potuque refecti . . . Alia. Gratia magna tibi, Pater et Rex inclyte rerum . . . Amen. Gratiarum actiones a cibo semper concludantur hac precatiuncula. Deus servet ecclesiam, regem vel reginam custodiat . . . Amen.
Capita quædam christianæ religionis &c. versibus comprehensa.
Oratio dominica. G. Æmylii. Summe Parens, qui tecta tenes sublimia cæli . . .
Symbolum apostolorum. Adami Siberi. Credo in Deum Patrem, creavit omnia . . .[6]
Decem mandata. Joh. Parkhursti. Unum agnosce Deum, colas et unum.[7]
Eadem breviss. compendio comprehensa. Unum crede Deum, nec jures vana per ipsum . . . (as in No. 124. A.D. 1536. page 162).

---

[1] Enchiridion preclaræ ecclesiæ Sarum. A.D. 1528. No. 83. page 135.
[2] J. Ludovicus Vives, Preces. (Brit. Mus. 1019. a. 6). A.D. 1539.
[3] Precationes Erasmi. (Brit. Mus. 3224. a. 58 (3)). A.D. 1537.
[4] Precationes Christianæ. (Brit. Mus. 843. b. 6.) A.D. 1536.
[5] See Sarum Horæ c. A.D. 1541. No. 161. page 154.
[6] See Delitiæ Poetarum Germanorum. ed. 1612.
[7] J. Parkhursti ludicra. ed. 1573.

De sacro baptismo. Joh. Sauromani. Christus ad æthereas, cum vellet scandere sedes . . .
De cæna domini. Andrea Ellingeri. Nocte qua Christus rabidis Apellis.
Hymnus matut. Ant. Flaminii. Jam noctis umbras Lucifer . . .[1]
Hymnus pænitent. Ant. Flaminii. Jesu benigne, fervidas Præcationes, et mea Ne, quæso, vota despice . . .[1]
Dei beneficia prædicantis. Ant. Flaminii. Jesu beate, numinis Æterna proles maximi . . .[1]
Pro felici in literis successu. G. Fabricii. Omnis in humanis vana est sapientia rebus . . .[2]
Hymnus meridianus. Ant. Flaminii. Jam sol, citato sidere, Suprema cæli culmina . . .[1]
Præcatio cubitum euntis. Ant. Flaminii. Jam vesper ortus incipit Diem tenebris condere . . .[1]
Meditatio cubitum euntis. G. Fabricii. Ut modo ponuntur languentia corpora somno . . .[2]
Hymnus ad Jesum servatorem. Antonii Flaminii. Te, sancte Jesu, mens mea, Amoris icta vulnere . . .[1]
Pro pia vita. Antonii Flaminii. Tutela præsens omnium, Qui mente pura te colunt . . .[1]
Pro pace. Joh. Stigelli. Da, Deus, lætæ bona sancta pacis . . .
Ad Deum patrem. Joh. Cellarii. Dona tui serva nobis, Deus optime, verbi . . .
Ad Deum filium. Joh. Cellarii. Tu quoque quem Dominum dominorum agnoscimus unum . . .
Ad Deum Spiritum S. Joh. Cellarii. Necnon, vere Deus, paracleteque Spiritus, adsis . . .
Pia admonitio ad pueros. Nic. Borbonii. In primis, pueri, Christum discamus amare . . .
Studiorum omnium scopus. Omnium in hoc uno versatur summa laborum . . .
Cursus vitæ Domini nostri Jesu Christi, a Joh. Parkhursto episcopo Nordovicensi, descriptus.[3] Adventus Christi in carnem. Absque viro facta est fæcunda Deipara, Natum. Nativitas. Purus homo ex pura Messias virgine natus. Circumcisio. Inditur, abscissa pueri cute, nomen Jesu. Epiphania. Munera grata ferunt longa regione profecti. Disputatio cum doctoribus. Disputat in templo bis senos circiter annos. Baptismus. Abluitur sacra Christus ter maximus unda. Tentatio. Hostis ter Christum petit, et ter vincitur hostis. Doctrina. Semen per varias sanctum disseminat urbes. Miracula. Omne genus morbos curat, dat lumina cæcis. Ingressus Hierosolymam. Ingressus Solymas pigram conscendit asellam. Lotio pedum. Vilia mendico præstemus munera fratri. Passio et mors. Plurima perpessus vitam cum sanguine fundit. Resurrrectio. Devictis Satana, peccato et morte resurgit. Ascensio. Astra petit Christus, nos astra

[1] M. Antonii Flaminii de rebus divinis carmina ed. 1550.
[2] G. Fabricius Chemnicensis. Odarum libri tres. ed. 1552.
[3] J. Parkhursti ludicra. ed. 1573.

petemus et ipsi. Spiritus sancti missio. Spiritus e rutilo sanctus delapsus Olympo. Judicium extremum. Adveniet Christus supremo tempore Judex. Decem plagæ Ægypti. Exod. 7. 8. 9. 10 et 11. J. Parkhursti. Primum sanguinei latices, post rana coaxans.[1] Modi quibus Christus se nobis exhibet. Se, nascens dedit in socium. De vita beata. Joh. Stigelli. Vitam quæ faciunt beatiorem. In eandem sententiam. G. Fabricii. Summam quæ doceant salutis hæc sunt.[2] In morbo. Ant. Flaminii. Jam quinta lunæ cornua.[3] De morte. Joh. Parkhursti. Certius incerta nihil est mortalibus ipsa.[1] Pro beato vitæ exitu. An. Flaminii. Rector beate cælitum.[3] De carnis nostræ resurrectione. Aur. Prudentius. Nosco meum in Christo corpus consurgere : quid me.[2] Finis.

*** *Ed. 1573 has the following Preces sacræ.*

Ex Psalmo I. Aufer a nobis, Deus optime maxime, prava consilia . . . Amen. Ex Psalmo II. Hoc tempore sentimus, Deus optime maxime non solum Antichristum . . . Amen. Ex Psalmo III. Supra modum auctæ sunt copiæ. Deus optime maxime, illorum qui adoriuntur ecclesiam tuam . . . Amen. Ex Psalmo LI. Misericordiam tuam, Deus optime maxime, conjunctis precibus imploramus . . . Amen. Ex eodem. Agnoscimus, omnipotens Deus, quam perniciosa labe peccatorum . . . Amen. Finis.

*** *These Preces sacræ are taken from " Preces sacræ ex Psalmis David desumptæ per D. Petrum martyrem Vermilium Florentinum, sacrarum literarum in schola Tigurina professorem. Tiguri excudebat Christophorus Froschouerus, Anno MDLXIIII. An english translation by Charles Glenham was published in* 1569.

*** *Ed. 1573 has the following in english and latin. Ed. 1564 is not so full as ed.* 1573.

Regna et regiones, quæ sunt juris et imperii Elizabethæ, reginæ Angliæ. 1573. Anglia. Francia. Hibernia. Idioma. Insulæ habitatæ. Vecta vel Vectis . . . Islands inhabited. Wight . . . Comitatus, seu Provinciæ, Angliæ xxxix. Cantium. Kent . . . Comitatus, seu Provinciæ, Walliæ xi. et Insula Angleseyæ supradicta. Brecnoca. Brecknock . . .

Civitates Angliæ et Walliæ. Canturia. Canterbury . . .

Archiepiscopatus in Anglia duo. Cantuariensis. Eboracensis.

Episcopatus in provincia Cantuariensi. Bishopricks in the diocese of Canterbury. Londinensis. London . . .

Episcopatus in provincia Eboracensi. Bishopricks in the diocese of York. Dunelmensis. Durham . . .

Præcipua flumina Angliæ. xiii. Thamesis. Thames . . .

Quinque portus (quos vocant) Dover . . .

Admonitio ad lectorem. Ubi in Calendario, singulis fere diebus uniuscujusque mensis, sanctorum (quos vocant) nomina apposuimus id eo fecimus, amice lector, non quod eos omnes pro divis habeamus, quorum aliquos

---

[1] J. Parkhursti ludicra. ed. 1573.
[2] G. Fabricius Chemnicensis. Odarum libri tres. ed. 1552.
[3] M. Antonii Flaminii de rebus divinis carmina. ed 1550.

ne in bonis quidem ducimus; aut quod alioqui (si sanctissimi sint) iis divinum cultum atque honorem tribuendum censeamus: sed ut certarum quarundam rerum, quarum stata tempora nosse plurimum refert, quarumque ignoratio nostris hominibus obesse possit, quasi notæ quædam sint atque indicia. Atque hæc quidem hujus facti et instituti nostri ratio esto. Vale.

Colophon. Londini . . . Anno domini 1564. & Reg. Reginæ nostræ Elizabethæ feliciss. memoriæ. 7. Cum privilegio ad imprimendum solum.

A.D. 1627, R. Young, London, 12o. English. No. 255.

*** *The title has "A collection of private devotions, in the practice of the ancient church, called the Hours of prayer. As they were much after this manner published by authority of Q. Elizabeth 1560.*[1] *Taken out of the Holy Scriptures, the ancient Fathers, and the divine service of our own church." A summary is given of all the contents of this book.*

The approbation. Febr. xxii. 1626. I have read over this book, which for the encrease of private devotions, I think may well be printed; and therefore do give licence for the same. Geo. London.

The Printer to the Reader. Gentle Reader. As it oftentimes falleth out in many occurrences and actions, that things are distasted before they are well known; and that, through false reports and mistakings in them that either judge before they see, or out of disaffection make sinister construction of that which deserveth better understanding, good intentions are wrested, and truth impeached: so hath it befallen this handful of collections for private devotions, which was compiled out of sundry warranted books for the private use of an honorable well-disposed friend, without any meaning to make the same publick to the world; though (to save the labor and trouble of writing copies to be sparingly communicated to some few friends) a certain number of them by leave and warrant of the Ordinary were printed at the charge of the party for whose only use the same was collected. It hath therefore seemed good to authority, to give leave to the re-printing thereof, and permitting the same to be sold, to such as please to buy it, only for private use, as in former times way hath been given to the printing of private prayer books. Whereby it is presumed, all well disposed christians may receive satisfaction, that there is not such cause of dislike as it seemeth hath been rumored. And for the avoiding of all mistakings hereafter, care is had to amend such escapes, as either by the printer's haste, or the corrector's over-sight were committed. Only the collector hereof, and others that were therewith acquainted before the printing of the book, who are as ready to engage their credits and lives in defence of the faith of the present Church of England, by law established, and in opposition of Popery; and Romish superstition, as any others, do with grief observe the malevolence of some dispositions of these times; with whom a slip,

---

[1] See Orarium. No. 244. A.D. 1560. page 253: and Preces privatæ. No. 247. A.D. 1564. page 257.

or misprision of a word or two, as liable to a fair and charitable understanding as otherwise, doth not onely lose the thanks due for all the good contained in the work, but also purchase to the author a reprochful imputation of way-making to Popish devotion, and apish imitation of Romish superstition. And howsoever he may be requited for his pains herein, he shall never depart from his good intention of wishing, that the reader may at all times, and for all occasions be assisted with divine grace, obtained by continual prayer. And as for the misdeeming censures and detractions of any, he feareth them not; but rather hopeth that his prayers to God for them will be more beneficial to them, than any their censures or detractions can be prejudicial to him: who doth in this, and in all things else, humbly submit himself to the judgment of the Church of England, whereof he is a member, and, though inferior unto most, yet a faithful Minister.

The preface, touching prayer and the forms of prayer; the fountain and wellspring from which they all proceed, being that perfect form of prayer which Christ taught his disciples. For the good and welfare of our souls, there is not in christian religion anything of like continual use and force throughout every hour of our lives as is the ghostly exercise of prayer and devotion. An exercise it was, which the holy Apostles had often observed their Lord and Master to use . . . The Apostles therefore desired of him to be taught a form of prayer . . . which, from him who made it then, was ever afterwards called the Lord's prayer . . . It is for this cause called by the Fathers, the Prayer of all prayers, and the rule or square whereby all our petitions are to be formed, having likewise been thus used in all ages of the church, not onely as a common part of her prayers and service, but as the chief and fundamental part of them, the ground whereupon she builds, the pattern whereby she frames, and the complement wherewith she perfects all the rest of her heavenly devotions; framing them all as this is framed with much efficacy, though not with any superfluity of words. Thus we begin at this day all our church services with the Lord's prayer, and lay it as a foundation whereon to build the rest of our petitions that follow . . . A part of which ancient piety are these daily devotions and prayers that hereafter follow; Prayers which for the most part, after the same manner and division of Hours[1] as here they are, having heretofore been published among us by high and sacred authority, are now also renewed and more fully set forth again; as for many other, so chiefly for these four reasons. 1. The first to continue and preserve the authority of the ancient laws and old godly Canons of the church, which were made and set forth for this purpose, that men, before they set themselves to pray, might know what to say, and avoid, as near as might be, all extemporal effusions of irksome and indigested prayers which they use to make; that herein are subject to no good order or form of words, but pray both what and how and when they list . . . 2. The second is to let the world understand;

that they who give it out, and accuse us here in England to have set up a new church and a new faith, to have abandoned all the ancient forms of piety and devotion, to have taken away all the religious exercises and prayers of our forefathers, to have despised all the old ceremonies, and cast behind us the blessed Sacraments of Christ's catholick church; that these men do little else but betray their own infirmities, and have more violence and will, than reason or judgment for what they say; the common accusations, which out of the abundance of those partial affections that transport them the wrong way, they are pleased to bring so frequently against us, being but the bare reports of such people, as either do not, or will not understand us, what we are. 3. The third is, that they who are this way already religiously given, and whom earnest lets and impediments do often hinder from being partakers of the publick, might have here a daily and devout order of private prayer; wherein to exercise themselves, and to spend some hours of the day at least (as the old godly christians were wont to do) in God's holy worship and service; not employing themselves so much to talk and dispute, as to practise religion and to live like christians; the continual and curious disquisition of many unnecessary questions among us, being nothing else but either the new seeds, or the old fruits of malice, and by consequence the enemy of godliness, and the abatement of that true devotion, wherewith God is more delighted, and a good soul more inflamed and comforted, than with all the busy subtilties of the world. In which sense S. Austin was wont to say, that: the pious and devout, though unlearned, went to heaven, whiles other men, trusting to their learning, disputed it quite away. 4. The last is, that those who perhaps are but coldly this way yet affected, might by others example be stirred up to the like heavenly duty of performing their daily and christian devotions to almighty God, as being a work of all others the most acceptable to his divine majesty. In so doing, we shall give evident testimony to the world, whose servants we are, and wherein our chief delight doth consist; we shall enjoy a perpetual communion with the Saints triumphant as well as militant, and we shall have just cause to conceive, that so much of our life is celestial and divine, as we spend in this holy exercise of prayer and devotion.

The Calender with the festivals and fasting days of the church, and the memories of such holy men and martyrs, as are therein registred.

Of the Calendar, and the special use thereof in the church of God.

The Calendar of the church is as full of benefit as delight, unto such as are given to the serious study and due contemplation thereof. For besides the admirable order and disposition of times, which are necessary for the better transacting of all ecclesiastical and secular affairs; it hath in it a very beautiful distinction of the Days and Seasons, whereof some are chosen out and sanctified, and others are put among the days of the week to number. But the chief use of it in the church (saith Saint Austin) is to preserve a solemn memory; and to continue in their due season, sometimes a weekly, and sometimes an annual commemoration of those excellent and high benefits, which God, both by himself, his Son, and his blessed Spirit, one undivided Trinity, hath bestowed upon mankind, for the founding and propagating of that christian faith and religion which we now profess. And, forasmuch as this faith of ours is no other than it was of old, even the very same, wherein the holy angels are set to succour us, and which the glorious company of the Apostles, the noble army of Martyrs, and the goodly fellowship of other God's Saints and servants, men famous in their generations before us, have some maintained with the sanctity of their lives, and some sealed with the innocency of their deaths ; it is for this cause, that the names of these holy and heavenly Saints are still preserved in the Calendar of the church, there to remain upon record and register (as of old time they did) where they might also stand, as sacred memorials of God's mercy towards us, as forcible witnesses of his ancient truth, as confirmations of the faith which we now profess to be the same that then was, as provocations to the piety which they then practised, and as everlasting records, to shew whose blessed servants they were on earth, that are now like the angels of God in heaven. Howbeit, forasmuch also as in process of time the multitude of men and women, reputed holy in this kind, became so exceeding numerous, that all the days of the year would not have been sufficient for a several commemoration of them ; it was the great wisdom and moderation of those religious grave Prelates, whom by God (of his special blessing unto our church above others) did reform such things as were many ways amiss among us, to choose one solemn day alone, (All Saints day) wherein to magnify God for the generality of all his Saints together ; and to retain some few selected days in every month for the special memory of others, both holy persons and holy actions, which they observed not our people alone, but the universal church of Christ also, to be most affected unto, and best acquainted withall ; hereby avoiding only the burthen, and the unnecessary number of Festival days, not disallowing the multitude of God's true martyrs and saints, whose memorials we are to solemnise ; howsoever in the general festival of All Saints day, as by the proper lessons, the collect, epistle, and gospel, then appointed in our publick Liturgy, doth most evidently appear.

The Calendar has those days printed in red for which there is an epistle and gospel in the Books of Common prayer A.D. 1559 and A.D. 1604. It also has other Saints days, with some account of each Saint, printed in black. The date of a particular year is assigned to each Saint's day, as well as to other events. It has " The day of K. Charles his inauguration. 1615." on March 27. " Powder-treason day. 1605." on November 5.

A table of the moveable feasts. Rules to know when the moveable feasts and holy days begin. The fasting days of the church, or days of special abstinence and devotion. The times wherein marriages are not usually solemnized.

The sum of the Catholick Faith, called the Apostles Creed: divided into twelve articles.

The Lord's Prayer divided into seven petitions. The preface. Our Father which art in heaven. Math. 6. The petitions. Hallowed be thy name . . . The Doxology. For thine is the kingdom . . .

The ten Commandments.

The duties enjoined and the sins forbidden in the ten commandments. Which may serve for a direction to know, or to make known our manifold offences against God and man. . . .

The two precepts of charity, or the laws of nature. To love God above all for his own sake. 2. To love all men as ourselves for God's sake: to do unto others, as we would they should do unto us.

The precepts of the church. The sacraments of the church. The three theological virtues. Three kinds of good Works. Seven gifts of the Holy Ghost. The Twelve fruits of the Holy Ghost. The Spiritual works of mercy. The Corporal works of mercy. The Eight beatitudes. Seven deadly sins, as they are commonly so called. The contrary virtues. Quatuor novissima, or the four last things that befall any men.

A collection of private devotions for the Hours of prayer.

Of the ancient and accustomed times of prayer in general. At all times and in all places to give thanks and praise unto Almighty God our heavenly father, with all manner of devout prayer and supplication, is no more than our very meet, right, and bounden duty. But inasmuch as the common employments of most, and the natural infirmities of all sorts of people be so great, that whiles they have this body of flesh upon them, they cannot possibly attend the heavenly exercise of prayer and thanksgiving without any intermission at all: it hath therefore been the custom of religious and godly persons in all ages, to appoint themselves certain set times and hours of the day, wherein to perform their devotions . . . The practise then of old hath been so to keep up prayer, that men might keep up themselves withall. Three times a day to perform this duty, and otherwhiles seven times a day to do it was King David's sacred resolution . . . From which holy examples it afterwards came to pass, that what was by them so religiously observed under the law, three times a day at least to offer up prayers and thanksgivings to almighty God besides the morning and evening sacrifice, was by christians as piously continued and practised under the gospel also; both Jews and Christians being in this duty but equal servants to the same Trinity, the God both of law and gospel. It is from the prophet Daniel, saith Saint Cyprian, that we christians have our Third, our Sixth, and our Ninth Hour of prayer which we duly observe in reverence of the blessed Trinity . . . Such are these Hours and Prayers that hereafter follow; which be not now set forth for the countenancing of their novelties, that put any trust in the bare recital only of few prayers, or place any virtue in the Bead-roll or certain number of them at such and such set-hours, but for the hearty imitation of that ancient and christian piety, to whom the distinction of Hours was but an orderly and useful, no superstitious or wanton performance of their duties. And surely so small a part of our time taken up from other common actions, if not perhaps from doing ill, or doing nothing; and so small a task, though but voluntarily imposed upon ourselves for God's service, will never undo us, nor never prove to be an abridgment of our christian liberty, who say our delight is to be numbered with the Saints of old, and profess every day, that God's service is perfect freedom.

Certain choice sentences out of Holy Scripture; whereby the frequency of prayer and devotion is highly commended unto us. Psal. 34. 15. The eyes of the Lord are over the righteous.

Pious ejaculations or short prayers; to be committed unto perfect memory for our first holy exercise in the beginning of the day. According to the direction of S. Ambrose in his third Book de virgin.

When we first awake. Lighten mine eyes, O Lord, that I sleep not in death. Psal. 13 . . .

At our uprising. In the name. Blessed be the holy and undivided Trinity . . . Or this. In the name of our Lord Jesus Christ who was crucified for me I arise from mine own rest to do him service . . . I laid me down and slept . . .

At our apparelling. According to the direction of S. Basil, orat. in Martyr. Julit. Clothe me, O Lord, with the ornaments of thy heavenly grace . . . Put ye on the Lord Jesus Christ . . .

At the washing of our hands. Wash me clean, O Lord, from my wickedness . . . Cleanse me, O God, by the bright fountain of thy mercy . . . And then humbly commending ourselves to God's protection upon our knees. Into the hands of thy blessed protection . . .

At our going abroad. Shew me thy ways, O Lord, . . . Lead me, O God, in the way of thy truth . . . O give thine angels charge over me . . .

When we hear the clock at any hour of the day. Teach me, O Lord, to number my days . . . Our time passeth away like a shadow . . . Have mercy upon me, O Lord, now and at the hour of death.

At our entrance into the church. As for me, I will go into thy house, O Lord, in the multitude of thy mercies . . . Lord, I have loved the habitation of thine house . . . My soul hath a desire and longing . . .

When we are come into the Quire. O how amiable are thy dwellings . . . Blessed are they that dwell in thy house . . .

When we fall down to worship, and adore before the presence of God. Holy, holy, holy, Lord God almighty . . . Thou art worthy, O Lord our God to receive glory . . .

A divine hymn preparative to prayer. When to thy God thou speak'st, O creature mean . . .

The Hours of prayer.

An advertisement concerning the division of the Hours following. It appeareth, both by the histories of the Jews, and by plain observations out of the New Testament, that the space of the day from the morning to the evening was solemnly divided into four equal parts, which they called Hours, to wit, the First, the Third, the Sixth and the Ninth . . .

The First Hour or the Morning prayers. Which have been distinquished but of late times, being anciently both one Hour of prayer. Radul. de Rivo. in lib. de. Can. observ. propos. 14.

The antiquity of the Mattins or Morning prayer, deduced as well from the testimony of the sacred scriptures, as from the holy fathers of the church. In the primitive church it was daily the first speech which those good christians used, and the first thing they did; Ante omnia adoremus Dominum, qui fecit nos. (1) Before we do anything, let us fall down and worship the Lord that made us: they would serve God first, and then serve themselves . . . From the Holy Scriptures. Exod. 36. 3. And they brought their offerings . . . From the Fathers. Const. Apost. lib. 8. cap. 34. Let every christian begin his day's work with devotion . . .

Preparatory prayers to all the Hours that follow. God be in my head and understanding . . . Amen. Prevent me, O Lord, in all my doings with thy most gracious favour . . . Amen. The confession. Almighty and most merciful Father, I have erred . . . Amen. The prayer. Almighty God, the Father of our Lord Jesus Christ, who desirest not the death of a sinner . . . Amen.

Mattins or Morning Prayer for the first Hour of the day . . . The Laudes or the praises at morning prayer . . . The Third Hour of prayers or the middle space between Sun-rising and noon. The ancient use of prayers at the third Hour. Prayers for the third Hour. The Sixth Hour of prayer or Mid-Day. The ancient custom of prayer at the Sixth Hour or Noon-day. Prayers for the Sixth Hour. The Ninth Hour of prayer or Mid-space between Noon and Sun-set. The ancient use of prayers at the ninth Hour. Prayers for the ninth Hour. Prayers at the Vespers or time of Evensong. The ancient use of Evening prayer. Prayers for the evening. The Compline or final prayers to be said before bed time.

Prayers at bed-time to be committed unto perfect memory. An admonition before we go to sleep. Permit not sluggish sleep to close your waking eye . . . When we enter into our bed. In the name of our Lord Jesus who was crucified . . . As we lie down to sleep. At night lie down, Prepare to have, Thy sleep, thy death, thy bed, thy grave . . . I. I will lay me down in peace . . . II. Have mercy upon me, O Lord, now . . . III. Preserve me while I am waking . . . Amen. Amen. Amen. The end of the last hour at night.

⁎ *The general arrangement of these Hours is that of devotions for the first, third, sixth, ninth Hours, Vespers or time of Evensong, and Compline. The first Hour includes Mattins and Lauds. The form of each of the Hours is that found in No. 244. A.D. 1560 (page 253): the component parts, with the exception of Matins, are different. Lauds and Compline end in the same way as Preces matutinæ, and Preces vespertinæ in No. 247 A.D. 1564 (page 258).*

The seven penitential psalms, with the Letanie and suffrages.

Seven penitential psalms, to be used in times of penance, fasting, affliction or trouble, or at any other time, as private devotion shall move us.

The Letanie to be used on Sundays, Wednesdays and Fridays after the Morning prayers, or any other hour of devotion. As also upon the Rogation and Fasting days: and in the time of plague, famine, war and other calamities. Such misery, as being present or imminent, all men are apt to bewail with their tears, they that be religious and wise will ever seek to prevent or avert with their prayers. In regard whereof these Letanies were at first composed by the Fathers in the primitive church, solemnly to be used for the appeasing of God's wrath in publick evils, and for the procuring of his mercy in common benefits. At the first they were not so large as now they are, being augmented by Mamercus Bishop of Uienia, and by Sidonius Apollinaris Bishop of Auerna, and afterwards by S. Gregorie the Great Bish. of Rome, in whose times there was much affliction and trouble throughout the whole world. From their days they have been brought down to ours; and in the meanwhile got some trust: the addition and invocation of the Saints names, which some men have thereunto annexed, being by Walafride Strabo's own confession, but a novelty; and therefore are not inserted into these our Letanies: which being lately by our own church brought into that absolute perfection, both for matter and form, as not any church besides can shew the like so complete and full, needs must they be upbraided with error or somewhat worse, whom in all parts this principal and excellent prayer doth not fully satisfy.

The Letanie. It has "Thy servant Charles, our most gracious King and Governour. Our most gracious Queen Mary, Frederick the Prince Elector Palatine, and the Lady Elizabeth his wife with their princely issue." It is the same as that in the Book of Common prayer A.D. 1604, omitting "That it may please thee to give to all nations unity, peace, and concord," leaving out all the collects after "We humbly beseech thee, O Father, mercifully to look upon our infirmities," and substituting "O God whose nature and property is ever to have mercy and to forgive".

The collects for the Sundays and Holy-days throughout the whole year.

⁎ *These collects are the same as those in the Books of Common prayer A.D. 1552 and A.D. 1604. Explanations are given before Advent Sunday. Septuagesima Sunday. The first day of Lent. The week before Easter. Easter-day. Monday and Tuesday in Easter week. Whitsunday or the Feast of Pentecost. Trinity Sunday.*

Devout prayers that may be used before and after the receiving of Christ's holy Sacrament, his blessed body and blood.

Prayers before the receiving of the blessed Sacrament. When we enter into the church. Lord, I have loved the habitation of thine house . . . I will wash mine hands in innocency . . .

When we are prostrate before the altar. Thou art worthy, O Lord, to receive glory . . . Blessing and glory and wisdom . . . Amen. Holy, Holy, Holy, Lord God almighty . . . Psal. 51. Have mercy upon me, O God . . .

At the consecration. Vers. I believe, Lord help my unbelief. The Hymn. A special theme of praise is read . . . The prayer. I. Almighty Lord, who hast of thine infinite mercy vouchsafed to ordain this dreadful sacrament for a perpetual memory of that blessed sacrifice . . . Amen. II. O Lord our heavenly Father, almighty and everlasting God, regard we beseech thee, the devotion of thy humble servants . . . Amen. III. Be pleased, O God, to accept this our bounden duty and service . . .

Heavenly aspirations immediately before the receiving of the blessed sacrament. I. Psal. I will go unto the altar of God . . . II. Psal. I will offer thanksgiving unto my God . . . III. Ex Letan. O Lamb of God, that takest away the sins of the world, have mercy upon us. IV. Ex Letan. O Lamb of God, that takest away the sins of the world, grant us thy peace. V. Ex Liturg. Grant me gracious Lord, so to eat the flesh of thy dear Son . . .

At the receiving of the Body. Lord, I am not worthy . . . Adding with the priest. The body of our Lord Jesus Christ, which was given for me . . . And answer. Amen.

At the receiving of the Cup. What reward shall I give unto the Lord . . . Ps. 116. Adding with the Priest. The blood of our Lord Jesus Christ which was shed for me . . . Ex Liturg. Answering again. Amen.

Thanksgiving after we have received the blessed Sacrament. I. O my God, thou art true and holy . . . II. O the depth of the wisdom and knowledge of God . . . Rom. 11. 33. III. Praise the Lord, O my soul . . . Psal. 103. 1. 2. IV. Glory be to God on high . . . Amen.

Meditations whilest others are communicated. Happy are those servants, whom when their Lord cometh . . . Ex Evang. II. Know ye not that ye are the temple of God . . . Ex S. Paulo. III. Behold thou art made whole . . . Joh. 5. 13. IV. The hour cometh and now it is . . . Joh. 4. 23. V. Be we followers of God . . . Ephes. 5.

At the end of the Communion. The doxology. To the King eternal . . . Amen.

Divers forms of devout and penitent confessions of our sins. To be used as at other times, so especially before the receiving of Christ's blessed Sacrament. According to the direction of the church. Exhortation before the Communion. If any require comfort and counsel for the quieting of his conscience . . . I. John 1. 9. If we confess our sins . . . The preparation. I. Almighty God, unto whom all hearts be open . . . Amen. II. Almighty and everlasting God, which hatest nothing that thou hast made . . . Amen. The confession. I confess &c. those sins, which if I would, I cannot hide from him . . . Amen. Other forms of general confessions. I. Almighty and most merciful Father, I have erred and strayed from thy ways . . . Amen. II. Almighty God, Father of our

Lord Jesus Christ, maker of all things . . . Amen. III. Forgive me my sins, O Lord, forgive me the sins of my youth . . .

A devout manner of preparing ourselves to receive absolution. I that am a wretched sinner, here personally appearing and prostrate before the presence of the everlasting God . . . Amen. The prayer. O God, whose nature and property is ever to have mercy and to forgive . . . Amen. After absolution. Blessed is he whose unrighteousness is forgiven . . . Blessed is the man unto whom the Lord imputeth no sin.

Prayers for the King and Queen.

Prayers for the King and Queen. Our Father. Vers. O God make speed . . . Resp. O Lord make haste . . . Glory be to the Father. Allelujah. Praise the Lord. The Hymn. Great God of Kings, whose gracious hand hath led our sacred sovereign Head . . . The antiphona. Behold, O God, our defender . . . Psal. 21. The King shall reign in thy strength. Psal. 61. Hear my prayer, O God. Psal. 89. Thou hast made a covenant O Lord. The antiphona. Behold, O God, our defender . . . The Lesson. I. Tim. 2. 1. I will therefore, that prayers and supplications . . . Vers. O Lord, save the King. Resp. And mercifully hear us . . . The prayers. Almighty God, whose Kingdom is everlasting . . . Amen. II. Almighty and everlasting God, we be taught by thy holy Word that the hearts of Kings . . . Amen. III. We beseech thee, O Lord, to save and defend all christian Kings . . . Amen. IV. O Lord our heavenly Father, high and mighty, King of Kings . . . Amen. V. Ex libro regali. O almighty and everlasting God, Creator and Lord of all things, give ear we beseech thee unto our humble prayers . . . Amen. VI. Lib. Reg. God the unspeakable author of the world, creator of men, governor of empires and establisher of all kingdoms . . . Amen. VII. Lib. Reg. Look down, almighty God, with thy favourable countenance upon thine anointed and our glorious King . . . Amen. VIII. Lib. Reg. Grant we beseech thee almighty God, that our sovereign Lord the King may be a most mighty Protector of his people . . . Amen.

Prayers for the Queen. I. Almighty God, the fountain of all mercy, we humbly beseech thee to pour down the riches of thine abundant goodness upon the head of thine handmaid our most gracious Q. Marie . . . Amen. II. Almighty God, our heavenly Father, we be taught by thy holy Word that the bringing forth of children . . . Amen. III. O God from whom all good graces do proceed, we beseech thee to multiply upon thy devoted handmaid our gracious Queen . . . Amen. IV. Almighty God, bless her with the blessings of heaven above . . . Amen.

Prayer for the Pr. Palat. with the Ladie Elizabeth &c. Almighty God the fountain of all goodness, hear our humble supplications which we make unto thee for thy blessings and favors upon Frederick, Prince Elector Palatine, and the Lady Elizabeth his wife with their princely issue . . . Amen. The Lord's name be praised.

Prayers for the four Ember-weeks.

Prayers for the four Ember-weeks. Among all the set fasts of the year Lent hath the first and these Ember days the second place; days of devotion and fasting, which were instituted of old and observed at the four seasons of the year . . . Vers. Our help . . . Resp. Who hath made . . . Vers. Blessed be the name . . . Resp. From henceforth world without end. Amen. The Psalms. Psal. 119. Beati immaculati. Legem pone. Appropinquet. After these Psalms, the Letany may be said.

The prayers common to all the Ember days, disposed according to the seven reasons before specified. I. For God's acceptance of our humiliation. Almighty God, who did'st command thy people Israel to afflict their souls . . . Amen. II. For consecrating the beginning of every season unto God. Almighty God, from whom we have the beginning and continuance of our life . . . Amen. III. For grace to spend the whole season aright. Almighty God our heavenly Father, we most humbly beseech thee, that we thy servants . . . Amen. IV. For the fruits of the earth. Almighty God, Lord of heaven and earth, in whom we live, move, and have our being . . . Amen. V. For pardon of sins past. Almighty and most merciful Father, who for our many and grievous sins . . . Amen. VI. For the health of our bodies. O God, the father of lights, from whom cometh down every good and perfect gift . . . Amen. VII. For the ordination of Priests and Deacons. Almighty God our heavenly Father, who hast purchased to thy self an universal church . . . Amen.

The prayers proper to the four several ember weeks. I. In the time of Advent. Grant, we most humbly beseech thee O heavenly father, that with holy Simeon and Anna . . . Amen. II. For the ember week in Lent. O Lord Jesus Christ, the Son of God and Saviour of the world, who did'st foretel to thine Apostles . . . Amen. III. For the ember week after Pentecost. O Lord Jesus Christ, the eternal Son of the eternal Father, who at the time of thy glorious ascension . . . Amen. IV. For the ember week in September. Almighty God, who givest to all life and breath and all things . . . Amen. Assist me mercifully, O Lord, in these my supplications and prayers . . . Amen.

Prayers for the sick.

Prayers for the sick. Our Father. Vers. Our help standeth . . . Resp. Which hath made . . . Vers. Blessed be the name . . . Resp. Henceforth . . . Glory be to the Father. Antiphona. Blessed are they whom thou chastenest . . . Psal. 25. Unto thee, O Lord, do I lift up my soul . . . Psal. 27. Hearken unto my voice, O Lord . . . Psal. 31. 34. In thee, O Lord, have I put my trust . . . Antiphona. Blessed are they whom thou chastenest . . . Seven penitential psalms. The Letanie. The confession. I confess unto almighty God those sins, which if I would I cannot hide from him . . . Amen. An humble protestation of free forgiveness to others. I do further most humbly desire all and every one whom I have offended ... Amen. The Creed. I believe in God. After the Creed. In this faith, which I do unfeignedly and wholly believe ... Amen. The prayers. Lord have mercy upon me. Our Father. Vers. O Lord save thy servant. Resp. Which putteth ... Vers. Send me help ... Resp. And evermore ... Vers. Let the enemy ... Resp. Nor the wicked one ... Vers. Be unto me, O Lord ... Resp. From the face ... Vers. O Lord, hear ... Resp. And let my cry ... I. God who declarest thy almighty power ... Amen. II. O God who seest that I put not my trust in any thing which I can do ... Amen. III. O Lord look down from heaven, behold, visit, and relieve me thy sick servant ... Amen. IV. Hear me almighty and most merciful God and Saviour, extend thine accustomed goodness unto me ... Amen. V. O sweet Jesus, I desire neither life nor death but thy most holy will ... Amen. VI. O God whose nature and property ... Amen. The blessing. The almighty Lord, who is a most strong tower ... Amen.

Prayers at the hour of death. Our Father. Vers. O Lord save thy servant. Resp. Which putteth ... Psalm 13 and 16. Consider and hear me. Psalm 23. The Lord is my Shepherd. Psalm 38 and 39. Put me not to rebuke. Psalm 102. Hear my prayer, O Lord. Job 14. Man that is born of a woman. Vers. O Lord hear my prayer. Resp. And let my cry ... The Letanie ... The peace of God ...

Prayers at the point of death. The manner of commending the soul into the hands of God, at the very point of time when it is departing from the body. We brought nothing into this world ... Into thy merciful hands, O Lord, we commend the soul of this thy servant ... God the Father who hath created thee, God the Son who hath redeemed thee ... Amen. Christ that redeemed thee with his agony ... Amen. Christ Jesus that rose the third day from death ... Amen. Christ that ascended into heaven ... Amen. God the Father preserve and keep thee ... Amen. Then let be said plainly, distinctly, and with some pauses these ejaculatory meditations, and prayers. Go to thy rest, O my soul ... Lord Jesus receive my spirit. And these with the prayers following to be repeated until the soul be departed. O thou Lamb of God that takest away the sins of the world, grant him thy peace. O Lord with whom do live the spirits of them that die ... Amen.

Prayers and thanksgivings for sundry purposes.

Prayer and thanksgiving for the whole estate of Christ's Catholick church. With a commemoration of the Saints before us. Ex Litur. Eccl. Almighty God, who by thy holy apostle hast taught us ... Our Father, &c.

For our parents. Almighty God, Father of our Lord Jesus Christ, of whom the whole family in heaven and in earth is named ... Amen. Another for our parents. Almighty God, who hast straightly commanded us to honour our father and our mother next unto thee ... Amen.

For our children. Almighty God the Father and maker of us all ... Amen.

Prayer to be used by women that travel with child. Almighty God, the father of all mercy and comfort . . . Amen. Another. Merciful Lord who when thou tookest upon thee to deliver man . . . Amen.

Thanksgiving after child birth. Gracious God, by whose providence we are all fearfully and wonderfully made . . . Amen.

Thanksgiving for recovery from sickness. Praise the Lord, O my soul, and all that is within me praise his holy name . . . Amen.

Prayer in the time of war. O almighty God, King of all Kings, and governor of all things . . . Amen.

Thanksgiving for peace and victory. O almighty God, who art a strong tower of defence unto thy servants . . . Amen.

Prayer in the time of any common plague. Almighty God, who in thy wrath in the time of King David . . . Amen.

Thanksgiving for deliverance from any plague. O Lord, who hast wounded us for our sins . . . Amen.

Prayer and thanksgiving for every true subject to use upon the anniversary day of the King's reign. Lord by whom Kings do reign . . . Amen.

Prayer and thanksgiving upon the anniversary day of our birth. Almighty God, the father and maker of all things . . . Amen.

Prayer and thanksgiving upon the anniversary day of our baptism. O Lord heavenly father, almighty and everlasting God, who of thine infinite goodness towards me . . . Amen.

Prayer wherewith St. Augustine began his devotions, admiring the unspeakable majesty and attributes of God. Conf. Lib. 1. Cap. 4. What art thou, O my God, what art thou . . . Amen.

Prayer wherewith to conclude all our devotions. Almighty God, who hast promised to hear the petitions of them that ask in thy Son's name . . . Amen.

The blessing. The peace of God which passeth all understanding . . . Amen.

Finis.

The table.

Finis.

A.D. 1671, London, for S.S. sold by Thomas Hartley, London. 8º. English. Nº. 258.

₊ *The title is " The King's Psalter containing psalms, and hymns with easy and delightful directions to all learners, whether children, youths, or others for their better reading of the english tongue. Also prayers for every day of the week, beginning with the letters of the name of our Sovereign Lord King Charles ; and other observable varieties, fit either for the school, or for the closet, all which are profitable, plain, and pleasant." A summary is given of all the contents of this book.*

The book is dedicated to his royal grace, Edgar Baron Dawntzey in the county of Wilts, Earl and Duke of Cambridge, son and heir apparent to the thrice illustrious Prince, the most highly magnanimous James Duke of York and Albany &c.

To the instructors of youth in His majesty's three kingdoms of England, Scotland, and Ireland &c. This treatise, entituled the King's psalter, is composed on purpose to succeed the King's Primer:[1] which Primer is of so excellent a use for young children that, with ease, the child, by learning that, will be prepared to improve himself in this. And since, as Solomon saith, instruction is the life of a man; and whoever loveth instruction loveth knowledge, it is very necessary, that likewise the art of giving instruction should be considered; wherefore with great care and industry you have now presented to you a method both easy and delightful; it being a mixture of prose and verse in divinity and morality, by which the youth is, as it were, enticed into a pleasant grove of profitable fancies; where by his meditations he may learn not onely to be a good son, but a good christian, according to that of the divine Herbert . . . Printed and published according to order, with his Majesty's special approbation.

Fifteen selected psalms with a hymn and an antiphon to each.[2]

The father's advice to his child. My son hear the instruction of thy father . . . Blessings of obedience. My son do thou observe my law, And slight not my decree . . . The prodigal son's return. A certain man had two sons. . . .[2] The son's experience. Vanity of vanities all is vanity . . . Solomon's seasons. Is there not an appointed time to man on earth . . . Blessed qualifications. Blessed, thrice blessed are the poor . . .

The Alphabet illustrated by texts: there are cuts at the left hand of the page: at the side of the cut a letter of the alphabet.

A Psalm or summary of God's providence.[3] Come now and hear, you that fear the Lord. Hymn. Jesu who from thy Father's throne. Antiphon. Blessed be the mercy of our God . . . A psalm of remembrance. Soon as his blest decree was made of sending the son of God to redeem mankind. Hymn. What can I crave, More than the Lord hath done. Antiphon. The Lord hath redeemed me from my sins. A psalm of our Saviour's sufferings. It was not thy joys alone O Lord that thou inspirest into thy holy prophets . . . Hymn. O thou God almighty . . . Antiphon. And now Lord what is my hope . . . A psalm of praise Praise the Lord all you nations of the earth, praise him with the voice of joy and thanksgiving . . . Hymn. Blessed Saviour Lord of all . . . Antiphon. Bless the Lord O my soul . . . A psalm of thanksgiving. We praise thee, O God . . . Hymn. Why do we seek felicity . . . Antiphon. Never can we say too much of this gracious subject . . . A psalm of adoration. Come let us adore our God that hath redeemed us, when O Lord we had sold ourselves in sin . . . Hymn. Come let's adore the King of love . . . Antiphon. Let us take up our cross . . .

Evening prayer. O Lord our heavenly father, almighty and everliving God by whose providence both the day and night are governed . . . Amen. Glory be to the Father. Hymn. Permit not sluggish sleep. To close

---

[1] Primer set forth by the King's majesty and his clergy. A.D. 1545. May 29. page 237.
[2] This does not occur in Bodl. copy, Bliss. 1524.
[3] This does not occur in Camb. Univ. copy.

your waking eye. . . . Down lying. At night lie down, Prepared to have, Thy sleep, thy death, Thy end, thy grave . . . Antiphon. I will lay me down in peace . . . Have mercy upon me, O Lord . . .

A prayer and thanksgiving for every true subject to use upon the anniversary day of the King's reign. O Lord by whom Kings reign . . . Amen. Hymn. Give to the King Thy judgments Lord, That he may justice do . . . Antiphon. Lord preserve the life of the King.

Catholick Faith, called the Apostles Creed, divided into twelve articles. The exposition of the Creed. The Lord's prayer. The doxology. The exposition of the Lord's prayer. The ten commandments. The exposition of the ten Commandments.

The three theological virtues. Faith. Hope and Charity. They are called theological, because the word signifieth a thing that belongeth to God . . . Of faith . . . Of hope . . . Of charity . . . Fasting. Prayer and Alms-deeds. Of fasting . . . Of prayer . . . Of alms-deeds . . . Pray and labour for the seven gifts of the Holy Ghost . . . To these add the twelve fruits of the Holy Ghost . . . Likewise let these seven spiritual works of mercy be in you . . . Together with these, six corporal works of mercy . . . There are seven capital sins, which are the fountains of all others, and to every one is opposite a contrary virtue . . . There are six sins against the Holy Ghost . . . There are four sins that cry to heaven for vengeance . . . The four last things . . . There were fifteen stages in our Saviour's pilgrimage from the womb unto his tomb . . .

When thou awakest say with the Psalmist. Lighten mine eyes, O Lord, that I sleep not in death. Or thus. Awake thou that sleepest, and arise from death and Christ shall give thee light. Or thus. Open thou mine eyes O Lord, that I may see the wonders of thy law.

At thy uprising say. In the name. Even blessed be the holy and undivided Trinity . . . I laid me down and slept . . .

Every morning, noon, and evening let us fall down to worship and adore before the presence of our God, saying. Holy, Holy, Holy, Lord God almighty which was and is . . .

A prayer for the morning. Into the hands of thy blessed protection . . . Amen. Glory be to the Father. Hymn. Sweet Jesus, why, why dost thou love . . . Antiphon. Thou art, O Lord, the true light of the world . . .

A prayer for the evening. O most blessed Saviour, whose sacred body after that thou had'st finished the work of our redemption . . . Amen. Glory be to the Father. Hymn. O Lord now night's returned again . . . Antiphon. He hath made the out-goings of the morning . . . Let the Priests, the ministers of the Lord, weep before the porch . . .

The altar. A broken altar, Lord, to thee I raise, Made of a heart to celebrate thy praise . . .

The youth's ejaculation. God be in my head and understanding . . . Hymn.

Oh that I once were in that city . . . Antiphon. The heavenly Jerusalem is the city of our God.

Preparatory prayers for morning and evening, beginning with the several letters of the name of our sovereign Lord King Charles. Begone profaneness come not near . . .

₊ *A prayer, hymn and antiphon is added to the six first letters of the King's name. The seventh and last letter has the following. A private prayer for all times. Say unto my soul, O God thou art my salvation . . . Glory be to the Father. Hymn. The sun by prayer. Did cease his course and staid . . . Antiphon. Prayer is the soul's artillery.*

An alphabet of lessons for the instruction of youth.

₊ *A lesson is added to each letter of the alphabet.*

Loyal prayers for every day of the week, beginning with the letters of the name of our sovereign Lord King Charles.

₊*₊ *There is a prayer, a hymn and an antiphon for each day.*

Meditations holy and humane on sundry occasions divided into chapters.

₊ *These are forty seven in number in Cambridge University copy, but fifty one in the Bodleian copy: each chapter is composed of texts of Holy Scripture and proverbs.*

A prayer for the King's most excellent majesty, the Queen, Queen mother, Duke of York, and the rest of the royal family.[1] O thou eternal Lord God, Kings of Kings, Lord of lords, and mighty ruler of princes . . . Amen. King Charles the second began his reign the thirteenth day of January 1648, at which time his royal father of glorious memory was most barbarously murthered.

The alphabet illustrated by a descriptive rhyme with a cut; a cut and a rhyme occur opposite to each letter of the alphabet. A. (a cut) "Unhappy chance! such fate should give . . ."

Words fitly spoken or apples of gold in pictures of silver.

₊ *This portion of the book is composed of fifty eight proverbs.*

The names of the Archbishopricks and of the several counties. The names of the several cities throughout England and Wales. In the year are these twelve months. Names in use for men. Names in use for women.[1]

Graces before and after meat. Grace before meat. Good Lord bless us and these thy good creatures to our use . . . Amen. Grace after meat. We thank thee, O Lord, for all thy benefits . . . Amen. Grace before meat. Lord be merciful unto us and bless us . . . Amen. Grace after meat. O Lord, we thank thee for the use of these thy good creatures . . . Amen. Grace before meat. O Lord bless us and this our store, And make us thankful evermore . . . Amen. Grace after meat. We praise thy name, for thou O Lord . . . Amen. Grace before meat. O Lord the merciful and good . . . Amen. Grace after meat. O Lord to whom all praise is due . . . Amen. Psalm 150. Praise ye the Lord God.

[1] This does not occur in Camb. Univ. Copy.

The Youth's Library.[1] The Book of common prayer. The practice of piety. The whole duty of man. Valentine's private devotion. The crums of comfort. The supplications of saints. The plain man's pathway to heaven. The doctrine of the Bible. The history of the Bible. Dr. Featley's devotions. The great assize. Bishop Andrew's catechistical doctrine. The help to discourse. The mother's blessing. David's repentance. Dr. Hewet's sermons &c.

On the reverse of the last leaf. A cut of the royal arms. Above the cut the words, " Fear God, and honor the King ". Underneath the cut and on either side of it, a cut of a small crown, underneath the cuts the letters C. R. " Dieu et mon droit." underneath these words: " And meddle not with them that are given to change. Be subject to all in authority, to the King as most excellent. Be subject not only for fear, but for conscience sake." Finis.

₊ *The following books belong to this class.*
A.D.
1545, May 29, Richard Grafton, London. 8º. English. Nº. 173.
1545, June 19, Edwarde Whitchurche, London. 4º. English Nº. 176.
1545, June 20, Edwarde Whitchurche, London. 8º. English. Nº. 177.
1545, June 20, Edwarde Whitchurche, London. 8º. English. Nº. 178.
1545, Sept. 6, Richard Grafton, London. 4º. English and Latin. Nº. 179.
1546, Jan. 6, Edward Whitchurche, London. 8º. English and Latin. No. 181.
1546, March 16, Richard Grafton, London. 16º. English. Nº. 182.
1546, April 1, Edward Whitchurche, London. 16º. English. Nº. 183.
1546, August 17, Richard Grafton, London. 4º. English. Nº 184.
1546, August 20, Edward Whitchurche, London. 8º. English. Nº. 185.
1546, Sept. 6, Richard Grafton (London) 8o. Latin. Nº. 186.
1548, Jan. 9, Edward Whitchurche, London. English and Latin. 8o. Nº. 189.
c. 1548, 16º. English. Nº. 190.
c. 1548, Richard Grafton, London. 8º. English. Nº. 191.
c. 1548, 8º, English. Nº. 192.
1552, Richard Grafton, London. 8º. English. Nº. 199.
1575, William Seres. London. 8º. English. Nº. 252.

[1] This does not occur in Camb. Univ. Copy.

A SUMMARY OF THE CONTENTS

OF

A PRIMER OR BOOK OF PRIVATE PRAYER

AUTHORIZED AND SET FORTH BY THE KING'S MAJESTY,
AGREEABLE TO THE SECOND BOOK OF COMMON
PRAYER

IN THE REIGN OF EDWARD VI.,

AND OF

KINDRED PRIMERS

IN THE REIGNS OF MARY, ELIZABETH, CHARLES II,
JAMES II, GEORGE II, GEORGE III, AND GEORGE IV.

A.D. 1553—A.D. 1825.

EXPLANATIONS.

1. The books which form this class are those in which the framework of the Order of private prayer for Morning and Evening is that of Matins and Evensong in the Book of Common prayer A.D. 1552: the earliest book of this class is No. 200. A.D. 1553.

2. A summary is given of all the contents of No. 200. A.D. 1553. as a standard of comparison for all the books in this class.

3. All fresh matter is given as it occurs, and all variations from the book which is the standard of comparison : in some cases it has been found convenient to repeat matter which had been already given: either in order to indicate the probable date of a book of which the title is wanting, or in general to facilitate comparison with some other book (see No. 202. c. A.D. 1553. No. 243. A.D. 1560. No. 248. c. A.D. 1564. No. 254. c. A.D. 1580. No. 257. A.D. 1670. and No. 264. A.D. 1758).

4. An index is given of the prayers and psalms. Groups of psalms such as the seven penitential psalms or those in the Hours are not indexed separately. Another index gives all the hymns. A general index refers to other matters of liturgical, devotional and general interest.

A SUMMARY OF THE CONTENTS

OF

A PRIMER OR BOOK OF PRIVATE PRAYER

AUTHORIZED AND SET FORTH BY THE KING'S MAJESTY,
AGREEABLE TO THE SECOND BOOK OF COMMON PRAYER

IN THE REIGN OF EDWARD VI,

AND OF

KINDRED PRIMERS

IN THE REIGNS OF MARY, ELIZABETH, CHARLES II, JAMES II,
GEORGE II, GEORGE III, AND GEORGE IV.

A.D. 1553—A.D. 1825.

A.D. 1553, William Seres, London, 8º. English. No. 200.

** *The title has " A Primmer or book of private prayer, needful to be used of all faithful christians. Which book is auctorised, and set forth by the King's majesty; to be taught, learned, read, and used of all his loving subjects . . . Cum privilegio ad imprimendum solum."*

An extract of the King's Majesty's privilege. Edward the VI by the grace of . God King of England, France and of Ireland &c. To all printers, stationers, booksellers ; and to all other our officers, and subjects these our letters hearing or seeing ; we do you to understand, that of our grace especial, certain science, and mere motion, we have granted and given privilege; and by these presents do grant and give privilege and licence to our wellbeloved subject William Seres and to his assignes, to print or cause to be printed all manner of books of private prayers, called and usually taken and reputed for Primers, both in great volumes and little, which are and shall be set forth agreeable and according to the Book of common prayers established by us in our high Court of Parliament, any other privilege or licence to the contrary notwithstanding. And furthermore, our mind and pleasure is, that the same William Seres and his assigns, shall and may have the only printing from time to time of the said primers aforesaid in all kind of volumes . . . In witness whereof, we have caused these our letters to be made patentes. Witnesseth our self. At Westminster, the sixth day of March, the seventh year of our reign. God save the King.

The order of the Kalender. First you shall have the golden number or prime printed with red ink . . . A brief declaration when every term beginneth and endeth. Be it known that Easter term beginneth always . . .

The Kalendar has those Saints days printed in red, for which there is an epistle and gospel in the Book of Common prayer A.D. 1552; except S. Barnabas which is printed in black: it has other Saints days printed in black: it has "Becket traitor" on July 7. "Assumptio ma" on August 15. Fast days are noted by the use of the word "Fish".

A Catechism, that is to say, an instruction to be learned of every child before he be brought to be confirmed of the bishop.

₊ *This catechism is that in the Book of the Common prayer. A.D. 1549.*

Graces to be said before dinner and supper.

Grace before dinner.[1] The eyes of all things do look up and trust in thee O Lord . . . Amen. The King of eternal glory make us partakers of thy heavenly table. Amen. God is charity . . . Amen.

Grace after dinner.[1] The God of peace and love vouchsafe alway to dwell with us . . . Amen.

Grace after supper.[1] Blessed is God in all his gifts . . . Our help . . . Who hath made . . . Blessed be the name . . . From henceforth . . . Most mighty Lord and merciful father, we yield thee hearty thanks for our bodily sustenance . . . Amen. Lord save thy church, our King, and realm; and send us peace in Christ . . . Amen.

Another grace before meat. At the beginning of this refection, let us reverently, and earnestly call to our remembrance . . . Answer. Laud, praise, and glory be unto God . . . So be it.

Thanks after meat. Forasmuch as you have well refreshed your bodies . . . Answer. Praise and thanks be to God, now and always . . . Amen.

Grace before supper. Christ which at his last supper promised his body to be crucified . . . Amen. (see No. 115. c. A.D. 1534 page 198).

Thanks after dinner or supper. All ye whom God hath here refreshed . . . Amen.

Grace before dinner. All that is, and shall be set upon the board . . . Our Father.

Thanks after dinner. We give thee thanks, O Father almighty, For thy graces and benefits manifold . . . Amen.

Grace before supper. He that is King of glory, and Lord over all, Bring us to the supper of the life eternal. Our Father.

Thanks after supper. O Lamb of God, Christ, which takest away The sins of the world and cleansest all thing . . . Amen.

Grace before meat. Pray we to God, the almighty Lord, That sendeth food to beasts and men . . . Amen.

Thanks after meat. Blessed be the Father celestial, Who hath fed us with his material bread . . .

A preparative unto prayer. Before thou pray. First, examine thine own con-

---

[1] See Primer. A.D. 1545. No. 174. page 239.

-1553] PRIMER OR BOOK OF PRIVATE PRAYER. 291

science with what kind of temptation or sin thou art most encumbered withal . . . Secondarily, upon consideration of thine own lack and the common lack of the congregation . . . Thirdly, consider that God doth not only command thee to pray, but also promiseth graciously to hear . . . Fourthly, thou must steadfastly believe God's promises, and trust undoubtedly . . . Fifthly, thou must ask of God all thy petitions and requests for his mercy and truth sake, for Christ Jesus sake . . . Sixthly, thou must ask all bodily, worldly, and corruptible things pertaining to this transitory life . . . Seventhly, thou must appoint God no certain time of granting thy requests . . . Finally, thou must in any wise take heed, when thou prayest, that thou be in love and charity with all men . . . And in thy faithful prayers remember Thomas Cottesforde the preparer of this preparative. Summa. Pray because. 1. Thou hast need. 2. God commands thee . . . 9. Ask things pertaining to thy salvation, remission of sin, and life everlasting without condition. For these hath God certainly promised to all them that with a true, faithful, and obedient heart doth come unto him in earnest and continual prayer.

Prayer containing in it all the aforesaid Preparative unto prayer. O gracious Lord and most merciful Father, which hast from the beginning of mine age . . . So be it.

At thine uprising in the morning, say. I enter into this day, to do all things in the name . . . So be it. Add this prayer following. After due examination of my former life, with an humble and contrite heart . . . So be it.

Going to thy rest, say. I lay me down to rest, in the name . . . So be it. Add this prayer following. O most gracious Lord, and merciful Father, I thy sinful creature . . . So be it.

Prayer for the morning.[1] O merciful Lord God, heavenly father, I render most high lauds . . . Amen. (as on pages 186. 246).

Prayer to be said at night going to bed.[1] O merciful Lord God, heavenly father, whether we sleep or wake . . . Amen. (as on page 246).

An order of private prayer for Morning and Evening every day in the week; and so throughout the whole year.[2]

At the beginning of morning and evening private prayer, thou shalt daily read, meditate, weigh, and deeply consider one of these sentences of holy scripture that follow. And then from the bottom of thine heart add the confession of thy sins, and the prayer following.

Sentences of holy scripture. If the ungodly will turn away from all his sins that he hath done . . .

A confession of sins.[2] Almighty and most merciful Father, I have erred and strayed from thy ways . . . Amen. Add to this confession this prayer.

---

[1] See Godly prayers. Book of Common prayer. A.D. 1552. E. Whitchurche. 4°; and Parker Soc. Liturgies. Elizabeth. p. 246.

[2] See the Book of Common prayer. A.D. 1552.

Almighty God, the Father of our Lord Jesus Christ, which desirest not the death of a sinner . . . Amen.

The beginning of morning prayer. Morning prayer for Sunday. The Litany. Evening prayer for Sunday. Morning prayer on Monday. Evening prayer for Monday. Morning prayer on Tuesday. Evening prayer on Tuesday. Morning prayer for Wednesday. Evening prayer on Wednesday. Morning prayer on Thursday. Evening prayer on Thursday. Morning prayer on Friday. Evening prayer on Friday. Morning prayer on Saturday. Evening prayer on Saturday.

₊ *This order of private prayer for morning and evening, every day in the week, includes the Litany on Sunday morning; the order for each day has the same framework as that of Matins and Evensong in the Book of Common prayer A.D. 1552: but the sentences of holy Scripture begin "If the ungodly will turn away . . ." and the Exhortation "Dearly beloved brethren . . ." does not occur. The collect for the King at Morning and Evening prayer has "Edward the sixth."*

The Litany which forms part of "Morning prayer for Sunday" has no invocations of Saints, it has "From the tyranny of the Bishop of Rome and all his detestable enormities"; and "That it may please thee to keep Edward the sixth thy servant our King and governour": it is the same as that in the Book of Common prayer A.D. 1552, except that at the end a collect, For one that is sore sick. "Hear us, almighty and most merciful God and Saviour." occurs, as well as the collects to be said after the Offertory, when there is no communion, in the Order for the Administration of the Lord's Supper in the Book of Common prayer. A.D. 1552.

The Collects for Sundays, and Holy days throughout all the year.

₊ *These collects are the same as those in the Book of Common prayer. A.D. 1552.*

Sundry godly prayers for divers purposes.

For the King.[1] Almighty God, whose kingdom is everlasting and power infinite . . . Amen.

Another for the King.[1] Almighty and everlasting God, we be taught by thy holy word . . . Amen.

For the King.[2] O almighty God, King of kings, and Lord of lords . . . Amen.

For the King's counsell.[2] It is written, O most mighty and everlasting King, that where many are that give good counsel . . . Amen.

For Judges.[2] O God, thou most righteous judge which commandest by thy holy word . . . Amen.

For Bishops, spiritual Pastors, and Ministers of God's word.[2] O Lord Jesu Christ, most true Pastor, Shepherd, and Herdman of our souls . . . Amen.

---

[1] The Book of Common prayer. A.D. 1552.
[2] T. Becon. The flower of godly prayers. Parker Soc.

For Gentlemen.[1] Albeit, whatsoever is born of flesh is flesh . . . Amen.
For Landlords.[1] The earth is thine, O Lord, and all that is contained therein . . . Amen.
For Marchauntes.[1] Almighty God, maker and disposer of all things . . . Amen.
For Lawers.[1] We know, O Lord, that the law is good if a man use it lawfully . . . Amen.
For labourers and men of occupations.[1] As the bird is born to fly, so is man born to labour . . . Amen.
For rich men.[1] Albeit, O Lord, thou art the giver of all good things . . . Amen.
For poor people.[1] As riches, so likewise poverty is Thy gift, O Lord . . . Amen.
The prayer of a true subject.[2] As it is thy godly appointment, O Lord God . . . Amen.
For fathers and mothers.[2] The fruit of the womb, and the multitude of children is thy gift . . . Amen.
Of children.[2] Thou hast given a commandment in thy law, O heavenly Father . . . Amen.
Of maisters.[2] Thy commandment is by thine holy apostle, O most merciful Lord Christ . . . Amen.
Of servauntes.[2] O Lord Jesu Christ, we are commanded by thy blessed apostles, that we should honour . . . Amen.
Of maydes.[2] There is nothing that becometh a maid better than silence . . . Amen.
Of syngle men.[2] Lord, thou hast commanded by Thy holy apostle, that we should abstain from fornication . . . Amen.
Of husbandes.[2] Forasmuch, O heavenly Father, as thou hast called me from the single life . . . Amen.
Of wyves.[2] O Lord, forasmuch as Thou of Thy fatherly goodness hast vouchsafed to keep me . . . Amen.
Of housholders.[2] To have children and servants is Thy blessing, O Lord . . . Amen.
Of all christians.[2] Albeit, O heavenly Father, all we that unfeignedly profess Thy holy religion . . . Amen.
A prayer meet for all men, and to be said at all times. Most merciful Father, grant me to covet with an ardent mind . . . Amen.
General prayers to be said.
For the grace and favour of God.[2] Whosoever liveth without Thy grace and favour, O most gracious and favourable Lord . . . Amen.
For the gift of the Holy Ghost.[2] So frail is our nature, so vile is our flesh . . . Amen.
For the true knowledge of ourselves.[2] It is written in Thy holy gospel most loving Saviour, that Thou camest into this world . . . Amen.

[1] T. Becon. The flower of godly prayers. Parker Soc.
[2] T. Becon. The pomander of prayer. Parker Soc.

For a pure and clean heart.[1] The heart of man naturally is lewd and unsearchable . . . Amen.
For a quiet conscience.[1] The wicked is like a raging sea which is never in quiet . . . Amen.
For faith.[1] Forasmuch as nothing pleaseth Thee that is done without faith . . . Amen.
For charity.[1] Thy cognisance and badge, whereby thy disciples are known . . . Amen.
For patience.[1] When Thou lived'st in this world, O Lord Christ . . . Amen.
For humility.[1] What have we, O heavenly Father, that we have not received . . . Amen.
For mercifulness.[1] Thy dearly beloved Son in his holy gospel exhorteth us to be merciful . . . Amen.
For true godliness.[1] In Thy law, O Thou maker of heaven and earth, Thou hast appointed us a way to walk in . . . Amen.
For the true understanding of God's word.[1] O Lord, as Thou alone art the author of the holy Scriptures . . . Amen.
For a life agreeable to our knowledge.[1] As I have prayed unto Thee, O heavenly Father, to be taught . . . Amen.
For the health of the body.[1] I feel in myself, O merciful Saviour, how grievous a prison . . . Amen.
For a good name.[1] Nothing becomes the professor of thy name better, O heavenly Father . . . Amen.
For a competent living.[1] Although I doubt not of thy fatherly provision for this my poor and needy life . . . Amen.
For a patient and thankful heart in sickness.[1] Whom Thou lovest, O Lord, him dost Thou chasten . . . Amen.
For strength against the devil, the world, and the flesh.[1] O Lord God, the devil goeth about like a roaring lion . . . Amen.
For the help of God's holy angels.[1] An infinite number of wicked angels are there, O Lord Christ . . . Amen.
For the glory of heaven.[1] The joys, O Lord, which thou hast prepared for them that love thee . . . Amen.
Thanksgiving unto God for all his benefits.[1] Thy benefits toward me, O most loving Father, are so great . . . Amen.
Prayer necessary to be said at all times.[2] O bountiful Jesu, O sweet Saviour, O Christ the Son of God . . . Amen.
Prayer of Jeremy. Jeremy xxxi.[2] O Lord, thou hast correct me, and thy chastening have I received . . . Amen.
Prayer when we are punished of God for our sins or trial. O Lord, thou art righteous, and all thy judgments are true . . .
Prayer of Jeremy. Jeremy xvii.[2] Heal me, O Lord, and I shall be whole, save thou me, and I shall be saved . . . Amen.

[1] T. Becon. The pomander of prayer. Parker Soc.
[2] See Primer. A.D. 1545. No. 174. pages 242, 243.

Blessing and thanksgiving that Toby the elder thanked God with at the end of his life. Toby xiii. a.[1] Great art thou, Lord God, for ever more ; and thy kingdom world without end . . .

Prayer of Salomon, for sufficing of livelode. Prov. xxx. a.[2] Two things I require of thee, that thou wilt not deny me before I die . . .

Prayer of Nehemias before God, for the sins of the people. ii Esdras i. a.[1] Lord God of heaven, thou great and terrible God, thou that keepest covenant . . . Amen.

Prayer for sin, which Jeremy teacheth the Iraelites to say. Jeremy iii. e.[1] Lo, we turn unto thee, we are thine, for thou art the Lord our God . . . Amen.

Prayer in prosperity. Most merciful Father, which hast of thy gracious mercy without my deserving . . . Amen.

Prayer in adversity. Almighty God, which for mine ingratitude and sinful life . . . So be it.

Prayer to be said when the sick person is joyful and glad to die. O Lord Jesu Christ, I beseech thy mercy and goodness, that thou wilt strengthen . . . Amen.

Prayer. Laud, honour, and thanks be unto thee, most merciful Lord Jesu Christ . . . Amen.

Prayer for them that lie in extreme pangues of death. O pitiful physician, and healer both of body and soul . . . So be it.

A general exhortation unto all men. Thou shalt reprehend thy brother when he sinneth . . .

Oration of Job in his most grievous adversity and loss of goods.[2] Naked came I out of my mother's womb . . .

The rulers of the people shalt thou not blaspheme. Fear the Lord and the King ; and keep no company with the slanderers, for their destruction shall come suddenly.

Thanks be given unto God ; Obedience unto our prince ; And love to our neighbours. Finis.

The table. The contents of this Primer or book of private prayer . . . Finis.

Colophon. These bookes are to be solde at the weste ende of Paules towarde Ludgate, at the signe of the Hedgehogge.

c. A.D. 1553, William Seres, London, 16º. English. No. 201.

*** *The title is the same as that in No.* 200. *A.D.* 1553. (page 289).

An extract of the King's majesty's privilege.[3] Edward the VI by the grace of God ; King of England, France, and of Ireland &c. To all printers, Stationers, Booksellers, and to all other our officers, and subjects ; these our letters hearing or seeing. Because it is requisite to have some uniform of daily prayers fit to be used privately, as of children and divers

---

[1] See Prayers of the Bible. (Lambeth. Archiep. 24. 9. 11. (1)). c. A.D. 1534 ; and Principal Prayers of the Bible. R. Taverner. (Brit. Mus. 1219 a. 34. (2)). A.D. 1539.

[2] See Primer. A.D. 1545. No. 174. pages 242. 243.

[3] See No. 200. A.D. 1553. page 289.

other our subjects, being not the Ministers or Curates of churches, shall have from time to time occasion to occupy: therefore we do you to understand . . . In witness whereof, we have caused these our letters to be made patentes. Witnesseth ourself. At Westminster, the syxte daye of Marche, the vii year of our reign. God save the Queene.

The Kalender has those Saints days printed in red, except " Conver. of Paule " which is printed in black, for which there is an Epistle and Gospel in the Book of Common prayer A.D. 1552: it has other Saints days printed in black: it has " Henry the eyght " on January 19: " King Edwarde began " on January 31: " Assumpt of Mary " on August 15: " Thomas Becket " on December 29: also the days and places at which fairs were held.

A catechism, that is to say, an instruction to be learned of every child, before he be brought to be confirmed of the bishop.

₊ *This Catechism is that in the Book of the Common prayer. A.D. 1549: and the same as that in No. 200. A.D. 1553.*

Graces to be said before dinner and supper (as in No. 200, A.D. 1553.) adding.

Grace before supper. O Lord Jesu Christ, without whom nothing is sweet . . . Amen. (as in No. 174. A.D. 1545. page 239).

A preparative unto prayer. (as in No. 200. A.D. 1553. page 290). except that it has " And in thy faithful prayers remember that thou pray for Mary, our most virtuous and sovereign Queen ": instead of " And in thy faithful prayers remember Thomas Cottesforde the preparer of this preparative ".

At thine uprising in the morning. Going to thy rest. Prayer for the morning. Prayer to be said at night going to bed.

₊ *These prayers are the same as in No. 200. A.D. 1553. (page 291).*

An order of private prayer for Morning and Evening, every day in the week, and so throughout the whole year.

₊ *This includes the Litany on Sunday morning; it is the same as in No. 200. A.D. 1533, substituting " Queen Mary " for " Edward the sixth ". " O Lord save the King " occurs as a Versicle in the Morning prayer for Sunday.*

The Litany which forms part of " Morning prayer for Sunday " is the same as in No. 200. A.D. 1553; substituting " Queen Mary " for " Edward the sixth."

₊ *The use of this order of private prayer is thus explained. " Thus endeth the Morning and Evening prayer for the Sunday. And the same order shall ye keep every day in the week in all points, except only psalms and lessons, which shall be proper for every day in the week, as shall appear by the order of this book following."*

The collects for Sundays and Holydays throughout all the year. These are the same as in No. 200. A.D. 1553. (page 292).

The Dirige is the same as in No. 174. A.D. 1545, except that after Psalm 145. Lauda anima mea. the collect " O merciful God the Father of our Lord Jesu Christ, who is the resurrection and the life." occurs instead of the two collects " O God whose nature and property." and " We beseech

-1553] PRIMER OR BOOK OF PRIVATE PRAYER. 297

    thee, O Lord, to shew upon us thine exceeding great mercy." At the end of the Dirige, the collect "Almighty God, we give thee hearty thanks for those thy servants whom thou hast delivered from the miseries of this wretched world." occurs instead of the two collects "Almighty eternal God to whom there is never any prayer made." and "Lord bow thine ear unto our prayers."

The Commendations. This psalm is the A.B.C. of godly love, the paradise of learning . . . shall be punished and destroyed. (as in No. 174. A.D. 1545. page 241).

    ₊ *This is all that is given of The commendations.*

Seven psalms (as in No. 174. A.D. 1545. page 240).

Sundry godly prayers for divers purposes.

    ₊ *These are the same as in No. 200. A.D. 1553 (page 292) substituting "Queen Mary" for "Edward the sixth."*

General prayers to be said.

    ₊ *These are the same as in No. 200. A.D. 1553. (page 293).*

The contents of this Primer or Book of private prayer. Finis.

Colophon. These bokes are to be solde at the weste ende of Paules towarde Ludgate, at the sygne of the Hedgehogge.

c. A.D. 1553, 8º. English. No. 202.

    ₊ *The title-page and colophon are wanting. The book begins with the Kalender. A summary is given of all the contents.*

The Kalender has those Saints days printed in red for which there is an Epistle and Gospel in the Book of the Common prayer. A.D. 1549. It has not any other Saints days.

The Catechism, that is to say, an instruction to be learned of every child before he be brought to be confirmed of the Bishop.

    ₊ *This Catechism is that in the Book of the Common Prayer. A.D. 1549. and the same as that in No. 201. c. A.D. 1553. (page 296).*

Graces before and after dinner, and before and after supper as in No. 195. A.D. 1551 (page 248); except that "Lord save thy church, our King, and realm, and send us peace in Christ" occurs, instead of "God save our King, and realm, and send us peace in Christ. Amen."

A prayer at your uprising.[1] O Lord Jesu Christ, which art the very bright sun of the world . . . Amen.

A prayer before ye go to bed.[1] O Lord which art only good, true, gracious and merciful . . . Amen.

The order to say Mattyns. When ye have said the Pater noster, and the Psalms for the day, then say Te Deum, which ye shall find in the end of the book, and then read the Lesson; after that is said, read the end of Mattins which ye shall find before the Litany in the middle of the book.

---

[1] See Primer. A.D. 1545. No. 174. page 242.

The collect for the day is that which ye say on Sunday, which serveth for all the week after, both at Mattins and Evensong, except it be a Saints day, and then ye shall find the collect thereof among the collects for Saints days. After ye have read the Collect of the day, read the other collects that follow in the end of the Matins, and the first collect for the King which ye shall find at the end of the book. The same order also shall ye follow at Evensong, saying last the second collect for the King, which ye shall find at the end of the book.

Mattyns for Sunday. Evensong for Sunday. Mattyns for Monday. Evensonge for Monday. Mattyns for Tuesday. Evensong for Tuesday. Mattins for Wednesday. Evensong for Wednesday. Mattins for Thursday. Evensong for Thursday. Mattins for Friday. Evensong for Friday. Mattins for Saturday. Evensong for Saturday.

₊ *This order of Mattins and Evensong is imperfect ; it is modelled on No. 200. A.D. 1553, but the psalms and lessons are for the most part different : one psalm only occurs on some of the days, and never more than one lesson.*

Collects for Sundays and Holy-days.

₊ *They are those in the Book of the Common prayer. A.D. 1549.*

The Litany is the same as in No. 188. A.D. 1547 (page 245) and in the Book of Common prayer. A.D. 1552, it has no Invocations of Saints: it has " From the tyranny of the Bishop of Rome and all his detestable enormities," but at the end it differs from the Book of Common prayer A.D. 1552, for only these two collects: "We humbly beseech thee, O Lord, mercifully to look upon our infirmities"; and "Almighty God which hast given us grace" occur: it has " Edward VI thy servant, our King and Governour ".

The end of Evensong through the whole week. Lord have mercy upon us &c. as before in the ende of Mattyns with the Collect of the day. Second collect at Evensonge. " O God from whom all holy desires ". Third collect for aid against all perils. " Lighten our darkness." [1]

Sundry godly prayers for divers purposes.

General confession to be made openly, of all them that receive the communion.[1] Almighty God, Father of our Lord Jesus Christ, maker of all things . . . Amen.

Before the receiving of the Communion.[1] We do not presume to come to this thy table, O merciful Lord . . . Amen. (Signs. L. 3. 4. 5. 6. and M. 1. are wanting).

For bishops and priests. O God almighty, which speaking to every preacher of the word . . . (Sign. L. 8ᵇ). (Sign. M. 1. is wanting).

For judges and magistrates. O Lord, who by thine infinite wisdom considering our frailty . . . Amen. (Sign. M. 2.) (Sign. M. 3. is wanting.).

In time of prosperity. Almighty God our heavenly father, which diddest create man to live eternally in Paradise . . . Amen. (Signs. M. 4ᵇ. 5. 5ᵇ.) (Sign. M. 6 is wanting).

---

[1] See Books of Common Prayer. A.D. 1549, and A.D. 1552.

Prayer fit to be said by men of low degree. O Lord God almighty, which by thine infinite wisdom disposest thy gifts . . . Amen. (Sign. M. 7b.).

Prayer necessary to be said at all times. O bountiful Jesu, O sweet Jesu, O Christ the son of God have pity upon me . . . Amen. (as in No. 200. A.D. 1553. page 294). (Sign. N. 3b).

Prayer to eschew the infection of worldly men. O good Lord, father almighty, I meekly beseech thee hear my prayer . . . Amen. (Sign. N. 5).

Against ungodly carefulness for worldly riches. O Lord God, who of thy most bountiful goodness dost daily feed fowls of the air . . . and all necessaries plentifully for me and my house. (Sign. N. 6b). (All the rest of the book is wanting).

A.D. 1560, William Seres, London, 8º. English. No. 243.

₊ *The title has " A Primer or Book of private prayer, needful to be used of all faithful christians. Which book is to be used of all our loving subjects . . . Cum privilegio ad imprimendum solum." A summary is given of all the contents.*

The order of the Kalender : as in No. 200. A.D. 1553 (page 289).

The Kalender has those Saints days printed in red for which there is an Epistle and Gospel in the Book of Common prayer. A.D. 1552: it has " St. George " printed in red on April 23 : it also has other Saints days printed in black, including " Tho. Becket " on July 8.

An Almanacke for x years. It begins 1560. Easter day xiiii of April.

A Catechism, that is to say, an instruction to be learned of every child before he be brought to be confirmed of the bishop.

₊ *This catechism is that in the Book of the Common prayer. A.D. 1549. and the same as that in No. 200. A.D. 1553. (page 290).*

Graces to be said afore dinner and supper: as in No. 200. A.D. 1553 (page 290).

A preparative unto prayer : as in No. 200. A.D. 1553 (page 290), except that it has " And in thy faithful prayers remember to pray for Elisabeth our most gracious Queen ": instead of " And in thy faithful prayers remember Thomas Cottesforde the preparer of this preparative ".

At thine uprising in the morning. Going to thy rest. Prayer for the morning. Prayer to be said at night going to bed.

₊ *These prayers are the same as in No. 200. A.D. 1553 (page 291).*

An order of private prayer for Morning and Evening every day in the week, and so throughout the whole year.

₊ *This includes the Litany on Sunday morning : it is the same as in No. 200. A.D. 1553, but the Sentences of holy Scripture " At what time soever a sinner . . ." and the Exhortation. " Dearly beloved brethren . . ." from the Books of Common prayer, A.D. 1552 and A.D. 1559, are added before the Sentences " If the ungodly will turn away . . ." At Morning prayer ; the fourth collect for the Queen has " Our most gracious sovereign Lady Queen Elisabeth." At Evening prayer. A prayer for the Queen : has " Elisabeth thy daughter and servant, and our Queen and governour."*

The Litany which forms part of Morning prayer for Sunday is the same as in
   No. 200. A.D. 1553. but omits as in the Litany in the Book of Common
   prayer. A. D. 1559. the words "From the tyranny of the Bishop of Rome
   and all his detestable enormities." It has "Elizabeth thy daughter and
   servant, and our Queen and Governour."
The collects for Sundays and Holydays throughout all the year.

*** *These collects are the same as those in the Books of Common prayer A.D. 1552, and A.D. 1559. and as in No. 200. A.D. 1553. (page 292).*

Seven penitential psalms (as in No. 201. c. A.D. 1553. page 297).
Sundry godly prayers for divers purposes.

*** *These are the same as in No. 200. A.D. 1553 (page 292) with these additions.*

Prayer for a woman to say travailing of child. O almighty and merciful
   father, which of thy bountiful goodness hast fructified my womb . . .
A woman with child's prayer. Father of mercy, and God of comfort and all
   consolation . . . So be it.
Prayer for a woman to say when she is delivered. O my Lord God, I thank
   thee with all my heart . . . So be it.
General prayers to be said.

*** *These are the same as in No. 200. A.D. 1553 (page 293).*

The contents of this Primer; or Book of private prayer . . . Finis.

c. A.D. 1560, 8º. English. No. 246.

*** *The title-page is wanting; the book begins with "Morning prayer for sondaye" on sign B1; it belongs to the same class as No. 200. A.D. 1553 (page 289), see explanations (page 288).*

c. A.D. 1564, 16º. English. No. 248.

*** *The title page and colophon are wanting: the book begins with the Kalender. A summary is given of all the contents.*

The Kalender begins with March 5: and wants all after November 16: it has
   those days printed in black, which are printed in black in No. 201. c. A.D.
   1553 (page 296); also the days and places at which Fairs were held.
An Almanacke for xv. yeares: it begins A.D. 1564. Easter day. 2 April.
The A. B. C. + A. a. b. c. d. e. f. g. . . . In the name.
The Catechism.

*** *This catechism is that in the Book of the Common prayer. A.D. 1549; and the same as that in No. 200. A.D. 1553. (page 290).*

Grace before dinner. O most gracious God, and loving father, which merci-
   fully feedest all living creatures . . . Amen.
Grace after dinner. Now you have well refreshed your bodies . . . Response.
   Grace and thanks be now unto him and always . . .
Grace before meat. Receive your meat without grudging, Take hede ye never
   abuse the same . . .
Grace before supper. Give thanks to God with one accord, For that shall be
   set on this board . . .

-1580] PRIMER OR BOOK OF PRIVATE PRAYER. 301

Grace after supper. Now that your bodies refreshed be, And that of food is left some store . . .

Prayer at your uprising.[1] O Lord God, my heavenly father, I most humbly thank thee that thou of thy fatherly goodness . . .

Prayer to be said when we go to bed.[1] I thank thee, O heavenly father, by thy dearly beloved son Jesus Christ our Lord and Saviour that of thy free mercy . . .

Morning prayer. Evening prayer.

∗ *This order of Morning and Evening prayer includes the Litany: it is the same as the Morning and Evening prayer for Sunday in No. 200. A.D. 1553; the sentences of holy Scripture before the exhortation begin "If the ungodly . . ." At Morning prayer the third collect for the Queen has "Our most gracious sovereign lady Queen Elizabeth." At Evening prayer. A prayer for the Queen has "Elizabeth thy daughter and servant, and our Queen and governour."*

The Litany which forms part of Morning prayer is the same as in No. 200. A.D. 1553; but omits as in the Litany in the Book of Common prayer A.D. 1559; and No. 243. A.D. 1560. (page 300). the words " From the tyranny of the Bishop of Rome and all his detestable enormities " : it has " Elizabeth our most gracious Queen and governour " : the following collects, which occur in No. 200, A.D. 1553, are omitted. In time of dearth, " O God, merciful father, which in the time of Heliseus: " For one that is sore sick, " Hear us, almighty and most merciful God and Saviour : " it has only one of the collects, to be said after the Offertory when there is no communion, in the Order for the administration of the Lord's supper in the Books of Common prayer, A.D. 1552, and A.D. 1559, " Grant we beseech thee almighty God, that the words."

Seven psalms (as in No. 201. c. A.D. 1553. page 297). down to " of thine hands are the heavens," in Psalm 102. Domine exaudi. on Sign L7b. (All the rest of the book is wanting).

c. A.D. 1566, 16o. English. No. 249.

∗ *The title has "A book of private prayer, necessary to be used of all christians with many godly prayers;" the book belongs to the same class as No. 200. A.D. 1553 (page 289), see explanations (page 288).*

A.D. 1568, 8o. English. No. 251.

∗ *The title has " A Primer, or book of private prayer needfull to be used of all faithful christians, which book is to be used of all our loving subjects"; the book belongs to the same class as No. 200. A.D. 1553 (page 289) see explanations (page 288).*

c. A.D. 1580, 16o. English. No. 254.

∗ *The title page and colophon are wanting, the book begins with June 13 in the Kalender. A summary is given of all the contents.*

The Kalender is printed entirely in black, and in columns which are across the page; those days for which there is an epistle and gospel in the Book of

---
[1] T. Becon. Governance of virtue. Parker Soc.

Common prayer A.D. 1552. are printed in Roman type, the rest of the Kalendar is in old English type: it has the days and places in which fairs were held, also the day and year on which english sovereigns began to reign, and the year in which they died : it mentions that the Thames was frozen over in 1564, and that Queen Elizabeth had reigned full twenty one years. It has a stanza of four lines at the beginning of each month, and one of two lines at the end: those for the month of November begin: "Now beginneth the season to sow wheat and rie ..." and "If stomach forsake thee, Then tart receits make thee."

An Almanack for ten years: it begins 1580. Easter day 3 April.

The four terms of the year. Days wherein the Queen Majesty's judges neither sit in Westminster hall, nor hear any matter pleaded. A rule to know, what the ordinary charges of a penny by the day cometh to in the year; and so from a penny a day to ten shillings. &c.

The Catechism, that is to say, an instruction to be taught and learned of every child before he be brought to be confirmed of the bishop.

₀ *This catechism is that in the Book of the Common prayer A.D.* 1549: *and is the same as in No.* 200. *A.D.* 1553. (*page* 290).

Certain godly graces to be said before and after meals.

Grace before dinner.[1] The eyes of all things do look up, and trust in thee . . . Amen. Our Father.

Grace after dinner [1] The King of eternal glory make us partakers of his heavenly table. Amen. God save his universal church, our Queen Elizabeth, the realm, and grant us peace and truth in Christ Jesus. Amen.

Grace before supper.[2] O most gracious God and loving Father, which mercifully feedest all living creatures . . . Amen.

Grace after supper.[2] Now you have well refreshed your bodies, remember the lamentable afflictions . . . Amen. Resp. Grace and thanks be now unto him and always . . . Amen.

Grace before meat.[2] Receive your meat without grudging, Take heed ye never abuse the same . . .

Grace after meat. As thou hast fed our bodies Lord, So feed our souls likewise . . .

Grace before meat. To eat and drink doth small avail, The world is all but vain . . . God save his church and eke our Queen, her enemies deface . . .

Grace after meat. Thou God be praised for the food which we receive from thee . . . God save his church, our Queen, and realm ; God send us peace in Christ Jesus. Amen.

Grace before meat. Bless us, O Lord, and these thy gifts, Whereof we now shall taste . . . Increase thy church, preserve our Queen . . .

---

[1] See Primmer. No. 200. A.D. 1553. page 290.
[2] See Primer. No. 248. c. A.D. 1564. page 300.

Grace to be said, before or after meat. Man's life preserved is by food, As God hath well decreed . . . We beseech thee Christ, thy church, Our Queen and realm to save . . .

Grace before supper.[1] Give thanks to God with one accord, For that shall be set on this borde . . . Praising God. &c.

Grace after supper.[1] Now that your bodies refreshed be, And that of food is left some store . . . Amen.

Prayer at your uprising.[1] O Lord God my heavenly father, I most humbly thank thee that thou of thy fatherly goodness . . . Amen.

Prayer to be said when you go to bed.[1] I thank thee, O heavenly Father, by thy dearly beloved Son Jesus Christ, our Lord and Saviour, that of thy free mercy . . . Amen.

Morning and Evening prayer.

∗ *This order of Morning and Evening prayer includes the Litany: it is the same as the Morning and Evening prayer for Sunday in No. 200. A.D. 1553. but the Sentences of holy Scripture " At what time soever a sinner . . .," and the Exhortation " Dearly beloved brethren," from the Books of Common prayer A.D. 1552 and A.D. 1559, occur before the General confession. " Almighty and most merciful Father." At Morning prayer; the fourth collect for the Queen has " Our most gracious sovereign Lady Queen Elizabeth." At Evening prayer. A prayer for the Queen has " Elizabeth thy servant and daughter and our Queen and Governour."*

The Litany which forms part of Morning prayer is the same as in No. 248 c. A.D. 1564 (page 301): it has " Thy servant Elizabeth our most gracious Queen and governour."

Seven psalms (as in No. 201. c. A.D. 1553. page 297) down to " thou not despise " in Psalm 51. Miserere mei. (All the rest of the book is wanting).

c. A.D. 1670, for Company of Stationers, London, 16º. No. 257.

∗ *The title is " The Primer, or Catechism set forth agreeable to the Book of Common Prayer, authorised by the King's majesty; to be used throughout his realms, and dominions, wherein is contained godly prayers, and graces, very meet and necessary for the instruction of youth. Cum privilegio." A summary is given of all the contents.*

A cut of a Master and scholars within a circle on which is the motto " Children obey your parents in the Lord, for this is right. Ephe. 6." Underneath the cut " Train up a child . . . depart from it."

The A. B. C. + A. a. b. c. d. e. f. g . . . In the name.

The Catechism.

∗ *This Catechism is the same as that in the Book of Common prayer A.D. 1662.*

Graces to be said before and after meat.

---

[1] See Primer. No. 248. c. A.D. 1564. pages 300, 301.

Grace before meat.[1] The eyes of all things do look up and trust in thee . . . Amen. God save his church, our King, Queen, and realm, and send us peace in Christ our Lord. Amen.

Grace after meat.[1] The King of eternal glory make us partakers of his heavenly table. Amen. God save his church &c.

Grace before meat. Whether ye eat or drink, saith S. Paul, or whatsoever ye do else . . . Amen. God save his church &c.

Grace after meat.[2] The God of all glory and power, who hath created, redeemed . . . Amen. God save his church &c.

Grace before meat. Christ, who at his last supper gave himself unto us . . . Amen. God save his church &c. (See No. 200. A.D. 1553. page 290).

Grace after meat. Grant, O most merciful Father, that our hunger and thirst being satisfied . . . Amen. God save his church &c.

Grace before meat.[2] Glory, honor, and praise be given to thee, O Lord, which dost feed us . . . Amen. God save his church &c. (as in No. 233. A.D. 1557. page 192).

Godly prayers.

Prayer to be said at your uprising.[1,3] O Lord God, my heavenly father, I most humbly thank thee, that thou of thy fatherly goodness . . . Amen.

Prayer to be said when you go to bed.[1,3] I thank thee, O Father, by thy dearly beloved son Jesus Christ that of thy free mercy . . . Amen.

Prayer for the whole state. God preserve our sovereign Lord King Charles, his royal consort Queen Katherine, and all the royal progeny . . . Amen.

Morning and Evening prayer.

.*. *This order of Morning and Evening prayer includes the Litany: it is the same as the "Morning and Evening prayer for Sunday" "When the wicked man . . .", in No. 200. A.D. 1553 with these exceptions. The sentences of holy Scripture, and the Exhortation "Dearly beloved brethren," are from the Book of Common prayer. A.D. 1662. The first lesson at Morning prayer is Genesis 21. "Now the Lord visited Sarah": instead of Exodus 20. "Remember that thou keep holy the Sabbath day." At Morning prayer the three collects are as in the Book of Common prayer A.D. 1662, the Litany then follows. At Evening prayer after the second collect and before the third collect against all perils, these two collects occur ; A prayer for the King's majesty "O Lord, our heavenly father high and mighty" which has "Our most gracious sovereign Lord King Charles;" and, For one that is sore sick "Hear us almighty and merciful God our Saviour, extend."*

The Litany which forms part of Morning prayer is the same as in No. 200. A.D. 1553. and No. 243. A.D. 1560. (page 300) omitting " From the tyranny of the Bishop of Rome and all his detestable enormities " : it has " Thy servant Charles, our most gracious King and Governour," also " Our gracious Queen Catherine, James Duke of York, and all the royal family." At the end the collects, In time of dearth " O God merciful Father who in

---

[1] See Primer. No. 254. c. A.D. 1580. pages 302. 303.
[2] See J. Knox. Book of Common Order. A.D. 1564.
[3] T. Becon. Governance of virtue. Parker Soc.

the time of Helisæus." and, For one that is sore sick " Hear us almighty and most merciful God extend." are omitted ; but, A prayer in the time of any common plague " O almighty God who in thy wrath did'st send a plague ". Prayers for the King's majesty " O Lord our heavenly father high and mighty." For the royal family " Almighty God the fountain of all goodness." For the clergy and people " Almighty and everlasting God, who alone workest great marvels." as well as some of the Thanksgivings upon several occasions, and the collect after the Offertory when there is no Communion " Grant we beseech thee that the words." occur from the Book of Common prayer. A.D. 1662.

Seven penitential psalms . . . The anthem. Remember not, O Lord God, our old iniquities . . . Let not the wicked people say, where is their God . . . Amen.

Godly prayers.

A godly prayer meet to be used of all christians.[1] O bountiful Jesus, O sweet Jesus, O Jesus that son of the Virgin Mary . . . Amen.

Prayer of Manasses, King of Judah.[2] O Lord almighty, God of our fathers Abraham, Isaac, and Jacob . . . Amen.

An oration of Job in his most grievous adversity, and loss of goods.[2] Naked came I out of my mother's womb . . . Amen.

A godly prayer to be said at all times.[3] Honour and praise be given to thee, O Lord God almighty . . . Amen.

Godly graces. Grace before meat.[4][5] Receive your meat without grudging, Take heed you never abuse the same . . .

Grace after meat.[4] Man's life preserved is by food, As God hath well decreed . . .

Grace before meat. Dust, earth and ashes is our strength, Our glory frail and vain . . .

Grace after meat.[4] To eat and drink doth small avail, The world is all but vain . . .

Grace before meat. As to the sick all pleasant things Have sharp and bitter taste . . .

Grace after meat.[4][5] Now that our bodies refreshed be, And that of food is left some store . . .

Colophon. London : printed for the Company of Stationers.
Finis.

c. A.D. 1685, 16º. English. No. 259.

The title is " The Primer, or Catechism set forth agreeable to the Book of Common Prayer ; authorized by the King's majesty to be used throughout his realms, and dominions. Wherein is contained Godly prayers, and Graces, very meet and necessary for the instruction of youth. Cum privilegio." The book

[1] See Primer. No. 200. A.D. 1553. page 294.
[2] See Primer. No. 174. A.D. 1545. page 242.
[3] See Godly prayers. Book of Common Prayer. A.D. 1552. and John Knox. Book of Common Order. A.D. 1564.
[4] See Primer. No. 254. A.D. 1580. pages 302. 303.
[5] See Primer. No. 248. 1564. pages 300. 301.

306   SUMMARY OF CONTENTS.   [1758-

belongs to the same class as No. 200. A.D. 1553. (page 289).   See explanations (page 288).

✱ *The contents of this book are the same as those of No. 257. A.D. 1670. (page 303). The following words occur in the Prayer for the whole state.*[1] *"God preserve our sovereign Lord King James, his royal consort Queen Mary, and all the royal progeny."*

A.D. 1758, London, for Company of Stationers, London, 16º. No. 264.

✱ *The title has "The Primer or Catechism, set forth agreeable to the Book of Common prayer, authorized by the King, to be used throughout his dominions. Containing godly prayers and graces . . ." (On the verso of the title page.) A cut of a master and scholar. A summary is given of all the contents. (Other editions of this book were printed in 1764, 1766, 1769, 1772, 1775, 1777, 1783.*

The A. B. C. + A B C D E F G . . . In the name.
The Catechism.

✱ *This Catechism is that in the Book of Common prayer. A.D. 1662.*

Graces to be said before and after meat.
Grace before meat.[2] The eyes of all things do look up and trust in thee, O Lord . . . Amen.
Grace after meat. To the great and good God be given all honour and praise for these and all other mercies we have received . . . God save the church, the King, and realm, Lord send us peace in Christ our Lord. Amen.
Grace before meat. O eternal God, in whom we live and have our being, we beseech thee bless unto us these good creatures . . . Amen.
Grace after meat.[3] The God of all glory and power, who hath created, redeemed and this time plentifully fed us . . . God save the church &c.
Grace before meat. Good Lord, pardon and forgive us all our sins, which make us unworthy of thy mercies . . . Amen.
Grace after meat.[3] Grant, O most merciful Father, that our hunger and thirst being satisfied . . . God save his church &c.
Prayer to be said at your uprising.[2] O Lord God, my heavenly Father, I most humbly thank thee that thou of thy fatherly goodness hast vouchsafed to defend me this night . . . Amen.
Prayer to be said before you go to bed. I thank thee, O Father, by thy dearly beloved Son Jesus Christ, that of thy free mercy thou hast preserved me this day . . . Amen.
Prayer for the whole state.[3] God preserve our most gracious sovereign Lord King George, and all the royal family . . . Amen.
Morning and Evening prayer.

✱ *This order of Morning and Evening prayer includes the Litany : it is the same as in No. 257. A.D. 1670 (page 304) with these exceptions. At Morning prayer.*

---

[1] James II. married Marie d'Este, November 21st, 1673.
[2] See Primer. No. 254. A.D. 1580. pages 302, 303.
[3] See Primer. No. 257. A.D. 1670. page 304.

-1825] PRIMER OR BOOK OF PRIVATE PRAYER. 307

Psalm 2. " *Quare fremuerunt gentes*" *is added. First lesson. Proverbs Chap.* 3. "*My son forget not my law.*" *occurs instead of Genesis Chap.* 21. "*Now the Lord visited Sarah;*" *there is no Benedicite. At Morning prayer the collects are the same as those in No.* 257. *A.D.* 1670, *the Litany then follows. At Evening prayer, the three collects as well as the Prayers for the King's majesty, the royal family and the clergy and people occur as in the Book of Common prayer. A.D.* 1662. *The prayer for the King's majesty has* "*Thy servant George, our most gracious King and governor.*"

The Litany which forms part of Morning prayer is the same as that in No. 257. A.D. 1670 (page 304): it has "thy servant George, our most gracious King and governor"; also "George Prince of Wales, the Princess dowager of Wales, the Duke, the Princesses, and the royal family".

The seven penitential psalms. The anthem. Remember not ... Let not the wicked people say, where is their God ... Amen.

Collect for Ash-Wednesday. Almighty and everlasting God, who hatest nothing that thou hast made ... Amen.

Collect. O Lord, we beseech thee mercifully hear our prayers, and spare all those who confess their sins unto thee ... Amen.

Another collect. O most mighty God and merciful father, who hast compassion upon all men ... Amen.

Collects for the sick.[1] O Lord, look down from heaven, behold, visit, and relieve this thy servant ... Amen. Another. Hear us, almighty and most merciful God and Saviour, extend thy accustomed goodness ... Amen.

Prayer for the whole state of Christ's church militant here on earth.[2] Almighty and everlasting God, who by thy holy apostle hast taught us ... Amen.

Collects to be said after any of the foregoing prayers.[2] Assist us mercifully, O Lord, in these our supplications and prayers ... Amen. O almighty Lord and everlasting God, vouchsafe, we beseech thee to direct ... Amen. Grant we beseech thee, almighty God, that the words which we have heard ... Amen. Prevent us, O Lord, in all our doings with thy most gracious favour ... Amen. Almighty God, the fountain of all wisdom who knowest our necessities before we ask ... Amen. Almighty God, who hast promised to hear the petitions of them that ask in thy Son's name ... Amen. The peace of God which passeth all understanding ... Amen. Finis.

A.D. 1825, London, for C. and J. Rivington, London; Deighton and Sons (Cambridge); and J. Nicholson, Cambridge. 12º. No. 265.

*** *The title is* " *The Primer, a book of private prayer needful to be used of all christians; which book was authorised, and set forth by order of King Edward VI to be taught, learned, read, and used of all his subjects.*"

The preface says, "that the edition of the Primer from which this book is taken seems to have been actually in the press when Edward the sixth expired; his sister Mary's name and title having been substituted for his," thus

---

[1] See No. 255. A.D. 1627. page 281.
[2] See Book of Common Prayer. A.D. 1662.

"Preserve King Edward thy servant, sow in him, good Lord, such seed of virtue now in his young age, that many years this realm may enjoy much fruit of this thy blessing in him" is altered to "Preserve Queen Mary now in her young age".[1] Another argument for fixing the date of the original edition may be formed from the existence of the following petition in the Litany "Good Lord deliver us, From all sedition and privy conspiracy, from the tyranny of the Bishop of Rome and all his detestable enormities"[2]; the publisher who claiming privileges on a royal grant, yet ventured to print such a prayer as this, could not have witnessed the first month of Mary's reign. There is another prayer which must soon have been known to be likely to give very great offence to this bigotted Queen; the words alluded to are these "We most humbly beseech thee favourably to behold Mary thy servant, our Queen and governess, and to breathe into her heart through the Holy Spirit, the wisdom that is ever about the throne of thy Majesty; whereby she may be provoked, moved, and stirred to love, fear, and serve thee, to seek thy glory, to banish idolatry, superstition, and hypocrisy out of this realm; and unfeignedly to advance thy holy and pure religion among us her subjects, unto the example of other foreign nations".[3]

* *The words of the prayers above quoted are in No. 201. c. A.D. 1553 295) on folios 65. 47. 156.*

[1] See Primer. No. 201. A.D. 1553. page 295. (Brit. Mus. c. 35. a. 9. folio 65.)
[2] See Primer. No. 201. c. A.D. 1553. page 295. (Brit. Mus. c. 35. a. 9. folio 47.)
[3] See Primer. No. 201. c. A.D. 1553. page 295. (Brit. Mus. c. 35. a. 9. folio 156.)

A SUMMARY OF THE CONTENTS

OF

JOHN AUSTIN'S DEVOTIONS IN THE ANCIENT WAY OF OFFICES.

FIVE EDITIONS.

A.D. 1668 — A.D. 1789.

THEOPHILUS DORRINGTON'S REFORMED DEVOTIONS.

NINE EDITIONS.

A.D. 1686 — A.D. 1727.

GEORGE WHELER'S PROTESTANT MONASTERY.

ONE EDITION.

A.D. 1698.

DEVOTIONS IN THE ANCIENT WAY OF OFFICES PUBLISHED BY GEORGE HICKES.

EIGHT EDITIONS.

A.D. 1700 — A.D. 1758.

A COLLECTION OF MEDITATIONS AND DEVOTIONS PUBLISHED BY N. SPINCKES.

ONE EDITION.

A.D. 1717.

THOMAS DEACON'S PRIMITIVE METHOD OF DAILY PRIVATE PRAYER.

TWO EDITIONS.

A.D. 1734 — A.D. 1747.

EXPLANATIONS.

. The books which form this class are those which follow John Austin's "Devotions in the ancient way of offices" No. 256. A.D. 1668; they are (*a*) Theophilus Dorrington's "Reformed devotions." No. 260. A.D. 1686. (*b*) George Wheler's "Protestant Monastery." A.D. 1698. (*c*) "Devotions in the ancient way of offices, reformed by a person of quality and published by George Hickes, D.D." No. 261. A.D. 1700. (*d*) "A collection of meditations and devotions, in three parts, by the first reformer of the devotions in the ancient way of offices, afterwards reviewed and set forth by the late learned Dr. Hickes, published by N. Spinckes, M.A." No. 263. A.D. 1717. (*e*) Thomas Deacon's "Primitive method of daily private prayer." A.D. 1734.

2. A summary is given of all the contents of the first edition of "John Austin's devotions." No. 256. A.D. 1668; all fresh matter, in the other editions, is given as it occurs; a summary is given of all the contents of ed. 1789, as this edition follows more than one of the former editions. Five editions of John Austin's devotions are known.

3. A summary is given of all the contents of the first edition of "Theophilus Dorrington's reformed devotions." No. 260. A.D. 1686. All fresh matter in the other editions is given as it occurs. Nine editions are known.

4. A summary is given of all the contents of George Wheler's "Protestant Monastery." A.D. 1698. One edition only is known.

5. A summary is given of all the contents of the first edition of "Reformed devotions published by George Hickes, D.D." No. 261. A.D. 1700. All fresh matter in the other editions is given as it occurs. Eight editions are known.

6. A summary is given of all the contents of No. 263. A.D. 1717. "A collection of meditations and devotions reviewed by Dr. Hickes and published by N. Spinckes." One edition only is known.

7. A summary is given of all the contents of Thomas Deacon's "Primitive method of daily private prayer." A.D. 1734. Two editions are known.

8. An index is given of the prayers and devotions; another index gives the hymns. A general index refers to other matters of liturgical, devotional and general interest.

A SUMMARY OF THE CONTENTS

OF

JOHN AUSTIN'S DEVOTIONS IN THE ANCIENT WAY OF OFFICES.

FIVE EDITIONS.

A.D. 1668 — A.D. 1789.

A.D. 1668, Paris, 8o. English. No. 256.

*** *The title is "Devotions in the ancient way of offices, with psalms, hymns, and prayers; for every day in the week, and every holiday in the year."*[1]

Directions. This book consists chiefly of eleven offices; one for each day in the week, one for our Saviour's feasts, one for the Holy Ghost, one for Saints, and one for the Dead. Each office has four parts; Matins and Lauds for the Morning, Vespers and Complin for the Evening. The manner of reciting these offices. When one says his prayers alone, the circumstances are free to be governed by his own devotion. · But if two say together, 'tis convenient they agree on some rules; for which purpose these following are proposed; yet so as to be altered by their own discretion as they please. The place, I suppose, will be their private oratory, or other convenient retirement.

*** *The rules for saying Matins, Lauds, Vespers, and Compline then follow.*

The Office of our Saviour is said on all the feasts of our Saviour and on all Sundays of Advent and Lent, as is noted in the Proper of festivals: where you will find sometimes a particular Invitatory which is to be recited with its psalm; and always three particular antiphons, one for each psalm of Matins, Lauds, Vespers, and Complin, and then the antiphons set down in the office are omitted; they being provided only for those who think the particular ones too troublesome, and such as chuse to say our Saviour's office sometimes on a day that is not of obligation. The same may be observed in the antiphons for Benedictus, and Magnificat, and in the prayer, whenever any particular ones are provided. All the rest, psalms, lessons, hymns, etc., say, as in the Office of our Saviour.

[1] See A few particulars of Austin's devotions. (Brit. Mus. 01903. e. 27 (1)).

The Office of the Holy Ghost is said on Whitsunday, and during the Octave, and on every first Wednesday of the month, unless it be a holiday; and then 'tis remitted to the next convenient day.

The Office of Saints is intended only for Feasts of obligation, but may be applied to others, according to particular devotion. In saying this office, the same method is to be observed as in that of our Saviour.

The Office of the dead is said every first Monday of the month unless it be a holiday, and then 'tis transferred to the next convenient day, as also at other times according to occasion or particular devotion. Whenever this office is said that of the day is omitted, only the ordinary Complin must be used, this having none of its own.

Alleluia. From Easter morning till the Octave of Corpus Christi be past, to every antiphon and invitatory is added one Alleluia, except at Matins and Vespers on Fridays. In Advent and Lent Alleluia is never said.

Of Concurrence of offices. If a holiday fall on a Sunday the office is said for the holiday, except Easter-day, Whitsunday, Trinity Sunday, and all the Sundays in Advent and Lent. Only, the Annunciation is preferred before the Sundays in Lent, unless it fall on Palm Sunday, and then 'tis omitted that year with a commemoration; if any Holiday happen on Thursday, Friday, or Saturday in Holy week, 'tis omitted that year without a commemoration; if any Holiday happen on Monday, or Tuesday in Easter or Whitsun week, 'tis omitted that year with a commemoration, on other days, within those Octaves, the Office of the Holiday is said; and so, in all other Octaves with a commemoration of the Octave. These Feasts only have Octaves; Christmas-day, Twelfth-day, Easter, Ascension, Whitsunday, Corpus Christi, Assumption of our B. Lady, All-Saints.

A Commemoration is made by reciting all that's set down in the Proper of festivals for the feast commemorated; and is to be made immediately after the prayer of the day whose office is actually said . . .

Holidays of obligation. All Sundays, New-Year's day, Twelfth-day, the Purification, Annunciation, Assumption, and Nativity of our B. Lady, all the twelve Apostles, S. Joseph, the Invention of the H. Cross, S. John Baptist, S. Ann the mother of our B. Lady, S. Laurence, S. Michael, All-Saints, Christmas-day, S. Stephen, Holy Innocents, S. Sylvester.

Moveable holidays. Easter-day with two days next following, Ascension-day, Whitsunday with two days following, Corpus Christi-day.

Fasting-days. All Lent except Sundays, the Ember-days, the Eves of Christmas and Whitsunday, the Eves of the Nativity, Purification, Annunciation (unless it fall in Easter-week) and Assumption of our B. Lady; the Eves of All-Saints, of all the twelve Apostles (except S. John Evangelist, and SS. Philip and Jacob) of the Nativity of S. John Baptist, and of S. Laurence; all Fridays, except in Christmas and between Easter and Ascension. As long as the Bridegroom is with us, Matt. 9. 15.

Days of abstinence. All Sundays in Lent; all Saturdays in the year; Monday, Tuesday and Wednesday before Ascension; and S. Mark's day if it fall not in Easter-week.

These Lessons are out of Holy Scripture; but sometimes the particular places not cited, because sometimes the Lesson is not taken out of one place, but composed of many.

Office for each day in the week. Office of our B. Saviour. Office of the Holy Ghost. Office of the Saints. Office for the Dead.

⁎ *The Offices, for each day in the week, of our B. Saviour, aud of the Saints, have Matins, Lauds, Vespers, and Compline: the Offices of the Holy Ghost and for the Dead have only Matins, Lauds, and Vespers. The Hours in these offices are composed of Invitatories, Hymns, Psalms of an original composition with antiphons, lessons, chapters, versicles and responses, and prayers. The introduction to Matins consists of the collect, "Prevent we beseech thee, O Lord, our actions," then, In the name. Blessed be the holy and undivided Trinity. Our Father. Hail Mary . . . Holy Mary, Mother of God pray for us sinners, now and in the hour of our death. Amen. I believe in God. V. O Lord open thou our lips. R. And our mouths . . . V. O God incline . . . R. O Lord make haste . . . Glory be to the Father. Sunday Matins has the Te Deum, Lauds the Benedictus, Vespers the Magnificat, and Compline the collect "Visit we beseech thee, O Lord, this habitation." The following commemorations occur at the end of Sunday Lauds. For the B. Virgin. For the Saints. For the church. For the King. "May the souls of the faithful departed through the mercy of God rest in peace" occurs at the end of Sunday Vespers. V. and Rs. prayers, hymns addressed to the Virgin Mary, and benedictions occur at the end of the Sunday office; they are for the seasons from Advent to Candlemas, Candlemas to Maundy-Thursday, Easter to Trinity Sunday, Trinity Sunday to Advent. The following collect occurs at the end of Vespers for the dead, "Behold with pity we beseech thee, O Lord, the soul of thy servant N for whom we humbly offer our prayers to thy divine majesty."*

Proper of Festivals. Sundays in Advent, St. Andrew, St. Thomas Apostle, Christmas-day and the fourth and fifth days in the Octave, S. Stephen, S. John Evangelist, SS. Innocents, S. Sylvester, New-years-day, Twelfth-day and during the Octave, Candlemas, Ash-Wednesday, Sundays in Lent, S. Matthias, S. Joseph, Annunciation, Passion Sunday, Palm Sunday, Maundy Thursday, Good Friday, Holy Saturday, Easter day and during the Octave, SS. Philip and Jacob, Invention of the H. Cross; Rogation Week, Monday, Tuesday, and Wednesday; Ascension and during the Octave; Whitsunday and during the Octave; Trinity Sunday, Corpus Christi and during the Octave; S. John Baptist, SS. Peter and Paul, S. James, S. Ann, S. Laurence, Assumption of our Lady and during the Octave; S. Bartholomew, Nativity of our Lady, S. Matthew, S. Michael, SS. Simon and Jude, All Saints and during the Octave. All Souls.

⁎ *Proper Invitatories, Antiphons, V. and R., and Collects are given.*

A prayer for a family at night.

⁎ *This office consists of: In the name. Blessed be the holy and undivided Trinity. Our Father. Hail Mary. I believe. Collect. "O eternal, infinite and*

almighty God whose gracious wisdom." Confession. *"I confess to almighty God, to the blessed Virgin Mary ..." and a Litany.*

A.D. 1672, Rouen, 12º. English. No. 256.

** The title is *"Devotions, first part in the ancient way of offices, with Psalms, Hymns, and Prayers; for every day in the week and every holiday in the year. Second edition, corrected and augmented."*

To the Honourable H. J., Esq. Sir. It may seem perhaps but a bad compliment, and no less unseasonable than unusual, to begin an address of this nature with an open declaration, that the present I offer neither needs nor courts any man's patronage to set it off ... Tis a book which Catholicks use with very great devotion and benefit; the moderate Protestant will find nothing in it he can with reason dislike, nor the passionate Zealot which he can justly traduce ... And now I have mentioned the Author,[1] be pleased to know that his quality makes this book particularly suitable to your self ... he had begun also an office of the B. Virgin,[2] intending to annex it to these devotions, which was so inimitably excellent, that scarce any will be found in all respects able to match his sense and expression, or finish it as it ought. The prayers throughout this book were by his desire writ by a worthy hand with which he joined his in a perfect friendship ... Your true Honourer and humble servant. J. S. (John Serjeant).

Directions. This book consists chiefly of eleven offices (as in No. 256. first ed., A.D. 1668. page 311).

Holidays of obligation. All Sundays ... S. Sylvester. (as in No. 256. first ed. A.D. 1668. page 311). To which are here added (for the devout) S. Mark, S. Mary Magdalene, S. Luke.

Ember days. Wednesday, Friday, and Saturday, next following the first Sunday in Lent. Whitsunday, the Exaltation of the H. Cross, and S. Lucy's day.

Office for each day in the week. Office of our B. Saviour. Office of the Holy Ghost. Office of the Saints. Office for the dead.

** These *Offices are the same as those in No. 256. first ed., A.D. 1668 (page 311).*

Proper of festivals. These are the same as in No. 256, first ed. A.D. 1668 (page 311). To which are added S. Mark Evan. S. Mary Magdalene. S. Luke.

After the prayer of the day at Lauds and Vespers, say on all week days in Lent till Passion Sunday ... On Fasting eves ... On ember days ... On Rogation days ...

** Each of these devotions consists of an Antiphon, hen a V. and R. and a collect.

Occasionals. To be used before the daily commemorations. In time of mortality ... War ... Persecution ... For a member of the family; Sick ... Recovered ... Deceased ...

---

[1] See Preface to ed. 1789. page 315.   [2] See third edition. A.D. 1684, page 315.

₊ *Each of these devotions consists of an antiphon, then a V. and R. and a collect. The daily commemorations occur at the end of Sunday Lauds and are; For the B. Virgin. For the Saints. For the Church. For the King.*

A.D. 1684, Rouen, 12º. English. No. 256.

₊ *The title is "Devotions, first part in the ancient way of offices, with Psalms, Hymns, and Prayers; for every day in the week, and every holiday in the year. Third edition, corrected and augmented."*

Directions. This book consists chiefly of twelve offices; one for each day in the week, one for our Saviour's feasts, one for the Holy Ghost, one for the B. Virgin, one for Saints, and one for the Dead. Each office has four parts; Matins and Lauds for the morning, Vespers and Compline for the evening.

The offices for the B. Virgin and Saints are intended only for feasts of obligation, but may be applied to others according to particular devotion. In saying these offices the same method is to be observed as in that for our Saviour.

An octave is the same day sennight after a feast, till which be past the feast is every day commemorated. These feasts have octaves; Christmas-day, Twelfth day, Ascension, Whitsun-day, Corpus Christi, Assumption of the B. Virgin, All Saints.

Office for each day in the week. Office of our blessed Saviour. Office of the Holy Ghost. Office of the blessed Virgin. Office of the Saints. Office for the dead.

₊ *These Offices are the same as those in No. 256, first ed., A.D. 1668 (page 811) with the addition of the Office of the blessed Virgin, which has Matins, Lauds, Vespers, and Compline.*

A.D. 1789, Edinburgh, 8º. English. No. 256.

₊ *The title is "Devotions in the ancient way of offices, containing exercises for every day in the week, and every holiday in the year. By Mr. John Austin. A new edition."*

Editor's preface. The work we here offer to the publick is too well known to need any recommendation. It has always been considered as a family-piece among Catholics, while the pious and judicious members of the Church of England have done justice to its merit. Hickes' devotions[1] deservedly continue to be held in high esteem; and it is somewhat singular that the Reformers of this excellent piece regretted, while making them, the alterations it underwent among their hands. In this edition we have restored the book to its original owners, hoping that the perusal thereof may still be beneficial to the liberal minded of all denominations. It is a debt we owe to the memory of the author to present the public with what account we can procure of him; and of this we acquit ourselves the more readily, as former editions have been silent on the subject. John Austin was born of a good family at Walpole in the county of Norfolk, and was educated in St. John's College in Cambridge, where he was contemporary with Mr. John Serjeant, who afterwards published

[1] See page 325.

the second edition of this work,[1] wherein he relates the circumstances of his death. About 1640 Mr. Austin became Catholic, and leaving the University, designed to follow the law, for which end he entered himself in Lincoln's Inn. He was for some time tutor to a gentleman, and it is probable he travelled in this capacity, for we find he did not neglect this source of improvement. He afterwards lived in London, spending his time wholly in books and learned conversation . . . The Devotions were at first published in two volumes. The second from what cause we know not is now almost neglected. It consisted of the four gospels reduced to the form of lessons, besides which a third volume remains in manuscript. The author was prevented from finishing the Office of the blessed Virgin which he intended to insert in the second edition, as has been done since . . . [2] He died in Bow Street Covent Garden anno 1669, and was interred in the Parish Church of St. Paul. . . . Such was the servant of God to whose enlightened piety we owe this inimitable production, the prayers excepted, which were composed by a friend of the author's at his desire . . . We do not pretend to ascertain how many editions it has gone through, but this we know that the present has been preceded by twenty impressions at least . . . We build our hopes of support from the religious part of society, and in particular from Catholics who have been for so many years calling in vain for an impression of a work so universally esteemed; May they who peruse it live the life, and die the death of the just man who composed it.

Office for each day in the week. Office of our blessed Saviour. Office of the Holy Ghost. Office of the blessed Virgin. Office of the Saints. Office for the Dead.

⁎ *These offices are the same as those in No. 256, third ed., A.D. 1684 (page 315) omitting the V. and Rs., prayers, hymns addressed to the Virgin Mary and benedictions which occur at the end of the Sunday office. Introduction to Matins called " Prayers to be said in secret " consists of, In the name. Blessed be the holy and undivided Trinity. Collect. " Prevent we beseech thee, O Lord, our actions ". Our Father. Hail Mary. I believe in God. An introduction to Vespers called " Prayers to be said in secret " also occurs ; it consists of, In the name. Blessed be the holy and undivided Trinity. Our Father. Hail Mary. etc.*

Festivals. These are the same as in No. 256, second ed., A.D. 1672 (page 314) omitting St. Sylvester.

On all week-days in Lent till Passion Sunday, after the prayer of the day at Lauds and Vespers . . . On Fasting eves . . . On Ember days . . . On Rogation days . . . (as in No. 256, second ed., A.D. 1672 page 314).

Occasionals. To be used before the daily commemorations. In time of mortality . . . Persecution . . . For peace . . . For a member of the family; Sick . . . Recovered . . . Deceased . . .

⁎ *Each of these devotions consists of an Antiphon, V. and R. and collect.*

Prayer at night for a family (as in No. 256, first ed., A.D. 1668, page 311).

---

[1] See page 314. [2] See third ed. A.D. 1684, page 315.

A SUMMARY OF THE CONTENTS

OF

THEOPHILUS DORRINGTON'S REFORMED DEVOTIONS.

NINE EDITIONS.

A.D. 1686 — A.D. 1727.

A.D. 1686, London, 12º. English. No. 260.

⁎ *The title is "Reformed devotions in meditations, hymns, and petitions; for every day in the week, and every holiday in the year. Divided into two parts."*

To the right honourable, the Lady Ann Boscawen . . . Madam. It is because I account this book very excellent in it's kind, and worthy to be recommended as such to the world, which makes me presume, Madam, to dedicate it to so high a person as your honour . . . Madam, your Honour's most humble, most obedient, and devoted servant. T. D. (Theophilus Dorrington.)

The Preface. Some account of the following book I am bound to give . . . It was a Book of devotions disposed into the form and method of the Roman Breviary; and though the matter of it was not the same with that, yet therein were the truths of christian religion frequently mixed, as in the belief of that church, with those erroneous doctrines which in latter ages have been added to christianity. What I thought to be such, by the direction of Holy Scripture and the Articles of our church which are drawn from thence, according to the usual interpretations made of it by the most pure and primitive ages of christianity, that I have taken away, and connected the sense with what those rules suggested to be truth. Therefore has this book the title of Reform'd devotions. And I dare say, if Holy Scripture may be the rule to judge by in these matters (as it must be in all such matters) the book is now more truly corrected and amended, than it was in any of the former editions, though it pretends to have been four times printed, and twice with that advantage.[1] In the fourth and last edition, which is dated Roan. 1685[2] it is said to be corrected and augmented; and there is added to it in that a whole Office for the Virgin Mary, which being very different from the former book,[3]

---

[1] See No. 256. 2nd ed. 1672. page 314 and 4th ed. 1685. page 87.

[2] Devotions in the Ancient way of offices. No. 256. 4th ed. 1685. page 87 and 3rd. ed. 1684. page 315.

[3] Devotions in the Ancient way of offices. No. 256. 1st. ed. 1668. page 311.

and much inferior to it in all respects and more corrupted, I have wholly left it out; and having made use of that part of the former book which provided for all the Saints days, I should have wanted a good reason for so regarding one particular Saint, if I had used that part of the book distinct; and there being enough of the other to serve my method, I did not trouble myself to pick out the best sentences of that to mix with the rest. This I did out of one office in the other book, because in the present method I had no occasion for it distinct, and because the greatest part of that office related to the souls supposed to be in purgatory. I am justified in the reforming of this book and purging out those fore-mentioned doctrines, by the authority of our nation which did for the sake of them, a few years ago, condemn the book to a publick burning; and because there was a great deal of it very good sense, and that composed in a very devout strain and an ingenious style, and mixed with several curious hymns, I thought it was worthy of a reformation; and as well too good to be thrown away whole, as too bad to be used whole, which I doubt not all ingenious and devout readers will acknowledge upon perusing what is here presented, when I shall have said that the most part of it is but what I found in that book. Yet I subscribe to the wisdom and justice of that condemnation which it underwent as it was; for the better it was in some respects (since many offensive things were contained in it, and they often with great artifice insinuated in very disguising terms) the more it did deserve that fate. Some passages there were in it capable of two interpretations which joined with false doctrines must be interpreted to an ill meaning; but joined with truths must be understood to mean well. And some of these do still remain here, because I was loth to throw out anything needlessly, and especially if there was wit and elegancy in the composure, that so this book might be in some respects better, and in others, at least, no worse than the former. There were in it Lessons to every office which I have left out, because they consisted of but some sentences of the truly Canonical Scripture joined without distinction with other sentences; and that translation which those Scriptures were in is different from that authentick among us; besides I did not always think them exactly suited to the places they held, and I think the absence of them may be reckon'd well enough supplied by the pertinent sentences of Holy Scripture which I have through the whole book frequently mixed with the matter of it; especially since those that will read Lessons in their private devotions have the holy Scriptures in their hands translated into the vulgar tongue. The hymns that were in the former book are all retain'd, and one is added to fill up the present method; but they are many of them alter'd, some to be corrected, some to be supplied with a few syllables, or a stanza here and there to fit them to the tunes of our singing psalms, as many of them were before and now they all are. The petitions here are gathered partly out of those parts of the former book, which in that were called Psalms, in this meditations, and partly from other places. The devotions for every day in the week are not so appropriated to those days of the week they are design'd for, but that they may be used on any other day, as indeed I know no reason for such appropriation; they are thus placed to dispose them in some method, that they might not lye together like a confus'd disorderly heap. Only those for the Lord's day are most proper for that: those set to Thursday, because all the subject of them is the Sacrament of the Lord's supper, are very fit to be used on any day when we receive that holy sacrament. To this, that some of the devotions are said to be designed for the Holy-days, I say, those that will be pleased to look beyond the title, will be as well satisfied with the matter of that, as of any other part of the book. I did not contrive the book so distinguished but found it so . . . I intended not to infect the book with controversy, and not to gratify but rather divert the contentious humour of the age; I would not engage the world more in controversy which perhaps is already too much engaged in it, but had rather possess men's minds with an affectionate powerful sense of those important truths which christians do generally assent unto, and which are of absolute necessity to be known and lov'd and obeyed; for which purpose this book is perhaps as well fitted now as any that can be met with, unless any one will except that incomparable book the Exposition of our church Cathechism lately composed for the use of the diocese of Bath and Wells;[1] I can readily assent to him that shall prefer that to this. In this following book I am sure no impartial and judicious reader can think, that the devout and serious expressions do want their foundation in reason by being separated from the principles that are purg'd out; many such expressions may be found in the writings of the devout and elegant Fathers, which could not be drawn from such principles, because they are of a latter invention; besides, the Holy Scripture and the fundamental truths drawn from thence and contained in the four first Creeds are foundation enough for such things. It were a mistake therefore to imagine, that we must needs be beholden to any peculiar or distinct principles, not held by the truly ancient and Apostolick church, for such a production as this. I think it may appear by the following book, that those principles are not necessary as a foundation, nor any ways advantageous to the superstructive . . . I shall not need to direct particularly on what days those parts of the book designed for the holy-days should be used; for that will be sufficiently suggested by the publick Liturgy of our church to those that are acquainted with it . . .

Devotions for every day in the week. The first part. Devotions for every day in the week. The second part. Devotions for the Holy-days. The first part. For the feasts of our blessed Saviour. For the feasts of the

---

[1] An exposition on the Church catechism, or the practice of divine love. A.D. 1685.

Holy Ghost. For the feasts of the Saints. Devotions for the Holy-days. The second part. For the feasts of our blessed Saviour. For the feasts of the Holy Ghost. For the feasts of the Saints.

₊ *Each of these devotions includes a form for the Morning and Evening; that for the morning is composed of A meditation, a Hymn, then two meditations, and petitions; that for the evening of three meditations, then petitions, and a hymn.*

A.D. 1700, London, 12°. English. No. 260.

₊ *The title is "Reform'd devotions in meditations, hymns, and petitions; for every day in the week and every holiday in the year. Divided into two parts. The fifth edition, revised and corrected. To which are added the Contents. And (to render the devotions complete and useful upon all occasions) a holy office, before, at, and after receiving the Holy sacrament, by Dr. Edw. Lake."*

Devotions for every day in the week. Part I. Devotions for every day in the week. The second part. Devotions for the Holy days in two parts. For the feasts of our blessed Saviour. For the feasts of the Holy Ghost. For the feasts of the Saints. Devotions for the Holy days. The second part. For the feasts of our blessed Saviour. For the feasts of the Holy Ghost. For the feasts of the Saints.

₊ *These devotions are the same as those in No. 260. A.D. 1686. page 320.*

Prayers before, at, and after the Holy communion, by Dr. E. Lake. At thy entrance into the Lord's house before the service of the church begins. Forgive me my sins, O Lord, forgive me the sins of my age . . . Amen. At thy approach to the Holy Table, say. O Saviour of the world, save me who by thy cross and passion . . . Amen. To the King eternal, immortal, invisible . . . Amen. Then kneel down and pray for devotion. Most great God, who hast not only permitted, but invited us . . . Amen. Whil'st others are coming up, and the Priest preparing to read the sentences, pray. Almighty God, who hast of thine infinite mercies vouchsafed to ordain this sacrament, for a perpetual memory of that blessed sacrifice . . . Amen. Be pleased, O God, to accept this our bounden duty and service . . . Amen. Whil'st upon your knees, cast in your offering, stop and say. Blessed Jesu, who did'st accept the poor widow's two mites . . . Amen. Whil'st the priest and others are communicating, say. Grant me gracious Lord so to eat the flesh of thy son . . . Amen. O Lord I am not worthy nor fit that thou should'st come . . . Amen. O Lord God, how I receive the body and blood of my most blessed Saviour . . . Amen. Upon the approach of the priest with the consecrated bread, say. Thou, O blessed Jesu, hast said, he that eateth thy flesh . . . When the priest offers thee the holy bread, say: The body of our Lord Jesus Christ which was given for me . . . Amen. Whil'st you eat it, say. By thy crucified body deliver me from the body of death. After receiving, say. By thine agony and bloody sweat . . . Upon the approach of the priest with the consecrated cup, say. What reward shall I give unto the Lord for all the benefits . . . Amen.

After you have received it. O my God, thou art true and holy, O my soul, thou art blessed and happy . . . Amen. Most blessed redeemer, I do truly believe that thy body was crucified . . . Amen. Almighty God, the fountain of all goodness, from whom every good and perfect gift proceedeth . . . Amen. When you are come home, make use of these prayers that follow. Most holy God, who art of purer eyes than to behold iniquity . . . Amen. O thou with whom is no variableness nor shadow of turning let thy holy Spirit direct me . . . Amen. O Lord, I do here humbly present unto thee my soul and body . . . Amen.

Thus have you chosen your Communion devotions; it only remains that you remember what a great business lies upon your hands in performing those promises that you made to God . . .

To your Evening prayer that Sunday night you receive, subjoin this collect. O blessed Jesus, who hast this day made me a partaker of thy blessed body and blood . . . Amen. God the Father bless me, God the Son defend me, God the Holy Ghost preserve me, God the holy Trinity be with me, now and for evermore. Amen.

A SUMMARY OF THE CONTENTS

OF

GEORGE WHELER'S
PROTESTANT MONASTERY.

ONE EDITION.

A.D. 1698.

A.D. 1698. 8º. English.

₊ *The title is "The Protestant Monastery, or christian œconomicks; containing directions for the religious conduct of a family. Printed in the year 1698."*

To the devout perusers of the following treatise. Dear friends, christian brethren, and fellow servants. I hope this my design and desire in publishing this small book, being to promote the glory of God among you, will not be unacceptable to you ; nor this method, I propose to do it, be disagreable or uneasie, when you shall have made trial of it, and been some time versed in it. It is not any new or unpracticable thing I propose to you, but what the primitive and most sincere christians were trained up in from their admission into the body of Christ. And the matter of the devotion I recommend to you, being chiefly taken out of our most excellent Liturgy, it will make the actual performance very easy to you. For it is what you are already acquainted with ; and what I hope both you and your households have already, for the most part, by heart ; (especially the Belief, the Commandments, the Lord's prayer, and suffrages, which is the substance of all the rest.) This your long and continued practice in the church must needs produce; where I am sure you are safe, and whereby you will be out of danger of error, if you firmly adhere to her doctrine and discipline, in these perilous times. And I trust the enlargements upon them are perfectly agreeable to the same analogy of doctrine. And so I hope they may assist you in the understanding the former, and in some measure enlarge your minds in the practise of them both . . . If the name of Monastery be offensive to any one as a Popish name, I answer, I have a very Revered and pious Bishop for my example, but applied to single persons *i.e.* Bishop Duppa. And it being joined with the protestant name, I doubt not but it may be as innocently used to distinguish it from the Romans, as the word Church or Faith may be in the like distinction of Popish and Protestant. And if I have not sufficiently declared my dislike to the Roman abuse of the thing; I know not how to do it more emphatically, than by such a distinction; it being the Romish abuses, and not the thing itself I dislike . . . I do not foresee any offence the devotions themselves can justly give to any devout person of the Church of England, for whom they are designed; as to others, they may bear with me, if they please; and if they raise captious disputes about them, they shall trouble themselves more than me. With respect to the practise of them; it may not be amiss to observe, that though they are principally designed for stated family devotions, yet they may also be used in private closets by single persons without any considerable alteration; especially the enlargements by those who have much time and leisure, since our Saviour has taught us to pray in the plural number in his most excellent pattern of all prayer. Thus widows, and virgins, and all single persons who have not the convenience and happiness of the united devotions of an unanimous family; thus the several offices for night would be pious employment and entertainment for soldiers, and such as watch with the sick, and the sick that cannot sleep themselves. The hymns if adapted to short chanting tunes, such as some I have added at the end, being most easy to be learned, may well suit a christian labourer's practice in the cornfields, meadows, and woods . . . I have added no Office for the sick, because it is the office of the master of the family then, to send to the Minister of the parish to pray with the sick; and to receive his directions therein. I shall only add by way of encouragement, that the practise of what is here proposed wants not a trial; it having been generally used in my family near twenty years last past . . . Your most affectionate friend, brother, and fellow servant in Christ. Geo. Wheler.

The Protestant Monastery or Christian œconomicks.

₊ *This portion of the book consists in the first place of ten chapters which treat I. Of a monastick life in general, sacred and prophane. II. Of the beginning and progress of monasteries in the christian church. III. The just censure of the Church of England; what they have done and do allow. IV. Of Monasteries for women. V. Of the design of this discourse. VI. Of paternal authority. VII. The paternal office. VIII. The duty of the wife. IX. The duty of children. X. The duty of servants towards their masters. Then follows The application. The several sorts of masters of families. 1. Of the husbandman or labourer. 2. Concerning those who live by the labour of others in general. 3. Concerning those of great estates and great quality. 4. Of watching. 5. Fasting. 6. Of alms. 7. Medicines. 8. Of hospitality.*

Forms of prayer for the use of private families. For all the Hours of prayer both night and day, taken out of the Common prayer; with other inlargements. Which may be abbreviated or inlarged, as more or less time and leisure will permit. For the use of a family, and alone, for all the Hours of prayer in the day.

The first Hour of prayer. Hora tertia. Nine O'Clock. Hora Sexta. At noon. Hora nona. Three O'Clock. The first watch. At six O'Clock at night. Second watch or Midnight watch. Nine at night or if that be late sooner.

A form of prayer taken out of the Common Prayer-Book, which may be used in part or in whole as time will permit, either night or morning. A prayer for midnight or after xii. of the clock, being the third watch, in private when we wake. The fourth watch or morning watch about three of the clock in the morning.

⁎ *These Hours and Forms of prayer are made up of devotions from the Book of Common prayer, as well as of other devotions which are called inlargements. The arrangement of the different parts of these Hours does not follow that of any office in the Book of Common prayer.*

An office for a woman in labour of child-birth. In the family or in private.

⁎ *This office consists of the Kyrie. Lord's prayer. V. and R. A prayer. Two petitions of a Litany. O Saviour of the world . . . The almighty Lord who is a most strong tower to all that put their trust in him . . . Unto God's gracious mercy . . . The grace of our Lord Jesus Christ . . .*

Thanksgiving after delivery of childbirth.

⁎ *This office consists of the Lord's prayer. V. and R. Thanksgiving. Almighty God, father of all mercies . . . Unto God's gracious mercy . . . The grace of our Lord Jesus Christ . . .*

Hymns suited to the several Hours of prayer and other occasions, for the use of a private family. To the right honourable and most excellent lady, the Lady Crew, my Lord Bishop of Durham, his most virtuous and most deserving consort. Madam. Your Ladyship's not long since countenancing one of these hymns with your approbation, both intitles you to the rest, and encourages me to present you with them . . . Ladyship's most obliged and most humble servant. George Wheler.

⁎ *This collection includes hymns for the Lord's day, to be used either in a family or at church. Paraphrases on the forty second and forty third psalms. Hymn called a lesson out of the gospel. Hymn called a lesson out of the Acts or Epistles. Penitential hymn in time of trouble or distress. Hymn of praise for mercy received. Hymn of praise for deliverance from trouble or sickness. A Sanctus.*

Short tunes to chant several of the hymns.

A SUMMARY OF THE CONTENTS
OF
DEVOTIONS IN THE ANCIENT WAY OF
OFFICES PUBLISHED BY
GEORGE HICKES.

EIGHT EDITIONS.

A.D. 1700—A.D. 1758.

A.D. 1700, London, 12º. English. No. 261.

₊ *The title has " Devotions in the ancient way of offices with psalms, hymns, and prayers, for every day of the week and every holiday in the year. Reformed by a Person of quality, and published by George Hickes, D.D."*

To the reader. It is not the respect for the reformer of these devotions,[1] which I acknowledge to be very great, nor any thoughts of advantaging the bookseller for which I write this preface, but a pure and uninterested desire to give some account and character of this book, which in one dress or other hath been sent abroad no less than nine times[2] into the world. It hath had four editions unreformed from the Roman Catholicks, in the last of which is added, The Office for the Blessed Virgin, which J. S.[3] in the epistle dedicatory, before the second edition, assures us was begun by the excellent author before he died who intended to annex it to his devotions; and truly I cannot but wonder who he was that durst undertake to finish a piece that this Apelles left imperfect, especially after so great a judge of sense and style as Mr. S. had said, that it was so inimitably excellent, that scarce any would be found in all respects able to match his sense and expression, or finish it as it ought. It hath had five editions more,[2] as it was reformed by the reverend and worthy Mr. Dorrington . . . It now presents itself again in a new reform unto the world in which I do not doubt but it will have many editions and perhaps as many as any book of devotion in what language soever, except the Psalter, ever had. For though Mr. Dorrington's reform of it hath very well deserved the good reception it hath found in the world; yet it was not altogether so acceptable to some discerning as well as devout persons who were skilful in divine offices . . . Wherefore to oblige those devout persons who desired another reforma-

---

[1] Mrs. Susanna Hopton. See page 335.
[2] See No. 256. John Austin's devotions. Four editions. 1668-1685. page 87. and No. 260 Theophilus Dorrington's devotions. Nine editions. 1686-1727. page 89.
[3] John Serjeant. See page 314.

tion of those devotions, another is here presented to them, in the author's own way, from the pen of a most pious as well as ingenious and ready writer[1] who hath not left out or altered anything but some few sentences and expressions which hindered those offices from being introduced into the closets and oratories of the more devout sons and daughters of the Church of England, especially of those who delight in the more Heaven-like way of worship, I mean in alternate or choral devotions . . . But of all others none have it in their power to practise this most delightful way of worship in the heaven-like fellowship of alternate devotion, to so much advantage as the religious societies, of whose rise and progress the world hath lately had an account by the Reverend Mr. Woodward, Minister of Poplar.[1] It is to the votaries of these, and such like Societies, that I particularly recommend this book of devotions, which in other forms hath already more than once been recommended to the whole christian world. J. S. who I suppose is Mr. John Serjeant, in the epistle dedicatory of the second edition[2] tells us that it is the most substantial part of divinity rendered usefully practical . . . The Reverend and most worthy Mr. Dorrington, to whom the world is so much obliged for the first reform of it, tells us in the Epistle Dedicatory[3] that it is a book very excellent in its kind . . . Know then, it consists of eleven offices, one for every day in the week, one for our Saviour's feasts, one for the Holy Ghost, one for Saints, and one for the dead, which the author of this reform hath entitled, "A preparatory office for death" . . . I hope, no man will be so uncharitable as to think, that while I thus recommend set Hours of devotion, I am so superstitious as to put any trust in the bare recital of a few psalms and prayers and hymns, at such and such prescribed times; but that I do it to restore the ancient practice of devotion, which was in use among the Jews and the primitive Christians, among whom the distinctions of Hours for prayer was not the effect of superstition but a rational institution, in which they agreed as it were by common inspiration, as the best means of advancing piety and devotion . . . As for directions in using these offices . . . First, as to the place; let it be some private oratory, if any such can be had, at least some retirement if the house where they meet will afford any such . . . It is incumbent upon masters of families . . . to be as far as they can priests in their own families, and those who think fit to use this book, by the benefit of it, will with great ease make their domesticks truly knowing christians; and if to the daily use thereof they please to add on the Lord's day the reading of the Church catechism as expounded by the R.R. the Bishop of Bath and Wells, Mr. Kettlewell's practical believer, and the Christian Monitor, they will in great measure make up the loss of parochial instruction, and thoroughly

---

[1] See An account of the rise and progress of the religious societies in the City of London by Josiah Woodward.
[2] See page 314. [3] See page 317.

furnish their younger dependants unto all good works. Among the latter I have more particularly commended it to those religious societies of which the Reverend Mr. Woodward hath given us an account . . . But all this while I have been speaking of the book, I had almost forgot the devout reformer of it, who is one that hath a mighty genius for divinity, and though never bred in scholastick education, yet by conversation with learned clergy-men and reading the best divinity books hath attained to a skill in the sacred science not much inferior to that of the best divines. It is one who hath already given the world one book of devotions[1] which hath been well received in three or four editions; and will leave it another for which posterity will bless the author's name . . . One who is a great example of christian piety, and a singular ornament to our communion in this degenerate age; and among the many and most serious good wishes I have for the Church of England this is and always shall be one, that all her sons and daughters were such. George Hickes.

Office for each day in the week. Office of our B. Saviour. Office for the Holy Ghost. Office for the Commemoration of Saints. Preparatory office for death by way of commemoration of the faithful departed.

₊ *The offices, for each day in the week, of our B. Saviour, for the Holy Ghost, for the Commemoration of Saints have Mattins, Lauds, Vespers, and Compline; but the Preparatory office for death has only Mattins, Lauds, and Vespers. The Hours in these Offices are mainly the same as those in No. 256. first edition. A.D. 1668. (page 311). except that the Commemorations at the end of Sunday Lauds, as well as the V. and Rs. antiphons, prayers, hymns addressed to the Virgin Mary, and Benedictions which occur at the end of the Sunday office are omitted, and also "May the souls of the faithful departed, through the mercy of God rest in peace. Amen." at the end of Sunday Vespers. At the end of Vespers for the dead the following collect occurs from the Book of Common prayer A.D. 1662. "O merciful God, the father of our Lord Jesus Christ who is the resurrection and the life." instead of "Behold with pity we beseech thee." The introduction to Mattins consists of the collect. "Prevent we beseech thee, O Lord, all our doings." then, In the name. Blessed be the holy and undivided Trinity.*

The Motto proper, not only for Ash Wednesday but for our whole lives . . . For ember-days . . . In time of persecution.

₊ *The motto for Ash Wednesday consists of texts of holy Scripture, a collect, antiphon, V. and R. and another collect: that for Ember-days, of texts of holy Scripture and a collect; that for time of persecution, of texts of holy Scripture, V and R. and a collect.*

Proper Festivals. Sundays in Advent, St. Andrew, St. Thomas the Apostle, Christmas-day, St. Stephen's Day, St. John Evangelist, Holy Innocents, New Year's day, Twelfth-day, The Conversion of St. Paul, Candlemas, Ash-Wednesday, The Annunciation, Passion Sunday, Palm Sunday, Easter-day, Easter Monday and Tuesday, and all Sundays after until the Ascension. St. Mark the Evangelist, St. Philip and James, Ascension

---

[1] Daily devotions by an humble penitent. 1673.

day, Whitsunday, Monday and Tuesday. Trinity Sunday. St. John Baptist, St. Peter, St. James, St. Bartholomew, St. Matthew, St. Michael, St. Luke, St. Simon and Jude, All Saints, Ember-days, Rogation days.

₊ *Proper Invitatories, Antiphons, V and R, and Collects are given.*

A.D. 1701, London, 12°. English. No. 261.

₊ *The title is "Devotions in the ancient way of Offices, with Psalms, Hymns, and Prayers, for every day of the week and every holiday in the year. Reformed by a Person of Quality and published by George Hickes, D.D. The second edition corrected and enlarged."*

I had here concluded my preface, but that I was desired to say something to an objection which some have made against the words, Mattins, Vespers, Lauds, and Compline, which denominate the four parts of every office in this book . . . Some it seems there are who to render this book of devotion suspect have said that those words carry with them a sound of popery, as if all words were popery that are used in the offices, or by writers of the church of Rome . . . The first of them is still used by the Church of England, the second, I hope, is a very harmless word, and needs no apology, the third was commonly used in our english books of devotion long after the reformation, and as for the last, which perhaps may sound like Popery in these nice gentlemens ears, I hope they will no longer be offended with it, when I have told them that Compline is a technical word of the latin church, formed from the latin word Complenda, which with Completa and Completorium signifies the concluding or last office in every day's devotion . . . Some others I hear there are who have no other objection against this book but that it is needless and superfluous, because, as they think, there are two many books of devotion already in the world, but are there not much greater numbers of books written in all arts and sciences suited in various styles and methods of writing to the several pallats and capacities of the great number of readers, some whereof are pleased with this book and others like that, and another perhaps prefers a third or fourth before them both . . . George Hickes.

Office for each day in the week. Office of our B. Saviour. Office for the Holy Ghost. Office for the Commemoration of Saints. Preparatory office for death by way of commemoration of the faithful departed.

₊ *These offices are mainly the same as in the first edition (page 325), but Sunday Lauds has the Benedictus, Vespers the Magnificat, and Compline the collect: "Visit we beseech thee, O Lord, this habitation." A prayer of commemoration for the saints departed; "Finally O Lord we beseech thee of thy goodness to accept of the high praise . . . Amen" occurs at the end of Vespers in the "Preparatory Office for death." as well as the collect "O merciful God, the father of our Lord Jesus Christ, who is the resurrection . . . Amen." The Collect, "Almighty God, with whom do live the spirits . . . Amen" occurs at the end of Lauds.*

Proper of Festivals. Sundays in Advent, St. Andrew, St. Thomas the Apostle,

Christmas day, St. Stephen's day, St John Evangelist, Holy Innocents, New Year's day, Twelfth day, Conversion of St. Paul, Candlemas, Ash Wednesday, St. Matthias, The Annunciation, Passion Sunday, Palm Sunday, Maundy Thursday, Good Friday, Holy Saturday, Easter day. Easter Monday and Tuesday and all Sundays after until the Ascension. St. Mark the Evangelist, St. Philip and James, Ascension-day, Whitsunday, Monday and Tuesday. St. John Baptist, St. Peter, St. James, St. Bartholomew, St. Matthew, St. Michael, St. Luke, St. Simon and Jude, All Saints. On the Saints eves which are kept with fasting. Ember days. Rogation days.

₊ *Proper Invitatories, Antiphons, V and R, and Collects are given.*

A.D. 1706, London, 8º. English. No. 261.

₊ *The title is "Devotions in the antient way of offices with psalms, hymns, and prayers, for every day of the week, and every holiday in the year. Reformed by a person of quality[1] and published by George Hickes, D.D. The III. edition more correct than the former."*

To the reader . . . In the last edition I added three prayers; one at the end of the Lauds, and two others at the end of the Vespers of the preparatory Office for death; and in this I have added, in the margin of those prayers, directions for the commemoration of our friends or relations of any sort, natural, civil, or spiritual, whom through exemplary holiness of life or penitence before death, we believe to have departed in the peace of God. This I took upon me to do, because I think such pious commemorations are of great use . . . In a word, I think to commemorate our dead friends and relations, especially in this devout way, is an office very agreeable to the nature of true friendship and affection; though we, who survive them, are apt to forget it because we too soon forget them . . . I think myself also obliged to give the reader notice, that in this edition I have made some alterations, particularly in the Thursday office, the Office of our Saviour, and the preparatory Office for death. I made them upon reading some observations and animadversions which a judicious and learned person, I suppose a Divine, sent me with a civil letter, for which I think myself here obliged to give him thanks; and I would have given them to him by name, but that he is pleased to conceal it from me; I also presumed to make them without the privity of the devout reformer,[1] whom being at a great distance from me I could not conveniently consult . . . George Hickes.

Office for each day in the week. Office of our B. Saviour. Office for the Holy Ghost. Office for the Commemoration of Saints. Preparatory Office for death by way of commemoration of the faithful departed.

₊ *These offices are the same as those in the first edition (page 325) with the additions and alterations mentioned in the preface to this book.*

[1] Mrs. Susanna Hopton. See page 335.

Prayer at night for a family, reformed.

⁎ *This is the same as that in No. 256. first edition. A.D. 1668 (page 311). omitting "Hail Mary" and "The confession." The Litany is different. The "Gloria in excelsis" is added.*

Prayers to be said in private by persons afflicted with great melancholy. O most blessed and gracious God, who only can'st heal a wounded spirit . . . Amen. O blessed Jesus who wast made man and who in our nature tookest our infirmities . . . Amen. Soliloquy of a troubled soul. Why art thou so vexed, O my soul . . .

A.D. 1712, London, 12º. English. No. 261.

⁎ *The title is "Devotions in the ancient way of offices with psalms, hymns, and prayers, for every day in the week and every holiday in the year. To which are added occasional offices, and other devotions in the same ancient way. Reform'd by a person of quality and publish'd by George Hickes, D.D. The ivth edition more correct than the former".*

To the reader. Know then, it consists of twelve offices; one for every day in the week, one for our Saviour's feasts, one for the Holy Ghost, one for Saints, and one for the dead, which the author of this reform hath entituled, "A preparatory office for death" and one for a family . . . In the office for a family is briefly comprehended all what relates both to the erudition and devotion of a christian family; and all the stages of human life are fitly represented, with the various dispensations of God toward mankind from the beginning to the end of all things, in order to our final and perfect restoration. And as families are founded in the society of man and woman, as first instituted by God; one main part of the service, proper for a family, turns upon a religious and useful discourse of the evil and good which have been derived to mankind by woman; being part of the reformation of the Office for the B. Virgin,[1] said to be written by the same author; and which in all the former editions was entirely left out . . . The office for a family is not confined to any time, but may indifferently be used at the discretion of the Master or Mistress thereof, upon such ordinary days when no proper service is appointed. This is the only office of the twelve which will not agree with solitary devotion, as well as with that which is social, as being calculated chiefly for the use of religious families . . . This is what I had publish'd in the former editions, being then obliged to silence, concerning the first reformer of these devotions;[2] of whom the world has now been already by me made acquainted, that it was a very devout gentlewoman of quality lately deceas'd who in her youth had been drawn away from the church of England to that of Rome; but return'd back to her first fold upon a fuller and more accurate review of the controversy betwixt the two churches; whereof a sufficient account is to be found in

---

[1] See John Austin's devotions, third ed. 1684. page 815.
[2] Mrs. Susanna Hopton. See page 335.

a letter of hers to Father Turbeville, which I have inserted in "A second collection of letters relating to the Church of England and the Church of Rome. p. 118. printed for R. Sare, 1710." under the title of "A letter written by a lady to a Romish Priest upon her return from the Church of Rome to the Church of England."[1] And in the preface to the said collection the reader may see a faithful relation concerning this honourable daughter of the Church of England . . . In this edition, there is added the greatest part of the Compline for the Office of the Holy Ghost, and the Compline for the preparatory Office for death ; also the Morning service for a family by which that Office is now made complete, that in all the former editions, both unreformed and reformed, was but half done, together with commemorations and occasionals upon most sort of emergencies of life, publick and private. In the psalms also there are made some considerable alterations and additions, and their number is increas'd from cxxxvii in the first number of the reform'd offices to cl according to the first number in the unreform'd Offices. Several new Hymns are likewise added in this edition, and even whole stanzas are supplied in some of the others which were before omitted. Moreover the prayers and collects apparently added by some other unequal hand, and wherein these offices were generally thought to be most defective, have been carefully revised and adjusted, and several new ones added where they did appear to be wanting. In the proper Offices or Commemorations for the Feasts and Fasts of the church very considerable alterations and additions have been made ; particularly a commemoration is here added for the Feast of St. Barnabas, which was wholly wanting in all the editions both reform'd and unreform'd ; that for St. John Baptist is in a manner new ; those for the Conversion of St. Paul, for St. Peter, for the Purification, and the Annunciation are much changed from what they were, and more accomodated both to the method of such offices, and to the principles and practice, both of the catholick and this particular church ; and that for any Sunday or Holy Day, when the Holy Eucharist is received, is also added for the use of devout communicants. In these that are proper for the Fasts and Vigils of the church, which are now distinguished from the former under the title of penitentials, the alterations and additions are no less considerable. Both of which in the general and particular offices for that great duty of humiliation and mortification are at first sight discernible. To these is also added a prayer to be said upon a fast before a battle, or even generally in time of war, taken from a manual of devotions printed at Lyons,[2] with a short service to be used in any imminent peril of death from what cause soever ; which last may serve for a supplement to the preparatory Office, and may be joined with any part of it as occasion shall be . . . The office

[1] See Dr. George Hickes second collection of controversial letters. 1710.
[2] See Precationes Christianæ. Lugduni. Joannes Frellonius. ed. 1548. page 250. and ed. 1586. Argentinæ. (Brit. Mus. C. 53. a. 36. page 169[b.])

for a family[1] is intended for the benefit of families; to be used, as has been said, at discretion, but more especially at the seasons of Advent and Lent, and upon days of particular commemoration for obtaining a blessing upon the family; as upon the anniversary day of marriage, or upon the first settlement of the married couple in any habitation, or upon the birth of every child in it, and the like. This office is not altogether in the method of the former; and is of a more general extent with respect both to time and persons; and it consists of no more than two parts or Morning and Evening prayer; whereas all the rest have four, each of which also may be abridg'd by the head of the family, observing but the rules laid down in the office itself . . . George Hickes.

Office for each day in the week. Office of our B. Saviour. Office for the Holy Ghost. Office for the Commemoration of Saints. Preparatory office for death by way of commemoration of the faithful departed.

. *These offices are the same as in the first ed. (page 325), with the additions mentioned in the preface to this book.* "*Nunc Dimittis*" *as well as Ps. 134.* "*Ecce nunc*" *are said at Sunday Compline.*

Office for a family. Morning prayer for a family. Evening prayer for a family.

. *This office is composed of psalms of an original composition with antiphons, hymns, lessons, collects, and a litany; it is fuller than* "*Prayer at night for a family, reformed.*" *in the third ed. A.D. 1706. (page 329); it has a form of morning prayer, as well as a form of evening prayer; an account of this office is given in the preface to this book.*

Commemorations. For the church. For the civil state. For all conditions of men. For enemies. For friends and natural relations. For the saints.

. *Each commemoration consists of an antiphon, V and R. and a collect.*

The Litany or general supplication to be said after Morning prayer; chiefly upon the days of fasting and humiliation, upon Trinity Sunday, and upon the Feasts of our blessed Saviour, and the Holy Ghost, and some of the Saints days; or according as discretion or devotion shall prompt, omitting the Commemorations which go before.

. *This Litany is of an original composition.*

Occasionals. To be used just before or after the daily commemorations. In time of mortality. When a member of the family is; Sick. Recovered. Deceased. Dearth. In time of war. Persecution.

. *Each of these devotions consist of an Antiphon, V and R. and a collect. Collects are added to be used as discretion shall direct.*

Festivals. Sundays in Advent. St. Andrew. St. Thomas the Apostle. Christmas-day. St. Stephen's day. St. John Evangelist. Holy Innocents. New-Year's day. Twelfth day. Conversion of St Paul. The Purification or Candlemas. St. Matthias. The Annunciation.

---

[1] See page 322, The protestant monastery containing directions for the religious conduct of a family. A.D. 1698.

Easter-day. Easter Monday and Tuesday, and all Sundays after until the Ascension. St. Mark Evangelist. St. Philip and James. Ascension Day. Whitsunday. Whit-Monday and Tuesday. Trinity Sunday. St. Barnabas. St. John Baptist. St. Peter. St. James. St. Bartholomew. St. Matthew. St. Michael and all Angels. St. Luke. St. Simon and Jude. All Saints. Proper for any Holy day or Sunday when the Holy Sacrament is received.

₀ *Each of these devotions consists of an Invitatory, Antiphon, V and R. and collect: the alterations and additions made to them are described in the preface.*

Penitentials or Invitatories, Antiphons, and Collects to be used on the fasts and vigils of the church; and all times of humiliations publick or private. General. Particular. Proper in Lent. First day of Lent called Ash-Wednesday. Passion Sunday. Palm Sunday. Holy Week. Maunday-Thursday. Good Friday. Holy Saturday. Fasting-eves. Ember-days. Rogation-days. Advent. On Wednesdays and Fridays.

₀ *Each of these devotions consists of an invitatory, an antiphon, V and R. and a collect; these devotions are referred to in the preface.*

A collect to be said in the time of war. Taken out of a latin Manual of prayers, which was printed at Lions, under the reign of Francis I when he was in war with the Emperour Charles V. Use this before a battel. Omnipotent king of hosts, the Lord of Sabaoth, who by thy angels for that end appointed doth administer both war and peace . . . Amen.

Proper in perils either at sea or land. O Saviour of the world, who by thy cross . . . In the midst of life . . . O spare me a little . . . O God make speed to save me. O Lord make haste to help me . . . Amen. Our Father. Lord help or we perish . . . Amen. If there be opportunity, here repeat, in faith, the XCIst. Psalm.[1]

A.D. 1765, Edinburgh, 12º. English. No. 261.

₀ *The title is " Devotions in the ancient way of offices, with psalms, hymns, and prayers for every day of the week, and every holiday in the year. To which are added occasional offices and other devotions in the same ancient way. Reformed by a person of quality and published by George Hickes, D.D."*

Advertisement. It is a common observation, and but too just; that errors increase in proportion to the number of editions made of a book . . . This consideration induced the present editors to seek for an old edition of these sublime devotions, and they had the good fortune to procure a copy of the fourth printed in 1712, while Dr. Hickes was yet alive. By carefully comparing every proof sheet of this edition with that of 1712, several errors have been corrected, some of them of importance. Two of these shall be pointed out as a specimen. In all the later editions, a

---

[1] See Precationes christianæ, Lugduni. Joannes Frellonius. ed. 1548. page 250. and ed. 1536. Argentinæ. (Brit. Mus. C. 53. a. 86. page 169[b].)

passage in the prayer when a sick member of a family is recovered, which begins p. 558. l. 20. runs thus: "Make therefore the thoughts he had in his health . . . now to pursue close that one necessary work," which is evidently neither sense nor grammar. This passage is now restored to its original correctness. The versicle "This day we have seen," p. 620. l. 6. 7. is altogether wanting in the later editions. And with respect to arrangement: upon the authority of an Erratum marked in the afore-mentioned edition 1712, the prayers appointed to be read when a member of the family is sick, recovered, or deceased, which are the last of the Commemorations in other editions, are in this put among the Occasionals. The editors therefore hope that this will be found the most correct edition extant of the book. Edinburgh, December 1764.

A SUMMARY OF THE CONTENTS
OF
A COLLECTION OF MEDITATIONS AND DEVOTIONS PUBLISHED BY N. SPINCKES.

ONE EDITION.

A.D. 1717.

A.D. 1717, London, 8º. English. No. 263.

₊ The title is "*A collection of meditations and devotions in three parts. I. Meditations on the creation. II. Meditations and devotions on the life of Christ. III. Daily devotions and thanksgivings, &c. By the first reformer of the devotions in the ancient way of offices; afterwards reviewed and set forth by the late learned Dr. Hickes. Published by N. Spinckes. M.A.*"

The preface.   Though I am not desirous to detain the reader with any long preamble, concerning the following meditations and devotions; I cannot but think it necessary however, to present him with some short account, both of the author of these religious and truly christian remains, and of the work itself.   The author of them was Mrs. Susanna Hopton, a person of quality, estate, and figure in her country; the ingeniously inquisitive, and truly devout and pious relict of Richard Hopton, Esq.; who had been one of the Welsh Judges in the reigns of King Charles II., and King James II.; his seat was at Kington in Herefordshire; and here she lived divers years after his death . . . She was the first reformer of the devotions in the ancient way of offices[1] sent up to the singularly learned and truly reverend Dr. Hickes, now with God; and by him review'd, improved, and communicated to the publick. . . . The reverend Mr. Theophilus Dorrington gives this account of that collection of offices as reformed by himself in his epistle dedicatory,[2] that it's beauty is not concealed and disguised by too much external ornament, nor exposed to contempt by too little, but it is fitted to possess mens minds with that pure and peacable wisdom which is from above . . . And the great and good man before mentioned, the late Dean of Worcester, thinks it, as it since appears, a just pattern for christian devotion in all it's offices[3] . . . Nor did Mrs. Hopton employ herself only in

---

[1] See Devotions in the ancient way of offices No. 256 A.D. 1668. page 311 and No. 261. A.D. 1700. page 325.
[2] See page 317.   [3] See page 325.

meditations and devotions, but in the argumentative way too. A very remarkable evidence whereof she has given in her controversy betwixt the Church of England and that of Rome[1] . . . Nor are these all the works of hers, that have been formerly published, though all that bear her name. For there was a piece of devotion which now makes a part of these remains, that was printed in 1673 for Jonathan Edwin, entituled " Daily devotions, consisting of thanksgivings, confessions and prayers by an humble penitent "[2] . . . This little book met with such reception, that by the year 1703, it had a fifth edition, and there the title runs thus " The humble penitent or daily devotions, consisting of thanksgivings, confessions, and prayers, with a preparatory exercise for a good death, to which is added the Sacrifice of a devout christian, or preparations to the worthy receiving of the blessed Sacrament by a Reverend divine of the Church of England." Where the preface to the reader begins with these words; "The following meditations, praises, prayers and confessions were the devotions of a most learned and pious divine of the Church of England." But the late learned and pious Mr. Dean Hickes assures us, in his "Preface to the reader" of his second collection of controversial letters, that this venerable and excellent gentlewoman was the true author of these devotions, as she herself owned to him . . .[3] They are now restored to the right owner, and together with a preparatory office for the blessed Sacrament, of which I shall give an account in its proper place, make up the last part of these remains . . . "The Sacrifice of a devout christian, or his preparation for a reception of the Blessed Sacrament" which going along with the "Daily devotions;" and no other author being named for it, but on the contrary being put into my hand as Mrs. Hopton's, I over easily believed it to be hers . . . but looking over Dr. Hicke's preface to his "Second collection of letters," I find that he attests the contrary from her mouth . . .

Meditations in the six days of the creation.

Meditations and devotions upon the life of Christ. On the incarnation. On the nativity. On the circumcision. On the epiphany. Of Christ's presentation in the temple. Purification of the Virgin and the presentation of our Saviour in the temple. Of our Saviour's flight into Egypt. Our Saviour's return out of Egypt to Nazareth. Our Saviour's disputation with the Doctors in the Temple where his Mother, after three days' seeking, found him. Of our Saviour's return from Jerusalem to Nazareth, and of his concealed life there. Our Saviour's inauguration into his priestly office. Of Christ's retirement to the desert. Of Christ's temptation and fasting. Of our Saviour's manifestation of himself to the world. Christ's sermon on the Mount. On the Lord's prayer.

[1] See page 331.
[2] See. Daily devotions by an humble penitent. (Brit. Mus. 3408. a. 11. (2) ed. 1673.)
[3] See Dr. George Hickes second collection of controversial letters. ed. 1710.

Christ's sermon on the Mount. Christ's preaching, works, and miracles. On the Sacrament. On Judas treachery after the sacrament. Reflections upon our Saviour's sermon after the Sacrament, before his passion. John 14. On our Saviour's prayer. John 17. Christ's passion. Christ's burial. Of Christ's descent into hell. Applicatory prayers upon the merits of our Saviour. Christ's resurrection. Promise of the Holy Ghost. Christ's Ascension. Of the coming of the Holy Ghost.

Daily devotions consisting of thanksgivings, confessions, and prayers with a preparative exercise to a good death;[1] to which is added, The sacrifice of a devout christian or his preparation for, and reception of the blessed Sacrament.[2] Devotions and meditations to be used as we go to church. I was glad when they said unto me let us go to the house of the Lord. Psal. 122. 1 . . . But oh, do thou deliver me, and be merciful to my sins for thy name's sake. Psal. 79. 9. Devotions in the church. O most holy God, who art glorious in holiness . . . Amen. After church. I praise and magnify thy great and glorious name . . . Devotions comprising all our duties. O Lord, hear my prayer, and let my cry come unto thee . . . Paraphrase upon the objective Hymn of praise. O my God, do all thy works praise thee and shall not I . . . Thanksgivings for all persons and times. Blessed art thou, O Lord God, who sustainest all things . . . Amen. Hymn to Jesus, wherein the soul may expatiate itself with delight in him. Jesus, the only thought of thee, Fills with delight my memory . . . Prayer for the third Hour. O blessed Jesus, seeing the third hour was devoted to thee by the ancient christians . . . Prayer to the Holy Ghost out of St. Augustine. O love of the divine power, the holy communication of the omnipotent Lord and Father . . . Amen. Prayer for the sixth Hour. O blessed Jesus, I now commemorate thy holy sufferings for me . . . Amen. Prayers for the ninth Hour. O blessed Jesus, I come now to commemorate thy holy death . . . Additional devotions for the evening. O blessed Jesus, by the eye of faith I now behold thee dead upon the cross for me . . . Compline or prayer before bed-time. Having now, dearest Lord, passed this day in health and safety . . . Amen. Prayer for Lent. Most holy and ever blessed Lord Jesus, who did'st fast forty days and forty nights . . . Amen. Daily thanksgiving. I praise thee for electing me before all time . . . Amen. Prayer for Christmas-day. Holy Jesus, who being infinitely higher than the heavens . . . Amen. Prayer for Easter-day. Eternal Son of the eternal Father, who wast a man of sorrows . . . Amen. Prayer upon the Day of Pentecost. O Lord, my light, my life and confidence, my love . . . Amen. Confession of sin. I confess, O Lord, that I was shapen in wickedness . . . Deprecations. O Lord rebuke me not in thy wrath, Cast me not off for ever . . . Intercessions for all

---

[1] See Daily devotions, by an humble penitent. (Brit. Mus. 3408. a. 11. (2) ed. 1673.)

[2] See The humble penitent or daily devotions. To which is added: The sacrifice of a devout christian. 5 ed. 1703.

mankind. I beseech thee, O Lord, for the conversion of Turks, Jews and Heathens . . . A christian's dedication of himself unto God. I that am a wretched sinner, here personally appearing . . . Prayer for acceptation of acts of humiliation or abstinence on fasting days. Lord Jesus, who both by thy word and thine own example hast taught us to deny ourselves . . . Amen. Evening thoughts and exercises before going to bed. The advice. Do not dare to go to bed in such a state with such a conscience in which you do not dare to die . . . Amen. Prayer to be used after the foregoing examination. O Lord, the author and giver of all good things, whose mercies are over all thy works . . . Amen. Prayer against affliction. Heavenly Father, be with us in all our streights and misfortunes . . . Amen. Brief soliloquy by way of admonition. Forasmuch as the violence of sickness, which ordinarily goes before death . . . Exercise preparative to a good death, consisting of several Acts of piety. 1. Submission to the sentence of death. O Lord my God, in most profound humility of soul and body . . . Amen. 2. Having accepted the sentence of death . . . Gracious God, the fountain of all goodness and all graces . . . Amen. 3. After thanksgiving for all benefits . . . Lord God who did'st make me for nothing else but to serve thee . . . Amen. 4. A prayer to die to sin. Lord Jesus Christ, who did'st die for me . . . Amen. 5. A petition for the virtues of the dying Jesus. Lord Jesus teach me when the time of my dissolution shall come . . . Amen. And now, my Lord, my Saviour, and my all, as having nothing . . . Amen.

The sacrifice of a devout christian, or his preparation for and reception of the blessed Sacrament.[1] Every good christian is presumed to understand that it is his indispensable duty, not only to appear as oft as he can at the Lord's table, but also to behave himself there with all the fervour and devotion that may be . . .

Preparation. The best and most effectual preparation for this sacrament is a holy life . . . Articles of self-examination preparatory to the receiving of the Blessed Sacrament. Examination upon the first commandment. Dost thou steadfastly believe there is a God . . . Prayer of humiliation and confession to be used before our approaches to the Holy Table. O eternal God, the supporter of all our hopes, our comfort in time of trouble, our life in death . . . Amen. Ejaculations immediately before your going to the Holy Table. O Lord I am not fit, nor worthy that thou shouldest come under the filthy roof of the house of my soul . . . Amen. At your approach to the Holy Table. Lord, I am not worthy, by reason of my sins, to appear before thee . . . Before receiving (out of the Liturgy). Grant, O most merciful Father, that I receiving these thy creatures . . . Amen. When thou givest thine alms. Here, O blessed Jesus, I give to thee, and to thy members for thee . . . Amen. When

---

[1] See The humble penitent or daily devotion. To which is added; The sacrifice of a devout christian. 5 ed. 1703.

you see the Bread broken. O vile wretch that I am, that I by my sins . . . When the Minister comes to distribute. Christ with the benefit of his death doth now come to sanctify . . . Adding with the Minister. The body of our Lord Jesus Christ . . . Amen. While you eat the bread. Blessed Jesus I do heartily believe that thou wast crucified on the cross . . . Immediately before receiving the cup. O blessed Jesus, let the blood that ran from thy blessed heart wash my soul . . . Adding with the Minister. The blood of our Lord Jesus Christ . . . After receiving the cup. It is finished, blessed be the name of our gracious God . . . Thanksgiving at home after the holy Communion. Blessed art thou, O Lord God, and blessed be thy holy name for ever . . . Amen. Another shorter thanksgiving after the communion. I give thee hearty thanks, O most merciful Saviour, for thine ineffable love . . . Amen. Brief recommendation of oneself to God. Into the hands of thy ineffable mercy, O Lord, I recommend my soul . . . Amen. The devout penitent's close of all. Let this day, O my God, be noted in thy book . . . Some farther directions how to demean yourselves before, and at the holy Communion. God being the majesty whom sin offends, of him pardon is to be sought. A hymn. Sweet Jesus why, why dost thou love Such worthless things as we . . .

A SUMMARY OF THE CONTENTS
OF
THOMAS DEACON'S PRIMITIVE METHOD OF DAILY PRIVATE PRAYER.

TWO EDITIONS.
A.D. 1734—A.D. 1747.

A.D. 1734, London. 8º. English.

⁎ *The title has "A compleat collection of devotions both Publick and Private. In two Parts. Part I. comprehending the publick Offices of the church taken from the apostolical constitutions, the ancient Liturgies, and the Common Prayer Book of the Church of England . . . Part II. Being a primitive method of daily private prayer, containing devotions for the morning and evening, and for the ancient Hours of prayer, Nine, Twelve, and Three; together with Hymns and Thanksgivings for the Lord's day and Sabbath; and prayers for Fasting days; as also, Devotions for the Altar, and Graces before and after meat. All taken from the apostolical constitutions and the ancient Liturgies, with some additions; and recommended to the practice of all private Christians of every communion."*

Advertisement. The publisher of these papers is not so sanguine as to imagine; that such a collection of devotions as the preceding, though unexceptionable because primitive and apostolical, will be acceptable to, or admitted into publick use by the present christian churches, which are unhappily prepossessed with such strong prejudices and miserably over-run with so many modern corruptions. However, till they can be so truly reformed as to be perfectly free from all novelty, and entirely conformable to antiquity, universality, and consent, which would be matter of rejoicing to all good men, and of terror to the wicked; that the Publisher might render his design as universally serviceable as possible, he has accomodated those parts of the foregoing devotions as are taken out of the apostolical constitutions (not of all them indeed, most of them however, at least as many as he conveniently could) to private use in this second part; which he earnestly recommends to the practice of all pious christians of every communion. He likewise takes this opportunity of advising the devout christian to follow the excellent counsel of Mr. Law in his "Serious call to a devout and holy life." p. 244 "If you was to use yourself (as far as you can) to pray always in the same place; if you was to reserve that place for devotion, and not allow yourself to do anything common in it, if you was never to be there your self, but in times of devotion; if any little room (or if that cannot be) if any particular part of a room was thus used; this kind of consecration of it, as a place holy unto God, would have an effect upon your mind, and dispose you to such tempers, as would very much assist your devotion.

For by having a place thus sacred in your room, it would in some measure resemble a chapel or house of God. This would dispose you to be always in the spirit of religion, when you was there; and fill you with wise and holy thoughts, when you was by your self. Your own apartment would raise in your mind such sentiments as you have when you stand near an altar, and you would be afraid of thinking or doing anything that was foolish near that place which is the place of prayer and holy intercourse with God."

Devotions for the morning.

₊ *These devotions consist of, Prayers at waking and first rising; then A form of morning prayer consisting of. In the name. Lord have mercy upon me. Ejaculation. Introit, composed of verses of the psalms. Hymn, Glory be to God in the highest . . . Intercession. Thanksgiving. Prayer for benediction. and Conclusion.*

Devotions for the evening.

₊ *These devotions consist of, Introduction. In the name. Lord have mercy upon me. Ejaculation. Introit composed of verses of the psalms aud texts of holy Scripture. Hymn, O Jesus Christ, thou joyful light of the sacred glory of the immortal . . . Intercession. Thanksgiving. Prayer for benediction. Conclusion.*

Note, great part of the foregoing devotions for the morning and evening being taken out of the Apostolical constitutions, and therefore the same with part of the Morning and Evening prayer prescribed above[1] in the publick Offices of the church; those persons who have the comfort and advantage of joining in the said publick offices, may use the following method in their private devotions. They may begin and proceed, according to the directions given in the devotions for the morning and evening, till they come to the hymn, and instead of those there prescribed, they may use the following.

₊ *Then follows Morning Hymn. Holy, Holy, Holy, Lord God almighty . . . Evening Hymn. O Jesus Christ, thou joyful light . . . and an Intercession.*

The Evening intercession may be the same with that which stands in the Devotions for the evening; and after the intercession they may use Bishop Andrew's private devotions, or any other that they like best; ending with the Lord's prayer and the conclusion, as before prescribed in the Devotions for the Morning and Evening.

Devotions for the ancient Hours of prayer. At nine in the morning. At twelve at noon. At three after noon.

₊ *Each of these devotions consists of: The Introduction, as in the Devotions for the Morning and Evening : then an Ejaculation, and prayers : the following words occur before the end of each Hour.*

On Sundays and every day between Easter and Pentecost; on Whitsunday, Monday and Tuesday in Whitsun-week; and on Christmas day; here shall follow the Hymn and proper Preface. On Mondays, Tuesdays and Thursdays, except in Holy week, and the week before, and except

---

[1] Part 1. of this book.

between Easter and Pentecost, and except Monday and Tuesday in Whitsun-week, here shall follow an Act of glorification of God. On Wednesdays, except between Easter and Pentecost, and on Monday, Tuesday, and Thursday in Holy week and the week before, here shall follow one of the Collects for Wednesdays; and on Fridays, except as above excepted, and on Easter eve, here shall follow one of the Collects for Fridays. And after the Collect on all the days above mentioned shall follow one of the prayers for Fasting days, and then one of the Penitential prayers. On all Saturdays, except that next before Easter, here shall follow one of the Thanksgivings for the Sabbath.

₊ *Each Hour ends with the following devotions.*

Prayer. O almighty God, Father of thy Christ thine only begotten Son, give me a body undefiled, a pure heart and a watchful mind . . . Amen. Then say the Lord's prayer, and end with the conclusion, as in the devotions for the morning and evening.

The Hymn with the Proper prefaces.[1] It is very meet . . . Here shall follow the Proper preface. Upon all Sundays, except the Sunday after Ascension day and Whitsunday, and upon every day between Easter and Ascension day. But chiefly am I bound to praise thee . . . Upon Ascension day and every day till after Whitsunday. Through thy most dearly beloved son Jesus Christ our Lord . . . Upon Whitsunday, and Monday and Tuesday in Whitsun-week. Through Jesus Christ our Lord, according to whose most true promise . . . Upon Christmas-day. Because thou dids't give Jesus Christ thine only Son . . . After the Preface shall follow. Therefore with angels . . .

Acts of glorification of God.

₊ *Then follow three Acts.*

Collects for Wednesdays. Collects for Fridays.

₊ *Each group consists of three collects.*

Prayers for Fasting-days.

₊ *Then follow three devotions. Each one consisting of a prayer, then a text of Holy Scripture in the form of a V. and R. and then another prayer.*

Penitential prayers.

₊ *Then follow three prayers.*

Note, the devout christian may easily accomodate to his private use the Penitential Office prescribed above among the publick Offices of the Church,[1] beginning with the following sentences of Scripture instead of those there ordered. O Lord correct me but with judgment . . . Jer. x. 24. I will arise and go to my father . . . S. Luke. xv. 18. 19. Immediately before the Confession the following Suffrages may be added. Have mercy upon me, O Lord for I am weak . . . After the prayer of Absolution may be added as followeth. Have mercy upon me, O Lord, have mercy upon me; for my soul trusteth in thee . . .

---

[1] See Book of Common prayer. A.D. 1662.   [2] Part I. of this book.

Thanksgivings for the Sabbath.

⁎ *Then follow three thanksgivings.*

Devotions to be used in the church. Before Morning and Evening service, and the Penitential office. O thou that hearest prayer . . . After Morning and Evening service, and the Penitential office. Grant I beseech thee, almighty God, that the words which I have heard this day . . . Amen.

Devotions for the altar. Before the Eucharistick service. To be said by the officiating Priest. I thank thee, O Lord, thou God of all powers . . . Amen. To be said by any other but the officiating Priest. The Lord hear thee. The name of the God of Jacob defend thee . . . O Lord, send forth thy power from thy high and lofty habitation . . . Amen. After the Nicene Creed. To be said by the officiating Priest. O God who art great in name . . . To be said by any other but the officiating priest. Merciful Saviour at this most noble and pious mystery . . . When you put your offering into the basin. I offer thee thine own out of thine own, O God . . . Amen. At the placing the offerings in the basin upon the altar. We offer thee thine own out of thine own . . . When the Priest washes his hands he may say. I will wash mine hands in innocency, O Lord . . . While the Priest is washing his hands, and he or the Deacon mixes the wine and water. Blessed art thou, O Christ our God, the Saviour of thy church, who through thy incomprehensible incarnation . . . O God who dids't wonderfully create the dignity of human nature . . . Amen. At the placing the elements upon the altar. We offer thee thine own out of thine own . . . After the placing the elements upon the altar, when the Priest is to pray secretly for a short space. To be said by the officiating Priest. O God, our God, who has sent our Lord and God Jesus Christ, the heavenly bread . . . Amen. No one immersed in carnal lusts and pleasures is worthy to approach . . . Amen. To be said by any other but the officiating Priest. O God, our God, who has sent our Lord and God Jesus Christ, the heavenly bread . . . Amen. Glory be to thee, O Christ our God, thou art our High-Priest . . . Amen. When the Priest signs himself with the sign of the cross upon the forehead, do you do the same, saying. God forbid that I should glory . . . Before communicating, to be said both by the officiating Priest, and others. Lord Jesus, I believe and confess, that thou art the Christ . . . Lord, I am not worthy that thou should'st come under the filthy roof of the house of my soul . . . Attend, O Lord Jesus Christ my God, from thy habitation . . . O Lord my God and Saviour, do thou teach me to render thee worthy praise for all the benefits . . . O Lord grant that though I am in myself most unworthy . . . Amen. Just before communicating. Lord, I believe help thou my unbelief . . . Before receiving the cup. What reward shall I give unto the Lord . . . At drinking of the cup. In the name of the Father . . . After receiving the cup. This hath touched my lips, and it will take away mine iniquities . . . After communicating. I have now, O Christ my God, finished

344   SUMMARY OF CONTENTS.   [1734-

and perfected according to my ability, the mystery of thy dispensation . . . I thank thee, O Lord my God, for admitting me to partake of thy holy, precious, and heavenly mysteries . . . Thou hast sanctified me, O Lord, by making me a partaker of the most holy body and precious blood of thine only begotten Son . . . Amen. After the Eucharistick Service. To be said by the officiating Priest. O God, great and wonderful, look upon us thy servants . . . Amen. To be said by any other but the officiating Priest. O God, great and wonderful, look upon me thy servant . . . Amen.

An office for the use of those who, by reason that the Holy Eucharist is not publickly celebrated in the church, communicate daily in private of the consecrated Eucharistick elements, which were reserved at the publick Communion.

Begin with the introduction as in the devotions for the morning and evening. Then say or sing standing. I will lift up my heart unto the Lord . . . Holy, Holy, Holy, Lord God of Sabaoth . . . Then say standing. I thank thee, O Father, for the life which thou hast revealed unto us by thy son Jesus . . . Then say the following prayer kneeling. O Lord and heavenly father, according to the institution of thy dearly beloved Son our Saviour Jesus Christ, I thy humble servant do celebrate . . . Amen. Then say the following prayer of intercession. Almighty and ever living God, who by thy holy apostle has taught us . . . Amen. Then say the Lord's prayer. Our Father. Then say the following prayers. I do not presume to come to this thy table . . . Amen. Lord Jesus, I believe and confess that thou art the Christ . . . Lord I am not worthy that thou should'st come under the filthy roof of the house of my soul . . . Attend, O Lord Jesus Christ my God, from thy habitation . . . O Lord, my God and Saviour, do thou teach me to render thee worthy praise for all the benefits . . . O Lord, grant that though I am of myself most unworthy . . . Amen. Then just before you communicate, say. Lord, I believe, help thou my unbelief . . . I believe that thy flesh is meat indeed . . . Let then thy body, O Lord Jesus Christ . . . Then receive the Sacrament of the body of Christ with reverence and devotion, saying. The body of Christ. Amen. Before you receive the cup, say. What reward shall I give unto the Lord . . . I believe that thy blood is drink indeed . . . Therefore I will feed on thy flesh . . . Let then thy blood, O Lord Jesus Christ . . . Then receive the sacrament of the blood of Christ with reverence and devotion, saying. The blood of Christ, the cup of life. Amen. While you drink of the cup, say within yourself. In the name of the Father . . . Amen. After you have received the cup, say. This hath touched my lips . . . Amen. After you have communicated, say the following thanksgivings. I have now, O Christ my God, finished and perfected, according to my ability, the mystery of thy dispensation . . . I thank thee, O Lord my God, for admitting me to partake of thy holy, precious, and heavenly mysteries . . . Thou hast

-1734]   PRIVATE PRAYER, T. DEACON.   345

sanctified me, O Lord, by making me a partaker of the most holy body and precious blood of thine only begotten Son . . . Almighty and ever living God, I most heartily thank thee for that thou hast vouchsafed to feed me with the most precious body and blood of thy Son our Saviour Jesus Christ . . . Amen. O God, great and wonderful, look upon me thy servant . . . Amen. Then end with the conclusion, as in the devotions for the Morning and Evening.

Commemoration of the dead. If you would commemorate any of the faithful departed in a solemn and particular manner, let it be done with almsgiving on the third, ninth, and fortieth days after the person's decease; and on the anniversary day of his or her death. In all the offices wherein you pray for the dead, on those days particularize the name of no one but the person whom you would commemorate. If the Eucharist be celebrated publickly on any of those days; before you communicate use the following prayers, omitting those above prescribed in the devotions for the altar to be said before communicating; unless there be time sufficient for them all. If you have the Eucharist reserved at home, use the foregoing office for private daily communicants; adding the following prayers immediately after the Prayer of intercession. But if you have no opportunity of receiving the Eucharist on those days; then add the following prayers to your private Morning and Evening devotions immediately after the intercession. The prayers. O thou, who art by nature immortal and everlasting, from whom everything mortal and immortal deriveth its being . . . Amen. O merciful God, father of our Lord Jesus Christ, who is the resurrection and the life . . . Amen.

Graces before and after meat. Grace before meat. Blessed art thou, O Lord, who hast fed us from our youth . . . Amen. Grace after meat. Glory be to thee, O Lord, glory be to thee, O holy king . . . Amen.

Instead of Bishop Andrews's, or any other private devotions, I conceive the following will be long enough for those who frequent the morning and evening prayer prescribed above in the publick offices of the church.[1] For the morning. I return thee my humble and hearty thanks, O Lord God, for thy preservation of me the night past . . . Father, forgive me the sins of the night past . . . Amen. O merciful God, preserve me from all sin and danger this day . . . Amen. Lord as thou hast awaked my body from sleep, so by thy grace awaken my soul from sin . . . Amen. Visit, I beseech thee, O Lord, this habitation; and drive far away all snares of the enemy . . . Amen. For the evening. I return thee my humble and hearty thanks, O Lord God, for thy preservation of me the day past . . . Father, forgive me the sins of the day past . . . Amen. O merciful God, preserve me from all sin and danger this night . . . Amen. O blessed Lord, the keeper of Israel, who neither slumberest nor sleepest . . . Amen. Visit, I beseech thee, O Lord, this habitation; and drive far away all snares of the enemy . . . Amen.

[1] Part I. of this book.

A.D. 1747, London, 8º. English.

⁎ The title is "*Devotions to be used by primitive Catholicks at church and at home. In two parts. Liverpool. Printed by J. Sadler in Harrington St. M.DCC.XLVII. Devotions to be used by primitive Catholicks at church. Part I. Printed in the year. M.DCC.XLVII.*"

⁎ Part I ends on Page 91, line 3. Sign H3. with the words "*or charitable uses, according to the direction of the Bishop*": it contains the private devotions to be used at the "*Office of the holy Liturgy*" from Part II. ed. 1734,[1] also "*A Litany for the use of those who mourn for the iniquities of the present times, and tremble at the prospect of impending judgments*";[2] together with "*Prayers in behalf of the Catholick church, and particularly of that part of it belonging to these kingdoms*":[2] and "*The form of admitting a convert into the communion of the church*".[2]

⁎ Part II of this book is not known.

[1] See page 340.   [2] See Brit. Mus. 3407. c. 3. ed. 1746.

A SUMMARY OF THE CONTENTS

OF THE

PRIMER OR OFFICE OF THE BLESSED VIRGIN MARY,

IN WHICH THE HOURS ARE IN LATIN, LATIN AND ENGLISH, OR ENGLISH,

ACCORDING TO

THE REFORMED LATIN OF THE ROMAN USE.

A.D. 1571—A.D. 1844.

EXPLANATIONS.

1. A summary of all the contents of No. 266, A.D. 1571 is given, because it is the first edition of the "Officium B. Mariæ Virginis" of the Roman use; revised by Pius V., according to the bull "Superni omnipotentis," published. A.D. 1571, April 14. Some of the contents of the following editions of the Pian revision are also given; namely of that of A.D. 1573: of A.D. 1607 "Cum Kalendario Gregoriano a Sixto PP. V. et S. D. N. Clemente VIII. Pont. Max. aliquot Sanctorum festis aucto": of A.D. 1627 "Cum indulgentiis et orationibus a Clemente VIII, ordinatis. Cum Kalendario Gregoriano:" of A.D. 1644. "Ad instar Breviarii Romani sub Urbano VIII recogniti. Cum indulgentiis": of c. A.D. 1687. "Ad instar Breviarii Romani sub Urbano VIII recogniti cum indulgentiis, orationibus, hymnis, et hujusmodi aliis."

2. A summary of all the contents of No. 267. A.D. 1599 is given, as a standard of comparison of the Primers in English and Latin, and in English; which followed the Pian revision.

3. The Primers in English and Latin, in English, and in Latin with rubricks in english fall into the following groups. (1) Those which have a preface by Richard Verstegen: they are No. 267. A.D. 1599. No. 268. A.D. 1604. No. 278. A.D. 1633. No. 280. A.D. 1650. and No. 281. A.D. 1658. (2) Those with or without the Preface which begins "This Office of our B. Lady being with licence of Superiors, to be printed in english alone . . ." they are No. 270. A.D. 1615. No. 271. A.D. 1616. No. 272. A.D. 1617. No. 273. A.D. 1621. No. 274. A.D. 1631. No. 275. A.D. 1632. No. 276. A.D. 1632. No. 277. A.D. 1633. (3) Those which have a preface by Thomas Fitzsimon, they are No. 282. A.D. 1669. No. 284. A.D. 1684. No. 291. A.D. 1720. No. 292. A.D. 1730. (4) Those which have a preface which begins "The Primer or Office of our B. Lady here presents itself to your devotion . . ." they are No. 283. A.D. 1673. No. 285. A.D. 1685. and No. 288. A.D. 1699. (5) Those which have "A short exposition of the Primer." which begins "The Office of Our B. Lady is of great antiquity." they are No. 286. A.D. 1687. No. 289. A.D. 1706. No. 290. A.D. 1717. No. 293. A.D. 1732. No. 295. A.D. 1770. No. 296. A.D. 1780. No. 296.* A.D. 1789. No. 297. A.D. 1817. (6) Those which have both the preface which begins "The Primer or Office of Our B. Lady here presents itself to your devotion." as well as "A short exposition of the Primer." they are No. 283. A.D. 1673. No. 285. A.D.1 685. No. 288. A.D. 1699. (7) No. 297.* A.D. 1844.

4. All fresh words in the titles and all fresh devotions in the Latin, English and Latin, and English Primers or Office of the Blessed Virgin Mary are given as they occur; as well as any variation in the component parts of a devotion.

5. An index is given of the prayers, psalms and benedictions. Groups of psalms such as the seven penitential psalms, or those in the Hours are not indexed separately. Another index gives all the hymns and rhythms. A general index refers to other matters of liturgical, devotional, and general interest.

A SUMMARY OF THE CONTENTS

OF THE

PRIMER OR OFFICE OF THE BLESSED VIRGIN MARY,

IN WHICH THE HOURS ARE IN LATIN, LATIN AND ENGLISH, OR ENGLISH,

ACCORDING TO

THE REFORMED LATIN OF THE ROMAN USE.

A.D. 1571—A.D. 1844.

A.D. 1571. Rome 12º. Latin. No. 266.

*** *The title is* "*Officium B. Mariæ Virginis, nuper reformatum, et Pii V. Pont. Max. jussu editum. Cum privilegio et indulgentiis. Romæ in ædibus populi Romani. M.D.LXXI.*"

Pius Episcopus servus servorum Dei, ad perpetuam rei memoriam (Exordium). Superni omnipotentis Dei providentiæ ac benignitatis exemplo excitati, qui ut humanum genus ab errorum tenebris vindicaret, et in veritatis semitam perduceret . . . et si quæ irrepserunt protinus evellantur. (Sec. 2. Concilium Tridentinum emendari jussit Cathechismum. Breviarium, et Missale; et emendata fuerunt). Cum itaque in executionem decretorum sacri Concilii Tridentini . . . ad pristinam sanctorum Patrum normam restituto. (Pontifex emendari postea fecit Officium B. Mariæ). Eamdem curam et operam adhiberi mandaverimus in emendando ac corrigendo gloriosissimæ Dei genitricis B. Mariæ Virginis Officio . . . Romæ imprimi, et impressum devulgari jusserimus, ut inde spiritualibus quam optamus Christi fidelium animabus proveniat consolatio. (Sec. 3. Et modo illud observari præcipit). Motu proprio, et ex certa scientia nostris, ac de Apostolicæ potestatis plenitudine; Officia quæcumque, in primis Italico, seu quovis alio vulgari idiomate et sermone quomodolibet composita; atque Officium anno proxime præterito 1570, Venetiis apud Junctas impressum, his verbis licet falso inscriptum "Officium beatæ Mariæ Virginis per Concilium Tridentinum Pio Quinto Pontifice maximo reformatum"; denique et omnia et singula alia officia hujusmodi etiam latino sermone sub Hortuli animæ seu Thesauri spiritualis compendii aut quovis alio titulo et nomine quomodolibet pervulgatum ; omnemque illorum usum approbatione apostolica ac consuetudine, et institutione (inveteratis infra dicendis semper salvis) harum nostrarum serie perpetuo, ab omnibus et singulis utriusque sexus Christi fidelibus, sæcularibus vel ecclesiasticis, etiam quorumvis Ordinum regularium, et militiarum Religiosis, qui de jure, consuetudine, usu, statuto, institutione, ac constitutionibus; etiam eorumdem Ordinum militiarum et regulæ, seu alias quomodolibet ad recitationem Officii B. Mariæ tenentur, et obligati sunt, tollimus et abolemus. (Sec. 4. Aliaque officia tollit et abolet, nisi in primæva institutione vel a consuetudine supra 200 annos approbatæ fuerint, et non sint vulgari sermone composita) Ipsisque in virtute sanctæ obedientiæ interdicimus . . . ut illud etiam in choro dicere et psallere possint permittimus. (Sec. 5. Hortatur omnes alios non obligatos recitare officium B. Mariæ, ut officio isto reformato uti velint) Ab eis vero qui ad ejusdem Officii B. Mariæ Virginis recitationem non aliqua obligatione tenentur . . . hoc nostrum officium non perlegant vel recitent. (Sec 6. Officiaque antiqua inquisitoribus con signari mandat) Ac ut ipsorum Officiorum vulgaris idiomatis et sermonis abusus re ipsa penitus aboleatur . . . consignari quam primum jubemus. (Sec 7. Officium vero reformatum, immutari non posse statuit.) Statuentes huic nostro Officio nuper edito . . . et neminem muneri suo nisi hac formula satisfacere posse. (Sec. 8. Indulgentias illud recitantibus concedit). Ac ut fidelium omnium voluntas et studium . . . recitantibus concedentur. (Sec 9. Prælatis etiam præcipit ut illud introducant.) Mandantes omnibus . . . semper salva. (Sec 10. Concionatoribus et Confessoribus idem præcipit). Concionatoribus quoque verbi Dei . . . superstitiones et errores in fide Catholica redolentia omnino delere. (Sec 11. Illudque Romæ tantum imprimi posse declarat). Quod nostrum B. Mariæ Virginis Officium . . . expressa licentia. (Sec 12 Clausulæ preservativæ). (Sec 13. Forma publicandi hanc constitutionem). (Sec. 14. Decretum irritans). (Sec 15. Clausulæ derogatoriæ). (Sec 16. Sanctio pænalis). Datum Romæ apud Sanctum Petrum, Anno Incarnationis Dominicæ millesimo quingentesimo septuagesimo, quinto Idus Martii, Pontificatus nostri anno sexto. Publicatio anno Incarnationis Dominicæ 1571, indictione 14 die vero 5 mensis Aprilis, Pontificatus Sanctissimi D.N.D. Pii divina providentia Papæ V anno 6.

Tabula litterarum dominicalium . . . Aureus numerus . . . Tabula perpetua . . . De anno et ejus partibus . . . Ex quot diebus constet unusquisque mensis . . . De numero Nonarum ac Iduum singulorum mensuum . . . Quando inchoatur Adventus domini . . . Quatuor tempora . . . Nuptiæ juxta decretum Concilii Tridentini . . . Modus inveniendi quota sit luna cujusque mensis per epactam . . . De Indictione . . .

Elucidatio Calendarii . . . Calendarius.

Institutio christiana. Symbolum apostolorum. Oratio dominica. Salutatio

angelica. Decem Dei præcepta quæ in decalogo continentur. Septem
ecclesiæ catholicæ sacramenta.   Virtutes theologicæ.   Virtutes car-
dinales.   Dona Spiritus sancti.   Fructus Spiritus sancti.   Præcepta
charitatis.   Præcepta ecclesiæ.   Opera misericordiæ, spiritualia, temporalia. Beatitudines. Quinque sensus corporis. Septem peccata
capitalia quæ communiter mortalia appellantur. Quatuor novissima
memoranda.

Passio Domini nostri Jesu Christi secundum Matthæum. Capit. 26. In illo
tempore dixit Jesus discipulis suis. Scitis quia post biduum pascha
fiet . . .

Passio Domini nostri Jesu Christi secundum Marcum. Cap. 24. In illo tempore erant Pascha et azyma post biduum . . .

Passio Domini nostri Jesu Christi secundum Lucam. Cap. 22. In illo tempore approprinquabat autem dies festus azymorum . . .

Passio Domini nostri Jesu Christi secundum Joannem. Cap. 18. In illo tempore, egressus est Jesus cum discipulis suis . . .

Officium beatæ Mariæ dicendum a die post Purificationem, usque ad Vesperas
Sabbathi ante primam Dominicam Adventus : præterquam quod in die
Annunciationis dicitur ut infra in Adventu.

Officium beatæ Mariæ dicendum a Vesperis Sabbathi ante primam Dominicam
Adventus, usque ad Vesperas Vigiliæ Nativitatis Domini, et in die
Annunciationis beatæ Mariæ.

Officium beatæ Mariæ dicendum a Vesperis Vigiliæ Nativitatis Domini, usque
ad totam diem Purificationis.

Officium Defunctorum.

Psalmi Graduales.

Septem Psalmi Pænitentiales.

Litaniæ, preces, et orationes.

Aliæ Preces et orationes dicendæ post Litanias pro diversitate temporum.
Litaniæ dicuntur usque ad Psalmum. Deus in adjutorium. Deinde.
℣. Ego dixi domine . . . ℟. Sana animam meam . . . ℣. Convertere
domine . . . ℟. Et deprecabilis . . . ℣. Fiat misericordia tua . . . ℟.
Quemadmodum . . . ℣. Sacerdotes tui . . . ℟. Et sancti tui . . . ℣.
Domine salvum . . . ℟. Et exaudi . . . ℣. Salvum fac . . . ℟. Et
rege . . . ℣. Memento congregationis tuæ. ℟. Quam possedisti
. . . ℣. Fiat pax . . . ℟. Et abundantia . . . ℣. Oremus pro fidelibus
defunctis. ℟. Requiem æternam . . . ℣. Requiescant . . . ℟. Amen.
℣. Pro fratribus nostris . . . ℟. Salvos fac . . . ℣. Pro afflictis . . .
℟. Libera eos . . . ℣. Mitte eis, domine, auxilium . . . ℟. Et de Sion
. . . ℣. Domine exaudi . . . ℟. Et clamor . . . Psalmus 78. Deus
venerunt gentes. vel Psalmus 45. Deus noster refugium. Psalmus 76.
Voce mea ad dominum. ℣. Domine Deus . . . ℟. Et ostende . . .
℣. Exurge Christe . . . ℟. Et libera . . . ℣. Domine exaudi . . . ℟. Et
clamor . . . Oremus. Ad poscenda suffragia Sanctorum. A cunctis
nos, quæsumus domine mentis et corporis defende periculis . . . Amen.

Pro ecclesia sancta Dei. Omnipotens sempiterne Deus, qui gloriam tuam ... Amen. Pro Papa. Deus omnium fidelium pastor et rector ... Amen. Pro omni gradu ecclesiæ. Omnipotens sempiterne Deus, cujus spiritu totum corpus ecclesiæ ... Amen. Pro quacunque necessitate ecclesiæ et re obtinenda. Deus refugium nostrum et virtus adesto piis ecclesiæ tuæ ... Amen. Contra persecutores ecclesiæ. Ecclesiæ tuæ, quæsumus Domine, preces placatus admitte ... Amen. Ad implorandum auxilium contra infideles. Pientissime Deus, qui iniquitatum ad te conversorum non recordaris ... Amen. Pro Imperatore. Deus regnorum omnium et christiani maxime protector imperii ... Amen. Pro Rege. Quæsumus omnipotens Deus ut famulus tuus N Rex noster ... Amen. Pro Catechumenis. Omnipotens sempiterne Deus, qui ecclesiam tuam nova semper prole ... Amen. Ut cunctis mundum purget erroribus. Omnipotens sempiterne Deus, mæstorum consolatio ... Amen. Pro hæreticis et schismaticis. Omnipotens sempiterne Deus, qui salvas omnes ... Amen. Pro perfidis Judæis. Omnipotens sempiterne Deus, qui etiam Judaicam perfidiam ... Amen. Pro paganis. Omnipotens sempiterne Deus, qui non mortem peccatorum sed vitam semper inquiris ... Amen. Tempore belli. Deus qui conteris bella et impugnatores ... Amen. Contra paganos. Omnipotens sempiterne Deus in cujus manu sunt omnium potestates ... Amen. Pro pace. Deus a quo sancta desideria, recta consilia ... Amen. Tempore famis et pestis. Da nobis quæsumus Domine, piæ supplicationis effectum ... Amen. Ad pluviam petendam. Deus in quo vivimus, movemur, et sumus ... Amen. Ad serenitatem petendam. Ad te nos Domine clamantes exaudi, et aeris serenitatem ... Amen. Pro quacunque tribulatione. Ne despicias, omnipotens Deus, populum tuum in afflictione clamantem ... Amen. Pro remissione peccatorum. Deus qui nullum respuis, sed quantumvis peccantibus ... Amen. Pro tentatis et tribulatis. Deus qui justificas impium, et non vis mortem peccatorum ... Amen. Pro iter agentibus. Adesto Domine supplicationibus nostris, et viam ... Amen. Pro infirmis. Omnipotens sempiterne Deus, salus æterna credentium ... Amen. Pro tribulatione peccatorum. Ineffabilem nobis Domine misericordiam tuam clementer ostende ... Amen. Pro peccatis. Exaudi quæsumus Domine supplicum preces ... Amen. Pro salute vivorum. Prætende Domine fidelibus tuis dexteram cælestis auxilii ... Amen. Pro vivis et defunctis. Omnipotens sempiterne Deus, qui vivorum dominaris ... Amen. ℣. Domine exaudi ... ℟. Et clamor ... ℣. Exaudiat nos ... ℟. Et custodiat nos ... Amen.

Preces dicendæ in principio congregationis. Veni sancte Spiritus reple tuorum corda fidelium ... Kyrie eleyson. Pater noster. ℣. Memento congregationis tuæ. ℟. Quam possedisti ... ℣. Domine exaudi ... ℟. Et clamor ... Oremus. Mentes nostras quæsumus Domine lumine tuæ claritatis illustra ... Amen.

Preces dicendæ in fine Congregationis. Kyrie eleyson. Pater noster. ℣. Confirma hoc Deus . . . ℞. A templo sancto tuo . . . ℣. Domine exaudi . . . ℞. Et clamor . . . Oremus. Præsta nobis, quæsumus Domine, auxilium gratiæ tuæ . . . Amen. ℣. Retribuere dignare Domine benefactoribus nostris vivis atque defunctis vitam eternam . . . ℞. Amen.

Ad invocandam gratiam Sancti Spiritus. Hymnus. Veni creator Spiritus. vel. Veni sancte Spiritus, et emitte cælitus lucis tuæ radium. ℣. Emitte Spiritum tuum . . . ℞. Et renovabis . . . ℣. Domine exaudi . . . ℞. Et clamor . . . Oremus. Deus qui corda fidelium . . . ℞. Amen. Alia oratio. Deus cui omne cor patet . . . Amen. Pro devotis amicis. Oratio. Deus qui charitatis dona per gratiam Sancti Spiritus . . . Amen. Pro inimicis. Oratio. Deus pacis, charitatisque amator . . . Amen. Ad repellendas malas cogitationes. Oratio. Omnipotens et mitissime Deus, respice propitius preces nostras . . . Amen. Ad postulandam charitatem. Oratio. Deus qui diligentibus te facis cuncta prodesse . . . Amen. Ad postulandam patientiam. Oratio. Deus qui unigeniti tui patientia antiqui hostis . . . Amen. Ad postulandam continentiam. Oratio. Ure igne sancti Spiritus renes nostros . . . Amen. ℣. Domine exaudi . . . ℞. Et clamor meus . . . ℣. Exaudiat nos Dominus. ℞. Et custodiat nos semper. Amen. Gratiarum actiones. Te Deum laudamus; vel Hymnus. Jesu nostra redemptio. ℣. Benedicamus Patrem . . . ℞. Laudemus et superexaltemus . . . ℣. Domine exaudi . . . ℞. Et clamor meus. Oremus. Deus cujus misericordiæ non est numerus . . . Amen. ℣. Domine exaudi . . . ℞. Et clamor . . . ℣. Benedicamus Domino. ℞. Deo gratias.

Hymni per totum annum.

Orationes Dominicales et Feriales cum suis Antiphonis et Versiculis per annum.

Orationes propriæ de Sanctis cum suis Antiphonis et Versiculis.

Orationes communes de Sanctis.

Officium S. Crucis.

Officium S. Spiritus.

Exercitium Quotidianum. Cum mane surgis muniens te signo sanctæ Crucis dic. In nomine. Deinde junctis manibus ante pectus; dic Amen. Benedicta sit sancta et individua Trinitas . . . Pater noster. Ave Maria. Credo in Deum. Confiteor Deo omnipotenti, beatæ Mariæ semper virgini . . . Misereatur nostri omnipotens Deus . . . ℞. Amen. Indulgentiam, absolutionem, et remissionem . . . ℞. Amen. Dignare Domine die isto sine peccato nos custodire. Miserere nostri Domine . . . Fiat misericordia tua . . . Domine exaudi . . . Et clamor meus . . . Oratio. Domine Deus omnipotens, qui ad principium hujus diei . . . Amen. Oratio. Dirigere et sanctificare, regere et gubernare . . . Amen. Angele Dei qui custos es mei . . . Amen. Benedictio. Dominus nos benedicat . . . Amen. Cum mane, meridie, et vesperi salutationis angelicæ signum datur. Angelus Domini annunciavit Mariæ . . . Ave

Maria. Ecce ancilla Domini . . . Ave Maria. Et verbum caro factum
est . . . Ave Maria. Oratio. Gratiam tuam quæsumus Domine mentibus
tuis infunde . . . Amen. Fidelium animæ . . . Ante inchoationem officii.
Oratio. Actiones nostras quæsumus Domine aspirando præveni . . . Amen.
Post officium. Oratio. Suscipe clementissime Deus precibus et meritis
beatæ Mariæ . . . Amen. Exeundo domum dic. Vias tuas Domine
demonstra mihi . . . Intrando ecclesiam. Domine in multitudine
misericordiæ tuæ . . . In aspersione aquæ benedictæ. Asperges me
Domine hyssopo . . . Ad sacrosanctum Eucharistiæ sacramentum.
Oratio. Ave verum corpus natum de Maria virgine . . . Amen. Oratio
ante missam. Clementissime pater misericordiarum . . . Amen. Benedictio mensæ pro sæcularibus. Benedicite. ℟. Benedicite. Oratio.
Benedic Domine nos et hæc tua dona . . . ℟. Amen. Gratiarum actio
post mensam. Benedicamus Domino. Deo gratias. Oratio. Agimus
tibi gratias omnipotens Deus pro universis beneficiis tuis . . . ℟. Amen.
Kyrie eleyson. Pater. ℣. Et ne . . . ℟. Sed libera . . . ℣. Sit nomen . . . ℟. Ex hoc nunc . . . Oremus. Retribuere dignare Domine . . .
℟. Amen. ℣. Et fidelium animæ . . . ℟. Amen. Cum vadis dormitum muniens te signo sanctæ Crucis dic. In nomine. Deinde junctis
manibus ante pectus, dic Amen. Benedicta sit sancta et individua
Trinitas . . . Pater noster. Ave. Credo. Confiteor. Hymnus. Te
lucis ante terminum. Salva nos domine vigilantes . . . Custodi nos
domine ut pupillam oculi . . . Dignare domine nocte ista sine peccato
. . . Miserere nostri domine . . . Fiat misericordia tua . . . Domine
exaudi . . . Et clamor . . . Oratio. Visita quæsumus Domine habitationem
istam . . . Amen. Angele Dei qui custos es mei . . . Amen. Benedictio. Benedicat et custodiat nos omnipotens et misericors Dominus . . .
Amen.

Oratio præparatoria ad confessionem sacramentalem. Conditor cæli et terræ
. . . Amen. Oratio ante confessionem sacramentalem. Suscipe confes-
sionem meam piissime ac clementissime Domine Jesu Christe . . .
Amen.

Oratio post confessionem. Sit tibi Domine obsecro, meritis beatæ semper
virginis . . . Amen.

Oratio ante sacram communionem. Ad mensam dulcissimi convivii tui pie
Domine Jesu Christe . . . Amen. Alia oratio Sancti Thomæ Aquinatis
ante communionem. Omnipotens sempiterne Deus ecce accedo ad
sacramentum unigeniti filii tui . . . Amen.

Oratio Sancti Thomæ Aquinatis post communionem. Gratias tibi ago Domine
sancte pater omnipotens æterne Deus, qui me peccatorem . . . Amen.
Alia oratio S. Bonaventuræ post communionem. Transfige dulcissime
Domine Jesu medullas . . . Amen. Alia oratio post communionem.
Ineffabilem misericordiam tuam Domine Jesu Christe humiliter exoro
. . . Amen.

Orationes seu Meditationes variæ de Passione Domini. Oratio de singulis arti-

culis passionis. Deus qui pro redemptione mundi voluisti nasci . . .
Amen. Alia oratio. Domine Jesu Christe in cujus ditione cuncta sunt
posita . . . Amen. Ad vulnera Christi. Oratio. Rogo te Domine Jesu
per illa salutifera vulnera tua . . . Amen. Meditationes piæ de passione
Christi. O Domine Jesu Christe, adoro te in cruce pendentem . . .
Amen. Pater noster. Ave Maria. O Domine Jesu Christe, adoro te
in cruce vulneratum . . . Amen. Pater noster. Ave Maria. O
Domine Jesu Christe, propter illam amaritudinem . . . Amen. Pater
noster. Ave Maria. O Domine Jesu Christe, adoro te descendentem ad
inferos . . . Amen. Pater noster. Ave Maria. O Domine Jesu
Christe, adoro te resurgentem a mortuis . . . Amen. Pater noster.
Ave Maria. O Domine Jesu Christe, pastor bone justos conserva . . .
Amen. Pater noster. Ave Maria. O Domine Jesu Christe, adoro te in
sepulchro positum . . . Amen. Pater noster. Ave Maria. De septem
verbis quæ Christus in cruce pendens dixit. Oratio. Domine Jesu
Christe fili Dei vivi, qui in cruce pendens dixisti . . . Amen. Saluta-
tiones ad omnia membra Christi et sui ipsius ad eum commendatio.
Salve tremendum cunctis potestatibus caput Domini Jesu Christi . . .
Amen.

Oratio ad beatam virginem Mariam. Obsecro te domina sancta Maria mater
Dei . . . Amen. Alia oratio ad eandem et simul ad B. Joannem evangelistam. O intemerata et in æternum benedicta . . . Amen. Planctus
beatæ Mariæ virginis. Stabat mater dolorosa . . . Amen. ℣. Tuam
ipsius animam . . . ℟. Et revelentur . . . Oratio. Interveniat pro
nobis quæsumus Domine Jesu Christe nunc et in hora mortis nostræ
. . . Amen. Commendatio ad virginem Mariam. O domina mea sancta
Maria, me in tuam benedictam fidem . . . Amen. Alia oratio ad virginem. O Maria Dei genitrix et virgo gratiosa, omnium desolatorum ad
te clamantium consolatrix . . . Amen.

Oratio divi Gregorii papæ, quæ habetur in fine explanationum septem Psalmorum pænitentialium. Bone Jesu, verbum Patris, splendor paternæ gloriæ
. . . Amen.

Oratio ad Jesum. O Bone Jesu, O piissime Jesu, O dulcissime Jesu, O Jesu
fili Mariæ Virginis . . . Amen.

Oratio beati Thomæ de Aquino. Concede mihi misericors Deus, quæ tibi
placita sunt ardenter concupiscere . . . Amen. Alia oratio S. Thomæ
de Aquino ante studium. Creator ineffabilis, qui de thesauris sapientiæ
tuæ . . . Amen.

Oratio in afflictione. O dulcissime Domine Jesu Christe verus Deus . . .
Amen.

Psalmus in tribulatione. Qui habitat in adjutorio. Oratio. Deus, qui contritorum non despicis gemitum . . . Amen.

Symbolum Athanasii. Quicunque vult . . .

Itinerarium. In ipso itineris ingressu, si solus fuerit, dicat in singulari; si cum
sociis in plurali. Antiph. In viam pacis. Canticum. Bene-

dictus dominus Deus Israel. An. In viam pacis et prosperitatis dirigat me (si fuit solus) nos (si fuerint socii). Omnipotens et misericors Dominus et angelus Raphael comitetur mecum (vel nobiscum) . . . Kyrie eleison. Pater noster. Secreto. ℣. Et ne nos . . . ℞. Sed libera . . . ℣. Salvos fac . . . ℞. Deus meus . . . ℣. Mitte nobis Domine . . . ℞. Et de Sion . . . ℣. Esto nobis . . . ℞. A facie inimici. ℣. Nihil proficiat . . . ℞. Et filius iniquitatis . . . ℣. Benedictus dominus . . . ℞. Prosperum iter . . . ℣. Vias tuas . . . ℞. Et semitas tuas . . . ℣. Utinam dirigantur . . . ℞. Ad custodiendas ustificationes tuas. ℣. Erunt prava in directa. ℞. Et aspera in vias plenas. ℣. Angelis suis Deus . . . ℞. Ut custodiant te . . . ℣. Domine exaudi . . . ℞. Et clamor meus . . . Oremus. Deus qui filios Israel . . . Deus qui Abraham puerum tuum de Ur . . . Adesto quæsumus Domine supplicationibus nostris . . . Præsta, quæsumus omnipotens Deus ut familia tua . . . ℞. Amen. ℣. Procedamus in pace. ℞. In nomine Domini. Amen.

Finis.

Index eorum quæ in hoc volumine continetur.

A.D. 1573. Plantinian Press, Antwerp. 8º.

₊ The title is "*Officium Beatæ Mariæ Virginis nuper reformatum, et Pii V. Pont. Max. jussu editum. Antwerpiæ ex officina Christophori Plantini. M.D. LXXIII. Cum privilegio et indulgentiis.*"

Summarium constitutionis, et indulgentiarum, ac decretorum S.D.N.D. Pii Papæ V. super recitatione Officii Beatæ Mariæ Virginis. Sanctissimus in Christo pater et D.N.D. Pius, divina providentia Papa V. per suas litteras in forma motus proprii, sub datum Romæ apud S. Petrum, anno incarnationis dominicæ 1570. V. Id. Martii, Pontificatus sui anno VI. et publicati die V. Aprilis, 1571 (Sec 3. Pontifex Officium B. Mariæ observari præcipit) Officia quæcumque in primis italico . . . tollimus et abolemus. (Sec. 4. Aliaque officia tollit et abolet; nisi in primæva institutione, vel a consuetudine supra 200 annos approbatæ fuerint, et non sint vulgari sermone composita). Ipsisque in virtute sanctæ obedientiæ interdicimus . . . ut illud etiam in choro dicere et psallere possint permittimus. (Sec. 5. Hortatur omnes alios non obligatos recitare Officium B. Mariæ ut officio isto reformato uti velint) Ab eis vero qui ad ejusdem Officii B. Mariæ Virginis recitationem non aliqua obligatione tenentur . . . hoc nostrum officium non perlegant vel recitent. (Sec. 6. Officiaque antiqua inquisitoribus consignari mandat) Ac ut ipsorum Officiorum vulgaris idiomatis et sermonis abusus re ipsa penitus aboleatur . . . consignari quamprimum jubemus. (Sec. 7. Officium vero reformatum, immutari non posse statuit) Statuentes huic nostro Officio nuper edito . . . et neminem muneri suo nisi hac formula satisfacere posse. (Sec. 8 Indulgentias illud recitantibus concedit) Ac ut fidelium omnium voluntas et studium . . . recitantibus conceduntur.

-1599] PRIMERS OF THE ROMAN USE. 357

Pius PP.V. Dilecto filio Christophoro Plantino, in civitate Antuerpiensi librorum impressori. Dilecte fili salutem et apostolicam benedictionem. Supplicari nobis nuper fecit dilectus filius noster Antonius Cardinalis Granuellanus, regni Neapolitani Prorex; ut pro publica Christi fidelium, et præsertim inferioris Germaniæ, et aliarum christianæ ditionis partium devotione spiritualique consolatione, Officium beatæ et gloriosæ semperque virginis Dei genitricis Mariæ, quod nuper in alma urbe nostra impressum est, a te imprimendi licentiam concedere de benignitate apostolica dignaremur . . . Datum Romæ, apud sanctum Petrum, sub annulo piscatoris, die xiii. Martii. M.D.LXXII. Pontificatus nostri anno septimo.

Initium S. Evangelii secundum Johannem. Gloria tibi domine. In principio erat verbum . . .

Sequentia S. Evangelii secundum Matthæum. Gloria tibi domine. Cum natus esset Jesus in Bethlehem Judæ . . .

Sequentia S. Evangelii secundum Marcum. Gloria tibi domine. In illo tempore recumbentibus undecim discipulis . . .

Sequentia S. Evangelii secundum Lucam. Gloria tibi domine. In illo tempore missus est angelus Gabriel a Deo . . . Deo gratias.

A.D. 1599. Arnold Conings, Antwerp. 12º. Latin and English. No. 267.

⁎ *The title is " The Primer or Office of the blessed Virgin Mary, in Latin and English, according to the reformed Latin, and with like graces privileged."*

To the christian reader. For the more utility of such of the english nation as understand not the Latin tongue; it hath been thought convenient to publish, in Latin and English, the Primer or Office of the blessed Virgin Mary; containing nothing but matter of prayer and devotion, and therefore not offensive to any except it be in respect of the service of God, according to the ancient faith of our christian forefathers who have continued in former ages (even as the most part of Christendom yet observeth) the worthy magnifying of His most blessed Mother, fulfilling therein her own prophesy of such generations of faithful people as ever should call her blessed. For unto her, to whom the almighty God of heaven did vouchsafe to send in ambassage his holy Archangel Gabriel, by whose mouth should first be pronounced " Hail Mary full of grace, our Lord is with thee blessed art thou among women, &c." Well may earthly creatures, following so worthy an example and president, often repeat this glorious salutation, and sue for her intercession unto him with whom she now liveth in everlasting glory, and cannot be unmindful of those generations that still must continue the remembrance of her blessedness, according as herself of such fore-told long before they were born. The due consideration whereof, as it must needs move these christians to the performance of like ancient devotion unto her, so our Lord vouchsafe that others thereby may be moved, not only to cease to hate them for the continuance of her praise, but also to unite themselves and concur in the honoring of that blessed mother, by whose intercession they may obtain mercy of that blessed fruit of her womb, her son, and our saviour Jesus Christ. The veneration of other Saints and desire of their intercession hath in like manner by devout christians been used: who knowing them to be united with God in such charity that they desire the salvation of all and rejoice at the conversion of sinners, do also know that God's will is such, that he will be praised and glorified in his Saints. In the translation of the psalms and other parts of Holy Scripture the direct sense, as is most requisite, hath more been sought to be observed than any phrases in our language more affected and pleasing. The hymns in the Office of our Lady, as also those for the whole year, notwithstanding the difficulty, are so turned into english meter as that they may be sung unto the same tunes in english that they bear in latin. I wish that all may be to the increase of thy devotion, to the supreme honor of the most holy glorious and undivided Trinity, God the Father, God the Son, and God the Holy Ghost, and to the laud of the blessed Virgin and all saints. R. V. [Richard Verstegen]. Vouchsafe good reader to remember in thy prayers such as have assisted to the furtherance of this work.

A Table of the moveable feasts, according to the reformed Kalender from the year of our Lord 1600 to the year 1625.

In the ensuing Kalender, besides the feasts of the Saints usually set down, the feasts of many notable Saints of England are also added. Then follows the Kalender.

An introduction to the Christian faith.[1] Symbolum Apostolorum . . . The Apostles Creed. Oratio dominicalis. Our Lord's prayer. Salutatio angelica. The angelical salutation. Decem Dei præcepta quæ in decalogo continentur. The ten precepts of God which are contained in the decalogue. The seven sacraments of the Catholick church. The theological virtues. The cardinal virtues. The gifts of the Holy Ghost. The fruits of the Holy Ghost. The precepts of charity. The precepts of the church. The spiritual works of mercy. The corporal works of mercy. The Beatitudes. The five bodily senses. The seven capital sins which are commonly called deadly. The four last things to be remembered.

The beginning of the gospel according to St. John.[2] Glory be to thee, O Lord. In the beginning was the word . . . Thanks be to God.

The office of our B. Lady to be said from the day after the Purification unto the Evensong of the Saturday before the first Sunday of Advent, saving that on the day of the Annunciation it is said as hereafter followeth in the Advent.

The Office of our B. Lady to be said from the Evensong of the Saturday

---

[1] The Apostles Creed. The Lord's prayer. The angelical salutation. The ten precepts of God are in Latin and English. The rest is in English only.

[2] This is in english only.

before the first Sunday in Advent, unto the evensong of Christmas eve ; and on the day of the Annunciation of our B. Lady.

The office of our B. Lady to be said from the Evensong of Christmas eve, unto the whole day of the Purification.

The Office or Service for the Dead.

The Gradual Psalms.

The Seven Psalms are to be said with the Litanies kneeling.

The Litanies and prayers.

The Office of the Holy Cross.

The Office of the Holy Ghost.

A daily Exercise. When thou risest in the morning, arming thyself with the sign of the cross, say. In the name. That done thy hands joined before thy breast, say. Amen. Blessed be the holy and undivided Trinity, now and ever, and world without end. Our Father. Hail Mary. I believe in God. I confess unto almighty God, to blessed Mary ever Virgin . . . Almighty God have mercy upon us . . . ℟. Amen. The almighty and merciful God give unto us pardon . . . ℟. Amen. Vouchsafe O Lord to keep us this day without sin. Be merciful unto us, O Lord . . . O Lord hear my prayer. And let my cry come unto Thee. A prayer. O Lord God almighty which hast caused us to come unto the beginning of the day . . . Amen. A prayer. Vouchsafe, O Lord God, King of heaven and earth to direct and sanctify . . . Amen. O angel of God, which art my keeper illuminate, guard . . . Amen. The blessing. Our Lord bless us and defend us from all evil . . . Amen. When at morning, noon-tide, and evening the sign of the salutation is given, say : The angel of God declared unto Mary . . . Hail Mary. Behold the handmaid of our Lord . . . Hail Mary. Behold the handmaid of our Lord . . . Hail Mary. And the word was made flesh . . . Hail Mary. A prayer. We beseech Thee, O Lord, pour forth Thy grace into our minds . . . Amen. The souls of the faithful . . . Amen. Before the beginning of any office. A prayer. Prevent we beseech Thee, O Lord our actions . . . Amen. After the office. A prayer. Accept O most clement God, by the prayers and merits of blessed Mary ever a virgin . . . Amen. In going forth of thy house, say : Shew me, O Lord, thy ways, and teach me thy paths . . . Entering into the church. O Lord, in the multitude of Thy mercies I will enter into thy house . . . In sprinkling of holy water. Thou shalt sprinkle me, O Lord, with hyssop . . . Unto the holy sacrament of the Eucharist. A prayer. All hail true body born of the virgin Mary . . . Amen. A prayer before Mass. O most clement Father of mercies, and God of all consolation . . . Amen. The blessing before meat for secular persons. Bless ye. ℟. Bless ye. The prayer. Bless us, O Lord, and these Thy gifts which we are to receive of thy bounty. ℟. Amen. Grace after meat. Bless we our Lord. ℟. Thanks be to God. The prayer. We give Thee thanks, O almighty God, for all thy benefits

... ℟. Amen. Lord have mercy upon us. Our Father. ℣. And lead us not ... ℟. But deliver us ... ℣. The name of our Lord ... ℟. From this time forth ... Let us pray. Vouchsafe, O Lord, to render to all our benefactors ... ℟. Amen. ℣. And the souls of the faithful ... ℟. Amen. When thou goest to sleep arming thee with the sign of the cross, say, In the name. Then thy hands joined before thy breast, say. Amen. Blessed be the holy and undivided Trinity ... Our Father. Hail Mary. I believe. With I confess &c. as before. The hymn. Before the lightsome day expire ... Amen. Save us, O Lord, waking ... Keep us, O Lord, as the apple of the eye ... Vouchsafe O Lord to keep us this night ... Have mercy upon us ... Let thy mercy, O Lord ... O Lord hear my prayer ... And let my cry ... The prayer. Visit we beseech Thee, O Lord, this habitation ... Amen. O angel of God which art my guardian, lighten, guard, rule ... Amen. The blessing. The almighty and merciful Lord ... Amen.

A preparatory prayer before sacramental confession. O maker of heaven and earth, King of kings ... Amen. A prayer before sacramental confession. Receive my confession, O most benign and most clement Lord Jesu Christ ... Amen.

A prayer after confession. I beseech Thee, O Lord, let this my confession be grateful ... Amen.

A prayer before receiving the B. Sacrament. O most benign Lord Jesu Christ, I a sinner presuming nothing ... Amen. Another prayer of S. Thomas of Aquine before receiving the B. Sacrament. Almighty and eternal God, behold I come to the sacrament of Thy only-begotten Son ... Amen.

A prayer after receiving the B. Sacrament by St. Thomas of Aquine. I give Thee thanks, O holy Lord, Father almighty ... Amen. Another prayer after receiving the B. Sacrament by Saint Bonaventure. Pierce through, O sweet Lord Jesu the marrow and bowels of my soul ... Amen. Another prayer after receiving the blessed Sacrament. O Lord Jesu Christ, I humbly beseech Thy unspeakable mercy that this sacrament of thy body and blood ... Amen.

Sundry prayers or meditations of the passion of our Lord. A prayer of the particular articles of the passion. O God, which for the redemption of the world would'st be born ... Amen. Another prayer. O Lord Jesu Christ, in whose power all things are put ... Amen. A prayer unto the wounds of Christ. I beseech Thee O Lord Jesu, by those Thy health-bringing wounds ... Amen. Godly meditations of the passion of Christ. O Lord Jesu Christ, I adore thee hanging on the cross wearing a crown of thorns on thy head ... Amen. Our Father. Hail Mary. O Lord Jesu Christ, I adore thee wounded upon the cross being given gall and vinegar to drink ... Amen. Our Father. Hail Mary. O Lord Jesu Christ, I beseech thee for that bitterness which thou en-

dured'st upon the cross . . . Amen. Our Father. Hail Mary. O Lord
Jesu Christ, I adore thee descending into hell and delivering the captives
Amen. Our Father. Hail Mary. O Lord Jesu Christ, I adore thee
rising from the dead . . . Our Father. Hail Mary. O Lord Jesu Christ,
the good shepherd, preserve the just . . . Amen. Our Father. Hail
Mary. O Lord Jesu Christ, I adore thee laid in the sepulchre . . .
Amen. Our Father. Hail Mary. Of the seven words which Christ
spake hanging on the cross, A prayer. O Lord Jesu Christ, Son of the
living God, which hanging upon the cross said'st . . . Amen. Salutations to all the parts of Christ, and recommendation of himself unto
Him. All hail, O head of our Lord and Saviour Jesu Christ . . .
Amen.

A prayer to the blessed Virgin Mary. I beseech Thee, O holy Lady Mary,
mother of God most full of pity . . . Amen. Another prayer to the
said Virgin and withall unto S. John the evangelist. O untouched and
for ever blessed, singular and incomparable Virgin Mary mother of God
. . . Amen. The plaint of the blessed Virgin Mary. The mother stood
in woful wise . . . Amen. ℣. The sword of sorrow hath passed
through thy soul. ℟. That cogitations may be revealed . . . A prayer.
We beseech Thee, O Lord Jesu Christ, that the blessed Virgin Mary thy
mother may be a mean for us . . . Amen. A recommendation unto the
Virgin Mary. O my Lady, holy Mary, I recommend myself into Thy
blessed trust . . . Amen. Another prayer unto the Virgin. O Mary
mother of God and gracious Virgin the true comforter of all desolate
persons . . . Amen.

A prayer of S. Gregory the pope which is in the end of the exposition of the
seven penitential psalms. O good Jesu, the word of the Father, the
brightness of fatherly glory . . . Amen.

A prayer unto Jesus. O good Jesu, O most benign Jesu, O sweetest Jesu, O
Jesu the Son of the Virgin Mary . . . Amen.

A prayer of St. Thomas of Aquyne. Grant unto me, O merciful God, ardently
to desire . . . Amen. Another prayer of St. Thomas of Aquyne before
study. O unspeakable Creator, which forth of the treasure of Thy wisdom . . . Amen.

A prayer in affliction. O most sweet Lord Jesu Christ, the true God who from
the bosom of the highest almighty father . . . Amen.

A psalm in tribulation. He that dwelleth in the help of the highest. A prayer.
O God, which despisest not the wailing of the contrite . . . Amen.

The Creed of Athanasius. Whosoever will be saved . . .

The Passion of our Lord Jesus Christ according to Matthew. Chap. 26. At
that time Jesus said to his disciples . . .

The Passion of our Lord Jesus Christ according to Mark. Chap. 14. At that
time the Pasche was . . .

The Passion of our Lord Jesus Christ according to Luke. Chap. 22. At that
time the festival day of the azymes approached . . .

XX

The Passion of our Lord Jesus Christ according to John. Chap. 18. At that time Jesus went forth with his disciples . . .
The antiphons, verses and prayers of the principal feasts of the whole year.
Prayers and orisons to be said after the Litanies, according to diversity of times. The Litanies are said unto the Psalm. O God incline thyself unto my aid, as before. Then the verse. I said O Lord have mercy upon me. ℞. Heal my soul . . . ℣. Turn unto us, Lord . . . ℞. And be thou intreatable . . . ℣. Let thy mercy O Lord light upon us. ℞. Even as we have hoped in thee. ℣. Let thy Priests . . . ℞. And let thy saints rejoice. ℣. O Lord save the King. ℞. And hear us . . . ℣. Save thy people, O Lord . . . ℞. And govern them . . . ℣. Be mindful of thy congregation. ℞. Which thou hast possessed . . . ℣. Let peace be made . . . ℞. And abundance . . . ℣. Let us pray for the faithful departed. ℞. Eternal rest . . . ℣. Let them rest . . . ℞. Amen. ℣. For our brethren absent. ℞. Save thy servants . . . ℣. For the afflicted and captives. ℞. Deliver them O God . . . ℣. Send them help . . . ℞. And from Sion . . . ℣. O Lord hear . . . ℞. And let my cry . . . The 78 Psalm. O God the gentiles are come. Or the Psalm. Our God is a refuge (as before leaf 60) The psalm being ended is to be said. ℣. Convert us . . . ℞. And shew thy face . . . ℣. Rise up, help us . . . ℞. And deliver us . . . ℣. O Lord hear . . . ℞. And let my cry . . . Let us pray. Prayer to require suffrages of saints. We beseech thee, O Lord, defend us from all perils . . . Amen. Prayer for the holy church of God. O almighty everlasting God which hast revealed thy glory . . . Amen. Prayer for the chief bishop. O God the pastor and governor of all faithful . . . Amen. Prayer for every degree of the church. O almighty everlasting God, by whose spirit the whole body of the church . . . Amen. Prayer for any necessity of the church and anything to be obtained. O God our refuge and strength, the very author of piety . . . Amen. Prayer against the persecutors of the church. We beseech thee, O Lord, admit being appeased the prayers of thy church . . . Amen. Prayer for the demanding help against infidels. O most merciful God, who remembrest not the iniquities . . . Amen. Prayer for the Emperor. O God protector of all kingdoms, and especially of the christian empire . . . Amen. Prayer for the King. We beseech thee, O almighty God, that thy servant N our King . . . Amen. Prayer for those that are to be catechised. O almighty everlasting God, which ever makest the church fruitful . . . Amen. Prayer that the world may be purged from all errors. O almighty everlasting God, the consolation of the sorrowful . . . Amen. Prayer for hereticks and schismaticks. O almighty everlasting God, which savest all men . . . Amen. Prayer for the unfaithful Jews. O almighty everlasting God, which repellest not from thy mercy . . . Amen. Prayer for the pagans. O almighty everlasting God, which desires not the death of sinners . . . Amen. Prayer in the time

of war. O God which dissolvest wars, and by the power of thy protection . . . Amen. Prayer against Pagans. O almighty everlasting God, in whose hand are the powers of all ˙. . . Amen. Prayer for peace. O God from whom all holy desires . . . Amen. Prayer in the time of famine and pestilence. Grant unto us we beseech thee, O Lord, the effect of our prayer . . . Amen. Prayer for rain. O God in whom we live, are moved and have our being . . . Amen. Prayer for fair weather. Hear us, O Lord crying unto thee and grant unto us, making supplications, fair weather . . . Amen. Prayer to be used in any tribulation. O almighty God, despise not thy people crying unto thee in affliction . . . Amen. Prayer for forgiveness of sins. O God, which rejectest none, but being pacified by merciful pity . . . Amen. Prayer for those that are tempted and troubled. O God which justifieth the wicked and wilt not the death of sinners . . . Amen. Prayer for such as are in journey. Hearken to our supplications, O Lord, and dispose the way of thy servants . . . Amen. Prayer for the sick. O almighty and everlasting God, the eternal health of them that believe . . . Amen. Prayer in tribulation of sins. Shew with clemency, O Lord, thy unspeakable mercy unto us . . . Amen. Prayer for sins. Hear we beseech thee, O Lord, the prayers of thy suppliants . . . Amen. Prayer for the health of the living. Stretch out, O Lord, the right hand of thy heavenly help to thy faithful . . . Amen. Prayer for the living and the dead. O almighty everlasting God, which hast power over the living . . . Amen. ℣. O Lord hear my prayer. ℟. And let my cry . . . ℣. Our Lord graciously hear us. ℟. And keep us evermore. Amen.

Prayers to be said in the beginning of the congregation. Come Holy Ghost, replenish the hearts of thy faithful . . . Lord have mercy upon us . . . Our Father. ℣. Be mindful of thy congregation. ℟. Which thou hast possessed . . . ℣. O Lord hear my prayer . . . ℟. And let my cry . . . Let us pray. Illuminate our minds we beseech thee, O Lord, with the light of thy clearness . . . Amen. At the end of the congregation. Lord have mercy upon us. Our Father. ℣. Confirm, O God, that which thou hast wrought on us. ℟. From thy holy temple . . . ℣. O Lord hear . . . ℟. And let my cry . . . Let us pray. Grant unto us, we beseech thee, O Lord the help of thy grace . . . Amen. ℣. Vouchsafe O Lord to render eternal life to our benefactors alive and dead. Amen.

To call for the grace of the Holy Ghost. The Hymn. Come Holy Ghost that us hath made. Or this sequence. Come unto us Holy Ghost, send us from the heavenly coast . . . Amen. ℣. Send forth thy spirit . . . ℟. And thou shalt renew . . . ℣. O Lord hear . . . ℟. And let my cry . . . Let us pray. O God, which by inlightening of the Holy Ghost . . . Amen. Another prayer. O God, to whom each heart is open . . . Amen. Prayer for devout friends. O God, which hast poured the gifts of charity by the grace of the Holy Ghost . . . Amen.

Prayer for our enemies. O God, the lover and keeper of peace . . . Amen. Prayer to repel wicked thoughts. O almighty and most mild God, mercifully regard our prayers . . . Amen. Prayer to require charity. O God, which makest all things to profit them that love thee . . . Amen. Prayer to require patience. O God, which hast broken the pride of the old enemy . . . Amen. Prayer to require continence. Kindle with the fire of the Holy Ghost our reins . . . Amen. ℣. O Lord hear . . . ℟. And let my cry . . . ℣. Our Lord graciously hear us. ℟. And keep us . . . Amen. Thanksgiving. We praise thee, O God, or the Hymn. O Jesus our redemption. ℣. Bless we the Father . . . ℟. Let us praise and extol him . . . ℣. O Lord hear . . . ℟. And let my cry . . . Let us pray. O God of whose mercy there is no number . . . Amen. ℣. O Lord hear . . . ℟. And let my cry . . . ℣. Bless we our Lord. ℟. Thanks be to God.

Prayers in journeys. In the beginning of thy journey, if thou be alone, say in the singular number; if with company in the plural. The Antiphona. In the way of peace. The song. Blessed be our Lord God of Israel. In the end. Glory. That done let the Antiphona be repeated. In the way of peace and prosperity let him direct me; if thou be alone [or us, if there be company] the almighty and merciful Lord and the angel Raphael accompany me [or us] in the way; that with peace, safety, and joy I [or we] may return home. Lord have mercy upon us. Our Father (in secret) ℣. And lead us not into temptation. ℟. But deliver us from evil. ℣. Make safe thy servants ℟. My God trusting in thee. ℣. Send us help . . . ℟. And from Sion . . . ℣. Be unto us . . . ℟. From the face . . . ℣. Let not the enemy . . . ℟. And let not the son of iniquity. ℣. Blessed be our Lord . . . ℟. The God of our salvation . . . ℣. Shew unto me . . . ℟. And teach me . . . ℣. O that our ways . . . ℟. To keep thy righteousness. ℣. The crooked . . . ℟. And the rough . . . ℣. God hath given charge . . . ℟. That they may guard thee . . . ℣. O Lord hear . . . ℟. And let my cry . . . ℣. Our Lord be with you. ℟. And with thy spirit. Let us pray. O God which did'st make the children of Israel to pass dry foot . . . Amen. O God, which hast preserved unhurt through all the ways of his peregrination thy servant Abraham . . . Hearken, O Lord, we beseech thee unto our supplications . . . Grant we beseech thee, O almighty God, that thy family . . . ℟. Amen. ℣. Let us proceed in peace. ℟. In the name of our Lord. Amen.

Finis.

A table of the contents of this book.
The manner how to serve the Priest at mass.[1]
The hymns through the whole year.[2]

---

[1] This is in Latin only.
[2] These hymns as well as the rest of the book are in english only.

PRIMERS OF THE ROMAN USE.

Prayers on Sundays and other days with their antiphons and versicles throughout the year.
The prayers proper to the Saints with their antiphons and versicles.
The prayers common to Saints.
The holy Gospel according to Matthew. Glory be to thee, O Lord. When Jesus was born in Bethlehem of Juda . . .
The holy Gospel according to Mark. Glory be to thee, O Lord. At that time Jesus appeared to the eleven disciples . . .
The holy Gospel according to Luke. Glory be to thee, O Lord. At that time the angel Gabriel was sent of God . . . ℟. Thanks be to God.
Finis.

A.D. 1604. Arnold Conings, Antwerp. 12º. Latin and English. No. 268.

⁎ *The title is " The Primer, or Office of the blessed Virgin Marie, in Latin and English : according to the reformed Latin, and with like graces privileged."*
In the ensuing Kalender, besides the feasts of the Saints usually set down, the feasts of divers notable Saints of England, Scotland, Ireland, and Wales are also added. Then follows the Kalender.

A.D. 1607. Plantinian Press, Antwerp, for John Moret, Antwerp. 8º. Latin. No. 269.

⁎ *The title is "Officium beatæ Mariæ Virginis. Pii. V. Pont. Max. jussu editum. Cum Calendario Gregoriano,[1] a Sixto PP.V. et S.D.N. Clemente VIII. Pont. Max. aliquot Sanctorum festis aucto . . . Cum gratia et privilegio."*
Summarium constitutionis et indulgentiarum ac decretorum S.D.N.D. Pii Papæ V. super recitatione Officii Beatæ Mariæ Virginis. Sanctissimus in Christo Pater, et D.N.D. Pius divina prouidentia Papa V. per suas litteras in forma motus proprii, sub Datum Romæ apud S. Petrum Anno incarnationis Dominicæ 1570. V. Id. Martii, Pontificatus sui anno VI. et publicati die v. Aprilis 1571. Officia quæcumque inprimis Italico . . . recitantibus conceduntur (as on page 356).
De indictione. Indictio est revolutio 15 annorum ab 1 usque ad 15 . . . cujus usus perpetuus est; initium tamen sumit ab anno correctionis 1582. Tabella indictionis ab anno correctionis. Nam si anno 1582 tribuas primum numerum qui est 10 et sequenti anno 1583; secundum numerum qui est II., et sic deinceps usque ad annum propositum . . . De anno et ejus partibus . . . Quando inchoatur Adventus Domini . . . Quatuor Tempora . . . Nuptiæ juxta decretum Concilii Tridentini . . . Ratio aurei numeri . . .
Tabula literarum dominicalium ab Idibus Octobris anni correctionis 1582 (detractis prius decem diebus) usque ad annum 1700 exclusive. Tabula literarum respondentium aureis numeris ab Idibus Octobris anni correctionis 1582 (detractis prius decem diebus) usque ad annum 1700 exclusive. Tabula temporalia festorum mobilium.

[1] See John J. Bond Handy-book, ed. 1875, page 6.

366 SUMMARY OF CONTENTS. [1615-

Clemens PP. VIII. ad futuram rei memoriam. Sinceræ fidei et devotionis affectus, quem dilecti filii hæredes quondam Christophori Plantini librorum impressores Antwerpienses, et nominatim Joannes Moretus ejusdem Christophori gener, ad nos et apostolicam sedem gerere comprobantur . . . præsertim vero Joanni prædicto, ut Missalia, Breviaria, et Diurna, necnon Officium parvum B. Mariæ juxta ritum et præscriptum Romanæ ecclesiæ, prout dictus Christophorus poterat, imprimere libere et licite possint, et valeant, auctoritate apostolica tenore præsentium licentiam concedimus et facultatem . . . datum Romæ apud S. Petrum, sub annulo Piscatoris, die VII. Martii M.D.XCII. Pontificatus nostri anno primo. M. Vestrius Barbeanus.

Summa privilegii regis catholici et Principum Belgarum. Philippus Dei gratia Hispaniarum, &c. Rex catholicus, diplomatibus suis sanxit ne quis citra voluntatem Joannis Moreti, Typographi Antwerpiensis, Missalia, Breviaria, Diurna, Officia B. Mariæ aut reliqua officia ad usum ecclesiæ catholicæ Romanæ edita: olimque a Christophoro Plantino p.m. dicti Moreti socero excusa, novisque officiis nunc aucta sive posthac augenda, mutanda, aut corrigenda ullo modo imprimat, aut alibi impressa in suas ditiones importet, venaliave habeat . . . Datis Bruxellæ, xvi Maii M.D.XCI et iisdem innovatis ac confirmatis, xxv Februarii MDXCVIII. Signat S. di Grimaldi et in Consilio Brab. J. de Buschere . . . Albertus et Isabella, Archiduces Austriæ, Duces Burgundiæ . . . approbarunt et confirmarunt litteris datis Bruxellæ xv Maii. M.DCI. Signat. I. de Buschere.

Colophon. Antwerpiæ, ex officina Plantiniana. Apud Johannem Moretum.

₊ *An earlier edition of this book is in the possession of the Rev: E. S. Dewick; the title is "Officium Beatæ Mariæ Virginis nuper reformatum et Pii V. Pont. Max. jussu editum. Cui accessit Kalendarium Gregorianum perpetuum, Parisiis, Apud Societatem Typographicum Librorum Officii Ecclesiastici ex Decreto Concilio Tridentino Via Jacobæa. Cum Privilegiis Pont. Max. & Franc. & Navarræ Regis Christianiss. M.D.XC.VII."*

₊ *The contents of this book are the same as those of No. 266, A.D. 1571 (page 349), with the exception of the kalendar, but the order of them is different.*

A.D. 1615. Henrie Jaey, Mackline, 16o. English. No. 270.

₊ *The title is "The Primer, or Office of the blessed Virgin Marie, in english. According to the last edition of the Romane Breviarie. Cum gratia et privilegio."*

Christian reader. This office of our B. Lady being, with licence of Superiors, to be printed in English alone after the example of the French and Flemish who have it so in their language: it was thought fit not to bind the printer to follow rigorously the late edition in Latin and English;[1] but to renew the whole work, and make it as it were a new translation; which hath been performed in this manner. The places of holy Scripture, which are the principal part of the book, are accorded with the

---

[1] Primer. A.D. 1599. No. 267. page 357.

authentical translation of the Bible in english, lately published at
Doway. The Hymns, most of which are used by the holy Church in
her public office, are a new translation done by one most skilful in
english poetry, wherein the litteral sense is preserved with the true
strain of the verse. The Antiphons and prayers for the Feasts, which
are also part of the public Office, and whatsoever else is taken thence
doth fully agree with the Breviary lately renewed and published by the
authority of Clement the eight.

If this work fall into the hands of any not catholicks, and therefore possessed
with a prejudicate conceit of the Roman church's idolatry : let them
know, that whatsoever is here demanded of the Mother of God or any
other Saint is asked of them, not as being able to give any thing of themselves, but as being friends of God, and therefore powerful to obtain any
good thing at his bountiful hands, who is the only fountain of all goodness. At whose mercies seat vouchsafe pious reader to remember all
those, who have laboured in the edition of this present work.

A.D. 1616. John Heigham, St. Omers, 12º. Latin and English. No. 271.

Summa Privilegii. Albertus et Isabella, Clara Eugenia Archiduces Austriæ,
Duces Burgundiæ, Brabantiæ etc Serenissimi Belgarum Principes,
Diplomatibus suis sanxerunt, nequis præter Joannis Heigham voluntatem,
Officia Beatæ Mariæ, Anglice et Latine, ullo modo imprimat, vel alibi
terrarum impressa, in earum ditiones importet, venaliave habeat. Qui
secus faxerit, confiscatione librorum, et alia gravi pæna multabitur, uti
latius patet, in literis datis. Bruxellæ, 1 Junii. 1612.

Signat. I. de Buschere.

A.D. 1627. 12º. Latin.

₊ *The title is "Officium B. Mariæ Virginis nuper reformatum, et Pii V
Pont. Max. jussu editum, ubi omnia suis locis sunt extensa. Cum indulgentiis
et orationibus a Clemente VIII ordinatis. Cum Kalendario Gregoriano.
Parisius apud Gabrielem Clopejav via Jacobæa, sub signo Annuntiationis.
M.DC.XXVII."*

Litaniæ augustissimi nominis Jesu.

Litaniæ antiquissimi Eucharistiæ sacramenti.

Litaniæ beatæ Mariæ Virginis quæ in æde Loretana recitantur.

Precatio pro rege. Psalmus IV. Exaudiat te Dominus in die tribulationis. ℣.
Domine salvum . . . ℟. Et exaudi . . . Oremus. Quæsumus omnipotens Deus ut famulus tuus rex noster . . . Amen.

A.D. 1632. 12o. English. No. 275.

₊ *The title is " The Primer or Office of the blessed Virgin Marie in english.
According to the last edition of the Roman Brevarie. Permissu Superiorum."*

Litaniæ in nomine Jesu.

Litaniæ quæ singulis diebus Sabbathi, et festis beatissimæ Mariæ canuntur in
sanctissima æde Lauretana.

A.D. 1632. Rouen, 12º. English. No. 276.

₀ The title is "*The Primer or Office of the blessed Virgin Mary in english. According to the Roman use.*"

In the ensuing Calendar are set down very many principal feasts of the Saints of England, Scotland, and Ireland, upon the days which the Roman Calendar hath left void.

Act of contrition to be made once a day, especially to bed-wards.   O my Lord Jesus Christ, true God and man, my Creator and redeemer . . . Amen.

A.D. 1644. Venice, apud Cieras, 4º. Latin. No. 279.

₀ The title is "*Officium B. Mariæ Virginis nuper reformatum, et Pii Quinti Pont. Max. Jussu editum. Ad instar Breviarii Romani sub Urbano VIII recogniti. Cum indulgentiis.*"

Ex bulla sanctissimi D.N. Papæ Pii V.   De recitatione Officii B. Mariæ Virginis.   (Sec. 8. Indulgentias illud recitantibus concedit) Ac ut fidelium omnium voluntas et studium . . . recitantibus conceduntur. (as on page 350).

Tabula litterarum dominicalium ab Idibus Octobris anni correctionis 1582 (detractis prius decem diebus) usque ad annum 1700 exclusive.

Tabella Epactarum respondentium aureis numeris ab idibus Octobris anni correctionis 1582 (detractis prius x diebus) usque ad annum 1700 exclusive.

Tabella temporalia.   Tabella festorum mobilium.

Tauola del far della Luna secondo il vero Computo.

Principiando il giorno secondo l'uso del l'horologio commune al tramantor del sole.

Tabella indictionis ab anno correctionis 1582.

De anni correctione, ejusque necessitate, ac Kalendario Gregoriano.

Oratio a sanctissimo domino nostro Urbano VIII edita.   Ante oculos tuos Domine culpas nostras . . . Amen.   ℣. Gregem tuum Pastor æterne . . . ℟. Sed per beatos Apostolos . . . ℣. Protege Domine populum . . . ℟. Perpetua defensione custodias.   ℣. Orate pro nobis sancti Apostoli . . . ℟. Ut digni . . . Oratio. Præsta quæsumus omnipotens Deus ut nullis nos permittas perturbationibus concuti . . . Amen. Implorent clementissime Domine nostris opportunam necessitatibus . . . Amen.

Della miracolosa solennita, et Festa del Santo Rosario.   Instituita da N. S. Papa Gregorio XIII. per la prima Dominica d'Ottobre . . . Datum Romæ apud Sanctum Petrum sub annulo Piscatoris.   Die primo Aprilis. M.D.LXXIII.   Pontificatus nostri Anno primo.

Rosario della Madonna.

Litanie della B. Vergine Maria.

Oratione alla regina di tutte le creature.   Serenissima Imperatrice del cielo, madre dell unigenito figliuolo dell eterno Padre . . .

A.D. 1650. Widow of John Cnobbaert, Antwerp, for James Thompson (London) 12o. Latin and English. No. 280.

⁎ *The title is "The Primer or Office of the blessed Virgin Mary in Latin and English. According to the reformed Latin, and with like graces priviledged."*

To the christian reader. For the more utility of such of the english nation as understand not the latin tongue, it hath been thought convenient to publish in Latin and English the Primer or Office of the blessed Virgin Mary . . . R. V. (Richard Verstegen) as in No. 267. A.D. 1599. (page 357).

Seven petitions. 1. The first is to beg of God efficacious grace, to love him most earnestly and most entirely with thy whole heart. 2. To love thy neighbour as thyself . . . Amen.

A daily devotion to our blessed Lady. O blessed Virgin Mary and eternal Queen of angels, I offer myself unto you . . . Amen.

A.D. 1669. Nicolas Le Tourneur, Rouen, 12o. Latin and English. No. 282.

⁎ *The title is " The Primer more ample, and in a new order ; containing the three offices of the B. Virgin Mary, in Latin and English, and all offices and devotions which were in former primers. In this last edition the hymns are in a better verse, and six offices newly added. I. Of the holy Trinity. II. Of the B. Sacrament. III. Of the holy name of Jesus, with a Letany. IV. Of the immaculate conception of our B. Lady, with a Letany. V. Of the Angel-Guardian. VI. Of S. Joseph. And sundry sweet devotions, and instructions taken out of the holy Scripture for to live a devout christian life. A large and short examen of conscience. To the Calender are annexed many English and Irish Saints. With permission."*

To the pious Reader. More ample and in a new order, Christian reader, I present to Thee the primer, containing the three offices of the blessed virgin Mary in Latin and English, and all Offices and devotions which were in the precedent and former primers printed in Antwerp. In this last edition are added six Offices, two Letanies, twenty-six Instructions taken out of the holy Scripture for to live a devout Christian life, a large and short Examen of conscience, and many other sweet devotions which never were set forth in the Primer. A Table of the moveable feasts for thirty years according to the English account. To the Calender are annexed many English and Irish Saints ; immediately follow the ordinary and moveable holy days, fasting, and Ember days throughout the year. The use and practice of this good book is commended to thy piety, and to thy prayers. Thine affectioned well-wisher in Jesus Christ. Thomas Fitz Simon, Priest.

A table of the moveable feasts according to the English account for thirty years. The Kalender.

Holy-days throughout the year, according to the last institution. The moveable holy-days. Fasting days. Ember days. Advent. The time of marriage.

Instructions for to live a christian life taken out of the holy Scripture. I. In those two commandments love God and your neighbour is comprehended the whole law. A Pharisen, doctor of law, asked of Jesus tempting him . . .

Brief exhortations to the often frequenting of the sacrament of penance by certain familiar examples. He that long defers the confession of his sins . . .

Instructions for examining our conscience, and for confession. Before we begin the examen itself . . .

An examen of conscience upon the ten Commandments.

A shorter method of confession for those that frequent the same often. He that is accustomed to confess often . . .

A short prayer to be said presently after absolution. Let, O Lord, I humbly beseech thee this my confession . . . Amen. Then say. Deus propitius esto mihi peccatori . . . or, God be merciful unto me a sinner.

Consideration of the horror of mortal sin. Saint Anselm, Bishop of Canterbury was often wont to say . . . Consideration upon the sad effects of mortal sin . . . Consider then these circumstances following . . . The application . . . An act of hope. I repose all my trust, hope, and affiance in the mercies of God.

A prayer to be said before we go to confession, or when we desire to have true contrition. O most worthy redeemer and Saviour of mankind, I a wretched sinner in hope of pardon and absolution . . . Amen.

A table of the contents of this book.

The three offices of our B. Lady.

Saturday. The little office of the immaculate conception of the ever B. Virgin Mary. To be daily said by such as are devoted to this divine mystery. The Litany of our blessed Lady. The little office of St. Joseph.

Sunday. The little office of the blessed Trinity.

Monday. The office of the Holy Ghost.

Tuesday. The little office of the Name of Jesus. The Litany of our Lord and Saviour Jesus Christ.

Wednesday. The little office of the Angel guardian.

Thursday. The little office of the blessed Sacrament.

Friday. The office of the holy Cross.

Short prayers taken out of the gospel. Lord if thou wilt thou canst make me clean . . .

A summary of such acts as every good Christian ought daily to practise, and may be enlarged according to every one's particular devotions. 1. Address to God. 2. Act of humility. 3. Adoration . . .

A Testament of the soul to be made by a good christian every day. In nomine Domini. Amen. I bequeath my soul to God, my body to the earth . . .

A meditation of judgment. Consider that instantly after death thy soul is to be presented before the bar of God's judgment . . .

A meditation of the blessed Sacrament. Consider that so often as thou dost communicate thou art made the tabernacle of the blessed Trinity . . .

A.D. 1673. St. Omers, 12º. English. No. 283.

∗ The title is "The Primer or Office of the Blessed Virgin Mary in english, exactly revised, and the new Hymns and Prayers added, according to the reformation of Pope Urban 8."

To the pious Reader. The Primer, or Office of our B. Lady here presents itself to your devotion, being thoroughly reformed according to the last corrected Latin of Pope Urban the VIII. now generally used in the church; wherein you shall find all the Hymns put into a true divine poetic strain, yet keeping close to the literal sense; of which there are some new ones, and many prayers which did never before speak english. The Calendar with the holy days in the rubricks is exactly modelled according to the last Roman institution. The prayers are rendred more harmonious and genuine, the references and directions are truly adjusted. In a word the whole book hath been with much care revised, and purged from many incongruities and solecisms; enlarged besides with such pieces of devotion, as the church hath recommended to the piety of her children. And, which was most necessary, a short exposition of the whole book is prefixed for the instruction of the ignorant. All which hath deservedly gained the approbation of the learned, and may prove a hopeful means to advance thy devotion. Which God of his mercy grant.

Kalender.

Introduction to the christian faith. The Apostles Creed. Our Lord's prayer. The angelical salutation. The ten commandments of God which are contained in the decalogue. The seven sacraments of the catholike church. The theological virtues. The cardinal virtues. The gifts of the Holy Ghost. The fruits of the Holy Ghost. The precepts of charity. The precepts of the church. The spiritual works of mercy. The corporal works of mercy. The eight beatitudes. The five corporal senses. The seven capital sins which are commonly called deadly. The four last things to be remembered.

Holy days throughout the year. New Year's day and Twelfth day, the Purification, Annunciation, Assumption and Nativity of our B. Lady. All the twelve Apostles. S. Joseph. The invention of the holy Cross. S. John Baptist. S. Anne the mother of our B. Lady. S. Laurence. S. Michael. All Saints day. Christmas day. S. Stephen. Holy Innocents and Sylvester; and one of the principal patrons of a city, province, or kingdom.

The moveable holy days. All Sundays, Easter-day and Whit-sunday with two days next following. Ascension day. Corpus Christi-day.

A table of the contents.

A short exposition of the Primer or Office of the blessed Virgin Mary. The Office of our B. Lady is of great antiquity, and was composed by the church, directed by the Holy Ghost; and this book is called the Primer from the latin word primo which signifies first of all; to teach us that prayer should be the first work of the day. And the office is divided into Psalms, Hymns, Canticles, Antiphons, Versicles, Responsories, and prayers, for order, beauty, and variety sake, and warranted by Scripture. Col. 3. 16. Sing you in your hearts unto our Lord in spiritual psalms, hymns, and canticles . . .

Litanies of our Lord and Saviour Jesus Christ.

Hymn to our Saviour Jesus, composed by S. Bernard. Jesu dulcis memoria. Jesu, the only thought of thee Fills with delight my memory.

A prayer composed by S. Augustine, and recommended to the devotion of all christians by Pope Urban VIII. Ante oculos tuos, Domine . . . Before thy holy eyes, O Lord, . . . The antiphon. We wait in expectation of our Saviour's coming . . . ℣. Behold, the God of heaven . . . ℟. In him without fear . . . The prayer. Almighty God, who for the redemption of mankind . . . Amen.

The manner how to serve a priest at Mass.[1]

Finis.

An antiphon and prayer in honour of our B. Lady to be said in honour of our B. Lady; to be said in time of plague. O star of heaven, whose Virgin breast Thy son our Lord did feed . . . Pray for us, holy mother of God, that we may be made worthy . . . Let us pray. O God of mercy, God of piety, God of pardon . . . Amen.

Another antiphon and prayer against the plague in honor of S. Roch. Venerable confessor of Christ, holy Roch . . . Let us pray. Omnipotent eternal God, who by the prayers and merits of thy blessed confessor St. Roch did'st stay a general pestilence . . . Amen.

Litanies of our B. Lady of Loretto. So called, for that they are usually sung in that sacred church of Loretto, upon all the Saturdays in the year, and feasts of the B. Virgin Mary.

Finis.

A.D. 1685. Antwerp, for T. D. (Antwerp). 12o. English. No. 285.

⁎ *The title is "The Primer, or Office of the blessed Virgin Mary in english exactly revised; and the new hymns and prayers added according to the reformation of Pope Urbans."*

Salutations to all the parts of Christ, and a recommendation of ones self to him. Hail, O head of our Lord and Saviour Jesus Christ . . . Amen.

The method of saying the Rosary of our blessed Lady; as it was ordered by Pope Pius the fifth of the holy Order of preachers. And as it is said in her Majesties Chapel at St. James. The fifteenth edition. Printed for T. D. in the year 1685. An advertisement concerning the following method of saying the Rosary. The devotion of the Rosary, so called because it is, as it were, a Chaplet of spiritual roses, that is, of most sweet and devout prayers, was first revealed by the B. Virgin to St. Dominick (the father and founder of the holy Order of preachers) as a

---

[1] This occurs in Latin in No. 267 A.D. 1599. page 364.

devotion most efficacious for the obtaining of all favours from God, and averting all evils from our selves. It consisteth of fifteen Pater nosters, and a hundred and fifty Ave Marys, and is divided into three parts; whereof each containeth in it five Decads, that is five Pater nosters, and fifty Ave Marys. To each of these Decads, in the following method, is assigned one of the principal mysteries of the life of our Saviour or his B. Mother, as matter of meditation; wherein the mind is to exercise itself while it prays, and therefore is prefixed before the beginning of each decade. The mysteries also in number fifteen are divided into three parts, answerable to the three parts of the Rosary; that is, into five joyful mysteries for the first part of the Rosary; five sorrowful for the second; and five glorious for the third. Now the use of the following method or manner of saying the Rosary consisteth in a devout application or attention of the mind to the mystery assigned while the Decade is saying; and raising correspondent affections in the will, such as the devotion and necessity of each one shall suggest: for example; in the first part, of joy and thanksgiving for the coming of our redeemer and the great work of our redemption: in the second, of compassion for the suffering of our Lord, and contrition for our sins which were the cause of them: in the third, of exaltation of the glory of our Saviour, and his B. Mother; and hope through the merits of his passion and her intercession to be made partakers of glory with them. He that shall say the Rosary with this attention of mind and affection of will shall undoubtedly give much glory to God, and reap much benefit to his own soul; which was the intention of Pope Pius the fifth (a most pious son of St. Dominick) in ordering, and is the endeavour at present of one of the meanest among the sons of so glorious a father in publishing the meditations and prayers, as they are set down in the following method. The joyful mysteries assigned for Mundays and Thursdays through the year, and Sundays in Advent and after Epiphany till Lent . . . The dolorous or sorrowful mysteries for Tuesdays and Fridays through the year, and the Sundays in Lent . . . The glorious mysteries for Wednesdays and Saturdays through the year, and Sundays after Easter until Advent . . .

Prayers for the King, Queen, and Queen dowager. Psalm xix. Our Lord hear thee in the day of tribulation. Vers. Lord save James our King. Resp. And hear us in the day . . . Let us pray. We beseech thee almighty God, that thy servant James our King . . . Amen.

To be added to the last collect at the end of mass. And defend thy servants Innocent the chief bishop, James our King, Mary our Queen, and Queen Catherine, together with ourselves . . . Amen.

A.D. 1687. Henry Hills, London, 8o. English. No. 286.

˛ *The title is "The Office of the B.V. Mary in english. To which is added the Vespers, or Even-Song in Latin and English, as it is sung in the Catholic church upon all Sundays and principal Holy Days throughout the whole year. With the Compline, Rosary, Hymn, and Prayers that are sung at the Benediction*

374 SUMMARY OF CONTENTS. [1687-

of the B. Sacrament. The prayers for the King, Queen &c. The Ordinary of the Holy Mass, the Sequence, Dies iræ, Dies illa, that is sung at Solemn Mass for the dead, and the Libera that is sung after Mass for the dead: all in Latin and English. Together with several other devout prayers in English."

A short exposition of the Office of the blessed Virgin Mary (as on page 371).

Vespers or Even-song, as it is sung in the Catholic church in Latin and English.

The method of saying the Rosary of our blessed Lady in Latin and English[1]; as it was ordered by Pope Pius the fifth of the holy Order of preachers, and as it is said in Catholic chappels.

The hymn and prayers that are sung at the Benediction of the blessed sacrament. Tantum ergo sacramentum. Let's then this sacrament adore. ℣. Panem de cælo . . . Thou hast given them bread . . . ℟. Omne delectamentum . . . Replenished with all sweetness . . . ℣. Dominus vobiscum. Our Lord be with you. ℟. Et cum spiritu tuo. And with thy spirit. Oremus. Let us pray. Deus qui sub sacramento mirabili . . . Amen. O God who in this wonderful sacrament . . . Amen. Ecclesiæ tuæ quæsumus Domine preces placatus admitte . . . Amen. Receive we beseech thee O Lord the prayers of thy church . . . Amen.

Prayers for the King, Queen, and Queen dowager. Pro rege. Ps. 19. Exaudiat te Dominus. For the King. The 19 Psalm. Our Lord hear thee. Oremus. Quæsumus omnipotens Deus, ut famulus tuus Jacobus rex noster . . . Let us pray. We beseech thee almighty God, that thy servant James our King . . . Pro Rege, Regina, et Regina Dotaria. Et famulos tuos summum Pontificem Innocentium, Regem nostrum Jacobum, Reginam nostram Mariam, Reginam Catharinam . . . For the King, Queen, and Queen-Dowager. And defend thy servants Innocent the chief Bishop, James our King, Mary our Queen, and Queen Katherine . . .

The Ordinary of the holy Mass in Latin and English according to the copy printed at Paris, Anno 1661, in French and Latin.

Short prayers during the time of mass, necessary for the better understanding thereof. The holy sacrifice of the mass is celebrated in memory of the passion of our Lord Jesus Christ, as he commanded his apostles; when giving them his body and blood he said, " Do this in remembrance of me " Luke xxii. 25. that is, Do this in remembrance of my passion, as if he should have said, remember that I suffered for your salvation; let therefore this mystery be brought in use by you, for the good of you and yours. (Albinus Flaccus Alcuinus, L. 8. de divinis officiis.) When the Priest goes to the altar. Jesus enters the garden. The prayer. Lord Jesus Christ, son of the living God, who when thy passion drew near . . . Amen . . . At the last Dominus vobiscum. Jesus ascends into heaven. The prayer. Lord Jesus Christ, who after the term of forty days did'st ascend glorious into heaven . . . Amen. At the sending of the holy

---

[1] See page 372.

-1687]　PRIMERS OF THE ROMAN USE.　375

> Ghost. The prayer. Lord Jesus Christ, who did'st send thine holy Ghost upon thy disciples ... Amen.
>
> The seven penitential psalms. The penitential psalms are so called because they contain many deep expressions of inward sorrow and repentance for sins committed, and many cries of supplications to God for mercy and forgiveness; and therefore are to be said with the Litanies kneeling.
>
> The Litanies of Saints in Latin and English. They are sung also in the catholic church on the three Rogation days.
>
> The hymn. Stabat mater dolorosa. Under the world-redeeming rood, The most afflicted mother stood.
>
> The conversion of a soul to God. Elevate thyself, O my soul, to thy creator and defer no longer thy conversion though but for a moment ...
> Finis.

A.D. 1687. Henry Hills, London, 16o. Latin. No. 287.

_{*} *The title is "Officium B. Mariæ Virg. nuper reformatum, et Pii V. Pont. Max. jussu editum. Ad instar Breviarii Romani sub Urbano VIII recogniti; cum indulgentiis, orationibus, hymnis, et hujusmodi aliis quæ in Indice notantur."*

> Urbanus Papa VIII. Ad perpetuam rei memoriam. Divinam psalmodiam sponsæ consolantis in hoc exilio absentiam suam a sponso cælesti decet esse non habentem rugam, neque maculam ... Quæ causæ quondam impulere summos Pontifices, prædecessores nostros felicis memoriæ, Pium hujusce nominis Quintum, ut Breviarium Romanum incertis per eam ætatem legibus vagum, certa stataque orandi methodo inlegaret; et Clementem VIII., ut illud ipsum lapsu temporis ac Typographorum incuria depravatum, decori pristino restitueret. Nos quoque in eamdem cogitationem traxere et solicitudo nostra erga res sacras ... Mandavimus dilecto filio Andreæ Brogiotto, Typographiæ nostræ Apostolicæ Præfecto, procurationem hujus Breviarii in lucem primo edendi, quod exemplar, qui posthac Romanum Breviarium impresserint, sequi omnes teneantur. Extra Urbem vero nemini licere volumus idem Breviarium in posterum typis excudere, aut evulgare, nisi facultate in scriptis accepta ab Inquisitoribus hæreticæ pravitatis, siquidem inibi fuerint; sin minus, ab locorum Ordinariis ... Sub iisdem etiam prohibitionibus, et pænis comprehendi intendimus et volumus, ea omnia quæ a Breviario Romano ortum habent, sive ex parte, sive in totum; cujusmodi sunt Missalia, Diurna, Officia parva beatæ Virginis, Officia majoris Hebdomadæ, et id genus alia quæ deinceps non imprimantur, nisi prævia illorum, et cujuslibet ipsorum in dicta Typographia per eumdem Andream impressione, ut omnino cum Breviario de mandato nostro edito concordent. ...
>
> Datum Romæ apud sanctum Petrum sub annulo Piscatoris, die xxv Januarii M.DC.XXXI. Pontificatus nostri anno octavo.
>
> Modus ministrandi et respondendi sacerdoti celebranti Missam ex præscripto Missalis Romani Clementis VIII. auctoritate recogniti,

Psalmi qui dicuntur ad Vesperas in Dominicis, in Nativitate Domini cum sua Vigilia et Octava, et in Festis Apostolorum et Evangelistarum; item ii qui per totum annum dicuntur ad completorium. Psalm. 109. Dixit Dominus. Psalmus. 110. Confitebor tibi. Psalmus. 111. Beatus vir. Psalmus 112. Laudate pueri. Psalmus 113. In exitu Israel. Canticum B. Mariæ Virg. Lucæ 1. Sequentes Psalmi dicuntur ad Vesperas in Vigilia nativitatis Domini. Dixit Dominus. Confitebor. Beatus vir. Laudate pueri. Psalmus 116. Laudate Dominum. Magnificat. Sequentes Psalmi dicuntur ad Vesperas in die Nativitatis Domini, et per totam Octavam ejusdem. Dixit Dominus. Confitebor. Beatus vir. Psalmi 129. De profundis. 131. Memento Domine. Sequentes Psalmi dicuntur ad Vesperas in Festis Apostolorum et Evangelistarum. Dixit Dominus. Laudate pueri. Psalmi 115. Credidi. 125. In convertendo. 138. Domine probasti. Psalmi qui dicuntur ad Completorium per totum annum. 4. Cum invocarem. 30. In te Domine. 90. Qui habitat. 133. Ecce nunc. Canticum Simeonis. Lucæ 2. c. Nunc dimittis.

A.D. 1732. (London) for Thomas Meighan (London) 12o. English. No. 293.

⁎ *The title is " The Primer, or Office of the B. Virgin Mary, with a new and approved version of the church hymns. To which are added the remaining hymns of the Roman Breviary."*

An universal prayer. O my God, I believe in you, but strengthen my faith, I hope in you, but confirm my hope, I love you, but redouble my love ... Amen.

A.D. 1780. J. P. Coghlan, London, 12o. English. No. 296.

⁎ *The title is " The Primer, or Office of the Blessed Virgin Mary, with a new and approved version of the church hymns. Translated from the Roman Breviary. To which is added a table according to the new regulations of the festivals of obligation, days of devotion, fasting, and abstinence, as observed by the Catholics in England."*

A thanksgiving. Hymn of St. Ambrose and St. Augustine. Te Deum laudamus. Thee sovereign God our grateful accents praise ... or the Hymn on the Ascension of our Lord. Æterne rex altissime. O Saviour Christ, O God most high. Then say. ℣. Let us bless the Father ... ℟. Let us praise and extol him ... ℣. Lord hear my prayer. ℟. And let my cry ... Let us pray. O God, of whose mercies there is no number ... Amen. ℣. Lord hear my prayer. ℟. And let my cry ... ℣. Bless we our Lord. ℟. Thanks be to God.

A method of examination of conscience, according to the threefold duty we owe to God, to our neighbour, and to ourselves. I. In relation to God. Have you through your own fault ... For superiors. Have you taken care that those under your charge ... II. Relation to your neighbour. Have you disobeyed your superiors.... For superiors. Have you been excessive in reprehending others under your care . . . III. In relation to yourself. Have you been over eager in following your own will . . .

A.D. 1817. Dublin, published by Coyne, Dublin, 12º. English. No. 297.

₀ *The title is "The Primer, or Office of the B. Virgin Mary. To which are added a new and improved version of the church hymns, and the remaining hymns of the Roman Breviary with many useful additions and amendments."*

An offering of the Office with all the intentions of the passion. O most divine and adorable Jesus, my blessed Saviour and Redeemer, I offer up to thy divine majesty this holy office . . .

Prayer before the Office. Open, O Lord, our mouths to bless thy holy name . . . Amen. At Matins. O most divine and adorable Jesus, I offer these Matins and Lauds . . . Hail Mary . . . pray for us sinners now, and at the hour of death . . . Amen.

The Crown of our blessed Lady . . . These beads or seven decads called the Crown of our blessed Lady are to be said in honour of the seventy two years she lived on earth, by saying which a plenary indulgence can be gained; as was granted by Pope Innocent the eleventh.

Prayers at mass.

The Litany of the blessed Sacrament.

Prayers to be said at the Novena of St. Joseph which commences on the eleventh of March.

Seven prayers in honour of the seven dolours and seven joys of St. Joseph.

A.D. 1844. P. J. Hanicq, Mechlin. 8º. Latin. No. 297*.

₀ *The title is "The Office of the Blessed Virgin Mary, for the three times of the year. According to the Roman Breviary. Permissu Superiorum."*

The rubricks to be observed in reciting the Office of the Blessed Virgin. 1. When Lauds are said immediately after Matins . . . 2. If the Office be said in private . . . when the Office is interrupted at the end of Prime, Tierce, Sext, None or Vespers . . . 3. When the Office is said without interruption . . .

Prayer of the church before Office. Open, O Lord, my mouth . . . Amen. Aperi, Domine, os meum . . . Amen. O Lord, in union with that divine intention . . . Domine, in unione illius divinæ intentionis . . .

Prayer after the Office. To the most holy and undivided Trinity . . . R. Amen. Sacrosanctæ et individuæ Trinitati . . . R. Amen. V. Blessed is the womb of the Virgin Mary . . . V. Beata viscera Mariæ Virginis . . . R. And blessed the breasts . . . Our Father. Hail Mary. R. Et beata ubera . . . Pater-noster. Ave Maria.

The sovereign Pontiff Leo X granted to those who say this prayer on their knees at the end of Office, the remission of the faults they commit through human frailty in reciting it. Pater noster. Ave Maria. Credo.

The Office of the Blessed Virgin Mary.

„ *The Office is in Latin, the rubricks are in english.*

Grace at meals. Before the midday repast the Priest (or other person) who is to say grace says, Benedicite. and the rest answer, Benedicite. The Priest says, ℣. Oculi omnium, and the rest continue. In te sperant . . . Et tu das escam . . . Aperis tu manum . . . Et imples . . . Gloria Patri. Kyrie eleison. Pater noster etc. in secret. Then the Priest says. Oremus. Benedic Domine nos . . . ℟. Amen. Then the Reader (or the person who represents him) says. Jube domine benedicere. The blessing. Mensæ cœlestis participes . . . ℟. Amen. After the repast grace is said, as follows. The Reader having said. Tu autem Domine . . . ℟. Deo Gratias, all rise. The Priest begins the ℣. Confiteantur . . . ℟. Et sancti . . . V. Gloria Patri. ℟. Sicut erat. Then the Priest will say, without any addition. Agimus tibi gratias . . . ℟. Amen. Then is said the Psalm Miserere. The Priest saying the first verse and the rest answering, and so on alternately; or else the Psalm 116. Laudate Dominum. Gloria Patri. Sicut erat. Kyrie eleison. The Priest says. Pater noster. ℣. Et ne nos . . . R. Sed libera . . . ℣. Dispersit . . , ℟. Justitia ejus . . . ℣. Benedicamus Dominum . . . ℟. Semper laus . . . ℣. In Domino . . . ℟. Audiant mansueti . . . ℣. Magnificate Dominum . . . ℟. Et exaltemus . . . ℣. Sit nomen . . . ℟. Ex hoc nunc . . . Then without Oremus. Retribuere dignare Domine . . . ℟. Amen. ℣. Benedicamus Domino. ℟. Deo gratias. ℣. Fidelium animæ . . . ℟ Amen. Pater noster etc. in secret. After which the Priest says. Deus det . . . ℟. Amen. Before the evening repast the Priest begins: Benedicite. and the rest repeat: Benedicite. Then the Priest begins the ℣. and the rest continue. Edent pauperes . . . Gloria Patri. Sicut erat. Kyrie eleison. Pater noster etc. in secret. ℣. Et ne nos. Oremus. Benedic Domine, as above at the midday repast. Jube Domine. The blessing. Ad cœnam . . . ℟. Amen. At the end of the evening repast is said. ℣. Memoriam fecit . . . ℟. Escam dedit . . . Gloria Patri. Sicut erat. The Priest says. Benedictus Deus . . . ℟. Amen. Then is said the Psalm. Laudate dominum. the Priest saying the first verse, the rest answering anthems, as above at the midday repast. When only one meal is taken, all is said as prescribed for the evening.

This manner of saying grace is followed throughout the year, except on the days mentioned below; on which nothing is changed but the ℣.

From Christmas to the evening repast on the Epiphany exclusively is said. ℣. Verbum caro . . . Alleluia. ℟. Et habitavit . . . Alleluia. Gloria Patri. At the end is said V. Notum fecit Dominus. Alleluia. R. Salutare suum. Alleluia. Gloria Patri. The rest as above. The Psalm. Cantate, or

Laudate Dominum. This last may be said every day even on solemn feasts.

The day of the Epiphany, and throughout the Octave is said. ℣. Reges Tharsis ... Alleluia. ℟. Reges Arabum ... Alleluia. Gloria Patri. At the end is said. ℣. Omnes de Saba ... Alleluia. ℟. Aurum et thus ... Alleluia. Gloria Patri. Psalm 71. Deus judicium tuum.

On Maundy Thursday is said in an under tone ℣. Christus factus est .. Then Pater noster, in secret, after which the Priest without saying anything blesses the table with the sign of the cross. Jube Domine, and Tu autem. Are not said. After the repast is said. ℣. Christus factus est ... Then the Psalm Miserere, without Gloria Patri. Then Pater noster etc. in secret. Then the Priest says. Respice quæsumus Domine ... After which Pater noster etc. is said in secret, and nothing more. Deus det. Is not added.

On Good Friday all as on Maunday Thursday, except the ℣. Christus factus est ...

On Holy Saturday before the repast is said. Benedicite. ℟. Benedicite. ℣. Vespere autem Sabbati ... Alleluia. Gloria Patri. Sicut erat. After the repast. ℣. Vespere autem, as above with Gloria Patri. Psalm. Laudate Dominum with Gloria Patri. Kyrie eleison etc. as above.

On Easter day, and till the evening repast the Saturday following, before meals is said. ℣. Hæc dies ... Alleluia. Gloria Patri. After meals. Hæc dies, as above.

On Ascension day, and till Witsun eve exclusively, is said ℣. Ascendit Deus ... Alleluia. ℟. Et Dominus ... Alleluia. Gloria Patri.

After meals is said the ℣. Ascendens Christus ... Alleluia. ℟. Captivam duxit ... Alleluia. Gloria Patri. Psalm. 46. Omnes gentes.

From Witsun eve till the evening repast the Saturday following is said. ℣. Spiritus Domini ... Alleluia. R. Et hoc quod continet ... Alleluia. Gloria Patri. After meals is said the ℣. Repleti sunt ... Alleluia. ℟. Et cæperunt ... Alleluia. Gloria Patri. Psalm 47. Magnus Dominus.

At collation. The blessing. Hoc donum charitatis ... ℟. Amen. After collation is said. ℣. Sit nomen ... ℟. Ex hoc nunc ...

A.D. 1867. John F. Fowler, Dublin. 8o. Latin and English. No. 297**.

*** *The title is " The Office of the Blessed Virgin Mary and the Office for the Dead. Same as in the Evening Office Book of the St. John's Society as established in Dublin."*

The little Office of the B. V. M. is of ancient usage in the church and was recited by the clergy and devout laity and practised by rule in religious monasteries even from the sixth and seventh centuries, and probably at a more early period, as Meratus observes in his annotations on Gavantus ... The little Office of the B. V. M. is always of a simple rite, and as such it should be recited every day and invariably observed the whole year round. The simple rite signifies, 1st: That the office commence at Vespers and terminate at None; 2nd: That there be said only one nocturn at Matins, the psalms are changed according to the order of the days, 3rd: That there be recited the common suffrage, or commemoration for the saints, after the prayer in Vespers and Lauds; and 4th: That the anthems of the Psalms be simple viz. that the first words only of the anthems be said before the psalms, but after the psalms the anthems recited entire. It is therefore a material fault in Church rites to subject the little Office of the Blessed Virgin Mary to the various changes of rites and ceremonies of what is called the Divine Office, and to recite the anthems entire before the psalms on feasts of a double rite; for the Office of the B. V. M. has no relation to the occurring festivals and transferred feasts of the Divine Office. The contrary practice is erroneous, and should be corrected, because repugnant to the sacred rite and order prescribed by the Church. Besides, there are many rubrical difficulties and absurdities, that would arise by changing thus the simple rite of the Little Office of the B. V. M. . . .

Vespers and Complin are usually said in the afternoon, Matins with Lauds late in the evening, or both Vespers and Matins can be recited together late in the evening for the convenience of those who cannot attend the choir more early on account of business, and the lesser hours of Prime etc., are said in the morning. In order to promote true piety towards the Blessed Virgin Mary, and to encourage the devout recital of her office, Pope Pius V., by his decree on the 9th July, 1558 has granted to those who are bound to say her little Office the indulgence of a hundred days every time they perform this duty at the prescribed times, according to church rites. His holiness has also granted fifty days of indulgence to those who are not bound to this office, each time they devoutly recite the little Office of the Blessed Virgin Mary.

Office of the Blessed Virgin Mary.
Office for the Dead.

₀ *An Appendix with continuous pagination consists of The Litany of Loretto. Acts of Contrition, faith, hope and charity. Litany of the holy name of Jesus. Litany for a happy death. Litany for the dead. Litany of the Saints. An act of adoration to the sacred heart of Jesus. Adorable heart of Jesus, hypostatically united to the eternal Word. . . Amen. An act of consecration to the sacred heart of Jesus. To thee, O sacred heart of Jesus, to thee I devote and offer up my life . . . Amen. The thirty days prayer to the B. V. Mary. In honour of the sacred passion of our Lord Jesus Christ. Ever glorious and blessed Mary, Queen of Virgins, mother of mercy . . . Amen. The thirty days prayer. Glory, honour, and praise be to our Lord Jesus Christ . . . Amen. Thirty days prayer to our blessed Redeemer in honour of his bitter passion. O dear Jesus, my blessed Saviour and Redeemer, the sweet comforter of all sad, desolate and distressed souls . . . Amen.*

INDICES.

I. INDEX OF LITURGICAL FORMS.
II. INDEX OF HYMNS AND RHYTHMS.
III. INDEX OF NAMES AND PLACES.
IV. GENERAL INDEX.

EXPLANATIONS.

1. The references in the Indices are to pages and not to numbers.
2. A word within round brackets is either an addition or substitution.

INDEX OF LITURGICAL FORMS.

	PAGE
A cunctis nos q. Dne. mentis et corporis defende periculis	351
A domo tuo q. Dne. nequitiæ repellantur	132
Ab initio (*Chapter*)	160
Ablue Dne. D. aqua tuæ divinæ gratiæ	258
Abluitur sacra Christus ter maximus unda	268
Above all things love God with all thy heart	221
Absolve	
Dne. animam famuli tui	129
q. Dne. animas famulorum	110
Absque viro facta est fœcunda Deipara	268
Accept O most clement God by the prayers and merits of b. Mary	359
According to the multitude of thy mercies, O Lord	247
Actiones nostras q. Dne. aspirando præveni	132. 354
Ad mensam dulcissimi convivii tui pie Dne.	135. 354
Ad te	
nos Dne. clamantes exaudi	352
s. Spiritus qui es Spiritus solatii	255
Adesto (quæsumus)	
Dne. supplicationibus nostris et viam	108. 352. 356
ut qui ex iniquitate nostra	139
Adonai Dne. D. magne rex admirabilis	119
Adorable heart of Jesus	380
Adoramus te	
Dne Jesu Christe et benedicimus tibi	136
s. Trinitas pater et fili et spiritus sancte	134
Adoro te devote latens Deitas	145
Adoro te Dne. Jesu Christe	
descendentem ad inferos	112
in cruce pendentem	112
in cruce vulneratum	112
in sepulchro positum	112
resurgentem a mortuis	112
Adoro te s. et individua Trinitas D. ineffabilis	151
Adsit omnibus gratia Dnm. n. Jesum Christum amantibus	262
Adveniet Christus supremo tempore judex	269
Aeterne ac misericors D. qui es D. pacis	255. 265

INDEX

	PAGE
After	
due examination of my former life	291
that he appeared unto the eleven (*Sequence*)	118. 162. 215
Agimus tibi gratias	
indulgentissime pater conditor cæli et terræ	266
omn. D. pro universis beneficiis tuis	154. 354. 378
Agnoscimus omn. D. quam perniciosa labe	269
Agnus Dei qui tollis peccata mundi	153
Ago Deo meo	
gratias per Jesum Christum de vobis omnibus	262
semper de vobis gratias	262
Ago tibi gratias	
Jesu Christe pro ineffabili caritate tua	265
pater cæli terræque Dne.	261
Ah Dne. D. fortis qui consilia impiorum	255
Albeit	
O h. Father, all we that unfeignedly profess thy holy religion	293
O Lord thou art the giver of all good things	293
whatsoever is born of flesh is flesh	293
All christian souls rest in peace	214
All hail	
most benign Jesu, full of mercy and grace	166. 210
O head of our Lord and Saviour Jesu Christ	361
true body born of the V. Mary	359
All holy	
angels and archangels	240
patriarchs and prophets	240
saints and the elect creatures of God	217
All that is and shall be set upon the board	290
All ye whom God hath here refreshed	290
Alme pater Augustine cum tuo collegio	149
Almighty and eternal God	
behold I come to the Sacrament	360
look mercifully upon our weakness	177
Almighty and eternal God which	
by the operation of the Holy Ghost	174
hast commanded the body of thy glorious v. and m. Katherine	164
vouchsafest that we as it were heavenly children	192
Almighty and everlasting God	
we be taught by thy holy word	251. 292
we most heartily thank thee	251
Almighty and everlasting God which	
hast granted to us thy servants	162. 215. 217. 230. 239
hatest nothing that thou hast made	278

	PAGE
Almighty and everlasting God who	
alone workest great marvels	305
by thy holy apostle hast taught us	307
hatest nothing that thou hast made	307
Almighty and everliving God	
I most heartily thank thee	345
which only workest great marvels	241
who by the holy apostle hast taught us	344
Almighty and merciful God	
behold mercifully thy people	182
having pity on us	180
of whose gift it becometh	179
Almighty and most merciful Father	
I (we) have erred and strayed	251. 276. 278. 291. 303
who for our many and grievous sins	280
Almighty eternal God	
to whom there is never any prayer made	256. 297
Almighty eternal God grant that we may	
bear ever a devout mind	178
so use the mysteries of the Lord's passion	178
Almighty eternal God which	
by the operation of the holy Ghost	164. 176. 230
hast given to thy servants	178
Almighty everlasting God	
give to us increase of faith	179
guide our doings in thy pleasure	177
Almighty everlasting God which	
governest both heavenly and earthly things	177
in the abundance of thy goodness	179
through thy grace healest both bodies and souls	180
wouldest that our Saviour	177
Almighty everlasting God which hast	
granted a generable and holy mirth	180
granted us godly to praise	181
Almighty God	
and most holy Father, Lord both of the living and of the dead	173
bless her with the blessings of heaven above	279
eternal Father we do remember	187. 242
father of all mercies	324
from whom we have the beginning	280
King and Lord of glory eternal	184. 222
Lord of heaven and earth	280
maker and disposer of all things	293
regard our infirmity	240

INDEX

	PAGE
Almighty God	
syth (since) thou of thine infinite benevolence	197. 203
unto whom all hearts be open	278
whose kingdom is everlasting	251. 279. 292
with whom do live the spirits	328
Almighty God father of our Lord Jesus Christ	
maker of all things	251. 278. 298
of whom the whole family	281
Almighty God have mercy	
on thy servant	182
upon us and all our sins being forgiven	359
Almighty God our heavenly father	
thy mercy and goodness is infinite	186. 241
we be taught by thy holy word	279
we beseech thy gracious goodness	186. 241. 254
we most humbly beseech thee	280
Almighty God our heavenly father which	
dids't create man	298
suffereds't Peter thy (the) apostle	187. 241
Almighty God our heavenly father who hast purchased	280
Almighty God the father	
of all mercy and comfort	281
of our Lord Jesus Christ	251. 276. 292
Almighty God the father and maker	
of all things	282
of us all	281
Almighty God the fountain	
of all mercy	279
of all wisdom	307
Almighty God the fountain of all goodness	
from whom every good and perfect gift	321
hear our humble supplications	279
we humbly beseech thee to bless	305
Almighty God the Saviour of souls	182
Almighty God we	
beseech thee vouchsafe that the merits	164
give thee hearty thanks	297
humbly beseech thy majesty	181
Almighty God which	
choosest the weak things	182
for mine ingratitude	295
hast given us grace	241. 245. 298
Almighty God who	
by thy holy apostle hast taught us	281

Almighty God who	
dids't command thy people Israel	280
for the redemption of mankind	372
givest to all life and breath	280
hast of thine infinite mercies vouchsafed to ordain	320
hast promised to hear the petitions	282. 307
hast straightly commanded us to honor	281
in thy wrath in the time of King David	282
Almighty Jesu and God in Trinity	222
Almighty Lord who hast of thine infinite mercy	278
Although I doubt not of thy fatherly provision	294
Amator humani generis Deus	172. 264
Among other innumerable pestilent infections of books	195
An infinite number of wicked angels	294
And	
defend thy servants Innocent the chief bishop	373. 374
from the very bottom of my heart	245
in thy faithful prayers	296. 299
now my Lord my Saviour	338
the souls of all true believers being departed	231
Angele	
Dei qui custos es mei	353. 354
qui meus es custos	107. 191
Angustiæ mihi sunt undique	263
Anima Christi sanctifica me	107. 174
Animabus q. Dne. omnium famulorum	134
Animae	
eorum in bonis demorentur	133
obscurus teterque carcer	156. 256. 267
omnium fidelium defunctorum	150. 154. 165. 217
Ante oculos tuos Dne. culpas nostras	368. 372
Aperi Dne. os meum	377
Apparuit Jesus undecim discipulis (*Lesson*)	259
Apply thy ears to our prayers	176
Apposita et apponenda benedicat Dei dextera (*Blessing*)	154
Appropinquet (*Psalm*)	280
Aqua benedicta sit mihi salus	108
Arise	
Lord let thine enemies (*Psalm*)	242
O God and let the enemies	247
As	
for me I will go into thy house	275
I have prayed unto thee, O heavenly father to be taught	294
it is thy godly appointment	293

388 INDEX

	PAGE
As	
riches, so likewise poverty	293
the bird is born to fly	293
thou hast fed our bodies Lord	302
to the sick all pleasant things	305
Ascendat ad te Dne. D. oratio mea	108
Asperges me Dne. hyssopo	354
Assist me (us) mercifully O Lord	280. 307
Assoyle we beseech thee the faults of thy people	180
At	
certain hours unto God for to pray	164
night lie down prepare (prepared) to have	276. 284
the beginning of this refection	252. 290
the last as the eleven sat at the table (*Lesson*)	183. 219. 228
what time soever a sinner doth repent	251. 299. 303
At that time	
Jesus appeared to the eleven disciples (*Sequence*)	118. 365
Jesus said to his disciples	361
Jesus went forth with his disciples	362
the angel Gabriel was sent of God (*Sequence*)	118. 365
the festival day of the Azymes approached	361
the Pasche was	361
Attend O Lord Jesus Christ my God	343
Audi preces meas æterna Patris sapientia	254. 264
Audivi vocem de cælo	262
Aufer a nobis	
D. optime maxime prava consilia	269
Dne. cunctas iniquitates	149
Auxiliare	
mihi et tu princeps obsecro eximie Raphael	114
nos deprecamur D. noster	114
Auxiliatrix sis mihi Trinitas	107. 162
Auxilientur	
mihi Dne. Jesu Christe omnes passiones tuæ	127
nobis pie Dne. Jesu Christe omnes passiones tuæ	127
Ave	
benigne Jesu gratia plenus	115. 166
caput Christi gratum	123
caro Christi cara	126
Dei patris filia nobilissima	128
domina sancta Maria mater Dei	130
Dne. Jesu Christe verbum Patris	149. 174
dulcis mater Christi	126
acies præclara	127

OF LITURGICAL FORMS.

	PAGE
Ave	
fuit prima salus	128
in ævum sanctissima et preciosissima caro	127
Jesu Christe verbum Patris	111
Jesu splendor paternæ gloriæ	135
manus dextera Christi	124
mundi spes Maria	126
regina cælorum	156
rex noster ave fili David	137. 187
rosa sine spinis	124. 201
sanctissima caro	145
vere sanguis	149. 174
verum corpus	111. 165. 217. 354
vulnus lateris	122
Ave Maria	
alta stirps	124
ancilla sanctæ trinitatis humilissima	131
ancilla trinitatis humilissima	201
gratia plena . . . et benedicta sit s. Anna	125
gratia plena . . . Jesus (Christus)	108, 118, 162
gratia plena . . . ora pro nobis peccatoribus	152
quem virgo carens vitio	122
Ave sanctissima Maria mater Dei	123
Avete	
fideles omnes animæ	117
omnes Christi fideles animæ	128
omnes sancti et electi Dei	137
Averte faciem tuam Dne. (*Psalm*)	259
Awake thou that sleepest	284
B. Johannis apostoli tui et evangelistæ	115. 166
B. Matthæi apostoli tui et evangelistæ	138
Be	
glad Jerusalem (*Chapter*)	249
pleased O God to accept	278. 320
we followers of God	278
Beati immaculati (*Psalm*)	280
Beatus vir qui non abiit (*Psalm*)	120
Because	
thou dids't give Jesus Christ	342
ye may understand the Pater noster	214
Before thy holy eyes O Lord	372
Begone profaneness come not near	285
Behold	
thou art made whole	278

	PAGE
Behold	
with pity we beseech thee O Lord	313
Benedic	
Dne. nos et dona tua	154. 155. 354. 378
igitur et nunc mihi	121
Benedicat	
et custodiat nos omn. et misericors Dnus.	136. 354
me D. pater qui cuncta creavit	130
me imperialis majestas	114
te D. pater qui in principio	129
Benedicite	205. 354. 378. 379
Benedicta sit	
s. et individua Trinitas	353. 354
summa et incomprehensibilis Trinitas	134
Benedictio	
Dei patris et filii et spiritus sancti	137
et claritas et sapientia	264
Benedictum sit dulce nomen Dni. n. Jesu Christi	115. 132. 191
Benedictus	
Deus in donis suis	154. 267. 378
Benedictus Dominus	
Deus (*Psalm*)	145. 205
Deus Israel	355
Deus qui non abstulisti misericordiam	121
die quotidie	145
Benigne salvator sinum tuæ pietatis	260
Benignissime	
Deus qui nos pascis	267
Dne. Jesu Christe respice	112
et indulgentissime pater defensor noster	156. 256. 265
Bless us O Lord and these thy gifts	
whereof we now shall taste	302
which we are to receive	359
Bless we our Lord which of his grace	214
Blessed	
are they that dwell in thy house	275
is God in all his gifts	173. 192. 239. 290
is he whose unrighteousness is forgiven	279
is the man	279
thrice blessed are the poor	283
Blessed art thou	
O Christ our God	343
O Lord who hast fed us	345
O Virgin (*Chapter*)	249

Blessed art thou O Lord God	
and blessed be thy holy name	339
who sustainest all things	337
Blessed be	
our Lord God of Israel (*Canticle*)	364
the father celestial	290
the Father the Son	186
the holy and undivided Trinity	275. 313. 316. 327. 359. 360
the sweet name of our Lord Jesu Christ	191. 231
thou O God which feedest us	198
Blessed be the Lord omnipotent	
that sendeth us plenty	214
with all faithful eyes that trust in him	214
Blessed Jesu who dids't accept the poor widow's mite	320
Blessed Jesus I do heartily believe	339
Blessing and glory and wisdom	278
Bone Jesu verbum Patris	355
Bountiful Lord God I pray thee	221
Break thou the bread and food to the poor	214
Burn our reins and thoughts	182
But oh do thou deliver me	337
But upon one of the sabbaths (*Lesson*)	183
By thine agony and bloody sweat	320
By thy crucified body	320
Cantate (*Psalm*)	378
Castigans castigavit me Dominus	264
Castigasti me Domine	255. 264
Celebremus conversionem s. Pauli apostoli	138
Certius incerta nihil est mortalibus ipsa	269
Christ that	
ascended into heaven	281
redeemed thee	281
Christ which (who) at his (the) last supper	
gave himself unto us	198. 220. 228. 233. 304
promised his body to be crucified	252. 290
Christ with the benefit of his death	339
Christ Jesus that rose the third day	281
Christi autem generatio (*Lesson*)	183
Christus	
ad athereas	268
resurrexit ex mortuis	262
Cibo spiritualis (*Blessing*)	154
Circumdederunt me dolores	263
Clamavi de tribulatione mea ad Dnm.	122. 172

INDEX

	PAGE
Cleanse me O God	275
Clementissime	
Deus qui per b. patriarchæ Joachim	138
et misericors D. concede mihi	267
pater misericordiarum	354
redemptor qui semper es misericors	255
Clothe me, O Lord	275
Coenam sanctificet qui nobis omnia præbet	154
Come	
Holy Spirit replenish the hearts	198
let us adore our God	283
now and hear	283
Concede mihi	
Dne. D. felicem ac salutarem vivendi ac moriendi horam	266
misericors D. quæ tibi placita sunt	130. 355
Concede q. omn. Deus	
ut nos unigeniti tui nova	144
ut qui hodierna die unigenitum tuum	143
ut sanctissima vulnera	124
ut sicut apostolorum tuorum	118
Concede q. omn. et misericors Deus	
ut qui b. Christofori	113. 151
Conditor cæli et terræ rex regum	118. 167. 189. 354
Confiteantur tibi (*Psalm*)	154
Confitebor tibi Dne. rex	255
Confitemini (*Psalm*)	146
Confiteor Deo	
b. Mariæ, omnibus sanctis, et vobis	153
cæli	152
omnipotenti, b. Mariæ	353
Confiteor tibi	
Dne. D. omnipotens creator	135
Dne. Jesu Christe omnia peccata mea	108. 155
Conform me my high sovereign Lord Jesu Christ	223
Conscientias nostras q. Dne. visitando purifica	144
Consider and hear me (*Psalm*)	281
Cor mundum crea in me Deus	263
Corpora qui solito satiasti nostra cibatu	267
Creator ineffabilis qui de thesauris	355
Creavit Deus cibos	267
Credere meruisse Christum	162
Credo	
in Deum	108
in Deum Patrem creavit omnia	267

	PAGE
Crucem tuam adoramus	107
Crux Christi sit mecum	124. 201
Crux triumphalis	
Dni. n. Jesu Christi	107
passionis Dni. n. Jesu Christi	107
Culter qui circumcidisti sacrosanctam carnem Christi	136
Cum	
cepisset agnus librum	262
natus esset Jesus in Bethlehem (*Sequence*)	118. 162. 357
Custodi nos Dne. ut pupillam oculi	354
Da	
Deus lætæ bona sancta pacis	268
Dne. ut tuis præceptis eruditus	263
mihi dona tria, sanctissima virgo Maria	143
pacem Dne. in diebus nostris	108
requiem cunctis D. hic et ubique sepultis	150
Da nobis q. Domine	
imitari quod colimus	109. 163. 216
piæ supplicationis effectum	352
Da nobis q. omn. D. vitiorum nostrorum flammas	109. 152. 163. 216
Da q. omnipotens Deus	
ut qui b. Huberti confessoris	146
vitiorum nostrorum flammas	140
De profundis	
clamavi ad te Dne. (*Psalm*)	110. 155. 165. 173
cordis clamamus ad te Dne.	260
Dearly beloved brethren the scripture moveth us	251. 292. 299. 303. 304
Deduc me (Dne.) in via tua	145. 266
Dele quæso iniquitates nostras	260
Deliver me O Lord from the ungodly (*Psalm*)	189. 242
Deo	
gloria supremis in locis	262
gratias	118. 161. 354. 357
Deus	
aeterne qui absconditorum cognitor	122
charitas est	154
Deus meus (*Psalm*)	133
illuminator omnium gentium	111
judicium tuum (*Psalm*)	379
mi pater mi et servator	253. 258
misereatur (*Psalm*)	205
misericordiæ D. pietatis	111. 165
noster refugium (*Psalm*)	351
omnium fidelium pastor	352

		PAGE
Deus		
pater n. qui ut oremus hortaris		108
patrum meorum (nostrorum)	156. 167. 211.	255
pius et propitius agnus immolatus		150
refugium nostrum		352
regnorum (omnium)	108.	352
rex gloriæ		259
tuorum gloria sanctorum		142
venerunt gentes (*Psalm*)		351
Deus a quo		
bona cuncta procedunt	132.	143
sancta desideria	110. 132. 164. 216. 258.	352
Deus ago tibi gratias quod non sum quales		262
Deus auctor pacis		
et amator quem nosse vivere		132
et concordiæ amator		258
Deus cui		
omne cor patet	120.	353
omnia vivunt		146
proprium est misereri semper		205
Deus cujus		
charitatis ardore b. Valentinus		139
claritatis fulgore b. Michael		137
dextera b. Petrum apostolum	109. 163,	216
dispositione mirabili corpus b. Jacobi		113
gratia b. Erasmus martyr et pontifex		139
misericordiæ non est numerus		353
præconium innocentes martyres		144
Deus det		379
Deus in		
cujus miseratione		130
quo vivimus		352
Deus pacis		
charitatisque amator	132.	353
et dilectionis maneat		154
Deus pro cujus		
ecclesia gloriosus martyr et pontifex Thomas	110.	187
legis defensione b. Georgius		139
sanctissimi nominis honore		142
Deus propitius esto mihi		
peccatori et custos meus sis		124
peccatori et esto custos mei	114. 116. 117. 189. 201.	211
sonti		262
Deus qui Abraham puerum tuum de Ur		356

Deus qui	
ad imitandum passionis tuæ exemplum	140
affluentissimæ bonitatis tuæ prudentiam	142
b. Annæ tantam gratiam donare	113
b. Armigillum confessorem	130
b. Augustinum pontificem tuum	141
b. Dionysium martyrem tuum	140
b. Erasmum martyrem	151
b. evangelistas tuos	150
b. Gertrudam piam virginem	142
b. Hieronymum hæreticorum malleum	141
b. Jacobum apostolum tuum	138
b. Lambertum pontificem tuum	146
b. Marcum evangelistam tuam	139
b. Mariæ Magdalenæ pænitentiam	142
b. Matthiam apostolorum tuorum collegio fecisti	138
b. Nicholaum (pium) pontificem tuum	110. 141. 163. 202
b. Petro apostolo tuo collatis clavibus regni	138
b. Sebastianum gloriosum martyrem tuum	113
b. Sitham virginem famulam tuam	126
b. virginem Margaretam ad cælos	110. 164. 216
beatissimam virginem Mariam	110. 164. 217
caritatis dona per gratiam S. Spiritus	353
concedis obtentu b. Anthonii confessoris tui	113. 140
conspicis quia ex nulla nostra virtute	113. 141
conteris bella et impugnatores	352
contritorum non despicis gemitum	117. 355
corda fidelium s. Spiritus illustratione	109. 162. 215. 259
culpa offenderis, pænitentia placaris	118
de b. Mariæ virginis utero	126. 133. 143
de vivis et electis lapidibus	144
dedisti legem Moysi	142
diligentibus te facis cuncta prodesse	353
ecclesiam tuam b. Dominici	141
ecclesiam tuam b. Francisci	113
es sanctorum tuorum ductor	145
filios Israel per maris medium	356
gloriosissimum nomen Jesu Christi	112
gloriosum confessorem tuum Hieronymum	115
hodierna die per unigenitum tuum	143
hodierna die unigenitum tuum	143
hominem de limo terræ	133
humilium vota respicis	129
illuminas noctem et lucem	135
in tuorum divisione apostolorum	143

	PAGE
Deus qui	
in vexillo sanctæ crucis	143
justificas impium	108. 352
justum apostolum tuum Jacobum	113
liberasti Susannam de falso crimine	111
manus tuas et pedes tuos	119. 129. 162
mira crucis mysteria	141
miro ordine angelorum ministeria	109. 114. 146. 163
nobis aeternæ salutis b. Wolfgangum pontificem	141
nobis dedisti b. Servatium prædicatorem	146
nobis famulis tuis lumine vultus tui signatis	135
nobis nati salvatoris die	143
nobis sanctam hujus diei solemnitatem	147
nobis signatis lumine vultus	127
nobis sub sacramento mirabili	120. 143
nos annua apostolorum tuorum	138
nos annua b. Galli confessoris solemnitate	141
nos b. egregii confessoris tui Theobaldi	146
nos b. Gregorii confessoris tui atque pontificis	140
nos b. Wilhelmi confessoris tui	125
nos conceptionis nativitatis	119
nos patrem et matrem honorare præcepisti	109
nos per b. apostolos tuos Symonem et Judam	139
novem spirituum ordines	125
nullum respuis	352
per crucem passionis tuæ	117
per electos famulos tuos	140
per orationem b. Blasii	139
per os b. Lucæ evangelistæ	139
per prothodoctorem nostrum Augustinum	149
per unigeniti tui gloriosam resurrectionem	259
per unigeniti tui passionem	149
populo tuo æternæ salutis b. Ambrosium	141
pro redemptione mundi voluisti nasci	355
recta petentibus	142
sanctam crucem (tuam) ascendisti	109. 130. 163. 215
sanctorum angelorum tuorum	112. 191
sperantibus in te misereri potius eligis	132
Spiritus s. gratia almam virginem Odiliam	142
sub sacramento mirabili	374
superbis resistis et gratiam paras humilibus	132
superbis resistis et humilibus das gratiam	111. 191
Susannam matronam honestam	266
tres magos orientales	107. 111

Deus qui	
unigeniti tui patientia	353
universarum nationum populos	147
universum mundum b. Pauli apostoli	131
Deus qui voluisti	
pro perditione mundi a Judæis reprobari	112
Deus sub cujus	
ineffabili providentia	152
nutibus vitæ nostræ momenta	129
Dignare Domine	
die isto sine peccato	353
nocte ista sine peccato	354
Dignare me	
Domine die isto sine peccatis custodire	258
laudare te benignissime Jesu Christe	136
Dilectio sit inter vos (*Lesson*)	258
Dirigere et sanctificare	353
Dirupisti Dne. vincula mea	127
Discedite a me maligni	108
Discipulis autem recumbentibus (*Lesson*)	183
Divine Spiritus qui abhorres	266
Divinum auxilium maneat	132
Do	
as thou wouldest be done to	5. 210
this in remembrance of me	374
Docuit nos O Pater cælestis	266
Dominator Dne. D. misericors	121
Dominator Dne. D. omnipotens qui es	
personarum trinitas	150
trinitas in filio	116
Domine	
da nobis auxilium	263
Dei patris et filii et spiritus sancti	128
in unione illius divinæ intentionis	377
libera animam meam	108
miserere nobis	114
noli in eos hoc vindicare peccatum	262
Domine Deus	
cæli fortis magne et terribilis	262
creator omnium	265
de Deo lumen de lumine	152
dominator omnium	108
gloriose ecclesiæ salus	151
patrum nostrorum	121

INDEX

	PAGE
Domine Deus	
rex Israel	121
sine cujus voluntate ne passer	256, 266
tu regnare fecisti servum tuum	264
Domine Deus meus	
da cordi meo pænitentiam	265
si feci	108
Domine Deus omnipotens	
a quo omnis est sapientia	150
cui omnia exposita	156, 254
Pater et Filius et Spiritus sanctus	116
patrum nostrorum Abraham	121
Domine Deus omnipotens qui	
ad imaginem	150
ad principium hujus diei	353
caritas es	265
me in hanc horam secundam	108
Domine Deus pater omn. immensæ pietatis	144
Domine Deus qui	
noctem destinasti	253
nos ad principium hujus diei	108
nos secundum te plurimum honoris	266
serenissimam nostram reginam	260
Domine dominus noster (*Psalm*)	116
Domine in multitudine misericordiæ tuæ	108, 170, 266, 354
Domine inventor factorque omnium	256
Domine Jesu	
accipe spiritum meum	185, 262
qui es unica salus	256, 267
redemptor et consolator	265
unica salus	255
Domine Jesu Christe	
aeterne salvator	266
apud me sis	117
clemens ac misericors Deus	265
cujus inexhaustæ bonitatis	264
ego cognosco me graviter peccasse	115
ego miser peccator rogo	127
exaudi orationem meam	130
fac quod amem te	130
in cujus ditione cuncta sunt posita	355
in summa potentia mitissime	256, 265
Paradisum tuum postulo	128
per agoniam et orationem tuam	114

	PAGE
Domine Jesu Christe	
propter illam amaritudinem	129
rex virginum integritatis amator	108
rogo et ammoneo te	127
salus et liberatio fidelium animarum	123
salvator et redemptor	127
Domine Jesu Christe fili Dei ac	
redemptor noster	184
Domine Jesu Christe fili Dei vivi	
creator et resuscitator	125
Deus omnipotens rex gloriæ	117
pone passionem crucem	123. 197
salvator mundi	127
te deprecor per sanctissiman carnem	127
Domine Jesu Christe fili Dei vivi qui	
es verus et omn. Deus	114
in cruce pendens dixisti	355
pro redemptione nostra	131
pro salute mundi	126
Domine Jesu Christe qui	
b. Brigittam . . . sponsam tuam	141
cum discipulis tuis cænans	150
Deus immortalis	134
dixeras unumquemque fratri suo irascentem	256. 265
dum hora sexta	108
es clarus mundi sol	156. 254
gloriosas manus tuas	112
gloriosum caput tuum	112
hanc sacratissimam carnem tuam	111
hora tertia diei ad crucis pænam	108
hora nona in crucis patibulo	108
omne genus humanum	144
per os prophetæ tui dixisti	114
per os s. Petri apostoli	156. 256. 267
pretiosos pedes tuos	112
pretiosum latus tuum	112
pro nobis mori dignatus es	114
redemisti nos pretioso sanguine tuo	114
septem verba	123. 161. 201
solus es medicus ægrotarum animarum	256
solus es sapientia	111
totum corpus tuum	112
verus es mundi sol	264
Domine non est apud te ulla distantia	156

	PAGE
Domine non sum dignus ut intres	108. 167. 175. 210. 217
Domine omnipotens Deus	
miserere nostri	255
patrum nostrorum Abraham	255. 263
qui es charitas	255
Domine pater	
cælestis rex regum	254
et Deus vitæ meæ	156. 256. 263
et dominator vitæ meæ	122
Domine qui	
es unus Deus verus	156. 254
fons es sapientiæ omnis	256
in terribili et tremenda majestate tua	260
Domine sancte Pater omn. æterne Deus	
in illa sancta custodia	117
qui coæqualem	114
qui nos ad principium	254. 258
Domine Spiritus sancte D. qui coæqualis	114
Domine tu	
Deus es qui cælum fecisti ac terram	255. 262
fecisti cælum et terram	172. 211
Dominus	
nos benedicat	353
Dominus noster Jesus Christus	
apud te sit	129
per suam misericordiam	145
Dona mihi quæso omn. D. ut per hanc sacrosanctam	115. 167
Dona tui serva nobis Deus optime verbi	268
Dulcissime Dne.	
da mihi cor mundum	133
Jesu qui splendor es Patris	265
Jesu Christe fili D. vivi qui beatissimam	110. 165
Dulcissime Jesu inspira cordi meo	117
Dulcissime salvator ac redemptor n. Jesu Christe	150
Duo rogavi te ne deneges mihi	167. 211. 218. 255. 263
Dust earth and ashes is our strength	305
Ecce	
mensurabiles posuisti dies meos	262
non dormitabit, neque dormiet	259
nunc benedicite Dominum (*Psalm*)	133
plasmator mei multa rogavi	264
Ecclesiae tuae q. Dne. preces placatus admitte	352. 374
Ecclesiam tuam	
fidelem q. Domine benignus illustra	216

Ecclesiam tuam	
q. Domine benignus illustra	109. 163
Edent pauperes (*Psalm*)	154
Ego	
autem constitutus sum rex	136
sum resurrectio et vita (*Lesson*)	262
Egressus est Dominus Jesus cum discipulis suis	118. 119. 162. 259
Ei qui vos confirmare potest	262
Elevate thyself, O my soul	375
En ad ostium tuum summe paterfamilias	264
Enter not into judgment with thy servant	247
Eripe me, Domine, a viris iniquis	254
Erravi sicut ovis quæ periit	263
Esto mihi Dne. in Deum protectorem	264
Et	
animæ omnium fidelium defunctorum	110
benedicta sit s. Anna mater tua	129
cum complerentur dies Pentecostes (*Lesson*)	259
radicavi (*Lesson*)	160
sic in Syon (*Lesson*)	160
Eternal son of the eternal Father	337
Ever blessed be the holy and undivided Trinity	284
Exaudi	
nos exaudi exaudi nos Christe	116
quæsumus Dne. supplicum preces	108. 252
Exaudiat te Dominus (*Psalm*)	367
Exercituum Dne. Deus Israel	263
Exhilirator omnium Christe	267
Exivi a Patre et veni in mundum (*Lesson*)	259
Expurgate vetus fermentum (*Lesson*)	155. 264
Exsurge Domine ut dissipentur inimici	254
Exultavit cor meum in Domino	176. 263
Fac mecum signum in bonum	127
Faith cometh of the word of God	175
Famulam tuam q. Dne. b. Wilgefortis	125
Famulis tuis q. Dne. cælestis gratiæ munus	134
Famulorum tuorum q. Dne. delictis ignosce	123. 128
Father	
forgive me the sins of the night (day) past	345
of mercy and God of comfort	300
the hour is come glorify thy son	172. 211
Fear the Lord and the King	295
Felix ille qui meretur esse terra bona	264
Fidelium animæ per misercordiam Dei	133. 354

	PAGE
Fidelium Deus omnium conditor	134
Fili redemptor mundi Deus	114. 120
Finally O Lord we beseech thee of thy goodness	328
First	
I knowledge myself guilty	133. 190
we believe in one God	246
when thou intendest to prayer	220
Forasmuch as	
nothing pleaseth thee	294
the violence of sickness	338
you have well refreshed your bodies	252. 290
we have now grievously offended	200
Forasmuch, O heavenly father, as thou hast called me	293
Forgive me my sins O Lord	
forgive me the sins of my age	320
forgive me the sins of my youth	279
Fortissime Deus spirituum universæ carnis	121
Fortitudo mea et laus mea Dominus	121
Fragilitatem nostram q. Dne. propitius respice	137
Frange esurienti panem tuum (*Lesson*)	154
Fraterna nos Domine	146
From the	
depth I called on thee, O Lord (*Psalm*)	173
fiery darts of the devil	192
tyranny of the Bishop of Rome	241. 298. 300. 301. 304. 308
Gaude	
flore virginali	110. 165
virgo mater Christi	110. 164
Give thanks to God with one accord	300. 303
Give us	
alway O Lord for thy mercy	179
peace O Lord in our days	247
Gloria in excelsis	204. 330
Gloria tibi	
Domine	118. 152. 357
Domine gloria tibi sancte	267
Gloriosa passio Domini nostri	115. 123. 166. 197
Glory be to God on high (in the highest)	278. 341
Glory be to the Lord	161
Glory be to thee	
O Christ our God	343
O Lord	198. 358. 365
O Lord glory be to thee	345
Glory honour and praise be given to thee O Lord	304

OF LITURGICAL FORMS. 403

	PAGE
Glory honour and praise	
be to our Lord Jesus Christ	380
be to thee O God	192. 239
Go to thy rest O my soul	281
God	
almighty father of all mercy	198. 220. 229. 233
be in my head	129. 174. 276. 284
be merciful unto me a sinner	370
forbid that I should glory	343
have mercy on all christian souls	110. 217. 249
is charity	173. 192. 239. 290
of our fathers	189. 243
our sovereign Lord knowledging the great fragility	149
God preserve our	
most gracious sovereign Lord King George	306
sovereign Lord King Charles	304
sovereign Lord King James	306
God save	
his church and eke our Queen	302
his (the) church our (the) Queen (King) and realm	302. 304. 306
his universal church our Queen Elizabeth	302
our King and the realm and send us peace in Christ	248. 252
our noble worthy King Henry and his gracious Queen Anne	214
the church our (the) King (Queen) and realm	173. 192. 239. 248
the King	185. 219
the King and bring us to the bliss	110
God setteth forth his incomparable love	197
God that hast caused the b. Virgin Margaret	164. 216
God the father	
bless me God the son defend me	321
preserve and keep thee	281
who hath created thee	281
God the illuminator of all heathen	177
God the unspeakable author of the world	279
God to whom it is appropried to be merciful	249
God which	
brightenest this day with the glory	178
hast left the remembrance of thy passion	178
God who declarest thy almighty power	281
Good Lord	
bless us and these thy good creatures	285
for thy grace meekly we call	214
pardon and forgive us all our sins	306
Good Lord God and sweet Saviour Jesu Christ	189

INDEX

	PAGE
Grace and thanks be now unto him	300. 302
Gracious God	
by whose providence	282
the fountain of all goodness	338
Grant	
I beseech thee Lord God that by the holy melody	167
good Lord that we may perfectly follow him	163. 216
Lord to thy servants the gift of heavenly grace	181
Grant me	
gracious Lord so to eat the flesh of thy (dear) son	278. 320
merciful Lord God to desire fervently	188
Grant O most merciful father	
that I receiving these thy creatures	338
that our hunger and thirst being satisfied	304. 306
Grant to us	
most merciful God that as Mary Magdalene	180
we beseech thee eternal God to rejoice	181
Grant to us almighty God that we	
may quench the flames of our vices	180
which know that thy glorious martyrs	240
Grant unto	
me O merciful God ardently to desire	361
us most merciful Father that like as b. Mary Magdalen	164. 216
Grant unto us we beseech thee O Lord	
the effect of our prayer	363
the help of thy grace	363
Grant us good Lord that all these prayers	197
Grant we beseech thee	
that both the course of this world	179
that the words	305
which have known	182
Grant we beseech thee Almighty God that	
as thy people devoutly observeth	181
our sovereign Lord the king	279
the brightness of thy clearness	178
the family may walk in the way of health	180
the new nativity	176
the words	301. 307. 343
we which be punished	177
we which fain	177
we which have known	182
Grant we beseech thee Lord	
that we may follow that that we greatly esteem	181
to thy people	180

OF LITURGICAL FORMS. 405

	PAGE
Grant we beseech thee O almighty God that	
thy family	364
we in our trouble	241
Grant we beseech thee O Lord God that thy servants	230. 254
Grant we most humbly beseech thee O h. Father that with h. Simeon	280
Grates Dno. Israelitarum Deo	262
Gratia Domini (nostri) Jesu Christi	
adsit animo vestro	262
et Dei charitas	262
vobis adsit	262
Gratia magna tibi Pater et rex inclyte rerum	267
Gratia misericordia pax	
a Deo patre et Domino	262
a Deo patre nostro	262
Gratia vobis et pax	
a Deo patre nostro	262
multa sit	262
Gratiam tuam q. Dne. mentibus nostris (tuis) infunde	120. 354
Gratias agimus Deus ac Pater de tot beneficiis	253
Gratias agimus tibi	
Domine Deus omnipotens qui es et qui eras	263
Pater cælestis qui tua ineffabili potentia	267
Gratias ago tibi (Dne.) D. omn. qui non solum	256. 266
Gratias ago tibi Dne. omn. æterne D. qui me in hac nocte	151
Gratias ago tibi Dne. Jesu Christe	
cujus gratia sum id quod sum	136
qui voluisti pro redemptione mundi	152
quod hanc noctem mihi volueris	258
Gratias ago tibi	
omnipotens et misericors Deus meus	127
Pater omnipotens æterne Deus	258
Gratias tibi ago	
benignissime Jesu Christe quod me	266
et laudes tibi refero Dne. D. meus	135
Gratias tibi ago Dne. D. omn. qui me per hujus diei cursum	108
Gratias tibi ago Dne. s. Pater omn. æterne Deus	
qui me dignatus es	136
qui me peccatorem	354
Great art thou Lord God for evermore	295
Hæc dies quam fecit Dominus	155
Hæc sunt convivia quæ tibi placent	130
Hail	
heavenly king father of mercy	176. 187. 230
Jesu Christ king of mercy	184. 199. 217

INDEX

	PAGE
Hail	
O head of our Lord and Saviour	372
queen mother of mercy	164. 174
very body incarnate of a virgin	165. 217. 231
Hail Mary full of grace	
blessed . . . fruit of thy womb	153. 173. 239. 246
blessed . . . fruit of thy womb Jesus Christ	162
blessed . . . pray for us sinners	131. 313
Happy are those servants	278
Haste thee Lord God which art great	200
Have mercy	
on me God according of thy great tenderness	246
we beseech thee Lord God through the precious passion	166
Have mercy upon me O God (*Psalm*)	278
Have mercy upon me O Lord	
for I am weak	342
have mercy upon me for my soul	342
now and at the hour of death	275. 276
Having now dearest Lord passed this day	337
He that	
dwelleth in the help of the highest (*Psalm*)	361
is King of glory	290
loveth God loveth his neighbour	211
He which of his inestimable goodness	198
Heal me	
(good) Lord and I shall be healed	172. 211
O Lord and I shall be whole	188. 243. 294
Hear	
Israel our Lord God is one Lord	168. 209. 232. 246
me almighty and most merciful God	281
my prayer O God (Lord) (*Psalm*)	279. 281
O Lord our prayers	182
our prayers we beseech thee Lord	177
we beseech thee (O) Lord the prayers	182. 363
Hear us	
almighty and (most) merciful God	292. 301. 304. 305. 307
O Lord crying unto thee	363
Hearken	
O Lord we beseech thee unto our supplications	364
to our supplications O Lord	363
unto my voice O Lord (*Psalm*)	280
Heavenly Father be with us	338
Here O blessed Jesus I give to thee	338
Hic et in perpetuum nos custodire digneris	116

	PAGE
His epulis donisque tuis benedicito Christe	267
Hoc	
donum charitatis	379
tempore sentimus Deus optime maxime	269
Holy holy holy Lord God	
almighty	278. 284. 341
of Sabaoth	344
Holy Jesus who being infinitely higher	337
Holy Lord almighty father everlasting God	249
Holy Mary mother of God b. virgin for ever	191
Holy Trinity be helping unto me	162. 186. 210
Honour and praise	
be given to thee O Lord God almighty	305
be unto (to) God the king everlasting	198. 220. 229. 233
How hàst thou O Lord humbled	188. 242
I am thy Lord God which hath brought thee	209
I believe	
that thy blood is drink indeed	344
that thy flesh is meat indeed	344
I believe in God (the) Father almighty	131. 153
I bequeath my soul to God	370
I beseech thee	
Lord Jesu cause me to have	166
O holy lady Mary mother of God	361
I beseech thee O Lord	
for the conversion of Turks	338
let this my confession	360
I beseech thee O Lord Jesu by those thy health bringing wounds	360
I confess	
and re-knowledge here before thee O heavenly Father	183
to (unto) almighty God to (the) b. Mary ever virgin	314. 359
unto almighty God those sins	278. 280
I confess O Lord that I was shapen in wickedness	337
I cry God mercy	113
I do	
further most humbly desire	280
not presume to come to this thy table	344
I enter into this day to do all things	291
I feel in myself O merciful Saviour	294
I give	
thanks unto thee O God almighty	188
thee hearty thanks O most merciful Saviour	339
I give thee thanks	
O God almighty which not a lonely	243

INDEX

	PAGE
I give thee thanks	
O holy Lord Father almighty	360
I have	
not given meat to the hungry	214
now O Christ my God finished	344
I laid me down and slept	275. 284
I lay me down to rest	184. 198. 220. 229. 233. 291
I (we) offer thee thine own	343
I praise	
and magnify thy great and glorious name	337
thee for electing me before all time	337
I repose all my trust	370
I return thee my humble and hearty thanks O Lord God	345
I salute thee Saviour of the world	187
I thank thee	
also with all my heart	116. 211
good Lord of thine infinite goodness	190
O Father for the life which thou hast revealed	344
O Lord and king and praise thee	188. 243
O Lord my God for admitting me	344
O Lord thou God of all powers	343
I thank thee my h. Father by thy (most) d. beloved son Jesus Christ	
that this day	184. 198. 220. 229. 233. 234
that this night	228. 233. 234
I thank thee O (heavenly) Father by thy d. beloved son Jesus Christ	
our Lord and Saviour that of thy free mercy	301. 303
that of thy free mercy	304. 306
I that am a wretched sinner	279. 338
I was glad when they said unto me (*Psalm*)	337
I will	
arise and go to my father	342
go unto the altar of God (*Psalm*)	278
lay me down in peace	276. 284
lift up my heart unto the Lord	344
love thee O Lord my strength	220. 247
offer thanksgiving unto my God	278
therefore that prayers and supplications (*Lesson*)	279
wash mine hands in innocency	277. 343
If	
a man say I love God	211
any require comfort and counsel	278
the ungodly will turn away from all his sins	291. 292. 299. 301
we confess our sins	278
Illumina oculos meos	114. 201. 259

Illumina quæsumus Dne. (Deus) tenebras nostras	135. 259
Illuminate	
mine eyes	166
our minds	363
Implorent clementissime Domine	368
In illo tempore	
apprehendit Pilatus Jesum	129
appropinquabat autem dies festus azymorum	351
cum natus esset Jesus (*Sequence*)	118
dixit Jesus discipulis suis	351
egressus est Jesus cum discipulis suis	351
erant Pascha et azyma	351
missus est (angelus) Gabriel (*Sequence*)	118. 161. 357
recumbentibus undecim discipulis (*Sequence*)	118. 162. 357
In manus	
ineffabilis misericordiæ tuæ commendo animam meam	137
tuas Dne. commendo spiritum meum	152. 185. 186. 259
In matutinis Domine meditabor	151
In mei sint memoria Jesu pie	136
In my affliction I cried unto the Lord	172
In noctibus extollam manus tuas	259
In nomine Domini nostri Jesu Christi	
crucifixi surgo	136
surgo	258
In omnibus requiem quæsivi (*Lesson*)	160. 226
In præsentia sacrosancti corporis	111
In primis pueri Christum discamus amare	268
In principio erat verbum	118. 161. 357
In quo instituet adolescens viam suam (*Psalm*)	256
In sanctas ac venerabiles manus tuas	137
In te Domine speravi (*Psalm*)	207 218. 260
In the	
beginning was the word	161. 209. 215. 358
latter days some shall depart from the faith	205
midst of life	333
name of our Lord Jesus Christ	275. 276
way of peace	364
In thee O Lord have I put my trust (*Psalm*)	280
In this faith which I do unfeignedly	281
In thy law O thou maker of heaven and earth	294
In tonso capite corruens	211
Inclina cor meum Deus in testimonia tua (*Psalm*)	267
Inclina Domine	
aurem tuam ad preces nostras	155. 165. 217

INDEX

	PAGE
Inclina Domine	
aurem tuam (*Psalm*)	117. 127
Increase thy church preserve our Queen	302
Incute Dne. Jesu terrorem hostibus meis	266
Indulgentiam absolutionem et remissionem	353
Ineffabilem misericordiam tuam Dne. Jesu Christe	145. 354
Ineffabilem nobis Dne. misericordiam tuam	352
Infirmitatem nostram q. Dne. propitius respice	116. 147
Initium ruinæ hominis sibi fidere	156. 254. 265
Intercessio (nos) quæsumus (Domine)	
b. Barbaræ virginis	107. 113. 142
b. Bernardi abbatis commendet	141
Intercessionibus b. Agathæ	141
Interveniat pro nobis (quæsumus) Dne. Jesu Christe	
apud tuam clementiam	115. 122. 166
nunc et in hora mortis	119. 355
Into the hands	
of thy blessed protection	275
of thy ineffable mercy	339
Into this day do I enter	184
Into thy merciful hands O Lord	281
Introibo in domum tuam Domine	149
Is there not an appointed time	283
It is	
finished blessed be the name	339
very meet	342
It is written	
in thy holy gospel	293
O most mighty and everlasting King	292
It was	
never ordained O good reader	203
not thy joys alone O Lord	283
Ite missa est	153
Jesu	
fons bonorum omnium	264
for thy holy name	116. 211
have mercy on me	187
Lord that madest me	218. 222
O Christ the son of God	199
qui post innumeros corporis tui cruciatus	134
Jesu Christ	
omnipotent Lord that yet hanging on the cross	192
our Lord which by the mouth of thy (the) h. apostle St. Peter	190. 244
Jesu Christe dux æternæ felicitatis	264

OF LITURGICAL FORMS. 411

	PAGE
Jesu fili Dei	
omnium conditor	115. 166
qui coram judice tacuisti	115. 166
qui ligatus fuisti	115. 166
Jesu (the) son of God	
(and) maker of all things	166, 187
which heldest thy peace	166
which kept silence	187
Jesu (the) son of God which was (wast) bounden	
govern my members	187
rule mine hands	166
Jesus	
ascends into heaven	374
autem transiens	117
enters the garden	374
Jesus Jesus esto mihi Jesus	108
quem de Spiritu sancto	118
Jesus Nazarenus rex Judæorum	
fili Dei miserere mei	107. 135. 189
rex omnium populorum	137
Job	
his head clipped	172. 211
tonso capite	172
Jonas prayed unto the Lord	199
Jube Domine benedicere	154. 378. 379
Justus es Dne. et omnia tua judicia justa (vera) sunt	121. 172. 211. 263
Keep	
thy family with continual mercy	180
us O Lord as the apple of the eye	360
Kindle with the fire of the holy Ghost our reins	364
Kirieleyson	114
Know ye not that ye are the temple of God	278
Largire	
clarum vespere	129
nobis clementissime Pater	110. 164. 216
Laud	
be to God	188
honor and thanks be unto thee	295
praise and glory be unto God	252. 290
Laudate Dominum	
Deum nostrum quem non deseruit	121
omnes gentes (*Psalm*)	154. 155. 378. 379
Laudo et glorifico te Dne. Deus meus	137
Laus honor et gloria et gratiarum actio	122. 129

INDEX

	PAGE
Lead me O God in the way of thy truth	275
Let	
every christian begin his day's work	276
O Lord I humbly beseech thee this my confession	370
the operation of thy mercy O Lord	180
the priests the ministers of the Lord	284
then thy blood O Lord Jesus Christ	344
then thy body O Lord Jesus Christ	344
Let this day, O my God, be noted in thy book	339
Let us give thanks unto the Lord God for he is right good	198
Levavi oculos meos (*Psalm*)	117. 260
Lighten	
mine eyes O Lord (*Psalm*)	275. 284
our darkness	298
Linguam fidelium tuorum et vota	132
Lo	
the Lord is yet alive	210
we turn unto thee	295
Look down almighty God with thy favourable countenance	279
Lord	
although I be not worthy to receive thee	190
as thou hast awaked my body	345
be merciful unto us	285
bow thine ear unto our prayers	297
by the abundance of thy mercy	170. 210
by whom kings do reign	282
give thy people (them) eternal rest	173. 205. 232
have mercy	173
of all power and might	254
Lord God	
eternal I humbly beseech thee that by the great virtue of patience	220
in good mind in which I hold me now	130
of heaven thou great and terrible God	295
we pray thee that the prayer of blessed St. John	166. 210
which dost punish and scourge thy people	189
who didst make me for nothing else	338
Lord God I beseech thee	
not to be long absent from me	133
that my heart may be inflamed	220
Lord hear	
my prayer (*Psalm*)	188. 242
thou my words	247
Lord hearken to my words	190
Lord help or we perish	333

	PAGE
Lord I am not worthy	
by reason of my sins to appear before thee	338
that thou should'st come under my roof	278. 343. 344
Lord I believe help thou my unbelief	343. 344
Lord I have loved the habitation of thine house	275. 277
Lord if thou wilt thou cans't make me clean	370
Lord incline thine ear unto our prayers	165. 217
Lord it is all one with thee	189. 242
Lord Jesu I believe and knowledge	222
Lord Jesu Christ	
God's son of heaven set thy passion	189
king of mercy and of pity	222
the only guardian of our mortality	247
we beseech thee of thy goodness	166. 210
Lord Jesu Christ son of the living God	
set thy holy passion	240
who when thy passion drew near	374
Lord Jesu Christ which	
nailed and hanged	178
saids't whosoever is angry	243
Lord Jesu	
king of glory and omnipotent I believe	222
receive my soul unto thee	185
Lord Jesu king of glory I believe and knowledge	
that thou thirsted	222
that when thou sawest	222
that when thou were yet hanging	222
Lord Jesu king of mercy and pity I steadfastly believe	222
Lord Jesus	
I believe and confess that thou art the Christ	343. 344
receive my spirit	281
teach me when the time of my dissolution	338
who both by thy word	338
Lord Jesus Christ	
most poor and mild of spirit	254
which of thine almightiness	243
who after the term of forty days	374
Lord Jesus Christ who did'st	
die for me	338
send thine holy Ghost	375
Lord look down (out) from heaven	190. 200
Lord of all power and might who art the author	249
Lord save	
James our king	373

INDEX

	PAGE
Lord save	
thy church our King (Queen) and realm	252. 290. 297
Lord send us peace in our days	240
Lord the inventor and maker of all things	243
Lord thou art God which hast made heaven	243
Lord thou hast	
commanded by thy holy apostle	293
made heaven and earth	172. 211
Lord we beseech thee	
keep thy church with perpetual mercy	
to give us grace for to quench	179
Lord we humbly beseech thy majesty	163. 216
Magna et mirabilia sunt opera tua Dne. D. omnipotens	163. 216
Magnificat animus meus Dominum	263
Magnus es Dne. in æternum et in omnia sæcula	261
Majestatem tuam Dne. suppliciter exoramus	121
Man that is born of a woman	109. 139. 163. 216
Man's life preserved is by food	281
Maria peperit Christum, Anna Mariam	303. 305
Mater ora filium ut post hoc exilium	120
May the souls of the faithful departed	154
Media vita in morte sumus	313. 327
Mediator Dei et hominum bone Jesu Christe	262
Memento mei	145
Deus meus in bonum	120
Domine cum ad tuum regnum perveneris	262
Memento obsecro dulcissima mater	126
Memoriam fecit mirabilium (*Psalm*)	154
Mensæ cælestis participes	154. 155. 378
Mentem sanctam spontaneam honorem Deo	142
Mentes nostras quæsumus Domine	352
Merciful	
Lord God omnipotent this day	221
Lord who when thou tookest upon thee	282
Saviour at this most noble and pious mystery	343
Meritis et precibus suæ piæ matris	154
Meruisti Christum portare	169
Militia est vita hominis super terram	262
Mi Pater	
si fieri potest evadam hoc poculum	261
si hoc evadere poculum non possum	261
Misereatur vestri (nostri) omnipotens Deus et dimittat vobis	153. 353
Miserere	
mei Deus (*Psalm*)	167. 185. 195. 200. 218. 378. 379

OF LITURGICAL FORMS. 415

	PAGE
Miserere	
mi Domine animabus	125
piissime Jesu per gloriosam resurrectionem tuam	130
quæsumus Dne. Deus per preciosam mortem	150. 166
Miserere Domine	
miserere pie et omn. Deus	265
per tuam gloriosam resurrectionem	118
Misericordia Dne. Jesu Christe erga nos te commoveat	255
Misericordiam tuam D. optime maxime conjunctis precibus	269
Misericors Deus	
ac cælestis Pater in cujus manu	266
concede ut quæ tibi placita sunt	156. 256
qui alis nos indies	267
Misericors et miserator Deus qui et barbaros salvari vis	132
Misericors Pater gratiam tuam nobis impertire	255
Missus est Gabriel angelus ad Mariam virginem (*Sequence*)	
	118. 119. 129. 161. 259
Mitissime Dne. Jesu Christe qui ex mera atque singulari gratia	265
Most dear Lord and Saviour sweet Jesu	116. 211
Most dearly beloved in God	214
Most gracious loving and merciful Father which did'st write	246
Most great God who hast not only permitted	320
Most holy	
and ever blessed Lord Jesus who did'st fast	337
God who art of purer eyes	321
Most meek Lord and Saviour which kneeled at the feet	221
Most merciful Father	
grant me to covet with an ardent mind	293
which hast of thy gracious mercy	295
Most merciful Lord Jesus Christ which was sent	188
Most mighty Lord	
and merciful father we yield thee hearty thanks	173. 192. 239. 290
which after thine ascension	221
Most sweet Lord Jesu son of the living God	165
Multi dicunt animæ meæ	263
My God I knowledge and confess	149
My heart	
hath rejoiced in the Lord	176
is pleasantly set at rest in the Lord	200
My high and most sovereign Lord Jesu Christ	222
My most dearly beloved christian people	214
My son	
do thou observe my law	283
hear the instruction of thy father	283

	PAGE
My son	
forget not my law (*Lesson*)	307
My soul hath a desire and longing	275
My sovereign Lord Jesu Christ I humbly beseech thee	222
Naked I came out of my mother's womb	188. 242. 295. 305
Nam et si ambulavero	137
Ne	
despicias omn. Deus populum tuum	352
memineris dulcissime Jesu	265
Necnon vere Deus paracleteque Spiritus	268
No one immersed in carnal lusts	343
Nomen Dei patris et filii et spiritus sancti	132
Non	
avertas Dne. tanquam offensus faciem	260
habebis Deos alienos	162
nobis Domine non nobis	116. 221
Non est	
ætati nostræ dignum	263
mirum O justissime Pater	266
Nos cum prole pia benedicat Virgo Maria	119. 166
Nos miseri	
et egeni homines	256. 267
peccatores	266
Nothing becomes the professor of thy name better	294
Now	
that your (our) bodies refreshed be	301. 303. 305
the Lord visited Sarah (*Lesson*)	304. 307
you have well refreshed your bodies	300. 302
Nudus egressus sum de utero matris mei	255. 263
Nunc dimittis tuum me Domine	262
O above all blessed and almighty Lord God	198
O all ye blessed saints of God	191
O all you saints the elect and chosen of God	191
O almighty and eternal God which vouchsafest	190
O almighty and everlasting God	
Creator and Lord of all things	279
the eternal health of them that believe	363
thy holy word teacheth us	189
which being benign	191
O almighty and merciful Father which of thy bountiful goodness	300
O almighty and most mild God mercifully regard our prayers	364
O almighty everlasting God	
by whose spirit the whole body of the church	362
in whose hand are the powers	363

OF LITURGICAL FORMS.

	PAGE
O almighty everlasting God	
the consolation of the sorrowful	362
O almighty everlasting God which	
desires not the death of sinners	362
ever makest the church fruitful	362
repellest not from thy mercy	362
savest all men	362
O almighty everlasting God which hast	
given us thy servants to knowledge	198
power over the living	363
revealed thy glory	362
O almighty God	
despise not thy people crying unto thee	363
father of thy Christ thine only begotten Son	342
King of all kings and governor of all things	282
King of kings and Lord of lords	292
our heavenly father I confess and knowledge	186
the keeper of souls which correctest	247
which knowest that we sit in so great jeopardies	247
O almighty God who	
art a strong tower of defence	282
in thy wrath dids't send a plague	305
O almighty Lord and everlasting God vouchsafe we beseech thee to direct	307
O amantissime Dne sancte Pater ego offero	136
O angel of God which art	
my guardian	360
my keeper	359
O beata (et benedicta) et gloriosa Trinitas	120. 191
O benignissime Dne Jesu Christe respice super me	145
O blessed	
lady mother of Jesu	116. 212
mirror of truth	116
Trinity Father Son and Holy Ghost	114
Virgin Mary and eternal queen of angels	369
O blessed Jesu	
beginning and ending	116
deepness of endless mercy	116
loveable king and friend	116
maker of all the world	116
most meekest lion	116
royal strength	116
sweetness of hearts	116
the only begotten Son	116
very and true plenteous vine	116

418 INDEX

	PAGE
O blessed Jesu	
well of endless pity	116
O blessed Jesus	
by the eye of faith I now behold thee dead	337
I come now to commemorate thy holy death	337
I now commemorate thy holy sufferings	337
let the blood that ran from thy blessed heart	339
seeing the third hour was devoted to thee	337
O blessed Jesus who	
hast this day made me a partaker	321
wast made man	330
O blessed Lord the keeper of Israel	345
O blessed Lord God	
look not at my defaults	221
omnipotent by whose wisdom all things ben created	221
O blessed Trinity, Father, Son, and Holy Ghost	114
O bone Jesu	
duo in me agnosco	127
illumina oculos meos ne unquam obdormiam	152
O dulcis Jesu, O Jesu fili Mariæ	112. 167. 218. 256
O piissime Jesu, O dulcissime Jesu	355
sint coram te præterita valde mala	130
tu novisti et potes et vis	108
O bountiful Jesu O sweet Jesu	
O Christ the son of God	299
O Jesu the son of the pure virgin Mary	167. 189. 204. 218. 231. 233. 243
O Jesu the son of the virgin Mary	247
O bountiful Jesu O sweet Saviour O Christ the Son of God	294
O bountiful Jesus, O sweet Jesus, O Jesus that Son of the virgin Mary	305
O clementissime Deus, qui (te) vitæ et mortis	128. 145
O creator	
et Domine cæli et terræ	144
et gubernator cæli et terræ	134
O dear Jesus my blessed Saviour and Redeemer	380
O Deus appositis apponendisque precamur	267
O domina	
dulcissima visceribus misericordiæ plena	137
mea sancta Maria me in tuam benedictam fidem	137. 355
gloriæ, O regina lætitiæ	126
O Domine	
Deus meus meipsum mihi eripe	265
non est apud te ulla distantia	263
O Domine Jesu Christe	
adoro te ad judicium progredientem	136

	PAGE
O Domine Jesu Christe	
adoro te descendentem ad inferos	355
adoro te in cruce pendentem	355
adoro te in cruce vulneratum	355
adoro te in sepulchro positum	355
adoro te resurgentem	355
aeterna dulcedo	111. 165
in tuam protectionem	120
pastor bone justos conserva	112. 355
(pater dulcissime) rogo te amore	122. 129. 132
(rogo te) propter illam (maximam) amaritudinem	112. 355
O Domine Jesu Christe fili Dei vivi	
crucifixe	137
qui mysterium	136
suscipe hanc orationem	145
O dulcissime atque amantissime Dne. Jesu Christe	145
O dulcissime Domine Jesu Christe	
omnipotens Deus aperi cor meum	136
qui es sponsus virginum	113
qui pro me indignissimo peccatore	149
verus Deus	355
O eternal infinite and almighty God whose gracious wisdom	313
O eternal God	
in whom we live and have our being	306
the supporter of all our hopes	338
O excellentissima gloriosissima atque sanctissima v. Maria	137
O Father	
deliver us from thy everlasting wrath	197
in heaven halowed be thy name	150. 162. 213
O fons totius misericordiæ	130
O give	
thanks unto the Lord	234
thine angels charge over me	275
O gloriosissima O optima O sacratissima v. Maria	120
O gloriosissime Sancte vel Sancta	129
O glorious	
angel to (unto) whom our blessed Lord	116. 212
cross that with holy blood	128
Jesu O meekest Jesu O most sweet Jesu	113. 187
king which amongst thy saints	167. 189. 204. 218. 231. 233. 247
Lord that straight after thy expiration	221
O God	
defender of all that trust in thee	220
for whose church sake Thomas	187

		PAGE
O God		
	great and wonderful	344. 345
	in thy name	210
	in whom we live are moved	363
	incline thyself unto my aid (*Psalm*)	362
	merciful pitiful and sufferable	165
O God almighty which speaking to every preacher		298
O God from whom		
	all good graces do proceed	279
	all good things proceed	178
	all holy desires all good counsels	164. 216. 233. 240. 298
O God merciful Father		
	which (who) in the time of Helisæus	301. 304
O God of		
	mercy God of piety	372
	powers whose are all things	179
	whose mercy there is no number	364
O God of whom		
	are all desires right counsells	247
	holy desires	182
O God our		
	God who hast sent our Lord	343
	refuge and strength	362
	succour and strength	180
O God protector of all kingdoms		362
O God that art creator and redeemer		249
O God the		
	defender of them that trust in thee	179
	Father of lights	280
	Gentiles are come (*Psalm*)	362
	lord of pardon	249
	pastor and governor	362
	protector of all that trust in thee	161. 209. 215
	strength of hopers	178
O God the lover		
	and keeper	182. 247. 364
	of mankind	172. 210
O God thou most righteous judge		292
O God to whom		
	each heart is open	363
O God to whose church thy glorious martyr St. Thomas		174
O God which		
	always makest thy church merry	178
	brightenest this day	178

OF LITURGICAL FORMS

	PAGE
O God which	
declarest thy power	179
despisest not the groaning (wailing)	182. 361
dissolvest wars	363
for the redemption of the world	360
in the humility of thy Son	178
justifieth the wicked	363
knowest that we being set	177
madest the most holy night	176
rejectest none	363
renewest the world	177
resistest the proud	182. 191
shewest the light of thy truth	178
teachest us in the books of the testaments	178
through thy only begotten hast opened	178
O God which by	
a wonderful order	163
enlightening of the Holy Ghost	363
the information of the Holy Ghost	239
O God which dids't	
loose from bonds	182
make the children of Israel	364
O God which hast	
ascended thy most holy cross	163. 215. 239
broken the pride of the old enemy	364
consecrated thy church	180
extolled Mark thine evangelist	181
glorified b. Nicholas thy holy bishop	163
granted us to come to thy knowledge	181
instructed the hearts of the faithful	162. 198. 215. 230
poured the gifts of charity	363
prepared invisible things	179
preserved unhurt	364
taught the whole world by the preaching of b. Paul	181
taught us by the mouth of holy Paul	181
O God which makest	
all things to profit	364
the souls of the faithful	178
us merry with the yearly solemnity	181
O God which seest	
that we have confidence	177
us to want all strength	177. 248
O God which sufferest not	
sinners to perish	247

	PAGE
O God which sufferest not	
them that sin to perish	177
O God which with	
a marvellous order	181
double joy	164. 174. 217
O God which wouldest	
that thy Son should hang on (upon) the cross	178. 248
that thy word should receive flesh	181
O God who	
art great in name	343
dids't wonderfully create	343
in this wonderful sacrament	374
seest that I put not my trust	281
O God whose	
nature and property	241. 249. 277. 279. 281. 296
pleasure is to have certain of the holy angels	191
praise this day innocent martyrs	181
providence in disposition of things	179
right hand did lift up (uplift) b. Peter	163. 216
Son ascended mightily into heaven	178
O good Jesu	
O most benign Jesu O sweetest Jesu	361
the very solatious comfort of all them that are laden	223
the word of the Father	361
O good Lord	
Father almighty I meekly beseech thee	299
receive my words	167
O good Lord Jesu hearken to my words	223
O good Lord Jesu Christ I pray thee to open my mouth	187
O gracious Lord and most merciful Father which hast from the beginning	291
O great and marvellous Lord Adonai	188
O heavenly Father	
God almighty I pray	190
which like a diligent watchman	186
O holy	
angel of God the minister	191
Trinity one God	191
O how amiable are thy dwellings	275
O illustrissima excellentissima et gloriosissima mater	128
O inflammati Seraphin	125
O intemerata et in æternum benedicta	111. 191. 355
O Jesu	
abyssus profundissime	111
alpha et omega	111

OF LITURGICAL FORMS. 423

	PAGE
O Jesu	
blessed mirror of endless clearness	116
cælestis medice	111
dulcedo cordium	111
dulcissime Jesu	135
endless sweetness of loving souls	116. 165
endless sweetness to all that love thee	231
fons inexhaustæ pietatis	111
heavenly leach	116
intra pectus meum	150
leo fortissime	112
mundi fabricator	111
our health and glory	199
qui post innumeros corporis tui cruciatus	150
regalis virtus	111
rex amabilis	111
salus mea, Deus dominus	150
speculum claritatis divinæ	111
the very repairer and edifier of all mankind	223
the very Son of almighty God and of the pure v. Mary	221
the very victorious and triumphant crown	223
unigenite altissimi Patris splendor	112
vera libertas angelorum	111
veritatis speculum	111
very freedom of angels	116
vitis vera et fecunda	112
O Jesu Christ the Son of God our redeemer	184. 187. 199. 217
O Lamb of God	
Christ which taketh away the sins	290
that takest away the sins	278
O Lord	
almighty, God of our fathers	188. 242. 305
and heavenly Father according to the institution	344
as thou alone art the author of the holy scriptures	294
bless us and this our store	285
by whom kings reign	284
correct me but with judgment	342
defend us alway through the continued succours of St. John B.	163. 216
favour with the heavenly mercy	177
for thy great mercy and grace	162. 219. 228
forasmuch as thou of thy fatherly goodness	293
grant that though I am in (of) myself most unworthy	343. 344
hear my prayer and let my cry come unto thee	337
heavenly father almighty and everlasting God	282

INDEX

	PAGE
O Lord	
I am not fit nor worthy that thou shoulds't come	338
I am not worthy nor fit that thou shoulds't come	320
I do here humbly present unto thee my soul and body	321
in the multitude of thy mercies	359
in union with that divine intention	377
into thy hands	185
look down from heaven	281. 307
make us to have the perpetual fear	220. 247
my light my life	337
our heavenly Father almighty and everliving God	283
rebuke me not in thy wrath	337
send forth thy power	343
to whom all praise is due	285
we thank thee for the use	285
with whom do live the spirits	281
O Lord Christ in most mighty power	243
O Lord God	
all my hope hath been even in thee	223
how I receive the body and blood	320
I am sick and weak in my spirit	222
my heavenly Father I most humbly thank thee	301. 303. 304. 306
that of thy mere mercy	221
the devil goeth about	294
which art the very high imperial protector	218. 221
who of thy most bountiful goodness	299
without whose will and pleasure	188. 243
O Lord God almighty	
all seeing all things	114
our heavenly Father and most merciful Lord	188
to whom and before whom all things are manifest	242
O Lord God almighty which	
by thine infinite wisdom	299
hast caused us to come	359
O Lord God omnipotent which not of our deserts	231
O Lord God our heavenly Father bless thou us	198. 220. 228. 233
O Lord Jesu	
thou art the very Lamb of God	222
which art the only health	182. 185. 243. 247
O Lord Jesu Christ	
I humbly beseech thy unspeakable mercy	360
in whose power all things are put	360
most true pastor	292
the good shepherd	361

O Lord Jesus Christ	PAGE
we are commanded	293
without whom nothing is sweet	173. 192. 239. 296
O Lord Jesu Christ I adore thee	
descending into hell	361
hanging on the cross	360
laid in the sepulchre	361
rising from the dead	361
wounded upon the cross	360
O Lord Jesu Christ I beseech	
thee for that bitterness	360
thy mercy and goodness	295
O Lord Jesu Christ I commend	
and betake my hands	187
my hearing	187
my heart	187
my sight	187
O Lord Jesu Christ son of the living God	
put thy passion	197
which hanging upon the cross	361
O Lord Jesu Christ which art	
our very bishop	231
the health of all men living	189
the (very) bright sun of the world	242. 297
O Lord Jesus Christ the	
eternal Son of the eternal Father	280
Son of God and Saviour of the world	280
O Lord Jesus Christ to whom and before whom	186
O Lord Jesus Christ which art the bright sun of the world	186
O Lord let	
the ears of thy mercy be open	179
the venerable feast of b. Mary	180
thy continual mercy cleanse and defend thy church	179
us have perpetual love	17
O Lord my God	
and Saviour do thou teach me	343. 344
in most profound humility	338
O Lord our heavenly Father	
almighty and everlasting God regard	278
almighty and everliving God by whose providence	283
high and mighty king of kings	279. 304. 305
O Lord the	
author and giver of all good things	338
merciful and good	285

FFF

O Lord thou	
art righteous	294
father and God of my life	183. 247
O Lord thou hast	
chastened me	188. 243
correct me	294
O Lord we beseech thee	
being pacified grant pardon	180
mercifully hear our prayers	307
O Lord which	
art only God true gracious	242. 297
hast displayed thine hands and feet	155. 162. 215. 219. 228
hast vouchsafed of thy unspeakable goodness	189
O Lord who	
by thine infinite wisdom	298
hast wounded us	282
O love of the divine power	337
O maker of heaven and earth	155. 167. 189. 203. 214. 231. 246. 360
O Maria Dei genitrix	355
O Mary mother of God	361
O merciful God	
grant me to covet with a fervent (an ardent) mind	243. 247
preserve me from all sin	345
(the) father of our Ld Jesus Christ who is the resurrection	296. 327. 328. 345
O merciful Lord God heavenly father	
I laud and praise thee	246
I render most high lauds	186. 246. 291
whether we sleep or wake live or die	291
O merciful Lord God our heavenly father	
I laud and thank thee	246
whether we sleep or wake live or die	246
O merciful Lord I am not worthy	167. 210. 217. 221
O mighty and dreadful and most merciful Lord	221
O most benign Lord Jesu Christ I a sinner	360
O most blessed	
and gracious God who only cans't heal	330
Saviour whose sacred body	284
O most clement Father of mercies	359
O most dear	
and tender Father our defender	189. 243
Lord and Saviour sweet Jesu	116. 211
O most divine and adorable Jesus	
I offer these Matins and Lauds	377

OF LITURGICAL FORMS.

	PAGE
O most divine and adorable Jesus	
my blessed Saviour and redeemer I offer up . . . this holy Office	377
O most excellent goodness withdraw not thy mercy	188
O most gracious	
God and loving Father which mercifully feedest	300. 302
Lord and merciful Father I thy sinful creature	291
O most high	
and meek Lord which by thy goodness	221
and mighty Lord God and King of peace	248
O most highest almighty and eternal God whose glory	182. 190. 220. 247
O most holy God who art glorious in holiness	337
O most loving and gentle God	186
O most sweet Lord Jesu Christ the true God	361
O most worthy Redeemer and Saviour	370
O most merciful	
and ever good of whose incomparable goodness	185
Father which by the mouth of our sweet Saviour	199
God who rememberest not the iniquities	362
Jesu my sweet Saviour	188
Lord God and most tender and dear Father	186. 244. 246
Redemptor which art alway bowed to pity	247
O most mighty	
and everlasting King that where many	292
God and merciful Father who hast compassion	307
O my God	
do all thy works praise thee	337
I believe in you but strengthen my faith	376
thou art true and holy	278
O my lady holy Mary I recommend myself	361
O my Lord and maker omnipotent	221
O my Lord God	
I beseech thee humbly of thy benign grace	221
I thank thee with all my heart	300
O my Lord Jesu with all my mind	190
O my Lord Jesus Christ true God and man	368
O my most merciful Father the father of (all) mercies	185. 195. 214
O my sovereign	
Lord and creator of all things	221
Lord Jesu the very Son of almighty God	116. 187. 211
O my special and most gracious Lord Jesu	222
O my sweet love and potential Lord Jesu Christ	223
O our Father which art in heaven	245
O Pater misericordiarum scio et vere agnosco	131
O Petre beatissime apostolorum maxime	139

428 INDEX

	PAGE
O pie crucifixe, redemptor omnium populorum	112
O pitiful	
Lord God alway showing thy mercy	187. 210. 221
physician and healer both of body and soul	295
O quam bonus et suavis est Dne. Spiritus tuus	122
O regina cælorum, mater misericordiæ	129
O rex gloriose inter sanctos tuos	112. 167. 218. 247
O salutifera vulnera dulcissimi amatoris mei Jesu Christi	128
O sancte angele, Dei minister cælestis imperii	112. 191
O saviour of the world	
save me, who by thy cross and passion	320
who by thy cross and precious blood	324. 333
O serenissima et inclita mater Dni. nostri Jesu Christi	124
O sovereign Lord God that wouldest vouchsafe	222
O spare me a little	333
O spiritus cælorum angeli beatissimi assistite mihi	129
O summa Deitas immensa bonitas	128
O sweet	
Jesu the very solatious comfort	223
Jesus I desire neither life nor death	281
O the	
depth of the wisdom and knowledge of God	278
God of our fathers God of mercy	167. 211
O the most	
delectable and quietness of my soul	223
delicious rose and sweetness	223
high eternal consummation	223
highest sapience divine	223
sweetest spouse of my soul	113
O the very	
celestial joy and liberty of angels	223
former and creator of all this world	223
fountain and sweet spring	223
hope and glory of all that believe	223
plentiful of all goodness	223
O thou	
eternal Lord God King of kings	285
good Jesu clarify me with the clerete	133
Lamb of God that takest away the sins of the world	281
Lord father and God of my life	243
most benign Jesu grant me I beseech thee of thy grace	133
my most special Lord God	222
that hearest (the) prayer	343
who art by nature immortal	345
with whom is no variableness	321

	PAGE
O undefiled and blessed for ever	191
O unspeakable Creator which forth of the treasure of thy wisdom	361
O untouched and for ever blessed . . . Virgin Mary	361
O vile wretch that I am	339
O vos omnes sancti et electi Dei	113. 191
Obsecro Domine Deus magne et terribilis	263
Obsecro te	
domina sancta Maria	111
Domine Jesu Christe ut passio tua	136
Oculi omnium in te sperant Domine (*Psalm*)	154. 267
Omnes	
gentes laudent Dominum (*Psalm*)	267. 379
sanctae virgines et matronæ orate pro nobis	120
Omnes sancti	
apostoli et electi discipuli Domini, orate pro nobis	120
beatorum ordines, orate pro nobis	120
confessores, orate pro nobis	120
innocentes, orate pro nobis	120
martyres, orate pro nobis	120
orate pro nobis	120
patriarchæ et prophetæ, orate pro nobis	120
Omnia ad te respiciunt Domine	253
Omnipotens ac benignissime pater non possumus	265
Omnipotens aeterne	
ac cælestis Pater	258
Deus qui escam das	267
Omnipotens Deus	
cælestis Pater creator cæli et terræ	264
qui unigenitum filium tuum nobis dedisti	259
unice prosperator actionum	266
Omnipotens Deus et cælestis Pater quem nulla nostra dignitas	259
Omnipotens Deus Pater Domini nostri Jesu Christi	
qui non vis mortem peccatoris	258
qui non vult mortem peccatoris	253
Omnipotens Domine Deus ex cujus ordine	254
Omnipotens Dominus Christus Messias	120
Omnipotens et clementissime	
Deus qui es medicus unus	264
Pater tanquam oves perditæ	253. 258
Omnipotens et misericors	
Dominus et angelus Raphael	356
sanctorum exercituum Deus	140
Omnipotens et misericors Deus	
ecce accedo ad sacramentum	145
Pater Dni. nostri Jesu Christi qui est resurrectio	262

	PAGE
Omnipotens et misericors Deus	
rex cæli et terræ	126
Omnipotens et misericors Deus qui	
hominem ad imaginem tuam	138
manus ineffabiles	141
sanctorum tuorum Dionysii	120
Omnipotens et mitissime Deus	
qui electos sanctos tuos	140
respice propitius (ad) preces nostras	108. 132. 353
te humiliter imploro	142
Omnipotens mitissime Deus	
qui sitienti populo	132
respice propitius (ad) preces nostras	108. 132. 353
Omnipotens rerum omnium innovator	266
Omnipotens sempiterne Deus	
altare hoc nomini tuo dedicatum	144
apud quem est continua semper sanctorum festivitas tuorum	124
benignissime Domine ac Pater	255
conservator animarum	129
dirige actus nostros	150
ecce accedo ad sacramentum	354
et Pater benignissime	265
immensam clementiam tuam	141
intercessione beatissimi Joseph	147
maestorum consolatio	352
majestatem tuam supplices exoramus	143
misericordiam tuam concede	132
misericordissime qui venisti	145
non me permittas perire	117
parce metuentibus	115
per istorum et omnium sanctorum merita	137
precor te ut non permittas	108
salus æterna credentium	108. 352
spes et corona	113
tibi gratias ago	135
Omnipotens sempiterne Deus cujus	
filius sumpta carne	142
ineffabili providentia gloriosi m. Thomas Alphegus	149
spiritu totum corpus ecclesiæ	352
Omnipotens sempiterne Deus da	
cordibus nostris	138
nobis illam sancti Spiritus gratiam	143
Omnipotens sempiterne Deus in cujus	
manu sunt omnium potestates	352

	PAGE
Omnipotens sempiterne Deus in cujus	
nomine gloriosa v. et m. Dorothæa	125
Omnipotens sempiterne Deus qui	
b. Blasium pontificem tuum	149
deprecantium voces benignus exaudis	113. 191
donasti beatissimo regi Edwardo	125
ecclesiam tuam nova semper prole	352
etiam Judaicam perfidiam	352
Ezekiæ regi Judæ	152
gloriam tuam	352
hodierna die	140
infirma mundi eligis	141
non mortem peccatorum	352
per gloriosi bella certaminis	140
primitias martyrum	140
salvas omnes	352
salvatorem nostrum tradi manibus innocentium	259
sanctam filii tui genitricem	144
subvenis in periculis	129
vivorum dominaris	109. 352
Omnipotens sempiterne Deus qui dedisti	
(nobis) famulis tuis	109. 137. 163. 215. 217. 260
nobis filium tuum	254
Omnipotens sempiterne Deus qui ex	
abundantia charitatis	143
nimia charitate	123
Omnipotens sempiterne Deus qui gloriosæ virginis	
et matris Mariæ	110. 164. 176
et martyris tuæ Katharinæ	110. 164
Omnipotens sempiterne Deus qui meritis	
(et precibus) S. Sebastiani	139. 151
et precibus beatissimi Rochi	117. 118
Omnipotens sempiterne Deus qui nos	
b. Adriani martyris	146
Omnipotens sempiterne et clementissime Deus inter multiplices disciplinas	255
Omnipotent and merciful God the Father eternal	187
Omnipotent eternal God who by the prayers . . . of thy b. confessor St. Roch	372
Omnipotent King of hosts the Lord of Sabaoth	333
Omnipotent Ld. Jesu Christ that yet hanging on the cross	161. 210. 215
Omnis	
anima potestatibus	253
qui credit Jesum esse Christum (*Lesson*)	260
Omnium	
in hoc uno versatur summa laborum	268

	PAGE
Omnium	
sanctorum tuorum q. Dne. intercessione placatus	110. 164. 216
Open	
O Lord our (my) mouths to bless thy holy name	377
thou mine eyes O Lord	284
Osanna in excelsis	153
Our	
blessed Saviour Jesus (Jesu) Christ which in that great heaviness	187. 242
bountiful Lord God hath made unto us all	214
time passeth away like a shadow	275
Our Father	
that art in heaven	131
which art in heaven	153. 173. 197. 203. 218. 228. 239. 246. 274
Our God is a refuge (*Psalm*)	362
Our gracious Queen Catherine James Duke of York	304
Our Lord	
bless us and defend us from all evil	359
hear thee in the day of tribulation (*Psalm*)	373
Our most gracious sovereign	
lady Queen Elizabeth	299. 301. 303
lord and King Henry the eighth his most gracious Queen Anne	204. 206
lord and King Henry the eighth and all his true subjects	209
Our Saviour and redeemer . . . which in thy last supper	187. 241. 249. 254
Our Saviour Christ at his last supper	197
Our time passeth away like a shadow	275
Out of the bottomless pit of my heavy trouble	165. 217
Parce mihi Dne. nihil enim sunt dies mei	122
Pater ago tibi gratias, qui me audias	262
Pater de cælis Deus miserere nobis	
Domine sancte Pater	114
qui mundum	120
Pater tibi in manus commendo spiritum meum	262
Pater venit hora clarifica filium tuum	172. 211
Patiens Dnus. et multæ misericordiæ auferens iniquitatem	262
Pax Domini nostri Jesu Christi	129
Peccavimus tibi quia dereliquimus te	263
Per	
crucem hoc fugiat procul	152
crucis hoc signum fugiat procul	153
hæc sancta evangelica dicta deleantur	123
sanctorum omnium angelorum	144
signum sanctæ crucis de inimicis	107
te redempti (*Lesson*)	169
tua Christe Jesu merita	145

OF LITURGICAL FORMS. 433

	PAGE
Permit not sluggish sleep	276
Perpetuis nos Dne. s. Johannis B. tuere	109. 163. 216
Peto Dne. Jesu (Christe) largire mihi	115. 166
Pientissime Deus qui iniquitatum	352
Pierce through O sweet Lord Jesu the marrow	360
Piissime Deus et clementissime Pater	107
Populo tuo Domine qui sacrosancti evangelii tui	162
Postea animadverti tantam turbam	262
Praesta nobis q. Dne. auxilium	353
Praesta q. Dne. famulo tuo consolationis auxilium	145
Praesta q. omnipotens Deus ut	
familia tua	356
nullis nos permittas perturbationibus concuti	368
sanctae Dei genitricis	147. 164
sicut b. Mauricius	140
Praesta q. omnipotens Deus ut qui	
b. Christofori martyris	140
b. Herasmi martyris	131
pro peccatis nostris	146
Praesta q. omn. Dne. ut b. Bartholomæus	138
Praesta q. omn. et misericors D. ut qui devotissimi regis	117
Praetende Domine fidelibus tuis dexteram	352
Praise and thanks be to God	252. 290
Praise the Lord	
all you nations of the earth	283
O my soul and all that is within me	278. 282
Praise ye	
the Lord	205
the Lord all Gentiles (*Psalm*)	198
the Lord God (*Psalm*)	285
Praising be to God, peace unto the living	231
Pray for us holy mother of God	248. 372
Pray we to God the almighty Lord, that sendeth food	290
Precor Jesu Christe ut quando ex nobis ipsi	264
Precor te	
amantissime Dne. Jesu Christe propter illam eximiam charitatem	123
et princeps egregie Gabriel	114
Preserve	
King Edward thy servant	308
Queen Mary now in her young age	308
me while I am waking	276
Pretiosa in conspectu Dni. mors sanctorum ejus	262
Prevent me (us) O Lord in all my (our) doings	276. 307
Prevent we beseech thee O Lord all our doings	327

GGG

Prevent we beseech thee O Lord our actions	313. 316. 359
Pride cometh only of man's high arrogant will	215
Pro tali convivio benedicamus Domino	154
Propitiare	
nobis Domine famulis tuis	151. 174
Prosperum iter faciat nobis	145
Protector et princeps egregie Gabriel fortissime agonista	152
Protector in te	
sperantium Deus familia tua	113. 116. 161
sperantium Deus sine quo nihil est validum	118. 132
Protege et salva benedic santifica Domine	114
Put	
me not to rebuke (*Psalm*)	281
ye on the Lord Jesus Christ	275
Quae	
lingua aut qui mens	185
nunc sumemus membris alimenta caducis	267
Quaeso Domine Deus cæli fortis	122
Quaesumus Dne. intellectum sapientiæ tuæ divinæ	260
Quaesumus omnipotens	
Deus ut famulus tuus rex noster	352. 367. 374
sempiterne Deus sicut precibus	147
Quare fremuerunt gentes (*Psalm*)	307
Quem virgo carens vitio de flamine concepisti	122
Qui habitat in adjutorio (*Psalm*)	134. 355
Quicquid appositum est et quicquid apponetur	267
Quicunque vult salvus esse	168. 217. 355
Quis ergo Domine Deus et quæ domus mea	121
Quod sumus utilibus dapibus potuque refecti	267
Quoniam in sæculum	153
Quotquot maris sunt guttæ et arenæ terræ granæ	125
Raise up we beseech thee Lord	
the wills of thy faithful	180
thy power	176
Receive	
my confession O most benign and most clement Lord Jesu Christ	360
your meat without grudging	300. 302. 305
we beseech O Lord the prayers of thy church	374
Recumbentibus undecim discipulis	118
Refresh the hungry and thirsty both	173
Regard we beseech thee Lord this thy household	166. 210
Regi sæculorum immortali invisibili	263
Regina cæli lætare	151
Rejoice O flower of virgins all	165

Rejoice O virgin Christ's mother dear	164. 217
Reminiscere clementissime Deus miserationum tuarum	130
Requiescant in pace	118. 130. 134
Respice	
ad me infelicem pietas immensa	130. 201
clementissime Dne. Jesu Christe nos miseros	134
custodi protege plasma tuum	145
Domine famulum tuum in infirmitate	129
Respice quæsumus Domine	
Jesu Christe animas omnium fidelium	130
super hanc familiam tuam	115. 166. 379
Respice quæsumus omnipotens Deus	
super animas famulorum	128
Retribuere dignare Domine omnibus nobis	154. 155. 354. 378
Rex Jaspar, rex Melchior, rex Balthasar	111
Rogo te	
dilectissime Deus ut mors tua amarissima	136
Domine Jesu per illa salutifera vulnera tua	355
Sacerdotes tui induant justitiam	264
Sacro munere sacrati supplices	151
Sacrosanctæ et individuæ Trinitati	377
Saluto te sancta Virgo Maria	133
Salva me (nos) Domine vigilantem	259. 354
Salvam fac Domine reginam	260
Salvator mundi salva nos qui per crucem tuam	114
Salve	
cælorum rex pater misericordiæ	176
Disma, fur optime, defendens benignissime	138
intemerata Virgo Maria, filii Dei genitrix	134
Joseph nutricie, Christi pater	138
lux mundi, verbum Patris	127
regina (mater) misericordiæ	110. 164. 202
rex Jesu Christe rex misericordiæ	184
salutaris hostia	127
salve rex sanctorum	115
sanguis preciosi Dni. nostri Jesu Christi	151
tremendum cunctis potestatibus caput	124. 355
Salve sancta	
caro Dei	151. 175
civitas benedicat te tota Trinitas	137
facies nostri redemptoris	125
Salvete	
vos omnes fideles animæ quarum corpora	125
Sana me Domine et sanabor	172. 255. 264

INDEX

	PAGE
Sancta Maria	
Dei genitrix semperque virgo benedicta	111. 191
mater Dei ora pro nobis	120. 189
perpetua virgo virginum	135
regina cæli et terræ	111
Sancta Trinitas unus Deus miserere	
nobis. O beata et (benedicta et) gloriosa	111. 120. 191
nobis. Te Deum Patrem unigenitum	137
nostri. Domine Deus omnipotens	150
Sanctae Dei genitricis Mariæ semper virginis	151. 174
Sanctae et individuæ Trinitati	115. 166. 191
Sancte	
Deus sancte fortis	135. 189
Herasme, martyr Christi preciose	118
martyr vel confessor Dei preces meas	142
Michael esto mihi lorica	117
Pater omnipotens æterne et clemens Deus	265
Paule apostole prædicator veritatis	138
Philippe apostole Domini	138
Symon per gratiam illius qui te elegit	138
Thoma qui propriis manibus latus redemptoris	139
Sancti	
Dei quorum corpora et reliquiæ	149
nominis tui Domine timorem	150
patriarchæ, sancti prophetæ quibus ab initio mundi	138
Sanctifica	
me Dne. Jesu Christe signaculo tuæ S. crucis	112
nos Domine signaculo S. crucis	114
quæsumus Domine famulum tuum	117. 127
Sanctissimae ac individuæ Trinitati	131
Sanctorum confessorum tuorum Augustini	149
Sanctus sanctus sanctus	153
Sanguis tuis Dne. Jesu Christe pro nobis effusus	127
Sapiens ille qui tibi a secretis fuit Pater cælestis	156. 255
Sapientissime	
gubernator ac moderator universi	266
mundi conditor et gubernator Deus	266
Saucia Dne. Jesu Christe cor meum vulneribus tuis	129
Save	
all them that glorify thee	169
thy people, O God	177
us, O Lord, waking	246. 360
Say unto my soul, O God, thou art my salvation	285
Scio Domine et fateor quod non sum dignus	265

OF LITURGICAL FORMS. 437

	PAGE
Scio quod redemptor meus vivit	262
Seeing that thou, O heavenly Father, art that one	186
Servator benignissime illumina oculos meos	263
Serenissima imperatrice del cielo madre del unigenito	368
Servus tuus ego sum da mihi intellectum Dne.	263
Shew	
me O Lord thy ways	359
me thy ways O Lord	275
with clemency O Lord thy unspeakable mercy	363
Si	
consurrexistis cum Christo	154
iniquitates observaveris Domine	264
Signum sanctæ crucis defendat me	117
Sic	
benedicetis filiis Israel	263
Deus dilexit mundum (*Lesson*)	258
Sit	
Domine quæsumus b. Johannes apostolus	139
laus Deo pax vivis et requies defunctis	150
obsecro misericordia tua ad consolandum me	264
tibi Dne. obsecro meritis beatæ semper virginis	354
So frail is our nature, so vile is our flesh	293
Soon as his blest decree was made	283
Spare O Lord spare our sins	182
Spes	
animæ meæ post Deum v Maria	137
nostra Jesus Maria	139. 144
Spiritum in nobis Dne. tuæ charitatis infunde	155
Spiritus	
sancte Deus miserere nobis. Qui in columbæ specie	120
sancti gratia illustret	107
Stabat mater dolorosa	119. 355. 375
Statis horis Deum orare	164
Stella cæli extirpavit	165. 169
Stir up	
O Lord our hearts	176
we beseech thee Lord thy power	176
Stretch out O Lord the right hand of thy heavenly help	363
Suffer me not to receive thy glorious body and blood	192
Summe	
parens qui tecta tenes sublimia cæli	267
præsul Augustine prothodoctor Angliæ	149
Supplicationum servorum tuorum Deus miserator	144
Supra modum auctæ sunt copiæ	269

INDEX

	PAGE
Surge Domine ut dissipentur inimici	156
Suscipe	
clementissime Deus precibus et meritis b. Mariæ	354
confessionem meam piissime ac clementissime Dne.	354
verbum virgo Maria	126
Suscipe Domine	
animam servi tui	146
piissime Deus in sinu patriarchæ tui Abrahæ	109
rosarium Virgo deauratum	122
Suscipere dignare Dne. Deus omnipotens has orationes	108. 128. 156
Sweet and bountiful Lord God I meekly pray thee	221
Sweet Jesu, I do knowledge and believe that while thou were yet hanging	222
Sweet merciful and bountiful Ld. Jesu, this day I beseech thee	220
Sweet Saviour and good Ld. God, Jesu Christ, the son of the living God	192
Taedet me omnipotens ac misericors Deus	266
Te	
deprecor ergo mitissimam	119
igitur Deus rogo te	151
sancte Jesu mens mea	268
Te Deum	
laudamus	204. 353. 376
Patrem unigenitum	137
Teach me O Lord to number my days	275
Thank we God	164
Thanks	
be given unto God obedience unto our prince	295
be to God	219. 358. 365. 376
That	
meat that goeth into the mouth	205
the ministers and governors may catholically rule	217
wise man which was privy of thy secrets	189. 243
That thou give peace concord and victory	233
That thou vouchsafe to give	
peace to our King Henry	210
universal peace to Cæsar	217
That thou vouchsafe to preserve our King Henry	217
The	
almighty Lord who is a most strong tower	281. 324
angel Gabriel was sent (down) from God (heaven)	161. 209
beginning of the fall of man	188. 242
birth of Christ was on this wise	183. 228
The almighty and merciful	
God give unto us pardon	359
Ld. the Father and the Son and the Holy Ghost bless and keep us	360

	PAGE
The blood	
of Christ the cup of life	344
of our Ld. Jesus Christ which was shed for me	278 339
The body	
of Christ	344
of our Ld. Jesus Christ which was given for me	278. 320. 339
The earth is thine O Lord	293
The effect of our faith standeth in three parts	197
The evangelist witnesseth that he saith	214
The eyes of all things	
(do) look up and trust in thee O Lord	173. 290. 302. 304. 306
look up and wait upon thee	198. 220. 228. 233
trust in thee O Lord	192. 239
The eyes of the Lord are over the righteous (*Psalm*)	275
The faithful souls that are hence passed rest they	214
The fruit of the womb and the multitude of children	293
The glorious	
blood of Christ Jesu	113
passion of our Lord Jesu Christ	166. 197. 210. 240
The God	
of all glory and power who hath created	304. 306
of peace and love vouchsafe alway	173. 192. 239. 290
The grace of our Lord Jesus Christ	324
The heart of man naturally is lewd	294
The holy	
body of Christ Jesu	113
name of our Lord Jesu be ever blessed	214
Trinity one very God have mercy on me	187
The hour cometh and now it is	278
The joyful passion of our Lord	189
The joys, O Lord, which thou hast prepared	294
The king	
of eternal glory make us partakers (partners)	173. 192. 239. 290. 302. 304
shall reign in thy strength (*Psalm*)	279
The kindness and love of God	248
The Lord	
hear thee, the name of the God of Jacob defend thee	343
is my shepherd (*Psalm*)	281
The mother stood in woful wise	361
The peace of God which passeth all understanding	251. 282. 307
The prophets as they were all taught	206
The rulers of the people shalt thou not blaspheme	295
The souls	
of all true believers	165

INDEX

	PAGE
The souls	
of saints rejoice in heaven	240
of the faithful through the mercy of God rest in peace	359
that be hence passed in Christ Jesu, rest they in peace	214
The star of the sea which the Lord fostered	165
The very true receiving of thy glorious body	167. 210. 217. 221
The virgin Mary with her holy son	166. 210
The wicked is like a raging sea	294
Thee sovereign God our grateful accents praise	376
Then said Mary (*Lesson*)	253
There	
is nothing that becometh a maid	293
were false prophets	233
Therefore	
I will feed on thy flesh	344
with angels and archangels	342
These are the words of the Lord God omnipotent	214
This day	
good Lord I beseech thee by thy great virtue	221
pitiful Lord I beseech thee by the merits	221
This favour this grace O Lord shew me	183
This hath touched my lips	343. 344
This my body is the very dark	188. 244
Thou art	
just Lord and all thy judgments are true	172. 211
worthy O Lord (our God) to receive glory	275. 277
Thou God be praised for the food	302
Thou hast	
done Lord with thy servant David	211
given a commandment in thy law	293
Thou hast made	
a covenant O Lord (*Psalm*)	279
Lord with thy servant David	167. 189
Thou hast sanctified me O Lord	344
Thou O b. Jesu hast said he that eateth my flesh	320
Thou O our God art sweet longsuffering	189. 242
Thou our God art gentle and true	172. 211
Thou shalt	
have none other Gods but me	153. 173. 185. 239. 252
not have strange Gods	162
reprehend thy brother when he sinneth	295
sprinkle me O Lord with hyssop	359
worship one God only	128
Threnosa compassio	169

OF LITURGICAL FORMS. 441

	PAGE
Thus most merciful Lord that doest all	222
Thy	
benefits toward me O most loving Father	294
cognisance and badge	294
commandment is by thine holy apostle	293
dearly beloved Son in his holy gospel	294
Tibi	
ago laudes et gratias	137
Domine Jesu Christe commendo egressum meum	266
Timor Domini initium	253
Titulus triumphalis	
defendat nos ab omnibus malis	135. 189
Jesus Nazarenus rex Judæorum	115. 118
To	
believe that Christ hath for us merited	162. 209
eat and drink doth small avail	302. 305
have children and servants is thy blessing	293
To the	
great and good God be given all honour	306
holy and indivisible Trinity	166. 191. 210. 231
king eternal immortal	278. 320
most holy and undivided Trinity	377
To thee	
I cry O Lord hear me speedily (*Psalm*)	189. 242
O sacred heart of Jesus	380
Tobias senior cum putaret (*Lesson*)	258
Transfige dulcissime Dne. Jesu medullas	354
Transivimus per ignem et aquam	263
Tres sunt qui testimonium dant	260
Trium regum trinum munus	111
Tu	
autem Domine	378
Deus noster suavis et verus (patiens) es	172. 211. 255. 262
Domine qui omnium mentes perspicis	262
factus es fortitudo pauperi Domine	264
fecisti Domine cum servo tuo David	167
per Thomæ sanguinem	202
quoque quem Dominum dominorum	268
Tua me	
Domine Deus cælesti armatura	258
Domine quæso gratia semper præveniat	142
Tuorum corda fidelium Deus miserator illustra	142
Tutela præsens omnium	268

HHH

INDEX

	PAGE
Two things	
I require of thee, that thou wilt not deny me before I die	243. 295
Lord I demand that thou wouldest (wilt) not deny me	167. 189. 218
Lord have I required thee	211
Una autem Sabbati	183
Under the world-redeeming rood	375
Uno die Sabbatorum Maria Magdalene (*Lesson*)	259
Unto	
God's gracious mercy	324
thee O Lord do I lift up my soul (*Psalm*)	280
Unum	
agnosce Deum colas et unum	267
crede Deum nec jures vana per ipsum	162. 267
Ure igne sancti Spiritus renes nostros	132. 353
Ut	
modo ponuntur languentia corpora somno	268
tu Domine humiliasti et afflixisti me	254
Utinam vere sim azymus purus	264
Valete vos omnes fideles animæ quæ jacetis	127
Vanity of vanities all is vanity	283
Varnish and brighten the church abundantly	181
Veneranda nobis q. Dne. hujus diei festivitas	144
Veni Sancte Spiritus reple tuorum corda fidelium	259. 352
unicum solatium afflictorum	255. 264
unicum solatium verus doctor veritatis	255
Vera perceptio corporis et sanguinis	108. 167. 175. 210. 217
Verba mea auribus percipe Domine	167
Verbum caro factum est	259
Vere dignum et justum est	152
Veritas tua q. Dne. semper maneat	136
Vias tuas Domine demonstra mihi	137. 263. 354
Virgin Mary rejoice alway	248
Visit we (I) beseech thee O Ld. this habitation	313. 328. 345. 360
Visita	
nos quæsumus Domine et habitationem istam	117. 247
quæsumus Domine habitationem istam	136. 354
Vita viventium Christe ab iniqua et subitanea morte	117
Voce mea ad Dominum clamavi (*Psalm*)	117. 351
Votum servorum benedicat rex angelorum	154
Vouchsafe O Lord	
God King of heaven and earth to direct	359
to keep us this day (night) without sin	359. 360
to render to all our benefactors	360
Wash me clean O Lord from my wickedness	275

OF LITURGICAL FORMS. 443

	PAGE
We beseech thee almighty God behold the wishes of the humble	177
We beseech thee almighty God that thy servant James our King	373. 374
We beseech thee Christ thy church	303
We beseech thee good Ld. that thou being pleased	164. 216. 230
We beseech thee Lord	
admit being pacified our prayers	182
let thy grace prevent	179
of thy benignity	163. 216
pour into thy servants the spirit of truth	182
that the prayer of thy suppliants	249
We beseech thee O almighty God that thy servant	362
We beseech O Lord	
admit being appeased the prayers	362
defend us from all perils	362
hear mercifully the prayers of thy people	177
keep thy family	177
pour forth thy grace into our minds	359
to save and defend all christian kings	279
to shew upon us thine exceeding great mercy	241. 249. 296
We beseech thee O Lord Jesu Christ	
that the blessed Virgin Mary thy mother	361
We brought nothing into this world	281
We do not presume to come to this thy table, O merciful Ld.	251. 298
We give thee thanks	
O Almighty God for all thy benefits	359
O Father almighty for thy graces	290
We have	
saith Paul one Ld. one faith one baptism one God	246
sinned with our fathers	247
We humbly beseech thee	
O Father, mercifully to look upon our infirmities	241. 245. 277
O Lord, mercifully to look upon our infirmities	298
We most heartily thank thee, O Lord God	190
We know, O Lord, that the law is good	293
We (I) offer thee thine own out of thine own O God	343
We ought to glory in the cross	239
We praise	
thee O God	283
thy name for thou O Lord	285
We thank thee	
O heavenly Father, which of thine infinite power	198
O Lord for all thy benefits	285
O Lord (God) our father	198. 220. 228. 233. 234
We worship thee Christ	189

444 INDEX OF LITURGICAL FORMS.

	PAGE
What	
have we O heavenly Father	294
reward shall I give unto the Lord 278. 320. 343.	344
tongue or what mind may worthily	185
What art thou O my God what art thou	282
When	
I conceived in my mind the great danger of hypocrisy	220
I considered in my mind the penitential psalms	223
Jesus had spoken these words 162. 183. 210. 215. 219.	228
Jesus was born in Bethlehem 162. 209. 215.	365
the wicked man	304
thou lived'st in this world O Lord Christ	294
Whether ye eat or drink	304
Whom thou lovest, O Lord, him dost thou chasten	294
Whosoever	
(he be that) will (willeth to) be saved 153. 168. 210. 217. 219. 228.	361
liveth without thy grace and favour	293
Why art thou so vexed O my soul	330
With	
an humble and a contrite heart	197
my voice I cry to thee (*Psalm*) 188.	242
Works are divers	183
Ye be they that have left all things	239

INDEX OF HYMNS AND RHYTHMS.

	PAGE
A broken altar Lord to thee I raise	284
A special theme of praise is read	278
Abluitur sacra Christus ter maximus unda	268
Absque viro facta est fœcunda Deipara natum	268
Adoro te devote latens Deitas	145
Adveniet Christus supremo tempore judex	269
Aeterne rex altissime	376
Ales diei nuncius	258
All that is and shall be set upon the board	290
Andreas Christi famulus, dignus Deo apostolus	109
Angele Dei qui custos es mei	353, 354
Angele qui meus es custos pietate superna	112
Anima Christi sanctifica me	107, 174
Anthoni pastor inclyte, qui cruciatos reficis	113
Aqua benedicta sit mihi salus et vita	108
As thou hast fed our bodies Lord	302
As to the sick all pleasant things	305
Astra petit Christus, nos astra petemus et ipsi	268
At certain hours unto God for to pray	164
At complin time this mother of mercy	183
At night lie down, prepare to have	276, 284
Ave	
amator quam famose Hieronyme gloriose	115
caput Christi gratum, duris spinis coronatum	123
caro Christi cara immolata crucis ara	126
cujus conceptio solenni plena gaudio	119
Dei patris, filia nobilissima	128
domina S. Maria, mater Dei, regina cœli	130
domine Jesu Christe, verbum Patris, filius virginis	149
dulcis mater Christi, quæ dolebas corde tristi	126
facies præclara quæ pro nobis in crucis ara	127
flos patriarcharum, Joachim, dos prophetarum	138
fuit prima salus, qua vincitur hostis malus	128
Gertrudis virgo grata, ex regali stirpe nata	142
manus dextera Christi, perforata plaga tristi	124

	PAGE
Ave	
mundi spes Maria, ave mitis, ave pia	126
praesul honestatis, martyr magnæ sanctitatis	139
regina cœlorum, ave domina angelorum	123
rosa sine spinis, tu quam pater in divinis	124. 201
sancte rex Edwarde, inter cœli lilia	125
sanctissima caro, summa vitæ dulcedo	145
Sitha famula sancta Jesu Christi	125
stella radiosa, solis luce clarior	142
verum corpus natum de Maria virgine	111. 165. 217. 354
vulnus lateris nostri salvatoris	122
Ave gemma	
clericorum jubar stella quam doctorum	141
speciosa mulierum sidus rosa	142
Ave Maria	
alta stirps lilii castitatis	124
ancilla, Trinitatis humilissima	124. 201
Ave martyr	
Adriane qui martyrium immane passus es in corpore	146
gloriosa, Barbara quam generosa Paradisum venerans	142
Ave sancta famula	
Sitha Jesu Christi	125
Wilgefortis Christi	125
Beatus Nicholaus, adhuc puerulus	110
Before the lightsome day expire	360
Benedictus Deus in donis suis	267
Bless	
us, O Lord, and these thy gifts	302
we our Lord which of his grace	214
Blessed	
be the father celestial	290
Saviour Lord of all	283
thrice blessed are the poor	283
Carnes torreo Janus et trementes	257
Celeste beneficium introivit in Annam	113
Certius incerta nihil est mortalibus ipsa	269
Charitate vulneratus castitate dealbatus	141
Christe qui lux es et dies	135. 258
Christus	
ad æthereas cum vellet scandere sedes	268
qui lux es et dies	135. 258
Circumcisio Magos mittit	257
Coelorum candor splenduit, novum sidus emicuit	141
Coenam santificet qui nobis omnia præbet	154

Come	
let's adore the king of love	283
unto us Holy Ghost, send us from the heavenly coast	363
Come Holy Ghost	
O creator eternal	210
that us hath made	363
Consors paterni luminis	258
Corpora qui solito satiasti nostra cibatu	267
Credere meruisse Christum ut æterni patris	162
Credo in Deum Patrem creavit omnia	267
Culter qui circumcidisti sacrosanctam carnem Christi	136
Da	
Deus lætæ bona sancta pacis	268
mihi dona tria, sanctissima Virgo Maria	143
pacem Domine in diebus nostris	110
requiem cunctis Deus hic et ubique sepultus	150
Deus qui voluisti pro perditione mundi nasci	112
Devictis Satana peccato et morte resurgit	268
Dies iræ, dies illa	100. 103. 374
Disputat in templo bis senos circiter annos	268
Dolos maligne qui struunt	257
Domine Jesu Christe apud me sis ut me defendas	117
Dona tui serva nobis, Deus optime, verbi	268
Dulcis	
amica Dei, rosa vernans, stella decora	144
Jesu, cœlica nutu, regna gubernans	257
Dust earth and ashes is our strength	305
Erat autem Margareta annorum quindecim	110
Exultet urbs Bethania quæ contulit immania	142
Franciscus vir catholicus et totus apostolicus ecclesiæ teneri	113
Gaude	
Barbara beata, summe pollens in doctrina	113
felix tota Hispania, digna Deo cantans præconia	113
flore virginali honoreque speciali	110. 165
pia Magdalena, spes salutis, vitæ vena	142
sacer Severine, pie præsul Agripine	147
Gaude virgo	
mater Christi quæ per aurem concepisti	110. 164. 217
Katherina, quam refecit lux divina	142
Georgi martyr inclite, te decet laus et gloria	113
Give	
thanks to God with one accord	300. 303
to the King thy judgments Lord	284
Glory be to God in the highest	341

448 INDEX OF

	PAGE
God be in my head, and (in mine) understanding	129. 174. 276. 284
God save	
his church and eke our Queen	302
the church, the king and realm	306
Good Lord for thy grace meekly we call	214
Gratia magna tibi, Pater et rex inclyte rerum	267
Great God of kings, whose gracious hand hath led	279
Hail	
Queen mother of mercy, our life, our sweetness, our hope	164. 174
very body incarnate of a virgin	165. 217
Has videas laudes, qui sacra virgine gaudens	133
He that is king of glory and Lord over all	290
His epulis donisque tuis benedicito Christe	267
Holy, holy, holy Lord God	
almighty, who was and is and is to come	341
of sabaoth, heaven and earth are full of thy glory	344
Hostis ter Christum petit, et ter vincitur hostis	268
I am Sunday honorable, the head of all the week days	147
If stomach forsake thee, then tart receits make thee	302
In	
Jano claris calidisque cibo potiaris	209
mei sint memoria, Jesu pie signacula	136
primis pueri Christum discamus amore	268
Increase thy church (flock) preserve our Queen	302
Inditur, abscissa pueri cute, nomen Jesu	268
Ingressus Solymas pigram conscendit asellam	268
Jam	
noctis umbras Lucifer	268
quinta lunæ cornua	269
sol citato sidere	268
vesper ortus incipit	268
Jesu	
beate numinis	268
benigne fervidas	268
dulcis memoria dans cordi vera gaudia	145. 372
nostra redemptio	353
redemptor optime ad Mariam nos imprime	143
Jesu Lord	
for thine holy circumcision	16
the only thought of thee	337. 372
that madest me	218. 222
who from thy Father's throne	283
Jesus	
pulcher in decore	136
the only thought of thee	337. 372

Laurentius bonum opus operatus est	109
Let's then this sacrament adore	374
Libera nos, salva nos, justifica nos O beata Trinitas	109
Man's life preserved is by food	303. 305
Maria plena gratia stirpe concepta regia	144
Martyr Christofore pro salvatoris honore	113
Michael archangele veni in adjutorium populo Dei	109
Munera grata ferunt longa regione profecti	268
My son do thou observe my law	283
Necnon vere Deus paracleteque Spiritus adsis	268
Nocte qua Christus rabidus Apellis	268
Nos cum prole pia benedicat virgo Maria	119
Nosco meum in Christo corpus consurgere quid me	269
Novae laudis adest festivitas	144
Now	
beginneth the season to sow wheat and rie	302
that your (our) bodies refreshed be	301. 303. 305
Numinis ira brevis bonitas pia gaudia præbet	257
O	
beata Brigitta late collaudata	141
blessed Christ these hours canonical	174
candor perpetuæ puræ castitatis	113
decus insigne nostrum pastorque benigne	124
Deus appositis apponendisque precamur	267
Georgi miles Christi Palestinum devixisti	139
gloriosum lumen, omnium ecclesiarum solum splendidius	131
glorious cross that with holy blood	128
Gregorii dulcissimum s. Spiritus organum	140
inflammati Seraphin ardentes dilectione	125
Jesu intra pectus meum	150
Jesus our redemption	364
Jesus Christ, thou joyful light of the sacred glory of the immortal	341
lux et decus Hispaniæ, sanctissime Jacobe apostole	113
Martine, O pie, quam pium est gaudere	113
praeclara Christi sponsa, insignis Odilia	142
praeclarae vos puellae nunc implere meum velle	142
praesul beatissime Ambrosi doctor maxime	140
pulchra præcipuum rosa dans odorem	107
S. Dominice, amator pacis, lumen ecclesiæ, doctor veritatis	141
Saviour Christ, O God most high	376
star of heaven whose virgin breast	372
thou God almighty	283
vos undena millia puellæ gloriosæ	113
Wilhelme pastor bone, cleri pater et patrone	125. 147

	PAGE
O Anthoni	
heremita, infirmorum spes et vita	140
pastor inclite qui cruciatos reficis	113
O Lord	
bless us and this our store	285
for thy great mercy and grace	162. 219. 228
now night's returned again	284
the merciful and good	285
to whom all praise is due	285
O quam	
gloriosa refulget gratia, Sebastianus Dei martyr inclitus	113
magnificum est nomen tuum beate Roche	117
Oh that I once were in that city	285
Omne genus morbos curat dat lumina cæcis	268
Omnes	
gentes laudent Dominum	267
sancti et electi Dei nostri memoramini	110
Omnis in humanis vana est sapientia rebus	268
Omnium in hoc uno versatur summa laborum	268
One God only thou shalt love, and worship perfectly	133. 162. 213
Per	
haec sancta evangelica dicta	123
tua Christe Jesu merita et crucis ampla trophæa	145
Permit not sluggish sleep to close your waking eye	276. 283
Plurima perpessus vitam cum sanguine fundit	268
Pray we to God, the almighty Lord	290
Primum sanguinei latices, post rana coaxans	269
Purus homo ex pura Messias virgine natus	268
Quae nunc sumemus membris alimenta caducis	267
Quod sumus utilibus dapibus potuque refecti	267
Receive your meat without grudging	300. 302. 305
Rector beate cœlitum	269
Refresh the hungry and thirsty both	173
Rejoice	
O flower of virgins all	165
O virgin Christ's mother dear	164. 174. 217
Rerum creator omnium	258
Rex Henricus sis amicus nobis in angustia	117
Salvator mundi Domine, qui nos salvasti hodie	258
Salve	
Disma fur optime defendens benignissime a consortis injuria	138
Joseph, nutricie Christi pater, et Marie conjux cum pudicitia	138
lux mundi verbum Patris	147
regina (mater) misericordiæ vita dulcedo et spes nostra salve	110. 160. 164
salve rex sanctorum, spes votiva peccatorum	115

		PAGE
Salve sancta		
Agatha, virgo et martyr Dei inclyta		141
caro Dei per quam salvi fiunt rei		151
civitas, benedicat te tota Trinitas		137
facies nostri redemptoris		125
Salve virgo		
Dorothea, audi quæso vota mea		125
virginum, stella matutina		133
Sancte		
Dei preciose advocate gloriose, confessor Armigile		129
Herasme martyr Christi preciose		118
Pantaleon martyr Christi		129
Se nascens dedit in socium		269
Semen per varias sanctum disseminat urbes		268
Spiritus e rutilo sanctus delapsus Olympo		269
Stabat mater dolorosa juxta crucem lachrymosa	119. 355.	375
Stella cœli extirpavit quæ lactavit Dominum	111.	165
Summam quæ doceant salutis hæc sunt		269
Summe		
parens qui tecta tenes sublimia cœli		267
praesul Augustine, prothodoctor Angliæ		149
Suscipe rosarium virgo deauratum		122
Sweet Jesus, why, why dost thou love	284.	339
Tantum ergo sacramentum		374
Te		
Deum laudamus	353.	376
lucis ante terminum		354
sancte Jesu mens mea		268
The		
first six years of man's birth and age		209
mother stood in woful wise		361
star of the sea which the Lord fostered		165
sun by prayer did cease his course and staid		285
Thee sovereign God our grateful accents praise		376
Thou		
God be praised for the food		302
shalt worship one God only		128
To		
believe that Christ hath for us merited		162
eat and drink doth small avail	302.	305
Trium regum trinum munus		111
Tu		
per Thomæ sanguinem quem pro te impendit		110
quoque quem Dominum dominorum agnoscimus unum		268

INDEX OF HYMNS AND RHYTHMS.

	PAGE
Tutela præsens omnium	268
Ubi caritas et dilectio, ibi sanctorum est congregatio	132
Under the world-redeeming rood	375
Unhappy chance such fate should give	285
Unum	
agnosce Deum colas et unum	267
crede Deum, ne (nec) jures vana per ipsum	162. 267
Ut modo ponuntur languentia corpora somno	268
Veni creator Spiritus mentes tuorum visita	120. 210. 353
Veni sancte Spiritus et emitte cœlitus	353
Viam qui liquisti pro Christo dulcis Alexi	141
Vilia mendico præstemus munera fratri	268
Virgo	
Christi egregia pro nobis Apollonia	113. 142
S. Katherina, Greciæ gemma, urbe Alexandrina	110
Vitam quæ faciunt beatiorem	269
We	
beseech thee Christ, thy church, our Queen and realm to save	303
give thee thanks, O Father almighty	290
pray thee through St. Thomas blood, which he for thee did spend	187
We praise	
thee O God	364
thy name, for thou O Lord	285
What can I crave, more than the Lord hath done	283
When to thy God thou speak'st, O creature mean	275
Why do we seek felicity	283

INDEX OF NAMES AND PLACES.

⁎ *This index includes those prayers and devotions which have a proper name in the title: the general index includes all others: the names of printers, and places where they printed are also to be found at the beginning of the book before the Hand-list.*

	PAGE
A.B.C. signum, in cimiterio S. Pauli	23
Advent	
collects	176
concurrence of offices	312
general rule to know	208
method of saying the rosary in	373
penitentials or invitatories	333
rule for saying the Office of our Saviour in	311
season	311. 312. 313. 332. 369
Advent, Sundays in	
festivals	332
proper of festivals	313. 327. 328
Adventus	
Christi in carnem	268
Domini, oratio	144
Domini, quando inchoatur	350. 365
Aegyptus, decem plagæ	269
Aemylius, G., oratio dominica	267
Albertus et Isabella, archiduces Austriæ	366. 367
Alcuinus, Albertus Flaccus, de divinis officiis	374
Aldersgate Street	55
Alexander sixtus, pope of Rome	125
All hallowen day, collect on	181
All Saints	
collect of	164
memory of	230
prayer to	113. 128. 191
All Saints day	
eve of, a fast	312

All Saints day	
festival	333
general festival	273
holiday	371
holiday of obligation	312
octave of	312. 313. 315
proper of festival	313. 328. 329
All Souls day	
collect on	181
proper of festival	313
Allemanus, Nicolaus Higman	21
Anastasius, pope	125
Andrewes, bishop	
catechistical doctrine	286
private devotions	341. 345
Angel, prayer to the proper	112. 116. 191. 212
Angelos, oratio ad	
omnes choros	125
omnes, et præsertim ad proprium	129
sanctos	120
Angelum, oratio ad proprium	112. 116. 120. 129. 137. 191. 212
Angleseya, insula	269
Anglia	
arhiepiscopatus in	269
Elizabetha regina	269
flumina præcipua	269
regina, petitio ad Gregorium papam	123
Anglia et Wallia, civitates	269
Anglicanus mos, horæ secundum	3. 20. 131
Anna	
canticum	263
oratio	176
prayer of	176
song of	200
Anne Bullen	
arms of	44. 45. 200
in a prayer	214
in the litany	204. 206
Anne of Cleves	183
Annunciatio beate Marie	
oratio de festo	143
signum, via Jacobæa, Parisius	367
Annunciation, the	
collect on	181

NAMES AND PLACES.

	PAGE
Annunciation, the	
commemoration of	331
concurrence of offices	312
cut of	13
eve of	312
festival	332
holiday	371
holiday of obligation	312
proper of festival	313. 327. 329
Antonius, cardinalis, Granuellanus	357
Antwerp	196. 202
Antwerpiensis civitas	357. 366
Apollinaris, Sidonius, bishop of Averna	277
Apostles	
collect on the	181. 239
creed	284. 358
days of, holidays of obligation	312
eves of, fasts	312
feasts of, holidays	229. 371
Apostolis, orationes de	118. 138
Apostolis et evangelistis, orationes de	139
Apostolorum	
oratio	262
oratio in divisione	143
psalmi ad vesperas, in festis evangelistarum et	376
symbolum, carmen	267
Apostolos et discipulos, oratio ad	120
Archangels and our Saviour, prayer to the	117
Asa, king, prayer of	189. 242
Asa, rex	
contra hostes veritatis, precatio	263
in tempore belli, precatio	156. 255
Ascensio Domini	
cursus vitæ	268
oratio in die	143
psalmi, lectiones, et preces	259
Ascension day	
collect on	178
festival	333
grace at meals on	379
hymn on	376
hymn with proper preface	342
meditation on	337
moveable holiday	312. 371

	PAGE
Ascension day	
octave of	312. 313. 315
proper of festival	313. 327. 329
Ash Wednesday	
collect for	307
penitential	313. 327. 329. 333
proper motto	327
Assumptio beatæ Mariæ	144. 290
Assumption of our Lady	
concurrence of offices	312
eve of, a fast	312
holiday	371
holiday of obligation	312
in kalender	237. 245
proper of festival	313
Assumption of the b. Virgin Mary	
collect on	180
in kalender	296
octave of	313
Austin, John	
devotions	311. 315. 325. 330
devotions, a few particulars of	311
life of	315. 316
Austriae archiduces, Albertus et Isabella	366. 367
Averna, Sidonius Apollinaris, bishop of	277
Babylon, captivity of	122
Balthasar, rex, prayers to	111. 143
Barsabas, Josephus, precatio	262
Bath and Wells	
bishop of	326
diocese of	319
Battely, John, London, imprimatur	89
Becket, Thomas. See S. Thomas a Becket	
Becon, T.	
flower of godly prayers	292. 293
governance of virtue	301. 304
pomander of prayer	293. 294
Belgarum principes, summa privilegii	366. 367
Bell, St. Paul's churchyard, sign of the	67. 90
Benedict, pope, prayer made by	152
Bible, St. Paul's churchyard, sign of the	55
Black boy, St. Alban, Wood St., sign of the	88
Black Friars	
church door	40. 43
ditch side	100

NAMES AND PLACES. 457

	PAGE
Blue Garland, Fleet St., sign of the	52. 53
Bonifacius, pope, indulgence	124
Borbonius, Nicolas	268
Boscawen, Lady Ann	317
Botolph (Botoll) lane	52. 57. 184. 233
Bow street, Covent garden	316
Bradshaw, Henry	3. 4. 9. 112. 116. 128. 136. 173. 176. 238
Brecnoca (Brecknock)	269
Brogiotto, Andreas, typographiæ præfectus	375
Brunet, J. C. Manuel de libraire	147
Bruxellae, literæ datæ	366. 367
Bull, Henry, christian prayers	253. 258
Burgundiae, Brabantiae, duces, Albertus et Isabella	366. 367
Byddell, John	43. 44. 45. 48. 195. 200. 205

Bynham
    monachus de, oratio   114
    monk of, prayer shewed to   5. 114
Caesar   217
Caesarius in miraculis, de S. Edmundo   135
Calisia, villa   14
Cambridge
    Edgar, Baron Dawntzey, earl and duke of   282
    St. John's college   93. 315
    universities of Oxford and   208
Candlemas
    festival of   313. 332
    proper of festival   313. 327. 329
Canterbury
    archbishop of   126
    Christchurch within   36. 149
    city of   149
    diocese of   269
    see Canturia
Cantium, Kent   269
Canturia, Canterbury   269
Canturiensis
    archiepiscopatus in Anglia   135. 269
    archiepiscopus, Edmundus   135
    episcopatus in provincia   269
Carolus magnus   124
Catharina, regina   374
Catherine (Katherine) queen   156. 241. 304. 373. 374
Caxton, William   1. 3. 107. 116
Celestinus, pope   126

KKK

	PAGE
Cellarius, Johannes	268
Charles, king	
day of his inauguration, 1615	273
king and governour	277. 304
sovereign lord	88. 282
the second	285. 355
Charles the fifth, emperor	333
Cheapside, St. Paul's gate	46
Childermas day, collect on	181
Christ	
catholick church of	281
collect of the cross of	239
comfortable words, and sayings of	214
commandments expounded by	168. 209. 232. 246
image of the cross of	171
meditation of the passion of	222
meditations and devotions on the life of	92. 336
memory of the passion of	230. 234
nativity of. See Nativity of Christ	
prayer for concord of the church of	242
prayer in the worship of the members of	124
psalms of the passion of	217
salutation to all the parts of	361. 372
sermon on the mount	337
the wisdom of the Father	226
Christ our Saviour	
meditation on the passion of	337
passion of. See General Index. Passion of our Saviour	
prayer of	230
prayer to	176. 184. 187. 222. 231
prayers of the passion of. See General Index. Prayers of the passion	
Christ, prayer	
against the enemies of the truth	189
before his passion, for his church	172. 211
for concord of the church of	242
in the worship of all the members of	124
on the ascension of	337
Christ, prayer to the	
cross of	107. 112. 115. 117. 128
image of the body of	167
Christ, prayer unto	155. 184. 222. 231
Christ, prayer unto the wounds of	11. 112. 123. 360
Christ and the Virgin his mother, praise of	170. 230
Christ-Church within Canterbury	36. 149

NAMES AND PLACES. 459

	PAGE
Christi	
cursus S. Bonaventuræ de passione	136
horæ de passione	134
precatio contra inimicos veritatis	254
salutatio vulnerum	128
salutationes ad omnia membra	355
Christi ecclesiae, precatio pro	
concordia	156. 254
concordia et unitate	265
Christi, oratio	
ad vulnera	355
de armis passionis	136
devota de plagis	123
in cruce pendentis	133
Christi, psalmi de	
ascensione	259
nativitate	259
passione	2. 115. 119. 146. 166. 254. 259
regno	260
resurrectione	259
Christians and Jews	274. 360
Christmas day	
festival	332
grace at meals	378
holiday	371
holiday of obligation	312
hymn and proper preface	341. 342
octave of	312. 313. 315
prayer for	337
proper of festival	313. 327. 329
Christmas eve, a fast	312
Christum	
oratio ad salvatorem	176. 184
precatio ad, diluculo	264
Circumcisio Domini	
cursus vitæ Dni. nri. Jesu Christi	268
oratio in die	143
stanza in kalender	257
Clemens octavus, papa	
breviary renewed by	367
indulgentiæ	136. 367
licentia et facultas imprimendi	366. 375
modus ministrandi missam	375
officium b. Mariæ virginis cum calendario Gregoriano	95

	PAGE
Cocleus, Johannes	202
Colet, John	
dean of St. Paul's, the Paternoster	150. 213
Knight's life of	254. 264
Lupton's life of	150. 213
Cologne, three kings of, prayers to	111
Coloniensis civis	15. 17. 18. 19. 20. 21. 23. 26. 30. 31
Compline	
objections against use of word	328
what is meant by word	171. 230
Conceptio b. Mariæ Virginis, oratio in festo	144. 237
Confessoribus, oratio de	120. 140
Confessors, collect of	182
Copland, Robert, printer at London	147
Corporis Christi, oratio	
ante imaginem	118. 167
ante sumptionem	127. 167. 217
de corpore Christi	120
in die	143
in elevatione	78. 111. 145. 150
in sumptione	167. 217
post sumptionem	127. 167. 217
Corpus Christi	
moveable holiday	312. 371
octave of	312. 313. 315
proper of festival	313
Cottesforde, Thomas	291. 296. 299
Cranmer, Thomas	
letter to Henry the eighth	240
see T. Tanner, bibliotheca	
Todd's life of	206
Crew, lady	324
Crumwell, Thomas Lord	51. 52. 55. 225. 230. 233
Cuthbert, bishop of Durham, prayers made by	150
D. T.	372
D. T. (Theophilus Dorrington)	317
Dance of death	23
Daniel	
oratio pro peccatorum remissione	263
prayer, for restoring Christ's church	200
set hours of prayer	170. 274
David, king	
oratio, 2 Regum VII.	121
prayer according to	188. 242

David, king	
repentance of	171. 286
sacred resolution of	274
David et Ezechie, oratio	121
Dawntzey, Baron Edgar	282
De Buschere, J.	366. 367
Deacon, Thomas, daily private prayer	340
Dedicatio	
altaris, oratio	144
ecclesiae, oratio pro indulgentiis	144
Dedication day	173
Deum	
benedictio et recommendatio ad	137
oratio ad, pro bono fine	137
Deum filium	
carmen ad	268
oratio ad	114. 120. 264
Deum patrem	
carmen ad	268
oratio ad	114. 117. 120. 264
Deum S. Spiritum	
carmen ad	268
oratio ad	114. 120
precatio ad	255. 264
Dies rogationes, collecta	143
Discipulos et Apostolos, oratio ad	120
Disma, bonus latro	138
Divisione apostolorum, oratio in	143
Domini	
carmen de cæna	268
quatuor evangelia, et passio	118
Dominicis diebus, psalmi ad vesperas	376
Dominum, oratio ad	117
Dorrington, Theophilus, reformed devotions	317. 325. 326. 335
Dover	269
Doway, bible published at	367
Dublin	
Parliament Street	104
St. John's Society	379
Duke St., Grosvenor Square	103
Dunelmensis, Durham	269
Duppa, bishop	322
Durham, lord bishop of	324
Easter day	
collect on	178

INDEX OF

	PAGE
Easter day	
concurrence of offices	312
festival	333
general rule for	208
grace on	379
moveable holiday	312. 371
octave of	312. 313
prayer for	337
proper of festival	313. 327. 329
use of versicles between Septuagesima and	183
Easter eve, collect	342
Easter, season of	
benedictions for	313
hymn and proper preface	342
method of saying the rosary	373
Eboracensem, horæ secundum usum	15. 19. 41. 46. 72. 76. 77. 78. 130. 131
Eboracensis	
archiepiscopatus	269
ecclesiae, legitimus ritus	131
episcopatus in provincia	269
provincia	269
Eckius, John, manipulus curatorum	202
Edmundus archiepiscopus Cantuariensis	135
Edward, prince	
in the bidding prayer	155. 156. 175. 183. 211. 228
in the litany	206. 241
Edward the sixth	
collect for	292
first year of reign	65. 66. 244
homilies, of works	223, 231
in the Kalender	296
in the litany	245. 248. 292. 296. 298
injunctions	67. 244
letters patent	289. 295
licence to print daily private prayers	289. 295
primer in the reign of	65. 68. 69. 70. 93. 239. 244. 307
third and fourth year of reign of	68. 69
visitation articles of	244
Edwin, Jonathan, daily devotions	336
Egyptiacae, decem plagæ	144. 269
Eleazar	
oratio	121
pia deliberatio	263
Elephas, Parisiis, signum	
e regione Maturinorum	38. 49. 51

NAMES AND PLACES.

	PAGE
Elephas, Parisiis, signum	
in vico S. Jacobi	29. 30. 31. 34. 35. 37. 39. 40. 41. 42. 44. 47. 49. 51
juxta templum Maturinorum	27. 37. 38. 39. 41. 47
Elizabeth, lady	245
Elizabeth, queen	
collect for	251. 301. 303
in a preparative unto prayer	299
in the kalender	302
in the litany	252. 253. 256. 300. 301. 303
of England	126
of England and France	4
primer published by authority of	82. 86. 270
visitation articles	331. 333
wife to Henry the seventh	126
Elizabeth wife to Frederick prince Elector Palatine	277. 279
Elizabetha regina	
Angliæ	83. 123. 269
in the litany	254
regna et regiones, quæ sunt juris	269
Ellingerus, Andreas	268
Ember days	
collects for	247. 280. 316. 333
devotions on	314. 316
fasting days	148. 312. 328. 329
general rule to know	209
motto proper for	327
penitentials	329. 333
what they are	314. 369
England	
bishops and clergy of the realm of	207
catholicks in	103. 376
church of. See General Index. Church of England	
saints of	358. 365. 368. 369
England and Ireland	
church of	250
saints of	98. 99. 101. 102. 369
England and Wales	
cities in	285
counties in	285
England, church of	
by law established	270. 271
member of	323. 326. 327. 330. 331. 336
offices of	328
supreme head. See General Index. Supreme head	

INDEX OF

	PAGE
England, France, and Ireland, king of	244. 250. 295
England, Scotland, Ireland, and Wales, saints of	365. 368. 369
English	
books of devotion	328
tongue	153. 160. 184. 251
Epiphania Domini	
cursus vitæ Dni. nri. Jesu Christi	268
oratio in die	143
Epiphany, the	
collect on	177
grace at meals	378. 379
method of saying the rosary after	373
Erasmus	
of Rotterdam in Kalender	206
precationes. See General Index. Precationes	
Erinacei signum, in cimiterio S. Pauli	83
Esay the prophet, prayer of	190. 200. 210
Europae signum, Venetiis	97
Evangelistae et apostoli	
orationes de	139
psalmi in festis, ad vesperas	376
Evangelists, the four	229
Exaltation of the holy cross	314
Fabricius G. Chemnicensis, odarum libri	268. 269
Featley, Dr., devotions	286
Fisherus, Johannes, episcopus Roffensis	261
Fitz Simon, Thomas, priest	369
Flaminius M. Antonius, de rebus divinis, carmina	268. 269
Fleet bridge	44
Fleet street, sign of the	
blue garland	52. 53
George	17. 173. 176
sun	16. 44. 45. 48. 62. 64. 65. 66. 72. 73
Fleet street, signum	
Georgii	17
solis	10. 11. 16. 17. 24. 25. 28
Flemish language, office of our b. Lady in	366
Francia, juris et imperii Elizabethæ reginæ	269
Francis the first	333
Frederick, prince, elector palatine	277. 279
French language, the	
office of our b. Lady in	366
stanzas in	119
Friday, a fast	312

NAMES AND PLACES. 465

	PAGE
Froschouerus, Christopherus	269
Gau, John, right way to the kingdom of heaven	195. 196. 197. 201. 202. 203
Gavantus, Meratus, annotations on	379
George	
king, in a prayer	306. 307
Prince of Wales	307
George, Fleet street, sign of the	17. 173. 176
Germania inferior	357
Gerson, John	
behoveful teaching	136. 149. 174
forma absolutionis	145
quatuor exhortationes	146
tres veritates	136. 149
Glenham, Charles	269
Good Friday	
grace on	379
penitential	313. 329. 333
Gowhe (Gowghe), Johan, printer	46. 213
Grafton, Richard, printer to Edward the sixth	65. 66. 244. 245
Grafton, Richard, and Edward Whitchurche	220. 244
Granuellanus, Antonius Cardinalis	357
Greenwich, manor of	244
Gregoriane præcatiunculae	36. 149
Gregorianum Kalendarium	95. 365. 366. 367. 368
Gregorius papa	
decimus tertius, rosarium	368
tertius, indulgentiæ	123
Grey Friars, dissolved house of	54. 60. 61. 62. 63. 64. 67. 91. 220
Guido di monte, manipulus curatorum	202
Half-moon, St. Paul's churchyard, sign of the	89
Harry	
the seventh	126
the sixth, prayers made by	2. 111
Hebraical psalter	227
Hebrews, manner of lamentation for the dead	219. 231
Hedgehog, St. Paul's churchyard, sign of the	70. 81. 84. 85. 295. 297
Helisaeus	305
Henricus, beatus rex, oratio de	117. 147
Henry, holy king, prayer to	117
Henry the eighth	
and Queen Anne	46. 214
arms of	44. 45. 200. 218
in the Kalendar	296
in the litany	204. 206. 209. 210. 217. 241

Henry the eighth	
injunction, for the use of the primer	237. 251
king of England, France, and Ireland	244. 250
king's highness bill	244
letters patent	205
preface to primer	250
primer set forth. See General Index. Primer	
raised up to set forth God's will	207
supreme head. See General Index. Supreme head	
Henry the seventh	126
Henry the sixth, prayers	111
Herbert, George	283
Herbert's Ames, typographical antiquities	9. 55
Hewet, Dr., sermons	286
Hibernia, juris Elizabethæ reginæ	269
Hickes, Dr. George	
devotions in the ancient way of offices	90. 92. 315. 325. 328. 329. 330. 333. 335
preface to the reader	325. 328. 329. 330. 333
second collection of letters	331. 336
Hieremias, oratio	172. 255. 264
Hieremy, prayer of	172. 188. 211. 243. 294. 295
Hierom (Jerom) of Farrarye (G. Savonarola)	
exposition upon psalm, Miserere	48. 167. 200. 218
expositiones in psalmos	167. 200. 218
meditation upon psalm, In te Dne. speravi.	48. 167. 207. 218
Hieronymus, psalterium. See S. Hieronymus	
Hieronymus de Ferraria	
expositio in psalmum, Miserere	167
meditatio in psalmum, In te Dne. speravi	167. 207. 218
Hilsey, John, bishop of Rochester	
preface to primer	225
primer, or manual of prayers	51. 52. 55. 183. 219. 225. 230. 233
Hochstratus, Jacobus	202
Hollybush, John, exposition upon Salve regina	176. 184. 199. 230
Holtrop, Monumens typographiques	3
Holy Cross, the	
blessing by the virtue of	117
chapel in Rome, prayers written in	127
collect of	163. 215. 239
exaltation of	314
invention of	312. 313. 371
office of. See General Index. Office of the holy cross	
orison to	128

	PAGE
Holy Cross, the	
prayer to	117
Holy Ghost, the	
collect of	162. 215. 239
devotions for feasts of	320
exhortation. If thou have grace	215
hours of. See General Index. Hours of the holy Ghost	
memory of	230
office of. See General Index. Office of the holy Ghost	
prayer for the gift of	293. 363
prayer to	198. 337. 374
prayer revealed to S. Augustine by	124
promise of	337
seven gifts of	133. 274. 284. 358. 371
six sins against	284
to call for the grace of	363
twelve fruits of	274. 284. 358. 371
Holy Innocents day	
festival	332
holiday	371
holiday of obligation	312
proper of festival	313. 327. 329
Holy Saturday	
grace on	379
penitential	333
proper of festival	313. 329
Holy Week	
collect in	342
concurrence of offices	312
penitential	333
proper preface	341
Holy Trinity, the	
collect of	162. 215. 239. 246. 247
invocation to	7. 13. 14. 107. 162. 210
memory of	230
office. See General Index. Office of the holy Trinity.	
prayer to	107. 111. 114. 116. 150. 166. 191. 198. 221
season of	313
Hopton, Mrs. Susanna	325. 329. 330. 335. 336
Innocent	
the chief bishop	373. 374
the eleventh, indulgence	377
Innocentius	
papa octavus	136

	PAGE
Innocentius	
papa secundus	122. 127
pontifex	374
Invention of the holy cross	
holiday	371
holiday of obligation	312
proper of festival	313
Ireland	
Edward the sixth, king of England, France, and	295
Scotland and Wales, saints of	365. 368. 369
Iron Cross, St. Rouen, sign of the Turner	99. 101. 102
J. H. esquire	314
Jacob, prayer of Loth, Moses, and	121
Jacobus, rex, in a prayer	374
James	
duke of York	285. 304
duke of York and Albany	282
king, in a prayer	306. 373. 374
the second	335
Janus, in a stanza	257
Jaspar, rex, prayer to	111. 143
Jeremy, prayer of. See Hieremy	
Jerom de Ferraria. See Hierom of Farrarye	
Jesu	
expirantis, oratio	262
horae dulcissimi nominis	123. 218
jubilus de glorioso nomine	145
litaniae nominis	367
missa de nomine	136
precatio, ex novo testamento	261
precatio, revocaturi Lazarum	262
Jesu Christi	
cursus vitæ	268
passio. See General Index. Passio Domini	
Jesu Christi, oratio	
ad quinque plagas	122. 129
de singulis articulis passionis	135. 354
Domini nostri	263
in honore passionis, et b. virginis Mariæ	135
Jesum	
crucifixum, precatio ante	134
hymnus ad	268
oratio ad	134. 355
precatio ad	134

NAMES AND PLACES. 469

	PAGE
Jesum Christum	
commendatio ad	137
precatio ad, carmen	257
Jesum Christum, oratio ad	132. 256
Jesus	
act of adoration to the sacred heart of	380
act of consecration to the sacred heart of	380
devout prayer of the names of	150
devout short prayer to	218. 222
hours of the name of	218
litany of the holy name of	380
matins with prime and hours and evensong	46. 213. 218
office of the holy name of. See General Index. Office of the holy name	
petitions for the virtues of	338
prayer in english to	113. 196. 199. 361
prayer in the worship of S. Anna, our Lady, and	125
prayer to, before the crucifix	150
psalter	40. 46. 150
Jesus Christ	
litany of our Lord and Saviour	370. 372
litany of the acts of	217
passion of. See General Index. Passion of our Lord	
prayer at levation of. See General Index. Levation	
prayer to	243
salutation of our redeemer	187
Jesus Christ our Lord	
passion of. See General Index. Passion of our Saviour	
prayer to	187. 188. 189. 222. 231. 233
prayer to the pity of	11
Jesus Christ our Saviour	
intercession and prayer to	188
prayer to	187. 188
Jesus, filius Sirak, oratio	50. 122. 255
Jesus, our Saviour, hymn to	372
Jesus, prayer to	
before the crucifix	150
before the image of	125. 167. 189
in english	113. 116. 190. 199. 218. 222
in latin. O bone Jesu	112. 167. 189. 204. 231. 233. 247. 256. 361
Jesus, prayer with a reward of our b. Lady and	124
Jesus, son of Sirack, prayer of	188. 243
Jews	
ancient practice of devotion	326
and christians	274

	PAGE
Jews	
histories of the	276
prayers for the unfaithful	362
Job	
lectio ex historia	262
oratio et benedictio	172. 263
oratio sancti	122. 255
oration of	188. 242. 295. 305
prayer and blessing of	172. 211
the prophet, lessons out of	204
Johannes papa	
duodecimus	123. 128
quartus	125
vicesimus secundus	130
John, late bishop of Rochester	233
John, pope, the XXII	
grant of days (years) of pardon	126. 127
prayer made by	125
Jonas	
propheta, oratio	122. 172
the prophet, prayer of	45. 172. 199
Josua, dux populi, oratio	121
Joye, George, preface to Jeremy the prophet	206
Judaeis, oratio pro	352
Judas' treachery, meditation on	337
Judith, oratio	121
Katherine, queen	
in bidding the beads	156
in the litany	241. 304
prayer for	373. 374
Katherine, queen dowager	245
Kent (Cantium)	269
Kettlewell, Mr., practical believer	326
King Street, Westminster	9
Kington in Herefordshire	335
Knox, J., Book of common order	304. 305
Lady Elizabeth, in the litany	245
Lady Marie, in the litany	245
Lake, Dr. Edward, holy office by	90. 320
Lambeth, ex ædibus. Imprimatur	89
Lanspergius J. Pharetra divini amoris	265
Latin	
primers translated into english	160. 369
tongue	43. 44. 45. 48. 97. 160. 195. 238. 251. 257. 357. 369

NAMES AND PLACES. 471

	PAGE
Latin and Greek tongue	44. 45. 48
Law, Mr., serious call to a devout life	340
Le Boucher, N. registraire des libraires	102
Lent	
collects in	177
concurrence of offices	312
ember days	314
method of saying the rosary in	373
penitential	333
prayer for	337
rule for saying the office of our Saviour in	311
season of	148. 332
sorrowful mysteries, to be said in	373
sundays in	311. 312. 313
week days, devotions on	314. 316
Leo	
papa decimus, oratio	136
pope, epistle of our Saviour	124
the first bishop of Rome	171
the tenth, indulgence	377
Lincoln's Inn	316
Londinensis, London, bishoprick	269
London	
diocese of	269
George, bishop of	270
horae b. Marie virginis impresse in civitate	26
predicatorum domus	43
Londoniensis mercator	14
Lord Protector	245
Lord's day, the	
hymns for	324. 340
thanksgiving for	340
Loretana aede, litaniae	367. 368
Loretto, church of, litany of our b. Lady of	372. 380
Loth, Jacob, and Moses, prayer of	121
Louis roi de France et de Navarre	101. 102
Lucifer	221
Ludgate, sign of the Hedgehog toward	70. 295. 297
Lutherus, Martinus	
enchiridion	240
opera	196. 197. 203. 240. 242
Lyons, manual printed at	331. 333
Maiden's head, St. Paul's churchyard, sign of the	57. 59. 60. 61
Mamercus, bishop of Vienne	171. 219. 231. 277

Manasses	
king of Judah, prayer	188. 242. 305
rex, oratio	121. 255. 263
Margaret	
countess of Richmond, memoir of	107
princess, mother to the king	4
Maria regina, in a prayer	374
Maria virgo. See S. Maria virgo	
Marshall, William	
arms of	48. 207
hours known as printed for	198. 203. 209. 210. 213. 215. 219. 246
primer printed by John Byddell for	43. 44. 195. 200. 206
Martyres	
oratio ad decem millia	139. 140
oratio de	120
Martyrs, collect of	182
Mary, lady	245
Mary, queen	
horæ in the reign of	186
in the litany	277. 296
letters patent	71. 190
prayer for	279. 297. 306. 307. 308. 373. 374
primer in the reign of	70. 295. 307
Mary the virgin, hymns to	313. 316
Mathurinorum templum, Parisiis	27. 31. 34. 37. 38. 39. 41. 47. 49. 51
Maundy Thursday	
benediction for	313
grace on	379
penitentials, etc.	313. 329. 333
proper of festival	313. 329
Mayler, John, printer	184
Melanchthon, Philippus, carmen	267
Melchior, rex, prayer to	111. 143
Meratus, annotations on Gavantus	379
Midsummer day, collect on	180
Moretus, Joannes, librorum impressor	366
Moses	
commandments of God given by	168. 209. 232. 246
oratio, pro peccato populi	262
prayer of Loth, Jacob, and	121
Moysi et populi, oratio	121
Nativitas beatæ Mariæ, in festo	133. 144
Nativitas Domini	
cursus vitæ	268
in festo, collecta	144

NAMES AND PLACES.

	PAGE
Nativitas Domini, psalmi	
ad vesperas in dominicis	376
lectiones, et preces	259
Nativity of Christ, the	
collect in the day of	176
eve of, a fast	312
subject of Matyns of our b. Lady	170
Nativity of Mary, collect on	181
Nativity of our b. Lady	
holiday	371
holiday of obligation	312
in the kalender	237
proper of festival	313
Nehemiah dux, oratio	122. 262
Nehemias, prayer of	295
New Year's day	
epistle and gospel of	183. 184. 220. 233
festival	332
holiday	371
holiday of obligation	312
proper of festival	313. 327. 329
Nicene Creed, devotions after	343
Nonae ac Idus, de numero	350
Nuremberg. See General Index. Hortulus animæ	
Our Lady	
assumption of	237. 245. 313
called our life and hope	160
chapters in praise of	160. 169
church of, at Rouen	190
conception of, in kalender	237
crown of	377
daily devotion to	369
declaration of the evensong of	171
devout prayers to	116. 212
feast of	229
five corporal joys of	110. 164. 174. 217
golden prayer showed by	124
honour that belongeth to	226
hours of. See General Index. Hours of our Lady	
hours of the compassion of. See General Index. Hours of the compassion	
hymns in the office of, adapted to tunes	358
intercession of	357
litany of	370

INDEX OF

	PAGE
Our Lady	
litany of Loretto	372. 380
matyns of. See General Index. Matins of our Lady	
memory of	182. 230
memory of the compassion of	183. 230. 234
nativity of. See Nativity of Mary	313
office of. See General Index. Office of our Lady	
preface to primer of	369. 371
primer of. See General Index. Primer or Office of the b. Virgin Mary	
psalter of	221
rosary of. See General Index. Rosary of our b. Lady	
salutation of	126. 197
seven sorrows of, prayer of the	26. 126
seven spiritual joys of	110. 165
three offices of	370
visitation of	185
worship of (honour to)	160. 161. 168. 170. 202. 203. 226
Our Lady and St. John evangelist, prayer to	111. 191
Our Lady of Loretto, litanies	372
Our Lady of pity	
prayer before image of	111. 201
sign of, Fleet street	44
Our Lady, prayer	
devout to	116. 126. 128. 212
in honour of	125. 126. 372
in the praise of	164
of the great sorrow of	126
of the seven sorrows of	26. 126
taught to St. Bridget by	115
to, against the pestilence	111. 165
to, in english	116
with a reward of	124
Our Lord	
at the levation of. See General index. Levation	
crucified, prayer to	12. 112
fifteen hours of the passion of	111
hours of the passion of	55. 109. 110
meditation of the passion of	360
prayer to	3. 149. 175. 189. 190
vernacle of	125. 127
Our Lord and Saviour Jesus Christ	
litanies of	370. 372
prayer devoutly beholding	127
thirty days' prayer to	380

NAMES AND PLACES.

	PAGE
Our Lord God	
prayer to	150. 189. 190
psalm of the sufferings of	283
Our Saviour	
and archangels, prayer to	117
devotions for the feasts of	319. 320
devout prayers to. See General Index. Devout prayers	
epistle of, sent by Pope Leo	124
exaltation of, in the rosary	373
fifteen stages in the pilgrimage of	284
intercession and prayer to	188
litany of our Lord and	370
mysteries of the life of	373
offices for feasts of. See General Index. Office of our b. Saviour	
prayer to	28. 117
Our Saviour Christ. See General Index. Passion of our Saviour Christ	
Our Saviour Jesu	
hymn to	372
three devout prayers in english to	116
Our Saviour Jesu Christ	
intercession and prayer unto	188
prayer to. Conditor cœli	189
prayers to	187. 189
Oxford and Cambridge, universities	208
Paganis, oratio pro	352
Pagans	
prayer against	363
prayer for the	362
Palatine, prince, prayer for the	279
Palatium regis, Paris, signum S. Margarete	32. 33. 35. 42
Palm Sunday	
concurrence of offices	312
penitentials, &c.	313. 327. 329. 333
Papa	
oratio edita, coram imagine b. Marie virginis	123
oratio post divinum officium	131
oratio pro	352
Papa Clemens octavus. See General Index. Officium b. Marie Virginis	
Papa sixtus quartus, oratiuncula	112
Papa sixtus quintus. See General Index. Officium b. Marie Virginis	
Papa Urbanus octavus. See Urbanus octavus	
Parasceves, in festo, psalmi, lectiones, et preces	259
Paris, ordinary of the holy mass printed at	374

	PAGE
Parisiensis	
civis	21
universitas	8. 14. 27. 28. 29. 30. 31. 34. 35. 37. 40. 42. 43. 44
Parisiis, vicus novus	22
Parisiorum, academia	15. 16. 17. 18. 19. 20. 21. 22. 23
Parkhurstus, Johannes	
cursus vitæ Dni. Jesu Christi	268
decem mandata, carmen	267
ludicra	257. 267. 268. 269
precatio ad Jesum Christum	257
Parliament street, Dublin	104
Pascha, festum	
benedictio mensæ, in die	155
oratio in	143
psalmi, lectiones, et preces in	259
Passion Sunday, penitential	313. 314. 316. 327. 329. 333
Passion week, collects in	177
Patriarchas et prophetas, oratio ad omnes	120. 138
Patronum, oratio ad unum sanctum	142
Pentecost, day of	
act of glorification of God	342
hymn, and proper preface	341
prayer upon	337
Penthecostes, festum	
oratio in die	143
psalmi, lectiones, et preces in	259
Petrus martyr, Vermilius, Florentinus	269
Pharisaei, precatio	262
Pharisee, a, doctor of law	370
Philippe J. device	7
Philippus, rex Hispaniarum	366
Pius papa quintus	
bulla, Superni omnipotentis	349. 356. 365. 368. 375. 380
indulgence	380
licentia imprimendi, C. Plantinus	357
method of saying the rosary	372. 373. 374
officium B.M.V. nuper reformatum. See General Index. Officium	
summarium constitutionis	350. 356. 365. 368
Pius papa secundus, indulgence	125
Plantiniana officina Antwerpiæ	95
Plantinus, Christophorus, librorum impressor	357. 366
Pole, the Lord Cardinal	71. 186
Popery, opposition to	270
Popish church	322

NAMES AND PLACES. 477

	PAGE
Powder treason day	273
Praesentatio b. Marie, oratio in festo	144
Prest, John, printer, Rouen	190
Prevost, Nicolaus, calcographus	30
Prince of Wales	
George	307
plume, cut of	244
Prophetae et patriarchae, oratio ad	120. 138
Protestant	
faith	322
monastery	322. 323
the moderate	314
Prudentius, Aurelius	269
Publicanus, precatio	262
Purificatio b. Marie	
benedictio candelarum	142
oratio in festo	143
Purification, feast of	
collect on	181
commemoration for	331
devotion for	332
eve of, a fast	312
holiday	371
holiday of obligation	312
Quatuordecim auxiliatores, oratio ad	140
Quentyn, John, doctor in divinity	147. 212
Quinquagesima Sunday, collect	177
R. P., primer reviewed and corrected by	101
Raymund, Cardinal, and Legate, days of pardon	125
Raynalde, Thomas. See S. Paul, churchyard	
Redman, Robert. See S. Dunstan, church	
Responsorium, warranted by Scripture	372
Resurrectio Domini	
cursus vitæ Dni. nri. Jesu Christi	268
psalmi, lectiones, et preces de	259
Ridley, bishop, visitation articles	250
Rochester, John	
bishop of	51
late bishop of	52. 55. 225. 233
Rogation days	
devotion on	314. 316
litany, sung on	277. 375
penitential	313. 328. 329. 333
Rogation week, proper of festivals	313. 329

INDEX OF

	PAGE
Rogationibus diebus, oratio in	143
Romae datum apud S. Petrum, bulla	350. 356. 357. 365. 366. 368. 375
Roman	
abuse of the word monastery	322
calendar, new modelled	365. 368. 371
catholick	325
institution, calendar modelled according to the last	371
missal	349. 366. 375
use, primer according to	97. 349. 368
Roman Breviary	
book in form and method of	317
hymns from, in primer	101. 102. 103. 104. 376. 377
office of the b. Virgin Mary according to the last edition of	95. 96. 366. 367
primer according to	95. 96. 366. 367. 377
renewed by Clement the eighth	367
Romans	322
Romanum Breviarium	
emendatum jussu concilii Tridentini	349. 356. 366. 367
Joannes Moretus impressor	366
officium B.M.V. recognitum sub Urbano VIII.	97. 100. 368. 375
Romanum Missale. See General Index. Missal.	
Rome	
chapel of the holy cross	127
church of	328. 330. 331. 336. 367
Leo, bishop of	124. 171
pope of	124. 125. 126. 127. 131. 136. 208
S. Gregory, bishop of	277
S. John's church at	223
S. Paul's church at	171
Rome, bishop of	
in the litany	241. 245. 252. 254. 292. 298. 300. 301. 304. 308
publications with regard to	207
saints canonised by	204
unlawful jurisdiction	208
with his adherences	233
Romish abuses (superstition)	270. 323
Rothomagi	
officina R. Valentini bibliopole	190
via magna horologii	53
Rouen, epistles and gospels printed by John Prest	190
Rue de leseureul, Rouen	18
S. J. (John Serjeant)	314. 315. 325. 326
S. S., bookseller, London	88
S. Adrianus, oratio de	146

NAMES AND PLACES.

	PAGE
S. Agatha	
oratio de	141
verba scripta super candelas in die	142
S. Agnes, oratio de	141
S. Alban, church, Wood St.	88
S. Alexius, oratio de	141
S. Alphege, in the kalender	237
S. Alphegus, martyr	149
S. Ambrose	
and S. Augustine, hymn	376
liber de virginibus	275
prayer made by	125
S. Ambrosius, oratio de	140
S. Ancelmus, oratio	108
S. Andreas, oratio de	109. 139. 163. 216
S. Andrew	
collect of	163. 216
feast of	208
festival	332
proper of festival	313. 327. 328
S. Angeli, oratio ad	120. 125. 129
S. Anna	
oratio de	113. 129
prayer before image of Jesus, our Lady, and	125
prayer in the worship of Jesus, our Lady, and	125
S. Anne (Ann)	
holiday	371
holiday of obligation	312
prayer to	113
proper of festival	313
S. Anselm, bishop of Canterbury	370
S. Anthonius, oratio de	113. 140
S. Anthony, prayer to	113
S. Apollonia, oratio de	113. 142
S. Apostoli, oratio de	118
S. Apostoli et Discipuli, oratio ad	120
S. Appollyn, prayer to	113
S. Armigillus, oratio de	129
S. Athanasius	
creed of. See General Index. Creed of Athanasius	
symbolum. See General Index. Creed of Athanasius	
S. Augustine, prayer	
made by	130
recommended by Urban VIII.	372

S. Augustine, prayer
    shewed unto   124
    to the Holy Ghost, out of   337
    wherewith he began his devotions   282
S. Augustine and S. Ambrose, hymn of   376
S. Augustinus
    liber soliloquiorum   264
    meditationes   242. 263. 264. 265. 266
    monasterium, Cantuariense   36. 149
    oratio   108. 122. 264. 265. 266
    oratio de   36. 141. 149
    signum, in S. Pauli cimiterio   35. 36
S. Austin (Austine) (Austin)
    epistles of   169
    on prayer   272
    on the kalender   272
    prayer of   108. 169. 172
S. Barbara, oratio de   1. 107. 113. 142
S. Barnabas
    commemoration of   331
    festival   333
    in kalender   245. 290
S. Bartholomaeus, oratio de   138
S. Bartholomew
    collect of   180
    festival   333
    in kalender   250
    proper of festival   313. 328. 329
S. Basil orat. in Martyr. Julit.   275
S. Benedictus, oratio de   140
S. Bernard
    hymn, Jesu dulcis memoria   145. 372
    prayer of   124. 167. 218
    verses of   5. 114. 166. 201
S. Bernardinus, oratio   12. 112. 167. 218
S. Bernardus
    jubilus de nomine Jesu   145
    oratio de   141
    versus   114. 152. 166
S. Bernardyn, prayer of   112
S. Blasius
    oratio ad   36. 149
    oratio de   139

S. Bonaventura	
cursus de passione Christi	136
oratio post communionem	354
S. Bonaventure, prayer after receiving the b. sacrament	360
S. Brigitta (Brigitte)	
oratio de	141
quindecim orationes	1. 3. 12. 19. 36. 111
S. Brygytte (Brygyde) (Bryget)	
see General Index. Fifteen Oos	
short prayers of	115
S. Christopher, prayer to	113
S. Christopherus (Christoferus)	
commemoratio de	151
oratio de	113. 140
S. Chrysostom	
oratio	267
prayer of	241
S. Claudius, Paris, sign of	21
S. Clement, parish, London	11
S. Cornelius et Cyprianus, oratio de	147
S. Crux	
officium	353
oratio ad	115
oratio de	36. 109. 117. 143. 163. 215
S. Cyprian (Cipriane), testimony of, to hours of prayer	171. 274
S. Cyprianus. See S. Cornelius	
S. Dionise and his fellows	237
S. Dionysius	
in a prayer	120
oratio de	140
S. Discipuli. See S. Apostoli et Discipuli	
S. Disma, oratio de	138
S. Dominick, rosary revealed to	372, 373
S. Dominicus, oratio de	141
S. Dorothea, oratio de	125. 142
S. Dunstan	
church, London	173. 176
parish, London	52
S. Edmundus Archiepiscopus Cantuariensis	135
S. Edward, prayer of	115
S. Edwardus, oratio de	117. 125. 147
S. Elizabeth, oratio de	142
S. Erasmus (Herasmus)	
oratio de	139. 151
prayer to	5. 118. 131

	PAGE
S. Erhardus, oratio de	140
S. Erkenwaldus, oratio de	124
S. Felix. See S. Nabor and Felix	
S. Franciscus, oratio de	113, 141
S. Gabriel	
missus est	118. 119. 129. 161. 259. 357
oratio ad	114. 152
salutation of	162
S. Gallus, oratio de	141
S. George	
feast of	229
holy day, in epistles and gospels	173
in kalender	173. 237. 245. 299
prayer of	191
prayer to	113
S. Georgius, oratio de	4. 113. 139. 191
S. Gertrude, oratio de	142
S. Gregorius	
indulgentia	136
oratio	12. 116. 355
oratio de	3. 140
S. Gregory (Gregorie)	
bishop of Rome	277
dirige ascribed to	171
five petitions and prayers made by	124
litanies augmented by	277
prayer of	361
prayer to the Trinity made by	116
S. Henricus, commemoratio de	152
S. Herasmus. See S. Erasmus	
S. Hiacinthe. See S. Prothe and Hiacinthe	
S. Hierom (Hierome) (Iherom)	
argument of the psalter of	172
collect of	115
prayer to	172. 210
psalter of	167. 172. 217
S. Hieronymus (Iheronimus)	
meditatio in psalmum. See General Index. Meditatio	
oratio ad	115. 172
oratio de	141
psalterium	115. 167. 217. 261
S. Hubertus, oratio de	146
S. Innocentes	
oratio ad	120
oratio in festo	144

NAMES AND PLACES.

	PAGE
S. Isidore, dirige ascribed to	171
S. Jacobus apostolus, oratio ad	112
S. Jacobus major, oratio de	138
S. Jacobus minor Alphæi, oratio de	113. 138
S. Jacobus vicus, Paris 21. 27. 29. 30. 31. 32. 34. 35. 37. 38. 39. 40. 41. 42. 43.	
	44. 47. 49. 51
S. James	
festival	333
her Majesty's chapel at	372
proper of festival	313. 328. 329
the less, prayer to	113
the more, prayer to	112
S. Jerome	
Hebraical psalter, translated by	227
(Hierom) psalter	6. 46. 167. 172. 217
S. Joachim, oratio de	138
S. Johannes baptista, oratio de	36. 109. 138. 163. 215
S. Johannes, evangelista	
et S. Maria, oratio ad	191. 355
in parochio S. Martini, signum	42
initium S. evangelii, secundum	14. 29. 33. 54. 77. 118. 161. 357
oratio de	2. 109. 139. 163. 166. 216
Paris, sign of	7. 8. 9. 10. 13. 15. 22
passio Dni. nri. Jesu Christi, secundum	118. 119. 129. 136. 162. 183.
	254. 351
sequentia S. evangelii, secundum	152
S. John baptist	
collect of	163. 215
commemoration of	331. 333
festival	333
holy day	371
holiday of obligation	312
nativity, eve of, a fast	312
proper of festival	313. 328. 329
S. John evangelist	
and our Lady, prayer to	111. 191. 361
beginning of the gospel, according to	54. 161. 209. 215. 358
church of, in Rome	223
collect of	2. 163. 181. 216
college, in Cambridge	93. 315
fasting days	312
festival	332
holy day	371
holiday of obligation	312

INDEX OF

	PAGE
S. John evangelist	
lesson of the gospel of the passion	183. 219. 228
proper of festival	313. 327. 329
passion, written by. See General Index. Passion written by S. John	
prayer of	166
society in Dublin	379
S. Joseph	
holiday of obligation	312. 371
office of	98. 99. 101. 102. 369. 370
oratio de	138. 147
prayers at novena of	377
proper of festival	313
seven prayers in honour of	377
S. Judas, oratio de	139
S. Katherina, oratio de	1. 36. 110. 142. 164
S. Katherine (Katheryne)	
collect of	36. 164
commemoration of, in kalender	219. 233
S. Lambertus, oratio de	146
S. Laurence	
collect of	163. 180. 216
eve of, a fast	312
festival	312. 371
holiday	371
holiday of obligation	312
paroisse, Rouen	18
proper of festival	313
S. Laurentius, oratio de	2. 109. 140. 152. 163. 216
S. Leonardus, oratio de	141
S. Lo, rue, Rouen	99
S. Lucas evangelista	
oratio de	139
passio Domini nostri, secundum	351
sequentia s. evangelii	14. 118. 357
S. Lucy, day of	314
S. Luke evangelist	
collect on	181
festival	333
(holy) gospel according to	161. 209. 215. 365
lesson of the gospel of, mentioning the resurrection	183. 219. 228
passion of our Lord Jesus Christ, according to	361
proper of festival	314. 328. 329
S. Machabaei martyres, oratio de	146
S. Machutus ecclesia, Rothomagi	46

NAMES AND PLACES. 485

	PAGE
S. Marcus evangelista	
oratio de	139
passio Domini nostri. See General Index. Passio Domini nostri	
sequentia s. evangelii	14. 118. 357
S. Margaret, collect	1. 164. 216
S. Margareta	
oratio de	1. 110. 142. 164. 216
Paris, signum	32. 33. 35. 42
S. Maria Magdalena, oratio de	1. 36. 110. 142. 164. 216
S. Maria Virgo	
carmen	261
commendatio ad	137. 355
de gaudiis corporalibus	164. 217
de gaudiis spiritualibus	165
de recitatione officii	350. 368
devota contemplatio juxta crucem	119
ecclesia, Rothomagi	7. 69. 71. 74. 75. 77
edes, Rothomagi	74. 75. 77. 190
horae b. Mariæ Virginis. See General Index. Horæ b. Mariæ Virginis	
litaniae in æde Loretana	367. 368
matutinae de, a natali Dni. usque ad purificationem	18. 128
officium b. Mariæ Virginis. See General Index. Officium b. Mariæ Virginis	
oratio in honore Jesu Christi, et	155
planctus	355
prayer before the image of Jesus, S. Anna, and	125
precatio, carmen	261
recommendatio sub protectione	137
rosarium (the rosare)	16. 118. 122. 368
septem salutationes ad	128
vespere de, per adventum usque ad vigiliam natalis Dni.	17. 18. 128
vicus novus, Parisiis	7. 8. 9. 10. 13. 15. 22
visio, ante diem exitus	123. 130
S. Maria Virgo, oratio	
coram imagine	123
die Sabbati, ad honorem	129
in honore, et passionis Jesu Christi	135
pro vitæ incolumitate	111
S. Maria Virgo oratio ad	120. 123. 129. 130. 133. 134. 144. 151. 355. 368
S. Maria Virgo, oratio ad	
contra pestem	165
honorem, die sabbati	119. 129
in carmine	143
laudem deiparæ virginis	164
post communionem	124

INDEX OF

	PAGE
S. Maria Virgo, oratio ad	
pro bono fine impetrando	137
S. Johannem et	191. 355
S. Maria Virgo, oratio de	119. 120. 131
S. Maria Virgo, oratio in festo	
annuntiationis	143
assumptionis	144
conceptionis	144
nativitatis	133. 144
praesentationis	144
purificationis	142. 143
visitationis	143
S. Maria Virgo, orationes de	110
S. Mark, evangelist	
collect on	181
day of abstinence	313
festival	333
holiday of obligation	314
holy gospel according to	365
lesson of the gospel of, mentioning the ascension	183. 219. 228
passion according to	361
proper of festival	314. 327. 329
sixteenth chapter of	162. 215. 365
S. Mark and Marcellian, day of	237
S. Martha, oratio de	142
S. Martin, prayer to	113
S. Martinus	
oratio de	113. 141
parochia, intersignium S. Johannis	42
S. Mary Magdalene (Magdalen)	
collect of	1. 164. 180. 216
feast of	229. 237. 245
in kalender	237. 245
proper of festival	314
S. Mary the Virgin	
and S. John, prayer to	361
assumption of, collect	180
Christ's birth of	170
commemoration for	313. 315
commendation to	147
declaration of the Ave Maria	131
honour due to	226. 357
hymns to	313. 316
intercession of	357. 367

S. Mary the Virgin
    invocation of   215. 219. 357
    lauds and praises of Christ and   170. 230
    litany of Loretto sung on feasts of   372
    many things ascribed to   169
    mother of God, prayer to   367
    nativity of, collect   181
    office. See General Index. Office
    plaint of   361
    prayer to   361
    primer. See General Index. Primer
    recommendation unto   361
    rosary revealed to S. Dominick by   372
    rubricks in reciting the office of   377
    salutation of the angel to. See General Index. Salutation
    short exposition of office of   371. 374
    thirty days prayer to   380
    true piety towards   380
S. Maternus, oratio de   147
S. Matthaeus
    oratio de   138
    passio Dni. nri. Jesu Christi   351
    sequentia s. evangelii   14. 118. 357
S. Matthew, evangelist
    festival   333
    gospel of, mentioning the incarnation   183
    holy gospel according to   365
    passion of our Lord Jesus Christ, according to   361
    proper of festival   313. 328. 329
    second chapter. When Jesus was born   162. 209. 215. 365
S. Matthias
    festival   332
    oratio de   138
    oratio super subrogatione Apostolorum   262
    proper of festival   313. 329
S. Mauricius, oratio ad   140
S. Michael
    collect of   5. 114. 163
    collect on   181
    festival   333
    holiday   371
    holiday of obligation   312
    oratio de   36. 109. 137. 163
    prayer to   117

S. Michael	
proper of festival	313. 328. 329
sign of	52. 53
S. Nabor and Felix in the kalender	206
S. Nicolas, collect of	163
S. Nicolaus	
oratio de	1. 110. 141. 163
parochia, Rothomagi	19. 20
S. Odilia, oratio de	142
S. Omers	95. 96. 99
S. Panthaleon, oratio de	129
S. Patriarchae et Prophetae, oratio ad	120
S. Paul	
church of, at Rome	171
gate, next Cheapside	46
parish church of, Covent Garden	316
S. Paul churchyard, Rivington C. and J.	93
S. Paul churchyard, sign of the	
bell, John Jones	90
bell, Robert Toye	67
bible, Richard Grafton and Edward Whitchurche	55
blue garland, John Wayland	52. 53
half-moon, Joseph Watts	89
hedgehog, William Seres	70. 81. 84. 85
maiden's head, Thomas Petyt	57. 59. 60. 61. 71
star, Thomas Raynalde	250
swan, W. Keblewhite	90
three crowns, D. Midwinter	92
white horse	52
S. Paul, conversion of	
collect on	181
festival	331. 332
in the kalender	296
proper of festival	327. 329
S. Paulus	
gratiarum actio pro conversione	263
oratio de	131. 138
oratio de conversione	138
S. Paulus cimiterium	
bibliopolae in	12. 15. 18. 19. 21
Franciscus Byrckman, mercator	19. 20. 21. 22. 23
Guilelmus Seres, signum Erinacei	83
horæ venduntur apud bibliopolas	12. 15. 18. 19. 21. 30. 31
intersignium S. Augustini	35. 36

	PAGE
S. Paulus cimiterium	
Ricardus Fakes, librarius, signum A.B.C.	23
Thomas Petit, impressor	57. 61. 63
S. Peter	
commemoration of	331
festival of	333
first pope of Rome	127
proper festival	328. 329
the apostle, hours of prayer	170
upon all states	233
S. Peter and Paul	
collect of	163. 216
collect on the day of	180
in the kalender	237. 248, 250
proper of festival	313
S. Petrus	
bulla. Datum Romæ, apud	350. 357. 365. 366. 368. 375
oratio de	138
S. Petrus et Paulus	
oratio de	36. 109. 163. 216
S. Philip and Jacob	
collect on	181
festival	312
proper of festival	313
S. Philip and James	
festival	333
proper of festival	327. 329
S. Philippus, oratio de	138
S. Prophetae et Patriarchae, oratio ad	120
S. Prothe and Hyacinthe, in the kalender	237
S. Quirinus, oratio de	147
S. Raphael	
oratio ad	114. 146. 356
oratio ad b. Rochum	118
S. Rochus	
commemoratio de	151
oratio ad	117. 118
oratio de	147
S. Rock, prayer	
in honour of	372
in the worship of God, and	118
to S. Rock	5. 117
S. Sebastian, prayer to	113

	PAGE
S. Sebastianus	
commemoratio de	151
oratio de	9. 113. 139
S. Servatius, oratio de	146
S. Severinus, oratio de	147
S. Simon and Jude	
collect on day of	181
festival	333
proper of festival	313. 328. 329
S. Sitha, oratio de	125
S. Sophia, oratio de	142
S. Spiritus	
de septem donis	145. 351
fructus	145. 351
missio, carmen	269
officium. See General Index. Officium	
peccata in	145
psalmi, lectiones, et preces de missione	259
septem dona	351
S. Spiritus, oratio ad	5. 114. 120. 255. 264
S. Spiritus, oratio ad invocandam gratiam	120. 353
S. Spiritus, oratio de	36. 109. 143. 162. 215
S. Spiritus, oratio de missione	259. 269
S. Stephanus, oratio de	2. 36. 109. 140. 163. 216. 262
S. Stephen	
collect of	2. 163. 181. 216
festival	332
holiday	371
holiday of obligation	312. 314
proper of festival	313. 327. 329
S. Sylvester	
holiday	371
holiday of obligation	312. 314. 316
proper of festival	313
S. Symon chananæus, oratio de	138
S. Theobaldus, oratio de	146
S. Thomas a Becket	
day of	173. 195. 296
translation, day of	290. 299
S. Thomas apostle	
festival	332
proper of festival	313. 327. 328
S. Thomas apostolus	
oratio de	139
signum, London	6

NAMES AND PLACES.

	PAGE
S. Thomas archiepiscopus Cantuariensis, oratio de	1. 2. 36. 110. 149. 187
S. Thomas de Aquino, oratio	130. 355
S. Thomas de Aquino, oratio	
ante communionem	354
ante studium	355
in elevatione corporis Christi	145
post communionem	354
S. Thomas of Aquine, prayer	
after receiving the b. sacrament	360
before receiving the b. sacrament	360
before study	361
S. Thomas of Aquine, prayer of	361
S. Thomas of Canterbury	
collect of	1. 2. 174. 187
in the epistles and gospels	173. 176. 183. 184. 185. 190. 220. 226. 230. 234
in the kalender	152. 159. 168. 173. 174. 175. 176. 184. 185. 186. 195. 203. 205. 206. 209. 213. 226. 234
in the litany	152. 159. 168. 173. 174. 175. 176. 183. 184. 185. 186. 203. 206. 209. 226
octave of	203. 205. 206. 213
prayer to	36. 149
translation of	173. 190. 195. 203. 205. 206. 209. 213
S. Trinitas	
gratiarum actio	137
invocatio	128. 132. 162
officium. See General Index. Officium	
oratio ad	38. 41. 116. 120. 137. 151. 166. 191
oratio de	36. 109. 162. 191. 215
precatio ad	134
psalmi, lectiones, et preces	259
S. Trinitas et S. Anna in S. Pauli cimiterio, signum	12
S. Valentinus, oratio de	139
S. Vincentius	
oratio de	139
parochia, Rothomagi	32. 47
S. Virgines, oratio de	120
S. Wilgefortis, oratio de	36. 125
S. Wilhelmus, oratio de	33. 125. 147
S. Wolfgangus, oratio de	141
Sabbath, thanksgiving for the	340. 342. 343
Sabbatum, oratio ad honorem virginis Marie	9. 22. 119. 129
Sadler, J., printer	346
Saints, the	
books of the lives of	196. 202

Saints, the
    collect of, whose relikes are in church   36. 164. 216
    collects of   202
    commemorations to (of)   112. 281. 313
    communion with   272
    devotions for the feasts of   320
    glorious orison to   128
    intercession of   357. 367
    invocation of angels and   204. 217. 231. 233. 234. 240. 245. 277. 298
    litanies of the   161. 375. 380
    memories of the   159. 227. 230
    of England. See England
    of Ireland. See Ireland
    of Scotland. See Scotland
    of Wales. See Wales
    office of. See General Index. Office
    see All Saints
    triumphant and militant   272
    veneration (worshipping) of   160. 168. 170. 226. 358
Saints days in Dorrington's reformed devotions   318
Saints days in kalender
    printed in black 237. 244. 245. 248. 253. 257. 273. 290. 296. 299. 300. 301
    printed in red   237. 244. 245. 248. 249. 250. 253. 256. 257. 273. 290. 296.
                                                                     297. 299
Saints, the, prayers
    common to   365
    in memory of   159. 168
Saints, the, prayers to
    in rhyme, in kalender   128. 131
    proper to   365
    treated of   196. 204. 227
Saliceto, N. de, antidotarius animæ   130
Salisbury use, primer of. See General Index. Primer of Salisbury use
Sancta crux
    officium. See General Index. Officium
    oratio ad   115. 117
    oratio de   109. 143. 163. 215
Sancti omnes
    in festo   144
    officium de   134
    oratio ad   113. 191
Sancti, oratio ad
    ab infirmo   129
    plures   142

NAMES AND PLACES. 493

	PAGE
Sancti, oratio de	
omnibus	110. 120. 164
quorum reliquiæ in ecclesia continentur	147. 164. 216
Sara filia Raguelis, oratio	121
Sare, R.	331
Sarum breviary	
collects translated from	246
hymns from	239
Sarum manuale, benedictiones mensæ	154
Sarum missal	173
Sarum use	
commendations	199. 217. 241
dirige	205. 232. 241
enchiridion. See General Index. Enchiridion	
horae. See General Index. Horæ b. Mariæ Virginis secundum usum Sarum	
hortulus animae	33. 135
in hours	183. 198. 209. 210. 215. 219. 230. 239
kalender	203. 213. 215. 234
litany	204. 217. 231. 233. 234
manual	154
missal	173
prime, and hours of our Lady	171
primer. See General Index. Primer	
primer for children. See General Index. Primer	
Saturday, day of abstinence	313
Sauromanus, Johannes, de sacro baptismo	268
Savonarola G. expositiones in psalmos	167. 200. 207. 218
Scotland, Ireland, and Wales, saints of	365. 368. 369
Septuagesima Sunday, collect on	177. 183
Seres, William	289
Serjeant, John	314. 315. 325. 326
Sexagesima Sunday, collect on	177
Siberus Adamus, symbolum apostolorum	267
Simeonis carmen	262
Sixtus	
papa quartus, oratio	123. 131
papa quintus, officium b. Marie Virginis. See General Index. Officium	
pope, indulgence	126
Solomon	
seasons of	283
words of	283
Solomon, prayer for	
a competency of living	167. 189. 211. 218. 243. 295
wisdom to govern	167. 189. 211

494 INDEX OF

	PAGE
Solomon, prayer to obtain wisdom	167. 189. 211. 243
Solomon regis, oratio	
ad exemplar, pro regina	260
O quam bonus et suavis	122
Solomon regis, oratio pro	
obtinenda sapientia	156. 167. 211. 255
principe adolescente	264
sapientia ad gubernandum	167
vitæ competentia (moderato victu)	167. 211. 218. 255. 263
Spinckes, Nathaniel, collection of meditations	92. 335
Star, S. Paul's churchyard, sign of the	250
Stigellius, Johannes	
de vita beata	269
oratio pro pace	268
Strabo, Walafride	277
Sun, Fleet Street, sign of the	10. 11. 16. 17. 24. 25. 28. 44. 45. 48. 62. 64. 65. 66. 72. 73
Sunday	
concurrence of offices	312
holiday of obligation	312
morning prayer	83
moveable holiday	371
prayers on	365
Sunday and Holyday	
collect for every	292, 300.
prayer for every	58
Susan, prayer of	122
Susanna, oratio	122. 263
Swan, St. Paul's churchyard, sign of the	90
Syon, mons	136
Tanner, T. bibliotheca	237. 238
Taverner, R.	
epitome of the psalms	183. 186. 188. 189. 242. 243. 244
principal prayers of the Bible	295
Temple bar	
St. Clement's parish without	11
St. Dunstan's parish next to	52
Thames, Thamesis	269. 302
Thebaeorum legionem, oratio ad	142
Thobias et Judith, figuræ	21
Thobias junior, et Sara, oratio	121
Thobias senior	
a lesson. Cum putaret	258
et Sara, oratio	121. 172. 263

NAMES AND PLACES.

	PAGE
Thobias senior	
oratio, Deo regratiatoria	121
Thobye the elder, blessing and thanksgiving of	295
Thobye the elder and Sara, prayer of	121. 172. 211
Thobye the younger and Sara, prayer of	121
Three crowns, St. Paul's churchyard, sign of the	92
Three Kings	
collect of the	107. 111. 143
London, sign of the	11
Tiguri, Christopherus, Froschouerus	269
Tridentinum concilium	
decretum	349. 366
nuptiae juxta decretum	350. 365
Trinity. See Holy Trinity	
Trinity Sunday	
benedictions on	313
collect on	178
concurrence of offices	312
festival	333
proper of festival	313. 328
Turbeville, Father	331
Turner, Iron Cross St. Rouen, sign of the	99. 101. 102
Tyndale, W., answer to More	150
Twelfth-day	
concurrence of offices	312
festival	332
holiday	371
holiday of obligation	312
octave of	313. 315
proper of festival	313. 327. 329
Unicornes duæ, signum, Rothomagi	46
Unicornis, signum, Parisiis	32. 39. 40. 43
Urban the eighth, reformed primer. See General Index. Primer or Office	
Urbanus octavus	
bulla. Divinam psalmodiam	375
hymni. See General Index. Hymns	
officium b. Mariæ Virginis reformatum	97. 100. 368. 375
oratio, edita ab	368
prayer recommended by	372
Valentine, private devotions	286
Valentinus, Robertus, bibliopola	190
Vecta vel Vectis, juris Elizabethæ reginæ	269
Venetiis, officium b. Mariæ Virginis impressum	
apud Cieras	97
apud Junctas	349

	PAGE
Vermilius, Florentinus. See Petrus martyr	
Verrepaeus, S., enchiridion	265
Verstegen, Richard	358. 369
Via magna horologii, Rothomagi	53
Vienne, Mamercus bishop of	171. 219. 231. 277
Virgin Mary. See S. Mary the Virgin	
Virgines et Viduae, oratio de	141
Virgines, oratio	
ad undecim millia	142
de sanctis	120
de undecim millia	113
Virgins	
collect of	182
prayer to the xi. thousand	113
Visitatio b. Mariæ, in festo	143
Visitation of our Lady	185
Vives Ludovicus J. preces	242. 243. 244. 265. 267
Wales, Scotland, England, and Ireland, saints of	365. 368. 369
Wallia, juris Elizabethæ reginæ	269
Walter, Rev. Henry	93
Waterloo place, C. & J. Rivington	93
Wayland, John, citizen and scrivener	190
Wednesdays and Fridays, collects for	342
Week days moralysed	54
Westminster	
at Westminster	1. 3. 190. 229. 289. 296
hall	229. 302
palace of	239
Wheler, George, Protestant monastery	322. 323. 324
Whitchurch, Edward, and Richard Grafton	220. 244
White bear, Botolph lane, sign of the	52. 57. 184
White horse, St. Paul's churchyard, sign of the	52. 53. 58. 60
Whitsun-day	
collect	178
concurrence of offices	312
festival	312. 333
hymn, and proper preface	341. 342
moveable holy-day	312. 371
octave of	312. 313. 315
proper of festival	313. 328. 329
Whitsun ember season	314
Whitsun-eve	
a fast	312
grace on	379

NAMES AND PLACES.

	PAGE
Whitsun week, hymn, and proper preface	341. 342
Wight, island inhabited	269
Wilhelmus, Cantuariensis Archiepiscopus, oratio	132
Woodward, Josiah	
account of rise of religious societies	326
minister of Poplar	326. 327
Worcester, Dr. George Hickes, dean of	335
York	
archbishop of	126. 269
archbishoprick	269
duke of, prayer for	285. 304
primer. See General Index. Primer according to Sarum and York uses	
use of	171
York and Albany, James duke of	282
Zacharias, carmen	261
Zachary, song of	205. 248
Zodiac, signs of	131

GENERAL INDEX.

⁎ *This index includes those prayers and devotions which have not a proper name in the title: the index of names and places includes those which have.*

	PAGE
A.B.C. in	
a book of private prayer	300
an injunction given by Henry VIII.	237
Hilsey's primer for children	233
Sarum horæ	152. 153. 155. 156
Sarum horæ pro pueris	128
Sarum primer in english for children	54. 173. 176
Sarum and Marshall primer	213
the primer or catechism	303. 306
A.B.C. of godly love	241. 297
Abrogation of the holydays, act for	56. 173. 175. 211. 219. 229
Absolution, prayer to be said after	342. 370
Absolution, the absolution	251. 253
Accidentia mortis	15. 22
Act for abolishing divers books and images	248. 249
Act of	
abrogation of the holydays. See Abrogation	
address to God	370
adoration	370
adoration to the sacred heart of Jesus	380
charity	380
consecration to the sacred heart of Jesus	380
contrition	368. 380
faith	380
glorification of God	342
hope	370. 380
humility	370
Acts	
litany of the acts of Jesus Christ	217
of contrition, faith, hope, and charity	380
of humiliation, prayer for accepting	338

GENERAL INDEX.

	PAGE
Acts	
of piety	338
summary of	370
Admonitio ad lectorem	135. 269
Admonition	
before we go to sleep	276
to the dirige	204
to the reader	201. 264
Adolescentes, tabula œconomica	257
Advertisement to the reader	96
Agnus Dei	150. 153
Agonizantes, orationes circa	129
Alleluia, rule as to use of	208. 312
Almanack	119. 159
Almsdeeds	284. 323
Alphabet	
a descriptive rhyme	285
illustrated by texts	283
of lessons for the instruction of youth	285
Altar, the	
blessed sacrament of	72. 191. 205. 214. 231
hymn to	284
Alternate or choral devotions	326
Anatomical man	13. 119. 175
Ancient	
(and apostolick) church	86. 270. 319
faith	357
fathers	86. 270
forms of piety and devotion	272
hours of prayer	340. 341
liturgies	340
practice of devotion	326
times of prayer	274
use of prayers at third, sixth, ninth hours, etc.	276
Ancient way of offices, devotions in	
containing exercises for every day in the week	315
with psalms, hymns, and prayers	87. 90. 92. 311. 314. 315. 317. 325. 328. 329. 330. 333. 335
Ancillarum, officium	257
Angelical salutation	152. 153. 162. 359. 371
Anniversary day of	
death	345
marriage	332
our baptism	282

GENERAL INDEX.

	PAGE
Anniversary day of	
our birth	282
the king's reign	282. 284
Anthems	163. 202
Antidotarius animæ	130
Antiphons	
particular ones	311
verses, and prayers of the principal feasts	362
Apostolical constitutions	340. 341
Approbation of the bishop	276
Archbishopricks	285
Archbishops, in an injunction of Henry VIII.	237
Archbishops and bishops granting days of pardon	126
Archdeacon in an injunction of Henry the eighth	237
Archiepiscopatus in Anglia	269
Argument of	
commendations	172
dirige	171
psalms of the passion	172
S. Hierome's psalter	172
Articles of	
our faith, ten commandments, etc.	78. 133
self-examination	338
the church	317
Aspectus duodecim signorum	28. 124
Aspirations before receiving the b. sacrament	278
Aureus numerus	350
Auxiliatores, oratio ad quatuordecim	140
Ave bell, prayers at the tolling	126
Ave Maria	
declaration of	131
occurrence of	108. 118. 230. 232
Bead-roll	274
Beads, form of the new	48. 207
Beatitudes, the eight	133. 253. 274. 358
Beatitudines, octo	145. 351
Beginning of the holy gospel after St. John	54. 161. 209. 215. 358
Behoveful teaching of Master John Gerson	136. 149. 174
Belief, the	322
Benedictio	129. 353. 354
Benedictio	
et oratio	263
et recommendatio ad Deum	137
super quolibet bono opere finito	132

GENERAL INDEX.   501

	PAGE
Benediction	313. 316. 327
Benediction	
of the blessed sacrament	100. 373. 374
prayer for	341
Benedictiones mensæ	152. 154. 156. 253. 267. 354
Benedictus qui venit	153
Bible, the	
doctrine of	286
history of	286
prayers of	159
published at Doway	367
Bibliopola	
in cimiterio S. Pauli	12. 15. 18. 19. 21
Rothomagi	19. 26. 53. 69. 71. 74. 75. 77
Bibliotheca, T. Tanner	237. 238
Bidding the beads	
form of	56. 155. 156. 175. 183. 211. 219. 228. 234
form of the new	48. 208
forms of, by O. H. C.	155. 156
Bishop, the	
according to the direction of	346
approbation of	270
in an injunction of Henry the VIII.	237
Bishop of Rochester. See Index of names. Rochester	
Bishop of Rome. See Index of names. Rome, bishop of	
Bishops and archbishops granting days of pardon	126
Bishops, prelates, and universities	208
Black and red letter, printing in	1. 3. 5. 240
Blessed	
qualifications	283
sacrament, prayers before and after receiving the	190. 336. 337. 360
Blessing, the	251. 281. 282. 359. 366
Blessing	
a devout	114
a good	130
and thanksgiving of Thobye	295
before and after collation	379
before meat for secular persons	359
by the virtue of the holy cross	117
of the table, or grace	198
Blessings of obedience	283
Book of common order	304. 305
Book of prayers or Primer	55. 234. 238
Book of private prayer or Primer	69. 70. 82. 84. 93. 289. 295. 299. 301. 307

		PAGE
Book of Common prayer, the		
catechism agreeable to		88. 92. 290. 297. 305. 306
form of prayer taken from		323. 324
forms of family prayer taken out of		323
in the youth's library		286
primer agreeable to		289. 305
publick offices of the church taken from		340
Books for those who can read		240
Books of		
passions and (or) saints lives		196. 202
superstitious prayers		202
Bookseller, John Growte, London		40. 43. 150
Booksellers		91. 289. 295
Breviarium		
concilium Tridentinum emendari jussit		349
licentia imprimendi		356. 365. 366
Breviary		
Roman. See Index of names. Roman breviary		
Sarum. See Index of names. Sarum breviary		
Brief		
declaration when every term beginneth		289
recommendation of oneself to God		339
soliloquy by way of admonition		338
Bulla		
Pii V. Superni omnipotentis Dei		349. 356. 365. 368. 380
Urbani VIII. Divinam psalmodiam		375
Calcographus, Nicolaus Prevost		30
Calendar according to Roman institution		371
Calendarium Gregorianum		95. 365. 366. 367. 368
Canon		
for letting of blood		124
of ebbs and floods		16. 123
Canonical Scriptures		318
Canons of the church		271
Capita quædam Christianæ religionis		267
Cardinal virtues		358. 371
Cardinal and legate, Raymund		125
Carmen		
decem mandata		267
Dei beneficia prædicantis		268
meditatio cubitum euntis		268
oratio dominica		267
precatio cubitum euntis		268
studiorum omnium scopus		268

	PAGE
Carmen	
symbolum apostolorum	269
Carmen ad	
Deum patrem	268
Deum filium	268
Deum spiritum	268
pueros, pia admonitio	268
Carmen de	
cena Domini	268
sacro baptismo	268
Carmen pro	
felici in literis successu	268
pace	268
pia vita	268
Carmina	257. 267. 268
Carnali dilectione, oratio pro	108
Casus	
episcopales	145
papales	145
Catechism	
a catechism	81. 151. 213. 234. 252. 253. 256. 258. 290. 296. 299
exposition of, or practice of divine love	319. 326
primer and	68. 69. 83. 85
primer or	88. 92
the catechism	82. 84. 250. 297. 300. 302. 303. 306
the short	256
Catechismus	253. 258. 349
Catholick	
chapel	374
church	100. 331. 346. 373. 374. 375
faith called the Apostle's creed	284. 358
roman	322. 325. 328
Catholicks	314. 315. 316
Catholicks	
in England	103. 376
primitive	346
Cautela servanda circa morituros	146
Certain prayers, and godly meditations	197. 200
Certain questions, what sin is	133
Changes of the moon	150
Chapel	
of the holy cross in Rome	127
or house of God	341

	PAGE
Charity	
of charity	224. 284
rule of	175. 210. 224
two precepts of	274
Childbirth	
office for	324
thanksgiving after	324
Children	
catechism for	85. 250. 252. 256. 290. 296. 297. 299. 300. 302. 303. 306
christian instruction for	197. 234. 238. 283
daily prayers for	295
dialogue of christian living	151. 199. 213
epistles and gospels set forth for	208
grace to be said by	198
king's psalter for	85. 282
lesson for	151. 213. 199
prayer for	281
primer and catechism to be taught unto	85
primer for education of	52. 67. 88. 233. 238. 245. 283
primer in english for	49. 54. 173. 176
Children and youths, directions to, for reading english	88. 282
Choral, or alternate devotions	326
Christian, dedication of a	338
Christian	
faith and religion	273
man's learning	205
monitor	326
oeconomicks	322. 323
prayers, Henry Bull	253. 258
primitive	322. 326
souls, prayer for all	117
Church, the	
commemoration for	313. 315. 332
holiday	229
hymns. See hymns	
militant, prayer for the good state of	126
prayer, when thou enterest	149. 170. 210
prayer of Christ for his	172
prayer of, for sins	172
of St. Paul's at Rome	171
the ancient and apostolic	319
Church of Christ, prayer for concord of the	242
Church of England	328. 330

GENERAL INDEX. 505

	PAGE
Church of England, the	
by law established	270
censure of monasteries by	323
collection of letters by Dr. G. Hickes, relating to	331. 336
custom and use of the dioceses in	171
devout sons and daughters of	323. 326. 327
epistles and gospels after. See Epistles and Gospels	
in form of bidding the beads	155. 156. 208. 228
judgment of	271
matins used by	328
minister of	271
secession from and return to	330
supreme head of	207. 228. 250
Church of England and Ireland, supreme head of	250
Church of Rome, the	330. 367
Church of Rome, the	
clerks and priests, regular and secular of	229
collection of letters by Dr. G. Hickes, relating to	331. 336
writers of	328
Cimiterium sive ecclesiam, oratio cuilibet transeunti	128. 150
Civitates Angliæ et Walliæ	269
Collation, blessing before and after	379
Collection of	
devotions, complete	340
meditations and devotions	92. 335
private devotions	86. 270
Collects	
after other prayers	307
for fasts and vigils of the church	
for Sundays and holydays	298
for the Queen	251
for the sick	307
for Wednesdays and Fridays	342
in the passion week	177
of saints	202
or prayers at matins	198
throughout the year	56. 176. 277. 292. 296. 298. 300
Collects at Lauds	
in english	230. 239
in english and latin	162. 174. 187. 215
Collects in the Book of (the) Common prayer	
of 1549	298
of 1552	277. 292. 296. 300. 301
of 1559	300. 301

GENERAL INDEX.

	PAGE
Collects in the Book of (the) Common prayer	
of 1604	277
of 1662	305. 307. 327
Comfortable words and sayings of Christ	214
Commandments	
of God, given by Moses and expounded by Christ	168. 209. 232. 246
the ten. See Ten commandments	
Commemoration of the (faithful departed) dead	313. 315. 328. 329. 345
Commemorations	
at Lauds	312. 313. 315. 316. 327
daily	314. 315
of saints	112. 151. 281. 327. 329. 332
Commemorations for	
all conditions of men	332
enemies	332
friends and natural relations	332
Commemorations for the	
church	332
civil state	332
feasts and fasts of the church	331. 332. 334
Commendatio	
ad b. Virginem Mariam	137. 355
devotissima	137
piorum	260
Commendationes animarum	3. 115
Commendations, the	
argument of	172
in english	199. 205. 206. 241. 252. 253. 297
in english and latin	166. 209. 217
preface to	241
Communio, oratio	
ante communionem	130. 135. 145. 265
post communionem	124. 127. 135. 145. 265
Communion, the	
confession before receiving	298
prayer after receiving	344
prayer before receiving	298. 344
Comparison between	
faith and unfaithfulness	224
faith, hope, and charity	175. 210. 224
Compline	
or prayer before bed-time	103. 337
what is meant by the word	171. 230. 328
Concurrence of offices	312

GENERAL INDEX. 507

	PAGE
Conditor cæli et terræ. See Index of forms. O Maker of heaven and earth.	
Confessio	
peccatorum, generalis	134. 135. 144. 253. 256. 262. 264
pia	258
qualis debeat esse	144
Confessio, oratio	
ante communionem	144
post communionem	145
Confession	
a general	46. 108. 185. 186. 195. 214. 244. 246. 251. 276. 280. 291. 298. 303. 342
a shorter method	370
before communion	298
before receiving the blessed sacrament	278
form of	28. 133. 190. 278. 314. 337
prayer before	370
rule for	148
Confessional, the	40. 43. 150
Confirmation, catechism before	252. 253. 256. 258. 290. 296. 297. 299. 302
Confitendi, modus et forma	144
Confiteor	
Deo coeli	152
Deo (omnipotenti), beatæ Mariæ	128. 153. 353
tibi Domine Deus omnipotens creator	135
tibi Domine Jesu Christe	108. 155
Congregation, the, prayers in the beginning and at the end of	363
Conjugum, officium	257
Consideration of the horror of mortal sin	370
Consolation of comfort in faith	222
Contemplation	
a devout	221. 222. 223
a lively	221
Contrary virtues, seven	274. 284
Contrition, prayer for	370
Conversion of a soul to God	375
Convocation, bishops and clergy assembled in	207
Convocations of both provinces	208
Credo	
as it ought to be said	131
in Deum	128. 162. 213
Creed, the	
apostles	358
declaration upon	246
exposition of	284

GENERAL INDEX.

	PAGE
Creed, the	
or Belief	197. 205
or Belief. The effect of our faith . . .	197
or twelve articles of the christian faith	153. 173. 228. 233. 239. 252. 274
to be said after. In this faith . . .	281
Creed of Athanasius	217. 361
Creed (or symbol) of Athanasius	
a ghostly psalm of the catholick faith	210
daily read in the church	153. 168. 219. 228. 233
symbolum Athanasii	168. 217. 260. 355
Creeds, the four first	319
Cross of Christ, the	
blessing with the sign of	234
collect of	239
prayer to	107. 112. 115. 117. 128
prayers of S. Brigide, before the image of	171
Crown of our b. Lady	377
Crucem, oratio ad sanctam	115. 117. 143
Crucifix, the, prayer to Jesus before	150
Crucifixus	234
oratio prætereundo imaginem	130
orationes ante	129. 134
Crums of comfort	286
Curates	
of mens souls	161
or ministers of churches	296
persons, vicars, and	153. 184. 237
shrift to	148
young curates	48. 207
Cursus	
S. Bonaventuræ de passione Christi	136
vitæ Dni. nri. Jesu Christi a Joh. Parkhursto	268
Cut of	
a master and scholars	303. 306
the royal arms	195. 200. 218. 286
Daily	
commemorations	314. 315
devotions and thanksgivings	92. 335. 337
devotions by an humble penitent	327. 336. 337. 338
exercise	359
private prayer	192. 340
Dance of death	23
Dates of moveable feasts	150

GENERAL INDEX.

Days	
of abstinence	313
of fasting, and abstinence	376
of the week moralysed	147. 168. 209
wherein the Queen majesty's Judges do not sit	302
De	
anni correctione	368
anno et ejus partibus	257. 350. 365
comestione notabili	136
decem præceptis, confessio	144
duodecim articulis fidei	145
indictione	350. 365
luna quæ est temporum mutationis significativa	136
minutione notabili	135
missa	145
novem peccatis alienis	145
numero Nonarum ac Iduum	350
octo beatitudinibus	145
omnibus membris et sensibus, confessio	144
origine celebrandi horas	164
profundis for all christian souls	110. 155. 173. 217
qualitate signorum	136
tribus regibus, oratio	I. III. 143
De festis	
immobilibus	257
mobilibus	257
De peccatis	
clamantibus in cælum	145
mutis	145
omissionis	144
De quatuor	
partibus anni	135
ventis	136
De septem	
donis Spiritus Sancti	145. 351
gaudiis spiritualibus deiparæ virginis	165
peccatis mortalibus	
sacramentis ecclesiæ	145
De septem operibus misericordiae	
corporalibus	144
spiritualibus	144
De septem virtutibus	
cardinalibus	145
theologicalibus	145

	PAGE
Dead, prayers for the	165. 227. 329
Dean, in an injunction of Henry VIII.	237
Decem	
mandata. Joh. Parkhursti	267
praecepta Dei	162. 351. 358
prosagiæ (plagæ) Egyptiacæ	144. 269
Declaration of	
ave maria	131
complyn	171
dirige	171
evensong of our Lady	171
lauds	170
matyns	170
seven penitential psalms	171
Declaration upon the	
creed	246
pater noster	246
Dedicatio	
altaris, oratio	144
ecclesiæ, oratio	144
Dedication day	173
Defender of the faith	237. 244. 250
Defunctis, oratio pro (fidelibus)	130. 133. 134. 150. 165. 166
Deliberatio pia Eleazari	263
Delitiae poetarum Germanorum	267
Departed, the	
commemoration of	328. 329. 345
prayers for	53. 150. 155. 156. 165. 166. 175. 204. 228. 232
Deprecations	337
Devotions	
and instructions out of holy scripture	98. 99. 102
as we go to church	337
comprising all our duties	337
daily	92
english books of	328
in the church	337. 343. 345
reformed, in meditations, hymns, and petitions	317. 320
morning and evening	345
to be used by primitive catholicks	346
Devotions after	
church	337
placing the elements on the altar	343
the Eucharistick service	343
the Nicene creed	343

GENERAL INDEX.   511

	PAGE
Devotions at placing	
the elements upon the altar	343
the offerings in the basin	343
Devotions before	
and after morning and evening service	343
at, and after communicating	343. 344
the eucharistick service	343
Devotions for	
ancient hours of prayer	341
every day in the week	319. 320
feasts of our Saviour	319. 320
holidays	319. 320
the altar	340. 343
Devotions in the ancient way of offices. See Ancient way	
Devotions, private, for	
evening	337. 341. 345
morning	341. 345
Devotions when	
the deacon mixes the wine and water	343
the priest signs himself with the sign of the cross	343
the priest washes his hands	343
you put your offering into the basin	343
Devout	
contemplation	221. 222. 223
daily prayer	114. 190. 192
fruitful and godly remembrance of the passion	197
Devout prayers	
to our Lady	116. 212
to our Saviour	28. 116. 117. 187. 188. 222. 230.
Dialogue of christian living	199. 213
Directions how to demean yourselves at the holy communion	339
Dirige, the	
and Commendations	148. 205. 206. 209. 249. 252. 253
and praying for the dead. The making of this service . . .	171
goodly pictures in. See Goodly pictures	
in english	205. 209. 227. 234. 241. 249. 250. 252. 256. 296
in english and latin	166. 219. 232
preface	204. 241
prologue	219. 227. 231
psalms of	2
Distinctiones, quatuor, complexionum hominum	124. 135
Diurna, licentia imprimendi	366. 375
Divers godly prayers at the hour of death	182

GENERAL INDEX.

	PAGE
Divine	
office	380
service	270
Divinum officium, oratio ante	131
Divisio symboli per duodecim articulos	145
Divisione apostolorum, orationes in	143
Doctrine of the Bible	286
Dominical letter	150
Dulia, hyperdulia, latria, distinction of	202
Duodecim	
articuli fidei	145. 155. 162. 213
fructus Spiritus Sancti	145. 351
signorum aspectus	28
Duty of	
a christian man, in metre	162. 209
children	323
servants	323
the husbandman	323
the wife	323
Eclipses	150
Eight beatitudes	133. 253. 274. 354. 371
Ejaculation for	
a youth	284
the morning	341
Ejaculationes piæ e sacris scripturis excerptæ	263
Ejaculations at	
apparelling	275
entrance into the church	275
going abroad	275
going to the holy table	338. 339
uprising	275. 341
washing of our hands	275
Ejaculations when we	
are come into the quire	275
fall down to worship	275
first awake	275
give alms	338
hear the clock strike	275
Elders or parsons, office of all estates	232
Elucidatio Calendarii	350
Enchiridion	
Eckius J.	202
piarum precationum. D. Martinus Lutherus	240
praeclaræ ecclesiæ Sarum	32. 34. 42. 134. 259. 266. 267

GENERAL INDEX. 513

	PAGE
English tongue	153. 160. 184
Episcopatus in provincia	
Cantuariensi	269
Eboracensi	269
Episcoporum et Pastorum, officium	257
Epistle of our Saviour	16. 124
Epistle, the, prayer before	131
Epistles and Gospels	
daily read in the church	55. 234
in the Book of the Common prayer, 1549	248. 250. 297
in the Book of the Common prayer, 1552	249. 256. 290. 296. 299. 302
in the Book of Common prayer, 1559	253. 273
in the Book of Common prayer, 1604	273
read in the church through the whole year	244
throughout the whole year	57. 59. 184. 185
Epistles and Gospels of every Sunday and holiday	
in the year	48. 58. 59. 60. 173. 175. 176. 184. 185. 190. 208. 209
throughout the whole year after the church of England	250
Epistles and Gospels of Sundays and festival holy-days	
newly corrected and amended	183. 184. 220. 226. 233. 244
revised and diligently corrected	48. 207
Eucharist, the	
celebration of	331. 345
prayer to the holy sacrament of	359
reservation of	344. 345
Eucharistiae sacramentum	
in elevatione, oratio	78
in ostensione, oratio	78
litaniæ	367
oratio ad	354
oratio ad levationem	134
Evening	
prayer	283. 301. 303. 304. 306
thoughts and exercises	338
Evensong	
explanation of	230
of our Lady. What is meant by it	171
Evil thoughts, prayer against	108. 133. 187
Ex quot diebus constet unus quisque mensis	350
Exaltation of the holy cross	314
Examen of conscience	
large and short	98. 99. 101. 102. 369
method of	376
upon the ten commandments	370

514　GENERAL INDEX.

	PAGE
Exercise preparative to a good death	338
Exercitium quotidianum	
cum mane surgis	353. 359
cum vadis dormitum	354. 360
salutatio angelica	353
Exeundo domum, dic	137
Exhortation	
a general	295
a good	221
before the communion	278
dearly beloved brethren	292. 299. 303. 304
for them that receive the blessed sacrament	205. 214
if thou have grace of the holy Ghost . . .	215
of christian living	46
unto prayer	240
Exhortations, brief, to the often frequenting the sacrament of penance	370
Expositio ac meditatio in psalmum	
In te Domine speravi	56. 167
Miserere mei	56. 167
Exposition of the	
church catechism	319
creed	284
prayer of the Lord	203. 284
primer, a short	371. 374
ten commandments	284
Exposition upon Salve regina	160. 176. 184. 199. 230
Exposition upon the	
fifty-first psalm	57. 58. 59. 60. 167. 183. 184. 185. 200. 218
thirtieth psalm	57. 60. 93. 167. 183. 184. 185. 207
Extract of the King's Majesty's privilege	289. 295. 307
Fairs, days and places of	85. 300. 302
Faith	
consolation of	222
hope, and charity, comparison between	160. 175. 210. 284
of faith	160. 200. 224. 284
power of	200
prayer for true	220
work of	200
works, and prayer	234
Faithful departed, the, prayers for. See Prayers for the dead	
Family prayers	323. 330
Fasting	
days of the church	273. 277. 312. 314. 316. 340. 342. 369. 376
eves	314. 316. 329. 333

GENERAL INDEX.

	PAGE
Fasting	
prayer, and alms-deeds	284. 323
rules for	148
Father and mother dead, prayer for thy	109
Father's advice to his child	283
Fathers of the church	271. 276. 277. 319
Feast of	
dedication	175. 229
obligation	103. 312. 315. 376
patron saint	229
Feasts of the church's year	319
Festivals	
book of	202
of saints	147
proper of	312. 313. 314. 316. 327. 328. 332
Festis, orationes de principalioribus	143
Fifteen	
hours of the passion of our Lord	111
prayers of St. Bridget	111. 165. 171. 196. 223
precationes D. Joan. Fisheri episcopi Roffensis	261
psalms	2. 165. 219. 231
selected psalms	283
stages in our Saviour's pilgrimage	284
Fifteen Oos	
in english	4. 40. 107. 116. 150. 165. 171. 211. 223. 231
in latin	43. 111. 201
Figurae	
apocalipsae	21, 22
e bibliae historiis	30
et caracteres	15
passionis	23
Five	
bodily senses	358. 371
bodily wyttes	133. 214
corporal joys of our Lady	110. 164. 174. 217
ghostly wyttes	133. 214
glorious mysteries	373
godly necessary prayers	189
joyful mysteries	373
petitions and prayers made by St. Gregory	124
sorrowful mysteries	373
wounds of our Lord, prayer of (to) the	11. 112. 123. 360
Flores psalmorum	261
Flower of godly prayers, T. Becon	292. 293

GENERAL INDEX.

	PAGE
Flumina præcipua Angliæ	269
Form of	
admitting a convert	346
confession	133. 190
the new beads	48. 208
Forma absolutionis Gersonis	145
Forms of prayer for the use of private families	323
Four	
gospels in english	215
last things	274. 284. 358. 371
sins that cry to heaven	284
terms of the year	302
Fratres minores, ædes et conventus	26. 32
Frequency of prayer	275
Friend, prayer for thy	
in sickness or necessity	108
living	108
that is dead	109
Fructus Spiritus Sancti	145. 351
Fruitful	
and christian instruction for children	197
meditation	188
prayer, Deus propitius	59
Fruits of the Holy Ghost	274. 284. 358. 371
Garden of the soul	196. 202
General prayers	293. 297. 300
General rule to know	
Advent, Easter, Ember days	208. 209
when Alleluia goeth out	208
when it is lawful to marry	209
when leap year shall be	250. 256
Gifts of the Holy Ghost	133. 274. 284. 358. 371
Ghostly psalm of the catholick faith	210
Gloria in excelsis	330. 341
Godly prayer	
to be said at all times	305
to be used of all christians	305
to desire the life to come	188
Godly prayers	73. 76. 80. 81. 84. 187. 192. 220. 246. 291. 301. 304. 305
Godly prayers	
and graces	88. 92. 303. 305. 306
and necessary, at the hour of death	182. 185. 247
for diverse (sundry) purposes	92. 292. 297. 298. 300
necessary for all faithful christians	83. 85. 256

GENERAL INDEX.   517

	PAGE
Godly prayers	
throughout the year, called collects	176
Godly and devout prayers	72. 79. 191. 192
Godly and devout prayers newly set forth	71. 186
Goest first out of thy house, prayer	13. 107. 137
Golden number	
and dominical letter	150
or prime	289
Golden prayer	124. 201
Good	
exhortation. Above all things love God, etc.	221
works. Among good works, etc.	200. 203. 214
Goodly	
and godly prayers	43. 195
and necessary prayers at the hour of death	185
devout prayer	188
interpretation, or declaration of Pater noster	197. 203
Goodly prayers	57. 59. 60. 184. 185
Goodly pictures in the	
dirige	31. 37-50. 68. 70-76. 134. 150
hours of the cross	31. 37-50. 68. 70-76. 134. 150
kalender	31. 37-50. 68. 70-76. 134. 150
matyns of our Lady	31. 37-50. 68. 70-76. 134. 150
seven psalms	31. 37-50. 68. 70-76. 134. 150
Goodly primer in english	
newly corrected	44. 45. 48. 200. 206
with the King's most gracious privilege	44. 45
Gospel of S. John	
a lesson declaring the passion	183. 219. 228
the beginning of the. In the beginning	161. 209. 215. 358
the passion. Jesus went forth	241. 252, 362
the passion. When Jesus had spoken	162. 210. 215
Gospel of S. Luke	
holy gospel. Luke i. The angel Gabriel	161. 209. 215. 365
lesson mentioning the resurrection	183. 219. 228
Gospel of S. Mark	
lesson mentioning the ascension	183. 219. 228
Mark xvi. After that he appeared	162. 215. 365
Gospel of S. Matthew	
lesson mentioning the incarnation	183. 228
S. Matthew ii. When Jesus was born	162. 209. 215. 365
Governance of virtue, T. Becon	301. 304
Grace, prayer to get	221

	PAGE
Graces	
after dinner	205
and godly prayers	88. 92. 303. 305. 306
at meals	378
for fish days	205
to be said of children	198
Graces before and after	
dinner	173. 192. 198. 214. 220. 228. 233. 234. 239. 252. 290. 296. 297. 299. 300. 302. 303
meat	84. 248. 250. 252. 256. 285. 290. 300. 302. 303. 304. 305. 306. 340. 345. 359
supper	173. 192. 198. 220. 228. 233. 234. 239. 252. 290. 296. 297. 300. 302. 303
Gratiarum actio	
communis pro cognitione donorum Dei	256
Gratiarum actio	
et laus Dei	260
post communionem	265
post mensam	354
post pastum	253
pro divinis donis et beneficiis	267
S. Pauli pro conversione sua	263
sanctae et individuae Trinitatis	137
Gratiarum actiones a cibo	267
Gratiarum actiones pro	
acceptis beneficiis	137. 353
variis donis	135
Great assize, the	286
Gregorianae precatiunculae	36. 149
Hail Mary, explanation of	197. 214
Help to discourse, the	286
History of the bible	286
Holy Communion, the	
devotions for	319. 320
directions how to demean yourselves at	339
general confession before	251
prayer before, at, and after	251. 320
thanksgiving after	251
Holy-days	
moveable	312. 369. 371
of obligation	312. 314
throughout the year	369. 371
Holy gospel according to Mark, Matthew, Luke	365
Holy Eucharist. See Eucharist	
Holy Office, before, at, and after receiving the holy sacrament	90. 320

GENERAL INDEX.

	PAGE
Holy sacrament. See Sacrament	
Holy Scripture	
and tradition	161. 168
antiquity of matins deduced from	276
(choice) sentences of	275. 291. 292. 301. 303, 304. 342
devotions, and instructions out of	98. 99. 101. 102
devotions reformed according to	317. 319
hours of prayer taken out of	86. 270
in the mother tongue	208. 318
lessons out of	313
portions of hours taken from	209
prayer before reading	185
rule of	161
texts of	195. 327. 342
to be read at matins	226
translation in english, published at Doway	367
translation of	358. 366
works agreeable to	232
Holy water, prayer when thou takest	14. 108
Homilies, Edward the VI.	223. 231
Hope, of hope	224. 284
Horae	
conceptionis b. Mariæ	133
deiparae virginis	164
die sabbati de virgine Maria	134
dulcissimi nominis Jesu	10. 11. 24. 46. 123. 218
pro defunctis	134
Horae de	
compassione	109. 150. 162
cruce	109. 150. 162
passione Christi	134. 136
sacramento	134
Horae beatæ Mariæ virginis	
a nativitate usque ad purificationem	18. 128
a purificatione usque ad adventum	109
conceptionis	133
diligenter emendatæ	6. 119
per adventum usque ad vigiliam natalis Domini	128
pro pueris	16. 128
Horae beatæ Mariæ virginis cum	
bibliæ historiis decoratæ	30. 134
devotis suffragiis	7
figuris passionis mysterium representantibus	23
illius miraculis, figuris apocalipsis, ac mortis accidentia	21. 22. 131

GENERAL INDEX.

	PAGE
Horae beatæ Mariæ virginis cum	
quatuor evangeliis, passione Domini, et horis nominis Jesu	10. 11. 122. 123
septem psalmis, letaniis, mortuorum vigiliis, recommendationibus,	
ac oratiunculis et utilitatibus	25
Horae b. Mariæ virginis cum indulgentiis	97. 100. 367. 368. 375
Horae b. Mariæ virginis cum indulgentiis et privilegio	94. 349. 356
Horae beatæ Mariæ virginis cum orationibus	
cuilibet devoto, et modis	24. 133
jam ultimo in fine adjectis	24. 25. 26. 28. 31. 32. 46
multum devotis (devotissimis)	23-58. 75
pulcherrimis	12-44
quæ indulgentiarum gaudent privilegio	149
Horae beatæ Mariæ virginis cum orationibus ante et post	
eucharistiæ receptionem	23
sanctam communionem	17. 130
Horae b. Mariæ virginis cum orationibus et indulgentiis	23
Horae b. Mariæ virginis cum orationibus et indulgentiis	
de novo adjectis (recenter insertis)	14. 15. 18. 19. 21
jam ultimo ac de novo adjectis	15. 18. 19. 21
jam ultimo adjectis cum tabula aptissima	19-44
jam ultimo (in fine) adjectis	17-46
jam ultimo recenter insertis	14
Horae beatæ Mariæ virginis cum orationibus et suffragiis	
noviter additis	5. 7. 118
noviter impressis	32
noviter superadditis	10. 11. 119. 123
Horae b. Mariæ virginis cum suffragiis	
ad diversos sanctos et sanctas	36. 149
et orationibus	32. 48
multis devotis	7. 8
sanctorum et sanctarum	10. 11. 12. 119. 122. 123
Horae beatæ Mariæ virginis secundum	
morem Anglicanum	3. 20. 131
usum Eboracensem	15. 19. 41. 46. 72. 76. 77. 78. 130. 131
usum Sarum	107. 159. 213
Hortulus animae	
in duytsche, Antwerp	196. 202
Nuremberg	138. 144. 145. 146. 258. 259
secundum usum Sarum	33. 135
seu Thesaurus spiritualis	349
Hospitality, of	323
Hours	
antiquity of the	276
division of the	275

… GENERAL INDEX. 521

Hours   PAGE
- how the saying of, first began   164
- in remembrance of Christ's passion   171
- in remembrance of the compassion of the Virgin   171
- prayers preparatory to the   276

Hours according to Sarum and York uses
- in english and latin   159. 213
- in latin   107

Hours of
- devotion   326
- our Lady   55
- prayer   86. 270. 271. 274. 323. 326. 341

Hours of the
- name of Jesus   218
- day, prayer for diverse   108
- Holy Ghost   55
- passion of our Lord   55. 109. 110
- passion of our Lord, fifteen   111

Hours of the compassion of our Lady
- in english   230
- in english and latin   162. 164. 174
- in latin   109. 110

Hours of the cross
- goodly pictures. See Goodly pictures
- in english   230
- in english and latin   164. 174. 215. 219
- in latin   2. 110

How the saying of hours first began   164. 170
Humble penitent, or daily devotions   336
Husbandman or labourer, of the   323

Hymn
- called a lesson   324
- of praise   337
- on the ascension   376
- penitential   324
- preparative to prayer   275
- to Jesus   337
- with proper preface   342

Hymni per totum annum   353

Hymns
- and prayers at benediction of the b. sacrament   100. 373
- and thanksgivings for the Lord's day and Sabbath   324. 340
- church hymns, new and approved version   101. 102. 103. 376
- church hymns, new and improved version   104. 377

SSS

GENERAL INDEX.

		PAGE
Hymns		
for every day in the week		90. 329. 330. 331
in a better verse		98. 99. 101. 102. 369
in ancient way of offices		87. 89. 90. 311. 325. 328. 329. 330
in king's psalter		88. 282
in reformed devotions		317. 318. 320
in the office of our Lady, adapted to tunes		358
new hymns reformed by Urban VIII.		99. 100. 371. 372
of the Roman breviary. See Index of names. Roman breviary		
suited to hours of prayer		324
translated by one skilful in english poetry		367
put into a true poetic strain		371
through the whole year		364
to the Virgin Mary		313. 316
tunes adapted to		323
Hymnus		
matutinus		268
meridianus		268
poenitentialis		268
Hyperdulia, dulia, and latria, distinction of		202
Iambicum carmen quid deceat Christianum		162
Idolatry, abominable		203
Image of		
pity, prayer before the		112. 136. 201
the cross, prayers before the		171
Imagine, oratio coram		
b. Mariæ virginis		123
crucifixi		123. 130. 167
Immaculate mother of God		226
Imprimatur, J. Battely		89
Indulgence		
granted by Pope Pius V.		380
plenary		377
prayers to the pity of our Lord, with		112
Indulgence and pardon		126
Indulgentiae		
anni		123. 130
dies		122. 123. 128. 130. 136. 146
duplicatio		136
in dedicatione ecclesiæ		144
orationes b. Brigittæ, cum multis		36
summarium, Pii papæ V.		350. 356. 365. 368
Indulgentiis, horæ b. Mariæ virginis cum. See Horæ b. Mariæ virginis		
Infirmitate, orationes in		128

GENERAL INDEX.

	PAGE
Infirmus	
oratio postquam conclusit	146
oratio si anxiatur	146
orationes circa	114. 129
Initium s. evangelii secundum Johannem	14. 29. 33. 54. 77. 118. 161. 357
Injunction	
given by the king (Henry VIII.)	237. 251
of Edward VI.	67. 244
Inquisitores hæreticæ pravitatis	375
Institutio christiana	350
Institution of a christian man	153. 197
Instruction	
christian for children	197
how and in what manner we ought to pray	203
of the manner in hearing mass	231
Instructions for	
examining our conscience	370
to live a christian life	369
Intercession	
and prayer unto our Saviour	188
of saints	357. 367
prayer of	341. 344
Intercessions for all men	337
Interrogationes apud morientes faciendæ	146
Introduction	
to all persons to fulfil the commandments	214
to the christian faith	358. 371
Introit	341
Invocatio S. Trinitatis	128. 132. 162
Invocation unto the Holy Trinity. See Index of names. Holy Trinity.	
Invocations of	
saints	217, 277
saints and angels	204. 217. 231. 233. 234
the Virgin Mary	215. 219. 357
Ira Dei adversus pios brevis	257
Isaiah 59th chapter. Lo the Lord is yet alive	210
Itinerarium	355
Jubilus S. Bernardi abbatis	145
Judicium extremum	269
Kalendarii, orationes de festis, secundum ordinem	138. 143
Kalender, the	
goodly pictures in. See Goodly pictures	
Gregorian	95. 365. 366. 367. 368
in rhyme	128. 131

GENERAL INDEX.

	PAGE
Kalender, the	
order of	289. 299
special use	272
King, the, prayer for	100. 108. 292
King and Queen, prayer for	100. 218. 221
King's	
grace's injunction	227
highness bill assigned (Henry VIII.)	65. 91. 244
majesty's privilege (Edward VI.)	289. 295
most gracious privilege	44. 45. 200. 206
primer	283
psalter	88. 282
King's commandment, the	
bidding of the beads, by	155. 156. 175. 183. 211. 219. 228. 234
the king's highness	153. 184
Lamentation for the dead, manner of	219. 232
Latria, dulia, and hyperdulia, distinction of	202
Latronis crucifixi, oratio	262
Lauds, explanation of	170. 230
Laus Dei, et gratiarum actio	260
Lavatory, the, to answer the priest after	107
Lay fee	238
Legenda aurea	196. 202
Legends or Legendaries	196. 202
Lents, and days of pardon	117. 124
Lessons	
in private devotions	318
of the gospels	183. 219. 228
Letters patent (Henry VIII.) (Edward VI.) (Mary.)	71. 190. 205. 289. 295
Levation	
of our Lord	107. 111. 126. 127. 149. 150. 151. 165. 174
of the chalice	149. 174
of the sacrament	13. 111. 165. 174. 217. 231
Liber festivalis	202
Liber precum publicarum	253. 254. 257. 258. 259. 262
Libera, the, after mass for the dead	100. 103. 374
Liberorum, officium	257
Libraria officina	31. 32. 36. 74. 76. 82
Librarius	9. 10. 13. 39. 40. 43
Librarius	
in atrio librariorum	20
juratus	14. 27. 28. 29. 30. 31. 34. 35. 37. 40. 42. 43. 44
Londonensis in domo predicatorum	43

GENERAL INDEX. 525

Librarius
    mercator   7. 8. 14
Licentia et facultas imprimendi missalia etc.   357. 365. 366. 367. 375
Litaniae
    antiquissimi eucharistiæ sacramenti   367
    augustissimi nominis Jesu   367
    b. Mariæ virginis in æde Loretana   367. 368
    della b. Virgine Maria   368
    in nomine Jesu   367
    preces, et orationes   351
Litanies of
    our b. Lady of Loretto   372. 380
    our Lord and Saviour Jesus Christ   370. 372
    the saints in latin and english   362. 375
Litanies and prayers   359
Litany   1. 114. 166. 174. 204. 209. 233. 240. 245. 249. 250. 252. 253. 254. 256. 277. 286. 292. 296. 298. 300. 301. 303. 304. 307. 324. 330
Litany
    and honouring of God and his saints   161
    or general supplication   332
    preface to   203
    signification of the word   171. 219. 231
    when used   277
Litany for
    a happy death   380
    the dead   380
    those who mourn for the iniquities of the present time   346
Litany in the Book of Common prayer
    of 1552   292. 298
    of 1559   300. 301. 303. 304
    of 1662   304. 305. 307
Litany of
    Jesus Christ's acts   217
    our Lord and Saviour Jesus Christ   370. 372
Litany of the
    blessed sacrament   377
    holy name   98. 99. 101. 102. 369. 370. 380
    immaculate conception   98. 99. 101. 102. 369. 370
    saints   161. 375. 380
Little metre containing the duty of a christian man   162. 209
Liturgy, the publick   217. 319. 322. 338
Living and dead, prayer for the   109
Lombardic capital letters   3
Lord Protector in the litany   245

GENERAL INDEX.

	PAGE
Lord's prayer, the	271. 322
Lord's prayer, the	
divided into seven petitions	153. 274
exposition of	284
prayer of all prayers	271
Loyal prayers for every day of the week	285
Ludicra, Parkhurstus J.	257. 267. 268. 269
Magistratus, officium	257
Manipulus curatorum	202
Manner	
how to serve the priest at mass	103. 364. 372
to live well devoutly	147. 174. 212
Manual, Sarum. See Index of names. Sarum use	
Manual of prayers or primer (Hilsey's)	
in english	52. 55. 225. 226. 233
in english and latin	51. 52. 233
Manual of prayers printed at Lyons	331. 333
Marriage, anniversary day of	332
Mass, the	
answer to the priest at	107
for the dead	100. 374
instruction of the manner in hearing	231
low mass	148
manner how to serve a priest at	103. 372
of the five wounds	201
ordinary of	100. 103. 374
plain and godly treatise concerning	72. 73. 191
presence at a low mass	148
sacring of	231
Mass, the, prayers	
after	231
before	231. 359
during	374
Mass, the, prayers at	
after the gospel	123
in english	127
in latin	174
the sacring of	127
to the sacrament at levation	111. 126. 127. 165. 217. 231
Masters of families, duties of	323. 326
Matins	
and evensong, order to say	297. 298
antiquity of	276
in honour of the name of Jesus	46. 213. 218

GENERAL INDEX.

	PAGE
Matins	
introduction to	316
Jesus matins	46. 213. 218
prime, and hours, saying of	148
vespers, lauds, and compline, objections against	328
what is meant by the word	171
Matins of our Lady	
goodly pictures. See Goodly pictures	
meaning of, declaring the birth of Christ	170
Matins of our Lady with prime and hours in	
english	219. 226
english and latin	160. 173. 215
latin	16. 109. 128. 134
Matins of the compassion of our Lady in	
english	174
english and latin	162
latin	110
Matins of the cross in	
english	174
english and latin	162
latin	2. 110
Matutinae de	
compassione	162
cruce	162
S. Maria a nativitate Dni. usque ad purificationem	18. 128
Medicines, of	323
Meditatio	
Ieronymi (Hieronymi) in psalmum In te Dne. speravi	93. 167. 207. 218
pia ante preces	258
pia Susannæ	122. 263
Meditation of	
Christ's passion	222
judgment	370
the blessed sacrament	370
Meditation on the thirtieth psalm	56
Meditationes piae de	
passione Domini	
spe resurrectionis	262
vitae hujus fragilitate	262. 354. 355
Meditations	
holy and humane	285
in reformed devotions	89
in the paradise of the soul	46
in the six days of creation	336

Meditations	
of the passion of our Lord	360
while others are communicated	278
Meditations and devotions	
collection of	92. 335
upon the life of Christ	92. 336
Memories of the saints	159. 227. 230
Memory of	
our Lady	182. 230
the compassion of our Lady	183. 230. 234
the passion of Christ	230. 234
Mercator	12. 14. 15. 17. 18. 19. 21. 23. 25. 26. 30. 32
Mercator librorum in Anglia	8
Mercenariorum, officium	257
Merchants, letters patents to	205
Minister	
and governor	217
of the Church of England	271
of the parish	323
or curate	296
Miserere mei Deus	
after a general confession	195
exposition upon	167. 200. 218
prayer upon	246
see also. Exposition upon the fifty-first psalm	
Missa	
de nomine Jesu	136
et primo, unde exordium sumpserit	145
in fine dicitur, Ite missa est	153
oratio in, post communionem	152
secretum	127
Missal (Missale)	
Roman	349. 366. 375
Sarum	173
Missale, licentia imprimendi	357. 365. 366. 375
Missam, praefationes ad	152
Modi quibus Christus se nobis exhibet	269
Modus	
et forma confitendi	144
inveniendi quota sit luna	350
ministrandi et respondendi sacerdoti celebrandi missam	375
Monasteries	
beginning and progress of	323
little office of B.V.M. used in	379

GENERAL INDEX.   529

	PAGE
Morientes	
exhortationes Gersonis faciendæ apud	146
interrogationes faciendæ apud	146
Morituros, cautela servanda circa	146
Morning prayer	
a general	186
and evening prayer	186. 292. 301. 303. 304. 306
for Sunday	83
or mattins, antiquity of	276
prayer for the morning	151. 186. 197. 220. 246. 252. 291. 296
Morning and evening, devotions for	341. 345
Morning and Evening prayer in the Book of Common Prayer	
of 1552	292. 299. 303
of 1559	299. 303
Morning and Evening Service, devotions before and after	343
Mortalitatem hominum, oratio contra	117
Mother tongue	168. 208. 250
Mother's blessing, the	286
Motto proper for	
Ash Wednesday	327
Ember days	327
time of persecution	327
Mysteries, the joyful, sorrowful, glorious	373
Names in use for men and women	285
Names of	
archbishopricks	285
Jesus, devout prayer of the	150
several cities in England and Wales	285
several counties	285
Necessary doctrine and erudition of a christian man	153
New Testament	208
Nominibus Dei, oratio de	69. 120
Nosegay, or posey of light	223
Novena of St. Joseph, prayers at	377
Nuptiae juxta decretum Concilii Tridentini	350. 365
Occasional offices in Devotions in the ancient way of offices	333. 334
Occasionals	
for a member of the family sick	314. 316. 332. 334
for peace	316
in dearth	332
Occasionals in time of	
mortality	314. 316. 332
persecution	314. 316. 332
war	314. 332

GENERAL INDEX.

	PAGE
Octave, what it is	315
Octo beatitudines	145
Octonaries, what they are	172
Office	
an offering of the	377
at the reservation of the eucharist	344. 345
before, at, and after receiving the holy sacrament	90. 320
penitential	342
prayer before, and after the	359. 377
preparatory for death	326. 327. 328. 329. 331. 332
Office for	
a family	330. 331. 332
a woman in labour of child birth	324
each day in the week	311. 313. 314. 315. 316. 326. 327. 328. 329. 330. 332
private daily communicants	345
the dead	379
the sick	323
thursday	329
Office of	
all estates	155. 168. 203. 214. 232
our blessed Lady	366. 371
our blessed Saviour	311. 313. 314. 315. 316. 326. 327. 328. 329. 330. 332
Saint Joseph	98. 99. 101. 102. 369. 370
Office of our blessed Lady	
from day after Purification to Advent	358
from evensong at Christmas to Purification	359
from evensong of Saturday before Advent to Christmas eve	358
prayers before, and after	377
three offices of	370
Office of (for) the	
angel guardian	98. 99. 101. 102. 369. 370
blessed sacrament	98. 99. 101. 102. 336. 369. 370
commemoration of saints	327. 328. 329. 332
dead	311. 312. 313. 314. 315. 316. 326. 327. 328. 329. 332. 359. 380
holy eucharist for those who communicate in private	344
immaculate conception	98. 99. 101. 102. 369. 370
saints	311. 312. 313. 314. 315. 316. 326. 330
Office of the blessed Virgin Mary	314. 315. 316. 317. 325. 330. 377. 379. 380
Office of the blessed Virgin Mary. See Primer or Office.	
Office of the blessed Virgin Mary	
as in the evening office book of S. John	379
of a simple rite	379
Office of the blessed Virgin Mary according to	
last edition of the Roman Breviary	95. 96. 366. 367. 377

GENERAL INDEX. 531

	PAGE
Office of the blessed Virgin Mary according to	
reformation of Urban VIII.	99. 371. 372
reformed latin	94. 95. 96. 97. 98. 357. 365. 369
Roman use	97. 368
Office of the blessed Virgin Mary in english with	
compline, rosary	100. 103
hymn and prayers at benediction	100
manner how to serve at mass	103
method of saying the rosary	103
ordinary of the holy mass	100. 103
sequence, dies iræ, and libera	100. 103
vespers or evensong	100. 103
Office of the blessed Virgin Mary in latin	
according to the Roman breviary	377
for the three times of the year	377
permissu superiorum	377
with the rubricks in english	97
Office of the blessed Virgin Mary in latin and english with office for the dead	379
Office of the holy	
cross	359. 370
Ghost 55. 311. 312. 313. 314. 315. 316. 326. 327. 328. 329. 330. 331. 332.	359. 370
liturgy	346
name of Jesus	98. 99. 101. 102. 369. 370
(blessed) Trinity	98. 99. 101. 102. 369. 370
Offices	
ancient way of. See Ancient way of offices	
concurrence of	312
manner of reciting	311
occasional	330. 333
publick of the church	340. 341
Officium	
defunctorum	351
divinum, oratio ante et post	131. 354
parvum	349. 356. 366. 375
S. crucis	353
S. Spiritus	119. 353
S. Trinitatis	134
Officium b. Mariae Virginis	
a nativitate Domini usque ad Purificationem	18. 94. 128. 349. 351
a purificatione usque ad Adventum	4-18. 94. 109-128. 349. 351
cum figuris ac mortis accidentia	15. 22. 128. 131
licentia imprimendi	350. 357. 366. 367. 375
per Adventum	18. 94. 128. 349. 351

GENERAL INDEX.

	PAGE
Officium b. Mariae Virginis	
revisum et correctum	8. 119
secundum usum Sarum	7
Officium b. Mariæ Virginis cum	
figuris apocalipsis, ac mortis accidentia addita	21
multis (devotis) suffragiis	7. 8. 119
multis orationibus et indulgentiis recenter insertis	14. 123
orationibus et contemplationibus impressum, caracteribus, figuris, ac mortis accidentia	15. 28
Officium b. Mariae Virginis nuper reformatum et Pii V. jussu editum	
ad instar breviarii Romani sub Urbano VIII. recogniti	97. 100
cum calendario Gregoriano a Sixto V. et Clemente VIII. festis aucto	95. 366. 367
cum gratia et privilegio	95
cum indulgentiis	97. 100. 367
cum privilegio (et indulgentiis)	94. 356. 366
de recitatione	350. 356. 365. 366. 379
Officium de	
omnibus sanctis	134
sacramento	134
sancto Spiritu	119. 353
Officium operariorum	257
Officium parentum erga liberos	257
Officium patrum et matrum	257
Old ceremonies	272
Old english type	302
Opera misericordiae	
corporalia	144. 351
spiritualia	144. 351
temporalia	351
Operariorum, officium	257
Orarium	32. 34. 42. 134. 135
Orarium seu libellus precationum	65. 82. 237. 251. 253. 254. 259. 270
Orate pro me fratres	107
Oratio	
afflicti in tribulatione	265
bona pro benefactoribus	122
brevis sed efficax	265
de facie nostri redemptoris	135
die Sabbati ad honorem V. Mariæ	9. 22. 119. 129
dominica G. Æmylius	267
dormituro	135. 136
dum es in via	266
edita ab Urbano VIII.	368

GENERAL INDEX.   533

Oratio
- exeundo domum — 137. 354
- intrando ecclesiam (templum) — 266. 354
- iter ingressurus — 266
- mandatum dni. Wilhelmi Cantuariensis archiepiscopi — 132
- populi ut liberetur ab hoste — 263
- prima legislatoris — 121
- pro omni gradu ecclesiæ — 352
- qua nos Deo commendamus — 265
- quam si quis dicat non morietur absque vera confessione — 137
- quoties horam sonare audis — 266
- quum adeunda est schola — 256
- resipiscentis — 264
- revalescentis — 264
- reversus domum — 266
- sub noctem — 264
- super quolibet opere finito — 132
- transeundo per cymiterium (sive ecclesiam) — 123. 128
- viri afflicti — 260
- viri fidelis de se humiliter sentientis — 265

Oratio ad
- crucem — 107
- Deum Filium — 114. 120. 264
- Deum Patrem — 114. 117. 120. 264
- Dominum — 117
- ingressum templi — 185
- invocandam gratiam — 358
- pluviam petendam — 352
- poscenda suffragia sanctorum — 351
- postulandam patientiam — 170
- receptionem sacramenti
- repellendas malas cogitationes — 353
- serenitatem petendam — 352

Oratio ad postulandam
- charitatem — 353
- continentiam — 353
- patientiam — 353

Oratio ante
- concionem — 265
- confessionem sacramentalem — 354
- divinum officium — 131
- imaginem pietatis — 136
- inchoationem officii — 354
- missam — 354

GENERAL INDEX.

	PAGE
Oratio ante	
phlebotomiam sive minutionem	145
sacram communionem	130. 135. 145. 265. 354
Oratio ante et post	
confessionem	354
(sanctam) communionem	127. 131. 135. 145. 152. 354
Oratio contra	
desperationem	263
infideles	352
malorum insectationem	264
mortalitatem hominum	117
paganos	352
persecutores ecclesiæ	352
superbiam	260
superbiam et impudicitiam	263
tempestates et tonitrua	132
temptationes	117
Oratio coram imagine	
b. Mariæ virginis in sole	123
crucifixi	123
Oratio cum	
mane surgis	136. 258. 353
vadis dormitum	135. 136. 354
Oratio de	
aeterna sapientia	137
extremo judicio	146
fiducia in Deum	260
pace	216
plagis Christi	123
septem verbis	161. 355
singulis articulis passionis	135. 354
tribus regibus	I. III. 143
vitae hujus miseriis	266
Oratio ecclesiae	
fidelium	172
pro peccatis	172
Oratio in	
aestate	266
afflictione	263. 355
angustiis	266
aspersione aquæ benedictæ	354
autumno	266
divisione apostolorum	143
elevatione corporis Christi	78. 111. 145. 150. 165

Oratio in	
hyeme	266
hora mortis	267
morbo	264. 267
mortis periculo	263
ostensione eucharistiæ	78
rebus adversis	266
rebus prosperis	266
sumptione corporis Christi	167
tribulatione	260
Oratio in dedicatione	
altaris	144
ecclesiæ	144
Oratio in tempore	
belli	352
famis et pestis	266. 352
pestilentiae	266
veris	266
Oratio inter	
lavandum manus	258
vestiendum	258
Oratio post	
auditam concionem	266
communionem	127. 135. 145. 354
confessionem	145. 354
ingressum ecclesiæ	137
officium divinum	131. 354
quatuor evangelia	150
Oratio pro	
alterius vitæ cupiditate	267
amico tribulato	145
benefactoribus	122
bono fine	137
carnali dilectione	108
castitate	132
catechumenis	352
charitate	132
christiana amore	265
christiana perfectione	265
cogitatione mundi	132
concordia et unitate ecclesiæ	265
consensu dogmatum	264
devicta tentatione	263
devotis amicis	353

GENERAL INDEX.

		PAGE
Oratio pro		
divina misericordia		264
docilitate (pietatis)		254. 263
ecclesia sancta Dei		352
fide, spe, et charitate		265
fidelibus defunctis		133. 134
fiducia in Deum		265
gaudio spirituali		265
haereticis et schismaticis		352
humilitate		132
imperatore		352
impetranda sapientia		167
infirmo		114. 352
inimicis		353
iter agentibus		352
locutione accepta		132
munditia cordis		263
omni gradu ecclesiæ		352
operatione justa		132
pace		110. 132
paganis		352
peccatis		132. 352
peccatorum remissione		263
perfidis Judæis		352
peste evitanda		128. 145
principe adolescente		264
rege		352. 367. 374
rege, regina, et regina dotaria		374
regina		254. 352
remissione peccatorum		
salute vivorum		352
statu ecclesiastico		264
temptatioue carnis		108
tentatis et tribulationibus		352
timore pio		263
tollenda morum pravitate		265
tribulatione peccatorum		352
venia delictorum		263
vera fide		265
vera pietate		264
vera poenitentia		108
verae fidei augmento		265
vitae competentia		167. 218
vitae incolumitate		111

GENERAL INDEX.

	PAGE
Oratio pro	
vivis et defunctis	352
Oratio pro quacunque	
necessitate ecclesiæ	352
tribulatione	352
Oratio, quicunque dixerit	
beatam virginem Mariam videbit	123
non morietur sine confessione	123. 137
promeretur indulgentiarum	130
quaecunque licita petierit obtinebit	135
quicquid debite et juste petierit obtinebit	120
subitanea morte non peribit	135
Oratio ut	
cunctis mundum purget erroribus	352
liberemur ab adversariis	263
Oration or sermon. How we ought to pray to almighty God	197
Oratione alla regina di tutte le creature	368
Orationes	
communes de sanctis	353
cum mane surgis	136
cum vadis dormitum	135. 136
de passione Domini	354
dominicales et feriales	353
in agonia mortis	114
in infirmitate	128
mane in aurora	78. 258
propriae de sanctis	353
quotidianae	109
speciales	119
Orationes ad	
poscenda suffragia sanctorum	351
quinque plagas Dni. nri. Jesu Christi	122. 129
vulnera Christi	355
Orationes ante	
crucifixum	129
imaginem pietatis	136
Orationes ante et post	
eucharistiæ receptionem	23
sanctam (sacram) communionem	17. 130. 145
Orationes et indulgentiae a Clemente VIII. ordinatae	367
Oratory, private	311. 326. 341
Order	
for morning prayer	251
to say mattyns	297

538   GENERAL INDEX.

	PAGE
Order of private prayer	
explained	296
for morning and evening	272. 291. 292. 296. 299
Order of the kalendar	289. 290
Ordinary of the holy mass	100. 103. 374
Ordinary, the, leave and warrant of	270
Ordines religiosi regularium et militiarum	350
Osanna in excelsis	153
Our Father. This is the meaning ...	214
Our Lord God, devout prayer to	112. 149. 150. 175. 189
Pace, oratio pro	110. 132
Paradise of the soul	46. 196. 202. 213. 218. 220
Paraphrase	
of the psalms	246
on psalms 42 and 43	324
Parliament	
authority of	207
high court of	289
Pardon	
days of	117. 124. 125. 126. 149. 152. 196
years of	112. 124. 125. 127
Pardons, pilgrimages, kissing of images, etc.	232
Parson (Person), Vicar, and Curate	153. 184
Passio Domini	
cursus de	136. 268
ex quatuor evangelistis	197
horae	134
meditationes. See Meditationes piæ.	
oratio de singulis articulis	135
oratio in honore	135
psalmi, lectiones, et preces selectæ	259
Passio Domini nostri Jesu Christi secundum	
Johannem. Egressus est Jesus 118. 119. 129. 136. 162. 183. 254. 259. 351	
Lucam. In illo tempore appropinquabat	351
Marcum. In illo tempore erant Pascha	351
Matthaeum. In illo tempore dixit Jesus	351
Passion of our Lord	
fifteen hours of	111
hours of	109. 110
Passion of our Lord Jesus Christ according to	
Luke. At that time, the festival day of the Azymes	361
Mark. At that time, the Pasche was	361
Matthew. At that time Jesus said to his disciples	361
Passion of our Saviour Christ	197. 206

	PAGE
Passion of our Saviour (Jesu) Christ	
devout, fruitful, and godly remembrance of	197
fifteen hours of	111
prayer of the particular articles of the	360
prayers of the	186. 240. 241. 249. 250. 252. 254. 257. 360
thirty days' prayer in honour of the	380
Passion written by St. John	
Jesus went forth	241. 252. 254. 362
when Jesus had spoken	162. 183. 210. 215. 219. 228
Pater noster	
by John Colet, dean of St. Paul's	150
containing all petitions	159. 168. 196. 201. 203
goodly interpretation, or declaration of	197. 203. 246
in english	131. 162. 184. 205. 213. 214. 228. 233. 239. 251
in english and latin	162
in latin	
spoken of the sinner	218
Pater noster, ave, creed, and ten commandments	
in english	153
in latin	238
title of a book	232
uniform translation of	184
Paternal authority, of	323
Patronum, oratio ad unum specialem	142
Pax, the, when thou receivest	108
Peace, prayer for	2. 110. 164. 182. 216. 233. 240. 363
Penance, sacrament of	370
Penitentials or invitatories, antiphons, and collects	331. 333
Persecution	203. 214
Person (Parson), Vicar, and Curate	153. 184. 237
Pestilent infections of books and learnings	195
Petitio divini auxilii	260
Petition	
for every day in the week	89. 90
for the virtues of the dying Jesus	338
Pia meditatio ante preces	258
Piae meditationes de vitæ fragilitate	262
Pilgrimages, pardons, etc.	232
Pious ejaculations	275
Plain	
and godly treatise concerning the mass	72. 73. 191
man's pathway to heaven	286
Poenitentia, oratio pro vera	108

GENERAL INDEX.

	PAGE
Pomander of prayer, T. Becon	293. 294
Pope	
of Rome	124. 125. 126. 127. 152. 207. 208
usurped power of	202
Popery	
and Romish superstition	270
distinction of popish and protestant faith	322
sound of	328
Post ingressum ecclesiæ, oratio	137
Practical believer by Mr. Kettlewell	326
Practice of	
divine love	319
piety	286
Pray, when thou beginnest to	108
Prayer	
an effectuous of Esaye	200
an universal	376
ancient times of	182. 220. 274. 284
and thanksgiving	247
and ye be sick, or in tribulation	189
composed by St. Augustine	372
devout in english	130
expressing how Scripture should be read	185
for such as are in jeopardy of death	257
fruitful prayer	243. 247
necessary to be said at all times	294
of prayer	284
on entering into the church	359
peaseth God's wrath	200
primitive method of daily private	340
sentences of holy scripture on the frequency of	275
that the world may be purged from all errors	362
to be said upon a fast before a battle	331
to live and do the pleasure of God	133
to thank God of his gifts	121
universal	376
Prayer after	
absolution	279
agnus Dei	150
an office	359. 377
confession	360
receiving the blessed sacrament	360
self èxamination	338

GENERAL INDEX. 541

	PAGE
Prayer against	
adversities	182
affliction	338
anger	243
envy	243
evil thoughts	108. 133. 187. 210. 221
pagans	363
pride	243
pride and unchasteness	243
sins	189
sudden death	182
temptation	117. 247
thunder and tempest	115. 118
ungodly (worldly) carefulness	189. 299
vain glory of this world	222. 223
worldly carefulness	189. 243
Prayer against the	
adversities of the church	182
devil	190. 244
enemies of Christ's truth	189. 242
persecutors of the church	362
pestilence	111. 117. 165
plague	372
Prayer and thanksgiving	
for the whole estate of Christ's church	281
to the heavenly father	182. 190. 220. 247
Prayer and thanksgiving on the anniversary of	
our baptism	282
our birth	282
the king's reign	282. 284
Prayer at	
bed time	184. 246. 276. 296. 337
beginning of devotions	14. 108
conclusion of devotions	341
entrance into the church	275
night for a family	313. 316. 330. 332
waking	275
your uprising	184. 242. 275. 296
Prayer at the	
consecration of the holy sacrament	278
end of the communion	278
hour of death	243. 281
point of death	281

GENERAL INDEX.

	PAGE
Prayer at the receiving of	
the body	278
the cup	278
Prayer before	
mass	359
receiving communion	298
receiving the blessed sacrament	251. 277. 360
sacramental confession	360
study	
ye go to bed	242. 337
Prayer before and after absolution	279
Prayer before the	
beginning of any office	359. 377
epistle	131
Prayer before the image of	
S. Anna, our Lady, and her son Jesus	125
the cross	171
Prayer for	
acceptation of acts of humiliation	338
all christian souls	117
all times	285
bishops, and priests	298
bishops, spiritual pastors, and ministers	292
carnal delectation	108
charity	182. 294
chastity	182
competent living	243
concord of Christ's church	242
consecrating every season	280
devout friends	363
diverse hours of the day	108
fair weather	363
faith	294
fathers and mothers	293
fear of God	189
forgiveness of sins	363
friends in sickness and necessity	108
gentlemen	293
God's acceptance of our humiliation	280
hearing	187
hereticks and schismaticks	362
humility	182. 294
Judges	292
Judges and Magistrates	298

GENERAL INDEX. 543

	PAGE
Prayer for	
labourers and men of occupations	293
landlords	293
lawyers	293
meekness and chastity	183. 243. 247
merchants	293
mercifulness	294
midnight	324
molifying and suppling hard hearts	199
morning	186. 246. 291. 296
obtaining of wisdom	189. 243
one that is sore sick	292. 301. 304. 305
our enemies	182. 247
pardon of sins past	280
patience (in trouble)	188. 294. 242
peace	182. 233. 363
poor people	293
prisoners	182
rain	363
rich men	293
sin (sins)	295. 363
soul falling into sin	121
speech	187
strength against the devil, the world, and the flesh	294
such as are in jeopardy of death	247
such as are in journey	363
temptation of the flesh	108
those that are to be catechised	362
thoughts	187
thy friend living	221
thy friend that is dead	109
to acknowledge the truth	182
to ask time of repentance	122
true faith	247
trust in God	188, 242
truth	
very penance	108
wayfaring men	108
wisdom	211. 243
women in childbirth	120. 300
works	187
Prayer for a	
competency (competent) of living	167. 189. 211. 218. 294
family at night	313

GENERAL INDEX.

	PAGE
Prayer for a	
good name	294
life agreeable to our knowledge	294
patient and thankful heart in sickness	294
pure and clean heart	294
quiet conscience	294
soul falling into sin	121
sweet and still heart	183
Prayer for any	
necessity of the church	362
that falleth in dysclaunder, reproof	121
Prayer for every	
day in the week	282
degree of the church	362
morning, noon, and evening	284
Sunday and holyday	58. 184
Prayer for grace	
and mercy of God	222
to observe the commandments	246
to spend ember season	280
Prayer for keeping	
a good name	189. 243
of the sight	187
Prayer for our	
children	281
enemies	182. 247. 364
parents	281
Prayer for the	
chief bishop	362
clergy and people	305. 307
demanding help against infidels	362
departed	150
desire of the life to come	244
emperor	362
evening	284. 291. 341
forgiveness of sins	247
fruits of the earth	280
gift of the holy Ghost	293
glory of heaven	294
good estate of the church militant	126
grace of the holy Ghost	363
hands	187
health of our neighbour	182
heart	187

	PAGE
Prayer for the	
help of God's holy angels	294
holy church of God	362
illumination of man's mind	133
king	362
king's most excellent majesty	285. 304. 307
living and the dead	109. 171. 363
morning	284. 291. 296. 299. 341
mouth and speech	187
ninth hour	337
ordination of Priests and Deacons	280
prince Palatine	279
Queen	279
royal family	305. 307
salvation of all christian souls	125
sick	363
sixth hour	337
third hour	337
whole state	304. 306
whole state of Christ's church militant	307
Prayer for the grace and	
favour of God	222. 293
mercy of God	184. 222
Prayer for the health of	
our neighbour	182
the body	280. 294
the living	363
Prayer for the King	108. 285. 292. 305. 307. 362. 374
Prayer for the King	
and for peace	248
and queen	218. 221. 279. 374
queen, and queen dowager	373. 374
Prayer for the king's counsell	292
Prayer for the peace of the	
church	243
congregation	247
Prayer for the Queen	279
Prayer for the true	
knowledge of ourselves	293
understanding of God's word	294
Prayer for them that	
have labour in temptation	121
have sickness or adversity	122
have taken any new great thing upon them	121

	PAGE
Prayer for them that	
intend to be married	121
lie in extreme pangs of death	295
stand in disease and distress	122
will praise God	122
Prayer for them that be	
a dying	182
in disease	122
laboured with sundry vices	122
maliciously accused	122
Prayer for those that are	
tempted	363
to be catechised	362
Prayer for true	
faith	220. 227
godliness	294
Prayer in	
adversity	188. 243. 295
affliction	361
behalf of the catholick church	346
going forth of thy house	359
great trouble of conscience	188. 242
necessity	243
prosperity	188. 243. 295
sprinkling of holy water	359
temptation	121
time of plague	282. 305. 372
tribulation of sins	363
trouble	247
Prayer in the	
beginning of thy journey	364
morning	151. 162. 186. 242. 252. 284. 299
wars	189. 242
worship of the members of Christ	124
Prayer in the time of	
any common plague	282. 305. 372
dearth	301. 304
famine and pestilence	363
plague, in honour of our b. Lady	372
prosperity	188. 295. 298
war	282. 331. 333. 362
Prayer meet	
for all men	293
to be used of all christians	305

GENERAL INDEX.

	PAGE
Prayer of	
a true subject	293
Anna	176
any captive	188. 242
children	293
commemoration for saints departed	328
householders	293
humiliation and confession	338
husbands	293
maids	293
masters	293
procession, or litany	240
servants	293
single men	293
wives	293
Prayer of all	
christians	293
prayers	271
Prayer of the church	
against sins	189. 242
for sins (sinners)	172. 211
of the faithful	172. 211
Prayer of the God names	41
Prayer of the great sorrow of our Lady	126
Prayer of the Lord	173. 239. 271
Prayer of the Lord	
called the Pater noster	197. 203
declaration of	197. 203
exposition of	203
Prayer of the seven	
sorrows of our Lady	126
words of our Lord on the cross	161. 192. 210. 215. 361
Prayer, the golden	124
Prayer to	
all saints	191
avoid the dangers of life	222
conclude devotions	282
desire the life to come	188
die to sin	338
eschew the infection of worldly men	299
get grace for sins	108. 221
have the fear of God before our eyes	189
keep the tongue	189. 242
live and do the pleasure of God	133

GENERAL INDEX.

	PAGE
Prayer to	
obtain (for) wisdom	167. 189. 211
repel wicked thoughts	364
speak the word of God boldly	243
Prayer to be said	
at all times	294. 299. 305
at night, going to bed	246
at the hour of death	185
by men of low degree	299
daily	190
in private by persons afflicted with melancholy	330
in the beginning of the congregation	363
upon a fast before a battle	331
Prayer to be used	
by women that travail with child	281. 300
in any tribulation	363
in secret	316
Prayer to require	
charity	364
continence	364
patience	364
suffrages of saints	362
Prayer to thank God, of	
deliverance out of tribulation	121
his gracious gifts	121
victory of enemies	121
Prayer when	
a sick member of a family is recovered	334
the priest turneth after the lavatory	107
the sick person is joyful and glad to die	295
Prayer when thou	
beginnest to pray	108
enterest into the church	13. 108. 149. 170. 210. 277. 359
hast received the body of our Lord	175
hast received the sacrament	108. 210. 221. 277. 278
receivest the pax	108
shalt arise	162. 275. 296
shalt receive the sacrament	108. 210. 221. 277. 278
takest holy water	108
Prayer when thou goest	
first out of thy house	13. 107. 359
to bed	184. 198. 220. 229. 233. 234. 246. 291. 296. 297. 299. 301. 303. 304. 306
to receive the body of our Lord	175

GENERAL INDEX.

	PAGE
Prayer when thou goest to sleep	360
Prayer when we	
do arise	151. 184. 228. 233. 234. 296. 297. 299. 301. 304. 306. 341. 359.
enter into bed	276
fall down to worship	275
first awake	275. 284. 341
hear the clock	275
lie down to sleep	276
Prayer when we are	
come into the quire	275
prostrate before the altar	277
scourged (punished) of God for our sins	172. 211. 294
Prayer when ye	
enter into the churchyard	125
go out of the churchyard	127
Prayers	
after receiving the holy communion (sacrament)	320
and orisons after the litanies	362
before receiving the holy communion (sacrament)	277. 320
certain prayers and godly meditations	197. 200
christian	253. 258
common to saints	365
daily	114
extemporal effusions of	271
goodly	59. 60
goodly and godly	43. 195
on Sundays and other days	365
penitential	342
preparatory	285
proper to saints	365
taken out of the gospels	370
two devout in english	114
Prayers and thanksgivings for sundry purposes	281
Prayers and thanksgivings on the anniversary of	
our baptism	282
our birth	282
the king's reign	282. 284
Prayers at	
apparelling	275
bed-time	184. 246. 276. 337
(during time of) mass	374. 377
going abroad	275
going to bed	198. 291

550 GENERAL INDEX.

		PAGE
Prayers at		
night		198
night for a family		330. 332
receiving the holy communion		320
uprising		184. 186. 284
waking		275. 284
washing of our hands		275
Prayers at the		
hour of death		281
point of death		281
Prayers for		
every day of the week	88. 89. 90. 186. 220. 282.	329
our children		281
our parents		281
persons afflicted with melancholy		330
sundry things		182
Prayers for the		
clergy and people		305. 307
dead (departed)	109. 150. 165. 227. 228.	329
King and Queen		279
King's majesty		305. 307
King, Queen, and Queen dowager		373. 374
molifying and suppling of our hard hearts		199
morning. See Prayers in the morning		
Queen		279
sick		280
use of families		323
Prayers in journeys		364
Prayers in the		
agony of death		114
morning	151. 186. 197. 220. 246. 252. 291.	296.
Prayers of the bible 159. 167. 172. 176. 183. 188. 189. 190. 199. 200. 242. 243.		295
Principal prayers of the bible		295
Prayers of the passion. See Passion of our Saviour Christ.		
Prayers preparatory		
for morning and evening		276
to the hours		372
Prayers to the honour of God, and memory of his saints		159. 168
Preachers		
of God's word		161
order of		372. 374
Precatio		
ante Jesum crucifixum		134
antequam petas tectum		156. 254

Precatio
- apud ægrotum — 255
- cum surgis — 156. 186. 242. 254
- de vitae hujus miseriis querela — 266
- dum es in via aut itinere — 266
- ecclesiae contra peccata — 242. 255
- efficacissima — 267
- fructuosa — 156. 256
- ingrediens templum — 266
- iter ingressurus — 266
- latronis cum Christo crucifixi — 262
- matutina — 253
- poenitentis, et divinam misericordiam implorantis — 264
- publicani — 262
- quoties horam sonare audis — 266
- quum adeunda est schola — 256
- reversus domum — 266
- sub noctem, quum iter dormitum — 253. 258. 264

Precatio ad
- Deum filium — 264
- Deum patrem — 264
- (Deum) Spiritum sanctum — 255. 264

Precatio adversus
- avaritiam — 267
- consilia inimicorum Dei — 255
- (contra) curam mundanam — 156. 255. 265

Precatio contra
- (adversus) curam mundanam — 156. 255. 265
- diabolum — 156. 256. 267
- inimicos veritatis Christi — 254
- invidiam — 243. 256. 265
- iram — 243. 256. 265
- superbiam — 256. 265
- superbiam et libidinem — 122. 156. 243. 256. 263

Precatio in
- aestate — 266
- afflictione — 255
- aurora — 156. 242. 254
- autumno — 266
- gravi morbo — 255. 267
- hora mortis — 243. 256
- hostium periculo — 266
- hyeme — 266
- tempore pestilentiæ — 266

GENERAL INDEX.

	PAGE
Precatio in	
tristitia, morbis, et adversitatibus	255
Precatio in rebus	
adversis	188. 243. 256. 266
prosperis	188. 243. 256. 266
Precatio pro	
alterius vitæ cupiditate	156. 188. 244. 256. 267
annunciando verbum Domini confidenter	255
augmento, et constantia in vera fide	255
bona fama conservanda (tuenda)	156. 189. 243. 255. 266
christiana perfectione	265
christianis magistratibus	266
concordia ecclesie	254
concordia et consensu in rebus divinis	255
consensu dogmatum	264
custodia pudicitiæ	266
docilitate	264
felici conjugio	266
fide, spe, et charitate	265
fidelibus ministris, et fructu evangelii	255
fiducia in Deum	156. 188. 242. 254. 265
gaudio spirituali	265
gratia, et misericordia	255
ministris verbi, et fructu evangelii	266
obtinenda sapientia	156. 167. 189. 211. 243. 255
parentibus nostris	266
patientia	188. 242. 254
rege	367
regina	260
tollenda morum pravitate	265
verae fidei augmento	265
vere christiano amore	255. 265
Precatio pro concordia	
ecclesiae Christi	156. 254
et consensu . . . in rebus divinis	255
et unitate ecclesiae Christi	265
Precatio pro vera	
fide	265
pietate	264
Precationes	
aliquot biblicæ sanctorum patrum	262
ante cibum	267
biblicae	167. 172. 176. 183. 188. 189. 190. 196. 197. 198. 199. 200. 203. 242. 243. 257. 260. 262. 263

GENERAL INDEX. 553

	PAGE
Precationes	
christianae	183. 188. 200. 242. 255. 256. 257. 258. 264. 265. 266. 267. 331. 333
de passione Christi	254
e sacris biblicis	183. 188. 189. 190. 200. 243
Erasmi	172. 186. 188. 189. 242. 243. 254. 255. 258. 263. 264. 265. 266. 267
ex novo testamento	261
Precationes piae	
ac necessariae in hora mortis	185
variis usibus accomodatae	264
Precepta	
charitatis	351
decalogi	78
ecclesiae	351
Precepts of	
charity	274. 358. 371
the church	274. 358. 371
Preces	
et orationes post litanias	351
matutinae	253. 258
noctu	
privatae in studiosorum gratiam collectæ	83. 257
sacrae ex psalmis David	269
vel ejaculationes piæ	263
vespertinae	253. 254. 258
Preces dicendae	
cum ad somnum te rursum componis	259
cum itur cubitum	258
in fine congregationis	353
in principio congregationis	352
noctu, si forte expergisceris	259
Predicatores, domus, London	43
Preface	
advertising the reader. Our master Christ . . .	159. 168
christian reader. This office of our b. Lady . . .	366
it was never ordained, O good reader . . .	196. 203
John late bishop of Rochester to Thomas Lord Crumwell	225
made by Henry the VIII. to his Primer book	250
touching prayer	271
Preface and	
introduction to the Pater noster	203
the manner to live well devoutly	147. 174. 212
Preface to	
Austin's devotions in the ancient way of offices	311. 315

YYY

554 GENERAL INDEX.

	PAGE
Preface to	
Deacon's primitive method of daily private prayer	340
Dorrington's reformed devotions	317
Hickes' devotions in the ancient way of offices 325. 328. 329. 330. 333	
Spinckes collection of meditations and devotions	335
Wheler's protestant monastery	322
Preface to the	
christian reader	357. 366. 369
commendations	241
creed. The effect of our faith . . .	197
dirige	204. 241
litany. Forasmuch good christian reader . . .	203
matins, and the other hours	170. 219. 229
Pater noster	197. 203
reader	195. 201. 203
seven penitential psalms	171. 231
ten commandments. See Ten commandments	
Preface to the pious reader	
more ample and in a new order	369
the Primer or Office of our b. Lady	371
Prefationes ad missam	152
Prelates, reforming	273
Preparation	
for a reception of the b. sacrament	278
to meditation and prayer	189
to receive absolution	279
Preparative	
exercise to a good death	338
unto prayer	290. 291. 296. 299
Preparatory	
office for death	331. 332
prayers for morning and evening	285
Priests, in an injunction of Henry VIII.	237
Priests and clerks	229
Prime and hours of our Lady in	
english	173
english and latin	164
latin	109
Prime and hours of our Lady instituted in England	171
Primer according to last edition of Roman breviary	
newly reviewed and corrected	96
printed with licence	96
Primer according to Sarum and York uses	1 . . . 60. 63. 68. 70 . . . 81

GENERAL INDEX. 555

	PAGE
Primer after Salisbury use in English	
cum privilegio ad imprimendum solum	81
diligently correct and newly imprinted	50
newly imprinted	54. 76. 81
set out at length with godly prayers	76. 81
Primer after Salisbury use in English with	
A.B.C. for children	54
godly prayers	81
Primer after Salisbury use in english and latin	
cum privilegio	72
cum privilegio ad imprimendum solum	80
newly imprinted	72. 75. 79. 80
set out at length	72. 75. 79. 80
Primer after Salisbury use in english and latin with	
godly prayers	80
prayers and goodly pictures	72. 75. 79. 80.
Primer after Salisbury use in latin	
cum privilegio ad imprimendum solum	79
newly enprynted	31 ... 50. 68. 70 ... 76
set forth with many prayers and goodly pictures	79
Primer after Sarum use in english	
cum privilegio per septennium	73
diligently correct and newly imprinted	50
for children	49
set out along	50
Primer after Sarum use in english with	
godly and devout prayers	72
plain and godly treatise concerning the mass	72
Primer after Sarum use in english and latin	
cum privilegio ad imprimendum solum	57. 59. 60. 79
newly translated after the latin text	46. 48. 50
set out along	49. 75. 77. 79
set out at length	57. 59
Primer after Sarum use in english and latin with	
epistles and gospels throughout the year	57. 59. 60
exposition of In te Domine speravi	57. 60
exposition of Miserere mei Deus	57. 60
godly and devout prayers	79
goodly prayers	57. 59. 60
Primer after Sarum use in latin and english	
cum privilegio per septennium	73
with a plain and godly treatise concerning the mass	73
with godly and devout prayers	73

	PAGE
Primer and catechism set forth at large	
cum privilegio ad imprimendum solum	85
necessary for all faithful christians to read	83. 85
with godly prayers	83. 85
Primer and catechism set forth by the King's highness and his clergy	
all other set apart	68. 69
corrected according to statute	68. 69
cum privilegio ad imprimendum solum	68. 69
to be taught, learned, and read	68. 69
Primer and catechism set forth by the Queen's majesty	
cum privilegio ad imprimendum solum	85
to be taught unto children	85
with the notable fairs in the Kalender	85
Primer books, diversity of	238
Primer goodly in english	
cum privilegio regali	48
newly corrected and printed	44. 45. 48
with godly meditations and prayers	44. 45. 48
with the King's most gracious privilege	44. 45
Primer in english	
for the education of children	52
or manual of prayers	52. 55
Primer in english cum privilegio	
ad imprimendum solum (Bishop Hilsey)	52. 53
regali, et gratia	44
Primer in english with	
epistles and gospels of every Sunday and holiday	48
form of the new beads	48
goodly and godly prayers	43
prayers, and godly meditations	43. 45
Primer in english and latin	
cum privilegio ad imprimendum solum	52. 54. 58. 59
newly corrected	51
newly translated after the latin text	46. 48. 50. 51
or manual of prayers	51
Primer in english and latin with	
epistles and gospels	57. 58. 59
exposition of In te Domine speravi	56. 58
exposition of Miserere mei Deus	56. 58. 59
Primer in latin. See Concise list	
Primer in latin and english, an uniform and catholick	
all other set apart	71
cum privilegio per septennium	72
newly set forth by certain of the clergy	71

GENERAL INDEX. 557

	PAGE
Primer in latin and english, an uniform and catholick	
to be used according to the Queen's letters patents	71
with assent of Cardinal Pole	71
with godly and devout prayers	71
Primer, meaning of the word	371
Primer more ample and in a new order with	
devotions and instructions out of holy scripture	98. 99. 101. 102
examen of conscience	98. 99. 101. 102
permission	98. 99. 101. 102
six offices newly added	98. 99. 101. 102
three offices of the b. Virgin Mary	98. 99. 101. 102
Primer of Salisbury use in english and latin	
cum gratia et privilegio regali	46
set out along without any searching	46. 58
Primer of Salisbury use in english and latin with	
a confession general	46
a prayer for every Sunday and holyday	58
exhortations of christian living	46
Jesus matyns	46
meditations and prayers	46
paradise of the soul	46
S. Jerome's psalter	46
Primer of Salisbury use in latin	
new corrected	43
newly enprynted	31 ... 50. 68. 70 ... 76
set out along with many prayers	47. 60. 63
Primer of Salisbury use in latin with	
fifteen Oos in english	40. 43
Jesus psalter	40
many prayers	47. 60. 63
prayers and goodly pictures	31 ... 50. 68. 70 ... 76
the confessional	40. 43
Primer or book of prayers in english set forth along	55
Primer or book of prayers in english with	
epistles and gospels daily read in church	55
hours of our Lady	55
hours of the holy Ghost	55
hours of the passion	55
prayers and ghostly meditations	55
Primer or book of private prayer	
authorised and set forth by the King's majesty	69. 70. 93
cum privilegio	85
cum privilegio ad imprimendum solum	69. 70. 82. 84
needful (necessary) to be used of all (faithful) christians	69. 70. 82. 84. 93

558   GENERAL INDEX.

	PAGE
Primer or book of private prayer	
to be taught, learned (read), and used	69. 70. 93
to be used of all our loving subjects	82. 84
with godly prayers	84
Primer or catechism	
authorised by the King's majesty	88. 92
cum privilegio	88
set forth agreeable to the Book of common prayer	88. 92
to be used throughout the King's (realm and) dominions	88. 92
with godly prayers and graces	88. 92
Primer or manual of prayers set forth by Bishop Hilsey	
cum privilegio ad imprimendum solum	52
in english	52. 55
in english and latin	51
Primer or Office of the b. Virgin Mary in english	
printed in 1699	100
short exposition of	371. 374
Primer or Office of the b. Virgin Mary in english according to the last edition of the Roman breviary	
cum gratia et privilegio	95. 96
newly reviewed and corrected	96
permissu superiorum	96
printed with licence	96
Primer or Office of the b. Virgin Mary in English according to the reformation of Urban VIII.	
exactly revised	99
with new hymns and prayers	99
Primer or Office of the b. Virgin Mary in english according to the Roman use	97
Primer or Office of the b. Virgin Mary in english revised with	
new and approved version of church hymns	101. 102. 103. 104
remaining hymns of the Roman breviary	101. 102. 104
table according to the new regulation of feasts	103
Primer or Office of the b. Virgin Mary in latin and english according to the reformed latin	
permissu superiorum	97
set forth by commandment of Pius V.	95
with like graces priviledged	94. 95. 96. 97.
with the calendar of Pope Gregory	95
Primer set forth at large	
cum privilegio ad imprimendum solum	81
with godly and devout prayers	81
Primer set forth by the King's highness and his clergy in english	
all other set apart	67. 68

GENERAL INDEX.

	PAGE
Primer set forth by the King's highness and his clergy in english	
corrected according to statute	68
cum privilegio ad imprimendum solum	67. 68
to be taught learned and read	68
to be taught unto children	67
Primer set forth by the King's majesty and his clergy in english	
cum privilegio ad imprimendum solum	61. 62. 64. 65. 66. 91
in the first year of Edward the VI.	65
none other to be used	61. 62. 64. 65. 66. 91
to be taught learned and read	61. 62. 64. 65. 66. 91
Primer set forth by the King's majesty and his clergy in english and latin	
cum privilegio ad imprimendum solum	63. 66
none other to be used	63. 66
to be taught learned and read	63. 66
Primer set forth in english	
by order of King Edward VI.	93
Primitive	
catholicks	346
christians	322. 326
church	276. 277
method of daily private prayer	340
Printer to the King's	
grace	67
majesty	66. 67. 68. 69
most excellent majesty	100
most royal majesty	65
Printer to the Prince's grace	60. 61. 62. 63. 64. 91
Printer to the reader	270
Private	
closets, and oratories	311. 323. 326
oratory	326
prayer books	270
Privilegium	
ad imprimendum solum	52 ... 70. 79-85. 91
cum gratia, et privilegio	44. 46. 95. 96
cum privilegio	38. 72. 85. 88
cum privilegio, et indulgentiis	94
per septennium	72. 73
regale	43. 45. 48
Pro peste evitanda, oratio	128
Procession or litany	171
Prodigal son's return	283
Prologue. Forasmuch as the laws and decrees	207

GENERAL INDEX.

	PAGE
Prologue to the	
dirige	219. 227. 231
kalendar	51. 226
matins, and the other hours	226
manual of prayers	226
Proper	
in perils either at sea or land	333
of festivals	311. 312. 313. 314. 327. 328. 333
preface. It is very meet	342
Protestant	
monastery	322. 323. 332
the moderate	314. 322
Protestation of free forgiveness	280
Provost, in an injunction of Henry VIII.	237
Psalm	
beati immaculati	46
commending frequency of prayer	275
de profundis	173
for women in childbirth. Beatus vir	120
in a journey	364
in great trouble of conscience	188
In te Domine speravi	56-60. 93
in tribulation	361
Miserere mei Deus	56 ... 60. 185. 195. 246
or summary of God's providence	283
to keep the tongue	
to our Saviour. Domine Dominus noster	116
Psalm for the	
ember weeks	280
king and queen	279. 374
Psalm of	
adoration	283
our Saviour's sufferings	283
praise	283
remembrance	283
thanksgiving	283
Psalmi	
ad completorium, per totum annum	376
ad vesperas, in Dominicis diebus	376
benedictiones mensæ	154
de passione Christi	2. 115. 119. 146. 166. 254. 259
expositiones in (Hieronimus Ferrariensis)	167. 207. 218
graduales (quindecim)	114. 165. 351
poenitentiales	1. 2. 114. 146. 165

	PAGE
Psalmi	
quindecim	114
si infirmus anxiatur	145
Psalmi, lectiones, et preces selectae de	
ascensione Christi	259
missione spiritus sancti	259
nativitate	259
passione Domini	259
resurrectione Domini	259
S. Trinitate	259
Psalmi selecti	
de passione Christi	254
pro rege, et regina	260
quotidianae orationi idonei	260
si infirmus anxiatur	146
Psalmi seu precationes D. Joan Fisheri	261
Psalms	
after the litanies	362
at the hour of death	281
epitome of the	183. 186. 188. 189. 242. 243. 244
fifteen, selected	283
fifteen, the	165
for the sick	280
gradual	359
in King's psalter	88
in devotions in Ancient way of offices	87. 96. 311
or prayers taken out of holy scripture	261
penitential. See Seven psalms	
translation of	358
with prayer to the holy Trinity	116
Psalms of the passion	
argument of	172
in english	166. 199. 210. 217. 237. 241. 248. 252. 253. 254
in english and latin	166. 199. 217
in latin	2. 114
Psalmus	
contra omnia adversa. Qui habitat	134
cum itur cubitum	258
de fiducia in Deum. Qui confidunt	260
de laudando Deo	133
de profundis	155. 173
implorat divinam misericordiam. Ad te levavi oculos	260
in quo monet ad orationem	127
in tribulatione	355. 361

	PAGE
Psalmus	
oratio Christi in cruce pendentis. Deus Deus meus	133
quum adeunda est schola	256
Psalmus movet ad	
laudandum Deum. Ecce nunc	133. 260
orationem	117. 127
unitatem fraternam. Ecce quam	260
Psalmus pro	
iter agentibus. Benedictus Dominus Deus	145
ope divina in adversis. Domine quid	260
rege. Exaudiat te Deus	367
Psalter	
argument of St. Hierome's	172
Hebraical, translated into english by S. Jerome	227
the usual, in latin	227
Psalter of	
David in english	176. 178. 180
Jesus	150
our Lady	221
S. Hierome in english and latin	167. 172. 217
Psalterium S. Hieronymi	115. 167. 217. 261
Publick	
liturgy	273. 319
offices of the church	340
Purgatory	171. 201. 231. 318
Qualis debeat esse confessio	144
Quando inchoatur adventus Domini	350. 365
Quatuor	
exhortationes Gersonis	146
novissima memoranda	274. 351. 358. 371
tempora	350. 365
Quatuor evangelia	
et passio Domini	118
oratio post	150
Queen	
collects for the	251
majesty's letters patent	190
prayer for	279
Quicunque vult salvus esse	168. 210. 217
Quindecim psalmi	114. 165
Quinque	
orationes ad quinque plagas Dni. nri. Jesu Christi	122. 129
portus	269
sensus corporis	351

	PAGE
Ratio aurei numeri	365
Recommendatio	
ad Deum	137
sub protectione b. V. Mariæ	137
Recommendation	
of oneself to God	339
unto the Virgin Mary	361
Red letters, printing in	196. 240. 244. 253. 256
Reformation of Pope Urban	371. 372
Reformation, the	328
Reformed devotions	89. 317
Regius impressor	17. 24. 68. 100
Regna et regiones quæ sunt juris et imperii Elizabethæ	269
Religious societies	326. 327
Relykes in the church	36. 151. 164. 174
Resurrectio Domini. See Index of Names	
Resurrection of our Lord	206
Right godly rule	186
Right way to the kingdom of heaven	195. 196. 197. 201. 202. 203
Roman	
breviary	96. 317
catholick	322. 325. 328
church	367
institution	371
Rosare	118. 122. 368
Rosario della	
Madonna	368
miracolosa solennita et festa del Santo	368
Rosarium b. Mariæ Virginis	16. 118. 122. 368
Rosary of our b. Lady	6. 7. 8. 10. 13. 15. 42. 100. 103. 118
Rosary of our b. Lady, method of saying	372. 374
Rota	
literae dominicalis	135
numeri aurei	135
Royal	
arms	43. 195
supremacy	207. 208. 228. 237
Rubricks to be observed in reciting the office of the b. Virgin	377
Rule	
a right godly	186
of charity	175. 210. 224
to know what a penny a day comes to in the year	302
Rules to know when the moveable feasts and holy days begin	273

	PAGE
Sacrament, the	
commemoration on any Sunday or holyday	331. 333
devout prayers before and after receiving	190. 277
exhortations for them that receive	205. 214
meditation on	337. 370
meditations while others are communicated	278
Sacrament, the, of penance	370
Sacrament, the, prayer at	
elevation of	111. 165. 174. 217
receiving	185
Sacrament, the, prayer when thou	
hast received	108. 167. 175. 192. 210. 217. 221. 277. 278
shalt receive	108. 167. 210. 217. 221
Sacrament of the altar, the	
declaration concerning	231
prayer before and after receiving	190. 360
prayer to	111. 151. 359
prayers when we receive	319
preparation for, and reception of	336. 338
thanksgiving after receiving	190. 278
treatise concerning	72. 73
Sacraments of the church	272. 274
Sacrifice of a devout christian	336. 337. 338
Salutatio	
ad Virginem Mariam	128
angelica	152. 162. 213. 353. 358
vulnerum Christi	128
Salutation	
angelique	152
of our most blessed lady	126. 197
of our redeemer Jesus Christ	187
of the angel to the b. Virgin Mary	153. 162. 173. 197. 213. 228. 233. 239. 248. 358. 371
to all the parts of Christ	361. 372
Salutationes ad omnia membra Christi	355
Salve regina	
exposition upon	160. 176. 184. 199. 230
with the verses	2. 110
Salve rex	199. 217
Sanctus, sanctus, sanctus	153. 324
Schoolmasters and teachers of young children	238
Self-examination, articles of	338
Sentences of holy scripture	251. 275. 291. 299. 301. 303. 304

GENERAL INDEX. 565

	PAGE
Septem	
peccata capitalia	351
psalmi poenitentiales	2. 114. 165. 254. 260. 351
sacramenta ecclesiæ	351
salutationes ad b. Mariam Virginem	128
verbis, oratio de	355
Septem opera misericordiae	
corporalia	144
spiritualia	144
Sequence	
come unto us holy Ghost	363
dies irae, dies illa	100. 103. 374
Sequentia per octavas missæ	136
Sequentiae S. Evangelii, secundum	
Johannem	152
Lucam. Missus est angelus	118. 357
Marcum. Recumbentibus undecim discipulis	118. 357
Matthæum. Cum natus esset Jesus	118. 357
Serious call to a devout life	340
Servorum, officium	257
Seven	
capital sins called deadly	284. 358. 371
contrary virtues	274. 284
deadly sins	133. 215. 274. 284
gifts of the holy Ghost	133. 274. 284. 358. 371
petitions of the Pater noster by John Colet	150. 213
prayers in honour of St. Joseph	377
sacraments	133. 358. 371
sorrows of our Lady, prayer of the	26. 126
spiritual joys of our Lady	110. 165
words on the cross, prayers on the	161. 192. 210. 215. 361
Seven petitions	369
Seven petitions of the Pater noster by John Colet	150. 213
Seven psalms	
goodly pictures in the. See Goodly pictures	
in english	199
in latin and english	209
penitential	165. 174. 217. 277. 280. 305. 307. 359. 375
penitential, why so called	171. 231
with an argument to each	240. 252. 254. 297. 300. 301. 303
Seven works of mercy	
bodily	133
ghostly (spiritual)	133. 214. 284

GENERAL INDEX.

	PAGE
Short	
conclusion of the ten commandments	196
exposition of the Primer	371. 374
Shrift, every week	148
Sick, prayers for the	114
Sins	
deadly	125. 127
four that cry to heaven for vengeance	284
venial	125. 127
Six	
corporal works of mercy	284
sins against the holy Ghost	284
Societas typographicus librorum	366
Soldiers, prayers for	323
Soliloquy	
by way of admonition	338
of a troubled soul	330
Sovereign Pontiff, Leo X.	377
Stanzas	
before the hours of compassion	134
before the hours of the cross	134
before the seven psalms	134
in english, in kalender	134. 147. 175. 209. 302
in french, in kalender	119
in latin, in kalender	118. 131. 209. 257
in the dirige	134
with a weather prognostication	131
Stationers, privilege to	289. 295
Stationers, company	88. 92. 303. 306
Subditorum, officium	257
Suffragia (collects) (memories)	
ad laudes	109. 118. 124. 125. 129. 131. 147. 149
at lauds	162. 174. 198. 215. 230. 239
Sum of the Catholick faith, called the Apostles Creed	274
Summa privilegii Principum Belgarum	367
Summarium constitutionis Pii Papæ V.	350. 356. 365. 368
Summary	
of God's providence	283
of such acts as every good christian ought to practise	370
Sundry	
godly prayers. See Godly prayers	
prayers or meditations of the passion	360
Superstitious books	225
Supplications of saints	286

GENERAL INDEX. 567

	PAGE
Supreme head	
of the church of England	207
of the churches of England and Ireland	237. 244. 250
Supreme head under God of the spirituality and temporality	155. 156. 157. 175. 208. 228
Symbol or Creed of Athanasius. See Creed of Athanasius	
Symbolum	
apostolorum	145. 267
Athanasii. See Creed of Athanasius	
Tabella	
epactarum respondentium aureis numeris	368
festorum mobilium	368
indictionis ab anno correctionis 1582	368
temporalis	368
Table	
of festivals of obligation, days of devotion, fasting, and abstinence	376
of moveable feasts	273. 358. 369
to know the full floods and ebbs of any haven. See Canon of ebbs and floods	
Tabula	
ad cognoscendum in quo signo sit luna	135
ad inveniendum festa mobilia	123
de indictione	365
de quatuor ventis	
indicat locum lunæ	124. 135
literarum dominicalium 1582-1700	365. 368
literarum respondentium aureis numeris 1582-1700	365
oeconomica in qua quisque sui officii commonetur	257
perpetua	350
signorum, et festorum mobilium	135
temporalis festorum mobilium	365
Tavola del far della luna secondo il vero computo	368
Temptatione carnis, oratio pro	108
Temptationes, oratio contra	117
Ten commandments	56. 133. 162. 185. 196. 205. 213. 274. 322. 371
Ten commandments, the	
according to the last setting forth	232
an introduction to fulfil them	214
compendiously extracted, and briefly set forth	232
creed, and Lord's prayer	196
duties enjoined, and sins forbidden	274
exposition of	284
fulfilling of	196
given by Moses, and expounded by Christ	168. 209. 232. 246

GENERAL INDEX.

	PAGE
Ten commandments, the	
in rhyme	133. 162. 213
of almighty God	153. 173. 233. 239. 252
of the law	128
of the old and new law	214
short conclusion of	196
transgression of	196
Ten precepts of God	358
Testament of the soul	370
Texts of holy scripture	327. 342
Thanks after meat	252. 290
Thanksgiving	341. 364. 376
Thanksgiving	
at home after the holy communion	339
daily	337
unto God for all his benefits	190. 294
Thanksgiving after	
childbirth	282. 324
receiving the blessed sacrament	278
Thanksgiving for	
all persons and times	337
deliverance from any plague	282
peace and victory	282
recovery from sickness	282
the Lord's day and Sabbath	340. 342. 343
Thoughts to have in the church	54
Three	
kinds of good works	274
theological virtues	274. 284. 358. 371
verities	38
Thunder and tempest, prayer against	115. 118
Tierce, saying of	148
Times	
of prayer	
wherein marriages are not usually solemnized	273. 369
Tota congregatio, officium	257
Tradition of our elders	168
Tres veritates Gersonis	136
Tunes to hymns	318. 324. 358
Typographus	65. 70. 76. 82. 83. 85. 100. 149
Typographus lectori	257
Twelve	
articles of the (christian) faith	153. 162. 173. 213. 228. 233. 239. 252
fruits of the holy Ghost	274. 284: 358. 371

GENERAL INDEX.   569

	PAGE
Understanding of the Lord's prayer	203
Universities of Oxford and Cambridge	208
Uprising, prayers at	8. 9. 107. 184. 186. 197. 242. 284. 291. 296
Use, Roman	97. 349. 368
Use, Sarum	
blessings at matins, and suffragia at lauds	198
english primer of	168
hymn, Veni creator spiritus	210
Hilsey's hours	230
hours in english and latin	183
Marshall's hours	198. 209
prime and hours according to	171
Sarum and Marshall's hours	213. 215. 219
the primer of the king and clergy	239. 241
litany, according to	217. 234
order of the commandments	232
Use, York	171
Veneration (worshipping, honouring), of saints	160. 168. 170. 358
Vernacle of our Lord, orison to	125. 127
Verses of S. Bernard. See Index of Names. S. Bernard.	
Versus S. Bernardi. See Index of Names. S. Bernardus.	
Versiculus tantæ veritatis	136
Versus pro tribulatione evitanda	137
Vesperae per adventum de S. Maria	17. 18. 128
Vespers	
for the dead	313. 327
in latin and english	103
introduction to	316
or Evensong	100. 373. 374
Vicar, Parson, and Curate	153. 184. 237
Viduae, officium	257
Vigiliae mortuorum	115
Vigils, fasting on	148
Virtutes	
cardinales	351. 371
theologicæ	351. 371
Virtutes et remedia contra vitia septem capitalia	144
Visitation articles,	
bishop Ridley	250
Edward VI.	244
Elizabeth	251
Vulgar tongue	238. 240
War, collect in time of	331. 333

GENERAL INDEX.

	PAGE
Watch	
first, at six of the clock at night	323
second, or midnight watch	323
third, after twelve of the clock	324
fourth, or morning about three of the clock	324
Watching, of	323
Wayfaring men, prayer for	108
Weather prognostication	131
Week days moralysed	54
When thou	
awakest, prayers	284. 341
enterest the church, prayers	13. 107. 149. 170. 210. 277
goest to bed, prayers	184. 198. 220. 229. 233. 234. 276. 283. 284. 291. 296. 297. 299. 301. 303. 304. 306. 360
risest in the morning, prayers	184. 186. 220. 228. 233. 234. 284. 291. 296. 297. 299. 301. 303. 304. 306. 359
Whole duty of man	286
Women in travailing of child, prayer for	120
Word of God	
in the mother tongue	208
to be preached	207
Words fitly spoken	285
Works	
are divers. Third part of Primer, treating of works	183. 220. 232
homilies of Edward VI.	223. 231
of works	224
Works of mercy	173
Works of mercy	
corporal	274. 284. 358. 371
spiritual	274. 284. 358. 371
Wounds of our Lord, prayer to	11. 112. 123. 360
Youth	
ejaculation of a	284
king's psalter for	88
library of a	286
primer for	88. 226. 238. 305

END OF INDICES.

A LIST

OF

PRINTERS AND BOOKSELLERS

WITH

A LIST OF PLACES.

EXPLANATIONS.

In the list of Printers and Booksellers, the dates placed after their names are those of the years during which they were in business.

In the list of places, the date which immediately follows the name of the town denotes the year when printing was introduced into that town.

A LIST

OF

PRINTERS AND BOOKSELLERS.

A. J. (London), 1687.
　No. 260.

Barbier, Jean. London, at the sign of St. Thomas, 1497. Westminster, 1498. Paris, at the sign of the Sword, 1500-1514.
　No. 14.

Basset, Richard. London, in Fleet Street, 1691-1704.
　No. 260.

Bernard, Guillaume. Rouen, rue St. Vivien, 1508-1517.
　Nos. 51. 52.

Bignon, Jean. Paris, 1512-1542.
　No. 60.

Bonham, William. London, at the King's Arms in Paul's Churchyard, 1542; at the Red Lion in Paul's Churchyard, 1542-1558.
　Nos. 165. 166.

Bonhomme, Yolande, widow of Thielman Kerver. Paris, at the Unicorn, 1525-1557.
　Nos. 82. 83. 103. 104. 114.

Bourman, Nicolas. London, in Aldersgate Street, 1539-1540.
　No. 152.

Bowyer, Jonah. London, at the Rose in Ludgate Street, 1703-1722.
　No. 255.

Bretton, William. London, 1506-1510.
　Nos. 31. 37.

Brotherton, John. London, in Threadneedle Street, 1724-1755.
　No. 260.

Byddell, John. London, at the sign of Our Lady of Pity in Flete-street, and at the Sun in Fleet-street, 1533-1544.
　Nos. 115. 117. 119. 120. 121. 129. 130.

Byrckman, Francis. Antwerp, and London, in Paul's Churchyard, 1504-1528.
　Nos. 39. 43. 45. 48. 50. 53. 54. 55. 58. 59. 67. 79. 82.

Cademan, William. London, at the Pope's Head in the Strand, 1664-1675.
　No. 255.

Caly, Robert. London, in the Grey Friars, 1553-1558.
　Nos. 209. 220.

Caxton, William. Bruges, 1475-1477. Westminster, at the sign of the Reed Pale, 1477-1491.
　Nos. 1. 2. 4. 5.

Churchil, William. London, at the Black Swan in Paternoster Row, 1717-1719.
　No. 255.

Cierae. Venice, at the sign of Europa, 1607-1685.
　No. 279.

Clark, Henry. London, at the White Hart in Paul's Churchyard, 1677-1696.
　No. 260.

Clements, Henry. London, at the Half-Moon in Paul's Churchyard, 1707-1719.
　No. 255.

Cnobbaert, widow of John (Marie de Man). Antwerp, at the sign of St. Peter, 1637-1671.
　No. 280.

Coghlan, J. P. London, Duke Street, Grosvenor Square, 1780-1789.
　Nos. 256. 296.

Conings, Arnold. Antwerp, at the sign of the Red Lion, 1579-1605.
　Nos. 267. 268.

Cousin, Jacques. Rouen, près les Cordeliers, 1508-1537.
Nos. 51. 52. 68. 84. 125.

Cowse, Benjamin. London, St. Paul's Churchyard, 1700-1722.
No. 255.

Coyne. Parliament Street, Dublin, 1817-1820.
No. 297.

Cumberland, Richard. London, 1692-1696.
No. 260.

D., T. Antwerp, 1685.
No. 285.

Deighton & Sons. Cambridge, 1813-1828.
No. 265.

Downie, D. Edinburgh, 1789.
No. 256.

Drummond. Edinburgh, 1741-1765.
No. 261.

Endoviensis, Christopher. Antwerp, 1523-1531.
Nos. 66. 67. 88. 92. 94.

F. J. London, 1664.
No. 255.

Fakes, Richard. London, at the Maiden's Head in Paul's Churchyard, 1508; at the ABC in Paul's Churchyard, and in Durham Rents, 1523-1530.
No. 60.

Gaultier, Thomas. London, in St. Martin's Parish, 1550-1553.
No. 194.

Godfray, Thomas. London, in the Old Bailey, 1532-c.1535.
No. 118.

Gostling, Robert. London, at the Mitre and Crown in Fleet Street, and at the Middle Temple Gate,1706-1741.
No. 255.

Gowghe, John. London, at the Mermaid in Cheapside, 1536-1543.
No. 122.

Grafton, Richard. London, at the Grey Friars, 1538-1559.
Nos. 151. 170. 173. 174. 175. 179. 182. 184. 186. 187. 188. 191. 193. 195. 196. 199. 262.

Growte, John. London, dwelling within the Black Friars, next the Church door, 1532-1534.
Nos. 103. 104. 114.

Grover, John. London, Angel Alley, Aldersgate Street, 1670-1676.
No. 255.

Groyat, Jean. Rouen, 1536.
No. 123.

Guerin, Pierre. Rouen, at the sign of La Hache, in the Rue Ganterie, 1505-1517.
No. 49.

H., I. London, at the sign of St. Thomas Apostle, 1497.
No. 14.

H., W. London, 1693.
No. 255.

Hardouyn, Germain. Paris, at the sign of St. Margaret, 1503-1538.
Nos. 85. 91. 110.

Hartley, Thomas. London, at the Black Boy, behind St. Alban's Church in Wood Street, 1671.
No. 258.

Hazard, Joseph. London, 1701-1739.
No. 260.

Heighan, or Heigham, John. Doway, 1613. St. Omers, 1616-1631. London, Drury Lane.
Nos. 271. 273. 274.

Hester, Andrew. London, at the White Horse in Paul's Churchyard, 1539-1564.
Nos. 143. 144.

Higman, Nicolas. Paris, 1516-1535.
Nos. 54. 56. 57.

Hills, Henry. London, in Black Friars, on the Ditch side, 1645-1713.
Nos. 286. 287.

Hopyl, Wolfgang. Paris, at the sign of St. Barbara, rue Saint-Jacques, 1489; at the sign of St. George, 1490-1524.
Nos. 31. 48.

Horne, Thomas. London, at the Royal Exchange, 1689-1719.
No. 255.

Innys, William. London, Westend of Paul's Churchyard, 1709-1719. Innys, W. & J. West end of Paul's Churchyard, 1720-1724; Prince's Arms, 1725-1726. W. Innys, Prince's Arms, 1730-1732.
Nos. 255. 261.

J., F. London.
No. 255.

PRINTERS AND BOOKSELLERS. 575

Jaey, Henrie. Mackline (Malines), 1615-1622.
  No. 270.
Jehannot, Jean. Paris, 1488-98; in the rue neufve Notre Dame, at the sign of the Shield of France, and at the sign of St. John Baptist, 1511-1521.
  No. 18.
Jenour, Matthew. London, in Giltspur Street, 1699-1737.
  No. 261.
Jones, John. London, at the Bell in Paul's Churchyard, 1696-1700.
  No. 261.

Kaetz, Pieter. London, in Paul's Churchyard, 1524; and Antwerp, in the " Huys van Delft ".
  Nos. 63. 66.
Keblewhite, William. London, at the Swan in Paul's Churchyard, 1687-1724.
  No. 261.
Kerver, Thielman. Paris, at the Unicorn, 1497-1505; at the Hurdle, 1506-1522.
  Nos. 15. 37.
Kerver, Thielman, widow of, see Bonhomme, Yolande.
Knaplock, Robert. London, at the Angel in Paul's Churchyard, and at the Bishop's Head, 1689-1740.
  No. 255.
Knapton, James. London, at the Crown in Paul's Churchyard, 1687-1737.
  No. 255.
Kyng, John. London, in Creed Lane, and at the Swan in Paul's Churchyard, 1555-1561.
  Nos. 214. 222.
Kyngston, John. London, in Paul's Churchyard, at the West Door, 1553-1583.
  Nos. 221. 233.

Lecomte, Nicolas. London, at the sign of St. Nicholas in Paul's Churchyard, 1494-1498.
  No. 18.
Le Cousturier, John. Rouen, 1633.
  Nos. 277. 278.
Leeu, Gerard. Gouda, 1477-1484. Antwerp, 1484-1493.
  No. 6.
Le Prest, Jean. Rouen, 1544-1555.
  Nos. 203. 215.

Le Roux, Nicolas. Rouen, in the Rue de Ruissel, 1530-1557.
  Nos. 117.* 123. 125. 132. 135. 138. 189. 197.
Le Tourneur, Nicolas. Rouen, rue S. Lo, opposite the door of the Palace, 1649-1684.
  No. 284.
Le Tourneur, Nicolas, widow of. Rouen, at the sign of the Turner in Iron Cross Street, 1720.
  No. 291.
Le Turner, Nicolas. Rouen, at the sign of the Turner in Iron Cross Street, 1730.
  No. 292.
Lobley, Michael. London, at the sign of St. Michael in Paul's Churchyard, 1539-1563.
  Nos. 143. 144.
Longman, Thomas. London, at the Ship in Paternoster Row, 1755-1795.
  No. 261.

Machlinia, William de. London, 1482-1486.
  No. 3.
Marchant, Jean. Rouen, at the sign of the Two Unicorns, 1536-1542.
  No. 123.
Marescalus Henricus, see Marshall, Henry.
Marshall, Henry (Marescalus Henricus). Rouen, c. 1539.
  No. 145.
Marshall, William. London, 1535-1542.
  Nos. 115. 117.
Maurry, David. Rouen, 1658-1673.
  No. 282.
Mayler, or Maylart, John. London, at the sign of the White Bear in Botolph Lane, 1539-1545.
  Nos. 143. 144. 158. 161.
Mead, E. London, 1706.
  No. 261.
Mead, Thomas. London, 1692-1754.
  No. 261.
Meers, William. London, Lamb without Temple Bar, 1707-1739.
  No. 255.
Meighan, or Meigham, Thomas. London, Drury Lane, 1717-1765.
  No. 290. 293.
Meredith, Luke. London, at the Star in Paul's Churchyard, 1684-1693.
  No. 255.

576 A LIST OF

Midwinter, Daniel. London, at Pye Corner, the Three Crowns in Paul's Churchyard, and the Rose and Crown in Paul's Churchyard, 1697-1757.
Nos. 255. 261. 263.

Moret, Balthasar. Antwerp, in officina Plantiniana, 1641-1674.
No. 281.

Moret, John. Antwerp, in officina Plantiniana, 1597-1610.
No. 269.

Mundell & Son. Edinburgh, 1789-1797.
No. 256.

N., R. London, 1681.
No. 255.

Nicholson, J. Cambridge, 1825.
No. 265.

Nicholson, John. London, at the King's Arms in Little Brittain, 1695-1717.
No. 261.

Nicholson, John, executors of. 1717.
No. 261.

Notary, Julian. Westminster, in King Street, 1498-1500. London, at the Three Kings without Temple Bar, 1503-1510; at St. Mark in Paul's Churchyard, 1515-1516; at the Three Kings in Paul's Churchyard, 1518-1520.
Nos. 21. 28.

Osborn, John, and Longman, Thomas. London, at the Ship and Black Swan in Paternoster Row, 1725-1734.
No. 261.

Petyt, Thomas. London, at the Maiden's Head in Paul's Churchyard, 1536-1554.
Nos. 159. 160. 167. 169. 171. 172. 180. 204.

Philippe, Jean. Paris, at the sign of the Trinity, 1494-1512.
No. 11.

Pigouchet, Philippe. Paris, in the Rue de la Herpe, devant St. Cosme, 1484-1512.
Nos. 10. 13. 17. 23. 24.

Plantin Press. Antwerp.
No. 269.

Plomier, Alard. Paris, 1528
No. 83.

Poitevin, Jean. Paris, in the Rue neufve Notre Dame, 1498-1520.
No. 20.

Prevost, Nicolas. Paris, 1527-1532.
No. 79.

Purfoote, Thomas. London, at the sign of Lucretia in Paul's Churchyard, 1562-1615.
No. 253.

Pynson, Richard. London, without Temple Bar, 1493-1501; at the George in Fleet Street, 1502-1528.
Nos. 12. 16. 22. 29. 35. 38. 42. 44. 47. 61.

Rastell, William. London, in Flete Street, in St. Bride's Churchyard, 1531-1534.
No. 101.

Redman, Robert. London, without Temple Bar at the sign of St. George, 1523-1527; Flete Street, at the sign of the George, 1528-1540.
Nos. 128. 140.

Regnault, Francois. Paris, at the sign of St. Claude, 1505-1524; at the sign of the Elephant, 1524-1541.
Nos. 54. 70. 71. 72. 75. 76. 77. 78. 80. 81. 89. 90. 93. 96. 97. 98. 99. 100. 102. 105. 107. 109. 113. 116. 117.* 126. 132. 133. 134. 135. 141.

Richard, Jean. Rouen, rue St. Nicholas, 1490-1515.
No. 15.

Rivington, C. & J. London, at the Bible and Crown in Paul's Churchyard, 1822-1827.
No. 265.

Robinson, Robert. London, 1691-1719.
No. 255.

Roper, Abel. London, at the Sun in Fleet Street, 1687-1721.
No. 260.

Royston, Richard. London, at the Angel in Ivy Lane, 1630-1686.
No. 255.

Ruddiman, Walter, & Co. Edinburgh 1757-1769.
No. 261.

Ruremundensis, Christopher. Antwerp, 1524-1531.
No. 95.

S., S. London, 1671.
No. 258.

PRINTERS AND BOOKSELLERS.

Seres, William. London, without Aldersgate, in the Ely Rents in Holborn, 1546-1548; at the Hedgehogge in Paul's Churchyard, 1553-1576.
Nos. 200. 201. 239. 243. 244. 246. 247. 249. 251. 252. 253.

Sprint, Benjamin. London, at the Bell in Little Brittain, 1730-1738.
No. 261.

Sprint, John and Benjamin. London, at the Bell in Little Brittain, 1707-1730.
No. 261.

Sprint, John. London, at the Bell in Little Brittain, 1694-1707.
No. 261.

Stationers, Company of. James I., 29th Oct., 1603, granted to the Company the exclusive right of printing all primers.
Nos. 257. 264.

Sutton, Henry. London, at the Black Boy in Paul's Churchyard, 1552-1557; at the Black Marion in Paternoster Row, 1553-1563.
Nos. 221. 233.

Taylor, William. London, at the Ship in Paternoster Row, 1705-1719; at the Ship and Black Swan in Paternoster Row, 1719-1724.
No. 255.

Thompson, James. London, 1650.
No. 280.

 y, Robert. London, at the sign of the Bell in Paul's Churchyard, 1541-1556.
Nos. 162. 168. 194. 208. 210.

Valentin, Florence. Rouen, 1553-1559.
No. 225.

Valentin, Robert. Rouen, at the door of St. Mary's Church, 1544-1559.
Nos. 197. 198. 203. 215. 216. 217. 218. 219. 223. 224.

Verard, Antoine. Paris, at the sign of St. John the Evangelist on the Pont Notre Dame, 1485-1499; Rue St. Jacques, 1500-1503; Deuant la rue neuve Notre Dame, 1503-1512.
Nos, 30. 32.

Vostre, Simon. Paris, in the rue neuve Notre Dame, at the sign of St. John the Evangelist, 1488-1520.
Nos. 17. 19. 23. 24. 33. 34. 40. 56. 57.

Waley, John. London, in Foster Lane, 1555-1580.
No. 214.

Watts, Joseph. London, at the Half-Moon in Paul's Churchyard, 1684-1687.
No. 260.

Wayland, John. London, at the Blue Garland in Fleet Street, next to Temple Bar, 1537-1541; at the Sun in Fleet Street, near the Conduit, 1541-1556.
Nos. 142. 143. 144. 207. 211. 212. 213.

Wayland, John, assigns of. 1557-1559.
Nos. 231. 232. 234. 235. 236. 237. 238. 239.

Whitchurch, Edward. London, at the Well and Two Buckets in St. Martin Le Grand, in St. Mary, Aldemary Churchyard, 1538; at the Sun in Fleet Street, 1545-1560.
Nos. 151. 176. 177. 178. 181. 183. 185. 189.

Wight, John. London, at the Rose in Paul's Churchyard, 1551-1584.
Nos. 221. 226.

Worde, Wynkyn de. Westminster, in Caxton's House, 1493-1500. London, at the Sun in Fleet Street, and at Our Lady of Pity in Paul's Churchyard, 1501-1534.
Nos. 7. 8. 9. 14. 25. 26. 27. 36. 41. 46. 62. 64. 73. 74.

Wyat, John. London, at the Rose in Paul's Churchyard, 1719-1730.
No. 255.

Wyer, Robert. London, at the sign of St. John Evangelist beside Charing Cross, 1530-1560.
No. 111.

Young, Robert. London, at the Bishop's Head in Paul's Churchyard, 1627-1639.
No. 255.

BBBB

A LIST OF PLACES.

Antwerp (Antverpia). 1482.
Nos. 6. 65. 66. 67. 88. 92. 94. 95.
163. 267. 268. 269. 280. 281. 285.

Cambridge (Cantabrigia). 1521.
No. 265.

Dublin (Dublinum, Eblana). 1551.
No. 297.

Edinburgh (Edinburgum). 1507.
Nos. 256. 261.

London (Londinium). 1480.
Nos. 3. 12. 14. 16. 18. 22. 25. 26.
27. 28. 29. 31. 35. 36. 37. 38. 39.
41. 42. 43. 44. 45. 46. 47. 48. 50.
53. 54. 55. 58. 59. 60. 61. 62. 63.
64. 66. 67. 73. 74. 79. 82. 92. 95.
101. 103. 104. 111. 114. 115. 117.
118. 119. 120. 121. 122. 128. 129.
130. 140. 142. 143. 144. 151. 152.
158. 159. 160. 161. 162. 165. 166.
167. 168. 169. 170. 171. 172. 173.
174. 175. 176. 177. 178. 179. 180.
181. 182. 183. 184. 185. 186. 187.
188. 189. 191. 193. 194. 195. 196.
199. 200. 201. 204. 205. 207. 208.
209. 210. 211. 212. 213. 214. 220.
221. 222. 226. 231. 232. 233. 234.
235. 236. 237. 238. 239. 243. 244.
246. 247. 249. 251. 252. 253. 255.
256. 257. 258. 260. 261. 262. 263.
264. 265. 280. 286. 287. 290. 293.
296.

Malines (Mechlinia). 1581.
No. 270.

Paris (Parisius, Lutetia Parisiorum).
1470.
Nos. 10. 11. 13. 15. 17. 18. 19. 20.
23. 24. 30. 31. 32. 33. 34. 37. 39.
40. 43. 45. 48. 50. 53. 54. 55. 56.
57. 58. 59. 60. 70. 71. 72. 75. 76.
77. 78. 79. 80. 81. 82. 83. 85. 89.
90. 91. 93. 96. 97. 98. 99. 100.
102. 103. 104. 105. 109. 110. 113.
114. 116. 126. 132. 133. 134. 135.
136. 141. 256.

Rome (Roma). 1467.
No. 266.

Rouen (Rotomagus). 1487.
Nos. 15. 49. 51. 52. 68. 84. 117.*
123. 124. 125. 126. 132. 134. 135.
137. 138. 139. 145. 164. 197. 198.
203. 215. 216. 217. 218. 219. 223.
224. 225. 256. 276. 277. 278. 282.
284. 291. 292.

St. Omers (Audomaropolis). 1601.
Nos. 271. 273. 274. 283.

Venice (Venetiæ). 1469.
No. 279.

Westminster (Westmonasterium). 1477.
Nos. 1. 2. 4. 5. 7. 8. 9. 14. 21.

THE END OF THE BOOK.

THE ABERDEEN UNIVERSITY PRESS LIMITED.

Milton Keynes UK
Ingram Content Group UK Ltd.
UKHW030809130224
437765UK00006B/357